A history of English law Volume 9 – Primary Source Edition

William Searle Holdsworth

A HISTORY OF ENGLISH LAW

A HISTORY OF ENGLISH LAW

IN NINE VOLUMES

For List of Volumes and Scheme of the History, see p. ix

A HISTORY
OF ENGLISH LAW

BY

Sir W. S. HOLDSWORTH, K.C., D.C.L.

VINERIAN PROFESSOR OF ENGLISH LAW IN THE UNIVERSITY OF OXFORD; FELLOW OF ALL SOULS
COLLEGE, OXFORD; LATE FELLOW OF ST. JOHN'S COLLEGE, OXFORD; FOREIGN ASSOCIATE
OF THE ROYAL BELGIAN ACADEMY; FELLOW OF THE BRITISH ACADEMY

VOLUME IX

*To say truth, although it is not necessary for counsel to know what
the history of a point is, but to know how it now stands resolved, yet it is a
wonderful accomplishment, and, without it, a lawyer cannot be accounted
learned in the law.*
ROGER NORTH

METHUEN & CO. LTD.
36 ESSEX STREET W.C.
LONDON

First Published in 1926

PRINTED IN GREAT BRITAIN

PREFACE

IN this last volume of my History the history of Status is carried on from the point at which it was left in the fourth chapter of the preceding Book ; the early history of the law of Evidence is related ; and the history of the law of Procedure and Pleading, both at common law and in equity, down to the statutory reforms of the last century, is completed.

These nine volumes contain a history of the sources and general development of English law down to 1700 ; and a history of the judicial system, and of very many of the principles and rules of the English common law, down to modern times. It is, therefore, not quite a complete history. There still remains to be related the history of the sources and general development of English law during the eighteenth and nineteenth centuries ; the history of substantive rules of equity, which became the definite system which we know to-day during those centuries ; the history of some parts of the common law—notably mercantile law, maritime law, and the law of evidence—which then assumed their modern form ; and the history of certain other branches of law—such as ecclesiastical law, prize law, and international law—which fall within the sphere of the civilian's practice. To complete the history as it ought to be completed will be a long task ; but I hope to be able to accomplish at least some part of it in the next few years ; and I am the more encouraged to begin this final portion of my task by the manner in which these volumes have been received.

The section on Evidence in this volume owes very much to Professor Wigmore's great treatise ; and I have to thank him for giving me a list of the sections in his book which deal with the history of the subject. I have to thank the Right Hon. Sir Frederick Pollock for permitting me to print in the Appendix "the Circuiteers," together with his father's note thereon, and for letting me see his father's MS., from which this piece was printed in the Law Quarterly Review. I have to thank Messrs. Butterworth for information as to the volume of Hayesiana, from which Crogate's Case and the ballad of John Doe and Richard Roe are taken, and for their permission (so far as they were able to give it) to print these pieces. As before, I have to thank Dr. Hazel, the Principal of Jesus College, Oxford, All Souls Reader in English Law in the University of Oxford, and Reader in Constitutional Law and Legal History in the Inns of Court, for the benefit of his criticism and his help in correcting the proof sheets ; and Mr. Costin, Fellow and Lecturer in History at St. John's College, Oxford, for making the list of statutes.

ALL SOULS COLLEGE
December, 1925

PLAN OF THE HISTORY

CONTENTS

BOOK IV (*continued*)

THE COMMON LAW AND ITS RIVALS

PART II (*continued*)

THE RULES OF LAW

CHAPTER VI

STATUS

CONTENTS

CHAPTER VII

EVIDENCE, PROCEDURE, AND PLEADING

CONTENTS

APPENDIX

LIST OF CASES

xxv

LIST OF STATUTES

xxxi

LIST OF STATUTES

BOOK IV (*Continued*)

(1485-1700)

THE COMMON LAW AND ITS RIVALS

A HISTORY OF ENGLISH LAW

PART II

THE RULES OF LAW (*Continued*)

CHAPTER VI

STATUS

DURING this period the law of status tended to shrink. Certain of the persons, who occupied a peculiar status in the mediæval common law, disappeared as the result of religious, social and industrial changes. Thus, although from some points of view the clergy still hold a peculiar status, it is not so peculiar as it was in the Middle Ages; and the status of the monk and the nun disappeared as the result of the Reformation. We have seen that the villeins disappeared during the course of the sixteenth century;[1] and that their place was taken by hired servants. The Jews had disappeared when they were expelled by Edward I.; and, when they returned, they suffered no disabilities other than those which nonconformity to the established church entailed.[2] At the same time the peculiar course of English political and constitutional history stopped the growth of some of those new forms of status, which were arising in the public law of continental states, and helped to perpetuate many of the mediæval forms of status. Thus the victory of the common law prevented the growth of any system of administrative law, and consequently the formation of the peculiar status of the civil servant; and no legal recognition was given to the status of the soldier till after the Revolution. On the other hand, the continuity of the development of English law made for the retention of such forms of status as those of the outlaw, the person attainted, and the excommunicate; the status of the married woman, of the lunatic, and of the infant were only just beginning to be modified by the growth of the equitable jurisdiction of the Chancellor; and there was very

---

[1] Vol. iii 507-508. [2] Vol. i 46; vol. viii 402 seqq.

little change in the status of the peerage. But the development of the state, and the results of the constitutional controversies of the seventeenth century, produced a considerable development in the law relating to the king. Social developments and commercial expansion helped to produce developments in the law relating to the incorporate person; and both political events and commercial necessities helped to elucidate the position of the British subject and the alien. I shall therefore deal with the history of the law of status during this period under these three heads :—The King; The Incorporate Person; and, The British Subject and the Alien.

§ I. THE KING

In the first Part of this Book I have given an account of those constitutional changes, which have given to the king and his prerogative their position in our modern law. Hence it will only be necessary to recall briefly their salient features, and show how they have given to the prerogative its peculiar features. I shall then say something of the history of the remedies which the law has provided for the subject who has some cause of complaint against the king. We shall see that the history of these remedies has to a very large extent been influenced, firstly, by the development of the law relating to the prerogative; and, secondly, by the development of other branches of English law. Like the legal conception of the prerogative itself, the law relating to these remedies was evolved by the courts, under the pressure of these two sets of influences, with very little interference by the Legislature. The result has been the formation of a body of legal doctrine which, in modern times, was found to be very inadequate for the protection of the subject; and we shall see that its unsatisfactory character has not yet been wholly remedied by the Legislature. This subject, therefore, will fall under the two following heads: The Development of the Legal Conception of the Prerogative; and, Remedies against the Crown.

The Development of the Legal Conception of the Prerogative

We have seen that the Tudors waged war against feudal ideas and institutions; and that, in consequence, the Tudor lawyers formulated a set of doctrines as to the king and his prerogative which were almost the exact contrary of the doctrines which prevailed in the mediæval period.[1] Instead of assigning the royal prerogatives to a natural man, they personified the kingly office. They said that the king was a corporation sole, immortal, omni-

[1] Vol. iii 458-469.

present, infallible.[1] They ascribed all these qualities to the natural person who was on the throne; and, giving a characteristically ingenious turn to the old doctrine that it was almost treasonable to separate the capacity of the king as man from his capacity as king,[2] they denounced, as a "damned and damnable doctrine," any attempt to deny that the present occupant of the throne was invested with these supernatural qualities.[3] But whereas in the Middle Ages this separation of the two capacities of the king had been forbidden, because no one wished to think of the king as being otherwise than a natural man;[4] at the later period it was forbidden, because it was wished to make the king something more than a natural man, by concentrating attention upon, and by attributing to him personally, the supernatural qualities with which his office was invested.[5] Some hoped, no doubt, that the king thus glorified would become an absolute ruler, the visible embodiment of the state. This danger was avoided because the Parliament could rely upon a store of mediæval precedents, which came from a time when the double capacity of the crown was hardly discovered, and taught that the king should be regarded simply as a natural man who, under and by virtue of the law, was the head and representative of the state, but not the sovereign power within it. The parliamentary lawyers agreed that no separation could be drawn between the natural and the politic capacity of the king—but it was for the earlier mediæval reason, and not for the reason given by the Tudor lawyers. It was because they thought of the king as a natural man subject to law, not because they thought of him as the sovereign embodiment of the state.[6] Thus, although the Tudor speculations as to the infallibility, the immortality, and the corporate character of the king remained part of the law, they remained as complimentary mystifications, and not as legal doctrines from which any real deductions were drawn. Though

---

[1] Vol. iv 202-203; see the case of the Duchy of Lancaster (1562) Plowden, 212, 213; Bacon's argument in Calvin's Case, Works vii at pp. 668, 669; Calvin's Case (1608) 7 Co. Rep. at p. 11.
[2] Vol. iii 290, 466-467.   [3] 7 Co. Rep. at p. 11.   [4] Vol. iii 466.
[5] As Bacon put it in his argument in Calvin's Case (Works vii at p. 670), "it is one thing to make things distinct, another thing to make them separable, *aliud est distinctio aliud separatio;* and therefore I assure myself, that those that now use and urge that distinction, do as firmly hold, that the subjection to the king's person and crown are inseparable, though distinct, as I do. And it is true that the poison of the opinion and assertion of Spencer is like the poison of the scorpion, more in the tail than in the body; for it is the inference that they make, which is, that the king may be deposed or removed, that is the treason and disloyalty of that opinion. But, by your leave, the body is never a whit the more wholesome meat for having such a tail belonging to it."
[6] See e.g. Whitelocke's argument in the case of Impositions, 2 S.T. at pp. 482, 483; vol. vi 84 87; cp. Bracton f. 5b, "Ipse autem rex, non debet esse sub homine, sed sub Deo, et sub lege, quia lex facit regem."

the king was said to be a corporation sole, though he was said never to die, it has been necessary to pass many statutes, from the sixteenth century to the twentieth, to make it clear that the king can own property in his private capacity as distinct from his politic capacity, and to prevent "all the wheels of state stopping or even running backwards" on a demise of the crown.[1] It has even been thought that, though "the king never dies," the maxim *actio personalis moritur cum persona* applies to prevent liabilities affecting him from affecting his successor.[2]

It would, however, be a mistake to suppose that the only effect upon modern law of the legal doctrines relating to the prerogative, which were evolved during this period, was the creation of a set of speculative tenets as to the infallibility, the immortality, and the corporate character of the king. In fact, these doctrines so developed the national ideas which, as we have seen, were present in the mediæval conception of the prerogative,[3] that they made the prerogative the executive authority in the modern English state. That that executive authority was proved not to be the sovereign power, and that it was subject to the law, was the result of the constitutional controversies of the seventeenth century. But, as the executive authority in the state, it came into the undisputed possession of a large and indefinite range of powers, which were undreamt of by the mediæval lawyers;[4] and the king thus got his modern position of representative of the state, and the visible and intelligible embodiment of the unity of Great Britain and her Dominions beyond the seas.

But these developments of the prerogative have had one unfortunate result. The combined effect of the doctrines of the Tudor lawyers, which made the king the executive authority in the state and its representative, and of the clash between the doctrines of the parliamentary and prerogative lawyers of the seventeenth century, has been to retard the attainment by the law and the lawyers of a clear conception of the state as a legal entity. The law recognizes, not the state, but only the king—a person still possessed of all those semi-feudal rights which the mediæval common law attributed to him, and still, as in the mediæval common law, possessed, very inconveniently both for himself and for the state, of the ordinary wants and feelings and limitations of a natural man; a person who is the representative of the state, and, as such, possessed of the many mystical qualities attributed to him by the Tudor lawyers; but, though the repre-

[1] Maitland, Collected Papers iii 253, L.Q.R. xvii 135-136.
[2] Tobin v. The Queen (1842) 4 S.T.N.S. at pp. 779-780 *per* Lord Lyndhurst.
[3] Vol. iii 453-469.
[4] See Blackstone's summary, Comm. i 231 seqq.; and cp. Bagehot, English Constitution Introd. xxxviii.

sentative of the state, not the sovereign power within it.[1] If the
Stuart kings and the prerogative lawyers had had their way, king
and state would really have been identified. Our legal thoughts
about the state might have been clearer. We might have been
saved the many strange shifts and circumlocutions and inelegancies
of legal thought and language, to which we have had recourse,
in our endeavours to make our constitutional king stand for our
state[2]—but there would have been no pattern of constitutional
government for the nations of the world.

Remedies against the Crown

This topic is only a part of the larger subject of the king's
prerogative in relation to legal proceedings brought by or against
him.[3] It is a subject, the history of which ought to be completely
written; for no body of law is more historically instructive, by
reason of the many survivals from all periods in the history of the
law of procedure which it contains. But it is too special and
lengthy a subject to be even lightly sketched here. All that I
shall attempt is to give a short historical account of that part
of the subject which is concerned with remedies against the
crown. It is of general constitutional importance; and it affords
an illustration and a commentary on the development of the
constitutional position of the king, and the legal conception of his
prerogative.

Already in the seventeenth century the law, to use Bacon's
picturesque expression, had woven a garland of prerogatives
around the pleadings and proceedings of the king's suits;[4] and

---

[1] Maitland says, Collected Papers iii 253, L.Q.R. xvii 136, "the worst of it is
that we are compelled to introduce into our legal thinking a person whose personality
our law does not formally or explicitly recognize. We cannot get on without the
State, or the Nation, or the Commonwealth, or the Public, or some similar entity,
and yet that is what we are professing to do"; cp. an article by Mr. Harrison Moore,
L.Q.R. xx 351, on the Crown as Corporation; and Salmond, Jurisprudence (2nd ed.)
297-301.

[2] See Maitland, Collected Papers iii 252-267, L.Q.R. xvii 136-144; Maitland
has shown that English law might have avoided many of these difficulties, if it had
regarded the state as a corporation composed of king and subjects, instead of borrowing an analogy from ecclesiastical law, and talking of the king as a corporation sole;
and he thinks that this is the result to which English law would have come, "had not
that foolish parson led it astray," ibid 144; cp. vol. iv 203; but I have tried to suggest that we must take some account of the fact that the idea of the crown as a corporation sole was never properly applied, owing to the constitutional and somewhat
mediæval theories of the common lawyers; the logical outcome of the idea that the
crown is a corporation sole is that the crown is the state; that it remained a corporation with many extraordinary qualities, without becoming co-extensive with the
state, is due to the successful resistance of Parliament and the common law. The
ambiguous position which the crown thus occupied between the old theories and the
new, accounts for the failure of the theory of the corporation sole, and the resulting
confusion.

[3] For the early history see Ehrlich, Vinogradoff, Oxford Studies vol. vi no. xii.

[4] Case de Rege Inconsulto, Works (Ed. Spedding) vii 693; for one of the results
of this fact in helping to give the law officers of the crown their modern position see
vol. vi 466-470.

this learning had become a very special subject.[1]   But, as Maitland
has said, "this garland is not woven all at once, and some of its
flowers were but buds in the days of Henry III."[2]   The history
of the manner in which this particular part of this "garland of
prerogatives" was gradually developed, will give some indication
of the manner in which this branch of the law has been gradually
and continuously elaborated, from the reign of Henry III. to our
own days.

We have seen that it was recognized in Henry III.'s reign
that the king could not be sued in his central courts of law,
because, like any other lord, he could not be sued in his own
courts.[3]   But it was admitted that the king, as the fountain of
justice and equity, could not refuse to redress wrongs when
petitioned to do so by his subjects.[4]   The procedure to be followed
in such cases was, like many other rules of English law, fixed in
outline in Edward I.'s reign.   It became an established rule that
the subject, though he could not sue the king, could bring his
petition of right, which, if acceded to by the king, would enable
the courts to give redress.[5]   But many steps must intervene
before the petition was brought before the courts; and, when it
came before them, infinite delays were possible.[6]   We have seen
that the procedure of the courts in those days, and especially the
procedure in the real actions, was noted for its technicality and its
dilatoriness;[7] and, as petitions of right were usually brought for
some grievance which would have been the subject of a real
action, if relief had been sought against anyone except the king,
the procedure on a petition of right, when it came before the
courts, tended to follow the example of these actions.   The result
was that the Legislature intervened, and in Edward III.'s reign
gave new facilities to aggrieved subjects in certain common cases,
by improving the remedy of traverse of office, and by introducing
in its later and settled form the remedy of monstrans de droit.[8]
But these two remedies were chiefly useful in the case of a demand
for property which would, if the king had not been a party to the
action, have been the subject of a real action, or in disputes
which turned on the king's rights to the incidents of tenure.
Hence, during the latter part of the seventeenth and eighteenth

[1] "His counsel shall be called to it, who are conversant and exercised in the
learning of his prerogative, wherein common pleaders, be they never so good are
to seek," Bacon, Works vii 693.

[2] P. and M. i 502.

[3] Vol. iii 465. It is for this reason that anyone else, including the queen
consort, could be sued by ordinary action, Y.B. 11 Hy. IV. Pasch. pl. 26; Staunford,
Prerogative f. 25b; but this seems to have been new law at the beginning of the
fifteenth century, Ehrlich, op. cit. 57, 206-209.

[4] Vol. i 352, 355, 401; vol. ii 310, 346-347.

[5] Below 11.

[6] Below 16-17, 22-24.

[7] Vol. iii 624-625; vol. vii 5-7.

[8] Below 24-26.

centuries, they tended, like the real actions, to drop out of use.

It had always been recognized that the petition of right was a far more general remedy, and the only remedy available when these two more specialized remedies failed. The fact that it was not very frequently used had prevented its scope from being very rigidly limited; and the fact that it was simply one of that large genus petition, by which remedies could be sought which were wholly outside anything that could be given by the existing forms of action,[1] made it possible to use it to give, as against the king, the new forms of redress, which the development of English law— and notably the development of the law of contract—was originating. There are signs, in the latter part of the seventeenth century, that it was coming to be thought that the Crown should extend to its subjects those larger measures of redress, which they had against their fellow subjects;[2] and the use of the petition of right for this purpose was sanctioned by the *Bankers' Case*, which was before the Courts between the years 1690-1700.[3] But, during the eighteenth century, there was little further development. In the nineteenth century, however, this remedy began to be developed.[4] But little or nothing had been done to remedy those procedural defects, which had caused it to be rarely used in the Middle Ages and later, till the Legislature intervened, and, by the Petitions of Right Act of 1860,[5] to a very large extent assimilated the procedure to be followed thereon to that of an ordinary action. This Act, however, has in no way changed the law as to when the remedy by petition of right is available.[6] That question depends wholly on decided cases, chiefly of the nineteenth century, which proceeded partly on the somewhat sparse authority as to the scope of a petition of right in earlier days, and partly on deductions from the legal position assumed by the crown and its prerogative as the result of the constitutional conflicts of the seventeenth century, and the elaboration of the results of those conflicts in the eighteenth century.

It follows that the history of the law on this subject falls into certain well-marked periods: (1) The thirteenth century; (2) The fourteenth to the middle of the seventeenth century; (3) The later seventeenth and the eighteenth centuries; and (4) the nineteenth century.

(1) The thirteenth century.

Bracton states quite clearly that the king cannot be sued by ordinary writs in his court, and that the aggrieved subject must

---

[1] Vol. ii 346.
[2] Below 30-32, 38-39.
[3] 14 S.T. 1; below 32-39.
[4] Below 39.
[5] 23, 24 Victoria c. 34.
[6] 23, 24 Victoria c. 34 § 7.

have recourse to a petition;[1] and the same proposition was made the basis of a judgment of the king's court in 1234.[2] This principle was applied, not only to proceedings begun against the king, but also to proceedings begun against a subject in which, for one reason or another, the defendant found it necessary to call on the king to intervene. The commonest of these cases was the case where the king had granted land to X, and Y brought some one of the real actions against X for this land. If X's grantor had been a subject, X could have vouched him to warranty; but he could not vouch the king to warranty, since no writ lay against the king.[3] All he could do was to pray aid of the king, by reason of the king's obligations set out in the charter of gift.[4] The court must then suspend the proceedings till the king's pleasure was known; and the same course was pursued in the case of proceedings brought against the king's servants for acts done in the king's name.[5]

But we have seen that it was well recognized in the thirteenth century and later that the king was subject to the law; and that, though ordinary writs did not lie against him in his court, he was morally bound to do the same justice to his subjects as they could be compelled to do to one another.[6] Indeed, as we have seen, there were many, including perhaps Bracton, who thought that the highest court of the realm—the assembly of the baronage— ought to have jurisdiction over him.[7] But the methods by which the king could be approached were as yet very informal;[8] and it is clear that, at a time when the competence of the courts of law was only vaguely defined, when the King's Bench, and the Council were not as yet clearly separated,[9] a request or petition for justice to the king, sent for consideration to a court, which might be regarded either as King's Bench or Council, would somewhat

---

[1] "Si autem ab eo petatur (cum breve non currat contra ipsum) locus erit supplicationi quod factum suum corrigat et emendet," f. 5b; "contra ipsum non habebitur remedium per assisam imo tantum locus erit supplicationi," f. 171b; P. and M. i 501.

[2] Bracton's Note Book, Case 1108.

[3] "Nullus vocatus ad warantum de aliqua terra teneatur respondere de warantya sine summonitione per breve Dom. Regis vel per preceptum justiciariorum suorum, et Dom. Rex non potest summoneri nec preceptum sumere ab aliquo cum non habeat superiorem se in regno suo," ibid.

[4] "Poterit etiam ipse rex inter alios ad warrantiam obligari rationibus supradictis, sed tamen non potest vocari sicut vocantur privatæ personæ, quia summoneri non potest per breve, et ideo dicere poterit ille cui rex warrantizare debeat, cum quadam curialitate, sic: quod sine rege respondere non poterit eo quod habet chartam suam de donatione vel confirmatione, per quam, si amitteret, rex ei teneretur ad excambium," Ibid f. 382b.

[5] P. and M. i 501 and references cited in n. 5; see also the case de Rege Inconsulto, Bacon, Works vii 695-696, 700-701.

[6] Vol. ii 253-254, 435.   [7] Ibid 255.
[8] Ehrlich, op. cit. 26, 33-36.   [9] Vol. i 209-211.

easily assume some of the characteristics of an ordinary action.[1]
As yet the line could not be so clearly drawn as in later law ; and
so, though it was well recognized that the king could not be
brought into court by a writ of summons, litigants would sometimes
vouch the king to warranty as if he were a common person.[2]
Indeed, as late as 1293, a reporter thought it worth while to note
that the king cannot be vouched to warranty.[3]

But the victory of Evesham, and the constitutional settlement
made by Edward I., had thrown into the background the revolutionary views of those who held that it was lawful to constrain the
king ;[4] and the legal changes which had defined more clearly the
competence of courts, and had settled the principles of many
branches of English law, tended to separate more clearly the
proceedings begun against the king by petition, from proceedings
begun against a common person by writ. We have seen, too,
that there had been a good deal of regulation of the multifarious
mass of petitions which were presented to the king, or to the
king and Parliament.[5]   It is not surprising, therefore, to find that,
in the eyes of the lawyers, this procedure for obtaining redress
against the king by petition was becoming a more settled and
regular procedure, and that it was developing characteristics very
different from those of an ordinary action.   In 1307 Passeley, in
the course of an argument before the court of Common Pleas,
said, "in old times every writ, whether of right or of possession
lay well against the king, and nothing is now changed except that
one must now sue against him by bill, where formerly one sued by
writ ";[6] and no one apparently contradicted this surprising statement.   Probably the points which Passeley wished to emphasize
were, firstly, the fact that the procedure by bill or petition was
now recognized as the regular method by which the subject must
proceed, if he had that kind of grievance against the king which,
as against a subject, was remediable by an ordinary writ; and,
secondly, the fact that the relief given on such a petition was
given under conditions similar to those applicable to proceedings
begun by ordinary writ.   If these were the two points which he
meant to emphasize, he in fact put his finger on two features in

---

[1] See a case of 1235 in which William of Longsword was plaintiff, cited Ehrlich,
op. cit. 36-37.

[2] " When the king appears as a plaintiff or submits to be treated as a defendant
the difference between him and a private person is less marked in the thirteenth
century than it is in later times. When he is a plaintiff he will often employ one of
the ordinary writs. A defendant instead of using what even in Bracton's day was
becoming the proper formula ' I cannot answer without the king ' will sometimes
boldly say ' I vouch the king to warranty,' " P. and M. i 501-502, citing Bracton's
Note Book, Case 1183; and see ibid, cases 1141 and 1136 cited Ehrlich, op. cit. 38
n. 1.

[3] Y.B. 21-22 Ed. I. (R.S.) 287.   [4] Vol. ii 255.
[5] Vol. i 354-355, 401-402.   [6] Y.B. 33-35 Ed. I. (R.S.) 470.

the subject's remedy against the crown which have ever since characterized it. We shall see that, from this period onwards, the remedy by petition was recognized as the general and normal remedy; and that this particular variety of petition, which came to be known as a petition of right, is differentiated from other petitions by the fact that, in respect of the conditions under which substantive relief can be got by its means, it follows the nature of the ordinary remedies provided by law.

But we have seen that there was no foundation for the view that in the good old days writs lay against the king.[1] Though the line between the procedure by petition and the procedure by writ may not have been so well defined as it had become in Edward I.'s reign, it seems quite certain that there was never a time when writs lay against the king. Passeley was careful, as Maitland says, "to leave the ancient times indefinite"; and "probably he was referring to the good old days of St. Edward, and, like Blackstone after him, saw 'our Saxon ancestors' impleading each other by writs of entry."[2] But it would seem that his remark gave rise to those tales, which appear in the Year Books of Edward III., that, down to Edward I.'s reign, the king was sued like an ordinary person.[3] These tales were repudiated both by Brooke[4] and Staunford.[5] They were, as Bacon called them, "old fables."[6]

Some of the leading principles, then, of the law on this subject were fixed by the end of the thirteenth century. We must now turn to the development of this remedy by petition, and the evolution of other remedies designed to correct some of its defects, which took place in the period between the beginning of the fourteenth and the middle of the seventeenth centuries.

(2) The fourteenth to the middle of the seventeenth century.

It is during this period that the nature of a petition of right is fixed, that some indications of its sphere of action begin to appear,

---

[1] Apart from the evidence from Bracton, above 9-10, the negative evidence is, as Maitland says, overwhelming—"if Henry III. had been capable of being sued he would have passed his life as a defendant. . . . Plea rolls from his reign there are plenty, and in the seventeenth century they were jealously scanned by eyes which did not look kindly upon kings. Where are the records of cases in which King Henry issued writs against himself?" P. and M. i 501.

[2] Ibid 500.

[3] Y.BB. 22 Ed. III. Hil. pl. 25; 24 Ed. III. Trin. pl. 40; 43 Ed. III. Mich. pl. 12; in Y.B. 24 Ed. III. Trin pl. 40 Wilby said, "J'ay view jadis tiel brief *Praecipe Henrico Regi Angliae, etc.*, in lieu de que est ore don peticion pur son Prerogative"; if he really saw such a writ it must have been, as Maitland says, "some joke, some forgery, or possibly some relic of the Barons' War"; cp. Ehrlich, op. cit. 24-25.

[4] "Quere de tyel briefe, car videtur quod numquam fuit lex, car le roye ne poet escrier ne contermaunde luy mesme," Bro. Ab. *Peticion* pl. 12.

[5] "I think the law was never so for that a man should have any such action against the king," Prerogative f. 42a; for authority he cites Bracton.

[6] Case de Rege Inconsulto, Works vii 694.

and that the procedure to be pursued by the suppliant is ascertained. As the result of these developments its defects began to be obvious; and, in consequence of these defects, we get the rise of certain other remedies which, because they were comparatively speedy, rendered a recourse to a petition of right unnecessary in a large class of cases. This development had two important results. In the first place, it gave rise to a certain number of rules of a very technical kind as to when it was and when it was not necessary to have recourse to a petition of right; and, in the second place, the comparatively small use made of the petition of right prevented any very accurate definition of its sphere of action —a fact which will have, as we shall see, very important effects upon its future history. The history, therefore, of this branch of the law during this period can be grouped under the three following heads :—The evolution of the petition of right; the rise of other remedies against the crown; and, the relation of the petition of right to these other remedies.

The evolution of the petition of right.

The petition of right is one species of that large genus "bill" or petition, so many of which were presented in the fourteenth century to king, Parliament, and Council. We have seen that, throughout the fourteenth century, many regulations were made for dealing with the flood of petitions which poured in from all sides.[1] We have seen, too, that, as the various institutions of government became more definitely organized, and as their spheres of action became better defined, these petitions fell naturally into distinct groups. There were the bills or petitions presented to Parliament, which will fall wholly within the competence of Parliament, and will emerge, if assented to by both Houses and the king, as Acts of Parliament.[2] There are the bills or petitions presented to the Council, or to the chancellor, or to the chancellor and Council, the hearing of which will give to the Council and Chancellor a special jurisdiction of an equitable kind.[3] There are the bills or petitions presented to the king which ask for some grace or favour. It is to this last group that the petition of right belongs;[4] and it is only gradually that it becomes a distinct species in that group.

A petition which asks the king for some grace or favour may contain any kind of request; and in fact the prayers of these petitions are most various. But it is clear that a distinction can be drawn between petitions which ask for something which the suppliant could claim as a right, if the claim were made against

[1] Vol. i 354-555, 401-402.
[2] Vol. ii 340, 437-440.
[3] Vol. i 401-404.
[4] Clode, Petition of Right 16, 17.

any one but the king, and petitions which ask only for some favour to which he could have no legal claim. Both these classes of petitions are, it is true, petitions of grace; for in both cases it is in the absolute discretion of the king to grant or not to grant the prayer of the petition. And the fact that both these classes of petitions were petitions of grace, and were treated in earlier days in a somewhat similar way, has caused many difficulties when attempts have been made to use these early petitions to throw light upon modern problems connected with petitions of right. It has always been possible to deny or explain away the authority of these earlier cases by saying that they were mere petitions of grace.[1] But, as a matter of fact, it is probably impossible to say whether certain specimens were petitions of grace or of right, because this distinction had not clearly emerged much before the end of the fifteenth century. But we shall see that, though this difficulty as to the character of certain of these earlier petitions has made the law vague and doubtful, it has not been without a compensating advantage. It has given to the sphere of action of the petition of right a capacity for expansion, which a more rigid definition of the law would have denied to it.[2] Here, as in other branches of our constitutional law, haziness and obscurity have spelt flexibility.

It was during the fourteenth and fifteenth centuries that this distinction between petitions of grace pure and simple, and that variety of these petitions which became petitions of right, was being evolved. It was coming to be recognized that some of these petitions asked for something which could be described as the legal right of the party, while others asked simply for some favour. This distinction was emerging in the fourteenth century;[3] and two cases, one of the early fifteenth and the other of the early sixteenth century, indicate the manner in which it was taking its technical shape. In a Year Book of 1408[4] it was alleged that the king had recovered the presentation of a church against the Prior of T., but that the Prior had had no notice of the proceedings, and had never been summoned to defend his right. Counsel was told that his only remedy was to sue by petition to the king; but he was advised to pray in his petition that the judges should at once proceed to examine the truth of his allegations, as they could then proceed immediately. If he merely prayed that right be done, then he would be obliged to get a commission to examine the facts by the inquest of a jury, and a further writ out of the Chancery to take action on the

[1] Below 36-37.
[3] Ehrlich, op. cit. 118-123.
[2] Below 37-39.
[4] Y.B. 10 Hy. IV. Mich. pl. 8.

findings of the commission.[1] Clearly a petition which asked simply that right be done, is being differentiated from a petition asking for a particular favour, by the difference of the procedure consequent on the granting of the petition; and this difference of procedure is founded on the idea that, if a petitioner asks simply for his "droit" or legal right, he must establish that legal right in a manner similar to that in which it must be established in an ordinary action.[2] In 1509 the same difference was clearly put by Fineux, C.J.[3] To a petition of right there must always be a reply—"let right be done," and the proceedings, if the petition is successful, will end in a judgment "quod manus domini regis amoveantur." But to a petition of grace there is merely an assent or a refusal, and no judgment, "because the ordinary course of the common law is not pursued." It followed that, though the king could rightfully refuse to grant a petition of grace, he could not rightfully refuse to do what justice required when judgment had been got on a petition of right.[4] Later in the century the results of this evolution appear in Staunford's definition.[5] "Peticion is al the remedy the subject hath when the king seiseth his land or taketh away his goods from him, havinge no title *by ordre of his lawes* so to do. . . And therefore is his peticion called a peticion of right because of the right the subject hath against the king, *by the ordre of his lawes*, to the thing he sueth for."

Thus the petition of right was differentiated from a petition of grace. But even in the sixteenth century, when it had become

---

[1] " Si vous sues per peticion, et faits vostre conclusion en vostre petition, que le Roy nous commaunda de proceder al examination, nous poyames bien sans briefe hors del Chancery, et si vous concludes generalment, que il vous face droit, andonques vous deves aver briefe hors del Chancery, et uncore avant que vous eyes le briefe, vostre droit covient estre trove per enquest per vertue d'un Commission," *per* Tirwhit, J.

[2] " Sometime billes of peticion be endorsed and sent into the kynges benche or common place and not into the Chancery, and that groweth upon a special conclusion in his peticion, and a special endorsement upon the same, for the general conclusion is *que le roy luy face droit et reason*, which is as much as if he had prayed restitucion of that that he sueth for: And there upon such a general conclusion the endorsement is *Soit droit fait als parties* which ever is delivered unto the Chancellor as is declared," Staunford, Prerogative f. 73a ; it is no doubt true, as Clode, op. cit. 24-25 says, that a subject had no strict right against the crown, if by right is meant right enforcible by action ; but, as we can see from Bracton and the Y.BB., what the lawyers meant by right was a claim which would have been a right, if it existed against anyone but the king; cp. Ehrlich, op. cit. 97-98, 186-188.

[3] Conyngesby and Mallom v. R. Keilway 154 at p. 158.

[4] " Le peticion de droit require toutz foits un respons, mes un peticion de grace est semble a un special livery, le queux poient este sue per common bil, et si le Roy graunt a eux lour desire et effect de lour bil, uncore ils naveront james ascun maner de judgment, pur ceo que ils ne pursuant l'ordre ne le cours del common ley, et pur cest cause le Roy poit eux denier droiturelment, mes sur peticion de droit et general livery, nemy," ibid ; I take general and special livery to mean a general or a special endorsement.

[5] Prerogative f. 72b.

fairly well defined, there were still abundant traces of the time
when petitions to king, Council and Parliament were not distinguished, and of the time when petitions of grace to the king
were not clearly distinguished from petitions of right. Thus
Staunford tells us[1] that these petitions of right could be presented
either to Parliament or to the king; and that they could, if
presented to Parliament, either "be enacted and passe as an act
of parlement, or els to be ordered in like manner as a peticion
that is sued out of the parlement." Similarly, if a petition was
presented to the king it could either be endorsed generally—let
right be done, or specially; and in the latter case the procedure to
be followed must be according to the endorsement.[2] Clearly,
petitions so treated approximate, as Fineux, C.J., had pointed out,[3]
to petitions of grace—though, as we shall see,[4] they could still be
treated as petitions of right by Lord Somers in the *Bankers' Case*.[5]
But, in spite of these survivals, it is clear that the petition of right
had assumed the character of a definite legal remedy against the
crown. As was the case with other leading legal distinctions, it
was technically worked out through the procedure applicable to
these two classes of petitions to the king; and this differentiation,
thus worked out through the law of procedure, resulted in the
evolution of rules as to the sphere within which the petition of
right was applicable. Let us glance briefly at the manner in
which these two sets of results were achieved.

(i) We have seen that, at the beginning of the fourteenth
century, the usual procedure on a petition was to endorse on it
a short note, which referred the petitioner to that one of the
existing tribunals which was competent to deal with his case.[6]
But, if there was no competent tribunal, this course could not be
followed. Now this was generally the case with all petitions to
the king or Parliament which asked for some favour from the
king; and we have seen that it was into this class that the
petitions, which ultimately became petitions of right, fell.[7] In
this case, therefore, it was necessary to create a special body to
look into the facts. Therefore, when the petition had been
endorsed, "let right be done," a special commission was issued
by the Chancery to investigate the case.[8] When the commission

---

[1] Prerogative f. 72b; cp. Coke, Fourth Instit. 11—"of Petitions in Parliament
some be of right, some of grace, and some mixt of both"; for an illustration of a
petition of right presented to Parliament see 33 Ass. pl. 10.

[2] Staunford, Prerogative, f. 73a, cited above 15 n. 2.

[3] Above 15 n. 4.   [4] Below 37.

[5] (1700) 14 S.T. at pp. 58-60.   [6] Vol. ii 419.   [7] Above 13.

[8] See Clode, op. cit. 9-13; 37 Ass. pl. 11; Staunford, Prerogative 72b, 73; for
some illustrations of fourteenth-century procedure see Ehrlich, op. cit. 188-200; if
the commission found for the king, the party could either apply for a new commission
or sue out a fresh petition, Y.B. 3 Hy. VII. Mich. pl. 19.

made its return to the Chancery, it was generally found to involve the determination of many questions of law, either between the king and the petitioner, or between the petitioner and the king's grantees. If the question was between the king and the petitioner, the king was then called on to plead to the questions of law involved; and the matter was then generally either heard on the common law side of the Chancery, or sent into the King's Bench to be tried.[1] If the title of a grantee of the king was involved, such grantee must be summoned by writ of scire facias to attend and plead.[2] If the case was determined in favour of the petitioner, he had judgment of "amoveas manus": if it was determined against him, he had judgment "nil capiat."[3]

This procedure seems to have been evolved during the mediæval period.[4] It was in full working order long before Staunford wrote; and it lasted till 1860.[5] It is clear that it emphasized the fact that the title of the applicant to relief depended upon the question whether he could establish a right which the law would recognize. That meant, in effect, that he must prove that he was suffering from a wrong which, if the case were between subject and subject, could be remedied by some one of the ordinary writs. Obviously this characteristic of the petition of right has a considerable bearing upon the question of the sphere within which it was applicable.

(ii) We have seen that in the mediæval common law the land law was by far the most important branch of the law.[6] We have seen too that it covered a very much larger field than that covered by the land law at the present day. Many objects which would now be effected by the making of a contract, and many wrongs which would now be redressible by an action in tort, were attracted to the law of property, and were redressible by real actions. For instance, where we should make a contract to pay a sum of money, the men of the Middle Ages granted an annuity or a corody;[7] and where we should bring an action on the case for a nuisance, the men of the Middle Ages would bring an assize of nuisance, or an assize of novel disseisin, or a quod permittat.[8] Now it is quite clear that the main use of the

[1] Staunford, op. cit. f. 77b; for the common law side of the Chancery see vol. i 452-453; if the trial involved the summoning of a jury it must be tried in the king's bench, Staunford, loc. cit.

[2] "It is a general rule that if the king have graunted the wardship of the landes over for any term certain, or graunted any other certain estate in the landes, he that sueth his peticion, *Monstraunce de droit*, or traverse, must sue a *Scire facias* against the king's patentee in such case," Staunford, op. cit. f. 76b; so also ibid f. 73b; the Sadlers' Case (1588) 4 Co. Rep. at f. 59b; Clode, op. cit. 171.

[3] Ibid 183.   [4] There is a good illustration of its working in 37 Ass. pl. 11.

[5] Clode, op. cit. 18.   [6] Vol. ii 590.

[7] Ibid 355-356; for annuities and corodies see vol. iii 152-153.

[8] For these actions see vol. iii 8-11, 20; see also vol. vii 329, 330, 340.

petition of right in the Middle Ages was to gain redress for wrongs which, if the case had been between subject and subject, would have been redressed by some one of the real actions. The majority of cases were cases in which the king had seized or otherwise got possession of land to which the petitioner was entitled; and many turned on abuses of his rights to the incidents of tenure. But there were also cases in which the king was asked to give compensation to his grantee, who had been evicted in consequence of the successful bringing of an action;[1] or which turned on the petitioner's duty to provide a corody,[2] or on his right to an annuity,[3] a franchise,[4] a rent,[5] or an advowson.[6] Therefore when it is argued, as it has often been argued in the nineteenth century,[7] that in the Middle Ages a petition of right only lay to recover property, it should be remembered that, in the Middle Ages, the law of property covered a far wider field than it covers in modern law; and that the modern distinctions between property, contract, and tort had hardly been arrived at.

Perhaps the best illustration of the difficulties, which have occurred through the non-recognition of this fact, is to be found in the case of Robert de Clifton, which was before the courts in 1325,[8] and the case of Gervais de Clifton, which was before the courts in 1349.[9] In the earlier case the petitioner complained that the wardens of Nottingham Castle had dug trenches and erected certain works on his land, which diverted the waters of the Trent, and caused them to overflow his property; and that turf and other things had been taken from the petitioner's lands to repair the the king's works. He asked for compensation for these wrongs. On the inquiry held to examine the truth of these allegations, it was found that the petitioner had suffered damage to a certain annual amount. The petitioner thereupon sent in a second petition, asking for the grant of the bailiwick of the honour of Peverell in recompense, on which a second commission issued to certify the

---

[1] Y.B. 9 Hy. VI. Pasch. pl. 7; Bro. Ab. *Peticion* pl. 1; Brooke's note is "cesty que est de recover in value vers le roy per cause de garrantie, ou clause de recompensacion avera son cause entre sur son ayde prayer de roye, et donque avera son recovery per peticion et aliter non, quod nota que il ferra peticion de ceo."

[2] Longo Quinto 118; and see another case cited by Choke, J., at p. 122.

[3] See a case of 18 Ed. I., cited from Ryley 52, by Lord Somers in the Bankers' Case 14 S.T. at p. 82.

[4] Coke, Second Instit. 497.

[5] Y.B. 9 Hy. IV. Mich. pl. 17 *per* Hankford, J.; Wicks and Dennis's Case (1590) 1 Leo. at p. 191.

[6] Y.BB. 2 Hy. IV. Hil. pl. 26 = Bro. Ab. *Peticion* pl. 5; 43 Ass. pl. 21 = Bro. Ab. *Peticion* pl. 18.

[7] See Thomas v. the Queen (1874) L.R. 10 Q.B. at p. 35; Clode, op. cit. 116 seqq.

[8] R.P. i 416-417 (18 Ed. II. no. 3); Ehrlich, op. cit. 123-124.

[9] Y.B. 22 Ed. III. Pasch. pl. 12; Ehrlich, op. cit. 124-126, 264-265.

king.[1] In the later case there was a similar allegation that the petitioner's lands had been inundated by the action of the wardens of Nottingham Castle. The commission appointed to inquire into the facts found that they were true. A second petition then prayed for restitution of his losses and redress; and a direction was given that it and the findings of the commission should be sent to the King's Bench. It was sent thither; but the case went off on a point of form, and nothing further was heard of it. These cases were not unnaturally adduced in the cases of *Viscount Canterbury v. the King*[2] and of *Tobin v. the Queen*,[3] to prove that a petition of right lay for a tort. But, in the case of *Tobin v. the Queen*, the court came to the very proper conclusion that the gist of the matter in *Gervais de Clifton's Case*, was the misuser or the wrongful assertion of an easement which had caused damage. It was, in other words, an encroachment on the petitioner's property, for which a real action could have been brought.[4] But, as I have already pointed out, these and other mediæval cases do prove that it would be wrong to say that a petition of right lay only for the recovery of property, if we use this expression in its comparatively narrow modern sense. No doubt the pleadings assume the form of a proprietary action; but these proprietary actions then covered a far wider field than such actions cover at the present day; and, as we shall see, we must not lose sight of this fact when we come to consider the question whether the extensions made in the scope of the remedy in later law can be technically justified.[5]

In addition to the wide field of wrongs redressible by the real actions a petition would lie for a chattel interest in land;[6] and, according to the better opinion, for chattels personal.[7] But it was always recognized that it would never lie for a pure tort. The

---

[1] "Por ceo que ceste chose touche si hautement le Roi, et la dite enqueste n'est que de office, soient asquns Grantz du Conseil le Roi assigne de surver, enquere, et certifier le Roi," R.P. i 417 (18 Ed. III. no. 3); see Tobin v. R. (1864) 16 C.B.N.S. at pp. 363-365.

[2] (1843) 4 S.T.N.S. 767.   [3] (1864) 16 C.B.N.S. 310.

[4] "The statement shews a dispute between the owners of a dominant and servient tenement in respect of the easement of bringing water to a mill. The petition seems to admit a right to the easement, but complains of an excess in the exercise of the right, whereby the lands of the suppliant had been drowned (or inundated) and prays a restitution of his damages. . . . The report is not, as we read it, a precedent for a claim of damages for a wrong, but a suit to try a right. . . . In each case (i.e. in the cases of Robert and Gervais de Clifton) the petition is for relief from the exaction of a servitude in excess beyond the right of the dominant tenant. Each is in effect a petition that the king would remove his hand from the property of the servient tenant, to the extent of the excess," ibid at pp. 363, 365 *per* Erle, C.J.

[5] Below 41-42.

[6] 37 Ass. pl. 11; Y.B. 7 Hy. VII. Pasch. pl. 2 (p. 11) *per* Brian, C.J.; Bro. Ab. *Peticion* pl. 2.

[7] This was asserted by the court in Y.B. 34 Hy. VI. Trin. pl. 18 (p. 51); Staunford, Prerogative ff. 75b, 76a; *contra per* Hussey, C.J., and Catesby, J., in Y.B. 1 Hy. VII. Mich. pl. 3—"Peticion al Common Ley n'est de chatel, car petition ne gist sinon de franktenement al moins."

idea that the king could not be sued if he did wrong,[1] so that if wrong was done the agent who did it was alone liable, was coming to be recognized at the end of the fifteenth century;[2] and it developed, in the sixteenth century, into the theory that the king could do no wrong.[3]   On the other hand, if the tort consisted in a disseisin or dispossession, it was by no means clear that it was not redressible by petition of right.   Staunford, following the Year Books of Henry IV.[4] and Edward IV.[5] asserts that a disseisin by the king was thus redressible while the lands were in the king's hands, and that an assize lay against any person to whom he conveyed them;[6] and we shall see that there is some reason to think that this rule applied also to the case where the king dispossessed another of his chattels.[7]   It is clear, too, that there is no instance in the Middle Ages of a petition of right for breach of contract. But that does not mean that petitioners had no alternative redress for grievances which, at the present day, would be regarded as breaches of contract.   We have seen that a petition lay for omission to pay an annuity or a corody, because such a proceeding was regarded as a proceeding to recover an incorporeal thing; and that judgment could be given against the king to give a recompense, if he had failed in his duty to warrant the title of his grantee.[8]   It was said also by the court in 1456 that, if the king had got judgment on a debt, and it then appeared that the debt had been pardoned, petition of right would lie to recover it;[9] and, according to Brooke, it was said in 1473 that, if the king grants a rent out of his manor, though the manor is not charged, the king is personally liable, and this personal liability can be enforced by

[1] See Y.B. 1 Hy. VII. Mich. pl. 5 *per* Hussey, C.J., cited vol. iii 388 n. 5.
[2] Ibid; cp. vol. ii 449.   [3] Vol. iv 202-203; above 4-5.
[4] Y.B. 9 Hy. IV. Mich pl. 17 *per* Gascoigne, C.J.
[5] " Per le comen ley, et uncore a cest jour, si le Roy moy disseisit, ou moy ouste ou entre sur moy, pur ce que en le ley il ne poit moy disseiser, ne il ne serra appelle disseisor, uncore que il n'ad nul title per office ne record mes solement per le entre, uncore jeo suis mis a peticion a Roy, mes en meme cel case lou le Roy entre sur moy sans title et enfeoffe un auter per patent, jeo la puis entrer sur luy, ou per le Stat. de E. 3 un home avera assize de novel disseisin en cel cas," Y.B. 4 Ed. IV. Mich. pl. 3; see also Y.B. 4 Ed. IV. Mich. pl. 1 (p. 22).
[6] " When his highness seiseth by his absolute power contrary to the order of his laws, although I have no remedy against him for it, but I peticion for the dignities sake of his person, yet when the cause is removed and a common person hath the possession, then is myne assize revived, for now the patentee entereth by his own wrong and intrusion, and not by any tytle that the king giveth him, for the king had never tytle nor possession to give in that case," op. cit. f. 74b.
[7] Below 42.   [8] Above 18.
[9] Y.B. 34 Hy. VI. Trin. pl. 18 *per* Danby, J.; Fitz. Ab. *Peticion* pl. 8 thus abridges the case: "nota par touts les Justices que home puit aver peticion de droit de reaver ses biens et chateux si come l'eschetour seisit biens virtute officii, et accompt pur eux en l'eschekar, ou ascun que est utlay, reverse son utlagarie et l'eschetour ad accoumpt de ces biens, en tiels cases home sue par peticion et aver remedy, et le roy dirra soit droit fait as parties en dett etc."

petition.[1] It seems to be fairly obvious from these cases that the fact that the form of the judgment in favour of a petitioner was "amoveas manus," was not considered to restrict the scope of the petition to the restoration of property. It is not till the nineteenth century that this contention was put forward to justify the restriction of the competence of the petition of right.[2]

It would seem to follow that a petition of right would lie against the king in circumstances which, in modern law, would be considered to give a cause of action in contract. Undoubtedly there is no authority for saying that a petition of right would lie for breach of contract as such. But this is partly due to the fact that the law of contract was not yet fully developed, and partly to the fact that petitioners had alternative remedies. We have seen that in certain cases as between subject and subject a real action for an incorporeal thing would serve ; and, in the case of ordinary money claims, a petition to the king for a writ of liberate, ordering the Exchequer to pay, or for a direction that the barons of the Exchequer should hear the petitioner's claim, was a far easier and more expeditious remedy.[3]

No doubt the chief use made of the petition of right in the Middle Ages was the redress of grievances which, as between subject and subject, would have been redressed by some one of the real actions ; and it is possible that, owing to the number of cases of this kind, the competence of the petition might have been limited to this class of cases. We have seen that there is a dictum in Henry VII.'s reign which points in this direction.[4] But it was never so limited. It was never forgotten that such a petition was a petition of right, that is a petition on which a subject was entitled to succeed if he could show a good legal claim. But, obviously, the circumstances under which a subject can show a good legal claim change with changes in the law, so that, if this

[1] " Nota fuit dit que ou le roy graunt rent hors de son mannor, le mannor n'est charge, mes le person le roy per peticion, ratio videtur eo quod assisa ne gist vers le roy," Bro. Ab. *Peticion* pl. 29 ; for this Y.B. 13 Ed. IV. 6 is cited, but nothing of this kind appears in the printed Y.B.

[2] See Thomas v. the Queen (1874) L.R. 10 Q.B. at p. 35 ; the argument had, however, been used by Lord Somers in a similar way to restrict the competence of a monstrans de droit, see 14 S.T. at p. 80, and this may have suggested the argument in Thomas v. the Queen ; it may be noted that the Articuli super Cartas, 28 Edward I. c. 19, and the statute De Escheatoribus, 29 Edward I., provided that, on a judgment of amoveas manus, the escheator must restore the mesne profits of the lands ; this rule was applied in all cases of petition of right and monstrans de droit, Coke, Second Instit. 572 ; but it did not apply if the money had got into the king's hands, ibid ; Ehrlich, op. cit. 138-139 ; the Bankers' Case (1700) 14 S.T. at p. 71 ; the rule thus applied to property in the hands of the royal officials, shows that the phrase " amoveas manus " must not be taken too strictly in the case either of petition of right or monstrans de droit—it clearly covered a duty to account for money received.

[3] Clode, op. cit. 20-22, 123-125 ; Ehrlich, op. cit. 55, 79, 80, 81, 162 ; see the case of Fraunceys (1328) ibid 121-123 ; below 35.

[4] Above 19 n. 7.

idea is adhered to, it will give an elasticity to the competence of
a petition of right, which will make it a useful remedy at all
periods in the history of the law. That this idea was adhered to
is perhaps due, to some extent, to the fact that, in the course of
the fourteenth century, this remedy of petition was to a large
extent superseded by the growth of alternative remedies. It
became an occasional remedy to be followed when no other remedy
was available. The result was that the circumstances under which
it could be brought never came to be defined with sufficient accuracy to obscure the principle that it ought to lie whenever the
subject could show a legal right to redress.[1]

The rise of other remedies against the crown.

The reason for the rise of these other remedies against the
crown was the great procedural defects of the petition of right.
These procedural defects can, I think, be grouped under four main
heads. In the first place, there was a lengthy preliminary procedure before the legal question at issue could be brought before
the court. The petition must be endorsed. A commission must
issue to take an inquest to find the facts.[2] If the facts were not
found satisfactorily, a second commission might issue to find them
again.[3] If they were found satisfactorily, it was sometimes necessary to put in a second petition to stir up the crown to take the
next step of answering the petitioner's plea, and coming to an
issue, which could be sent to the King's Bench for trial;[4] and in
all cases begun by petition the crown could delay the petitioner
by instituting a search for records which would support his title.[5]
In the second place, that "garland of prerogatives" in "the pleadings and proceedings of the king's suits," placed a very heavy
burden on the petitioner. "Note," says Brooke,[6] "that in a petition all conveyances and acts which give possession to the king
ought to be expressly stated, and in it the king ought to be informed of all his titles, and that in certain, and not generally, as
by saying that diverse persons were seised or the like, and otherwise the petition is worthless." When this fence had been suc-

---

[1] " Thus have I opened and declared the manner of suing a peticion, but to declare specially when it lieth and when not, it were a long matter to entreat of. But
generally and by general rules a man may briefly declare it, that is to say, in all
cases where a party hath a right against the king, and yet no traverse or *Monstrans
de droit* will serve, then is he driven to his peticion," Staunford, op. cit. f. 74a.

[2] Above 16-17.   [3] Above 16 n. 8, 18.

[4] See the case of Robert de Clifton, above 18.

[5] See Y.B. 24 Ed. III. Mich. pl. 69 for a search ordered by the king; in Y.B.
9 Ed. IV. Hil. pl. 13 the question when a search could be granted was discussed, and
Spilman at p. 52 said that, if a man " sue per peticion le nature est d'aver serch,
come en breve de droit d'aver ession *de malo lecto* et auters delayes, mes en ce nature
de monstrans de droit serch n'est pas bon, car il n'est pas le nature d'icel "; Staunford, op. cit. ff. 73b, 74a.

[6] Ab. *Peticion*, pl. 21.

cessfully surmounted, the petitioner was further handicapped by the fact that the king had many advantages in pleading which he had not. "The king," says Bacon,[1] "shall be informed of all his adversary's titles; the king's plea cannot be double, he may make as many titles as he will; the king's demurrer is not peremptory; he may waive it and join issue, and go back from law to fact :— with infinite others."[2] At any time he could stop the proceedings by the issue of a writ rege inconsulto;[3] and the judges could not then proceed without an order from the king.[4] Indeed, it would seem that in any litigation in which it appeared that the king's interests were involved, though only indirectly, the judges would stay the proceedings till they got an order to go on.[5] In the third place, when the petition of right turned, as was usually the case, upon a complaint redressible by real action, all the causes which made these actions so dilatory applied to these proceedings.[6] In the fourth place, it was not sufficient for the petitioner merely to show that the king had no right, unless he could prove that he was entitled. It would seem, therefore, that the rule that a demandant could recover if he could show a better right than the tenant,[7] did not apply to the king.[8] To recover against the king an absolute right must be shown—a rule which, as we have seen, was not applied as between subject and subject till much later.[9] It is not surprising, therefore, that the lawyers should compare the procedure by petition of right to a writ of right.[10] It depended

[1] Case de Rege Inconsulto, Works vii 693-694 ; cp. Staunford, op. cit. f. 65a.

[2] As an example of these others we may take what was said by Sottell *arg.* in Y.B. 9. Ed. IV. Hil. pl. 14 (p. 52), " si jeo sue per peticion al Roy, et issue est prise enter le roy et moy, et est trove ove moy, le Roy serra conclude a touts jours a claimer per ascuns des points contenues en le peticion, mes s'il ad auter title que n'est compris, il ne serra conclude per cel, car le jugement est *salvo jure regis etc.*, mes s'il soit trove encontre moy, jeo serra conclude de touts maners de titles devant, car cest peticion est mon breve de droit."

[3] Case de Rege Inconsulto, Bacon, Works vii 701, 703.

[4] See e.g. 37 Ass. pl. 11, where the issue of the writ procedendo is stated in the report.

[5] Y.BB. 15 Ed. III. (R.S.) 142—Hillary, C.J., says he has had an order to proceed; ibid 198—direction to sue to the king as an interest of his lessee was involved; ibid 280—" so long as the tenements are in the king's hand, we will not hear the plea without the king's special command," *per* Hillary, C.J.; 18 Ed. III. (R.S.) 44-46.

[6] Vol. iii 8, 11; vol. vii 5-7.   [7] Vol. iii 89-90.

[8] Thus in Y.B. 18 Ed. III. (R.S.) 46 it was unsuccessfully argued that an office, which found that the ancestor of the petitioner died seised of no lands, was sufficient to show title against the king; similarly in Y.B. 24 Ed. III. Trin. pl. 40, where three offices had found that the petitioner held no land by knight-service of the king. Thorp *arg.* said, "cel n'est nient pluis pur vous que pur moy, car per eux n'est pas vostre droit trove"; in 37 Ass. pl. 11 Fulthorpe says, "quant il est trove que nous fuimus ouste sans cause, et le Roy nul droit ad, il est reason que nous sumus restitute," to which Grene replied, "vous n'averez restitution si vous ne purrez monstrer que vous avez droit"; as Staunford says, op. cit. f. 63a, " no man shall traverse the office unless he make himself a title, and if he cannot prove his title to be true, although he be able to prove his traverse to be true, yet this traverse will not serve him."

[9] Vol. vii 62-68, 426-430.

[10] See Y.B. 9 Ed. IV. Hil. pl. 13 cited above 22 n. 5; below 26 and n. 4; for the writ of right see vol. iii 5-8.

essentially on the right of the parties; and it set on foot an inquiry at large into the titles of the king and the petitioner. It resembled it also in its lengthy procedure. Hence, just as between subject and subject there was a demand for a less dilatory remedy, which was met by the creation of the writs of entry,[1] so, as between the king and subject, there was a demand for a less dilatory remedy which was met in a different, but not wholly dissimilar manner.

A very usual way in which the king got the property of his subjects into his hands, was by the holding of an inquest on the death of his tenant, or on the attainder or lunacy of any person whether tenant or not, to inquire what property such persons held. When the inquest found that the person in question was possessed of certain property, the king seized it; and he was then said to be entitled by office found.[2] Now it might well happen that the terms of the office so found did not, if construed properly, entitle the king, or that the facts so found were not true, or that the proof of additional facts would put a different complexion on the matter. In all these cases it might well be that the king seized property to which he was not entitled. What then was the position of the person thus ousted of his property? The answer is that he was generally compelled to resort to the tedious process of a petition of right. But, in one or two cases, it would seem that he might get a more speedy remedy by being allowed to traverse the facts found by the office and show his own right, or, without denying the facts, show that they gave the king no title to seize. Thus, in the case of an office finding that the king was entitled to chattels by attainder or outlawry, he could traverse the facts and show his own right.[3] But he had no such right at common law in the case of land, if the king was found to be entitled to the possession.[4] He could only show, if he could, that the facts as found made in law a title for himself.[5] In the case of land, it was only if the king was

---

[1] Vol. iii 12.

[2] As Maitland has said, Alston's Ed. of Smith, De Republica App. A 149, this term is "an instance of tight compression. An office found is the verdict of an inquest taken *ex officio* by a royal officer for the ascertainment of the king's rights."

[3] "A man is attaynted of treason or felony or outlawed in a personell accyon, and after by office it is founde that he was possessed of a horse or anye other goodes as hys owne proper cattell, where indeede they be the goodes of a straunger, in thys case the sayde straunger shall traverse thys office wyth the kyng," Staunford, op. cit. f. 67a, citing Y.B. 4 Ed. IV. Mich. pl. 1 p. 24; for another case allowed by a statute of 1301 see Ehrlich, op. cit. 74, 75.

[4] Y.BB. 17 Ed. III. (R.S.) 186-188; 4 Ed. IV. Mich. pl. 1.

[5] "If office be found for the king, and in the same office the title or interest of the party be found, then the party grieved might at the common law have his *monstrans de droit*, because his title appears by the same record, whereby the king is entitled," the Sadlers' Case (1588) 4 Co. Rep. at f. 55a; Lord Somers objects to calling this a monstrans de droit, but does not dispute the law laid down, the Bankers' Case (1700) 14 S.T. at pp. 78, 79.

found not to be entitled to take immediate possession, but only to take further proceedings by way of scire facias to get possession,[1] that the facts found could be traversed. That this was the common law on this topic, before it was changed by the statutes presently to be mentioned, is the view of Staunford, Coke, and Lord Somers; and, their view is borne out by the Year Books.

The Legislature in Edward III.'s reign considered that an extension of the cases, in which a person could traverse the facts found by an office entitling the king to possession, would be the most convenient method of providing a speedier remedy against the crown. It was enacted in 1360 that the person aggrieved should, in certain special cases, be allowed to traverse the facts found by an office;[2] and in 1362[3] this permission was greatly extended. It was provided that, "if there be any man that will make claim or challenge to lands so seized (i.e. seized by virtue of an inquest of office) that the escheator send the inquest into the Chancery within the month after the lands so seized, and that a writ be delivered to him to certify the cause of his seisin into the Chancery, and there he shall be heard without delay to traverse the office, or otherwise shew his right (*ou autrement monstrer son droit*), and from thence sent before the king to make a final discussion, without attending other commandments." This statute both gave to the traverse an extended sphere of application,[4] and was the origin of the remedy of "monstrans de droit."[5] It allowed the subject, not only to traverse the title found for the king,[6] but also to confess and avoid it by showing his own right.[7] Thus, in cases to which the

---

[1] Staunford f. 55a, 55b; the Sadlers' Case (1588) 4 Co. Rep. at f. 56a; Coke's statement is borne out by 30 Ass. pl. 28, and Y.B. 14 Hy. VII. Pasch. pl. 4 (p. 23), which are cited by him; and it is accepted by Lord Somers 14 S.T. at p. 78; in Reynel's Case (1612) 9 Co. Rep. at f. 96b Coke uses an analogy taken from the real actions, and says that, "in all cases when a common person is put to his action; there upon an office found the king is put to his *sci. fa.* . . . . But when a common person may enter or seize, there an office without a *sci. fa.* shall suffice for the king"; see below 26 and n. 4, 28 n. 2 for other uses made of an analogy taken from these actions to explain the relation inter se of the different remedies against the crown.

[2] 34 Edward III. c. 14; the Sadlers' Case (1588) 4 Co. Rep. at ff. 56b, 57a Ehrlich, op. cit. 175-176.

[3] 36 Edward III. st. 1 c. 13; the Sadlers' Case (1588) 4 Co. Rep. at f. 57a.

[4] Staunford, op. cit. ff. 60a seqq.

[5] This was the view of Staunford, op. cit. ff. 70b, 71a; of Anderson, C.J., and all the judges except two in the Sadlers' Case 1 And. at p. 181; and of Lord Somers 14 S.T. at pp. 77-79.

[6] " By the common law before the making of these statutes a man had no other remedy to avoid a false office, but only his peticion," Staunford, op. cit. f. 60b; above 24 n. 3; Y.B. 2 Hy. IV. Mich. pl. 47.

[7] "If the king be entitled by office or other matter of record which is traversable, howbeit there is no cause of traverse for that the office or record is true, in this case any man that hath right to the possession of the freehold of this land, which in shewing of his right is able to confess this office and avoid it, shall be received . . . to come into the Chancery and shew his said right," Staunford, op. cit. f. 71a; there is a statement by Keble in Y.B. 3 Hy. VII. Hil. pl. 10 of the difference between a Traverse, a Monstrans, and a Petition; though some of the statements are obscurely

statute was applicable, the subject got, either by means of a traverse or a monstrans de droit, a far speedier remedy than the remedy by petition; and though there are some signs of attempts to construe the statute restrictively, they did not succeed.[1] It was construed liberally, and further extended by an Act of 1548;[2] so that the traverse and the monstrans de droit became valuable remedies, whereby many of the delays incident to a petition of right could be avoided.

The advantages of these remedies over a petition of right were mainly three. In the first place, they cut out all the preliminary stages of the procedure on a petition of right—the presentation of the petition, the issue of a special commission, searches for evidence for the king. In the second place, it was not necessary to get the king's special permission to go on with the hearing of the case.[3] In the third place, the remedy of monstrans de droit substituted for an inquiry at large into the titles of the parties, an inquiry into a specific defect in the office, suggested by the process of showing the right of the complainant. It was probably this characteristic feature of the monstrans de droit, which led the lawyers to compare the relation between a petition of right and a monstrans de droit, with the relation between a writ of right and a writ of entry.[4] Just as in the writ of entry the proceedings were shortened by tying down the parties to the discussion of the particular fault in the title suggested by the demandant,[5] so in the monstrans de droit the proceedings were shortened by tying down the discussion to the defect in the office shown by the complainant. We shall now see that this analogy had some influence upon the rules which were evolved during this period as to the spheres of action of these two remedies.

---

expressed, it is said quite truly that " en *Monstrans* il confesse l'office et monstre son droit ouster."

[1] Thus Babington is reported to have said in 1431 that the statutes did not give a traverse if an office were found entitling the king to fee or freehold, Fitz. Ab. *Travers* pl. 47; but this, it would seem, was not accepted as law in Edward IV.'s reign, see Y.BB. 13 Ed. IV. Pasch. pl. 1, and 3 Hy. VII. Hil. pl. 10; and Coke, in the Sadlers' Case (1588) 4 Co. Rep. at f. 58a, said that "the book in 8 H. 5 is to be intended at the common law before the said Act"; this wider interpretation was also favoured by Staunford, op. cit. 61a, who cites a case of 19 Rich. II.; and see Y.B. 12 Rich. II. 19, 20.

[2] 2, 3 Edward VI. c. 8—passed just after the time when Staunford wrote his book; Coke's account of the law in the Sadlers' Case deals with the law before that Act, see note at the end of the case.

[3] 36 Edward III. st. 1 c. 13 cited above 25; "they shall proceed to judgment without any procedendo." the Sadlers' Case (1588) 4 Co. Rep. at f. 57a.

[4] " Also it is a general rule that where a straunger that hath title cannot enter upon a common person but is driven to his action, there hee can have no remedy against the king, but only a peticion," Staunford, op. cit. ff. 74a, 74b; and Coke repeats this in the Sadlers' Case (1588) 4 Co. Rep. at f. 58b.

[5] Vol. iii 12.

The relation of the petition of right to the other remedies open to a complainant.

This matter gave rise to an intricate body of rules which were based on several distinct principles.

(i) In order that a party aggrieved might take advantage of a traverse, the king must have got possession by an office found.[1] We have seen that if without any office found the king had entered wrongfully on another's land, the aggrieved party could only sue by petition, though he had his ordinary rights of entry or action against the king's grantee.[2] Similarly, in order to take advantage of a monstrans de droit, the king must have got seisin by office found, or in some other way which could not be traversed; and the subject must be able to confess the king's right, and avoid it by showing his own right.[3] "As for an example, it is found by office that the king's tenant by knight service in chiefe died seised of certain lands which are descended to his heire, being within age, where in dede in his life time I recovered this land against him, and, suyng no execution, suffered him to die seised thereof; now upon this office retourned into the Chancery, shal I come and shew my right, that is to say this recovery, and averre that this land found by office is the land that I recovered or parcel thereof, which being so proved and tried I shall have an *ouster le main*."[4] But the statutes were largely construed, so that, if the king got possession without office found, and afterwards an office was found, these remedies were held to be available;[5] and if an office was found, though the party was not ousted as the result of the finding of the office, they were likewise available.[6] (ii) The statutes allowed the complainant to traverse the record found for the king, or to confess and avoid it by showing his right. But if the king was entitled, not only by the office found, but by another title of record, the subject could not until 1548,[7] traverse or confess and avoid both. "These statutes are intended when the king is entitled by office only; for if his highness be entitled by another recorde beside the office, and entitled as it were by double matter of recorde, the party shall never have his traverse. As take the case to be this, a man is attainted of treason by act of parlement or otherwise by verdict, and afterwarde it is founde by office that the saide person attainted was seised the day of the treason committed of certaine lands, which in deede were never his lands but mine; in this case, if I be put out of my land by this office, I cannot traverse

---

[1] Above 24.   [2] Above 20.
[3] Above 25.   [4] Staunford, op. cit. f. 71a.
[5] The Sadlers' Case (1588) 4 Co. Rep. at f. 59a.
[6] Ibid.   [7] 2, 3 Edward VI. c. 8.

it."[1] (iii) The analogy of the case where a disseisee's right of entry was tolled and turned to a right of action, was applied to determine the question whether a complainant could sue by monstrans or petition of right. Thus, "it is found by office that the king's tenant in chief died seised, his heir within age, when indeed the said tenant had nothing but by disseisin done to me, and I suffered him to die seised without any claim made; in this case I get no remedy by *monstrans de droit* or traverse, but am driven to my petition. And so in all cases like, when myne entry should be tolled if the lands were in the hands of a common person."[2]

So long as matters falling within the sphere of the real actions, and matters connected with the incidents of tenure, were the chief cases in which these remedies against the crown were used, these remedies by traverse and monstrans de droit were useful, because they were less complicated and more speedy than the petition of right. In this respect the analogy between the writs of entry and the writ of right held good; and Blackstone can still repeat the language used by the older writers as to the advantages of using them.[3] In fact, long before Blackstone's day, they had almost superseded the petition of right.[4] Nevertheless the petition of right was destined in its turn to supersede them. They were very special remedies, and were more closely identified than the petition of right with the real actions. But we have seen that the petition of right, because it was a general remedy, had retained a certain

---

[1] Staunford, op. cit. ff. 61b, 71b; the Sadlers' Case (1588) 4 Co. Rep. at f. 57b gives an explanation of this very technical rule, which is probably in substance historically correct—"in the case of attainder and office the king is entitled by double matter of record, wherefore the party grieved ought to avoid it by double matter of record, and not by single traverse or *monstrans de droit*; for it was said, *nihil tam conveniens est naturali aequitati, unumquodque dissolvi eo ligamine quo ligatum est*, and therefore he shall be put to his petition"; we have seen, vol. ii 277 and n. 10, that the idea embodied in this maxim was known to the mediæval common lawyers; see also Y.B. 4 Hy. VII. Pasch. pl. 6. On the other hand, in Y.B. 9 Hy. IV. Mich. pl. 17, Gascoigne seems to state that there could be no traverse if the king was seised by judgment of record; if an office was always founded on such a judgment, this rule as to a double matter of record may have been a later explanation of the effect of a judgment; the rule seems, however, to be well established in Y.B. 4 Hy. VII. Pasch. pl. 6, though the expression "double matter of record" does not occur in the case; it is, however, introduced by Brooke, Ab. *Peticion* pl. 23.

[2] Staunford, op. cit. f. 74b; in the Sadlers' Case (1588) 4 Co. Rep. at f. 58b the analogy was used to extend the scope of the remedy; it was being used to illustrate the relation of the two remedies in 1406, Y.B. 7 Hy. IV. Mich. pl. 19 (p. 33) *per* Thirning.

[3] "These traverses as well as the monstrans de droit were greatly enlarged and regulated for the benefit of the subject by the statutes before mentioned, and others," Comm. iii 260; there is a reference to a Monstrans de droit in 1668, S.P. Dom. 1667-1668 358.

[4] Coke, Third Instit. 216, mentions a petition of right in 1583; Dyer at ff. 102a, 274a, mentions petitions in 1553 and 1568. There seem to be no instances of petitions in the reports in the seventeenth century; but we get incidental references elsewhere, e.g. in 1663, S.P. Dom. 1663-1664 413, lxxxviii 138.

elasticity.[1] Its scope was not precisely defined ; and it was not
forgotten that it was a remedy, which could give to the subject
redress against the crown, where he would have been entitled to
redress against a fellow subject.   The fact that the subject was
entitled to such redress was recognized in the Tudor period, not
only by the statute of 1548 which improved the remedy by
monstrans de droit,[2] but also by the extended powers of relief
against the crown available to the subject in the new courts of
Augmentations, Wards, and Surveyors, which were created in
Henry VIII.'s reign.[3]   In fact we shall see that these powers, and
the way in which they were used, had some influence, in the
following period, in making the courts willing to extend the
remedies of the subject, both by way of petition of right and otherwise.[4] It was recognized that the subject ought to have a remedy ;
and so, when the incidents of tenure were abolished, when the
real actions became obsolete, and when the cases in which the
subject asked for redress against the crown ceased to be chiefly
cases which fell within the sphere of these actions, it was to the
petition of right that the subject naturally turned.   The history of
this process of the revival of the petition of right will be the
subject of the two following sections.

(3) The later seventeenth and the eighteenth centuries.

The sixteenth and early seventeenth centuries are the period
of transition from the mediæval to the modern law.   After the
Restoration this period of transition is over, and the development
of the modern law is begun.   We begin to see the modern relations
between law and equity ; with the abolition of the incidents of
tenure, and the disuse of the real actions, many of the technical
rules and doctrines of the mediæval land law become obsolete ;
and other branches of the law—notably the law of contract—begin
to assume a new importance.[5]   These developments necessarily
affected the law as to the remedies available against the crown.
In the first place, we can trace the beginnings of the idea that the
subject should be able to get some sort of equitable relief against
the crown.   In the second place, the *Bankers' Case*[6] showed that
the principle underlying the petition of right—that the subject
ought to get the same sort of legal redress against the crown as
he had against a fellow subject—was still a living principle, and
capable of being applied in the modern, as it had been applied in
the mediæval common law, to safeguard the subject's rights.

---

[1] Above 21-22.   [2] Above 26.
[3] 27 Henry VIII. c. 27 (Augmentations); 32 Henry VIII. c. 46 (Wards);
33 Henry VIII. c. 39 (Surveyors); cp. vol. iv 271, 466.
[4] Below 34-35.   [5] Vol. vi 624-640.   [6] (1700) 14 S.T. 1.

Equitable relief as against the crown.

It would seem that it was in the case of *Pawlett v. the Attorney-General* in 1668,[1] that it was first clearly recognized that the subject was entitled to this relief against the crown. In that case the plaintiff had mortgaged property to a mortgagee. The legal estate had descended to the mortgagee's heir, who had been attainted of treason. The king had therefore seized his property; and the plaintiff brought his bill in the Exchequer against the attorney-general for redemption. It was argued that the plaintiff could not proceed in this way, but must petition the king to allow him, as a matter of grace and favour, to redeem.[2] But the court held that the plaintiff was entitled to succeed. Hale, C.B., grounded his judgment partly on the statute of 1541-1542 which created the court of Surveyors, and gave extended powers to the court of Augmentations to settle claims by or against the crown, in respect of property which was placed under the jurisdiction of that court.[3] But Atkyns, B., put the jurisdiction on a much broader basis. "The party," he said,[4] "ought in this case to be relieved against the king, because the king is the fountain and head of justice and equity; and it shall not be presumed that he will be defective in either. And it would derogate from the king's honour to imagine that what is equity against a common person, should not be equity against him." Probably, however, the decision owed something to the larger powers which the court of Exchequer had inherited, when these statutory courts of Henry VIII.'s reign were merged in it;[5] and for some time the jurisdiction to give equitable relief against the crown was supposed to be peculiar to the court of Exchequer. The law was so stated by Lord Hardwicke in 1741,[6] by Lord Northington in 1759,[7] and by Blackstone.[8] But later

---

[1] Hardres 465; in the case of Barnes v. Barnes (1568), mentioned in Dyer 236a, it is said that the court of Wards held that the mortgagor, after payment, could get the land from the queen by monstrans de droit, " without being driven to his petition "; but probably in this case the mortgagor had a legal right to redeem, and in such a case he clearly had this remedy, see the Sadlers' Case (1588) 4 Co. Rep. at f. 55b.

[2] Hardres at p. 466.

[3] 33 Henry VIII. c. 39 § 38; for the analogous influence of the practice of this court in inducing the judges to take a liberal view of the subject's right to *legal* redress see below 34, 35.

[4] Hardres at p. 469; or as it was put in the argument, ibid at p. 466, "no more than the king can deny justice in his own case, no more can he deny common equity; and common equity is as due to the subject against the king, as justice is."

[5] Above 29; below 34, 35.

[6] Reeve v. the Attorney-General (1741) 2 Atkyns 223—the question was whether a trust to sell and pay legacies and debts out of an estate escheated to the crown could be enforced; Lord Hardwicke said, "no I cannot, but the court of Exchequer may, as it is a court of revenue."

[7] " It is observable that there is in that case (*Pawlett v. Attorney-General*) a recognition of the equity without any declaration of the remedy. Whether this remedy has since been settled in the *Exchequer*, where alone it can, I really do not know; but I hope it is so settled; for I see a great deal of equity to support the opinion of Hale and Atkins," Burgess v. Wheate 1 Eden at pp. 255-256.

[8] " Nor can chancery give any relief against the king, or direct any act to be done

cases have distinguished the manner in which such relief can be
got in different circumstances; and have, in substance, put the
subject's right to this relief upon the broad basis suggested by
Atkyns, B.

We have seen that in the latter half of the fifteenth century it
was an established rule that the king could not be a feoffee to
uses;[1] and in 1610 it was said that he could not be a trustee.[2]
But the relief given by the court of Exchequer on bills against the
attorney-general, seems to have got rid of this idea that the king
could not be a trustee.[3] The question remained, How was his
liability as a trustee to be enforced? In 1741 Lord Hardwicke
held that he could not make a decree against the crown for the
performance of a trust, on a bill brought against the attorney-
general;[4] and in 1750 this case was used to show that, in these
circumstances, the subject must proceed against the crown by
petition of right.[5] It would seem, therefore, that in the eighteenth
century the court of Chancery could only administer relief on a
petition of right, while the court of Exchequer might give relief
on a bill filed against the attorney-general. In two cases of
1834[6] and 1837[7] the device was adopted of suing by a petition of
right, and praying that the plaintiff might proceed against the
attorney-general; and, since the Petitions of Right Act of 1860,
several petitions praying for equitable relief have been brought
against the crown under the provisions of that Act.[8] But the rule
that equitable relief could be given without a petition of right, on
a bill filed against the attorney-general, was stated perfectly
generally in 1835.[9] It was said also that this method of obtaining
relief was a convenient method, and that no difficulties should be
interposed by the crown to its adoption, when matters requiring a
judicial decision arose for discussion.[10] From this statement, and,
possibly, owing to a confusion with cases in which this procedure
had been followed after the presentation of a petition of right, the

by him, or make any decree disposing of or affecting his property; not even in cases
where he is a royal trustee. Such causes must be determined in the court of Exchequer, as a court of revenue; which alone has power over the king's treasure, and
the officers employed in its management," Bl. Comm. iii 428-429.
    [1] Vol. iii 467; vol. iv 427.   [2] Wikes' Case Lane 54.
    [3] Penn v. Lord Baltimore (1750) 1 Ves. Sen. at p. 453; Bl. Comm. iii 428;
Robertson, Civil Proceedings by and against the Crown 482-483. *Quære*—Should
not this jurisdiction be referred to the peculiar jurisdiction which the court of
Exchequer had as a court of revenue (vol. i 238-239), rather than to its general equitable jurisdiction?
    [4] Reeve v. the Attorney-General 2 Atkyns 225; Burgess v. Wheate, cited above
30 n. 7.
    [5] Penn v. Lord Baltimore (1750) 1 Ves. Sen. at p. 446.
    [6] Clayton v. Attorney-General Coop. t. Cott. 97; Clode, op. cit. at 143-144.
    [7] Taylor v. Attorney-General 8 Sim. 413; Clode, op. cit. 144-146.
    [8] Ibid 146-153; Robertson, op. cit. 368.
    [9] Deare v. Attorney-General 1 Y. and C. (Ex.) at p. 208.
    [10] Ibid.

deduction has been recently drawn that this method of giving relief was not simply a branch of the jurisdiction of the court of Exchequer as a court of revenue, but was a branch of its equitable
jurisdiction; and that it was not peculiar to the equity administered in that court.[1]   It is now settled law, therefore, that any court
administering an equitable jurisdiction can give relief in this way.
The further question as to the relation of this method of obtaining
relief, to the method of obtaining it by petition of right, is as yet
an open question.   It has been said that if the subject is claiming
equitable relief directly against the crown, he must proceed by
petition of right; but that, if the crown's rights are only indirectly
affected, he can proceed by an action against the attorney-
general.[2]   But it is by no means clear that the earlier cases, which
proceed rather on the line of the distinction between the Exchequer
and Chancery jurisdiction, bear out this distinction; and there is
weighty authority against it.[3]   But, however this question may be
decided, it seems clear that the general statement of Atkyns, B., in
Pawlett v. the Attorney-General,[4] as to the right of the subject to
equitable relief against the crown, has been of considerable historical importance, because it has supplied a clear recognition of the
principle that such relief should by some method be given.   We
shall now see that the lengthy discussion of the different possible
remedies against the crown, to which the *Bankers' Case* gave rise,
has had a similar but a far greater importance.

The BANKERS' CASE *and its influence on the development of
the petition of right.*

The facts leading up to the *Bankers' Case*[5] were as follows:
After the Restoration the bankers were accustomed to accommo-
date the king with loans on the security of the taxes or the
hereditary revenue.   The king was accustomed to give orders to
the barons of the Exchequer to pay the principal and interest from
the fund thus pledged as security;[6] and in 1667 he promised that
he would not postpone such payments.[7]   In 1671 he did postpone
these payments in order to get money for the war with Holland.[8]

---

[1] Dyson v. Attorney-General [1911] 1 K.B. at p. 416 *per* Cozens-Hardy, M.R.;
cp. Esquimalt and Nanaimo Railway Co. v. Wilson [1920] A.C. at pp. 367-368.
    [2] Dyson v. Attorney-General [1911] 1 K.B. at p. 421 *per* Farwell, L.J.; Robertson,
op. cit. 477; the distinction seems to rest ultimately on a passage in Mitford, Pleading
(2nd ed.) 29-30.
    [3] Dyson v. Attorney-General at p. 415 *per* Cozens-Hardy, M.R.; note that the
Privy Council in Esquimalt and Nanaimo Railway v. Wilson [1920] A.C. at p. 368
reserved their opinion as to the correctness of the decision in Dyson v. Attorney-
General, but whether because they questioned the correctness of this distinction, or
its application to the facts of that case, is not clear.
    [4] Above 30.   [5] (1690-1700) 14 S.T. 1.
    [6] See vol. viii 186-188 for this practice and its history; cp. also vol. vi 173, 252.
    [7] The text of this declaration is printed in 14 S.T. at p. 1 n.
    [8] Vol. vi 181.

This ruined several of the bankers who were unable to pay their depositors. In 1677 the king granted to these bankers annuities charged on the hereditary excise, to an amount which was equivalent to six per cent. interest on the principal of his debt. These annuities were paid till 1683. They then got into arrear, and were still in arrear in 1688.

After the Revolution the bankers took legal proceedings to recover these arrears. The course which they adopted was the presentation of a petition to the barons of the Exchequer for payment; and the case turned on the question whether this was a proper method of procedure. The court of Exchequer held that it was a proper method of procedure, and gave judgment for the bankers. In the Exchequer Chamber the majority of the judges were of the same opinion. But Lord Somers and Treby, C.J., held that a petition to the barons of the Exchequer was not warranted by the course of the Exchequer, because the barons could not command the Treasurer and the Chamberlains to make payments. According to their view, the proper method of procedure was a petition of right. As in the branch of the court of Exchequer Chamber which heard appeals from the Exchequer, the Treasurer and the Chancellor were sole judges, and were not bound by the opinions of the other judges whom they had called in to assist them,[1] the judgment of the court of Exchequer was reversed. In the House of Lords this judgment was reversed, and the judgment of the court of Exchequer was restored. But the bankers were never paid; and it was provided by a statute of 1701 that the hereditary excise should be charged with perpetual annuities at the rate of three per cent. in their favour, redeemable on payment of a moiety of the principal sums advanced.[2]

The actual decision in this case gave to creditors of the crown an alternative method of procedure—a petition to the barons of the Exchequer; and the fact that it sanctioned this procedure may, as we shall see, account partially for the disuse into which the remedy by petition of right fell during the eighteenth century. But the historical importance of the case is due, not so much to the actual decision, as to the exhaustive discussion of the nature and competence, both of the petition of right, and of other remedies against the crown. It provided an authority in which these remedies, and more especially the remedy by petition of right, were discussed from the point of view of the modern common law. Hence, when, in the nineteenth century, the remedy of petition of right was revived, the manner in which the mediæval

---

[1] Vol. i 244; this rule was assented to in this case by eight judges to three, 14 S.T. 105.

[2] 12, 13 William III. c. 12 § 24.

precedents had been interpreted in this case exercised a large influence on the modern development of the law. Let us therefore look at the case from these two points of view—the actual decision, and the views expressed in it as to the competence of the position of right.

(i) *The actual decision.*—It would seem that Holt, C.J., was of opinion that the Bankers could have proceeded, either in the way in which they did actually proceed, i.e., by petition to the barons of the Exchequer, or by way of monstrans de droit or petition of right.[1] In coming to the conclusion that they could proceed by petition to the barons of the Exchequer, Holt, and doubtless the other judges, were influenced by the cases of *Nevil* and *Wroth.* In *Nevil's Case*[2] the plaintiff petitioned the barons of the Exchequer for payment of a rent charge out of land, which had come into the hands of queen Elizabeth. The court gave judgment[3] that the sum should be paid to him, and issued a writ to the Treasurer and Chamberlains of the Exchequer to pay the sum so recovered.[4] In *Wroth's Case*[5] a similar judgment was given, and a similar writ was issued, on a petition made to the barons for the payment of an annuity for life granted to the petitioner by Henry VIII. Holt considered that these, and other cases which he cited, proved that money could be issued out of the Exchequer by order of the court of Exchequer;[6] and he held further that, so soon as such a writ to the Treasurer and Chamberlains was issued, these officials became debtors for the amount named in the writ to the petitioner, just as the sheriff became a debtor to the judgment creditor, when goods were taken and sold under a writ of fieri facias.[7] But Treby, C.J., did not agree to the latter proposition; and he was perhaps right.[8]

[1] 14 S.T. at p. 34.   [2] (1570)Plowden 377.   [3] Ibid 382.
[4] Ibid 382-383.   [5] (1573) Plowden 452.
[6] 14 S.T. 36-37; "there are several other records which have been already quoted, but I shall not trouble you with the repetition of them. . . . In all these records it appears that money issued out of the Exchequer by order of the court of Exchequer, and it is highly reasonable that they should have such a power," ibid at p. 37.
[7] "I do think that as soon as the writs are delivered to the officers of the exchequer, I mean the treasurer and chamberlain, the property is altered, and the officers become debtors to the parties. . . . So soon as a *fieri fac.* is delivered to the sheriff and upon it goods are levied, the property of the goods is altered, and the sheriff becomes a debtor to the plaintiff," ibid at p. 38.
[8] There was authority to the effect that if a writ of Liberate was delivered to the clerk of the hanaper, and he had assets, he became a debtor to the party in whose favour the writ of Liberate was issued, Y.B. 2 Hy. VII. Hil. pl. 1, which was cited by Plowden at pp. 36, 186; but Treby, C.J., pointed out, 14 S.T. at p. 24, that this doctrine had never been applied to the Treasurer and Chamberlains of the Exchequer; even if these officials came within the principle of this case, it does not follow that the same reasoning would apply to a writ issued by the court of Exchequer as was applied in the case cited to a writ of Liberate; the parallel drawn by Holt, C.J., with the sheriff and the writ of fi. fa., is an illustration of the same sort of fallacy as led him into error in the case of Lane v. Cotton (1701) 1 Ld. Raym. 646, vol. vi 267-268;

Lord Somers, on the other hand, explained these cases of *Nevil* and *Wroth* by showing that they both concerned property which came under the survey of the court of Augmentations; that the statutes creating the courts of Wards, Augmentations, and Surveyors gave these courts power to order such payments on a petition to them; that in these cases the court of Exchequer was only exercising the powers of the court of Augmentations after it had been united to the court of Exchequer; and that it had no power to make these orders in any cases except in those which fell under the survey of these courts.[1] Probably Lord Somers was right in the explanation which he gave of those cases. But his opinion was reversed; and so we have another instance of the manner in which the powers given to these new courts by the statutes of the Tudor period, materially helped the development of the remedies of the subject against the crown.[2] For, it followed from this decision that the subject could now, not only, as under the old practice, petition for a writ of Liberate,[3] but also petition the barons of the Exchequer for relief. One of the reasons assigned for the writ of error, on which Lord Somers' judgment was reversed by the House of Lords, was the allegation that, if the judgment stood, all who claimed under tallies or orders upon the Exchequer would be placed in a very much worse position.[4] It seems to me, therefore, that the sanction given to this procedure by the House of Lords, goes some way to account for the small use made of the petition of right during the eighteenth century.

(ii) *The views expressed as to the competence of the petition of right.*—Though all the judges were not agreed that the Bankers could have proceeded by way of monstrans de droit,[5] all agreed that they could have proceeded by way of petition of right. No doubt they were helped to this conclusion by the fact that the demand

the position of officers acting as the direct agents of the crown was not quite the same as that of a sheriff acting by virtue of the statutory or common law duties attaching to his office.

[1] 14 S.T. at pp. 84-102; the following sentence at p. 101 contains the gist of his argument :—"As the annuities were payable before by the treasurer of the court of Augmentations, by the order of that court; so, by the special authority given by this Act (1 Mary c. 10 which gave power to dissolve the court), the court of Exchequer might direct the same to be paid by the treasurer of the Exchequer; and such direction in those particular cases would be a good warrant in point of law. And yet no argument would be deducible from thence to maintain the judgments now before us, which relate to grants which were never under the survey of the court of Augmentations."

[2] Above 29.   [3] Above 21.

[4] "This cause in consequence must affect all persons claiming under the crown, or having any tallies or orders upon or payments out of the Exchequer; for all those will be made much better or worse by the judgment of the lords in this case," 14 S.T. at p. 109.

[5] Ibid at pp. 79-82 *per* Lord Somers.

of the Bankers could be represented as a proprietary claim.[1] They
were claiming an annuity ; and there is no doubt that in the Middle
Ages such things as rents or annuities, for which there was a real
action, could be recovered in this way.[2] These annuities were
said by Lord Somers to stand on the same footing as rents ; from
which he drew the conclusion that, just as no monstrans de droit
lay for a rent while the land out of which it issued was in the
possession of the crown, so it could not lie for the payment of
these annuities.[3]

If the reasoning in the case had stopped here, the case would
have lost a great deal of its historical importance ; for it would
have proceeded simply on mediæval lines. But we have seen
that at this period the law of contract was taking over much of
the territory formerly occupied by the law of property.[4] These
annuities were beginning to be regarded from the modern point
of view, and to be considered as rights against the crown resting
on contract. There is no doubt that Lord Somers, though he
enforced his opinion by mediæval precedents which regarded them
as property, regarded them as contracts made by the crown.[5] It
was because he so regarded them that he introduced a number of
petitions from Edward I.'s reign, taken from Ryley's Placita, which
showed that subjects had in fact petitioned the crown for the
payment of their debts. The question is, Was he justified in
relying on these precedents ?

Recent writers on this subject have maintained that he was
not justified, on the ground that these petitions were not petitions
of right, but rather petitions asking for some favour from the king.[6]

---

[1] " In the present suits we are in the case of a freehold," ibid at p. 84 *per*
Lord Somers.

[2] Above 18 ; vol. iii 151-153.

[3] " As the law is plainly so, where a person has a title to a rent by grant of a
subject out of lands which come to the possession of the king ; so the case is to all
purposes the same where he has a title to a rent or yearly sum by letters patent from
the crown. . . . By all these authorities and by many others which I could cite,
both ancient and modern, it is plain that if the subject was to recover a rent or
annuity or other charge from the crown ; whether it was a rent or annuity originally
granted by the king, or issuing out of lands, which by subsequent title came to be
in the king's hands ; in all cases the remedy to come at it was by petition to the
person of the king ; and no other method can be shown to have been practised at
common law," 14 S.T. at p. 82.

[4] Vol. iii 454 ; vol. vii 312 ; above 29.

[5] 14 S.T. at pp. 83-84 ; as Blackburn, J., said in Thomas v. the Queen (1874)
L.R. 10 Q.B. at p. 39, " the reasons given by Lord Holt in favour of the judgment
which was ultimately adopted by the House of Lords, as well as the reasons given
by Lord Somers for reversing it, both lead to the conclusion that a petition of right
lies in such case as the present "—i.e. for breach of contract.

[6] Clode, op. cit. 120-131. from which he deduces the conclusion that Thomas v.
the Queen (1874) L.R. 10 Q.B. 31, below 41, was wrongly decided ; Mr. Robertson,
Judicial Proceedings by and against the Crown 339, is inclined to agree with this
view, though, as he says, " if the decision had been to the contrary clearly a remedy
for such cases must have been made by legislation."

Lord Somers, on the other hand, maintained that, since the petitioners were only asking for what was due to them, their petitions
were not petitions of complaint,[1] and were therefore petitions of
right.   His view was that it was impossible to say that only those
petitions were petitions of right on which the general indorsement
was made—"soit droit fait al parties," and on which the regular
procedure of a commission from the Chancery, and further pleading
on the facts found by the commission, was followed.[2]   "The truth
is, the manner of answering petitions to the person of the king
was very various: which variety did sometimes arise from the
conclusion of the party's petition; sometimes from the nature of
the thing; and sometimes from favour to the person; and according as the indorsement was, the party was sent into Chancery, or
the other courts."[3]   Now it seems to me there is a good deal to
be said for the view taken by Lord Somers.   No doubt in normal
cases there was, as we have seen,[4] a fixed and settled procedure
on a petition of right.   But we have seen also that Staunford
admits that such a petition might be specially indorsed, and that
the procedure must follow the indorsement; and that these petitions
might sometimes be presented in Parliament.[5]   We have seen,
too, that Coke admits that some of these petitions presented in
Parliament were petitions of right.[6]   No doubt it is difficult to
draw the line between petitions "of grace," that is petitions which
merely ask for some favour, and petitions of right, largely because
the latter are an offshoot from the former.[7]   But it seems to me
that Lord Somers was substantially correct in treating as petitions
of right, petitions which asked for something which the petitioner
could have enforced if his claim had been against a subject.[8]

In truth the petition of right had never been completely
differentiated from other petitions "of grace"; and the fact that
the monstrans de droit and traverse of office had largely superseded it in the fifteenth and sixteenth centuries had prevented it
from being exactly defined.   Because its competence was vague,
it was possible to adapt it to the new claims which, owing to the
development of the law, the subject might have against the crown.
It was possible to make it a remedy by which the subject could
get his legal rights, though the extent and definition of those
rights had altered their form and content by reason of the

---

[1] 14 S.T. at pp. 58-59.   [2] Ibid.   [3] Ibid.   [4] Above 16-17, 22-24.
[5] Above 16.   [6] Above 16 n. 1.   [7] Above 13-15.
[8] Thus the petition in Everle's Case (1305), where the petitioner prayed Edward I.
for the payment of annuity granted to him by Henry III. and confirmed by Edward
himself, and for which he had a writ of Liberate, was said to be a petition of
complaint; but Lord Somers held it to be a petition of right on the ground that the
petitioner only asked for his rights—"no body is complained of in this petition, and
no body is blamed in the answer; a writ is to go, the charter is to be seen, and
justice is to be done," 14 S.T. at pp. 57-59.

development of the law. Just as the vagueness of the mediæval precedents helped the Parliaments of the seventeenth century to assert the new powers and privileges needed for the constitutional government of a modern state; so, a similar vagueness, which even in the sixteenth century still characterized the petition of right, enabled the early precedents of these petitions to be used to give a remedy to the subject, which was capable of enforcing his rights in the modern system of the common law.

But, it may be said, all this proves too much. If these early petitions are to be taken as precedents which prove the competence of a petition of right, it will, in the first place, be difficult to distinguish between a petition of grace and a petition of right; and, in the second place, it might be proved that a petition of right will lie for a tort.[1] But, in answer to the first objection, I think that it might be said that Lord Somers is careful only to cite those petitions which show that the suppliant had something in the nature of a legal claim;[2] and that it is easy enough to distinguish those petitions which ask for something for which the petitioner could have brought an action against a subject, from those which ask for something for which no action would lie. In answer to the second objection, it can, I think, be asserted that no one ever thought of petitioning the king for redress for a tort committed by the king himself; and that, in respect of torts committed by the king's servants, the rule that a petition of right will not lie for a tort must be taken with considerable limitations. We have seen that it lay for a disseisin,[3] and to recover a chattel wrongfully taken by the crown;[4] and we shall see that the modern rule in its modern shape is the result of cases decided in the nineteenth century, which adopt a theory of the principle underlying the modern doctrine of employers' liability which is now generally discarded.[5]

But, whether the view taken by Lord Somers was right or wrong, it is clear that the treatment by the judges of the remedy by petition of right in the *Bankers' Case*, had sanctioned the principle that it was an elastic remedy, which should, so far as possible, be allowed whenever the subject had a claim against the crown which could be enforced by action against the subject. "It would be a hard thing," it was said in the reasons given to the House of Lords for reversing the judgment of the Exchequer Chamber, "that the court of Exchequer can relieve the king against the subject, and not help and relieve the subject when he produces a legal title against the king";[6] and this salutary

---

[1] See Clode, op. cit. 129.   [2] 14 S.T. at pp. 57-63, 83-84.
[3] Above 20.   [4] Above 20; below 42.   [5] Below 43-44.
[6] 14 S.T. at p. 109.

principle, which had inspired legislation in the sixteenth,[1] and induced the court to give equitable relief in the seventeenth centuries,[2] was not lost sight of in the eighteenth century. Buller, J., and Lord Mansfield were of opinion that the subject could sue by petition of right for breach of contract.[3] But it was not till the remedy by petition of right was revived in the nineteenth century that the full effect of this principle was manifested.

4. The nineteenth century.

The reason why the remedy by petition of right was revived in the nineteenth century, was partly due to the fact that the manifold activities of the modern state necessitated some remedy against the crown for breaches of contract and other wrongs committed by its agents; and partly to the fact that the old remedy of suing for a writ of Liberate, or petitioning the barons of the Exchequer, had become obsolete with changes in the fiscal machinery of the state.[4] When once the remedy had been revived, litigants naturally tried to use it whenever they thought that they had a claim against the crown, for which they could have brought an ordinary action against a fellow subject.   Hence the question of the competence of the remedy was forced upon the attention of the courts; and this question became more pressing than ever when, in 1860, the Petitions of Right Act,[5] by reforming the procedure on such a petition, made it a more generally available remedy.

In the absence of recent precedents the lawyers were naturally led to theorize upon this question.   From the discussions in the courts and elsewhere in the first three quarters of the century, it may, I think, be said that three views emerge.   Firstly an unduly liberal theory, secondly an unduly restrictive theory, and thirdly an intermediate theory which the courts have in the main adopted.

(i) It was maintained by T. C. Anstey[6]—a counsel who had appeared for petitioners in many cases of this kind in the earlier part of the nineteenth century—that a petition of right would lie whenever a suppliant could show that justice demanded that a remedy should be provided for a wrong which he had suffered;[7]

---

[1] Above 26, 29.   [2] Above 30.

[3] Macbeth v. Haldimand (1786) 1 T.R. at p. 176.

[4] Mr. Clode, op. cit. 125, says of the mode of payment by writ of Liberate, "this form of payment lasted down to the reign of William IV., the two last people who received money in this way being the Master of the Rolls, for whose benefit a writ of Liberate passed under the Great Seal as late as 1837, and the Usher of the Exchequer, who received payment in this way in 1844."

[5] 23, 24 Victoria c. 34.

[6] Letter to Lord Cottenham as to the Petition of Right (1845).

[7] "To determine whether such a petition will lie there is but one criterion:—the justice of the case as stated by the suppliant," op. cit. 8; "whatsoever the

and that the grant by the crown of its fiat was as much a matter of right as the issue of a writ of subpœna.[1] It is clear that the latter proposition was not and never had been law, as, from the earliest times, the grant or refusal to grant the prayer of a petition has always been in the absolute discretion of the crown. It is clear also that the former proposition was far too widely stated, as, at no period in the history of the law, could a petitioner claim a right or invoke a remedy against the crown, unless he could show that he would have had a right and a remedy against a subject.

(ii) We have seen that Lord Somers made use of the fact that the form of the judgment on a monstrans de droit was "amoveas manus," to prove that this remedy only lay when the crown was in the possession of property, from the possession of which it could be directed to withdraw;[2] and that therefore this remedy was not available for the recovery of an annuity. We have seen, too, that the same argument was put forward in *Thomas v. the Queen*[3] to prove that a petition of right did not lie for breach of contract. Since the form of the judgment was the same on a petition of right and on a monstrans de droit, it is clear that both arguments are entitled to equal weight. But we have seen that the form of the judgment was not allowed, in the mediæval period, to fetter unduly the competence of the petition of right; and that it lay in cases, e.g. where the petitioner wished to recover a rent charge or an annuity, to which this form of judgment was not strictly applicable.[4] It follows that the admission of this argument would have circumscribed the competence of the petition of right within even narrower limits than those which circumscribed it in the Middle Ages.

(iii) The view which the courts have taken is an intermediate view, and one which is, on the whole, in accord with the principle that a petitioner should get a remedy if he would have had a remedy against a fellow subject. That the competence of a petition of right should be limited to legal claims of this kind was stated by Maule, J., in 1848;[5] and that the extent of the remedy of the subject against the crown should be no less than

nature of the demand which the subject hath—if there be none of the ordinary remedies available to him for the recovery thereof, he shall not on that account fail of his right—for he may sue to the Crown by petition of right, and the Crown is bound to provide the remedy," ibid 16; much the same view seems to have been put forward by Serjeant Manning *arg.* in Baron de Bode v. the Queen, but it was denied by Maule, J., who said that, "neither the Queen's Bench nor any other Court of Law administers justice in general; and that if the suppliant's claim was not cognisable by the Queen's Bench as a claim in law, it might be that the Court had no power to give any judgment at all," 13 Q.B. at p. 387 *n.*

[1] Letter to Lord Cottenham 42. [2] Above 21 n. 2, 36.
[3] (1874) L.R. 10 Q.B. at p. 35; above 21 n. 2. [4] Above 18, 21.
[5] Above 39 n. 7.

the extent of his remedy against a fellow subject, was equally clearly stated by Lord Denman, C.J., in 1845,[1] and by Cockburn, C.J., in 1865.[2] But the acceptance of this principle necessarily involves the consequence that the competence of the petition of right must develop and vary, with developments and variations in the rights and remedies of one subject against another. It has so varied; nor is there any historical ground for objecting to this variation. For, though it may be proved that a petition of right now lies for causes of complaint for which it did not lie in the Middle Ages, that fact merely shows that modern judges have faithfully adhered to the principle which right down the ages has governed the competence of this remedy—the principle that it should be available against the crown where the subject has a cause of action against a fellow subject.

Let us glance briefly at the way in which the courts have applied this principle.

We have seen that the *Bankers' Case* took a very long step towards adapting the petition of right to the needs of the modern common law, by sanctioning the principle that it lay for breach of contract;[3] and we have seen that this principle was accepted in the eighteenth century.[4] In all the earlier cases of the nineteenth century it was assumed;[5] and so, when the question was brought directly before the courts in 1874,[6] it was inevitable that it should be adopted. If it had not been adopted, it would both have been productive of the grossest injustice, and it would, as we have seen, have run counter to the principle which has governed the scope of this remedy throughout its history. That it lay for the recovery of property has never been doubted; and, owing to the wide sphere occupied by property law in the Middle Ages, this sphere of its competence covered much ground. Thus we have seen that there is clear authority for the proposition that it lay for a disseisin,[7] and for the recovery of chattels real or personal to which a subject could show a right.[8] Nor, it seems to me, ought the

---

[1] "We may here observe that there is nothing to secure the Crown against committing the same species of wrong, unconscious and involuntary wrong, in respect of money, which founds the subject's right to sue out his petition when committed in respect to lands or specific chattels; and there is an unconquerable repugnance to the suggestion that the door ought to be closed against all redress or remedy for such wrong," Baron de Bode's Case (1845) 8 Q.B. at pp. 273-274.

[2] "The petition of right, unlike a petition addressed to the grace or favour of the sovereign, is founded on the violation of some right in respect of which, but for the immunity from all process with which the law surrounds the person of the Sovereign, a suit at law or equity could be maintained," Feather v. the Queen 6 B. and S. at p. 295.

[3] Above 36.   [4] Above 39.

[5] See the cases summarized in Thomas v. the Queen (1874) L.R. 10 Q.B. at pp. 43-44.

[6] Thomas v. the Queen L.R. 10 Q.B. 31.

[7] Above 20.   [8] Above 21.

courts to hesitate to allow it to be extended to the recovery of compensation or damages for conversion. There is both mediæval [1] and modern [2] authority in favour of this proposition. Nor is the fact that the action of trover is in form an action in tort a very weighty argument; for, as we have seen, it was recognized in the eighteenth century that trover was in substance an action to recover property; [3] and the delictual element in a disseisin is at least as pronounced as in a conversion. [4]

The one respect in which the courts have, it seems to me, given inadequate recognition to the principle that the subject should have a remedy against the crown where he has a remedy against a fellow subject, is in their treatment of petitions of right for torts. But, to understand the modern law on this point, we must begin by examining the meaning and extent of the rule that no petition of right will lie for a tort. In the first place, no one has ever supposed that it lay for a tort committed by the king himself—the king can do no wrong. [5] All the cases concern torts committed by the king's servants. In the second place, it follows that, as the king can do no wrong, he cannot authorize wrong. If wrong is done apparently by his authority the law presumes that he has not authorized it, and the servant who does it is personally liable for his own wrong-doing. [6] In the third place, these principles are modified by the rule that a petition does lie for a tort to property which consists in its wrongful abstraction; [7] and it would seem that it lies also for certain cases of undue user of the property of the crown which damage the property of the subject. [8] These were causes of com-

---

[1] " *Danby.* Vous pouvez avoir votre remedy per un peticion de droit au Roy. *Wangford.* Ceo ne poimes avoir mesques fuit un plee de terre. *Quod fuit negatum per omnes justitiarios*, que disoient que en plusors cases on suera per peticion de reavoir son biens et chateux. Come si Eschetor *virtute officii* seisi biens et accompt pur eux en l'Exchequer, ou autrement que ascun que est utlage reverse son utlagarie, et l'Eschetor ad counte de ses biens," Y.B. 34 Hy. VI. Trin. pl. 18 (p. 51); Staunford, op. cit. 75b, 76a—in such cases compensation was clearly recoverable.

[2] " The only cases in which the petition of right is open to the subject are where the land or goods or money of the subject have found their way into the possession of the Crown, and the purpose of the petition is to obtain restitution, or, if restitution cannot be given, compensation in money," Feather v. the Queen (1865) 6 B. and S. at p. 294 *per* Cockburn, C.J.

[3] Vol. vii 442-444.

[4] The question is still an open one, Robertson, op. cit. 336; but Mr. Robertson " inclines to the opinion that the remedy by petition of right should, in strictness, be limited to specific property, though such a limitation would no doubt involve hardship," ibid.

[5] Above 19-20.

[6] Feather v. the Queen (1865) 6 B. and S. at pp. 295-296.

[7] Above 18, 20, 41-42.

[8] The cases of Gervase and Robert de Clifton, above 18-19, point in this direction; and it seems to be assumed by Erle, J., in Tobin v. the Queen that a petition would lie in such cases, 16 C.B.N.S. at pp. 363, 365, cited above 19 n. 4; moreover, the assize of nuisance, by which such causes of action as between subjects were remedied, vol. iii 11, was the complement of the assize of novel disseisin, ibid;

plaint for which a real action lay; and, if I am right in thinking that in the Middle Ages a petition would lie for any cause of complaint which would have supported a real action against a subject, it ought to lie now, not necessarily for mere trespasses, but for similar complaints of encroachment on the property of the subject, and for nuisance—though whether it would be held to lie in these cases is highly doubtful.[1]

I think that the mediæval precedents would justify the courts in allowing a petition of right in such cases. If it does not lie, there is, it seems to me, an obvious failure of justice. But the most obvious failure of justice arises from the undoubted rule that the modern doctrine of the employer's liability for the torts of his servants is not applicable to the crown. I think that the cases show that this rule is largely due to the view that the tort of the servant is imputed to the employer, in the same way as it is imputed to a person who has authorized a tort.[2] This view seems to run through the cases, and is characteristic of the period when, as we have seen,[3] the true basis of this liability was not properly understood. But if in fact the basis of this liability is, not the fact that the employer has authorized and therefore committed a tort; if it results rather from the imposition by law of a duty "analogous to the duties imposed with various degrees of stringency on the owners of things which are or may be sources of danger to others,"[4] there seems to be no reason why the crown should not be subject to the same duties. It seems to me that the House of Lords went some way towards the recognition of this principle,

and if a petition of right lay for a disseisin, there seems no reason why it should not lie for a nuisance.

[1] It may be noted that, in a case which turned on the construction of the Indemnity Act, 1920, the question whether a subject, from whom money had been illegally extorted, could waive the tort and sue on a quasi-contract, has divided the court of Appeal, Brocklebank v. the King [1925] 1 K.B. 52; the dissenting judgment of Scrutton, L.J., at pp. 67-70, which would allow such a course of action, seems to me to be not only more just to the subject, but also more in accord with the historical development of the remedy by petition of right. It is of course possible that, if the judges were considering, not the interpretation of the Indemnity Act, but the question whether a petition of right would lie for a quasi-contract, they might come to a different conclusion.

[2] Thus in Viscount Canterbury v. the King (1843) 4 S.T.N.S. at p. 778 Lord Lyndhurst said, "it is admitted that for the personal negligence of the sovereign neither this nor any other proceedings can be maintained. Upon what ground then can it be supported for the acts of the agent or servant? If the master or employer is answerable upon the principle that *qui facit per alium facit per se* this would not apply to the sovereign, who cannot be required to answer for his own personal acts. If it be said that the master is answerable for the negligence of his servant, because it may be considered to have arisen from his own misconduct or negligence in selecting or retaining a careless servant, that principle cannot apply to the sovereign"; this view of the case was followed in Tobin v. the Queen (1864) 16 C.B.N.S. 310; and in Feather v. the Queen (1865) 6 B. and S. at pp. 295-296, Cockburn C.J.'s reasoning applies only to wrongs authorized by the crown.

[3] Vol. viii 477-478.

[4] Pollock, Essays in Jurisprudence and Ethics 128; vol. viii 478-479.

when, in 1920, it held that a petition of right would lie to enforce
a statutory duty to pay compensation;[1] and that the court of
Appeal in 1925 has gone even further in the same direction, by its
decision that a petition of right would be to enforce the right
which a neutral has, by the rules of international law, to be com-
pensated for property taken by virtue of the prerogative right of
angary.[2] Obviously it is difficult to distinguish between a duty
imposed by statute or by international law, and a duty imposed by
the common law. In fact the crown should be liable for the torts
of its servants, just as it should be liable if, by the user of its property, it encroaches upon or causes a nuisance to the property of
a subject. To hold that the crown is liable for the torts of its
servants on the same principle as an ordinary employer, would
infringe the maxim that the king can do no wrong as much and
as little as to hold the crown liable for a disseisin, or a nuisance or
an encroachment on the subject's property.

In fact, the refusal of the courts to apply the doctrine of
employer's liability to the crown is the most important case
where the courts have refused to give the subject a remedy
against the crown, when he would have had a remedy against a
fellow subject. It is the most important case in which the
development of the competence of the petition of right has not
followed the development of the law as to the remedies available
to one subject against another. The subject's rights against the
crown are therefore, as we have seen,[3] governed by the inadequate
rules of the mediæval common law. That injustice results is
obvious. The subject is in this respect worse protected in this
country than in some foreign countries;[4] and in some of the
colonies this injustice has been so obvious, that it has been removed
by enlarging the competence of the petition of right. It was said
in 1887, in the case of *Farnell v. Bowman*,[5] "that the local governments in the colonies, as pioneers of improvements, are frequently
obliged to embark in undertakings which in other countries are
left to private enterprise, such, for instance, as the construction of
railways, canals, and other works for the construction of which it
is necessary to employ many inferior officers and workmen. If,
therefore, the maxim that "the king can do no wrong" were
applied to Colonial Governments . . . it would work much greater
hardship than it does in England." It is obvious that this reasoning applies with great force to the activities of our modern social-
istic state; and that, in consequence, a reform of the law on the

---

[1] Attorney-General v. De Keyser's Royal Hotel [1920] A.C. 508.
[2] Commercial and Estates Co. of Egypt v. Board of Trade [1925] 1 K.B. 271.
[3] Vol. iii 388; cp. vol. vi 268.
[4] W. H. Moore, Liability for Acts of Public Servants, L.Q.R. xxiii 12, 13.
[5] 12 A.C. at p. 649.

lines of these colonial statutes is urgently needed in the interests of the public at large.   Indeed the Legislature has recently recognized this fact by providing in § 26, 1 of the Ministry of Transport Act 1919,[1] that the minister shall be responsible for the acts and defaults of the servants and agents of the ministry as if they were his servants.   This clause produces in another way the same results as the colonial statutes which have enlarged the scope of the petition of right ; and it should obviously be extended to many other ministries.   Such an extension would be in entire conformity with the principle which has guided the development of the subject's remedies against the crown throughout their history —the principle that their competence should, so far as possible, be coextensive with the remedies available to one subject against another.

§ 2. THE INCORPORATE PERSON

During this period the mediæval principles which regulated this branch of the law were worked out in considerable detail. The largest part of the law still centres round the boroughs, and various ecclesiastical corporations sole or aggregate.   But hospitals[2] and colleges had begun to increase ; and, at the end of this period, commercial corporations were, as we have seen,[3] assuming a position of great importance.   We have seen, too, that they would have continued to increase more rapidly, and that, in consequence, the law on this topic would have developed much more quickly, had not the Legislature, as a result of the episode of the "South Sea Bubble," deliberately made the assumption of corporate form by these societies difficult.[4]   In fact the law developed very much on the mediæval lines; and, in describing it, I shall adopt a similar arrangement to that which I have adopted in the preceding Book of this History.   I shall consider the Creation of Incorporate Persons; their Powers, Capacities and Liabilities; their Dissolution; and, the Nature of Corporate Personality.

The Creation of Incorporate Persons

The rules as to the creation of the incorporate person had been ascertained in the mediæval period.[5]   Coke summed up the

---

[1] 9, 10 George V. c. 50.

[2] "The legal sense of the word hospital is a corporate foundation, endowed for the perpetual distribution of the founder's charity, in the lodging and maintenance of a certain number of poor persons, according to the regulations and statutes of the founder.   Such institutions are not necessarily connected with medicine or surgery, and in their original establishment had no necessary reference to sickness or accident," Grant, Corporations (ed. 1850) 567; as is there pointed out, they did not differ very materially from colleges ; in the case of the college, education of poor persons was the main object, and in the case of the hospital, their maintenance, ibid.

[3] Vol. viii 199-219.   [4] Ibid 219 221.   [5] Vol. iii 475 479.

mediæval rules, and laid down the modern rule, when, in the *Case of Sutton's Hospital*, he stated that the first essential for a valid corporation was a "lawful authority of incorporation"; and explained this to mean that a corporation must be created either by the common law, by authority of Parliament, by royal charter, or by prescription.[1] To this we must add that, as in the mediæval period, a corporation for a limited purpose could be created by implication.[2]

The need for the sanction of the state for the creation of a corporation was steadily adhered to in this period, and it has never been abandoned. It was adhered to on those grounds of public policy which I have explained in the preceding Book of this History;[3] and their existence is assumed in all the cases of this period. Perhaps the earliest case in which they are explicitly stated, is the case of the quo warranto proceedings against the City of London in 1682.[4] Sir Robert Sawyer, the attorney-general, was arguing that corporations which abuse their power could be seized into the king's hands. If, he said, it were impossible to proceed thus against corporations, and to punish them for their misdeeds, "it were to set up independent commonwealths within the kingdom and (this) . . . would certainly tend to the utter overthrow of the common law, and the crown too, in which all sovereign power to do right both to itself and the subjects, is only lodged by the common law of this realm."[5] A mere permission to aggrieved individuals to sue the corporation would be of little avail, "whilst the cause still remains and is in as great power to oppress as before." Indeed, "the law would be deficient if such inferior jurisdictions, or corporations, were not subject to the common law upon the like conditions, as other liberties franchises and inferior jurisdictions are."

That is really the gist of the matter. The same reasons which make it necessary for the law to recognize the crime of conspiracy, make it necessary to regulate these groups of men, who, when they act in combination, have far more power for good or evil than any single man. The failure to recognize this principle in the case of Trade Unions of workmen or masters, and the abandonment by the state of any control over their activities, have shown that Sir Robert Sawyer was a true prophet; for the abandonment by the state of its sovereignty has in effect set up a new feudalism, which is every whit as retrogressive in its ideas, and as mischievous, as the feudalism of the Middle Ages. Our modern

---

[1] "Lawful authority of incorporation; and that may be by four means, sc. by the common law, as the King himself, etc.; by authority of Parliament; by the King's charter (as in this case); and by prescription," (1615) 10 Co. Rep. at f. 29b.

[2] (1553) Anon. Dyer 100. [3] Vol. iii 478-479.

[4] 8 S.T. 1039. [5] Ibid at p. 1178.

experience is a striking illustration of the political wisdom of the Roman lawyers when they taught the expediency of " keeping the corporate form under lock and key."[1] In fact, creation by and subordination to the state are the only terms upon which the existence of large associations of men can be safely allowed to lead an active life.

It is, it is true, a favourite theory among our modern teachers of jurisprudence, that the life of these associations of men is a real living thing, quite independent of the permission to exist as an incorporate person given to them by the state; and a survey of the various groups which flourished in the Middle Ages, a consideration of the great freedom with which groups may incorporate themselves at the present day, may lead to the view that these incorporate groups have, and always have had, a life of their own, independent of the sovereign state—just as the custom which is at the back of law is independent of the command of the sovereign. The practical inference, sometimes drawn, seems to be that the law should recognize the personality of all such groups. But it is obviously inexpedient to limit unduly the sovereign's power to impose conditions upon such recognition. The sovereign may be willing to recognize many various groups, just as he may be willing to recognize as law many reasonable customs. But a civilized state cannot dispense either with the need for that recognition or with the power to impose conditions, any more than it can dispense with some test as to the reasonableness of the customs which it admits as laws. The somewhat anarchic theory that the sanction of the state could or should be dispensed with, has gained more favour in Germany and other continental countries than in England, because the attainment of corporate form was, as Maitland has shown, more eagerly desired in countries which had not the expedient of the trust.[2] We have seen that much can be done under cover of a trust without the necessity for a grant of incorporation.[3] And though it has been necessary to control the formation of these trusts in certain respects, a greater liberty of forming them can more safely be allowed than a large unregulated liberty of association, because the

---

[1] Political Theories of the Middle Age, xxx.

[2] " Behind the screen of trustees, and concealed from the direct scrutiny of legal theories, all manner of groups can flourish : Lincoln's Inn or Lloyds' or the Stock Exchange or the Jockey Club, a whole Presbyterian system, or even the Church of Rome with the Pope at its head. But, if we are to visit a land where Roman law has been 'received,' we must leave this great loose 'trust concept' at the Custom House, and must not for a moment suppose that a meagre *fidei-commissum* will serve in its stead. Then we shall understand how vitally important to a nation—socially, politically, religiously important—its Theory of Corporations might be," ibid xxix, xxx.

[3] Vol. iv 478-479.

capacity for action of a group of men, who depend for their life upon a body of trustees acting under a trust deed which defines and stereotypes their powers, is far more limited, both for good and evil, than the capacity for action of an incorporate person.[1]

Corporate life and form, therefore, cannot exist without the permission of the state, express, presumed, or implied.   But the incidents and the continuance of that life are not equally dependent on the state.   An Act of Parliament can of course do anything; so that it can give a corporation powers which, without such a sanction, would infringe the principles of the common law, or it can vary its powers, or dissolve it at pleasure.   But it was well recognized in the seventeenth century that the law cannot be changed by royal charter,[2] so that a charter, which purported to give a corporation powers which infringed the principles of the common law, would be void.[3]   It would seem, for instance. that a charter, which permitted a corporation to deprive at will any of the corporators of his freehold rights in the corporation, would be void;[4] and it was held after the Revolution that new charters, granted after an attempted surrender of the old charter, which could not take legal effect, were void.[5]   It would seem, too, that the king could not at his pleasure vary the rights of those upon whom he had conferred privileges by his charter,[6] nor could he dissolve the corporation which he had created.[7]

These principles are clearly the consequence of the definition of the constitutional position of the king in the state.   Obviously they made for the independence of the corporate life which these incorporate persons enjoyed, just as they made for the freedom of the natural persons who were the subjects of the state.   We shall see in the following section that they have had some influence on the character of the powers, capacities, and liabilities, which the law attributed to them.

Powers, Capacities and Liabilities

We have seen that in the Middle Ages the lawyers were beginning to deduce from the nature of corporate personality certain conclusions as to the powers, capacities and liabilities of corporations.[8]

---

[1] Vol. iv 479-480.

[2] " The king cannot by his charter alter the law," Anthony Lowe's Case (1610) 9 Co. Rep. at f. 123a; vol. iii 476-477.

[3] We have seen, ibid 477, that in the Middle Ages this principle had been applied to a charter which it was alleged had infringed a statute.

[4] See Warren's Case (1620) Cro. Jac. 540; Grant, Corporations (ed. 1850) 22.

[5] Piper v. Dennis (1692) Holt 170; Grant, op. cit. 21-22.

[6] City of London's Case (1610) 8 Co. Rep. at f. 126b, citing a record of 32 Ed. III.

[7] Hayward v. Fulcher (1624) Palmer at p. 501 per Whitelocke, J.

[8] Vol. iii 487-489.

This process was pursued during this period; and, in consequence, we find certain rules laid down as to activities from which the nature of that personality debarred corporations, and as to activities which were naturally incident to corporate life. But we shall see that, though it is possible to say that the nature of corporate personality debars corporations from certain activities, it is difficult to draw the line in particular cases; and that, from that time to this, there has been considerable fluctuation of opinion as to whether certain activities are or are not permissible. Similarly there has been considerable difficulty in determining what activities are or are not incident to corporate life; and in the evolution of the law on this matter, the disturbing influence of semi-political considerations may be suspected. Most corporations at this period were created by royal charter; and, as we have seen,[1] to allow a royal charter to vary the incidents annexed by the common law to corporate capacities, appeared to contravene the principle that a royal charter cannot change the law. Hence there was a tendency to define corporate powers and capacities somewhat rigidly, and to deny that the crown could limit the powers naturally incident to a corporation. But it was obviously desirable to maintain some measure of control over corporate activities. This fact was recognized by the law; and it soon became apparent that, as the purposes for which corporations were formed were very various, it was hardly possible to maintain that all corporations created by royal charter must have the same powers and capacities. Hence, in addition to older modes of controlling corporate activities, we begin to see the beginnings of a limitation on these activities based upon the purposes for which a corporation is created—a limitation which, in later law, will assume enormous importance. Though it may not be within the competence of the crown to change the incidents annexed by law to corporate personality, it is competent to the crown to define the purposes for which a corporation is created; and if the corporation tries to effect purposes other than those for which it was created, its acts will be ultra vires and void.

I shall therefore deal with the history of this subject under the following three heads: (1) activities impossible to a corporation; (2) powers and capacities incident to a corporation; and (3) limitations on the powers and capacities incident to a corporation.

(1) *Activities impossible to a corporation.*

The deductions which the mediæval lawyers had drawn from the nature of corporate personality, as to the activities which were impossible to a corporation, were summed up by Coke in the *Case*

---

[1] Above 48.

of Sutton's Hospital,[1] and passed on into modern law. "A corporation aggregate of many," he said, "is invisible, immortal, and rests only in intendment and consideration of law; and therefore a dean and chapter cannot have predecessor or successor. They cannot commit treason, nor be outlawed nor excommunicate, for they have no souls, neither can they appear in person but by attorney. A corporation aggregate of many cannot do fealty, for an invisible body can neither be in person nor swear. It is not subject to imbecilities, death of the natural body, and divers other cases."[2] In 1682 it was said by counsel, arguing for the corporation of London, that a corporation "is but a name, an *ens rationis*, a thing that cannot be seen, and is no substance."[3] It followed that it could not either do or suffer a personal wrong, so that it could not commit or suffer a battery; nor could it have a traitorous or a felonious mind, so that it could not commit treason or felony.[4] In the eighteenth century Blackstone summarized the older authorities as to the disabilities of a corporation which could be deduced from the nature of its corporate personality;[5] and in 1915 substantially the same views were expressed by Lord Wrenbury. "The artificial legal person called the corporation," he said, "has no physical existence. It exists only in contemplation of law. It has neither body, parts, nor passions. It cannot wear weapons nor serve in the wars. It can be neither loyal nor disloyal. It cannot compass treason. It can be neither friend nor enemy."[6]

But it is one thing to draw abstract conclusions from the nature of corporate personality, as to the powers and capacities and liabilities of a corporation: it is another thing to translate these conclusions into concrete rules. If these conclusions were pushed to their logical consequences, it would follow that a corporation could not, as a corporation, be held liable for tort or crime. These consequences followed from the arguments addressed to the court on behalf of the City of London in 1682.[7] But the court was swift to reject them;[8] and, in effect, held that a corporation could be guilty of a seditious libel and other misdemeanours.[9] In more

---

[1] (1613) 10 Co. Rep. 23a.

[2] At f. 32b; cp. Bevil's Case (1575) 4 Co. Rep. at f. 11a; Co. Litt. 66b.

[3] 8 S.T. at p. 1137.　　　　[4] Ibid at pp. 1137-1138.　　　　[5] Comm. i 464-465.

[6] Continental Tyre and Rubber Co. v. Daimler Co. [1915] 1 K.B. at p. 916.

[7] See 8 S.T. at pp. 1137-1140.

[8] "That bodies politic may offend and be pardoned appears by the general article of pardon 12 Car. 2, whereby corporations are pardoned all crimes and offences. And the Act for regulating corporations, 13 Car. 2, which provides that no corporation shall be avoided for anything by them misdone or omitted to be done, shows also that their charters may be avoided for things by them misdone or omitted to be done," *per curiam* 8 S.T. at pp. 1266-1267.

[9] As Sir F. Pollock says, L.Q.R. xxvii 232-233, "Treby's interest, of course, was to suggest every possible objection, technical as well as substantial, to penal pro-

modern times the courts have held a corporation liable even for malicious torts, committed in the course of acts which are within the scope of the powers of a corporation.[1] No doubt the theoretical difficulties of imputing malice to a corporation, which were felt by some judges,[2] and given effect to in some decisions of the nineteenth century,[3] have been slurred over by the modern doctrine of the employer's liability for the torts of his agent.[4] The human agent can be guilty of malice; and, if he is acting in the course of his employment, there is no reason why his master should escape liability for his acts because he is a corporation.[5] It would thus seem that, so far as criminal or civil liability is concerned, the courts have always been prepared to hold that a corporation is as capable of being held liable as a natural person. It is true that it cannot be punished in the same way as a natural person. It cannot be corporally punished; but its liability can be brought home to it in a manner which is appropriate to such a person. As we shall see, it can be dissolved or suspended;[6] and, as the cases show, it could always be made to pay compensation for the trespasses,[7] and in our modern law even for the malicious torts,[8] committed by it through its agents.

The manner in which the law has dealt with the liability of a corporation for wrong-doing, is typical of the manner in which it has reconciled the incapacities of a corporation, which flow from the conception of corporate personality, with considerations of practical convenience. At an earlier period in the history of the law, when as yet the idea of a corporation was new, the lawyers were inclined to lay more stress upon wide general deductions from the nature of corporate personality. Thus they said that a

ceedings against a corporation. The King's advisers, on the other hand, were prepared to go very far in ascribing both wrongful acts and wrongful intention to a corporate body, for they charged the City of London with a malicious and seditious libel. No general inference can be drawn, except that there was no settled rule either way to prevent either argument from being plausible."

[1] Barwick v. English Joint Stock Bank (1867) L.R. 2 Ex. 259; Citizen's Life Assurance Co. v. Brown [1904] A.C. at p. 426 per Lord Lindley.

[2] See e.g. Lord Branwell's judgment in Abrath v. the N.E.R. (1886) 11 A.C. at pp. 250-254.

[3] See e.g. Stevens v. Midland Counties Rly. (1854) 10 Ex. at p. 356 per Alderson, B.; Western Bank of Scotland v. Addie (1867) L.R. 1 Sc. and Div. App. at p. 167 per Lord Cranworth.

[4] Note e.g. that in Stevens v. Midland Counties Rly. (1854) 10 Ex. at pp. 356-357 Platt, B., thought that a corporation would be responsible for a malicious act of its servant which it had authorized.

[5] As Sir F. Pollock has said, L.Q.R. xxvii 235, "as for the question ' utrum universitas delinquere possit,' our modern way has been to circumvent it. The real difficulty was to make out how any man, any natural man, could be vicariously liable to pay damages for the wrongful act or negligence of his servant, which he had in no way authorized and might even have expressly forbidden. When this was overcome, the difficulty of ascribing wrongful intention to an artificial person was in truth only a residue of anthropomorphic imagination."

[6] Below 65-67.   [7] Vol. iii 488.   [8] Above n. 1.

corporation could not be seised to a use,[1] either because a corporation had no conscience, or because the process of the court of Chancery could not issue against it,[2] or because it had no capacity to take to another's use;[3] and Blackstone stated that it could not be a trustee.[4] Because it could hold only in its corporate capacity for the purposes of the corporation, it was said that a gift to a corporation and another person or another corporation jointly, would create, not a joint tenancy, but a tenancy in common; for in such a case the two co-owners held in different capacities.[5] No doubt these were legitimate deductions from the vague and wide premises on which they were founded. But they were found to be inconvenient in practice. And so, on grounds of practical convenience, they have been evaded or altered. Equity, contrary to Blackstone's dictum, found no difficulty in ruling that a corporation could be a trustee;[6] and the Legislature has recently enabled a corporation to hold jointly with another person or corporation.[7]

In fact, though these wide deductions drawn from the nature of corporate personality have called attention to salient incapacities of corporations as compared with natural persons, they have never been able to stand any severe strain. Practical convenience rather than theoretical considerations have, from the days of the Year Books onward, determined what activities are possible, and what are impossible to a corporation. And because the law has always followed this course, it was the more possible in these last days, in the supposed interests of national defence, to sacrifice the central doctrine of corporation law—the distinction between the corporation and its members—in order to affect a British corporation with the consequences of possessing an enemy character.[8] No doubt there is Year Book authority for the proposition that matters affecting individual corporators may affect the validity of corporate acts;[9]

---

[1] Fulmerston v. Steward (1554) Plowden at p. 103; Chudleigh's Case (1589-1595) 1 Co. Rep. at f. 122a; cp. Sanders, Uses (5th ed.) ii 27 n.

[2] "It was said that no corporation can be seised to a use, for none can have confidence committed to him but a body natural, who hath reason and is capable of confidence, and may be compelled by imprisonment by order of the Chancellor of England to perform the confidence, for that is the way the party shall take to have it performed, and no corporation which consists of many can be imprisoned, and their natural body shall not be imprisoned for the offence of their body corporate, which is another body," Croft v. Howel (1578) Plowden at p. 538.

[3] Abbot of Bury v. Bokenham (1539) Dyer at f. 8b.

[4] Comm. i 464.   [5] Litt. § 290; Co. Litt. 189b, 190a.

[6] Attorney-General v. Landerfield (1744) 9 Mod. 286, where the chancellor said that "nothing was clearer than that corporations might be trustees."

[7] 62, 63 Victoria c. 20.

[8] Daimler Co. v. Continental Tyre and Rubber Co. [1916] 2 A.C. 307; at p. 344 Lord Parker said, "the truth is that considerations which govern civil liability and rights of property in time of peace differ radically from those which govern enemy character in time of war."

[9] Vol. iii 485-486.

but this goes far beyond these decisions.   Here we need only
note that, historically, the fact that such a decision was possible,
illustrates the comparatively small importance which doctrines,
derived from the nature of corporate personality, have had on the
law as to what activities are impossible to a corporation.   We
shall see later that this decision has also some bearing on the
theory or want of theory as to the nature of that personality,
which has always been a characteristic feature of English law.[1]
But at this point we must turn from the consideration of the things
which a corporation cannot do to the things which it can do.
Here, too, we shall see that the wide general rules with which the
law started have been modified to meet practical needs.

(2) *Powers and capacities incident to a corporation.*

Already in the Middle Ages the lawyers were coming to the
conclusion that certain powers and capacities were incident to a
corporation.   It was assumed in 1481 [2] that a corporation could
take a grant of property or a franchise, for that was the purpose
for which the corporation had been created; and Fitzherbert, in
abridging this case, laid it down that, if a corporation were created,
it had by implication the capacity to sue and to be sued.[3]   Coke,
improving upon these authorities, laid it down that other powers
and capacities belonged to a corporation by necessary implication.
For instance, the power to acquire or alienate property, and to
have a seal, and the right of the survivors to succeed to the
corporate property—were all incident to a corporation.[4]   Further,
other powers might be given to a corporation, which were necessary
to enable it to carry out the purposes for which it was created.
Thus it might be given the power to acquire lands in mortmain,
or to make bye-laws for the better carrying out the purposes for
which the corporation was created.[5]   Blackstone, while admitting
that there were distinctions between corporations sole and corporations aggregate, and between ecclesiastical and eleemosynary
corporations and others,[6] lays it down that to every corporation
aggregate there is inseparably annexed as of course the following

---

[1] Below 69-71.   [2] Y.B. 21 Ed. IV. Mich. pl. 28.

[3] Fitz. Ab. *Grant* pl. 30, where he makes Brian and Choke say, " que le roy puit
faire corporacion sauns rien reserver ou riens dire que il serra pled ou empleder, quar
le si le roye graunte a moye licens de fayre une chaunterye pour une prest chaunterye
en certeyne lieu, et doner a luy et ces successours certeyne terre al value de certeine
somme, et jeo face, issint il est bone corporacion sauns pluis parolx et sauns riens
reserver etc."

[4] (1613) 10 Co. Rep. at f. 30b, cited below 55; as Sir F. Pollock says,
L.Q.R. xxvii 229, " Coke appears to go a little beyond Fitzherbert, and Fitzherbert a
little beyond the book at large."

[5] 10 Co. Rep. at f. 31a; Norris v. Staps (1617) Hob. 211.

[6] Comm. i 465-466.

five incidents: 1. To have perpetual succession. 2. To sue or be sued, implead or be impleaded, grant or receive, by its corporate name, and do all other acts as natural persons may. 3. To purchase lands and hold them, for the benefit of themselves and their successors. 4. To have a common seal. 5. To make bye-laws or private statutes for the better government of the corporation, which are binding upon themselves unless contrary to the laws of the land.[1]

It was settled before the sixteenth century,[2] and recognized in that century,[3] that any of the powers belonging to a corporation could be exercised by a majority of the corporators—a principle which an Act of 1541-1542 enforced on corporations, notwithstanding any directions to the contrary contained in their foundation statutes.[4] Similarly, the mediæval rule that an act of the corporation must be under the corporation seal,[5] and the mediæval exceptions to that rule,[6] were recognized and reasserted; and it was laid down at the end of the seventeenth century that the seal must be affixed by the proper officer,[7] and that the seal was not needed for acts which, being matters of record, the corporation was estopped from denying.[8]

All these powers, whether incident or not to a corporation, were giving rise to a large mass of case law. With the detailed rules which resulted we are not here concerned. But we are concerned with the manner in which the law regarded these powers, as it has a considerable bearing upon the view which the law took of corporate powers generally.

It would seem that, just as the law regarded certain powers and capacities to be impossible to a corporation owing to the nature of its corporate personality, so it regarded certain powers and capacities as incident to that personality, and as inseparably annexed to it as to a natural person. This view of the nature of corporate capacities had not emerged in the Middle Ages. It was

---

[1] Comm. i 463-464.

[2] Y.B. 21 Ed. IV. Mich. pl. 53 (p. 70) cited vol. iii 485.

[3] See the Chamberlain of London's Case (1591) 5 Co. Rep. at f. 63a; cp. R. v. Bailiffs of Ipswich (1706) 1 Salk. at p. 435; Grant, Corporations 68.

[4] 33 Henry VIII. c. 27—a necessary act for avoiding questions as to the validity of the surrenders of the monastic property.

[5] Vol. iii 489; Grant, op. cit. 55, and cases there cited.

[6] But the authority on this matter is scanty; besides the Y.BB. cases, vol. iii 489, Grant, op. cit. 62, only cites Randle v. Dean (1701) 2 Lut. 1496, which has not much bearing on the matter, and Blackstone does not mention these exceptions in his treatment of the subject in Bk. I; but the exception seems to have been recognized in Cary v. Matthews 1 Salk. 191, it had got into the Abridgments, and, as Grant points out, it was revived and given its modern importance by the decisions of the nineteenth century.

[7] (1702) Anon. 12 Mod. 423 per Holt, C.J.

[8] Mayor of Thetford's Case (1702) 1 Salk. 192—"the reason is, because they are estopped by the record to say it is not their act,"

said, it is true, that a power to sue or be sued was naturally incident to a corporation; and it was assumed that a power to hold property or make contracts was also naturally incident.[1] But it was not till the sixteenth century that these and the like powers were said to be inseparably annexed, and therefore tacitly incident, to all corporations. We may perhaps suspect that the analogy of developments of the law relating to the prerogative has had some influence. Talk about inseparable prerogatives was very much in the air;[2] the king had been endowed with a corporate capacity;[3] the law had, as we have seen, already drawn the conclusion that certain activities were impossible to a corporation, and that certain capacities were obviously and naturally incident to it. Was it not therefore natural to argue that these capacities were not only naturally incident to a corporation, but as inseparable as similar capacities were to a natural man? And another consideration, of a semi-constitutional kind, no doubt helped the judges to come to this conclusion. It was well recognized that the king's charter could neither change the common law, nor alter the rights and duties of private persons as fixed by law.[4] To hold, therefore, that the king could neither give nor take away powers from a corporation, which he could not give or take away from a natural man, was quite in accordance with this constitutional doctrine.[5] But, if this were so, it followed that these powers and capacities were not only incident, they were also inseparably annexed to a corporation. The result was that any attempt on the part of the crown to restrict these powers could have no legal effect.

This doctrine, and its practical results, are clearly expressed in the following passage in the *Case of Sutton's Hospital*:[6] "When a corporation is duly created all other incidents are tacite annexed . . . and therefore divers clauses subsequent in the charters are not of necessity, but only declaratory, and might well have been left out. As 1. By the same to have authority ability and capacity to purchase, but no clause is added that they may alien etc., and it need not, for it is incident. 2. To sue and be sued, implead and be impleaded. 3. To have a seal, that is also declaratory. 4. To restrain them from aliening or devising but in a certain form; that is an ordinance testifying the king's desire, but it is but a precept, and doth not bind in law." This doctrine was, according to Lord Raymond's report, partially at any rate accepted by Holt, C. J.,

---

[1] Above 53.   [2] Vol. iv 204-206; vol. vi 28.   [3] Above 4-5.
[4] Above 48; cp. the Prince's Case (1606) 8 Co. Rep. at f. 16b.
[5] Cp. Pollock, L.Q.R. xxvii 230.
[6] (1613) 10 Co. Rep. at f. 30b. On this question see P. T. Carden, Limitations on the Powers of Common Law Corporations, L.Q.R. xxvi 320, which contains a very full and suggestive account of the evolution of the law on this matter.

in 1694;[1] and the same view is stated even more strongly by Blackstone.[2]

Now it is clear that this doctrine gives to corporations great liberty of action. It means, for instance, that they have the same free power to alienate real and personal property as a natural person; and this consequence has, in spite of adverse criticism of the rule as to free alienation of realty,[3] been admitted by the courts.[4] Similarly, they have the same freedom of contract, provided that the contract is in the proper form. In 1874, in the case of *Riche v. The Ashbury Carriage Co.*,[5] Blackburn, J., after citing the passage just quoted from the *Case of Sutton's Hospital*, said,[6] "this seems to me an express authority that at common law it is an incident to a corporation to use its common seal for the purpose of binding itself to anything to which a natural person could bind himself, and to deal with its property as a natural person might deal with his own. And further, that an attempt to forbid this on the part of the King, even by express negative words, does not bind at law. Nor am I aware of any authority in conflict with this case." It is often said that the effect of these and similar dicta is to give complete corporate autonomy to a common law corporation; and that, though a restriction contained in a charter may give the crown the right to annul the charter if it is disregarded, "it cannot derogate from that plenary capacity with which the common law endows the company."[7] But, as we shall see, it may perhaps be open to doubt whether so extensive effect can be given to these dicta.[8]

It is clear that to allow corporations this great liberty of action is not without its dangers. The logical result of allowing it is to give them powers to do acts, which may be wholly beyond, or even contrary to the purposes for which they were created. It was probably due to these rules of law that, at the end of the seventeenth century, companies were able to cite the opinion of eminent counsel to justify their acts in carrying on trades or businesses, or pursuing activities, wholly outside the scope of their charters, so that, for instance, a company formed for the manufacture of hollow

---

[1] "There are two sorts of corporations. The one constituted for public government, the other for private charity. The first being duly created, although there are no words in their creation, for enabling their members to purchase, implead, or be impleaded, yet they may do all these things, for they are all necessarily included in and incident to the creation," Philips v. Bury 1 Ld. Raym. at p. 8; but this passage does not occur in Skinner's report of this case at p. 482.

[2] "These five powers (above 53-54) are inseparably incident to . . . every corporation aggregate," Comm. i 464.

[3] Grant, Corporations (ed. 1850) 129 seqq.; Brice, Ultra Vires (3rd ed.) 74-78.

[4] Baroness Wenlock v. River Dee Co. (1883) 36 C.D. at p. 685 *n. per* Bowen, L.J.

[5] L.R. 9 Ex. 224.

[6] At p. 263.

[7] Palmer, Company Law (12th ed.) 3.

[8] Below 61-62.

sword blades, proceeded to carry on a banking business.[1]   It was probably also a perception of the inconveniences which so unrestricted a power would give to corporations, that has induced eminent authorities to question the rule that a corporation may freely alienate its real property.[2]   But in fact, though corporations had these large powers at common law, the law has always provided some measure of control over their exercise.   To the consideration of the forms which this control has taken at different periods, and in different circumstances, we must now turn.

(3) *Limitations on the powers and capacities incident to a corporation.*

Just as all natural persons are subject to the common law, so, from the earliest times, the common law has enforced its rules on all groups and communities of persons.   We have seen that, in the early days of the common law, this control had a considerable share in moulding these various groups and communities, through which the local government of the country was carried on.[3] Naturally it exercised the same control over some of these groups when they became municipal corporations.   These corporations were simply the old borough communities incorporated.[4]   They could not be said to have any distinct founder ; and so they were said to be subject only to the "general and common laws of the realm."[5]   This expressed the historic truth as to the form of control to which these corporations had been subject from time immemorial.   Taken in connection with the doctrine as to the wide powers inseparably incident to a corporation, it in practice left these corporate bodies an undue freedom, which produced that state of mind which is illustrated by the defence of the Cambridge common councilman, to the charge that the corporation had been selling pieces of the corporation land to corporators at unduly low prices—"he thought that the property (of the corporation) belonged *bona fide* to the corporation, and that they had a right to do what they pleased with their own."[6]   In later law, this rule was expressed in the unhistoric form that these corporations, not being subject to any visitor, were subject to the visitation of the king, which was exercisable only in the court of King's Bench.[7]

---

[1] Vol. viii 215-216.   [2] Above 56 n. 3.
[3] Vol. ii 401-405.
[4] Vol. i 140; vol. iv 131-134; cp. Maitland, Township and Borough 19-20.
[5] Philips v. Bury (1694) 1 Ld. Raym. at p. 8 *per* Holt, C.J.
[6] Municipal Corp. Report iv 2199, cited Maitland, Township and Borough 12.
[7] "In general the king being the sole founder of all civil corporations . . . the right of visitation . . . results . . . to the king.   The king being thus constituted by law the visitor of all civil corporations, the law has also appointed the place, wherein he shall exercise this jurisdiction : which is the court of king's bench ; where, and where only, all misbehaviours of this kind of corporations are enquired into and redressed, and all their controversies decided," Bl. Comm. i 468-469.

And this rule was extended to all civil corporations; so that a clause in letters patent, subjecting a corporation to the visitation of others, was held in 1753 to be void.[1]

This somewhat unhistoric manner of stating the law was due to the fact that ecclesiastical and eleemosynary corporations were always subject to the control of a visitor. They were the earliest corporations;[2] and, till the modern growth of trading corporations, they were perhaps the most numerous, and not the least important of corporations. During this period, the law was well established that ecclesiastical corporations were liable to visitation by the bishop; and that, subject to any other appointment by the founder, lay corporations of an eleemosynary type were subject to the visitation of the founder and his heirs.[3] The powers and duties of these visitors were settled, and put on their modern basis, by the decision of Holt, C.J., in the case of *Philips v. Bury* in 1694,[4] "The office of visitor by the common law is to judge according to the statutes of the college, to expel or deprive upon just occasions, and to hear appeals of course. And from him, and him only, the party grieved ought to have redress; and in him the founder hath reposed so entire confidence that he will administer justice impartially, that his determinations are final, and examinable in no other Court whatsoever."[5] The control exercised by the visitor was supplemented by the control which, as we have seen, the court of Chancery exercised, from the sixteenth century onwards, over charitable trusts.[6] In fact, whenever a trust could be established, the court of Chancery could intervene to compel a corporation, as it could compel an individual, to carry it out.[7]

But this control was only exercisable when a trust could be established. And in the case of many corporations—municipal corporations and trading corporations for instance—there was no trust which entitled the court of Chancery to interfere. In fact, none of these methods of control were applicable to lay corporations of a non-eleemosynary type. This fact is illustrated by the provisions of the statute of 1437,[8] which gave the justices of the peace control over ordinances made by gilds and other similar bodies; and by the statute of 1504,[9] which required the consent of the chancellor, the treasurer, the chief justices or judges of assize, or any three of them, to ordinances made by crafts, gilds, mysteries, or fraternities. But these statutes went a very little

---

[1] Bl. Comm. i. 469. [2] Vol. iii 471.
[3] Case of Sutton's Hospital (1613) 10 Co. Rep. at f. 31a; Eden v. Foster (1725) 2 P. Wms. at p. 326; Bl. Comm. i 468.
[4] 1 Ld. Raym. 5. [5] Ibid at p. 8.
[6] Vol. iv 398-399; cp. Eden v. Foster (1725) 2 P. Wms. 325.
[7] See Attorney-General v. Foundling Hospital (1793) 2 Ves. 42.
[8] 15 Henry VI, c. 6; vol. iv 322. [9] 19 Henry VII, c. 7; vol, iv 322-323.

way towards controlling the activities of these corporations.   What was wanted was a control which should ensure that they used their powers in furtherance of the purposes for which they had been created.   Having regard to the doctrines as to the large powers incident to a corporation, the construction of such a body of doctrine was not easy; for, as we have seen, it seemed to follow from this doctrine, that restrictive clauses in their charters, which purported with this object to restrain their powers, would be void.[1]

We can see the remote origins of the method which will ultimately be devised to deal with this difficulty, in a dictum of Brian, C.J., in 1481.   "If," he said, "the king grants to the men of Islington that they shall be discharged of toll, that is a good corporation for this purpose; but it will not give them power to purchase, etc."[2]   Similarly, in 1553, it was said that, "if the queen at this day would grant land by her charter *to the good men of Islington*, without saying, *to have to them their heirs and successors*, rendering a rent, this is a good corporation for ever to this intent alone, and not to any other."[3]   At the time when these statements were made, it is probable that the idea that a corporation must have certain powers inseparably incident to it, had not yet been laid down so rigidly as it was laid down subsequently.[4]   We may therefore regard the idea that the powers of a corporation were limited by the purposes for which the corporation was created, as an idea which was accepted by the law, before the idea that certain powers were inseparably incident to a corporation became an accepted legal doctrine.   Historically, therefore, it can be maintained that the latter idea must be understood to be subject to the former, and that the former idea consequently qualifies the generality of the latter.   The former idea was understood to operate in this way by Rolle, who states it as a proposition which qualifies the general proposition that, when a corporation is created, all other incidents are tacitly annexed.[5]   It followed, therefore, that though a corporation has a general power of contracting and of dealing with property like a natural

---

[1] Above 55-56; cp. L.Q.R. xxvi 324-326.

[2] "Si le Roy grant hominibus de Islington que ils seront discharges de toll, cest bon corporacion a cest entent, mes nemy a purchaser etc," Y.B. 21 Ed. IV. Mich. pl. 28 (p. 59).

[3] Dyer at f. 100a.   [4] Above 54-55.

[5] "Quant un corporation est duement create touts auters incidents sont tacite annexe.   Come si le Roy fait un generall Corporation per un certein nosme, sans ascun parolls de licence a purchaser terre, ou implede ou destre implede, uncore le Corporation poet purchace, implede ou d'estre implede assets bien, pur ceo que per fesans del Corporation touts ceux necessarie incidents sont included.   Mes le Roy poet faire per special parolls un limited Corporation ou un Corporation pour un special purpose, come sil grant *probis hominibus de Islington et successoribus suis* rendant rent; Ceo est un Corporation a render le rent al Roy et nemy autrement," Rolle, Ab. *Corporations* G, 1-3.

man, which cannot be restrained by royal charter, yet, the fact
that it is created for certain purposes, will limit its general powers
and capacities, by avoiding acts done which are not in furtherance
of these purposes.

But though the law was accepted in this sense in the sixteenth
and seventeenth centuries, it rested on somewhat slender authority ;
it had not as yet been appealed to to invalidate corporate acts ;
and, in view of the much greater stress laid upon the doctrine of
powers inseparably incident to a corporation, it was largely
ignored ; and, as we can see from the Parliamentary inquiry
which followed upon the bursting of the South Sea Bubble, even
denied to be law.[1] We have seen, however, that the principle
was asserted, and given somewhat of its modern importance on
that occasion ; for it was clearly laid down that a corporation
could not engage in activities which were wholly foreign to the
purposes for which it had been incorporated.[2]

This view of the capacities of corporations was also being
reached by a consideration of the limitations on the power, incident to a municipal corporation, to make bye-laws. We have
seen that the common law had long been accustomed to super-
vise the law administered in the boroughs, and to pronounce upon
the reasonableness of their customs and bye-laws.[3] It is clear
that, during this period, the court, in considering the validity of
these bye-laws of boroughs, had begun to lay stress, not only on
their reasonableness, but also on the question whether these bye-
laws came within the scope of their corporate powers. Thus in
1682, in the case against the City of London, Sir Robert Sawyer,
the attorney-general, speaking of municipal corporations, said,[4]
" the limits and extents of their corporations and jurisdiction are
limited by their charters . . . the power of making bye-laws,
which is incident to a corporation, is only for better government ;
and by that rule they must be judged." Substantially the same
law was laid down by Holt, C.J., in 1700 ;[5] and, during the
eighteenth century, it was held both in Chancery and at common
law that, if a charter gave a corporation power to make bye-laws,
it could only make them in the cases in which they were enabled
to make them by charter, " for such a power given by the charter
implies a negative that they shall not make bye-laws in any other
cases."[6] " Corporations," said Yates, J., in 1766, " cannot make

---

[1] Vol. viii 216 and n. 5. [2] Ibid and n. 4.
[3] Vol. ii. 400. [4] 8 S.T. 1158-1159.
[5] " The corporation having power to make bye-laws for the well governing of the
city, that ought to be the touchstone, by which their bye-laws ought to be tried ; and
if it be for their benefit, the bye-law will be good." City of London v. Vanacker 1 Ld.
Raym. at p. 498.
[6] Child v. Hudson's Bay Co. (1723) 2 P. Wms. at p. 209 per Lord Macclesfield.

bye-laws contrary to their constitution. If they do they act without authority."[1]

Thus the principle that the activities of corporations must be restrained to the fulfilment of the purposes for which they were created, was made to limit the doctrine that certain powers were necessarily incident to a corporation. That doctrine, as we have seen, has resulted in giving to corporations a large freedom of action; but the growth of this limiting principle has imposed upon it a necessary and salutary restraint; and the growth in the number and variety of corporations, not otherwise restrained, showed the courts, at the end of the seventeenth century, that it was absolutely essential to insist upon it. We can say, therefore, that corporations hold their powers and capacities subject to what, in later law, will be known as the doctrine of ultra vires. The germs both of the law as to the powers and capacities naturally incident to a corporation, and of the supplementary doctrine of ultra vires, have been implicit in the law from an early period. Both began to be developed during this period and in the eighteenth century; but they were not as yet highly developed. It will not be till the nineteenth century that the doctrine of ultra vires will develop into a large body of complex rules;[2] and then it will be in relation rather to new statutory corporations than to these older common law corporations. Even at the beginning of the twentieth century, the application of the doctrine to the powers of these common law corporations will give rise to some legal problems to which the authorities give no very certain answer.[3]

We have seen that modern authorities contain some very general statements as to the inoperative character of limitations of powers contained in charters of incorporation.[4] But it may perhaps be contended that there is an over-riding common law rule to the effect that the undertaking of activities, which is wholly foreign to the purposes for which a corporation has been created, is void. This limitation upon the powers of these common law corporations would of course apply whether or not there is an express mention of it in the charter. It would follow, firstly, that a limitation of this kind contained in a charter would be valid, because it would merely enforce a common law rule; and, secondly, that the rule laid down by the modern cases must be taken to apply to a general limitation of activities, which is not necessarily contrary to the purposes for which the corporation was created—a general limitation, for instance, of the right to alienate property or to contract.

---

[1] R. v. Spencer 3 Burr. at p. 1839. [2] See Brice, Ultra Vires (3rd ed.) 37.
[3] See P. T. Carden's article on Limitations on the Powers of Common Law Corporations, L.Q.R. xxvi 320.
[4] Above 56.

Such a limitation would be invalid.   It might well be, however, that, in any given case, an alienation or a contract might be held to be void, if it was directed to give effect to purposes wholly foreign to those for which the corporation was created.   If this be the law, it is not correct to say that the capacity of a common law or chartered corporation is wholly unrestricted.   It is restricted, in a less definite way it is true, but in a somewhat similar way, to that in which a statutory corporation or a registered company is restricted.

We shall now see that these rules as to the extent of the powers of a corporation have some bearing upon some of the modes in which a corporation can be dissolved.

Dissolution

I shall consider, firstly, the various modes in which a corporation may be dissolved; and, secondly, the effect of dissolution on corporate rights and liabilities.

(1) *Modes of dissolution.*

The modes of dissolving a corporation, which were recognized during this period, were, firstly, the disappearance of all its members or of an essential member; secondly, surrender by the corporation of its charter; and, thirdly, forfeiture.

(i) The view that, if all the members of a corporation disappeared, the corporation came to an end, was the best supported view in the Middle Ages;[1] it was assumed to be correct by Coke;[2] and it has therefore become an accepted principle of the modern law as to common law corporations.[3]   It is, however, by no means a self-evident rule;[4] and it was not the rule of Roman law.[5]   It seems also to have been accepted as a rule of law that, if an essential member of a corporation disappeared, and there was no power in the others to replace him, the corporation was dissolved.   This was the view taken by Rolle in the seventeenth century;[6] and it seems to have been the view taken by Parker, C. J., in 1712,[7] and by Comyns in his Digest.[8]   So far was this carried that it was held that, if a municipal corporation omitted to elect its mayor on the right day, so that it lost all power to provide

---

[1] Vol. iii 489.

[2] "If land holden of J.S. be given to an Abbot and his successors; in this case if the Abbot and all the convent die, so that the body politick is dissolved, the donor shall have again the land, and not the lord by Escheat," Co. Litt. 13b.

[3] Bl. Comm. i 473 ; Grant, op. cit. 303.

[4] Salmond, Jurisprudence (2nd ed.) 268.

[5] Dig. 3. 4. 7. 2 ; Girard, Droit Romain 231.

[6] Ab. *Corporation* I. pl. 1.

[7] R. v. Bewdley (1712) 1 P. Wms. at pp. 210-211.   [8] *Franchises* G. (4).

itself with a head, the corporation was dissolved.[1] This was remedied by an Act of 1724;[2] and the fact that this Act was needed, is good evidence that, at common law, the loss of an essential member of the corporation, without power of replacement, operated as a dissolution. The Act only remedied one consequence of this doctrine in the case of one kind of corporation. But we shall see that the dissolution of a corporation entailed the very inconvenient consequence that all its rights and liabilities disappeared.[3] It was therefore obviously impolitic to allow corporations to be dissolved by carelessness or accident; and so, in the eighteenth century, the courts, in order to avoid this result, extended the older cases which, firstly, laid it down that acceptance of a new charter did not destroy the old corporation;[4] and, secondly, recognized that the crown by a new grant could revive an old corporation thus dissolved.[5]

(ii) During the whole of the sixteenth and seventeenth centuries, the effect of a surrender by a corporation of its possessions or its charter was extremely doubtful. The fact that the law was doubtful is illustrated by the care which Henry VIII. took to get the surrenders of the monastic and chantry lands confirmed by Act of Parliament;[6] and, at the end of the seventeenth century, the attack by Charles II. and James II. on the charters of the municipal corporations, and the surrenders of the charters which they procured, gave the law as to the effect of such surrenders a political interest.[7]

At the outset we must distinguish between a surrender by a corporation of its property, and a surrender of its charter.

It seems to have been the opinion of Fitzherbert that a surrender by a monastery of its lands did not extinguish the corporation; but Brooke took the opposite view;[8] and of his opinion were

---

[1] Case of the Corporation of Banbury (1716) 10 Mod. 346; Bl. Comm. i 473.
[2] 11 George I. c. 4.   [3] Below 69.
[4] Haddock's Case (1681) T. Raym. at p. 439; Mayor of Scarborough v. Butler (1685) 3 Lev. 237.
[5] Mayor of Colchester v. Seaber (1766) 3 Burr. 1866; R. v. Passmore (1789) 3 T.R. at p. 241; Grant, op. cit. 304-305, says, "there seems to be a difficulty in reconciling the doctrine of dormancy, or dissolution for some purposes only, with strict principles of corporation law; on the other hand, however, the inconvenience of holding that a corporation in such circumstances is wholly dissolved, so that their leases would be disturbed . . . and persons having debts due to them from the corporation could not recover them . . . is manifestly so great, that the doctrine . . . must probably be considered as almost established."
[6] 31 Henry VIII. c. 13; 37 Henry VIII. c. 4.   [7] Vol. vi 210-211, 503-504.
[8] "Labbe et touts les moygnes devie, le Corporation est dissolve, et le terre eschetera, tamen 32 H. 8 per Fitzherbert, si ils vend tout les terres et labbey uncore le corporation remayn, quære de que il serra abbe, car la est nul eglise ne monastarie, quære si labbe devye si ils poyent eslire auter, le meason estant dissolve, moigne et chanon sont capaces des spiritualities come destre vicar executor et hujusmodi," Bro. Ab. Corporations pl. 78; the meaning of the last sentence would seem to be that, the monastery being dissolved, the monks are no longer dead persons in the law.

Popham, C.J., and the court of Queen's Bench, in the *Dean and Chapter of Norwich's Case* in 1590. They held that "by the grant of all the possessions of a dean and chapter their corporation is determined, inasmuch as they ought to have a place for their assembling."[1]   But, according to Coke's report, on a reference to Egerton, the two chief justices, and the chief baron, it was held in 1598, in accordance with what would seem to have been Fitzherbert's opinion, that if the corporation had duties to perform, which they could perform without possessions, the mere surrender of their possessions did not dissolve the corporation;[2] and this is the view which has prevailed.   Thus Holt, C.J., pointed out in 1692 that a surrender of liberties and privileges did not dissolve a municipal corporation, as it still had duties to fulfil, i.e. the government of the town.[3]   If, on the other hand, the surrender of its property entailed the total impossibility of carrying out the purpose for which the corporation was created, the surrender of the property might mean the dissolution of the corporation.[4]

Right down to the Revolution the question of the effect of a surrender by a corporation of its charter was very uncertain. Two cases of 1568[5] and 1569,[6] reported by Dyer, could be cited for the proposition that a surrender of the charter would dissolve the corporation.   The first case is not very strong, because the point was rather assumed than decided, and there had been legislation confirming the surrender; but, in the second, four judges gave it as their deliberate opinion that a surrender of its charter by a corporation dissolved it.   Later, however, the current of opinion set the other way.   In 1598 the inference drawn from the case of 1568 was, that the surrender "was not thought sure, till the grant and surrender was established and confirmed by Act of Parliament";[7] and in 1628 Whitelocke, J., differing from Jones, J., was strongly against the view that a corporation could dissolve itself by such a surrender—a corporation which did such an act would, he said, be "as it were a felo de se, which is against nature."[8]   Naturally these different opinions were the subject of

---

[1] Dyer 273b.

[2] Dean and Chapter of Norwich's Case 3 Co. Rep. 73a; see at ff. 75a, 75b; followed by Hayward v. Fulcher (1628) W. Jones at p. 168.

[3] R. v. The Mayor of London (1692) 12 Mod. at p. 19.

[4] "He agreed that if a corporation were made to a particular purpose, and they devest themselves of all right, so that they cannot answer the end of their institution, it is thereby dissolved," ibid; so Coke said, 3 Co. Rep. at f. 75a, "there cannot be a warden of a chapel, if the chapel and all the possessions be aliened . . . because he cannot be warden of nothing."

[5] Walrond v. Pollard, Dyer 273a.

[6] Archbishop of Dublin v. Bruerton, ibid 282b.

[7] Dean and Chapter of Norwich's Case 3 Co. Rep. at f. 75b.

[8] Hayward v. Fulcher Palmer at p. 501; see a discussion of these and other relevant authorities in 8 S.T. at pp. 1283-1288.

much argument in the proceedings against the City of London in 1682;[1] and, since many corporations were induced to surrender their charters to James II. and accept new ones, the question of the effect of a surrender assumed and become a question of political importance. That the law was very doubtful, and that most of the judges could not wholly free themselves from their political prepossessions, is clear from the opinions which they gave to the House of Lords in 1690, when a bill for the restoration of corporations was before the House.[2] Most of the judges held that a corporation could not surrender;[3] but Holt, C.J., followed by Eyre, J., held that it could. "Whether," he said,[4] "a corporation may be legally surrendered is a question that has lately been debated in Westminster Hall. I am of opinion that a corporation may surrender, and thereby the corporation is dissolved. I take it to be a franchise from the crown and may be surrendered. It is a creature created by policy. Where is the harm if the king consents and the corporation too? A corporation is made for need; in times they are not fit." Then, after citing the two cases reported by Dyer, he proceeded, "some say this (i.e. a corporation) is but a capacity. This is more; this is an entity; they have power to act." As was generally the case, it is Holt's view that has prevailed;[5] but with this qualification that, if the corporation is a corporation by prescription,[6] or created under the authority of an Act of Parliament,[7] it cannot dissolve itself by the surrender of its charter. In the first case it has no charter to surrender, and in the second it does not derive its being from the charter.

(iii) That a corporation could be suspended or dissolved, on proceedings taken against it by the crown for misuse or abuse of its privileges, was a very old principle of the common law.[8] The two methods used to effect this object were, as in the preceding period, Scire Facias and Quo Warranto; but for the old writ of Quo Warranto an information in the nature of a Quo Warranto had been substituted.[9]

As in the case of a surrender, so in the case of a forfeiture or suspension of a corporation, the proceedings taken by Charles II. and James II. against the municipal corporations, occasioned much dispute as to the possibility of forfeiture. Those who argued for the City of London maintained the thesis that a corporation could not be "discorporated" as the result of an information in the

---

[1] 8 S.T. at pp. 111-113 *per* Treby *arg.*
[2] Hist. MSS. Comm. 12th Rep. App. Pt. vi no. 208 at pp. 429-432.
[3] See the views of Pollexfen, C.J., at pp. 429-430. [4] At p. 429.
[5] Butler v. Palmer (1700) 1 Salk. 191; Grant, op. cit. 46.
[6] Ibid 296, 306-307. [7] Ibid 46, 308.
[8] Vol. ii 396-397, 398; vol. iii 489-490.
[9] The chief difference between the two seems to have been in the meane process see Grant, op. cit. 298.

nature of a quo warranto;[1] and, after the Revolution, the same judges who denied that a corporation could be dissolved by surrender, maintained that it could not forfeit its existence, while the judges who took the opposite view on the question of surrender, also took the opposite view on the question of forfeiture.[2] Here too it is the view of the last named judges which has prevailed.[3] And it has rightly prevailed for those reasons of public policy, which were successfully urged by the counsel who argued for the crown in the case against the City of London in 1682.[4] It is a great hiatus in our modern company law, a hiatus which has recently been the cause of considerable difficulty,[5] that when once a company has been validly created, the Act provides no procedure by which it can be disincorporated.[6] It is true that dicta of great weight assert that the crown might institute proceedings to attack the validity of its creation, because the crown is not bound, as the subject is bound,[7] by § 17 of the Companies (Consolidation) Act 1908, which makes the certificate of the registrar absolutely conclusive as to the fact of incorporation.[8] But as yet there has been no direct decision on the question whether the crown possesses even this modified power.

A distinction as to when the proceedings by scire facias, and when the proceedings by quo warranto, were appropriate, was drawn at the end of the eighteenth century. Ashhurst, J., said in 1789[9] that, "a scire facias is proper when there is a legal existing body, capable of acting, but who have been guilty of an abuse of the

[1] 8 S.T. at pp. 1115, 1245.

[2] Hist. MSS. Comm. 13th Rep. App. Pt. v no. 269 pp. 72-73.

[3] R. v. Mayor of London (1692) 12 Mod. at p. 18; Grant, op. cit. 295; cp. Halsbury, Laws of England viii 397-398, 400.

[4] Above 46.   [5] Below 71, 103 n 3.

[6] "If created there is no power given in this Act of Parliament, nor in any other Act of Parliament that I am aware of, by which through any result of a formal application, like an application by scire facias to repeal a charter, the company can be got rid of, unless it can be got rid of by being extinguished through the effect of the Act of Parliament, which provides for the winding up of companies," Princess of Reuss v. Bos (1871) L.R. 5 H. of L. at p. 192 per Lord Hatherley; "It might have been a very wise provision of the Legislature to say that in a case of that kind—a case where there was an abuse of the Act of Parliament going on, a case where, if it had been a matter of royal grant, there would have been what is termed a forfeiture of the franchise by reason of nonuser or misuser—it might have been a very wise thing for the Legislature to say that . . . there should be some summary . . . mode of . . . getting rid of the incorporation. . . . However, the Legislature has not thought fit to provide any means . . . for getting rid of an incorporation in such circumstances," ibid. at p. 202 per Lord Cairns.

[7] "The section does preclude all His Majesty's lieges from going behind the certificate or from alleging that the society is not a corporate body with the status and capacity conferred by the Acts," Bowman v. the Secular Society [1917] A.C. at p. 439 per Lord Parker.

[8] Bowman v. the Secular Society [1917] A.C. at pp. 439-440 per Lord Parker; Cotman v. Brougham [1918] A.C. at p. 519 per Lord Parker; cp. the remarks of Lord Halsbury in Salomon v. Salomon [1897] A.C. at p. 30.

[9] R. v. Pasmore 3 T.R. at pp. 244-245.

power entrusted to them; for as a delinquency is imputed to them, they ought not to be condemned unheard; but that does not apply to the case of a non-existing body. And a quo warranto is necessary where there is a body corporate de facto, who take upon themselves to act as a body corporate, but from some defect in their constitution they cannot legally exercise the powers they affect to use." This seems to be the distinction recognized in modern law;[1] but it may be doubted whether it was recognized in the sixteenth and seventeenth centuries or earlier.[2] There is no doubt that quo warranto proceedings were taken against existing corporations in Edward I.'s reign; and these proceedings were taken against the City of London in 1682.[3] It is true that Treby, in his argument for the City, maintained that the procedure adopted was impossible, because it assumed that the City was a corporation, and yet charged the City with having usurped the name of a corporation;[4] and he cited a commonplace book of Hale for the proposition that, if a quo warranto was brought for usurping the name of a corporation, it must be brought against individuals, though it might be against a corporation for usurping particular liberties to which they were not entitled.[5] This distinction has not been upheld;[6] but it may be that the arguments in the City of London Case, and the subsequent discussions of that case, have had something to do with fixing the modern law.

If judgment is given for the crown on a scire facias the charter is repealed, and the corporation disappears.[7] On a quo warranto the crown, if successful, gets judgment that the corporation be seized into the king's hands. This does not necessarily dissolve, but may only suspend the corporation. If the crown chooses to take advantage of the seizure, and does not restore its rights, the corporation will be dissolved. But he may restore its rights or revive them by a new charter, in which case the result of the seizure will only be suspension; and this in fact has been the usual course pursued in such cases.[8] We shall now see that some of the effects of dissolution supply a very good reason why the king should, in such cases, choose to revive the old corporation, rather than let it be dissolved, and then create a wholly new corporation.

(2) *The effect of dissolution on corporate rights and liabilities.*

We have seen that, at the close of the Middle Ages, it was doubtful whether, on the dissolution of a corporation, its real

---

[1] Grant, op. cit. 296; Halsbury, Laws of England viii 400.
[2] Grant, op. cit. 296-298.   [3] Ibid 297-298.
[4] 8 S.T. at p. 1116.   [5] Ibid at p. 1117.
[6] Grant, op. cit. citing R. v. Amery (1788) 2 T.R. at pp. 547-549.
[7] Ibid 295.   [8] Ibid 295, 301; cp. 8 S.T. 1340-1343.

property escheated, or whether it reverted to the donor.[1] There is no doubt that the former view is the more logical; and there is reason to think that this view was taken in 1622.[2] The latter view was probably, in origin at least, based upon the case where the corporation held land in frankalmoin of the donor, in which case it would escheat to the donor.[3] But there was a disposition in the sixteenth century to apply this rule to all the real property of a corporation.[4] Coke took this view both in his commentary on Littleton,[5] and in a case which he decided in 1613;[6] and he repeated, or invented as the cause for the existence of the rule, the a priori reason that to all gifts of such property to corporations the law annexed a condition of reverter to the donor.[7] In this, as in many other cases, Coke fixed the modern law. This rule of reverter to the donor was stated to be law by Lord Hardwicke in 1740;[8] Blackstone repeated it, and added the new reason that, as a corporation can have no heirs, a gift to a corporation was in effect a gift to it during its life, and so was analogous to an estate for life;[9] and it has been accepted by the writers of text-books on corporation law,[10] and applied in a modern case.[11] Clearly Coke's reason applied with even greater force to the leasehold interests held by corporations; for in these cases there was a tenure between them and the lessor. It was assumed, in the sixteenth century, that a statute was required to prevent the leasehold property of the dissolved monasteries from reverting to the donors.[12] Blackstone stated the rule that they would revert,[13] and this rule also has been applied in a modern case.[14] The dissolution of a corporation, therefore, causes the lease to terminate, and the land to revert to the lessor.

The effect of the dissolution of a corporation on its chattels personal was long unsettled. When Grant wrote, in the middle of the nineteenth century, opinion was tending in the direction of

---

[1] Vol. iii 490.

[2] In Johnson v. Norway (1622) Winch 37, Hobart, C.J., said that he and the judges would consider whether the land escheated or reverted to the founders; in the Hale MSS., cited in Hargrave's note to Co. Litt. 13b, it is said that it was finally determined that the land escheated, Gray, Perpetuities 46-47.

[3] Vol. iii 490.   [4] (1590) Moore at p. 283, cited Gray, op. cit 46.

[5] Co. Litt. 13b.   [6] Dean and Canons of Windsor v. Webb Godbolt 211.

[7] Co. Litt. 13b.   [8] Attorney-General v. Gower 9 Mod. at p. 226.

[9] " The grant is indeed only during the life of the corporation; which *may* endure for ever: but, when that life is determined by the dissolution of the body politic, the grantor takes it back by reversion, as in the case of every other grant for life," Comm. i 472.

[10] Grant, op. cit. 303.

[11] Re Woking Urban Council [1914] 1 Ch. 300; cp. Hastings Corporation v. Letton [1908] 1 K.B. at p. 387 *per* Phillimore, J.

[12] Above 63.   [13] Comm. i 472.

[14] Hastings Corporation v. Letton [1908] 1 K.B. 378.

allowing the crown to take these chattels as bona vacantia;[1] and this would seem to be the rule now accepted.[2] It may be that the acceptance of this rule was due to a following of the analogy of the rule that, if chattels real or personal are vested in a trustee on trusts which fail, and the settlor's next-of-kin also fail, they are considered to be bona vacantia, and are therefore held by the trustee on trust for the crown. Obviously the analogy between such a case, and the case where chattels are held on trust for a corporation which has been dissolved, is close; and the same rule is applied in this case.[3] This made it the easier to apply the same rule to the chattels personal, which the dissolved corporation held in its own right.

From a very early date it was held that the personal rights and liabilities of a dissolved corporation disappeared. Thus rent-charges and annuities payable to and by them disappeared;[4] and a fortiori the same rule applied to such purely personal rights as debts.[5] It was probably these inconvenient results which followed on a dissolution that induced the courts to hold, wherever possible, that a new charter, given by the crown to a corporation which had become extinct, operated as a revival, so that the rights and liabilities of the old corporation remain.[6] It is for the same reason that the modern Company Acts make careful provision for the disposal of the company's property, and for the satisfaction of debts due by and to it, before it can be dissolved. The result is that the law on the subject of the effect of dissolution on a corporation's proprietary position, was, and still is, comparatively meagre.

The Nature of Corporate Personality

The genius of Maitland has popularized in this country the continental speculations on this topic. The question whether the personality of the corporation is fictitious or real is no doubt an interesting philosophical speculation; and it can easily be turned to political account in countries in which, because the trust is unknown, a larger liberty of incorporation is eagerly desired.[7] But these speculations are, for the most part, foreign to the province of the lawyer;[8] and, except so far as such speculations

---

[1] "The personal estate of a dissolved corporation seems to vest in the crown as *bona vacantia*," op. cit. 304.

[2] Re Higginson and Dean [1899] 1 Q.B. at p. 333 *per* Wright, J.; as he points out, at p. 331, this contention was made in the argument for the plaintiff in Corporation of Colchester v. Seaber (1766) 3 Burr. 1866.

[3] Re Higginson and Dean [1899] 1 Q.B. at p. 329.

[4] Y.B. 20 Hy. VI. Mich. pl. 17 *per* Paston and Newton, JJ.; Bishop of Rochester's Case (1596) Owen 73; Grant, op. cit. 303.

[5] Edmunds v. Brown (1668) 1 Lev. 237.

[6] Above 67.   [7] Above 47 and n. 2.

[8] This is well put in Prof. H. A. Smith's Law of Associations 128 seqq.

and theories have helped to make our law, they are equally foreign to the province of the legal historian. It will I think be clear from the history of the incorporate person, which I have narrated in this and in the preceding Book of this History,[1] that English law has, at all periods of its history, been very lightly touched by these speculations. No doubt in the Middle Ages, when the idea of an incorporate person was new, and the law relating to it was meagre, the lawyers do occasionally indulge in speculations of a crude and somewhat anthropomorphic kind, to help themselves out of the difficulties which they were experiencing in distinguishing this new entity from the human persons who composed it, or, more especially, from the human person who presided over it.[2] They were hampered both by the novelty of the conception, and the survival of older ideas, dating from a time when this distinction had not been clearly grasped. But, during this period, these causes of confusion were rapidly passing away. Such rules, for instance, as the rule as to the incapacity of a corporation to act while it was without a head, which historically can be traced back to a survival of some of these older ideas, had been placed on a new basis, logically consistent with the separate existence of the incorporate person. No doubt the lawyers still occasionally indulge in somewhat vague generalities as to the invisibility, immortality, and other non-natural qualities of this new entity. But they lay no great stress on them. They recognize that, by reason of its nature, some activities which are possible to the natural man are impossible to it; they are beginning to recognize that, as a matter of public policy, its activities should be limited to the purposes for which it was created; but, subject to these disqualifications, they have equated it as far as possible with the natural man.

This idea that the corporation is to be treated as far as possible like a natural man is the only theory about the personality of corporations that the common law has ever possessed. It is a large and a vague idea; but, on that very account, it is a flexible idea. It has made it possible to develop the law as to the powers and capacities of corporations according to the needs and public policy of the day.[3] It has made it possible to discipline them, and render them liable criminally or civilly for their wrongful acts, in ways which are appropriate to the artificial character of their personality. And the fact that it has thus been

---

[1] Vol. iii 469-490.   [2] Ibid 485-487.

[3] A good illustration of the way the lawyers went to work to determine what rules of law, applicable to natural men, should apply to corporations, can be seen in the reasons of expediency advanced in Croft v. Howel (1578) Plowden at p. 538, for the view that corporations, though not named, are included in Henry VII.'s statute of fines.

possible to make them liable for their wrongful acts, has enabled the law to adhere firmly to the central theory of corporation law, that the corporation is an artificial entity quite distinct from its members. It has been found possible to punish a corporation by dissolution or suspension of its existence; and it is not the case, as the counsel for the City of London argued in 1682, that a corporation cannot be punished; and that, if wrong is done, the individual corporators are alone liable in their individual capacity.

In these last days, the danger that an incapacity to deal with a corporation whose activities are mischievous, will induce the courts to tamper with this central theory of corporation law, is illustrated by the decision of the House of Lords in the *Daimler Case*.[1] This corporation, being a limited company, it was not possible to attack it, as it might have been possible to attack a common law corporation, on the ground that its activities were, in the circumstances, contrary to public policy.[2] And so the House of Lords, with an eye to national defence, and in order to do substantial justice, deliberately disregarded the distinction between the corporation and its members; and ruled that, in time of war, the character of its members might, for certain purposes, affect the character of the company. Foreigners might say that the corporation law of a country, in which such a decision is possible, is as yet in a rudimentary state, as it shows that the distinction between the personality of a corporation and that of its members is very lightly held. That would not be perhaps a wholly fair criticism; for the decision was largely due to the absence of any power in the crown to proceed against a company, as it might possibly have proceeded against a common law corporation.[3] In fact, the elastic theory of corporate personality, which the common law was developing and applying to common law corporations during this period, was in theory adequate to deal with corporate shortcomings. In practice, it is true, it had its defects, as the Municipal Corporations Report of 1833 was to show.[4] But the view that the corporation was to be given, so far as was consistent with its artificial nature and with the purposes for which it was created, the capacities and liabilities of the natural man, is probably as workable a theory of the nature of corporate personality as can be devised,—provided that the means of enforcing corporate liabilities civil or criminal are adequate, and provided that the law is enforced with vigilance.

---

[1] [1916] 2 A.C. 307.   [2] See Grant, op. cit. 42.
[3] See Mr. McNair's very pertinent criticisms on this decision in his Essays upon some Legal Effects of War 117-120; and see below 103 n. 3 for a criticism of one of the main reasons given for the decision.
[4] Above 57.

§ 3. The British Subject and the Alien

I propose to deal with this topic under two heads. In the first place, I shall say something of the history of the rules which define the persons who come under the category of British subjects, and of the position of the alien; and, in the second place, I shall deal with the history of the most important of the rights of the British subject—the right to personal liberty.

Subjects and Aliens

The beginnings of the modern rules of the common law, which define the persons who are to be accounted as British subjects, do not make their appearance till England, in the course of the thirteenth century, had lost the greater part of her continental possessions. These rules centre round the doctrine of allegiance; for it is the duty of allegiance, owed by the subject to the crown, which differentiates the subject from the alien. This doctrine has its roots in the feudal idea of a personal duty of fealty to the lord from whom land is held; and, though it has necessarily developed with the development of the position of the king, its origin in this idea has coloured the whole modern law on this topic. From the alien no such allegiance was due; and there can be little doubt that, in the thirteenth and fourteenth centuries, English law, reflecting insular prejudices, treated aliens as almost, if not wholly, rightless. But the king, from commercial and other reasons, gave them protection; and, by the close of the mediæval period, commercial reasons were differentiating the alien friend from the alien enemy, and were giving to the former definite though restricted rights in English private law. The law, as thus developed during the fifteenth and sixteenth centuries, was summed up, restated, and adapted to the conditions of the modern territorial state, in *Calvin's Case* in 1609. In the law of the seventeenth century we can see a development of the principles laid down in that case, along somewhat the same lines as are discernible in the fifteenth and sixteenth centuries. That development consisted in the elaboration both of the mediæval rules which centred round the doctrine of allegiance, and of the rules which defined the position of the alien friend.

At the close of the seventeenth century the more elaborate organization of commerce, and the closer intercourse between nations which came in its train, introduced a modification of the rules relating to alien enemies. It was recognized that they might be allowed to remain in England, and that, if so allowed to remain, they must be accorded the rights of alien friends. The recognition of this fact marks the beginning of a new set of principles. These principles cut across the old rules based on the personal tie of allegiance, which made birth within the territory of a given nation the test of whether or not a man was a subject or an alien, and across the distinction between alien friends and alien enemies. It came to be seen that, for commercial purposes, the law must look, not so much at the question of the nationality of a person, as at his residence, or the place at which he carries on his business; and, if we adopt this test, it may well be that enemy character will attach to a subject, and, conversely, that an enemy subject must be regarded as an alien friend. These new principles introduced a new test for distinguishing between friends and enemies. It was making its influence felt during the eighteenth and nineteenth centuries; and its meaning and consequences have been strikingly developed during the late war.

This summary will indicate the main lines of division for the historical treatment of this topic. I shall deal, in the first place, with the definition of the class of subjects; secondly, with the disabilities of aliens; and, thirdly, with enemy character.

(1) Who is a subject?

Ancient law, as Maitland has said, "will lay more stress upon purity of blood than on place of birth; it will be tribal rather than territorial law."[1] But feudalism introduced a new order of ideas. It is essentially territorial and personal. All rights and duties are bound up with and dependent upon the holding of land, and there is a personal tie of fealty between the tenant and his lord. These two ideas underlie the doctrine of allegiance, by which the later law will define both the class of persons who are to be reckoned as subjects, and the modes in which this status can be acquired and lost. But it was long before these ideas could make themselves felt. England was conquered by a foreign duke and an army of foreigners. The foreign duke and his descendants became kings of England and the ultimate lord of all the land in the country, without ceasing to be the duke of wide continental domains; and the leaders of the conquering army became the owners of much of the land of England, without ceasing to be lords of great estates on the continent. But so long as the king of England held these vast continental domains, and so long as his feudatories holding English land were as much French or Scotch as English, political conditions made the growth of anything like the rules of our modern law impossible. Till the boundaries of England were ascertained, till the great feudatories were reduced to the position

---

[1] P. and M. i 443.

of English landowners, English nationality could hardly emerge.[1] But, with the loss of Normandy, and the beginnings of the national enmity to France on the one hand and Scotland on the other, we can see the growth of the political conditions which will give birth to the modern rules. The doctrine of allegiance and its consequences can be more strictly applied to all Englishmen; and from this doctrine and its consequences the modern rules begin to emerge in the fourteenth and fifteenth centuries. The loss of Normandy, therefore, marks the beginning of the modern law; and we shall see that the circumstances attending on that loss long left their mark on that part of the law which relates to the disabilities of aliens.[2]

The history of the application of the doctrine of allegiance to determine the status of the subject, falls into three well marked periods: (i) the development of the law down to *Calvin's Case* in 1609; (ii) the restatement of the law in *Calvin's Case;* and (iii) the later developments.

(i) *The development of the law down to* CALVIN'S CASE.

The two sides of the feudal tie which existed between lord and man—its territorial basis, and its note of personal connection through the oath of fealty and the ceremony of homage[3]—reappear in the view which the law takes of the subject's duty of allegiance to the king. We shall see that the territorial basis of this tie has strongly influenced the rules as to the definition of the class of persons whom the law will account as subjects; while the personal obligation of fidelity has influenced no less strongly the rules as to how this status can be acquired and how it can be lost. But, necessarily, the contents of these rules were modified when they were transferred from their original application to the relation of lord and tenant, to their new application to the relation of king and subject—for the king is prerogative;[4] and these modifications will grow with time—for the exceptional character of the prerogative and the rules of law relating to it also grow with time. Let us see how these two aspects of the conception of the feudal tie—the territorial and the personal—helped to develop the mediæval law as to the acquisition and the loss of the status of a subject.

---

[1] P. and M. i 443-444—"the law even of Bracton's day acknowledged that a man might be a subject of the French king and hold land in France, and yet be a subject of the English king and hold land in England. It was prepared to meet the case of a war between the two kings: the amphibious baron must fight in person for his liege lord, but he must also send his due contingent of knights to the opposite army. In generation after generation a Robert Bruce holds lands on both sides of the Scottish border; no one cares to remember on which side of it he was born."

[2] P. and M. i 444-445; below 92.

[3] For fealty and homage see vol. iii 54-57.   [4] Ibid 56, 288-289.

The acquisition of the status of a subject.—The relation between the king and his subjects was never quite the same as the relation between the lord and his tenants. The tie of tenure played no part in it, and therefore the personal element was emphasized. But, for all that, the territorial element continued to be the most important element in the acquisition of the status of the subject. Though the duty of allegiance was dissociated from the tie of tenure, another and a wider territorial test became possible because it was the king—the ruler of all England—to whom allegiance was due. It could be laid down that all persons born on English soil, no matter what their parentage, owed allegiance to, and were therefore subjects of the king.[1] It is not surprising, therefore, that, at the beginning of the fourteenth century, the lawyers were beginning to think that birth within the king's allegiance signified birth within a defined "geographical tract."[2]

But did not this involve the consequence that all persons born outside that tract were aliens? Though it might be true that a person born a subject did not lose that character by residence abroad, what of the children of these persons born abroad? Were they necessarily aliens? And if so, did this rule apply to the king's children born abroad? If it did, it might affect even the succession to the crown. There was a debate on these matters in 1343.[3] It was stated as clear law that birth abroad cannot affect the position of the king's children, and cannot therefore have any application to the succession to the throne; and it was resolved that children born abroad to parents in the king's service were subjects. But on the general question nothing was then settled. In 1351, however, the matter came up again, and this time it was settled by statute.[4]

The statute recites the preceding debate, and states that, in order to put an end to all doubts on this matter, the king has charged the bishops and peers and other wise men of his council to deliberate upon the question, and that they have agreed to the following propositions: Firstly, that "the law of the Crown of England is, and always hath been such, that the children of the kings of England, in whatsoever parts they be born . . . be able and ought to bear the inheritance after the death of their ancestors." Secondly, that "all children inheritors, which from henceforth shall be born without the ligeance of the king, whose fathers and mothers at the time of their birth be and shall be at

---

[1] That this was assumed to be the rule in 1290 is clear from a case which arose out of the fraudulent dealing of Elyas de Rababyn, P. and M. i 446, R.P. i 44; it was also assumed to be the rule when, in 1343, the question of the status of those born beyond the sea was raised, R.P. ii 139 (17 Ed. III. no. 19).

[2] P. and M. i 442 and authorities cited in n 2.

[3] R.P. ii 139.   [4] 25 Edward III. stat. 2.

the faith and ligeance of the king of England, shall have and enjoy the same benefits and advantages . . . as the other inheritors afore said in time to come; so always that the mothers of such children do pass the sea by the licence and wills of their husbands." Parliament thus settled a debateable point in the law, by extending the status of a subject to persons born abroad of English parents.[1] In 1368 it was declared by Parliament, in accordance with precedents which came from the time when the king had large continental possessions,[2] that persons born, not only in England, but also in any territory belonging to the king, were subjects.[3]

Thus the rules as to the acquisition of the status of a subject by birth were fixed. It had also become clear, during this period, that the status could be acquired by statute, and that some of the incidents of the status could be acquired by an act of the prerogative.

It was recognized, certainly as early as, and probably before,[4] the beginning of the fifteenth century, that an Act of Parliament was needed to give to an alien the full status of a subject;[5] and this was accepted as a settled rule of law in *Calvin's Case*.[6] It may be that the national jealousy of royal favourites of foreign extraction,[7] and the growth of the legislative power of Parliament, have had something to do with the establishment of this rule of law; for it would seem that, though at the end of the thirteenth century the king claimed to be able to do what in later law could only be done by an Act of Parliament,[8] in a little more than a

---

[1] It was said by Huse, C.J., in Y.B. 1 Rich. III. Mich. pl. 7, that this was the common law rule, and that the statute was declaratory; but it would seem that the law was really doubtful, and that opinion was rather in favour of the view that those born abroad were aliens; see the case of Elyas de Rababyn, where the court, though it held that a particular person born abroad should be held as a subject, said that the case was not to form a precedent, R.P. i 44 (1290)—"quod de cetero non trahatur in consuetudinem quoad alios alienigenas."

[2] See Calvin's Case (1609) Co. Rep. at ff. 19a, 23a.   [3] 42 Edward III. c. 10.

[4] This rule seems to be in effect recognized in the case of Molyns v. Fiennes (1365) Select Cases before the Council (S.S.) 48-53; to a plea that the plaintiff was born out of the ligeance of the king, and so could not take as heir, the answer was given that, by treaty of peace, it was agreed that those disinherited by reason of the war should be restored; the plaintiff got judgment by reason of the treaty of peace "*exhibited in the same Parliament*"—an early authority for the modern rule of constitutional law that a treaty which changes or modifies the law needs the sanction of Parliament.

[5] "A ceo disons nous que meme cel Alice vient en Angleterre ove Beatrice Comtesse d'Arundel, . . . et puis nous disons que en le Parliament tenu tiel an en temps le Roy H. 4, la dit Alice per autorite del dit Parliament fuit fait person able a purchaser terre et tenements enheritances, come chescun auter legal home que fuit deins le Royaume, et mettra avant l'Act del dit Parliament," Y.B. 3 Hy. VI. Trin. pl. 30.

[6] 7 Co. Rep. at f. 6a; Bacon's Argument, Works (Ed. Spedding) vii 649.

[7] P. and M. i 446.

[8] Ibid 446-447, citing R.P. i 135, which shows that in 1295 Edward I. granted that Elyas Daubeny, born beyond the sea, should be held as "Anglicum purum," and should be able to sue in all courts.

century it is settled that the king's act can only have a much more limited effect.[1] He cannot make an alien a subject; for that might involve an alteration of the rights of other persons, which only Parliament can effect.[2] He can only make him a denizen. This means that by his letters patent he could give to an alien the right to hold and acquire land, and to sue all manner of actions.[3] This right was apparently looked upon as a species of franchise, and, like other franchises, could be regarded as a species of property; so that it could be granted to a man and his heirs, or to a man and the heirs of his body, or for life.[4] But it gave no rights in public law, and it had no retrospective operation. Thus, though it gave the person himself and his heirs the right to acquire land, neither the issue he had before the grant, nor any of his relations, other than his issue born after the grant, could inherit from him.[5] The status of a denizen thus gave only certain of the rights of the subject in private law.

The loss of the status of a subject.—The conception of allegiance had its personal as well as its territorial side. The subject owed faith and duty to the king who, throughout the mediæval period, was, as we have seen, regarded as a natural man.[6] As early as Edward I.'s reign, it would seem that a plea that a plaintiff was "not of the ligeance and faith of England," was held to be insufficient; and counsel was obliged to amend his plea, and say that the plaintiff was "not of the ligeance of England nor of the faith of the king."[7] We shall see that much reliance was placed on this ruling in *Calvin's Case*, because it was held to show that allegiance was a personal tie between the subject and the natural man who was king.[8] No doubt the fine-drawn speculations as to the differences between the king's politic and natural capacity,

---

[1] Above 76 nn. 4 and 5.

[2] " Nota pro lege Anno 36 H. 8, que ou alien nee vient en Angleterre et amesna son fitz ove luy que fuit nee ultra mare, et est alien come son pere est, la le roy per ses lettres patents ne poet faire le fitz heyre a son pere, ne a chescun auter, car il ne poet alterer son ley per ses letters patents nec aliter nisi per parliament, car il ne poit disinheriter le droit heire ne disapoynt le seignior de son eschete," Bro. Ab. *Denizen* pl. 9.

[3] "If made denizen by the king's letters patents, yet cannot he inherit to his father or any other. But otherwise it is if he be naturalized by Act of Parliament, for then he is not accounted in law alienigena, but indigena," Co. Litt. 8a; see ibid 129a; "the king only without the subject may make . . . letters patent of denization to them how and how many he will, and enable them at pleasure to sue any of his subjects in any action whatsoever," Calvin's Case (1609) 7 Co. Rep. at f. 25b; the distinction between a subject and a denizen seems to have been recognized in Edward IV.'s reign; Y.B. 9 Ed. IV. Trin. pl. 3 pp. 11-12; Plowden at f. 130, where this Y.B. is cited; see also Cockburn, Nationality 28.

[4] Calvin's Case (1609) 7 Co. Rep. at f. 6a.

[5] Co. Litt. 8a, 129a.   [6] Vol. iii 463-468.

[7] Cobledike's Case, cited in Calvin's Case (1609) 7 Co. Rep. at ff. 9b, 10a; for the stress laid on this case by Ellesmere, see Ellesmere's judgment in 2 S.T. at p. 688.

[8] Below 81-82.

which play so great a part in *Calvin's Case*, would have been un-intelligible in Edward I.'s reign, because the king was then re-garded simply as a natural man. But the earlier case does, it seems to me, emphasize the personal aspect of allegiance, and prove that it was then regarded as a personal tie between king and subject.

But this conception of the duty of allegiance gave it a permanent character, which it would have lacked if it had rested merely upon a territorial basis. If it had rested merely upon a territorial basis, it might have been argued that it, and with it the status of a subject, were lost, certainly if the territory ceased to form part of the dominions of the crown, and possibly so soon as the subject left the territory. But because it rested also on a personal basis, the latter conclusion would have been untenable. The personal tie of faith between king and subject, which had once attached by birth or otherwise, was independent of boundaries. And so we find that no one has ever supposed that mere depar-ture from the king's dominions can cause the loss of the status of a subject. This is assumed in the debates in Parliament in 1343, and in the debates which led up to the passing of the statute of 1351. No question is raised as to the status of the parents: the only doubt is as to the status of the children born abroad, as between whom and the king there is, by reason of their foreign birth, no personal tie. Whether this reasoning applied also to the loss of territory, so as to prevent persons in that territory who had once been subjects from losing that status, was not then settled; and, as we shall see,[1] it awaited a settlement till quite modern times.

This reasoning clearly involves the consequence that the tie of allegiance is indissoluble, and that therefore the status of the subject is permanent. This is, I think, assumed by mediæval lawyers; and was, as we shall see,[2] very clearly stated in the following period. That it was assumed in the mediæval period is, I think, a fair inference from the rule that the king could command any of his subjects abroad to return;[3] and from the statement of Fortescue, C.J., in 1454, that the king, without Parliament, cannot deprive his subject of the benefit of the common law;[4] for that would be, in effect, as much an alteration of the rights of the subject, as a grant of full naturalization which affected the rights of third persons.[5] It is true that a man could be outlawed or attainted by due process of law; but, subject to this, the tie of allegiance with all its consequences could neither be created nor

---

[1] Below 84-86, 87. [2] Below 84.

[3] Dyer 128b, citing a case of 19 Ed. II.; cp. Forsyth, Leading Cases 181.

[4] Y.B. 32 Hy. VI. Hil. pl. 13—"Le Roy sans Parlement ne poit prendre son lige home de droit."

[5] Above 77 and n. 2.

dissolved at the will of king or subject. The status of a subject is indissoluble—nemo potest exuere patriam.

Thus, in the case of the loss, as in the case of the acquisition, of the status of a subject, the root principles of the common law were ascertained in the mediæval period. But the consequences latent in these principles were not yet deduced and stated in detailed rules. The political history of England during this period had provided the raw material for these rules. But it was not till some time after the establishment of the modern territorial state that this raw material was used to establish them. The problems raised by the accession of James VI. of Scotland to the English throne, and the unwillingness of the Legislature to make a statutory settlement of these problems,[1] at length gave the judges their opportunity. They made the most of it, and, by their judgments in *Calvin's Case*, they put the law on this subject on its modern basis.

(ii) *The restatement of the law in* CALVIN'S CASE.[2]

The facts of *Calvin's Case* were simple. Calvin complained that he had been disseised of his free tenement in Haggerston in the parish of Shoreditch. The defendants pleaded that Calvin was an alien born in Scotland in the year 1606, and that he was therefore unable to hold freehold land; to which plea Calvin demurred. Simultaneously proceedings were begun in equity for detaining the evidences, and taking the profits, of land in the parish of St. Botolph in the city of London belonging to Calvin. To this suit the same plea was pleaded, and there was the same demurrer. Thus the question whether the post-nati, that is persons born in Scotland after the accession of James to the throne of England, were to be regarded as aliens in England or as subjects, was brought before the courts both of law and equity; and both cases were adjourned into the Exchequer Chamber, " to the end that one rule might overrule both."[3]

The judges were fully conscious of the importance of the principle involved. " I found the case," said Lord Ellesmere,[4] " to bee rare, and the matter of great import and consequence, as being a special and principall part of the blessed and happy union of Great Britaine." "The case," says Coke,[5] "was as elaborately substantially and judicially argued by the Lord Chancellor and my brethren the judges, as ever I heard or read of any; and so in mine opinion the weight and consequence of the cause, both *in praesenti et perpetuis futuris temporibus* justly deserved: for though it was

---

[1] Vol. vi 12. [2] (1609) 7 Co. Rep. 1. [3] 7 Co. Rep. at f. 2b.
[4] 2 S.T. at p. 659. [5] 7 Co. Rep. at f. 3b.

one of the shortest and least that ever we argued in this Court, yet it was the longest and weightiest that ever was argued in any Court, the shortest in syllables and the longest in substance; the least for the value . . . but the weightiest for the consequent, both for the present and for all posterity." This view of the case was very true—truer even than the judges who decided it imagined; for, as we shall see,[1] the result of the decision was to make a uniform status for natural-born subjects, not only in England and Scotland, but also in the many lands which, in the succeeding centuries, were added to the king's dominions.

The lord chancellor and all the judges, except Walmsley and Foster, JJ., held that the post-nati were natural born subjects. In fact the decision was inevitable;[2] for it could be supported by reasons drawn both from the territorial and from the personal view of the tie of allegiance. But we shall see that far more stress was laid, and rightly laid, on the latter view; and that it is the use made of deductions drawn from this view which gives the case its importance in later law. Let us examine the question from these two points of view.

(a) It was laid down that a person cannot be a natural-born subject, unless the place of his birth, at the time when he was born, was within the king's dominions. Hence the ante-nati could not be natural-born subjects, because they were not born in England, and at the time of their birth they were not under the allegiance of the king of England.[3] This was a conclusion which followed from the territorial principle. If the personal principle alone had been considered, it might well have been held that, since that the ante-nati owed allegiance to the same man James, who was king both of England and Scotland, they too were subjects. It was admitted that there were exceptions created by statute and otherwise, which allowed children born of English parents out of the king's dominions to be subjects;[4] and that it was possible that children born in England, e.g. of alien enemies in hostile occupation of English soil, were not subjects.[5] But generally any one born in England was

---

[1] Below 83.

[2] "The decision was one which pleased the king and displeased many of his subjects; but no other judgment could have been given unless many precedents derived from times when our kings had large territories on the continent of Europe had been disregarded," P. and M. i 441.

[3] "There be regularly (unless it be in special cases) three incidents to a subject born. 1. That the parents be under the actual obedience of the King. 2. That the place of his birth be within the King's dominion. And 3. the time of his birth is chiefly to be considered; for he cannot be a subject born of one kingdom that was born under the ligeance of the king of another kingdom, albeit afterwards one kingdom descend to the king of the other. . . . And that is the reason that *ante-nati* in Scotland (for that at the time of their birth they were under the ligeance and obedience of another King) are aliens born, in respect of the time of their birth," 7 Co. Rep. at ff. 18a, 18b.

[4] Ibid at f. 18a.   [5] Ibid at ff. 18a, 18b.

an English subject. And this did not apply to those born in England alone. Even before 1609 England was not the only country subject to the king of England. It was proved that the law had always regarded persons born in Wales, Ireland, the Channel Isles, and Calais, as subjects of the king.[1] But, if that was the law, what possible reason could be alleged for not regarding the post-nati as subjects? The fallacies underlying the reasons alleged for this distinction were fully exposed by Bacon.[2] Moreover, the judges took occasion to recognize a consequence of the territorial principle, which had been laid down in the sixteenth century.[3] For some purposes even an alien residing in England must be regarded as a subject, who owed a local and temporary allegiance to the king.[4]

(*b*) But far greater stress was laid on the conception of allegiance as a personal bond between the king and his subjects. This was due to the fact that, since the union between England and Scotland was as yet only a personal union of the crowns, the judges found it logically necessary to show that the duty of allegiance, and consequently the status of a subject, were attached, not to the corporate, but to the natural capacity of the king. The reasons why they found it necessary to show this were somewhat as follows: We have seen that it was well recognized that the king of England had, according to English law, a corporate or politic capacity.[5] But the king in his capacity of corporation sole was a purely English entity, wholly dependent on the rules of English law. If, therefore, it had been ruled that allegiance was due to the king in his corporate or politic capacity, it would have followed that it was only the persons subject to the rules of English law which defined that capacity, who had the status of a subject. Thus a Scotchman, who was a subject of the man James, would not be a subject of James king of England, because, not being subject to rules of English law, he owed no allegiance to the purely English corporation sole who occupied the English throne.[6] If, on the other hand, allegiance was due to the man James, then all those who owed this allegiance, whether subject to English or

---

[1] 7 Co. Rep. at ff. 19a-23b.   [2] Works (Ed. Spedding) vii 650-663.
[3] Sherley's Case (1557) Dyer 144a.
[4] 7 Co. Rep. at ff. 6a, 6b; see Kelyng 38; R. v. Tucker (1695) 1 Ld. Raym. at pp. 1-2; Locke, Two Treatises on Government Bk. ii § 122, puts this rule into theoretical shape.
[5] Vol. iv 202-203; vol. vi 20-22; above 4-5.
[6] Thus it appears to have been argued that, "whatsoever is due to the King's several politic capacities of the several kingdoms is severed and divided: but ligeance of each nation is due to the King's several politic capacities of the severed kingdoms; *ergo* the ligeance of each nation is severed and divided, and consequently the plaintiff is an alien"; and that "every subject that is born out of the extent and reach of the laws of England, cannot by judgment of those laws be a natural subject to the King in respect of his kingdom of England," 7 Co. Rep. at f. 3a.

Scotch law, were his subjects.   It was therefore successfully contended that as the obligation of allegiance involved the taking of
an oath and the doing of acts such as homage, which could not be
done to a corporate body, these obligations attached to the king
in his natural capacity.[1]   "The bond of allegiance," said Lord
Ellesmere,[2] "of which we dispute is *vinculum fidei*; it bindeth the
soul and conscience of every subject severally and respectively, to
be faithful and obedient to the king: and as a soul or conscience
cannot be framed by policy; so faith and allegiance cannot be
framed by policy, nor put into a politic body.   An oath must be
sworn by a natural body; homage and fealty must be done by a
natural body, a politic body cannot do it. . . . As the king nor his
heart cannot be divided, for he is one entire king over all his
subjects, in whichsoever of his kingdoms and dominions they were
born, so he must not be served or obeyed by halves; he must have
entire and perfect obedience of all his subjects . . . and he that is
born an entire and perfect subject ought, by reason and law, to
have all freedoms privileges and benefits pertaining to his birthright in all the king's dominions."   In support of this thesis plenty
of mediæval precedents could be adduced.[3]   They all presupposed
that allegiance was due to the natural man sitting on the throne,
because the distinction between the two capacities of the king had
not then emerged.[4]

The speculations as to the king's corporate and natural
capacities which the development of this thesis involved, may seem
to us to be far fetched, and to savour at times of the mystical.
But in fact they were necessary to establish firmly and upon a
broad basis of principle, the rule that the status of a subject
belonged to all those who owed allegiance to the king.   Parliament had prevented the attainment of the full benefit which might
have been expected from the union of crowns by refusing to
sanction any closer union of the two kingdoms.   The benefit
derived from that union would have been still further curtailed, if
a Scotchman and an Englishman had continued to be considered
as aliens by the laws of the other's country.   The principles upon
which the decision in this case was based prevented this unfortunate
result, and went some way to correct the narrow view taken by
Parliament.   They were, as we have seen, a logical development
from the mediæval law and history.   But, as thus developed and
applied to the new situation of the English state, they have affected
the whole future history of the law as to the status of the subject,

---

[1] 7 Co. Rep. at ff. 10a, 10b.   [2] 2 S.T. at p. 691.
[3] Especially Cobledike's Case, above 77 and n. 7, 7 Co. Rep. at f. 9b; 2 S.T. at
p. 688.
[4] Vol. iii 463-468.

and have, incidentally, helped to establish an important principle of colonial constitutional law. Their consequences can be summed up as follows :—

(a) The first and most important effect of the decision in *Calvin's Case* was the fact that it made a general rule for the acquisition of the status of a natural-born subject, which was applicable to all persons born within the king's dominions. This was a result of great importance when, in the eighteenth century, these dominions began to expand. It gave a uniform status to all persons born within these dominions ; it made this uniform status depend on the personal tie of allegiance to the crown ; and it thus played no small part in consolidating the position of the king as the head and main bond of union between the confederation of independent communities, which now constitute the British Empire. The opposite decision would have had an effect upon the status of natural-born subjects, similar to the effect upon the status of naturalized subjects, which followed from allowing each of these communities to establish its separate naturalization laws.[1] Just as a person naturalized in one of the Dominions does not necessarily have the status of a subject in another, so the status of a natural-born subject would have varied in different parts of the empire. The uniformity of status, which one of the most recent statutes dealing with the subject of naturalization attempts to accomplish for the naturalized subject,[2] was secured for natural-born subjects by this decision.

(b) In the second place, the decision laid down definite rules as to the acquisition of the status of a subject. The mediæval precedents made it clear that no distinction could be drawn between the inhabitants of the different dominions of the crown in respect of their status as subjects.[3] It was obvious, for instance, that Irishmen were as much subjects of the king as Englishmen. But it followed from this that, if the king acquired a new dominion either by conquest or by title of descent, the inhabitants necessarily became his subjects. It is true that the king's position in dominions thus acquired differed according to his title. If the dominion was acquired by conquest it might be either an infidel or a Christian kingdom. If it was an infidel kingdom its laws were abrogated ipso facto ; but if it was a Christian kingdom its laws remained till altered by the king ; for in all these dominions

---

[1] See McNair, Legal Effects of War 11 ; cp. the King v. Francis *ex parte* Markwald [1918] 1 K.B. 617 ; Markwald v. Attorney-General [1920] 1 Ch. 348 ; it is interesting to note that it was argued unsuccessfully in the latter case that doctrine of personal allegiance, laid down in Calvin's Case, operated to widen the effect of a colonial certificate of naturalization.

[2] British Nationality and Status of Aliens Act 1914, 4, 5 George V. c. 17 §§ 8, 9.

[3] Above 76.

acquired by conquest the king could change the laws as he pleased.[1] If the dominion was acquired by descent, the king must respect the laws of the dominion by virtue of which he had acquired it, and therefore could not change them without Parliament.[2] But, in spite of these differences, all the inhabitants of dominions so acquired were the king's subjects. These distinctions as to the prerogative of the king in relation to dominions acquired by conquest were followed in the latter part of the seventeenth century; but Coke's view that the laws of an infidel country were wholly abrogated, was limited to such as were against the law of God; and the principles which he applied to dominions acquired by descent were applied to dominions acquired by settlement.[3] Coke's rules, as thus modified and extended, were made the basis of the distinction drawn by Lord Mansfield between settled and conquered colonies.[4] A settled colony was a colony founded by Englishmen, who possessed all the rights and privileges secured to subjects of the king by English law. Therefore the king could no more acquire new rights over them in their new abode than he could alter the laws of a kingdom acquired by descent. They remained the king's subjects, and the rules of English law applied to them. Probably the application of these principles to colonies acquired by settlement was assisted by the fact that the prominence given to the personal aspect of allegiance by *Calvin's Case*, had emphasized the indelibility of the status of a subject.

(c) Thirdly, we have seen that, even in the Middle Ages, the personal aspect of allegiance was tending to establish the rule that the status of a subject was indelible.[5] This was acted upon in *Story's Case* in 1571;[6] it was accepted as good law in *Calvin's Case*;[7] and from it the consequence was drawn that, if the king lost any of his dominions, those born in them while he was king still retained their status as subjects, even though they might acquire a new status as the subjects of the ruler to whom these dominions had passed.[8] This conclusion was justified on two

---

[1] 7 Co. Rep. at f. 17b.   [2] Ibid.
[3] Blankard v. Galdy (1694) 2 Salk. 1.
[4] Campbell v. Hall (1774) 20 S.T. 239.
[5] Above 78-79.   [6] Dyer 300b.
[7] 7 Co. Rep. at f. 9b.
[8] " As the ante-nati remain aliens as to the Crown of England because they were born when there were several kings of the several kingdoms . . . so albeit the kingdoms . . . should by descent be divided and governed by several kings; yet it was resolved that all those that were born under one natural obedience while the realms were united under one sovereign should remain natural-born subjects and no aliens; for that naturalization due and vested by birthright cannot by any separation of the Crowns afterward be taken away: nor he that was by judgment of law a natural subject at the time of his birth, become an alien by such a matter *ex post facto*. And in that case, upon such an accident, our *post-natus* may be ad fidem utriusque Regis, as Bracton saith," 7 Co. Rep. at f. 27b; for the passage from Bracton see below 86 n. 4.

grounds—firstly by reference to historical precedents, and secondly on logical grounds.

The historical precedents were taken from the rules made in the thirteenth century at the time of the loss of Normandy. As Maitland has shown, the law for some time took the view that the loss of Normandy was temporary; and, therefore, unless a French landowner adhered to the French king, in which case his lands were forfeit for treason, the sequestration of his lands was considered to be only temporary. It was considered that he might well resume his possession if peace and a final settlement ever came.[1] But since he was thus capable of owning English land, he must, according to the settled principles of the later law, be a subject. It is true that these precedents came from a time when the settled principles of the later law as to the status of a subject, and the incapacity of an alien to own English land, were not as yet fixed. We shall see that, historically, this reasoning, to some extent, inverts the order of cause and effect—it was because the king had seized the lands of these Normans, that the common law arrived at its settled rules as to the right of the king to the lands of aliens, and the incapacity of the alien to hold English land.[2] But these are considerations which neither then, nor at any time, have weighed much with a law court in search of a precedent to justify a rule. It is clear that this piece of history did supply a precedent, which proved that loss of territory did not render those who dwelt within that territory incapable of holding English land. That they were thus capable of holding English land is assumed both by Bracton,[3] and the so-called statute Prærogativa Regis;[4] so that, having regard to the settled principles of the later law that capacity to own land connoted the status of a subject, the conclusion drawn from these thirteenth-century precedents was inevitable. It was drawn by Staunford,[5] it was skilfully

---

[1] P. and M. i 444-445.　　　　　　　[2] Below 92.

[3] Ff. 298a, 427b, and the other references cited P. and M. i 445; Bracton's Note Book, Cases 110, 1396, there cited.

[4] "Item habet esccatas de terris Normannorum de cujuscumque feodo fuerint, salvo servitio quod pertinet ad capitales dominos feodi illius, et hoc similiter intelligendum est si aliqua hereditas descendat alieni nato in partibus transmarinis, cujus antecessores fuerint ad fidem Regis Franciæ ut tempore Regis Johannis, et non ad fidem Regis Angliæ, sicut contingit de baronia Monemuth," c. 12; on which Bacon, in his argument in Calvin's Case, makes the apposite comment that from this, "it appears plainly, that before the time of King John there was no colour of any escheat, because they were the king's subjects in possession, as Scotland now is; but only it determines the law from that time forward," Works (Ed. Spedding) vii, 675.

[5] "By this branch it should appeare that at this tyme men of Normandy Gascoiyn Guyon Angeo and Brittain were inheritable within this realme as well as Englishmen, because that they were sometime subject unto the king of England, and under their dominion untill king Jhons time as is afore sayd, and yet after his time those men (saving such whose landes weare taken away for treason) weare still inheritable within this realme till the making of this statute," Prerogative f. 39a.

developed by Bacon in his argument in *Calvin's Case,*[1] and it was assented to by the court in that case.[2]

No doubt it was the more readily assented to because it was a rule which followed logically from the personal basis, upon which allegiance and the status of a subject were grounded in *Calvin's Case.* All the reasoning which justified the claim of the post-nati to be British subjects, on the ground that the personal bond of allegiance was created between them and the natural man James, king of England and Scotland, went to show that mere loss of territory could not dissolve the obligations of that personal bond. And just as those born before the union of the crowns remained aliens because born aliens;[3] so persons born before a separation of territory must remain subjects because they were born subjects. In such a case they would, like the Normans in the thirteenth century, be, as Bracton said, "ad fidem utriusque regis."[4]

But though this doctrine of a double allegiance followed logically from the principles laid down in *Calvin's Case*, though it was a doctrine which harmonized well enough with the loosely knit monarchies of Bracton's day, it was practically very inconvenient when applied to modern territorial states. The conclusion that loss of territory meant loss of subject status, which followed from adopting the territorial principle as the basis of that status, was far more convenient. We shall now see that the question whether, on grounds of convenience, this concession would be made to the territorial principle, was not settled till quite modern times.

(iii) *The later developments.*

The history of the later developments of the law on this subject can be grouped under two heads: (*a*) the development of the law as to loss of the status of a subject by reason of a loss of territory; and (*b*) the changes in the common law doctrines made by statute.

(*a*) The rule that the status of a subject is indelible, that "nemo potest exuere patriam," continued to be the rule of English law down to 1870. It was recognized by Hale;[5] and it was applied in the case of Æneas Macdonald in 1747.[6] "It is not," said the court in that case,[7] "in the power of any private subject to shake off his allegiance, and to transfer it to a foreign prince. Nor is it in the power of any foreign prince, by naturalizing or employing a subject of Great Britain, to dissolve the bond of allegiance be-

---

[1] Works (Ed. Spedding) vii 674-677.
[2] At ff. 27a, 27b.   [3] Above 80 n 3.
[4] " Sed tamen sunt aliqui Francigenae in Francia qui sunt ad fidem utriusque, et semper fuerunt ante Normanniam deperditam et post, et qui placitant hic et ibi ea ratione quia sunt ad fidem utriusque," f. 427b, cited 7 Co. Rep. at f. 27b.
[5] P.C. i 68.   [6] 18 S.T. 858.   [7] At p. 859.

tween that subject and the crown." But the question whether this principle should operate so as to prevent persons, resident in territory ceded by the crown, from losing their status as subjects, was raised by the recognition of the independence of the United States. Chalmers took the view that the principle had no application to such a situation;[1] but Reeves, the author of the history of English law, stoutly maintained the opposite conclusion, and insisted on a literal following of the dicta in *Calvin's Case.*[2] Obviously Chalmer's view is the more rational. It was approved by the law officers of the crown in 1824,[3] by the court of King's Bench in the same year,[4] and by the King's Bench Division in 1886.[5]

(*b*) Down to the beginning of the nineteenth century the statutory changes in the common law doctrines had been small. We have seen that the statute of 1351 made children born abroad, of parents who were English subjects, capable of inheriting English land.[6] On that statute two questions arose. Firstly, were these children not only rendered capable of inheriting, but also given all the other privileges of British subjects? As to this no hesitation seems to have been felt in placing upon the statute the more liberal construction;[7] and any doubt which there may have been was put an end to by the statute of 1708, which enacted that the children of natural-born subjects born abroad should be deemed to be natural-born subjects "to all intents constructions and purposes whatsoever."[8] Secondly, in order to take the benefit of the statute, must both the parents be subjects? The words of the statute of 1351 seem clearly to say that they must.[9] But in cases of the seventeenth century it was held that it would suffice if the father was a natural-born subject, though the mother was a foreigner. It was said that, the woman being "sub potestate viri," both must be deemed to owe allegiance to the king;[10] and for this

---

[1] Forsyth, Leading Cases 257 seqq. [2] Ibid 286 seqq.
[3] Joint opinion of the Attorney and Solicitor-General, Sir John S. Copley and Sir Charles Wetherell, on the status of a citizen of the United States born before the peace of 1783, and resident in Canada; and also on the status of his son, born in the United States after that date, ibid 324-325.
[4] Doe d. Thomas v. Acklam (1812) 2 B. and C. 779; cp. Auchmutz v. Mulcaster (1826) 5 B. and C. 771.
[5] Isaacson v. Durant 17 Q.B.D. 54. [6] Above 75-76.
[7] See Bacon's argument, Works (Ed. Spedding) vii 652; in Doe d. Duroure v. Jones (1791) 4 T.R. at p. 308 Lord Kenyon, C.J., said, " I cannot conceive that the Legislature in passing that Act (25 Ed. III.) meant to stop short in conferring the right of inheritance merely on such children, but that they intended to confer on them all the rights of natural born subjects."
[8] 7 Anne c. 5; 10 Anne c. 5. [9] Above 75.
[10] R. v. Eaton (1627) Litt. Rep. at pp. 28-29; Bacon v. Bacon (1641) Cro. Car. 601—" and it is not material although his wife be an alien, for she is as Berkley said, *sub potestate viri*, and *quasi* under the allegiance of our king "; Hale, C.B., said in Collingwood v. Pace (1664) 1 Vent. at p. 428 that, in his remembrance, this case had been several times followed, see below 88 and nn. 2-4.

construction there was some mediæval authority.[1]   Hale, however, was aware that this was a forced construction;[2] but he seems to have acquiesced in it on grounds of public policy;[3] so that it followed that the child of an English father born abroad, though not of an English mother, was a British subject.   But this construction was opposed to the literal words of the statute of 1351;[4] nor was the doubt cleared up by the statute of 1708, which spoke only of the children of "natural-born subjects born out of the ligeance of her Majesty."   To clear it up, it was enacted, in 1730, that the children born abroad, whose fathers were natural-born subjects, should be natural-born subjects;[5] and in 1773 it was enacted that the children of children who were natural-born subjects by virtue of the provisions of the Act of 1730, should be natural-born subjects.[6]   But it should be noted that it is now settled that the privilege conferred on these persons by these Acts was only a personal status, and it was not, as is the case with persons who are by virtue of their birth natural-born subjects, transmissible to their descendants.[7]   There were, it is true, a few dicta which pointed to the contrary conclusion, that persons made subjects by these statutes could transmit the status to their descendants ad infinitum.[8]   But it is clear that that interpretation was not the interpretation accepted in the eighteenth century, as, if it had been, the Act of 1773 would have been unnecessary.[9]

During the nineteenth century these common law rules were

[1] "Vide le printed livre dabridgment dassizes, Engloys passa le meere et mary feme alyen, per ceo le feme est dallegeans le roy, et son issu enheritera," Bro. Ab. *Denizen* pl. 21.

[2] "The statute de Natis ultra mare 25 E. 3 declares that the issue born beyond sea of an Englishman upon an Englishwoman shall be a denizen, yet the construction hath been, tho' an English merchant marries a foreigner, and hath issue by her beyond the sea, that issue is a natural born subject," 1 Vent. at p. 427.

[3] "The case of the post-nati commonly called *Calvin's Case*, the report is grounded upon this gentle interpretation of the law, tho' there were very witty reasons urged to the contrary ; and surely if ever there were reason for a gentle construction even in the case in question, it concerns us to be guided by such an interpretation since the union of the two kingdoms, by which many perchance very considerable and noble families of a Scottish extract may be concerned in the consequence of this question both in England and Ireland, that enjoy their inheritances in peace.   I spare to mention particulars," 1 Vent. at p. 428.

[4] In Doe d. Duroure v. Jones (1791) 4 T.R. at p. 308 Lord Kenyon, C.J., said that, "if we were now called upon for the first time to put a construction on the words of this statute, I should not think that they ought to be extended further than the natural import of the words, but that in order to be entitled to the privileges and benefits of that Act the children must be born of natural born parents, both father and mother, within the faith and ligeance of the king."

[5] 4 George II. c. 21.   [6] 13 George III. c. 21.

[7] De Geer v. Stone (1882) 22 C.D. 243.

[8] This was Bacon's view of the effect of the Act of 1351, Works (Ed. Spedding) vii 652; and it follows from the view held by some, above 76 and n. 1, that the Act was merely declaratory of the common law; see the unsuccessful argument in De Geer v. Stone (1882) 22 C.D. at p. 248.

[9] De Geer v. Stone at pp. 252-253.

found to be inconvenient, largely because, in the light of the newer ideas as to the acquisition and loss of subject status to which other nations were giving effect, they had become quite unsuited to the new political and economic conditions of the day. They were, in fact, too restrictive in respect both to the acquisition and to the loss of the status of a subject. It was becoming evident (i) that conflicting claims to allegiance resulted from the rule that all persons born on territory within the allegiance of the crown, no matter what their parentage, were British subjects; (ii) that some better mode of acquiring the status of a British subject than by the cumbersome process of an Act of Parliament was desirable; (iii) that the doctrine of the indelibility of the status of the subject sometimes gave rise to serious international complications; and (iv) that the law as to the national status of married women was very unsatisfactory. Let us glance briefly at these four defects in the law.

(i) The commissioners on the laws of naturalization and allegiance, who reported in 1869, pointed out that, though the place of birth as a test of nationality was favoured by the law of Great Britain and the United States, the nationality of the father was adopted as the test by the law of France, and of most other European nations. While admitting that the rule was open to objections, they considered that it had such real advantages in the provability of the test, and the speedy obliteration of racial disabilities, that it ought not to be abandoned. On the other hand, they thought that it " ought not to be, as it now is, absolute and unbinding. In the case of children of foreign parentage it should operate only where a foreign nationality has not been chosen. Where such a choice has been made, it should give way." [1] In this way, it was thought, some of the objections, [2] arising from conflicting claims of different states to the allegiance of the same person, would be obviated.

(ii) We have seen that, in general, naturalization required a special Act of Parliament. [3] Even then the person so naturalized was never, after 1714, [4] allowed to become a privy councillor, a member of Parliament, the holder of a public office, or capable of receiving from the crown a grant of land in Great Britain or Ireland; and the same restrictions were imposed on persons, such as certain traders or foreign Protestants, who were from time

---

[1] Report of the Naturalization Commission, Parliamentary Papers (1868-1869) xxv. viii; for some dissentient views see ibid xi-xv; and cp. Cockburn, Nationality 190 seqq.

[2] For a concrete illustration of the hardships which might arise from this cause see Cockburn, Nationality 68.

[3] Above 76.   [4] 1 George I. c. 4; 12, 13 William III. c. 2.

to time granted the privileges of naturalization by general Acts.[1] A special naturalization Act cost about £100, and was condemned in 1843 as a costly and cumbersome process.[2] In 1844 an Act was passed empowering the crown to grant certificates of naturalization to aliens who had been resident in Great Britain for five years.[3] An alien thus naturalized became a subject, but not for all purposes. He was still left incapable of becoming a privy councillor or a member of Parliament; he was subject to any other restrictions which might be imposed by his certificate of naturalization; and the power to impose these restrictions was used to limit the effect of naturalization to the dominions of the Crown.[4] This Act almost entirely put an end to the grant of letters of denization, and the passing of special naturalization Acts.[5] But the Act was only intended to apply to persons who were bona fide residents in Great Britain, and, as we have seen, it did not make those naturalized under its provisions British subjects for all purposes.[6] The commissioners, while recommending the retention of the rule that the alien must have resided for five years, suggested that service under the crown should be accepted in lieu of residence, and that a certificate of naturalization should make the recipient a British subject for all purposes.[7]

(iii) We have seen that though, as the result of a cession of territory, a subject who continued to reside in the ceded territory ceased to be a subject,[8] the status of a subject was otherwise indelible. It was this rule which had no small share in bringing about war between England and the United States in 1812. British seamen serving on board American vessels were impressed by the British government, although naturalized as American citizens; and the practice was justified by this doctrine of the indelibility of allegiance.[9] Though peace was made with America in 1814, this principle was never in theory departed from; but the war had shown that it was impossible to enforce it

---

[1] E.g. 15 Charles II. c. 15; 7 Anne c. 5, repealed by 10 Anne c. 5; 13 George II. c. 7; 22 George II. c. 45; 2 George III. c. 25; see Parliamentary Papers (1868-1869) xxv 6-7; for attempted legislation in 1672-1673, see Hist. MSS. Com. 9th Rep. App. Pt. ii 19 no. 72; for the attempt to naturalize foreign Protestants in 1693 see L.Q.R. xl 22-23, and Macaulay's History chap. xx.

[2] Parliamentary Papers (1868-1869) 8.　　　　　[3] 7, 8 Victoria c. 66.

[4] Cockburn, Nationality 115-116.

[5] Special Acts were sometimes asked for in order that the applicant might become a subject for all purposes; this was then possible as 1 George I. c. 4 had been repealed by 7, 8 Victoria c. 66, Parliamentary Papers (1868-1869) 8.

[6] Ibid 9.　　　　[7] Ibid x.　　　　[8] Above 87.

[9] A good account of these disputes will be found in Cockburn, Nationality 70 seqq.; Mr. H. J. Randall has pointed out, L.Q.R. xl 25, that it was the reluctance to abandon the right to impress emigrant seamen that led English statesmen to adhere to this view that allegiance was indelible—just as continental states now, in the interests of military service, make not the *jus soli*, but the *jus sanguinis* the test of nationality.

strictly. Hence it is not surprising to find that it was condemned by the Naturalization Commissioners. "It is," they said,[1] "at variance with those principles on which the rights and duties of a subject should be deemed to rest; it conflicts with that freedom of action which is now recognized as most conducive to the general good as well as to individual happiness and prosperity; and it is especially inconsistent with the practice of a state which allows to its subjects absolute freedom of emigration. It is inexpedient that British law should maintain in theory, or should by foreign nations be supposed to maintain in practice, any obligations which it cannot enforce and ought not to enforce if it could; and it is unfit that a country should remain subject to claims for protection on the part of persons who, so far as in them lies, have severed their connexion with it." They therefore recommended that a British subject should, on naturalization in a foreign country, cease to be a British subject.

(iv) Contrary to the rules of continental law, marriage had no effect on the nationality of the woman.[2] "An English woman marrying an alien still remained a British subject: an alien woman marrying a British subject remained none the less an alien."[3] The latter branch of the rule was changed in 1843;[4] but the doctrine of the indelibility of allegiance had prevented any change in the former branch. This change was recommended by the Naturalization Commissioners in 1869.[5]

The recommendations of the Naturalization Commission were carried out by the Naturalization Act 1870.[6] Natural-born British subjects, who at birth were subjects of a foreign state by the law of that state, and persons born out of the dominions of the crown of a father who was a British subject, were allowed to make a declaration of alienage;[7] the law as to the conditions and effect of naturalization were modified on the lines suggested by the commissioners;[8] British subjects who had become naturalized in a foreign state, were allowed to renounce their allegiance;[9] and the changes recommended by the commissioners were made in the law as to the effect of marriage on the national status of the woman.[10] With the enactment of this statute we have reached the period of the modern law.

(2) The disabilities of aliens.

It was recognized from a very early period that an alien had none of the capacities to hold official positions, and none of the

---

[1] Report p. v.
[2] So that " if a man taketh an alien to wife and dyeth she shall not be indowed," Co. Litt. 31b; Forsyth, Cases in Constitutional Law 340.
[3] Cockburn, Nationality 11, 12.   [4] 7, 8 Victoria c. 66 § 16.
[5] Report p. v.   [6] 33 Victoria c. 14.
[7] § 4.   [8] § 7.   [9] § 6.   [10] § 10.

franchises of the subject.   A case decided in 1413 is in effect an
application of this principle.[1]   In that case a juror was challenged
because he was a Fleming and born out of the king's allegiance.
It was admitted that this was the fact; but it was said that he
ought to be sworn because he had lived all his life in England, and
had sworn allegiance—it would seem, in the leet.[2]   But it was held
that this did not make him competent.   "Though," said Hankford, J., "an alien be sworn in the leet or elsewhere, that does not
make him a liege subject of the king, for neither the steward of a
lord nor any one else, save the king himself, is able to convert an
alien into a subject."

In private law his disabilities were, in the eyes of many of the
mediæval common lawyers,[3] almost as complete as his disabilities
in public law.   The reasons which had led them to this conclusion
are curious.   They hinge partly upon the measures adopted by the
king at the end of the thirteenth century with respect to lands in
England belonging to Norman landowners, and partly upon the
manner in which, in the Middle Ages, the rules of the land law
influenced other branches of the common law.

We have seen that, in the earlier part of the thirteenth century,
the king seized the lands of Normans and Frenchmen, subject to
a reconsideration of their rights if a permanent peace ever came.[4]
If, therefore, such an alien claimed land he was not met, as in the
later common law, by the peremptory plea that, being an alien,
he could not hold land; but by the dilatory plea that he was a
Frenchman and could not be answered here till Englishmen were
answered in France.[5]   But "that permanent peace never comes,
and it is always difficult to obtain a restoration of lands which
the king has seized. . . . And so Bracton's dilatory exception
becomes a peremptory exception.   'You are an alien and your
king is at war with our king' becomes 'you are an alien.'"[6]
This episode explains, as Maitland has pointed out, how it came
to be the law that an alien cannot hold English land, and that if
he in fact purchases such land the purchase is not a mere nullity,
but operates to divest the land from the conveyor, to convey it to
the alien, and therefore to give the king the right to seize it on
the ground that the alien is incapable of holding it.[7]

---

[1] Y.B. 14 Hy. IV. Hil. pl. 23.   [2] For the leet see vol. i 135-137.
[3] Below 93-94.   [4] Above 85.
[5] P. and M. i 445; above 85 n. 3; see the case of Boistard v. Cumbwell (1243)
Select Cases before the Council (S.S.) 1-2, and Introd. xlvii-ix, where the question
was raised, but not settled, whether, in the event of the next heir being an adherent
of the king of France, the lord could seize, or whether the heir next in succession,
being an adherent of the king of England, could take.
[6] P. and M. i 446.
[7] "To us it seems that the king's claim to seize the lands of aliens is an
exaggerated generalization of his claim to seize the lands of his French enemies.
Such an exaggerated generalization of a royal right will not seem strange to those
who have studied the growth of the king's prerogatives," ibid i 445-446.

Once the law had reached this position the consequences of the alien's incapacity to hold land were, like other branches of the mediæval land law, very fully worked out. As he cannot hold land he cannot inherit it,[1] nor can any claim to inherit through him.[2] If he were made a denizen he could hold land; but he could not inherit from his father, and only his issue born after he had become a denizen could inherit from him.[3] The rule that no inheritance could be traced through an alien was modified in 1700;[4] but the main principle of the law, which made an alien incapable of holding land and gave the king the right to seize, remained till 1870.[5] It was justified in *Calvin's Case* on grounds of public policy. If the law were otherwise, "the secrets of the realm might thereby be discovered. The revenues of the realm (the sinews of war and the ornament of peace) should be taken and enjoyed by strangers born. It should tend to the destruction of the realm."[6] It was approved by Blackstone;[7] nor can we, who have seen some of the results of the German policy of commercial penetration of friendly states in time of peace, say as decisively as our immediate ancestors that these reasons are wholly mistaken.

This disability of the alien to hold land has had important effects upon the development of the law. We have seen that it has, more than any other single cause, helped to elucidate the law as to the persons whom the law will account as subjects. It inspired the Act of 1351,[8] and it was a main cause for the enactment of the other eighteenth-century statutes, which extended the status of a British subject to other persons born abroad.[9] It was the means by which the status of the post-nati was submitted to the adjudication of the courts in *Calvin's Case*. Similarly we shall now see that it had, in the Middle Ages, a considerable influence in determining the view which some of the common lawyers took of the position of the alien.

Littleton laid it down that an alien could bring no action real or personal.[10] This in substance amounts to denying an alien any

---

[1] "A man seized of lands in fee hath issue an alien that is born out of the king's ligeance, he cannot be heir, *propter defectum subjectionis*, albeit he was born within lawful marriage," Co. Litt. 8a.

[2] "If an alien cometh into England, and hath issue two sons, these two sons are *indigenae* subjects born, because they are born within the realm. And yet if one of them purchase lands in fee, and dieth without issue, his brother shall not be his heir, for there was never any heritable blood between the father and them," ibid.

[3] Ibid, and 129a.   [4] 11, 12 William III. c. 6.

[5] See Report of the Naturalization Commission, Parliamentary papers (1868-1869) xxv 137.

[6] (1609) 7 Co. Rep. at f. 18b.   [7] Comm. i 360.

[8] Above 75-76.   [9] Above 88.

[10] "If such alien will sue an action real or personal, the tenant or defendant may say, that he was born in such a country which is out of the King's allegiance, and ask judgment if he shall be answered," § 198.

rights at all in private law; and that such a rule of law was laid down is probably, it seems to me, due in part to the extensive influence upon the mediæval common law exercised by the real actions. It is obvious that an alien could not bring a real action because he was incapable of holding land; and Littleton's rule seems to be the result of transferring ideas originating in the sphere of the real actions to the other actions. It was a mistake which a common lawyer like Littleton, who was especially learned in the land law, was likely to make; and the more so because, during the greater part of the mediæval period, the rights which aliens had were protected in courts and by remedies which were outside the sphere of the common law. And it was followed by other common lawyers. In 1503 Marowe said than an alien could not ask that others should be bound over to keep the peace to him, but that he could be bound over to keep the peace to others.[1] We shall now see that, even when Littleton and Marowe were writing, it was a view of the law which was being repudiated by the courts, and that it is very doubtful if it was ever fully accepted as law.

It is obvious that a law which denies any rights to aliens will discourage trade; and to the interests of trade the Legislature during the mediæval period was by no means indifferent. Magna Carta had enacted that, "all merchants shall have safe and secure exit from England, and entry to England, with the right to tarry there and to move about as well by land as by water, for buying and selling by the ancient and right customs, quit from all evil tolls, except, in time of war, such merchants as are of the land at war with us."[2] It is true that the rights and privileges of the boroughs very considerably restricted the freedom thus conferred on the alien;[3] but it is by no means clear that they were deprived of all rights in the courts of common law;[4] and it is certain that they got protection through agencies which operated outside the

---

[1] " Item si une alien que fut nee hors del liegeaunce nostre seigneur le Roie et nient fait denizyn voet demander sureti de peas de ascun autre il ne avera ceo, mes sureti del peas serra demande envers luy assetz bien," De Pace, Oxford Studies in Social and Legal History vii 324; note also that another MS. adds, " Mesne le ley est de enymy le Roy "—a comparison which is a striking illustration of the rightlessness of the alien.

[2] "Omnes mercatores habeant salvum et securum exire de Anglia, et venire in Angliam, et morari et ire per Angliam, tam per terram quam per aquam, ad emendum et vendendum, sine omnibus malis toltis, per antiquas et rectas consuetudines, preterquam in tempore gwerre, et si sint de terra contra nos gwerrina," §41.

[3] P. and M. i 447-448; and see L.Q.R. xxxvi 403 seqq. for a good account of the effect of the jealousy of the native trader in depressing the alien. They were fettered by rules as to "hostage," i.e. the hosts with whom they must stay, by restrictions as to the length of their stay, and by restrictions on their right to carry on their trades.

[4] " We may perhaps regard Coke's doctrine that the alien friend is protected by ' personal actions ' as ancient common law," P. and M. i 448.

sphere of the common law. In 1303 they got from the king many privileges by the Carta Mercatoria;[1] in the courts of the fairs, of the staple, and other courts which administered the law merchant, their rights were protected;[2] and the king's Council and the court of Admiralty also protected them.[3] It is no doubt true that, owing to the difficulties thrown in their way by the privileges of the boroughs, who were jealous of the foreign merchant, they were in practice forced to rely upon the special courts where the law merchant was administered, and on the king's extraordinary jurisdiction; so that it is not altogether surprising that it should be said in 1473 that alien merchants ought to sue in the Chancery, and that their cases ought to be determined there, not according to the law of the land, but according to the law of nature.[4] But it is possible that this result had been produced, not because the courts of common law had ever held that they would give them no remedy, but because the privileges of the boroughs made it in practice difficult for them to get a remedy—indeed, the Chancellor in 1473 assumed that an alien could sue, if he liked, at common law.[5] As Maitland says, "they can but seldom make their way to the king's justices because the courts of the towns in which they live claim an exclusive cognisance of actions brought against the burgesses, and when they do get to the royal courts there is a contest between privilege and privilege."[6] If this is correct, it may well be that Coke was right when, in commenting on Littleton, he maintained that at common law the incapacity of the alien to bring any kind of action applied only to alien enemies, and that alien friends were only incapacitated from bringing real or mixed actions.[7] On the other hand, both Littleton and Marowe would, as we have seen, have denied this distinction.[8] But whether Littleton and Marowe correctly laid the earlier common law, or whether they were only laying down the law of their own

---

[1] P. and M. i 448; L.Q.R. xxxvi 404-405. [2] Vol. i 535-543; vol. v 104-112.
[3] Vol. i 405, 548, 552; vol. v 136-139; Select Cases before the Council (S.S.) xxvii-xxviii, lxx, lxxvi-lxxvii, xcviii-c.
[4] "Le Chancelor. Cest suit est pris par un marchant alien, qui est venus per safe conduit icy, et il n'est tenus de suer solonques le ley del terre a tarier le trial de XII homes, et auters solempnities del ley de terre, mes doit suer icy, et sera determine solonque le ley de nature en le Chancery, et il doyt suer la de heur en heur et de jour [en jour] per le spede des marchants," Y.B. 13 Ed. IV. Pasch. pl. 5 (p. 9).
[5] Ibid.   [6] P. and M. i 449.
[7] "In this case the law doth distinguish between an alien that is a subject to one that is an enemy to the king, and one that is subject to one that is in league with the king; and true it is that an alien enemy shall maintain neither real nor personal action. Donec terrae fuerunt communes, that is, until both nations be at peace; but an alien that is in league shall maintain personal actions; for an alien may trade and traffick, buy and sell, and therefore of necessity he must be of ability to have personal actions, but he cannot maintain either real or mixt actions," Co. Litt. 129b; above 94 n. 4.
[8] Above 93 n. 10, 94 n. 1.

day, as it had come to be shaped under the influence of the real
actions, it is clear that, even when they were writing, the law was
developing in the direction indicated by Coke; and that, by the
middle of the sixteenth century, his statement was substantially
correct.

The reason for this development must be sought in the
beginnings of the rivalry between the common law courts and
the Council and the Chancery,[1] and in the desire of the common
lawyers to compete with these courts by extending the jurisdiction
of their own courts. We have seen that, towards the end of the
fifteenth century, they were already thinking of modifying their
strict rules of venue, so as to make it possible to hear cases which
turned upon transactions entered into abroad;[2] that the development of the action on the case was supplying a more adequate
remedy for breaches of contract and for tort;[3] and that, in consequence, the common law courts were absorbing much of the
business formerly done by the courts of fairs and other mercantile
courts, which, in the earlier mediæval period, administered justice
to the foreign merchant.[4] The effect of these developments was
soon visible in the manner in which the courts treated the alien
merchant; and, as all substantial distinction between merchants
and other classes of the community tended to disappear with the
absorption of the law merchant into the common law, the rules
made for the alien merchant soon became the rules for all aliens.[5]

So soon as the common law courts began to think of giving
some protection to alien merchants, the distinction between alien
friends and alien enemies, which is hinted at in Magna Carta,
reappears. At first it seems to have been assumed that the alien
friend must have come by licence and with a safe conduct—otherwise he was, as Marowe says, treated like an alien enemy.[6] In
fact this was a necessary corollary from the view that an alien as
such had no rights. Thus, in 1454 it was said that an alien who
had come by licence and with a safe conduct, unlike an alien
enemy, could bring an action of trespass against one who had
broken into his house.[7] But in 1480 it was assumed that any

---

[1] Vol. i 459, 486-489. [2] Vol. v 117-119.

[3] Vol. ii 455-456; vol. iii 318-360, 371-388, 428-454.

[4] Vol. i 539-540; vol. v 116-117.

[5] Coke said that it was only an alien merchant who could take a lease for years
for his habitation, Co. Litt. 2b; below 97 n. 10; and the law is so stated in Bacon, Ab.
Aliens i 81; but probably the rule, even in the sixteenth century, applied to all aliens,
see Dyer f. 2b n. (8); 7 Co. Rep. at f. 17a; it certainly applied to all aliens later,
Bl. Comm. i 360.

[6] Above 94 n. 1.

[7] "Si un alien come Lumbard, Galiman, ou tiel marchant que vient icy per
licence et sauf conduit et prend icy en Londres, ou ailours, un meason pro le temps,
si ascun debruse le meason, et prend ses biens, il aura action de trespass: mes s'il
soit enemy le Roy, et vient eins sans licence ou sauf conduit auter est," Y.B. 32
Hy. VI. Hil. pl. 5 *per* Ashton, J.; cp. Y.B. 13 Ed. IV. Pasch. pl. 5 (p. 9) cited
above 95 n. 4.

alien friend could maintain an action of debt upon an obligation.[1]
In 1484 it was said that if he were robbed he should have
restitution;[2] and in 1545 it was held that he could maintain all
personal actions.[3] In 1547 it was said that he could bring any
personal action, own property, and buy and sell;[4] in 1552 "it was
the opinion of the judges of the Common Bench that an alien,
who is not an enemy of the king, can have goods and leases in
England, and can make his will of them, though he be not a
denizen";[5] and it was settled in the mediæval period that he
might be tenant by statute merchant or staple,[6] for the purpose of
both the statute merchant and staple was to encourage trade, by
providing, both for subjects and aliens, a sure way of recovering
their debts.[7] But the law was very jealous of allowing the alien
to acquire any other interest in land; and it had been made more
strict by a statute of 1541.[8] Though in 1552 the judges said that
the alien could own leases, it would seem from *Croft's Case* in
1587,[9] that his right to take a lease was strictly limited to a lease
of a house for his habitation, and for the time during which he
inhabited it.[10] But, subject to this qualification, it would be true
to say that, by the end of the sixteenth century, the alien friend
could bring personal actions and could own personal property just
as a subject. We have seen that an Act of 1623 provided that
aliens could be made bankrupts, and that they could prove as
creditors in bankruptcy proceedings.[11] Conversely, we have seen
that it was recognized in the sixteenth century that they owed a
local and temporary allegiance, and could therefore be punished
for any crimes which they committed while in England.[12]

This admission of the capacity of alien friends to bring personal
actions for torts has had one very important consequence in our
constitutional law. It follows that they have gained the same

---

[1] Y.B. 19 Ed. IV. Hil. pl. 4.
[2] Y.B. 2 Rich. III. Mich. pl. 4; Bro. Ab. *Denizen* pl. 8.
[3] Dyer 2b.   [4] Bro. Ab. *Denizen* pl. 10.
[5] Benloe 36; S. C. Anderson 25.
[6] For these interests in land see vol. iii 131-132.
[7] Dyer 2b n. (8), citing Pasch. 11 Ed. III. Rot. 87.
[8] 32 Henry VIII. c. 16 § 4; cp. Pilkington v. Peach (1680) 2 Shower 135; Bacon,
Ab. *Aliens* i 82.
[9] Co. Litt. 2b.
[10] "But as to a lease for years, there is a diversity between a lease for years of a
house for the habitation of a merchant stranger being an alien, whose king is in
league with ours, and a lease for years of lands, meadows, pastures, woods, and the
like. For if he take a lease for years of lands, meadows, etc., the king shall have it.
But of a house for habitation he may take a lease for years as incident to commerce.
. . . But if he depart or relinquish the realm the king shall have the lease. So it
is if he die possessed thereof, neither his executors or administrators shall have it,
but the king; for he had it only for habitation as necessary for his trade or traffick.
. . . But if the alien be no merchant then the king shall have the lease for years,
albeit it were for his habitation, and so it is if he be an alien enemy," ibid.
[11] Vol. viii 237.   [12] Vol. v 45 and n. 6, 49 and n. 6; above 81.

protection as that accorded to subjects, not only against private persons, but also against the king and his servants. This is the logical and inevitable result of the establishment, in the seventeenth century, of the doctrine of ministerial responsibility; for, as we have seen,[1] the essence of that doctrine is that, if wrong is done by the king or his servants, that wrong cannot be regarded as done by a king who can do no wrong, but must be regarded as done by his servants, who therefore can be made personally liable, just like any other private persons. Since alien friends can sue for torts committed against them, it is obvious that they have the same rights of action as subjects in such cases. The result is that the definition of an "Act of State," for which the courts can give no remedy, is limited in respect to alien friends residing in this country, in just the same way as it is limited in respect to subjects.[2] Just as the law recognizes that there can be no such thing as an Act of State as between the king and his subjects,[3] so it recognizes that the same proposition is equally true as between the king and alien friends living within the jurisdiction of the British courts. It is only if a tortious act is committed against an alien in a place outside the jurisdiction of the British courts, and if that act has been previously authorized or subsequently ratified by the crown, that the defence of "Act of State" is available.[4] It is available because the alien in such a case owes no allegiance of any kind, and so is not entitled to the protection of the British courts.

On the other hand, all the cases which we have just been considering show that the alien enemy remained rightless. He could bring no action in the courts, and his property and choses in action could be seized by the king;[5] being "an enemy of our lord the king he could have no benefit from his laws."[6] It was only if, having a safe conduct from the king, he was, as Coke calls him, an "inimicus permissus," that he had any rights of action.[7] The only doubtful question which was never quite settled, was

---

[1] Vol. iii 465-466; vol. vi 101-103, 111, 266-267.

[2] Johnstone v. Pedlar [1921] 2 A.C. 262. If the crown authorises or ratifies the commission of a tort against a British subject in a place outside the jurisdiction of the British courts, could the defence of Act of State be set up? It is submitted that it could not; and that if the cause of action were transitory, e.g. for a trespass to the person or to chattels, an action would lie; but that if the cause of action were local, e.g. for a trespass to land, no action would lie, not because the act was an Act of State, but because the courts have no jurisdiction to try such causes of action, see British South Africa Co. v. Companhia de Mocambique [1893] A.C. 602.

[3] Stephen, H.C.L. ii 65.   [4] Buron v. Denman (1848) 2 Ex. 167.

[5] See Y.B. 19 Ed. IV. Hil. pl. 4; Hale, P.C. i 95; the best modern account of the position of the alien enemy at common law is contained in Lord Sumner's dissenting judgment in Rodriguez v. Speyer Bros. [1919] A.C. at pp. 115 seqq.

[6] Dyer 2b.

[7] Calvin's Case (1609) 7 Co. Rep. at f. 18a, citing Y.B. 32 Hy. VI. Hil. pl. 5, cited above 96 n. 7.

whether an alien enemy, who was an executor or administrator to a subject, could sue in his representative capacity.[1] That, like the outlaw or the attainted person, he could be sued was probably always the law;[2] but it was not finally settled till quite recently.[3] Probably the reason why this question remained so long unsettled is to be found in the fact that, till recently, most alien enemies worth suing were outside the jurisdiction of the English courts. The closer connection between the nations, under the changed commercial conditions of our own day, and changes in the law of procedure, have made it necessary to decide formally that an alien enemy can be sued.[4]

We shall now see that this closer connection between the nations, arising mainly from the growth of international trade, and the social changes which have come in its train, have set in motion a course of legal development which has, in relation to civil rights and liabilities, substituted for the old lines of division between subjects and aliens and between alien friends and alien enemies which were based on nationality, a new line of division which is based on enemy character.

(3) Enemy Character.

Lord Lindley, speaking of rights and liabilities arising under a contract with persons who subsequently become alien enemies, said:[5] "When considering questions arising with an alien enemy, it is not the nationality of a person but his place of business during war which is important. An Englishman carrying on business in an enemy's country is treated as an alien enemy in considering the validity or invalidity of his commercial contracts. Again, the subject of a state at war with this country, but who is carrying on business here or in a foreign neutral country, is not treated as an alien enemy; the validity of his contracts does not depend on his

---

[1] The cases are conflicting; the cases against allowing the right of action are Anon. (1589) Owen 45; Anon. (1589) Cro. Eliza. 142; but the authorities in favour of allowing the right of action are more numerous, see Brocks v. Phillips (1599) Cro. Eliza. 683; Caroon's Case (1625) Cro. Car. 8; Richfield v. Udell (1667) Carter 191; Villa v. Dimock (1694) Skin. 370; the weight of authority was considered to be in favour of the view that the enemy alien had a right of action in such a case by Bacon Ab. i 84, by Sir E. V. Williams, and by Lord Finlay, see Rodriguez v. Speyer Bros. [1919] A.C. at p. 70.

[2] Thus Coke says, Co. Litt. 129b, that "an alien that is condemned in an information shall have a writ of error to relieve himself: et sic de similibus"; it was also assumed by Marowe that the subject had the same remedies against him as he had against another subject, above 94.

[3] All the authorities will be found in the Attorney-General's argument and the judgment of the court in Porter v. Freudenberg [1915] 1 K.B. at pp. 864-865, 880-883; apparently the first statement of this rule, apart from Coke's statement cited in the last note, is Bacon's statement in his Abridgment (7th ed.) i 183, cited ibid at p. 881.

[4] Porter v. Freudenberg [1915] 1 K.B. 857.

[5] Janson v. Driefontein Consolidated Mines [1902] A.C. at pp. 505-506.

nationality, nor even on what is his real domicile, but on the place or places in which he carries on his business or businesses." It is clear from this passage that modern law has evolved a test of enemy character for the purpose of civil rights and liabilities, which is independent of the question of nationality. When and how did this new conception come into the law?

The first step towards its adoption was taken at the close of the seventeenth century. Technically it took the form of an extension of the rule that an alien enemy, if allowed by the crown to reside in this country, had the position of an alien friend. The underlying reasons why the courts made this extension were due certainly to the closer intercourse between nations which was the result of the growth of modern conditions of commerce, and probably also to the fact that, at that time, a number of French Protestants, who were technically but only technically alien enemies, were allowed to reside in England. Both these reasons seem to have weighed with the court in the case of *Wells v. Williams*,[1] which must be regarded as the starting-point of the development of the modern conception of enemy character, because it was the first case in which the rule as to the circumstances under which alien enemies could be held to be residing here by permission of the crown was extended.[2]

The action in this case was an action of debt on a bond. The defendant pleaded that the plaintiff was an alien enemy born in France of French parents, and that he came to England without a safe conduct. The plaintiff replied that he was in England by the licence and under the protection of the king. It was argued that, though this was so, he could maintain no action unless he had an actual safe conduct. But the court held "that the necessity of trade has mollified the too rigorous rules of the old law in their restraint and discouragement of aliens. . . . Commerce has taught the world humanity." If the plaintiff came here before the war he had no need of a safe conduct. Even if he came here since the war, "yet if he has continued here by the king's leave and protection ever since, without molesting the government or being molested by it, he may be allowed to sue, for that is consequent to his being in protection." Treby, C.J., further pointed out that the king, in his declaration of war, excepted all the French Protestants.[3] The later cases have made some variations

---

[1] (1697) 1 Ld. Raym. 282.   [2] See McNair, Legal Effects of War 31.

[3] "And Treby Chief Justice said in this case last Trinity term that the king may declare war against one part of the subjects of a prince, and may except the other part. And so he has done in this war with France, for he has excepted in his declaration of war with France all the French Protestants," 1 Ld. Raym. at p. 283; note that in 1708 Parliament passed an Act to naturalize foreign Protestants generally, 7 Anne c. 5, which was repealed in 1711, 10 Anne c. 5.

in the rules as to what facts will amount to residence in this country with the implied sanction of the government; but it has never since been doubted that, if such sanction can be shown, the alien enemy is put into the same position as an alien friend.[1]

The cases which establish this principle thus show that the principle of nationality is disregarded in considering the position of alien enemies allowed to remain in this country. Their enemy character is purged. The converse proposition, that enemy character will attach to a subject or a neutral who carries on business in an enemy's country, was probably also recognized in the latter part of the seventeenth century;[2] but, as a definite legal principle, it was not established till the following century. It would seem that the technical reasoning, by means of which this position was established, was based on the principle that British subjects are forbidden, without the licence of the crown, to have any commercial intercourse with the enemy. The classical exposition of this principle was given by Sir William Scott in the case of *The Hoop* in 1799;[3] and it was natural that it should have fallen to him to state this principle, because the question of what amounts to trading with the enemy, so as to render the goods of the trader liable to seizure, necessarily comes frequently before a court which is exercising a jurisdiction in Prize. The application of the principle is of course not confined to the Prize court; and it was again clearly enunciated by Willes, J., in 1857.[4] As the court of Appeal has pointed out in the case of *Porter v. Freudenberg*,[5] the principle was, in earlier days, based on "the conception that all subjects owing allegiance to the Crown were at war with the subjects of the States at war with the Crown"; but that later "it was based upon public policy which forbids the doing of acts which will be or may be to the advantage of the enemy State, by increasing its capacity for prolonging hostilities, in adding to the

---

[1] See Sylvester's Case (1702) 7 Mod. 150; George v. Powel (1717) Fort. 221; stricter proof as to the sanction of the crown seems to have been required in Boulton v. Dobree (1808) 2 Camp. 163, and Alciator v. Smith (1812) 3 Camp. 245; but, as Mr. McNair says, op. cit. 33 n. 1, Wells v. Williams was not cited in either of these cases; the modern rule is laid down in Porter v. Freudenberg [1915] 1 K.B. at pp. 870-871.

[2] In S.P. Dom. 1677-1678, 246 there is an opinion, probably by the law officers, given in answer to inquiries by Sir R. Lloyd and Sir Th. Exton, to the effect that "a natural-born subject having his fixed abode beyond the seas loses the privileges of an Englishman, and subjects his own estate to the same forfeitures as the subjects of that place are liable in time of war."

[3] 1 C. Rob. 196.

[4] "It is now fully established that, the presumed object of war being as much to cripple the enemy's commerce as to capture his property, a declaration of war imports a prohibition of commercial intercourse and correspondence with the inhabitants of the enemy's country, and that such intercourse, except with the licence of the Crown, is illegal," Esposito v. Bowden 7 E. and B. at p. 779.

[5] [1915] 1 K.B. at pp. 867-868.

credit money or goods or other resources available to individuals in the enemy State." It was because the principle was placed upon this new basis, that the courts were able to come to the conclusion that enemy character attached both to subjects and neutrals who carried on business in any enemy state. This conclusion had been reached at the beginning of the nineteenth century.

It had been laid down in 1799 that a British subject, who was naturalized and carrying on trade in the United States, had the commercial privileges of a citizen of the United States, though, in his capacity of British subject, he was not entitled to these privileges.[1] This showed that the courts were beginning to lay stress upon the consideration of commercial domicile. Three years later this consideration was applied to attach enemy character to a British subject, who was residing and carrying on trade in an enemy's country;[2] and it is clear, firstly, that the judges based their reasoning on the same ground of public policy as that upon which the prohibition of trading with the enemy was based;[3] and, secondly, that they recognized that this attribution of enemy character to the subject, who resided and carried on trade in the enemy's country, really rested on a principle similar to that which denied enemy character to the alien enemy, who resided in this country under the protection of the king.[4] And, though the principle upon which enemy character was attributed or denied to any given person, was reached mainly by reference to cases connected with subjects trading in hostile territory, or alien enemies trading in this country, it is not confined to traders. It was formally decided in 1915[5] that it applies equally to residents who are not traders. Here, as in other cases, law made primarily for traders has become the common law for all.

During the century which had elapsed from the close of the Napoleonic wars to the outbreak of war in 1914, the international character and organization of trade had become more

---

[1] Marryat v. Wilson 1 B. and P. 430.

[2] M'Connell v. Hector (1802) 3 B. and P. 113.

[3] " Every natural-born subject of England has a right to the King's protection so long as he entitles himself to it by his conduct; but if he live in an enemy's country he forfeits that right. Though these persons may not have done that which would amount to treason, yet there is an hostile adherence and a commercial adherence; and I do not wish to hear it argued that a person who lives and carries on trade under the protection and for the benefit of a hostile state, and who is so far a merchant settled in that state that his goods could be liable to confiscation in a court of prize, is yet to be considered as entitled to sue as an English subject in an English court of justice," ibid at p. 114 *per* Lord Alvanley, C.J.

[4] " It is well known that if an alien enemy be residing here under the king's protection he may sue; but if an Englishman be resident in a hostile country the king cannot enable him to sue," ibid at p. 114 *per* Rooke, J.

[5] Porter v. Freudenberg [1915] 1 K.B. at p. 869.

pronounced; and the disabilities of aliens in private law had almost vanished after the passing of the Naturalization Act of 1870.[1] Those who initiated and pursued the German commercial policy of peaceful penetration in preparation for the German war for world empire, had made skilful use of the weakening of national barriers, which had followed upon the growth of the international character and organization of trade, and upon the growing cosmo-politan habit of mind in the leaders of industry and commerce. For that reason the commercial facts, to which the courts were called upon to apply the existing principles as to the attribution of enemy character, presented problems of a far more complex character than had ever been known in any former war. On the whole the existing principles proved themselves capable of solving the problems which were thus set to them; but necessarily these principles gained in precision; and were, in some respects, modified in their application to new facts. For, as we might expect, the re-moval of the disabilities of aliens in private law, and the growth of the international character and organization of trade, have caused the question of enemy character to become, from some points of view, more important than the question of enemy nationality. This fact is illustrated by very many cases which have come before the courts. But it perhaps comes out most strongly in two leading cases—the case which turns on the enemy character of a corpora-tion, and the case which settles the manner in which the law will regard the plea of alien enemy.

It was held by Lords Parker and Sumner in the *Daimler Case*[2] that, just as in the case of an individual, his nationality is, from the point of view of his civil rights and liabilities, unimportant as compared with the place of his residence; so, in the case of a corporation, its place of incorporation is unimportant as compared with its real character, as disclosed by the sympathies and activities of the men who control it.[3] It was held in the case of *Rodriguez*

---

[1] Above 91.

[2] Daimler Co. v. Continental Tyre and Rubber Co. [1916] 2 A.C. 307 at pp. 338 seqq.

[3] But, obviously, the working out of this parallel involves the drawing aside of the corporate screen, and confusing the corporation with the natural men who com-pose it. In point of fact the parallel thus drawn between disregarding the nationality of a British subject, and disregarding the nationality of a British corporation, situated as this corporation was situated, is not exact. We attribute enemy character to, that is we disregard the nationality of a British subject, if, being resident abroad, he trades with the enemy. If he tried to pursue this course of conduct in a place within the jurisdiction of the British courts he could be proceeded against criminally. His nationality would certainly not be disregarded in such a case. Surely in these rules no warrant can be found for disregarding the nationality of a corporation who, being resident within the jurisdiction of the British courts, pursues enemy activities. If the parallel is to be pursued exactly the conclusion would be, not that its nationality can be disregarded, but that it should be punished. In fact, as I have already suggested (above 66, 71), it was probably the absence of power to dissolve, or otherwise punish such a corporation, which inspired this misleading parallel. As we have seen

v. Speyer Bros.[1] that, just as in attributing or denying enemy character to an individual we must look mainly at the rule of public policy, which renders it illegal to trade with the enemy; so, in considering whether we should apply to a firm, in which one of the partners is an alien enemy, the rule which absolutely prohibits an alien enemy from suing, we must look at the facts, and consider whether, as a matter of public policy, it is expedient in any given case to allow the alien enemy to join with the other partners in suing. In both cases the facts which were once thought to be all important—the place of incorporation in the case of a company, the nationality in the case of an individual—must give way to considerations based on the activities of the corporation or the individual, and the expediency of encouraging or discouraging such activities on grounds of public policy.

The Right of Personal Liberty

Whether or not the famous clause of Magna Carta, which enacted that " no free man shall be taken or imprisoned or disseised or exiled or in any way destroyed except by the lawful judgment of his peers or by the law of the land,"[2] was intended to safeguard the principle that no man should be imprisoned without due process of law,[3] it soon came to be interpreted as safeguarding it.[4] Because it was interpreted in this way, it has exercised a vast influence, both upon the manner in which the judges have developed the writs which could be used to safeguard this liberty, and upon the manner in which the Legislature has assisted that development. Without the inspiration of a general principle with all the prestige of Magna Carta behind it, this development could never have taken place; and, equally, without the translation of that general principle into practice, by the invention of specific writs to deal with cases of its infringement, it could never have taken practical shape. It is with the history of the manner in which the common lawyers gave it practical shape, by the invention and development of appropriate writs, that I shall deal in this section.

In the first place, I shall say something of certain old writs which, in the earlier mediæval period, were generally used to protect the liberty of the subject. Secondly, I shall describe the origin and early history of the writ which was destined to supersede them—the writ of *Habeas Corpus*. Thirdly, I shall show how

---

(above 50, 71), the confusion thus introduced between the corporation and the natural men who compose it, is contrary to the most fundamental of all the principles of corporation law.

[1] [1919] A.C. 59. [2] § 39 (1215).
[3] Vol. i 59-63; vol. ii 215. [4] Ibid 215 n. 3.

that writ came to be used to protect the liberty of the subject, and how the Legislature in consequence took a hand in its development, and made it the most efficient protector of that liberty that any legal system has ever devised.

(1) The older writs used to protect the liberty of the subject.

There were three of these writs which could be used to protect the liberty of the subject.

De Homine Replegiando.[1]—This was, in substance, the process of replevin, applied to the purpose of rescuing a person from imprisonment. Just as chattels unlawfully distrained could be recovered by their owner by the action of replevin,[2] so a person unlawfully detained could recover his liberty by this writ. Since it appears in Bracton,[3] it is at least as old as the earlier half of the thirteenth century. It was directed to the sheriff, and ordered him to replevy a man who was in prison, or who was detained in the custody of some person named in the writ. If the sheriff returned that the prisoner had been "eloigned," that is carried away to a place where he could not be found, he was directed to take in "withernam," i.e. by way of reprisal, the person holding the prisoner in custody, till he produced the prisoner. The chief use made of this writ was to compel the sheriff or other gaoler to release on bail a prisoner whom it was his duty to release.[4] As we have seen, the law as to what prisoners ought to be thus released on bail was laid down in 1275, and rendered more precise by later statutes.[5]

Mainprize.[6]—This writ, says Fitzherbert,[7] lies "where a man is taken for suspicion of felony, or indicted of felony, for the which thing by the law he is bailable, and he offereth sufficient sureties unto the sheriff or others who have authority to bail him, and he or they do refuse to let him to bail." The object of this writ was to get the release of the prisoner on mainprize, just as the object of the writ *de homine replegiando* was to get the release of the prisoner on bail. The difference between bail and mainprize seems to have been this—the prisoner is actually in the custody of the person who has given bail for him, so that technically he is still in prison; but if mainprize has been given he is not in custody at all, as the mainpernors are only sureties for his appearance. Thus, for instance, the justices of gaol

---

[1] F.N.B. 66 E.; Hale, P.C. ii 141; Bl. Comm. iii 129; Stephen, H.C.L. i 240; P. and M. ii 583; Jenks, Essays A.A.L.H. ii 533-534.
[2] Vol. iii 283-285. [3] At f. 154, cited P. and M. ii 583.
[4] P. and M. ii 583. [5] Vol. iv 526-528.
[6] F.N.B. 249 G.; Hale, P.C. ii 141-143; Bl. Comm. iii 128; Stephen, H.C.L. i 240-241; P. and M. ii 582; Jenks, Essays A.A.L.H. i 534.
[7] F.N.B. 249 G.

delivery could try a prisoner who was released on bail, because, in contemplation of the law, he was still in gaol; but they could not try a prisoner who had been released on mainprize.[1] But, as Maitland says,[2] this distinction soon became obscured. The statutory rules applicable to bail were applicable to mainprize; and, in fact, the writ of mainprize, at any rate in its later form, was framed on the clause of the statute of 1275, which regulated the conditions under which prisoners could be released on bail.[3] It would seem, however, that, in addition to this regular use of the writ of mainprize, the king would issue a special warrant for the issue of this writ in special cases, e.g. "to deliver persons in prison for felony upon mainprize to go into foreign parts in the king's wars, as Gascoigne and elsewhere at the king's wages."[4]

Both these writs thus had a somewhat similar scope. But of neither was very much use made after the mediæval period. The writ *de homine replegiando*, together with the writ *de odio et atia*,[5] was mentioned by Selden in 1628 as two of the remedies "for enlarging of a freeman imprisoned."[6] The *de homine replegiando* was used in 1677 to recover an heiress, who had been taken from her guardian;[7] in 1682 to get back a boy who had been "spirited" away to Jamaica;[8] in the same year it was made use of in the course of the proceedings against Lord Grey and others for debauching Lady Henrietta Berkely, in order to compel Lord Grey to produce the lady;[9] and we shall see that in 1758 Wilmot, C.J., suggested that it might still be a useful remedy, if a sufficient but false return were made to a writ of *Habeas Corpus*.[10] The writ of *mainprize*, so far as it applied to arrest and detention by the sheriffs or his bailiffs, was rendered obsolete by statutes of 1354[11] and 1460,[12] which deprived these officials of their power to arrest persons indicted for felony.[13] But it could still be used in the case of prisoners committed by others, e.g. by the justices of the peace.[14] There was an attempt to use the writ in the course of the proceedings taken for the release of Jenkes in 1676;[15] and many mediæval precedents were produced of prisoners released by its means in the reigns of Edward III. and Richard II., all of which were probably cases in which the king had directed a special issue of the writ.[16] Lord Nottingham refused to issue the writ,

[1] Coke, Fourth Instit. 178, 179-180; Hale, P.C. ii 124-125; P. and M. ii 587-588.
[2] Ibid 587; Hale, P.C. ii 124, says that the terms bail and mainprize "are used promiscuously often times for the same thing, and indeed the words import much the same thing . . . but yet in a proper and legal sense they differ"; cp. Select Cases before the Council (S.S.) 45n. 38.

[3] F.N.B. 249 G.　　　　[4] Hale, P.C. ii 143.　　　　[5] Below 107-108.
[6] 3 S.T. 95.　　　　[7] Jennings's Case 2 Free. 27.　　　[8] 8 S.T. 1347-1355.
[9] 9 S.T. 183-185.　　　[10] Below 120.　　　　[11] 28 Edward III. c. 9.
[12] 1 Edward IV. c. 2.　　　[13] Coke, Second Instit. 190; Hale, P.C. ii 142.
[14] Ibid.　　　　[15] 2 Swanst. 83-91.　　　[16] Above n. 4.

partly on the untenable ground that, though it might still be applicable to persons imprisoned on civil process, it no longer existed in criminal cases;[1] and partly on the much stronger ground that its disuse, especially in the earlier part of the seventeenth century, showed that it was not applicable to a case of commitment by the Council.[2] We have seen that at common law it is the better opinion that those so committed were not entitled to be released on bail.[3] We shall see that the statutes which altered the law on this point did so by enlarging the scope of the writ of *Habeas Corpus*.[4] Therefore, as the writ of mainprize was left as at common law, it is probable that Jenkes was not entitled to obtain his release by its means. In fact neither of these writs were of much use to a person imprisoned by the king's command.[5] They were directed rather to the securing of the provisional release of persons imprisoned by private persons, or by inferior officers of justice. We shall see, therefore, that when the need was felt for a remedy to compel the speedy release of persons imprisoned by the king or the executive government, they naturally gave place to another remedy which had a wider scope.[6]

De Odio et Atia.[7]—As early as Glanvil's day, the man who was appealed of homicide was not entitled to be released on bail or mainprize. To meet the case where a man was appealed of this crime, or probably of any other felony,[8] "from hatred and malice," this writ was provided.[9] It directed that an inquest should be taken to decide this issue. If the inquest found that the prisoner was not appealed "from hatred and malice," he remained in prison. If it found the contrary, he was released on bail. So popular was the writ that Magna Carta ordered that it should issue as of course without fee.[10] Though sometimes used by persons indicted,[11] it seems to have been used chiefly by persons appealed of felony; and, when the criminal appeal ceased to be a common remedy,[12] this writ lost much of its former importance. It merely, as Maitland has said,[13] "enabled a man

---

[1] 2 Swanst. 86, citing Fitzherbert and Coke; note that he cites also Hale's short treatise on the pleas of the crown; the finished treatise, in which Hale shows that the writ is not taken away in criminal cases, was not then published.

[2] Ibid 89-91.   [3] Vol. vi 32-37.   [4] Below 115.

[5] Jenks, Essays A.A.L.H. ii 534.   [6] Below 112 seqq.

[7] P. and M. ii 585-587; Bracton f. 123; Coke, Second Instit. 42; Hale, P.C. ii 148; Bl. Comm. iii 128-129; Stephen, H.C.L. i. 241-242; Jenks, Essays A.A.L.H. ii 534-535; Winfield, History of Conspiracy 15-22.

[8] Winfield, op. cit. 19, points out that the issue of the writ was not originally limited, as Blackstone states and as Coke and Hawkins imply, to homicide.

[9] P. and M. ii 585; Winfield, op. cit. 16-17, thinks that it was originally valued as a means of avoiding trial by battle, but that, with the spread of trial by jury, and the power to plead exceptions to an appeal, it came to be valued as a writ which secured a provisional release.

[10] § 36 (1215); Bracton ff. 121b, 123.   [11] Winfield, op. cit. 19-20.

[12] Vol. ii. 256-257, 360-364.   [13] P. and M. ii 587.

who is imprisoned on a charge of homicide to obtain a provisional release on bail, when an inquest has found that the charge has been preferred against him 'of spite and hatred.'" So useless did it become, both on account of the disuse of appeals, and on account of the cumbersome character of the procedure upon it,[1] that its ultimate fate has been a matter of controversy.[2] Foster,[3] followed by Stephen,[4] held that it was abolished by the statute of Gloucester of 1278;[5] but the statute hardly bears out this view.[6] Coke[7] held that it was abolished by a statute of 1354,[8] but revived by the statute of 1369 which repealed all Acts made contrary to Magna Carta;[9] and both Coke and Hale treat it as an existing writ. But Hale says that it was disused in his day, and points out that, by reason of the greater frequency of gaol deliveries, the prisoner was tried more quickly than he could get provisionally released by this writ.[10]

Thus all these writs had, for different reasons, become ineffective to safeguard the liberty of the subject. A new remedy was needed; and, at the end of the sixteenth and the beginning of the seventeenth century, this new remedy was found in the writ of *Habeas Corpus.* Of the origins of this writ, therefore, and of its early development, which made it possible to use it as a remedy for the protection of the liberty of the subject, I must now speak.

(2) The origin and early history of the writ of *Habeas Corpus.*

From Edward I.'s reign onwards different writs of *Habeas Corpus* were known to the law; and they were all connected with the law of procedure. Thus, in Edward I.'s reign, the issue of a writ of *Habeas Corpus ad respondendum* was one of the steps in that lengthy mesne process which could be taken to secure the appearance of a defendant.[11] The issue of this writ for this purpose seems to have been superseded by the practice of inserting a habeas corpus clause in the writ of distringas.[12] But, from an early date, we can see the germs of the writ of *Habeas Corpus ad subjiciendum,* by which a sheriff or a private person could be ordered to produce a person under his control;[13] and writs of

---

[1] "It has been disused by reason of the great trouble in the attaining and execution of it, for, 1. there must be a writ to enquire *de vita et membris*. 2. There must be an inquisition taken. 3. He was to be bailed by twelve persons," Hale, P.C. ii 148.

[2] P. and M. ii 587 n. 2.   [3] Crown Law 285.   [4] H.C.L. i 242.

[5] 6 Edward I. c. 9, which dealt with homicide by misadventure, see vol. iii 312.

[6] P. and M. ii 587 n. 2; Winfield, op. cit. 21-22.

[7] Second Instit. 43.   [8] 28 Edward III. c. 9.   [9] 42 Edward III. c. 1.

[10] "And now the justices of gaol delivery usually going their circuits twice a year, unless in the four northern counties, a prisoner comes to his trial as soon, if not sooner, than such inquisition and mainprize can be taken," Hale, P.C. ii 148.

[11] P. and M. ii 591.   [12] L.Q.R. xxxix 53.   [13] Ibid 58-59.

Habeas Corpus to summon the four knights for the purpose of the Grand Assize, or to summon a jury, have long been known to the law.[1]

So far the writ is a merely procedural writ. But even in the mediæval period it was beginning to be something more. The cause of this development must, I think, be sought in the desire of the courts of common law to extend their jurisdiction at the expense of rival courts. The use thus made of the writ can be divided into two distinct periods. Firstly, there is the mediæval period in which the contest of the common law courts was mainly with the local and franchise courts; and, secondly, there is the period which begins at the latter part of the fifteenth century, and continues throughout the sixteenth century, in which this contest was with rival central courts, such as the Chancery, the Council and Star Chamber, and the Admiralty. It was in the first period that the writ of *Habeas Corpus* became a weapon by which the courts of common law could both defend their own jurisdiction, and increase it at the expense of rival jurisdictions. It was in the second period that the power of this weapon was seen on a larger stage, and that the course of the struggle with some of these rival courts showed that it could be used in a new way to protect the liberty of the subject.

(i) During the fifteenth century the writ of *Habeas Corpus* was used, as an accompaniment of the writ of certiorari, to bring the proceedings in, and the parties to, an action in an inferior court, before the courts of common law;[2] and, as an accompaniment to a writ of privilege, to release a litigant in one of the central courts of law, who had been arrested by the process of an inferior court.[3]

There is an instance in 1412 of the issue of a writ (probably of certiorari), together with a *Habeas Corpus cum causa*, to the staple court of Chichester.[4] But, as might naturally be expected in that unscrupulous and litigious age,[5] this method of defeating the proceedings of inferior courts was abused. A statute of 1414[6] recites that persons, taken in execution on judgments recovered against them in the courts of the city of London and other cities, have, by means of writs of certiorari and corpus cum causa, got their release in the Chancery, whereby the

---

[1] Jenks, Essays A.A.L.H. ii 536; cp. Bl. Comm. iii 130; Sir John Charles Fox has shown, L.Q.R. xxxix 46-59, that Reeves and Dr. Jenks are mistaken in identifying writs of *capias* with writs of *habeas corpus*. The former writs are directed to the arrest and imprisonment of a defendant: the latter to his production before a court, ibid 53-54.
[2] Jenks, op. cit. 538.
[3] Ibid 539-541.
[4] Y.B. 13 Hy. IV. Mich. pl. 4.
[5] Vol. ii 415-416.
[6] 2 Henry V. st. 1 c. 2.

judgment creditors remain unsatisfied. It was therefore enacted that if, on the return to these writs, it was certified that the prisoners were condemned by judgment, they should be remanded. It would seem also from a statute of 1433[1] that a similar device was used by persons taken in execution for non-payment of the amounts due on statutes staple. At a later period the same device was used to hinder the proceedings of inferior courts. A statute of 1601 tells us that a defendant would wait till an issue had been reached, a jury sworn, and the case opened, and then get a writ of *Habeas Corpus* or other similar writ to remove the cause to Westminster.[2] It prohibits these practices; and further limitations were put on the issue of such writs by a statute of 1624.[3] At that time the victory of the common law courts over the local courts had long been complete, and the former desired to rid themselves of the mass of petty litigation with which they were embarrassed.

The issue of a writ of privilege, accompanied by a *Habeas Corpus*, to get the release of a litigant in one of the superior courts, who had been arrested by an inferior court, rested in substance on the same principle of asserting or safeguarding the superiority of the courts of common law. This device was also made use of for purposes of chicane; and the courts found it necessary to lay down strict conditions for the issue of such a writ. It would not lie for a person imprisoned at the suit of the king,[4] if the proceedings in the superior court were clearly collusive,[5] or if they had been begun after the arrest complained of.[6]

Both these classes of cases become of comparatively minor importance in the later law; but, towards the end of the fifteenth century, the principle upon which they rested, and the machinery by which this principle was asserted, were turned to a new use.

(ii) It was towards the end of the fifteenth century that the rivalry of the courts of common law and the court of Chancery began;[7] and, almost immediately, the courts of common law began to think of using the *Habeas Corpus* to assert their jurisdiction. In 1484 Huse, C.J., said that, if the chancellor committed a suitor for breach of an injunction not to sue at common law, the court would release him by *Habeas Corpus*.[8]

---

[1] 11 Henry VI. c. 10 § 2.   [2] 43 Elizabeth c. 5.

[3] 21 James I. c. 23; cp. vol. i 74.

[4] Y.B. 22 Hy. VI. Hil. pl. 34 *per* Newton.

[5] Y.BB. 39 Hy. VI. Hil. pl. 15; 2 Hy. VII. Mich. pl. 6; Worlay v. Harrison (1566) Dyer 249b.

[6] Y.B. 8 Ed. IV. Mich. pl. 23.   [7] Vol. i 459.

[8] " Et quant a ce si le Chancelor commande un home al Fleet, tantost que vous soies la si voillez faire conusans a nous, nous voillomus faire un *Habeas Corpus* retornable devant nous, et quant il veigne devant nous, nous voillomus luy dismisser," Y.B. 22 Ed. IV. Mich. pl. 21.

During the sixteenth century the common law courts found themselves under the necessity of defending their jurisdiction against many rival courts; and therefore this use of the writ of *Habeas Corpus* became very common. In *Glanvil's Case*[1] several precedents of Elizabeth's reign were cited for the release, by means of this writ, of persons committed to prison by the chancellor or by the Council;[2] and there is plenty of evidence that it was used to release persons committed by the court of Requests,[3] by the Admiralty,[4] and by the court of High Commission.[5] Naturally these cases became more numerous when the common law courts, under the leadership of Coke, entered upon their contest for supremacy with these rival courts.[6]

It was probably owing to its extensive use by the common law courts to defend their jurisdiction, that the writ had, at the close of the sixteenth century, become an independent writ, and not a mere satelite to a writ of certiorari or privilege;[7] and that, as so used, it was branching out into three distinct species. It is clear that, by the end of the sixteenth century, the *Habeas Corpus ad respondendum*—the form used "when a man hath a cause of action against one who is confined by the process of some inferior court,"[8] was distinct from the *Habeas Corpus ad subjiciendum et recipiendum*—the form used when a person was detained on a criminal charge;[9] and a little later the form *ad faciendum et recipiendum* became appropriated to the case where a defendant in a civil action, in an inferior court, wished to remove the action into a superior court.[10]

It was the application of the *Habeas Corpus ad subjiciendum et recipiendum* to the case of persons committed to prison by the Council, which suggested the use of the writ for the protection of the liberty of the subject. But, when it came to be so used, men naturally connected it with those clauses of Magna Carta which prohibited imprisonment without due process of law. The

---

[1] (1615) Moore 838.   [2] At p. 839.

[3] Select Cases in the Court of Requests (S.S.) xxxix, xlii.

[4] Select Pleas of the Admiralty (S.S.) ii xlvi-xlvii; Hawkeridge's Case (1617) 12 Co. Rep. 129.

[5] Coke, Fourth Instit. 333-334; cp. Jenks, op. cit. 544.

[6] Vol. i 414, 553, 610; vol. v 429, 432.   [7] Cp. Jenks, op. cit. 544.

[8] Bl. Comm. iii 129; this must have been the form of the writ in Worlay v. Harrison (1566) Dyer 249b.

[9] This was the form used in Darnel's Case (1627) 3 S.T. 11.

[10] There is a precedent of such a writ before 1510 cited by Jenks, op. cit. 541-542, from Pynson's Book of Entries f. 25 ; Jones's Case (1677) 1 Mod. 235 shows that by that time these differences were well settled; as that case shows, the distinction between the *Habeas Corpus ad subjiciendum* and the other varieties, was emphasized by the distinction drawn between the courts which, before the Act of 1679, had power to grant them; according to one view the *Habeas Corpus ad subjiciendum* could only be granted by the King's Bench, while the others could be granted by the Common Pleas, below 115-116.

history which I have just narrated shows that there is no historical connection between Magna Carta and this writ. But as the writ was now being used to give effect to the principle contained in Magna Carta, a substantial connection had in fact been created, which was too obvious to be overlooked. We shall now see that that connection was the more obvious, partly by reason of the shape which the struggle for the principle of the liberty of the subject had taken in the Middle Ages; and partly by reason of the shape which this same struggle was taking at the close of the sixteenth and the beginning of the seventeenth century.

(3) The writ of *Habeas Corpus* as the protector of the liberty of the subject.

We have seen that, during the mediæval period, the clause of Magna Carta which prohibited arrest without due process of law, and the other statutes which confirmed or amplified it, were used to show that arrests by the Chancery and Council were illegal.[1] Due process of law was interpreted by the House of Commons to mean due process of the common law; and Magna Carta and these later statutes were supposed to prove that arrests by order of the king or Council were illegal. But we have seen that this interpretation was never acquiesced in by the crown; and that the mediæval protests and mediæval legislation never succeeded in limiting the large and vague power of the king or his Council to make arrests.[2] This power was used extensively all through the Tudor period; and it was acquiesced in, because it was necessary for the safety of the country in its struggle with its foreign foes and its own rebellious subjects. We have seen also that this interpretation, which the mediæval Parliaments put upon this clause of Magna Carta, naturally commended itself to the common lawyers; for it magnified their jurisdiction at the expense of the Council and Chancery.[3] Hence we get mediæval precedents for resistance by the judges to arbitrary acts which were contrary to the principles of the common law.[4] But we have seen that the precedents were conflicting, and, naturally, during the greater part of the Tudor period, the judges did not desire to hamper the executive by an unseasonable insistence upon the technical rules of the common law. We sometimes hear faint echoes of those mediæval precedents—but that is all.[5] During the latter part of the Tudor period the growth of a parliamentary opposition helped to revive the mediæval feeling

[1] Vol. i 487.   [2] Ibid 488-489.   [3] Ibid 486.
[4] Vol. ii 561-564.   [5] Vol. i 509; vol. v 348.

against arbitrary power; and that feeling took the mediæval form of a protest against arbitrary imprisonment except under the process of the common law, and a demand for the observance of Magna Carta and of those other mediæval statutes by which this principle was guaranteed. But the form which this demand took naturally connected itself with the struggle of the common law courts for supremacy.[1] We have seen that the common law judges, though they might be willing, in the interests of national safety, to allow great freedom of action to the executive, were always jealous of their own privileges and jurisdiction.[2] The fact that protests against the imprisonment by the Council, and the fact that the assertion that such imprisonment was contrary to the common law, magnified their jurisdiction, made them the more ready to listen and accede to arguments that writs of *Habeas Corpus* should issue to question the legality of such imprisonments; for it was a mode of keeping the jurisdiction of the Council within due bounds, which they were using against the Chancery, the court of Requests, the Admiralty, and the High Commission.[3]

Two cases heard in 1588 illustrate the application of these ideas. In *Searche's Case*[4] a *Habeas Corpus* was issued to the Steward and Marshall on the application of Searche, who was detained by them in custody. The cause of his detention was certified as follows: The queen by her letters patent had taken into her protection one Mabbe and his sureties, and had stated that, if any should arrest or cause to be arrested Mabbe or his sureties, the Marshall of her house should arrest such persons and detain them till they had answered to the Council for their contempt; it was further stated that Searche had arrested one of Mabbe's sureties, and that that was the reason for his detention. The Court ordered Searche to be discharged; and, on his rearrest, it issued an attachment against those who had rearrested him. *Howel's Case*[5] was another case of detention by the Steward and Marshall. In this case the return was that Howel had been committed "per mandatum Fransisci Walsingham Militis Principalis Secretarii et unius de privato concilio dominae reginae"; and, "that return was by the Court holden insufficient, because the cause upon which he was committed was not set down in the return."

It was obvious, however, that the Council could not acquiesce

---

[1] Thus we find that in 1594 it was said that a contumacious defendant in the court of Requests, "in further manifestacion of his contemptuous disposicion preferres an Informacion into his (sic) Maties Court of Common Pleas agst. the Plaintife upon the statute of Magna Charta and divers other statutes in that case made," Select Cases in the Court of Requests (S.S.) xxxvii.

[2] Vol. i 260-261.

[3] Above 111.

[4] 1 Leo. 70.

[5] 1 Leo. 70·71.

in the deliverance of its prisoners by writs of *Habeas Corpus*. We have seen that an attempt was made to settle the rules applicable to such cases by the resolution of the judges in 1591; and that that resolution, which recognized the validity of commitments by the whole Council or by the king's special command, probably represented truly the existing law.[1]   But the result of these cases and of this resolution was to advertise, so to speak, the writ of *Habeas Corpus* as the best remedy available for those who considered that they had been unlawfully imprisoned by the crown. It is not surprising, therefore, that, when the contest with the prerogative began in the following century, it at once took its place as the great constitutional weapon for the protection of the liberty of the subject.   We have seen that it assumed this position in *Darnel's Case;*[2] and still more prominently in the subsequent debates in Parliament on the liberty of the subject.[3]   It was, said Selden in 1628, "the highest remedy in law for any man that is imprisoned."[4]   And, after the Great Rebellion, it assumed this position without question.   It is, says Hale,[5] "a writ of a high nature, for if persons be wrongfully committed, they are to be discharged upon this writ returned; or if bailable, they are to be bailed; if not bailable, they are to be committed."   "It is now," said Vaughan, C.J.,[6] "the most usual remedy by which a man is restored again to his liberty, if he have been against the law deprived of it."

But when a remedy which was originally devised for one purpose, has come to be used for a different purpose, it will generally be found that difficult questions will arise as to its application.   Its new use will raise all sorts of problems as to its competence, to which no certain answer can be given.   And these difficulties were aggravated in the case of the writ of *Habeas Corpus*, because the question of its competence was merged in the political controversies which were convulsing the state.   The king was interested in not allowing too wide a scope to the writ.   The Parliamentary opposition, in alliance with the common lawyers, wished to make it easily accessible to all who alleged that they had been unlawfully imprisoned.   They wished to make it an efficient protector of the principle that no man should be imprisoned without due process of the common law.   They effected their object by direct legislation; and it is this legislation, which extends from the Petition of Right to 1816, that has given to the writ its great place in our modern constitutional law.

Selden in 1628 asserted, not only that the writ of *Habeas*

---

[1] Vol. v 348 and App. I.; vol. vi 32-37.   [2] (1627) 3 S.T. 1; vol. vi 34-37.
[3] Vol. vi 37-38.   [4] 3 S.T. 95.   [5] P.C. ii 143.
[6] Bushell's Case (1670) Vaughan at p. 136.

Corpus was "the highest remedy in the law for any man that is imprisoned," but also that it was "the only remedy for him that is imprisoned by the special command of the king, or the lords of the Privy Council, without shewing cause of the commitment."[1] That the latter assertion was not law was decided in *Darnel's Case*.[2] But we have seen that that decision was declared not to be law by the Petition of Right; and that, as a result of that enactment, the king lost his right to imprison "per speciale mandatum" without showing cause.[3] The application of the writ to commitments by the Council was dealt with by the Act for the abolition of the Star Chamber and other courts exercising a like jurisdiction. That Act provided that, if any person should be imprisoned by any court exercising a jurisdiction similar to that of the Star Chamber, or by the command of the king or of the Council, he should, on application to be made to the judges of the King's Bench or Common Pleas, have a writ of *Habeas Corpus;* that the gaolor should bring his prisoner before the judges of the court from which the writ issued, with a certificate of the true cause of his imprisonment; and that the court should, within three court days after such return, examine the return, "and thereupon do what to justice shall appertain either by delivery, bailing, or remanding the prisoner."[4]

These enactments dealt with the defects in the writ which the constitutional conflicts of the earlier part of the seventeenth century had disclosed. But after the Restoration other, and, in some respects, more serious defects were disclosed. We have seen that the later Stuarts, being debarred from the more direct expedients for securing the maintenance of their authority which were open to their predecessors, were obliged to resort to more devious methods.[5] They found it possible to make use of some of the defects which still existed in the writ, to imprison persons they objected to for considerable periods. Thus it was by no means certain what courts had power to issue the different forms of the writ; and whether, assuming that any given court had power to issue it, that court could issue it in vacation as well as in term time. Hale thought that the writ could issue from either the Common Pleas or the Exchequer; but that "that is or ought to be always when a person is privileged or to charge him with an action"; so that it would seem that they could only issue the writ *ad faciendum et recipiendum* and not the writ *ad subjiciendum*.[6]

[1] 3 S.T. 95.   [2] (1627) 3 S.T. 1; vol. vi 34-37.   [3] Ibid 38.
[4] 16 Charles I. c. 10 § 6; cp. Jenks, op. cit. 547.   [5] Vol. vi 208-209.
[6] P.C. ii 144; Jones's Case (1677) 1 Mod. 235; from S.C. 2 Mod. 198 it appears that the opinions of the judges as to the right of the Common Pleas to issue a *Habeas Corpus ad subjiciendum* were conflicting; it appears from Anon. (1671) Carter 221 that Vaughan, C.J., was against the issue of this form of the writ by the Common Pleas, but that the three other judges of the Court were against him; see vol. i 202-203.

The King's Bench could issue the former form of writ in vacation or term time;[1] but some thought that it could issue the latter form only in term time;[2] and it is probable that on this matter there was no certain rule.[3] The Chancery could issue the latter, but not the former form of writ; but, according to Hale,[4] only in the vacation. Coke thought that the Chancery would issue this form of the writ either in vacation or in term time;[5] but Lord Nottingham, in *Jenkes's Case*, held that there were no precedents for the issue of such a writ by the Chancery in the vacation, and refused to grant it.[6] Then, too, if the writ was issued, the gaolor might wait for an *alias* or *pluries* writ, move the prisoner about to evade service of these writs, and, in the last resort, remove him out of the jurisdiction of the court.

Some of these defects in the writ of *Habeas Corpus* were illustrated by the arbitrary proceedings of Clarendon, who, in 1667, was accused of sending persons to "remote islands, garrisons, and other places, thereby to prevent them from the benefit of the law, and to produce precedents for the imprisoning of any other of his majesty's subjects in like manner."[7] Other defects were illustrated by the manner in which persons imprisoned by the Council were obliged to bribe courtiers to obtain their liberty.[8] That such illicit methods were a speedier way of gaining liberty than a recourse to the law is shown by *Jenkes's Case* in 1676.[9] Jenkes had made a speech at a Common Hall held in the Guildhall in the City of London, in which he had advocated a petition to the king for summoning a new Parliament. For making this speech he had been summoned before the Council, and committed to the Gatehouse prison. As it was the vacation, he moved Lord Nottingham, the lord chancellor, for a writ of *Habeas Corpus;* but, as we have seen, without success. He then applied to the quarter sessions held for the liberty of Westminster (within which the Gatehouse prison was) to be admitted to bail; but equally without success. He then applied to the lord chancellor to be released on mainprize; but, as we have seen, the lord chancellor

---

[1] Hale, P.C. ii 145.   [2] Ibid.

[3] Thus in 1759 Wilmot, C.J., said, after an inquiry into the records of the King's Bench, "no information is to be had from the records; but there are traces from the cases in print, and from fiats since the Restoration, and before the 31st Car. II, that there had been a kind of unsettled practice for the Chief Justice and Judges of the Court of King's Bench, granting them in vacation," Wilm. at p. 94.

[4] P.C. ii 147.   [5] Second Instit. 55; Fourth Instit. 81.

[6] (1676) 2 Swanst. 12-14; Wilmot, C.J., approved the decision, Wilm. at p. 101; but Lord Eldon disapproved, see 2 Swanst. at pp. 36-65.

[7] 6 S.T. 330.

[8] See the case of Moyer narrated by Pepys, Diary (Wheatley's ed.) vi 322, May 16, 1667; vii 12, July 7, 1667.

[9] 6 S.T. 1190; and see the extracts from Lord Nottingham's MSS., 2 Swanst. 12-14, 83-91.

held, probably rightly, that this remedy was not available.[1] Application was then made to Rainsford, C.J., who had just returned from his circuit. Finally, after he had interposed many delays, Rainsford, C.J., intimated to the lord chancellor that Jenkes ought to be released on bail ; and so he finally got his release.

The year after the impeachment of Clarendon the House of Commons had begun to consider the question of making better provision for securing the liberty of the subject. A bill to prevent the refusal of the writ of *Habeas Corpus* was considered by the House in 1668, but it failed to pass the committee stage.[2] In 1669-1670 another bill, which passed the House of Commons by a majority of one vote (100 to 99), but failed to pass the House of Lords, attempted to prevent the transportation of prisoners beyond the seas, or out of the jurisdiction of the English courts, except in the case of convicted felons who had consented to be transported as a condition of getting a pardon.[3] In 1673-1674 this bill again passed the Commons, and reached the committee stage in the House of Lords ;[4] and, in the same year, another bill for the improvement of the procedure on writs of *Habeas Corpus* passed the House of Commons, but was stopped in the House of Lords by a prorogation.[5] Bills similar to this last-mentioned bill passed the Commons in 1675 and 1676-1677, but dropped with the ending of the session in the House of Lords.[6] In 1679 the clauses of the bills which were designed to prevent the imprisonment of subjects beyond the seas, and of the bills which were designed to improve the procedure on the writ of *Habeas Corpus*, were combined in one bill, which became the famous Habeas Corpus Act.[7] Having passed the House of Commons, it was sent up to the House of Lords, where it was fully considered, and eventually passed its third reading with amendments.[8] After several conferences between the Houses, they at length came to an agreement on these amendments. But it was only on the last day of the session that this agreement was reached at a final conference ;[9] and the decision to hold this conference, on which the fate of the bill depended, was only carried by a majority of two (57 to 55), under circumstances which lend some colour to Burnet's tale that that majority was arrived at by a miscount.[10]

---

[1] Above 106-107.
[2] Hallam, C.H. iii 11 ; Commons' Journals, April 10th, 1668.
[3] Hist. MSS. Com. 8th Rep. App., Pt. i 142 no. 276.
[4] Ibid 9th Rep. App. Pt. ii 42 no. 161.   [5] Ibid 46 no. 184.
[6] Ibid 65 no. 279 ; 88 no. 388.   [7] 31 Charles II. c. 2.
[8] Lords' Journals xiii 549 ; Hist. MSS. Com. 11th Rep. Pt. ii 132 no. 163.
[9] Lords' Journals, xiii 595.
[10] In Hist. MSS. Com. 11th Rep. Pt. ii 136 it is pointed out that only 107 peers are entered as present, and that, in a previous division on this day, only 101 peers took part ; Burnet's tale, History of My Own Times (folio ed.). i 485, is as follows : " Lord

This Act made the writ of *Habeas Corpus ad subjiciendum* the most effective weapon yet devised for the protection of the liberty of the subject, by providing both for a speedy judicial inquiry into the justice of any imprisonment on a criminal charge, and for a speedy trial of prisoners remanded to await trial.   It seems to have made the *Habeas Corpus ad subjiciendum* the only form of the writ used for the purpose of protecting liberty; for we shall see that when, in the eighteenth century, it was desired to make still ampler provision for its protection, this object was achieved by an extension of this form of the writ as improved by this Act.[1]   The following summary of the provisions of the Act will illustrate the defects in the writ which the experience of the past nineteen years had disclosed, and will indicate the manner in which they were successfully remedied :—The lord chancellor and any of the judges of the superior courts must issue the writ in vacation or in term, unless the prisoner is committed for treason or felony plainly expressed in the warrant of commitment, or is in prison on conviction for crime, or by some legal process.[2]   The time is specified within which the return of the writ must be made, and within which the court or judge must adjudicate on the writ.[3]   Gaolers must deliver to prisoners a true copy of the warrant of commitment.[4]   No persons released by writ of *Habeas Corpus* may be again committed for the same offence.[5]   Prisoners indicted for treason or felony must be tried at the next sessions or bailed ; but if it appear that the king's witnesses cannot be ready at that time, they may be committed till the following term ; if not tried, then they must be discharged.[6]   No persons are allowed to alter a prisoner's place of confinement, except in certain specific cases defined by the Act.[7]   No prisoners may be sent to Scotland, Ireland, or parts beyond the seas.[8]   The writ is to run into the counties palatine and all other privileged places.[9]   The success of the Act in effecting its object is illustrated by the desire of James II. to get it repealed.[10]   His judges did their best to evade it by requiring prisoners, entitled to bail, to find security in such excessive sums

Grey and Lord Norris were named to be the tellers : Lord Norris, being a man subject to vapours, was not at all times attentive to what he was doing.   So a very fat Lord coming in Lord Grey counted him for ten, as a jest at first : But seeing Lord Norris had not observed it, he went on with this misrekoning of ten :   So it was reported to the House, and declared that they who were for the bill were the majority, Tho' indeed it went on the other side :   And by this means the bill past."   If only 101 peers really voted on the Habeas Corpus Bill, this would make a mistake of eleven ; but not much stress can be laid on the exact numbers ; probably there was a mistake, and this tale was very soon afterwards invented and embellished to account for it.

[1] Below 121-122.   [2] §§ 3 and 10.   [3] §§ 2 and 3.   [4] § 5.
[5] § 6.   [6] § 7.   [7] § 9.   [8] § 12.   [9] § 11.
[10] In Oct., 1685, Barillon wrote to Louis XIV. that James "designed to obtain from the Parliament a repeal of the Test and Habeas Corpus Acts, the first of which is the destruction of the Catholic Religion, and the other of the royal authority," cited Foxcroft, Life and Letters of Halifax i 450.

of money that they were unable to furnish it.   This abuse was the subject of one of the clauses of the Bill of Rights;[1] and the law as thus settled by the Act and by the Bill of Rights was not altered for more than a century.

But, in the course of the eighteenth century, two defects were disclosed in the existing law.   Firstly, the court had no power to examine the truth of any return made by a gaolor.   Secondly, the Act of 1679 did not apply to a detention which was not a detention on a criminal charge.   Till 1679 attention had been concentrated almost exclusively upon the assertion of the liberty of the subject against arrest and detention by the crown on criminal charges.[2] It was not till after that date that the writ of *Habeas Corpus* began to be commonly used to get relief from imprisonment by private persons, or from imprisonment on other than a charge of crime.[3] But the improvements made by the Act of 1679 did not apply to writs issued for these purposes.   They were therefore subject to the inconvenient common law rules, which that Act had been passed to reform.

Attention was called to these defects chiefly by the Acts which had allowed impressment for military service.   To some extent also they were illustrated by the existing bankruptcy law and practice; for we have seen that that law, by giving incompetent commissioners large powers to commit bankrupts, provided occasions for many applications to the chancellor to issue writs of *Habeas Corpus* for their release.[4]   It seems to have been the first of these causes which gave rise to a bill which was considered by the House of Lords in 1758.[5]   The object of the bill was to extend the Act of 1679 so as to give the benefit of the writ of *Habeas Corpus ad subjiciendum*, as improved by that Act, to persons who were imprisoned otherwise than on a criminal charge.[6]   But the Lords took the opportunity to get the opinion of the judges, not

---

[1] 1 William and Mary Sess. 2 c. 2 § 1 (10).   [2] See Wilm. at pp. 85-87.

[3] Wilmot, C.J., in 1758, Wilm. at pp. 95-96, said, " as to writs of Habeas Corpus in cases of private custody, I cannot ascertain the commencement of their being first issued by the Court. . . . The writ of homine replegiando . . . was the only specific remedy provided by the common law for the protection and defence of his liberty against any private invasion of it. . . . The first case is the case of *Sir Philip Howard*, mentioned in *Lord Leigh's Case*, and therefore must have been before that time. *Lord Leigh's Case* was in the 27 Car. II. where habeas corpus was granted to bring up his wife.   And the case of *Viner and Emmerton* was in the 27th year of Car. II. where a habeas corpus was granted to Viner to bring up his daughter-in-law, viz. his wife's daughter by a first husband.   From that time to this the Court has constantly granted them '; for the cases here cited see 2 Lev. 128-129.

[4] Vol. i 472; Crowley's Case (1818) 2 Swanst. 1 was a bankrupt's case; in the report at pp. 30-31 several cases were cited where the chancellor discharged bankrupts who had been committed; rules were made for the procedure on writs of habeas corpus brought by bankrupts thus committed by 5 George II. c. 30 §§ 18, 19.

[5] See Wilm. 81 *note*, where the resolutions of the judges on this point are given.

[6] For the bill see Wilm. 77 *note*.

only on the question of the law as to the issue of writs of *Habeas Corpus ad subjiciendum* not falling within the Act of 1679, but also upon the question whether a judge, before whom such a writ was returned, had power to examine the truth of the facts stated in the return.[1]

To some extent the views of the judges were in conflict; but there was a very substantial measure of agreement. It was agreed by all that the truth of the return was not examinable by the court, because it was a question of fact for a jury to be ascertained in other proceedings. The court, it was said, were concerned, not with the truth of the return, but with its sufficiency in point of law to justify a detention.[2] A series of precedents from the Year Books onwards proved that this was the law;[3] but there can be no doubt that it worked hardship. It had been proposed to allow such inquiry to be made in 1688; but this was one of the proposals which did not find its way into the Bill of Rights.[4] To some extent, however, the judges had mitigated its harshness by adopting the practice of making a rule that a person holding another in his custody should show cause for his detention, and of discharging such person if no cause were shown. In that way the merits of the case could be gone into.[5] It was suggested also by Wilmot, C.J., that a person, who could not get relief on a writ of *Habeas Corpus* by reason of the return being false but sufficient, could get relief by the writ *de homine replegiando*.[6] But no one seems to have tried to adopt this course; nor is this surprising if

[1] See the questions put to the judges, Wilm. 77-81; their opinions will be found in the Lords' Journals xxix 337-341, 344-347.

[2] "The Court says, 'Tell us the reason why you confine him.' The Court will determine whether it is a good or bad reason; but not whether it is a true or false one. The judges are not competent to this enquiry; it is not their province, but the province of a jury, to determine it. . . . The writ is not framed or adapted to litigatory facts: it is a summary short way of taking the opinion of the Court upon a matter of law," Wilm. at p. 107.

[3] Ibid at p. 108, citing Selden's argument in 3 S.T. at p. 96; ibid at p. 112, citing Y.B. 9 Hy. VI. Mich. pl. 24; Bagg's Case (1616) 11 Co. Rep. at f. 99b; Hawkeridge's Case (1617) 12 Co. Rep. at p. 130.

[4] "It appears by Sir G. Treby's report, February, 1688, that the House of Commons came to twenty-eight resolutions, to be carried into the Bill of Rights. Many of them were afterwards dropped, and amongst the rest the twenty-fifth which was, 'that the subject should have liberty to traverse returns to writs of habeas corpus and mandamus,'" Wilm. at p. 112.

[5] See the resolution of the judges in 1758 on the Act for impressment, Wilm. 81 *note;* it was clearly an established practice at the beginning of the nineteenth century, see the argument in Cox v. Hakes (1890) 15 A.C. at p. 509; but 1810—the date there assigned for the beginning of the practice—is obviously too late, having regard to the note in Wilmot.

[6] "If the case were ever so remediless, I think we are not warranted to impeach by affidavits the truth of the return of an officer, acting under an Act of Parliament, which the law says ought to be impeached by a verdict. But the case is not a remediless one; by the common law, the writ of de homine replegiando will clearly relieve him," Wilm. at p. 123; a more feasible suggestion was that made at p. 124, that an appeal should be made to the summary jurisdiction which the King's Bench could exercise over all inferior jurisdictions.

we consider the lengthy and cumbersome nature of the proceedings on such a writ. It was also generally agreed that, in some respects, the practice upon writs of *Habeas Corpus* not falling within the Act of 1679, had been improved by the judges. Thus these writs were issued in vacation as well as in term time,[1] and they could be issued returnable immediately, so as to avoid the delay of waiting for an *alias* and a *pluries* writ, and enforced by attachment.[2] But in other respects the provisions of the Act of 1679 did not apply. Thus the judges were agreed that they had a certain amount of discretion as to whether they would or would not issue the writ in vacation;[3] and that a person could get no relief against a judge who refused to issue a writ.[4]

The House of Lords rejected the bill, in spite of the objections[5] of those who pointed out that it appeared, from the opinion of the judges, that the practice of issuing the writ in vacation rested upon a very uncertain basis;[6] and that some definition of what should be deemed to be a sufficiently probable cause to compel a judge to issue the writ was desirable.[7] But, though the House rejected this bill, it ordered the judges to prepare a bill to extend the power of granting these writs in vacation to all the judges of the common law courts, to provide for the issue of process in vacation to compel obedience to such writs, and, if this was possible, to give the court power to inquire into the truth of the return.[8] The Judges prepared a bill; but nothing further was done till 1816, when this draft bill became the foundation of the Act[9] which effected the objects outlined by the House in 1758.[10] By this Act, "for more effectually securing the liberty of the subject," it was provided that the Act of 1679 should apply to persons deprived of their liberty otherwise than by reason of a charge of crime, unless they were imprisoned for debt or on process in a civil suit;[11] that the judges should be bound, on complaint made by or on

---

[1] Wilm. at p. 103.   [2] Ibid at p. 104.
[3] Ibid at pp. 81-94.   [4] Ibid at p. 104.
[5] The arguments appear in the Protest contained in the Lords' Journals xxix 352-353.
[6] Ibid 352.
[7] "It is now become of indispensable necessity to define with precision what shall be deemed a probable cause, under which the judges at all times shall be bound to issue the writs aforesaid, that they may not in bad times . . . assume an arbitrary discretion destructive of the personal liberty of the subject. . . . And because the general doctrines and opinions laid down in the course of this debate, that neither a judge nor the Court are bound to grant this great remedial writ to the subject, upon proof of actual confinement verified by affidavit, are not supported by any single determination of any one Court of Justice, and are directly repugnant to the reason and genius of the law of this free country," ibid.
[8] Ibid 353.
[9] 2 Swanst. 60 note 15, where it is pointed out that a copy of the draft is to be found in Dodson, Life of Sir Michael Foster 68-72.
[10] 56 George III. c. 100.   [11] § 1.

behalf of a person deprived of his liberty, if it appeared by affidavit that there was a probable ground for such complaint, to award a writ of *Habeas Corpus ad subjiciendum;*[1] and that, in the civil cases to which the Act applied, a judge should have power to inquire into the truth of a return to the writ.[2]

After the Revolution, the efforts of the Legislature to improve the writ of *Habeas Corpus* were seconded by the judges. In fact the judges have always been ready, except in the period of acute constitutional controversy immediately preceding the Revolution, to interpret the rules of the common law and the statute law in such a way that they made for the greater efficiency of the writ. This was due to two causes. In the first place, the tradition, which dated from the days when the writ was used by the common law courts to protect their own jurisdiction from the encroachments of rival courts,[3] supplied precedents for rules which made the writ both an effectual and a speedy remedy. We have seen that in 1588 it had been settled that any one again imprisoning a person released by the writ was liable to attachment for contempt;[4] and in 1610, in the *City of London's Case,*[5] the speediness and the informality of the process thereon were emphasized by Coke.[6] In the second place, the tradition, dating back to the Middle Ages, which made the common law the protector of the liberty of the subject, was intensified after the Revolution; and, in respect to the writ of *Habeas Corpus,* it was further strengthened by the legislation which we have just been considering.

I have already given some illustrations of the practical effect of this attitude of the judges in the eighteenth century.[7] In the nineteenth and twentieth centuries, the most striking illustration of the maintenance of this attitude is to be found in the rules which were evolved, as to the manner in which the correctness of decisions upon applications to issue the writ, could be questioned. Before the Judicature Act no provision was made (except in the case of the writ of prohibition[8]) for questioning the decision of a court to issue or not to issue any of the prerogative writs.[9] But the clauses of the Acts of 1679[10] and 1816,[11] providing that the

---

[1] § 1. [2] §§ 3 and 4. [3] Above 109-111.
[4] Above 113. [5] 8 Co. Rep. 121b.
[6] "To which it was answered and resolved, that this is not on a demurrer in law, but a return on writ of privilege, upon which no issue can be taken, or demurrer joined, neither upon our award herein doth any writ of error lie, and therefore the return is no other but to inform the court of the truth of the matter, in which such a precise certainty is not required as in pleading"; ibid at ff. 127b, 128a; for the meaning of the term writ of privilege, and its connection with the writ of Habeas Corpus, see above 109, 110.
[7] Above 120-121. [8] As to this see vol. i 229 and n. 4.
[9] Barnardo v. Ford [1892] A.C. at p. 337 *per* Lord Herschell.
[10] 31 Charles II. c. 2. [11] 56 George III. c. 100.

writ of *Habeas Corpus* could be issued by the lord chancellor or by any of the judges or barons of the exchequer "of the degree of the coif,"[1] and that no person released upon a writ of *Habeas Corpus* should be again imprisoned for the same offence,[2] gave what was in effect a right of appeal against a decision not to issue the writ; for it enabled a prisoner to "make a fresh application to every judge and every court in turn, and each court or judge was bound to consider the question independently, and not to be influenced by the previous decisions refusing to discharge."[3] The clause of the Judicature Act which provides for an appeal to the court of Appeal from any order of the High Court,[4] and the clause of the Appellate Jurisdiction Act which provides for an appeal to the House of Lords from any order of the court of Appeal,[5] raised difficult questions as to their effect upon the existing law. It was clear that the Acts gave an appeal from a decision granting or refusing to grant such prerogative writs as mandamus or prohibition.[6] Did they also give an appeal from a decision granting or refusing to grant a writ of *Habeas Corpus?* It was held in the case of *Cox v. Hakes,*[7] that the wide powers of appeal given by those Acts do not operate to upset the rule in force before their enactment, that there can be no appeal from a decision discharging a prisoner upon a writ of *Habeas Corpus;* and it was held in the case of *Secretary of State for Home Affairs v. O'Brien*[8] that the same rule applies to a decision awarding the writ, even though no actual order of discharge has been made. The main reason for these decisions was, that a contrary conclusion would have materially diminished the efficacy of the writ in protecting the liberty of the subject, by delaying a final decision upon the lawfulness of his imprisonment. It is only in cases like that of *Barnardo v. Ford*[9] and *R. v. Barnardo*[10] where, as Lindley, L.J., said,[11] the

---

[1] 31 Charles II. c. 2 § 3; for the meaning of the phrase "degree of the coif," see vol. i 237.

[2] 31 Charles II. c. 2 § 6.

[3] Cox v. Hakes (1890) 15 A.C. at p. 514 *per* Lord Halsbury, L.C.; Ex pte. Partington (1845) 13 M. and W. at p. 684.

[4] 36, 37 Victoria c. 66 § 19.   [5] 39, 40 Victoria c. 59 § 3.

[6] Barnardo v. Ford [1892] A.C. at p. 337 *per* Lord Herschell.

[7] (1890) 15 A.C. 506; the decision was in effect based on two grounds: a narrower ground that if a prisoner had been discharged there was no machinery for his rearrest, and a wider ground that any other decision would impair the liberty of the subject.

[8] [1923] A.C. 603.   [9] [1892] A.C. 326.   [10] [1891] 1 Q.B. 194.

[11] Ibid at p. 210; Lord Esher, M.R., said, ibid at p. 204, "the procedure generally and originally has been used for the purpose of bringing up persons whose liberty was alleged to be actually interfered with; but the writ has also been used with respect to the custody of infants, in order to determine whether the person who has the actual custody of them as children shall continue to have the custody of them as children. In such cases it is not a question of liberty, but of nurture, control, and education"; both these passages were cited with approval in Secretary of State for Home Affairs v. O'Brien [1923] A.C. at pp. 613, 620.

question at issue was not whether or not a person was to be set at liberty, but which of several persons ought to have the custody of a child, that any appeal is allowed from a decision awarding the writ. On the other hand, except in the case where a judgment refusing to issue the writ is a judgment in a criminal cause or matter,[1] an appeal lies from a decision not to issue the writ to the court of Appeal and the House of Lords. This question, which was left open by Lord Herschell in the case of *Cox v. Hakes*,[2] was decided in 1923 by the case of *Secretary of State for Home Affairs v. O'Brien*.[3] This power to appeal obviously gives, in another form, the power which prisoners formerly had of questioning a refusal to grant the writ, by applying in turn to different courts and different judges. The fact that these rules as to appeals from decisions granting or refusing to grant the writ are not wholly logical,[4] is the best evidence of the maintenance of the old tradition that the effectiveness of the writ must at all costs be maintained.

In this way the writ of *Habeas Corpus ad subjiciendum*, having in the seventeenth century been rendered an efficient means of securing the liberty of the subject imprisoned on a charge of crime, was, in the nineteenth century, not only rendered still more effectual for this purpose, but also extended to almost all other cases of imprisonment. Only in one instance has it been found necessary to restrict the scope of the writ. It was a well-established principle that, though the writ could not issue into the foreign dominions of a prince who succeeded to the throne of England, and therefore not into Scotland or Hanover, it could issue into any other part of the king's dominions.[5] It was held, therefore, in 1861 in *ex parte Anderson*[6] that it could issue into Canada. But, as the court in that case pointed out, its issue to Canada was inconvenient, because there might be difficulties in enforcing obedience to the writ; unnecessary, because the Canadian courts had power to issue it; and, "inconsistent with that higher degree of colonial independence both legislative and judicial which exists in modern times."[7] The result was that in the following year it was enacted that no writ of *Habeas Corpus* should be issued

---

[1] Ex pte. Woodhall (1888) 20 Q.B.D. 832; that is in a criminal case where a person has been committed to prison by a court having jurisdiction, not in a criminal case where, as in Secretary of State for Home Affairs v. O'Brien, there was a wholly illegal imprisonment.

[2] (1890) 15 A.C. at pp. 535-536.

[3] [1923] 2 K.B. 361; [1923] A.C. 603, at p. 610 *per* Lord Birkenhead.

[4] In Cox v. Hakes Lords Morris and Field, and in Secretary of State for Home Affairs v. O'Brien, Lord Atkinson, were dissentients.

[5] R. v. Cowle (1759) 2 Burr. at pp. 855-856; and cp. the authorities cited in Ex parte Anderson (1861) 3 El. and El. at p. 494.

[6] 3 El. and El. 487.   [7] Ibid at p. 495.

out of England by any English judge or court, into any colony or foreign dominion, where there existed a court having authority to issue and enforce obedience to the writ.[1]

At this point I close the history of substantive legal doctrine in this period. It now only remains to give some account of the developments in adjective law—in the law, that is, of evidence, procedure and pleading.

[1] 25, 26 Victoria c. 20.

CHAPTER VII

EVIDENCE, PROCEDURE, AND PLEADING

WE have seen that the beginnings of the practice of summoning witnesses to testify to the jury in the sixteenth century, profoundly modified the mediæval system of oral pleading at common law, and helped to introduce the modern system of written pleadings.[1] The change in the character of the jury,[2] which had made the presence of these witnesses necessary, had an effect upon the law of evidence as profound as it had upon the law of pleading. Now that the verdict of the jury was based, not on their own knowledge, but on the evidence produced to them in court, some law about this evidence became necessary. This law was beginning to be developed during the sixteenth and seventeenth centuries ; and, as the result of this development, we begin, at the end of the seventeenth century, to see in outline some of the main principles of our modern law of evidence. Older rules as to the production and effect of written evidence began to combine with newer rules as to the competency of witnesses, and as to the admissibility of their evidence, to produce this result. Of the beginnings of the modern law of evidence therefore I shall speak in the first place. I shall then say something of the development of the common law rules of procedure and pleading—a development which produced the artificial system, which lasted, with but little change, till the reforms of the second quarter of the nineteenth century. Lastly, I shall say something of the development of the rules of equity procedure and pleading. Like the common law rules, they were developed in most of their essential features during the sixteenth and seventeenth centuries, and remained unchanged for the same length of time. I shall therefore deal with them at this point, both because they afford an instructive parallel to and contrast with the common law rules, and because they will help us to understand the development of the modern system of equity which took place in the eighteenth century. The subject of this chapter therefore will be divided as

[1] Vol. iii 648-650.　　　　　[2] Vol. i 332-337.

follows: § 1. Evidence; § 2. Common Law Procedure and Pleading; and § 3. Equity Procedure and Pleading.

§ 1. EVIDENCE [1]

The form which the English law of evidence has assumed, is perhaps the most striking proof of the manner in which the ideas and principles of the common law have dominated the whole of the English legal system. The most characteristic rules of this branch of the law—the rules which exclude certain kinds of testimony—are due, as Thayer has pointed out,[2] to the existence of the jury; and have been evolved by the judges, partly to prevent the jury from being mis-led by the testimony produced, and partly to keep them to the issue defined by the pleadings of the parties. But, though those rules lose much of their point when applied by tribunals which do not work with a jury,[3] yet they are applied by these tribunals. Thus, by the middle of the eighteenth century, they had, with certain limitations, been accepted by the court of Chancery;[4] and at the present day they are applied in all Divisions of the High Court.

It was during the course of the sixteenth and seventeenth centuries that the jury definitely assumed its modern function as the judge of the facts on the evidence produced to it in court.[5] It follows, therefore, that the rules which regulate the admissibility of evidence, and exclude certain kinds of it, are a comparatively late development. In fact, their accurate definition, and the limitation of the sphere of their applicability, were the work of the eighteenth and nineteenth centuries.[6] But it was during the sixteenth and seventeenth centuries that the foundations of this superstructure were laid; and the rules so laid down are historically connected with still older rules, which, even in the Middle Ages,

---

[1] The leading authorities are Thayer, A Preliminary Treatise on Evidence at the Common Law; and more especially the sections dealing with the history of various parts of the law in Professor Wigmore's monumental treatise on the System of Evidence in Trials at Common Law, on which I have mainly relied; *my references are to the first edition of this work;* a useful short account of some aspects of the subject is given by Salmond, Essays in Jurisprudence and Legal History 3-69.

[2] Evidence, Introd.

[3] "Wherever evidence is taken by commission or deposition, the rules of exclusion largely break down; that is to say, in a great proportion of trials where there is no jury, namely in equity patent and admiralty cases," ibid 529; for the manner of taking evidence in the Chancery see below 353-358.

[4] Thus in the case of Manning v. Lechmere (1737) 1 Atk. 453, Lord Hardwicke said, "the rules as to evidence are the same in equity as at law, and if A was not admitted as a witness at the trial there, because materially concerned in interest, the same objection will hold against reading his deposition here"; but necessarily there were certain modifications of the common law rules, below 198; and see Maddock, Chancery ii 331-334.

[5] Vol. i 334-336.

[6] Thayer, op. cit. Introd. 2; Stephen, Digest of the Law of Evidence (4th ed.) Introd. viii.

had begun to regulate the treatment of documentary evidence of various kinds submitted to the court by the parties to an action. Thus, although large parts of the law of evidence are modern, other parts have old roots; and the older ideas which they have preserved have not been without their influence in shaping the modern rules.[1] Therefore we must, as Thayer has pointed out, take account, not only of that logical doctrine of relevancy, which Stephen treated as the core and centre of the whole matter, but also of primitive ideas preserved in some of the older rules, and of the need to guide the jury, which led to the exclusion of much testimony which should have been admitted if logical relevancy had been taken as the single test of admissibility.[2]

In fact, the rules of evidence, with which the law has been concerned all through its history, have never been solely dependent upon the logical doctrine of relevancy. They have never been solely rules for the conduct of the processes of reasoning. Rather they assume the existence of these processes.[3] They are concerned primarily with the selection of the material on which these processes operate. "When one offers evidence . . . he offers, otherwise than by reference to what is already known, to prove a matter of fact which is to be used as a basis of inference to another matter of fact. He offers, perhaps, to present to the senses of the tribunal a visible object which may furnish a ground of inference; or he offers testimony, oral or written, to prove a fact; for even direct testimony, to be believed or disbelieved, according as we trust the witness, is really but a basis of inference. In giving evidence we are furnishing to a tribunal a new basis for reasoning. This is not saying we do not have to reason in order to ascertain this basis; it is merely saying that reasoning alone will not, or at least does not, supply it. The new element thus added is what we call the evidence."[4] In this sense the term "evidence" is a term of "forensic procedure," and "imports something put forward in a court of justice."[5] The law about evidence of this kind is concerned with the mode of its production, with the qualifications of witnesses, and with the classes of evidential matter which for one reason or another are excluded.[6]

The law of evidence, then, is distinct from the logical processes of reasoning; but it is based upon and assumes the existence of these processes. And because they are assumed three consequences follow. In the first place, the rules of the law of evidence often take the negative form of exceptions to these assumed processes of reasoning, and lay it down that this or that

---

[1] See Salmond, op. cit. 14, 15.
[2] Ibid 263.
[5] Ibid 264.

[2] Thayer, Evidence 266-269.
[4] Ibid 263-264.
[6] Ibid; cp. Salmond, op. cit. 3, 4.

fact, which on the general principles of reasoning has an evidential value, shall not be admissible in a court of law.[1] In the second place, a large number of matters are settled by means of these principles of reasoning without the need for specific rules of law. Thus, from the earliest period, the court has taken judicial notice of certain obvious facts, and acted on what is obvious to its intelligence.[2] It is only when the law of evidence begins to be elaborated, that the need for distinguishing between cases in which it can thus act, and cases in which it cannot, arises; and that, in consequence, a body of rules as to what facts the court can judicially notice, and what it cannot, springs up.[3] Similarly, from the earliest period it has been obvious that the existence of certain facts creates a presumption as to the existence of other facts.[4] But this, again, is a matter which depends upon the principles of reasoning, and not upon specific rules of a law of evidence. It is only at a later period in the history of the law, that the function of these presumptions, in relation to the burden of proof, is analysed and reduced to rule. But, in the third place, these presumptions have given rise to a large body of rules which, on account of the form in which they are expressed, have been supposed to be part of the law of evidence.[5] This is due, partly to a natural confusion between the principles of reasoning and the rules of evidence, and partly to the fact that these presumptions are often expressed in the form of a prima facie rule—"this evidential form of statement leads often to the opinion that the substance of the proposition is evidential; and then to the further notion that, inasmuch as it is evidential, it belongs to the law of evidence."[6] The fact is that many of these presumptions are part of the substantive law. But here, as in other cases, the substantive law has been evolved through the law of procedure; and, in these cases, through a part of the law of procedure which, being concerned with the manner of proof, naturally connects itself with the law of evidence.

The principles of reasoning thus are and always have been the ground work of the law of evidence; and, as the legal system grows more elaborate, some of the results of these principles become the subject matter of specific rules, which are sometimes more and sometimes less closely connected with that law. But these rules, though based upon the principles of reasoning, have been shaped and fashioned into various technical forms by the changing ideas as to the nature of a trial, as to the procedure on a trial, and as to the manner in which the parties must present their cases to the

---

[1] See Stephen, Digest, Introd. ix, x.
[2] Below 135.
[3] Below 135-139.
[4] Below 139-143.
[5] Below 143-144.
[6] Thayer, Evidence 315.

court. Primitive ideas on these matters have been the parents of long lived technical rules, which have only gradually changed their shape, as these primitive ideas have given place to changed conceptions and new rules more fitted to them. Thus the rules which flow obviously from the principles of reasoning have been overlaid by a mass of technical rules, which represent the ideas and needs of many different periods in the law of procedure. It is for this reason that the contents of the law of evidence present a variegated mass of rules which can be traced historically to all periods in the history of the law. A rapid glance at the historical sequence of these ideas and needs will show us how and why different sets of these rules grew up, and will therefore indicate the manner in which the history of the origins of the modern law must be treated.

We have seen that the oldest forms of trial were not trials in the modern sense of the word. They were not rational adjudications upon evidence. They were methods of proof; and the party who went through the form of proof—witnesses, battle, compurgation, or ordeal—won his case.[1] Clearly there was little room left for a law of evidence, because, except in the manner of awarding proof, or later, in cases which turned on written documents,[2] there was little opportunity for passing a rational judgment on the facts. But when the jury superseded these older methods of proof, when pleas began to be recorded, and writing became more general, we can see some indications of the beginning of a law of evidence. It is true that the jury was at first treated as one of the older methods of proof. The reasons for its verdict might be as inscrutable as the results of one of the older methods of proof.[3] But, in spite of this, the jury was a body of reasonable human beings; evidence in the shape of records and documents could be put before them; and, under the influence of Roman ideas, man's legal conceptions were rapidly becoming more mature. At first, however, the records and documents adduced by the parties were treated as being themselves a form of proof. The record of a court, and a document under seal, were treated as conclusive; and thus we get the rise of the doctrine of estoppel by record or deed, which, historically, is the oldest part of the law of evidence.[4] This easily led to the development of another form of estoppel—estoppel by matter in pais—which was created by the doing of some notorious act of which the "pays" could have cognisance.[5] Then it began to be seen that writings of various kinds, though they could not create an estoppel, might be used by the parties to prove or disprove the facts in issue.[6] But, during the mediæval

---

[1] Vol. i 302-311.
[2] Vol. ii 109-110, 112, 115-116.
[3] Vol. i 317.
[4] Below 147-159.
[5] Below 159-161.
[6] Below 164-167.

period, the law did not advance much beyond this point. No extensive use was made of the oral evidence of witnesses. There was no means of compelling a witness to come forward to testify;[1] and, if he came forward voluntarily, he might expose himself to an action for maintenance.[2] As a rule oral evidence was averred in the pleadings;[3] for, at that period, the pleadings and the evidence in support of the pleadings were not accurately distinguished. The rule that evidence could not be pleaded had not as yet arisen.

The reason for this relatively late appearance of oral evidence in the common law, was due to the firmness with which the common law adhered to the view that the jury were as much witnesses as judges of fact. They could and did decide the question at issue from their own knowledge, with the assistance of the documents put in as evidence, and the averments of counsel. But, in the course of the sixteenth century, it was becoming obvious that juries could not decide the questions at issue from their own knowledge.[4] Witnesses giving oral evidence were well enough known in the Chancery and the other courts which administered justice outside the sphere of the common law;[5] and they were becoming increasingly frequent in the common law courts. The fact that they were a necessary part of a trial was recognized by the statute of 1562-1563 which provided a process for compelling their attendance, which was borrowed from process of sub-pœna which the Chancery had always used.[6] Thus, side by side with the older documents which either created an estoppel or furnished evidence, there arose the oral evidence of witnesses summoned to testify. It became possible to separate the averments of the pleader from the evidence for those averments;[7] and so the law of evidence gradually became a very distinct branch of the law of procedure.

But the admission of oral evidence raised many problems for the judges. In the first place, it raised the question of the competency of witnesses; and, seeing that as a general rule the witnesses were compellable to testify, the question whether under any, and if so, under what circumstances, a witness might be excused from testifying.[8] In the second place, it raised the far more important question of the nature of the control which the judges should exercise over the evidence offered by these witnesses. That they should exercise some control was inevitable. They already decided as a matter of law whether any documents or facts

---

[1] Below 177-178, 179-180.   [2] Vol. i 335.   [3] Vol. iii 635, 638.
[4] Vol. i 335.   [5] Vol. v 181-182, 281, 332-333.
[6] 5 Elizabeth c. 9; vol. iii 649; vol. iv 518; below 185.
[7] Vol. iii 650, 651.   [8] Below 185-203.

put forward operated to produce an estoppel; and we shall see
that, by the end of the sixteenth century, their decisions on these
matters had already created a very complex body of law.[1]
Similarly, we shall see that they began also to insist that
documents given in evidence to the jury must be put in in open
court, and not given to the jury privately;[2] and this enabled the
judges to exercise some control over the relevancy of the evidence
thus offered.   Moreover, the court had always had an absolute
discretion as to what averments made by counsel it would
admit; and, in the days when evidence was thus brought to the
notice of the court, this meant that the court had an absolute discretion as to the admission and rejection of evidence.   It was only
natural, therefore, that the court should assume the same control
over the evidence given by witnesses.   This control laid the
foundation of the rules excluding certain kinds of testimony, which
are the most characteristic feature of the English law of evidence.[3]
In the third place, this admission of oral evidence raised the
question of the relation of documentary to oral evidence—the
question how far, if at all, oral testimony should be admitted to
vary, add to, or explain matters which the parties have reduced
to writing.[4]

It was the rules laid down to solve these problems which laid
the foundation of the most modern part of the law of evidence;
and, as the rules laid down were common law rules, they were,
as we have seen,[5] formed mainly with an eye to the needs of a
tribunal which worked with a jury.   But we shall see that, though
the court of Chancery for the most part accepted these rules, it
also contributed something to their enlargement and modification.
In the admission of the oral evidence of sworn witnesses, in the
process by which they could be compelled to testify, in the ra-
tionalizing and enlargement of the principle of estoppel, in the
admission of the evidence of the defendant to a suit—we can see
influences which have helped to shape the law as we know it
to-day.   Similarly we shall see that the other great influence
which helped to enlarge and liberalize the common law—the
influence of mercantile custom—has not been without its influence
on this part of the common law.   But these influences were, for

---

[1] Below 144-162.   [2] Below 167-173.

[3] "The greatest and most remarkable offshoot of the jury was that body of excluding rules which chiefly constitute the English 'Law of Evidence.'   If we imagine what
would have happened if the petit jury had kept up the older methods of procedure, as
the grand jury in criminal cases did, and does at the present day—if, instead of hearing
witnesses publicly, under the eye of the judge, it had heard them privately and without
any judicial supervision, it is easy to see that our law of evidence never would have
taken shape; we should still be summing it all up, as Henry Finch did at the beginning
of the seventeenth century, *L'evidence al jurie est quecunque chose que serve le partie
a prover l'issue pur luy*," Thayer, Evidence 180-181.

[4] Below 219-222.   [5] Above 127.

the most part, not fully felt till the eighteenth and nineteenth centuries. They cannot therefore be fully dealt with at this point. Here I must confine myself mainly to the history of the manner in which the common law courts were laying the foundation of the common law rules, partly on the basis of the mediæval rules as to estoppel and the documentary evidence of sealed documents; partly by the development, from the basis of these mediæval rules, of new rules as to documentary evidence in general; and partly by the construction of new rules which were necessitated by the rise of the oral evidence of witnesses summoned to testify.

This complex growth of rules I shall deal with under the following heads: The Basis of the Law in the Principles of Reasoning; Estoppel; Documentary Evidence; Witnesses—how far Competent and Compellable; Oral Evidence; The Relations between Documentary and Oral Evidence.

The Basis of the Law in the Principles of Reasoning

"The law," says Thayer,[1] "has no mandamus to the logical faculty." At all periods it must use and apply the ordinary processes of reasoning, recognize the obvious facts of life, and draw the obvious inferences from those facts which ordinary experience teaches. But when these ordinary processes of reasoning, and this recognition of obvious facts and inferences, come to be applied to the proof of matters at issue in a law suit, they must necessarily adapt themselves to the technical ideas which, at any given period, govern men's notions as to the conduct of law suits. We have seen that, in the primitive period when the decision of the facts at issue in a law suit was left to be decided by such methods of proof as compurgation battle or ordeal, there was little scope left for the operation of the ordinary processes of reasoning.[2] But we have seen that even in this period these processes made themselves felt in the manner in which the proof was awarded by the medial judgment;[3] and it was partly due to these processes of reasoning, that it was even then recognized that the existence of certain facts created an absolute or rebuttable presumption of guilt.[4] They had many more opportunities to assert their influence when the jury took the place of these older methods of proof. Proof ceased to be something which could be " made" by mechanical tests, and became a process by which a rational body of men could be convinced. It ceased to be the privilege of the defendant, and became a burden which lay on the

---

[1] Evidence 314 n.　　　　　　　[2] Vol. i 299.
[3] Vol. ii 109-110, 112, 115-116; P. and M. ii 600.
[4] Vol. ii 106; below 142 and n. 3.

plaintiff;[1] and this burden could only be discharged by convincing the reason of this body of men. It is true that this body of men might decide the matter by the help of their own knowledge, and irrespective of the matters urged by the parties who were litigating before them. But, as this possibility grew more and more remote, more and more scope was left for the operation upon the minds of the jury of facts adduced by the parties in court ; and therefore in the conduct of litigation more and more play was given to the operation of the ordinary processes of reasoning, and the recognition of obvious facts and inferences. Hence we get the rise of maxims which embody the truisms which elementary reason and elementary experience teaches—"ea quæ manifesta sunt non indigent probatione,"[2] and "de quolibet homine præsumitur quod sit bonus homo donec probatur in contrarium,"[3] are early instances; and before the days of Coke, who was a great inventor of these maxims, the common law had already acquired a considerable number.[4]

But, when this stage has been reached, the fact that the court must be credited with knowing certain matters of common knowledge, and with possessing the power to draw obvious inferences, comes more prominently into notice than in the earlier period of mechanical proofs. "In conducting a process of judicial reasoning," says Thayer,[5] "as of other reasoning, not a step can be taken without assuming something which has not been proved ; and the capacity to do this, with competent judgment and efficiency, is imputed to judges and juries as part of their necessary mental outfit." They must be presumed to bring to their task the common knowledge of the day, and they must take judicial notice of matters of common knowledge. They must draw the inferences and make the presumptions from facts which common experience teaches. Thus the knowledge of the court, and its power to draw inferences, come to be matters of some importance. The question when it can act on its own knowledge or when it must act only on evidence adduced, and the question when it may draw an inference which will create a presumption more or less cogent as to the truth of the facts at issue, gradually become the centre of bodies of technical rules. Thus such topics as the sphere of the operation of judicial notice, and presumptions, give rise to bodies of legal doctrine more or less closely connected with the law of evidence. These two topics are intimately allied, for, as Thayer has pointed out, presumptions "furnish the basis of many of those spontaneous recognitions of particular facts and conditions which make up the

---

[1] See Thayer, Evidence 354.   [2] Bracton, Note Book, Case 194.
[3] Bracton f. 193a.   [4] Thayer, Evidence 335.   [5] Ibid 279-280.

doctrine of judicial notice."[1] Both topics also illustrate the manner in which the law of evidence is based fundamentally on the ordinary processes of reasoning. Let us therefore look at the manner in which, in these two cases, the working of these ordinary processes of reasoning has been technically developed.

Judicial notice.[2]

The technical working out of the doctrine of judicial notice is concerned, firstly, with defining the matters which are so notorious that the court can notice and act upon them without further proof; secondly, with defining the matters which require proof, whatever private knowledge the court may possess; and thirdly, with distinguishing cases where the court acts upon what has been called "real evidence," i.e. upon evidence submitted directly to its senses, and not through the medium of a witness or a document.

(i) From the days of the Year Books the courts have noticed judicially facts of many different kinds which they have considered to be notorious. On one occasion in 1302 it took judicial notice that the name of a defendant was John de Willingtone, and not John de Wilton;[3] but this was perhaps an extreme instance of the application of the doctrine, unless, as the judges intimated, John de Willingtone was a very notorious person at that time.[4] Generally the matters thus noticed were ordinary facts of common knowledge. Thus in 1456 the court took judicial notice of the fact that the county of Hereford bordered on Wales.[5] It noticed the order of months weeks and days as stated in the calendar, and especially the dates of the ordinary feast and saints' days, by reference to which many legal acts were dated. As Coleridge, J., pointed out in *Lumley v. Gye*,[7] "we find in the Year Books the judges reasoning about the ability of knights, esquires, and gentlemen to maintain themselves without wages; and distinguishing between private chaplains and parochial chaplains from the nature of their employments." Similarly the court has, from an early period, taken judicial notice of the ordinary meaning of words, and even of well-known usages as to the meaning of those words in particular cases;[8] and

---

[1] Op. cit. 314. [2] See Thayer, Evidence chap. vii.
[3] Y.B. 30, 31 Ed. I. (R.S.) 256-259.
[4] "*Brompton.* He is known all over England as Willingtone, and by no other name, and that we well know; and therefore as to John, you shall take nothing by the writ."
[5] Y.B. 35 Hy. VI. Mich. pl. 35.
[6] Y.B. 9 Hy. VII. Hil. pl. 1; see Thayer, Evidence 292 n. 3, for a translation and comment on this case; cp. Harvey v. Broad (1705) 6 Mod. 159.
[7] (1853) 2 E. and B. at p. 267.
[8] Thayer, op. cit. 287-288, citing Y.B. 27 Hy. VIII. Mich. pl. 12; Hewet v. Painter (1611) 1 Bulstr. 174; and cases of 1613 and 1623 from Rolle, Ab. *Court* C. 6, 7.

this is naturally extended to a recognition of ordinary literary allusions known to all educated men. The mediæval lawyers generally knew their Vulgate well ; and in later days the courts have "taken judicial cognizance of the moral qualities of Robinson Crusoe's 'man Friday' and Æsop's frozen snake."[1]

These are cases of the application of the doctrine to facts actually known to all educated men. The doctrine tends to take upon itself a more artificial, and a more technical tinge, when it is applied to a knowledge of such facts as the contents of statutes, the practice of the courts, acts of state, and the status of foreign sovereigns, because the court may as a fact have no actual knowledge of these matters. We can see the beginnings of this extension in 1537[2] and 1553,[3] when it was said that the judges must take judicial notice of the contents of statutes. Later cases have both added the other matters of state which will thus be noticed, and enlarged the list of matters which the courts will deem to be matters of notoriety, until the learning on this topic has become an important body of legal doctrine.[4] As we shall now see, this doctrine has been continually growing more precise by the parallel growth of the law as to the matters which the courts will not judicially notice.

(ii) It was an old question among the civilians and canonists "utrum judex secundum allegata judicare debeat an juxta conscientiam."[5] In other words, could a judge have recourse to his private knowledge to decide cases judicially before him? It was well established from an early date in English law that the judge must decide, not upon his own private knowledge, but upon the matters proved before him. In 1332-1333 Herle refused to go outside the record and recognize that a defendant was dead, merely because his death was alleged to be a notorious fact ;[6] and Coke in 1588-1589 argued that facts judicially noticed must be strictly confined to the facts appearing on the record, and

---

[1] Lumley v. Gye (1853) 2 E. and B. at p. 267 *per* Coleridge, J., citing Forbes v. King, 1 Dowl. P.C. 672, and Hoare v. Silverlock (1848) 12 Q.B. 624; in the last cited case at p. 633 Coleridge, J., said, "we ought to attribute to the court and jury an acquaintance with ordinary terms and allusions, whether historical or figurative or parabolical."

[2] "And also the statute is in the care of the judges whereof they are bounden to take notice," Dyer at f. 28b.

[3] Partridge v. Strange Plowden at pp. 83-84 *per* Saunders *arg.* ; the case went off on a point of pleading, but the court assented to this doctrine, see ibid at p. 84 ; cp. Thayer, op. cit. 283-284.

[4] See Halsbury, Laws of England xiii 484-497.

[5] Thayer, op. cit. 291 n. 2.

[6] "*Trewe.* La ou notice vient que home est mort, home ne ira my a jugement counter luy; mes notorious chose est que le Dean est mort, per que vous ne devez pas aler a jugement counter luy. *Herle.* Nous ne poiomus pas aler a jugement sur notorie chose, eins solonque ce que le proces est devant nous memes," Y.B. 7 Ed. III. Hil. pl. 7.

that the legal inferences, drawn from those facts, must not be influenced by the court's private knowledge of facts outside the record.[1] This was in accordance with a famous dictum of Gascoigne, C.J., which was often cited in subsequent cases, to the effect that if a jury found a man guilty of murder whom the judge knew privately not to be guilty, the proper course was to respite judgment and ask the king for a pardon.[2] That this principle was well enough recognized and acted on by the judges, is shown by the tale told by Roger North about his brother's manner of conducting cases, when chief justice of the Common Pleas:[3] "I wondered once to find him, after an hour's sticking and picking upon an evidence, at last all at once give it up. I asked him, 'Why he left off so abruptly?' He told me that he discerned a roguery; but the evidence was not sufficient to justify him to direct the jury to find it; and thereupon he directed, as the strength of the evidence required to find, even contrary to his own private judgment. For, in points of fact whereof he was neither judge nor witness, he must have warrantable reasons for what he said, or insinuated to the jury, who only were the proper judges."

The decision of the question what facts could not be noticed by the judge and made a basis of his decision, obviously helped to bring into clearer relief the facts which could be thus noticed. But we have seen that, though the judge could not notice many matters within his own private knowledge, the jury had the right to use their private knowledge, as a basis of their decision. As late as *Bushell's Case* Vaughan, C.J., recognized their right to do so;[4] and it is not till the beginning of the nineteenth century that there is authority for the proposition that the fact that a verdict has been given on this knowledge, is a good reason for granting a new trial.[5] Possibly the remembrance of this power of the jury to give a verdict from their private knowledge, was one of the causes which has retarded the clear recognition of the difference between facts which could be made the basis of a decision without

---

[1] " Here in our case is a variance in substance betwixt the name given to the hospital . . . and the name usurped in the lease. And . . . if the name given to the hospital upon the foundation of it, and the name usurped in the lease be not unum in sensu (not in your private understanding as private persons, but in your judicial knowledge upon the record . . .) then this lease is void ; for although you as private persons, otherwise than by record, know that the hospital of Savoy, and the hospital vocat Le Savoy, are all one hospital, you ought not upon your private knowledge to give judgment, unless also your judicial knowledge agree with it ; that is the knowledge out of the records which you have before you," Marriot and Pascall's Case 1 Leo. at p. 161 ; and see Thayer's account of this case, Evidence 284-285.

[2] Y.B. 7 Hy. IV. Pasch. pl. 5 ; Partridge v. Strange (1553) Plowden at p. 83 ; Marriot and Pascall's Case (1588-1589) 1 Leo. at p. 161.

[3] Lives of the Norths i 145.   [4] Vol. i 336, 346.

[5] R. v. Sutton (1816) 4 M. and S. 532 at p. 541, cited vol. i 336 n. 5.

formal evidence as to their existence, and facts which could not; and so delayed the growth of a specific body of doctrine upon the topic of judicial notice till the beginning of the nineteenth century.[1] Another cause may possibly be found in the erroneous idea that it is the jury and not the court which can decide all the facts arising in the course of a litigation. We shall now see that the power of the court to decide certain facts upon "real evidence," without reference to the jury, taken in connection with the general rule that it is for the jury to find the facts in issue, has tended to confuse the cases where the court decides facts on such evidence, with the cases where it acts upon its judicial knowledge.

(iii) Thayer has pointed out that though the issues of fact were matters for the decisions of the jury, the questions of fact which fall to be decided in the course of a trial, are by no means limited to these issues. "The courts settled a great many questions of fact for themselves; they could not take a step without passing upon such questions. Was the deed that was put forward in pleading 'rased' or not?[2] If a party claimed the right to defend himself as a maimed person, was it really mayhem? Was a person who presented himself and claimed to be a minor really under age? A stream of questions as to the reality, the *rei veritas*, the fact, of what was alleged before the justices, was constantly pouring in. A prisoner for example had confessed; on being brought into court, he declared that it was by duress of his jailer. Was this so? To find this out the justice took the short cut of sending for several of the fellow prisoners and the jailer, and questioning them all in the prisoner's presence; and he found that it was not true.[3] This is just as it is to-day. Courts pass upon a vast number of questions of fact that do not get on the record or form any part of the issue."[4] In many of these cases, e.g. as to the appearance of a deed, or as to age, or as to the capacity of a person, they decided by the mere appearance of the document or the person—the "real evidence" so presented satisfied them.[5] In others they might call for other evidence—a case in which the court ordered a plaintiff to prove his age by twelve selected witnesses occurred as early as 1219;[6] and in later law it was said

---

[1] "It was not until Starkie printed his book on evidence in 1824 that any special mention of this subject occurs in legal treatises on evidence; and this writer has very little to say about it," Thayer, Evidence 279.

[2] See vol. ii 250.   [3] Y.B. 30, 31 Ed. I. (R.S.) 543.

[4] Thayer, Evidence 184-185.

[5] In Y.B. 21, 22 Ed. I. (R.S.) 146 Metingham, C.J., said, "Where a man comes into court by warrant to make an acknowledgement, the condition of the person is judged of by inspection; that is to say whether he be or be not in a state to make the acknowledgement."

[6] Bracton's Note Book, Case 46—"Et Iohannes dicit quod habet ætatam quia ipse est xxii annorum vel prope xxii annorum, et quod habeat ætatem ponit se super visum et consideracionem justiciariorum, et si justiciarii inde dubitent probabit ætatem

that this question might either be decided by the judge, or submitted to the jury.[1] Another tale of Roger North's shows how a piece of real evidence, noted by the judge, convinced both judge and jury.[2]

Presumptions.

In the course of a trial facts may be proved which will give rise to an inference of law or of fact sufficient, if nothing else is proved, to decide the issue. As cases are decided, and the law gets more elaborate, a large number of these presumptions will arise in connection with different branches of the law, which will sometimes be treated by the courts as proving conclusively, sometimes as giving rise to an inference as to, the facts in issue. In some cases it will be enacted by the Legislature that the proof of certain facts shall be a conclusive proof. In this way the law as to presumptions of different kinds comes to contain a confused and heterogeneous mass of rules, relating to many different legal topics. In so far as the courts or the Legislature treat these presumptions as conclusive, they cannot at the present day be regarded as parts of the law of evidence. They are rather rules of substantive law. And many other presumptions of fact, which arise in the course of the trial, are rather instances of the operation of the ordinary processes of reasoning than rules of the law of evidence.[3] But all these rules are connected with the conduct of litigation, and more especially with that part of the law of procedure which is concerned with evidence; for they all have the effect either of proving conclusively, or of furnishing prima facie proof, of the issue before the court; they all dispense the party in whose favour they exist with the task producing further evidence;[4] and, if they are conclusive, they decide the case in his favour. Therefore it is not surprising to find that, throughout the history of the law, all these presumptions have, owing to the manner in which they are used in practice, retained their connection with the law of evidence, and have been supposed to belong peculiarly to that branch of the law. We thus have, as I have already pointed out,[5] a striking example of the manner in which the substantive law has been developed by means of the law of

---

suam vel per matrem et parentes suos vel alio modo sicut curia consideraverit. Et quia justiciarii et preterea magnates dubitant de ætate sua consideratum est quod probet ætatem suam per xii legales homines et veniat cum probacione sua in crastinum animarum ; " this case is cited and explained by Thayer, Evidence 19.

[1] " En touts cases ou la matiere puit esse trie per l'examination ou discretion des justices ils purront, s'ils sont en doubt, ceo refuser, et compeller le party de ceo mettre en trial del pais," Y.B. 21 Hy. VII. Mich. pl. 58.

[2] Lives of the Norths i 147, cited vol. vi 389 n. 3.

[3] Thayer, Evidence 314-315. [4] Cp. ibid 337.

[5] Above 129.

procedure; and, in cases where the courts have established a conclusive presumption without any facts at all to justify it (e.g. the
presumption of a lost grant),[1] a striking example of the manner in
which the law has been developed by means of legal fictions.[2]

From time to time the ordinary processes of reasoning have
suggested various inferences, which have been treated by the
courts in different ways. Sometimes they are treated as more or
less probable inferences of fact; and it is possible, though by no
means certain, that in the remote past most presumptions originated
as mere presumptions of fact. Just as in the case of judicial notice,
the courts, as a matter of common sense, assumed the existence of
matters of common knowledge without further proof;[3] so they
easily drew an obvious inference from facts proved or admitted, and
thus created a presumption, as common sense dictated. And just
as the truisms which elementary experience teaches came to be
embodied in maxims which illustrate the origins of the doctrine
of judicial notice, so other maxims arose which illustrate the
origins, in that same elementary experience, of some of the
commonest of the presumptions known to the law.[4] But it was
inevitable that, as the law developed, some of these presumptions
should be so frequently drawn that they took upon themselves the
character of rules of law; and we shall see that, owing to the
exigencies of primitive methods of trial, the Legislature and the
courts were active in creating them.[5] Some of them were made
or became only prima facie rules—rules, that is, which were
rebuttable by further evidence. Others were made or became
irrebuttable, and therefore, in effect, rules of law. Others hovered
uncertainly on the border line of rebuttable and irrebuttable
presumptions. Let us look at one or two illustrations.

I have already said something of the manner in which, at the
close of the mediæval period, an irrebuttable presumption had
arisen that a child below the age of seven was not *doli capax*, and
so could not be convicted of a crime; and that a rebuttable
presumption to the same effect had arisen in the case of a child
under the age of fourteen.[6] I have already traced the history of
the way in which the presumption of a lost grant was developed,
in order to cure the defects of prescription at common law, until
it has probably become something very like an irrebuttable presumption.[7] On the other hand, the presumption of law or fact
that, if an angle of forty-five degrees of light were left by a
defendant's building, there was no interference with a plaintiff's

---

[1] Vol. vii 345-349.   [2] See Salmond, Essays in Jurisprudence, 9, 10.
[3] Above 135-136.
[4] Above 134; other illustrations are the two maxims cited by Thayer, op. cit.
335—omnia præsumuntur rite esse acta, and, probatis extremis præsumuntur media.
[5] Below 141-142.   [6] Vol. iii 372.   [7] Vol. vii 345-349.

light, though it was for a short time recognized, has been held to give rise to no sort of presumption;[1] and the conclusive presumption of guilt, which in early law was attached to the possession of stolen goods,[2] has in modern times ceased to exist, and become "a mere judicial recognition of a permissible inference."[3] From a very early date the fact that a child was heard to cry was taken as a conclusive presumption that it was alive, so much so that some thought that its life could be proved in no other way.[4] But historically, the most interesting of these presumptions is the presumption of the death of a person who has not been heard of for seven years. It shows both the very gradual way in which a presumption of law may spring up, and the complex causes which may give rise to it. The growth of this presumption has been so admirably described by Thayer[5] that it is only necessary to summarize briefly his account of this piece of history.

A statute of 1603 had exempted from the punishment of bigamy those marrying again, whose spouses had been seven years beyond the sea, or had not been heard of for seven years.[6] Another statute of 1667 enacted that, if an estate depended on the life of a person who remained beyond the seas, or elsewhere absented himself within the kingdom for seven years, in an action begun by a lessor or reversioner to recover the estate, such person was to be accounted dead, unless proved to be alive.[7] Thus, for this particular purpose, after absence for seven years without having been heard of a person was presumed to be dead. This statute was probably extensively construed[8]; but there is no suggestion of a general presumption of death from such absence till the case of *George v. Jesson* in 1805.[9] The existence of such a presumption was suggested in that case by Lord Ellenborough, C.J., on the analogy of these two statutes; and he gave effect to this presumption in 1809.[10] These statutes and cases were the foundation of the rule, first stated in 1815 by Phillips in his book on Evidence, that if the issue is the life or death of a person, the presumption of a continuance of his life "ceases at the end of seven years from the time when he was last known to be living."[11] This rule was accepted by succeeding writers on the law of evidence,

---

[1] Thayer, Evidence 324-326, citing Beadel v. Perry (1866) L.R. 3 Eq. 465; City of London Brewery Co. v. Tennant (1873) 9 Ch. App. 212; Ecclesiastical Commissioners v. Kino (1880) 14 C.D, 213.

[2] Vol. ii 258; vol. iii 319-320.

[3] Thayer, Evidence 328, citing Stephen, Digest of the Criminal Law Art. 308; cp. R. v. Schama and Abramovitch (1914) 11 Cr. App. Rep. at p. 49.

[4] Litt. § 35; Paine's Case (1587) 8 Co. Rep. at ff. 34b, 35a.

[5] Evidence 319-324.   [6] 1 James I. c. 11.

[7] 19 Charles II. c. 6.

[8] See Holman v. Exton (1693) Carth. 246, where Holt, C.J., held that a remainderman was within the equity of Charles II.'s statute.

[9] 6 East 80.   [10] Hopewell v. De Pinna 2 Camp. 113.

[11] Thayer, op. cit. 323, citing Phillips, Evidence (2nd ed.) i 152.

and was thus stated by Stephen in his Digest in 1876: "A person shown not to have been heard of for seven years by those (if any) who if he had been alive would naturally have heard of him, is presumed to be dead, unless the circumstances of the case are such as to account for his not being heard of without assuming his death."[1]

The history of this particular presumption shows that the Legislature has had some share in creating these presumptions. In fact it has been creating them from a very early period. There are, as Thayer has pointed out,[2] several illustrations of their creation by the Legislature in the Anglo-Saxon laws;[3] and they have been thus created all through our legal history. Thus a statute of 1604[4] provided that, if one person stabbed another, who had not then any weapon drawn, or who had not given the first blow, and the person stabbed died within six months, the stabber should be held to be guilty of murder, though malice aforethought could not be proved—that is, there was to be a conclusive presumption of malice aforethought; and in 1624[5] it was enacted that the concealment by a woman of the death of her bastard child should give rise to a presumption that she had murdered it, unless she could prove that it was born dead. The courts also acted on very similar principles. Thus we have seen that in construing the statute of 1584-1585,[6] directed against conveyances made with the intent to defraud purchasers, they laid it down that the fact that a voluntary conveyance had been made, created an irrebuttable presumption that it had been made with intent to defraud a subsequent purchaser of the same land.[7]

The fact that the Legislature and the courts took hold of the natural conception of a presumption, which is simply an inference from one fact to another which the ordinary processes of thought suggest, and, from an early date, used it artificially to develop the law, is due historically to the ideas of primitive peoples as to the proper methods for arriving at a decision upon the facts at issue in a case. We have seen that under the primitive systems of trial there was little or no opportunity for hearing evidence, and coming to a rational adjudication upon the facts.[8] Such a process would then have been inconceivable and impossible. These so-called trials were in reality mechanical methods of proof,

[1] Art. 99.   [2] Evidence 327-328.
[3] "If a far-coming man or a stranger journey through a wood out of the highway, and neither shout nor blow his horn, he is to be held for a thief, either to be slain or redeemed," Laws of Ine, Thorpe i 115-117; the laws of Cnut provide that if a man bring stolen property to his house, and it is put under lock and key by his wife, she is guilty, Thorpe i 419.
[4] 1 James I. c. 8.   [5] 21 James I. c. 27.   [6] 27 Elizabeth c. 4.
[7] Vol. iv 481-482.   [8] Vol. i 299-311.

not methods of trial—the party who successfully went through the form of proof selected won his case. Under these conditions, therefore, it would have been impossible to prove or disprove such a thing as a guilty intent; and therefore the Anglo-Saxon laws fix on some provable fact which is thought to lead to the inference of the fact sought to be proved—the commission of theft or some other crime—and enact that it shall be a conclusive proof of the commission of the crime. And this mode of legislating lasted long in the common law because, owing to the fact that the jury were put into the place of the older modes of proof, and expected to find a verdict from their own knowledge, the growth of a system of rules for the management of oral testimony was slow,[1] and the proof of intent therefore continued to present almost insoluble difficulties. It is for this reason that we get those enactments of James I.'s reign cited above, and the growth of a wholly artificial presumption for determining the question of the existence of an attempt to defraud a purchaser. And, even in our modern law, the inconvenience of existing rules of law or the difficulty of proof, sometimes leads the courts to evade their difficulties by this means. The growth of the presumption of a lost grant to meet the difficulties of prescription at common law, and the unsuccessful attempt to create the presumption that there was no interference with light if an angle of forty-five degrees was left, are obvious illustrations.

Thus the difficulty of proving the facts needed to establish legal liability under the older modes of trial, the slow growth of our modern mode of trial, the same difficulties even under our modern procedure, and sometimes the wish to modify an inconvenient law—have all at different periods led both legislators and courts to adopt the expedient of inventing a presumption of law which is sometimes rebuttable and sometimes irrebuttable. These rebuttable presumptions of law no doubt belong primarily to those particular branches of the substantive law with which they are concerned; but they are all connected with that part of the adjective law which is concerned with evidence; for they direct the court to deduce particular inferences from particular facts till the contrary is proved.[2] Irrebuttable presumptions of law, on the other hand, belong at the present day more properly to the substantive law than to the law of evidence. But they are rules of substantive law which borrow the terminology and adopt

---

[1] Vol. iii 638-639; below 178, 180-183.
[2] Stephen, Digest of the Law of Evidence, Art. 1; see, however, Thayer, op. cit. 316-317; but he admits that "a rule of presumption does not merely say that such and such a thing is a permissible and usual inference from other facts, but it goes on to say that this significance shall always, in the absence of other circumstances, be imputed to them," which does not much differ from Stephen's statement.

the disguise of that branch of the law of evidence which is concerned with presumptions ; and, historically, they originate in the period when the law, not having arrived at the conception of a trial by the examination of the evidence produced by the contending parties, aimed at obtaining a conclusive proof which could settle the controversy.   It might therefore be said that these irrebuttable presumptions have never been part of the law of evidence, in the sense which we give to the term "law of evidence" in modern systems of law.   This would be true ; but perhaps it would be better to say that, historically, they supplied the place of evidence, at a period when man's ideas as to legal procedure precluded the existence of a law of evidence in the modern sense of that term.   We shall now see that it is to these primitive ideas that we must look for the origin of the doctrine of Estoppel.

Estoppel

An estoppel in our modern law has been defined to be " an admission, or something which the law treats as equivalent to an admission, of an extremely high and conclusive nature—so high and so conclusive that the party whom it affects is not permitted to aver against it or offer evidence to controvert it."[1]   It is clear from this definition that there is much in common between an irrebuttable presumption of law and an estoppel.[2]   In both cases there is no need for further evidence ; for the party to a litigation who can show that such a presumption exists in his favour, or who can show that his opponent is estopped, will win his case.   Their effect is the same.   The difference between them seems to consist in the fact that, while an irrebuttable presumption is in effect a rule of substantive law, to the effect that when certain facts exist a particular inference shall be drawn, an estoppel is a rule of evidence that when, as between two parties to a litigation, certain facts are proved, no evidence to combat these facts can be received.[3]

But this view of the nature of an estoppel is essentially a modern view.   It was not the view which prevailed when the doctrine of estoppel first made its appearance in the law.   In the

---

[1] Smith, Leading Cases (10th ed.) ii 726.

[2] In the essay on Presumptions of Law and Presumptive Evidence, Law Magazine vi 348 (1831), printed as App. A to Thayer, Evidence (pp. 539-550), it is said at p. 540 that, "in some cases of conclusive legal presumption a party is said to be *estopped*, and to have created an estoppel against himself.   An estoppel is when a man has done some act which affords a conclusive presumption against himself in respect of the matter at issue " ; so too Stephen, Digest of the Law of Evidence, devotes chap. xiv to " Presumptions and Estoppels."

[3] " Estoppel is only a rule of evidence ; you cannot found an action upon estoppel. Estoppel is only important as being one step in the progress towards relief on the hypothesis that the defendant is estopped from denying the truth of something which he has said," Low v. Bouverie [1891] 3 Ch. at p. 105 *per* Bowen, L.J.; see however a dictum of Vaughan Williams, L.J., in Williams v. Pinckney (1898) 67 L.J. Ch. at p. 37, to the effect that in equity it is possible to found an action on an estoppel.

twelfth and thirteenth centuries cases were decided, not by a process of reasoning from evidence offered to the court, but by modes of proof selected by the parties or ordered by the court. In those days the matters relied upon to create an estoppel were regarded as operating as modes of proof, which settled the case in much the same way as battle compurgation or ordeal. Probably the earliest way of proving one's case by means of an estoppel, and therefore the earliest form of estoppel, is that which is known as estoppel by matter of record; and it is a direct result of that machinery for the enrolment of pleas which was instituted in the twelfth century.[1] In the thirteenth century statements made by a person under his seal were allowed an effect very similar to the statements contained in a record;[2] and at the close of the mediæval period, certain acts, such as the giving of livery of seisin, entry on property, or acceptance of an estate—acts of which the *pays* or jury might be expected to know something—were given the same effect as statements in a deed.[3] They created an estoppel "by matter in pais."

We have seen that during the Middle Ages the land law, and the real actions which protected various rights in the land, were the most important part of the common law.[4] It is therefore chiefly in connection with the land law and the real actions that these varieties of estoppel were developed. And partly owing to the complexity and technicality of these actions, and partly owing to the growing elaboration of the system of pleading, the law as to estoppels became very complex. Coke called this learning "excellent and curious."[5] As to its curiosity there can be no question; but later lawyers have expressed doubts as to its excellence, and have spoken rather of its "absurd refinements."[6] But, in spite of the curiosity which was becoming characteristic of it in the mediæval period, we can see that the modern ideas as to the nature of a trial, which were coming with the development of the jury system, were introducing the modern conception of the nature of an estoppel. Lawyers were ceasing to regard the facts which created the estoppel as a mode of proof, and were beginning to regard them as a conclusive presumption which was raised either by a statement in a record, or by the parties' own words or acts. It was becoming clear that estoppels of the latter sort—estoppels by deed and by matter in pais—depended ultimately on the words or acts of the parties; and, since a trial was coming to be regarded as an adjudication upon the facts in issue by the light of the evidence offered, they were regarded as operating, not as modes

---

[1] Vol. ii 180-181, 185-186.
[2] Below 154-156.
[3] Below 159-161.
[4] Vol. ii 590.
[5] Co. Litt. 352a.
[6] Smith, Leading Cases (10th ed.) ii 726.

of proof, but as conclusive presumptions which precluded the necessity of offering further evidence.

The growth of this modern view as to the nature of an estoppel comes out clearly enough in Coke's well-known description—" it is called an estoppel or conclusion because a man's own act or acceptance stoppeth or closeth up his mouth to alledge or plead the truth."[1]   In other words, it is an admission which creates so conclusive a presumption that no further evidence is admissible, even though that evidence could prove that the real truth was contrary to the presumption.   But, when this point had been reached, it was inevitable that the principle should be further developed. There are signs of this development in the common law during the mediæval period and later.[2]   But at common law the doctrine long continued to be involved in the technicalities which had gathered round it in the Middle Ages, and to be applied mainly in the sphere of the land law.   It was developed and broadened mainly by equity,[3] and by its application in the sphere of mercantile law.[4]   As the result of these new applications, the common lawyers began to see that the doctrine depended on the fact that the party estopped had so conducted himself that another, in reliance on that conduct, had acted in a manner in which, but for that conduct, he would not have acted.   But it was long before the principle in this generalized form found expression.   It was not till 1837 that Lord Denman, C.J., stated it in this way in the case of *Pickard v. Sears*,[5] and so rendered possible the development of the modern doctrine of estoppel by conduct.[6]   This doctrine, as Thayer points out,[7] "has broadened the law by a direct application of the maxims of justice"; and it has in many cases obviated the necessity for the creation of those irrebuttable presumptions, which the Legislature and the courts created at an earlier stage of legal development.

Thus the doctrine of estoppel has accommodated itself to the gradual changes of men's ideas as to the nature of a trial.   Originating in an age where the main interest of the trial centred round the modes of proof, it was at first regarded simply as a

---

[1] Co. Litt. 352a.   [2] Below 157-160.
[3] Below 161-162.   [4] Below 162.

[5] "Where one by his words or conduct wilfully causes another to believe the existence of a certain state of things, and induces him to act on that belief, so as to alter his own previous position, the former is concluded from averring against the latter a different state of things as existing at the same time," 6 Ad. and E. at p. 474.

[6] This case seems to be considered by Lindley, L.J., to be the starting-point of the modern development of this branch of the law, Low v. Bouverie [1891] 3 Ch. at p. 101.

[7] Speaking of the development by the judges of presumptions, he says, op. cit. 318, "in such cases the judges accomplish through the phraseology, and under the garb of evidence, the same results that they have long reached, and are now constantly reaching, by the directer means of estoppel.   The modern extensions of this doctrine broaden the law by a direct application of the maxims of justice."

mode of proof.   But, now that the main interest of the trial centres round the evidence produced to prove the issues, it is, in its most important modern form, simply a rule of evidence.[1]

This summary shows us that, in tracing the history of the doctrine, we must first deal with the older modes of estoppel by record, by deed, and by matter in pais; and, secondly, with the evolution, from the basis of estoppel by matter in pais, of the modern doctrine of estoppel by conduct.

(1) *The older modes of estoppel.*

The first of the older modes of estoppel is, as I have already said, estoppel by matter of record.   Estoppel by deed comes a little later, and then comes estoppel by matter in pais.   The mediæval development of these three forms of estoppel gave rise to certain general rules relating to them, which were summarized by Coke;[2] and a very large number of cases which illustrated their application, and laid down special rules for each variety.   All these rules have been elaborated by modern cases, but while the rules as to estoppel by deed and by matter in pais were, in their earlier days, mainly influenced by the principles which were established in relation to estoppel by matter of record; as we approach modern times, these two later forms of estoppel show increasing signs of the influence of the conception which gave rise to the modern doctrine of estoppel by conduct.   This will appear from a sketch of the history of these three forms of estoppel in their chronological order.

(i) *Estoppel by matter of Record.*

The general principle upon which estoppel by matter of record depends is that matters solemnly recorded by the king's court must be accepted as proof, so that no averment to contradict them can be received.   This conclusive quality of the matters recorded by the king's court, and its absence in the case of matters transacted in other courts, was beginning to emerge in the early years of the twelfth century.[3]   It is said in the *Leges Henrici Primi* that a record of the king's court cannot be denied, though the judgments of other courts can be denied by men who were present and understood the plea;[4] and the same distinction is drawn by Glanvil between the record of the king's court and the judgments of other courts.[5]   This distinction is the foundation

---

[1] Above 144 n. 3.   [2] Co. Litt. 35a and 35b.
[3] See Salmond, Essays in Jurisprudence 61-64; P. and M. ii 666, cited vol. v 157.
[4] " Recordacionem curie regis nulli negare licet; alias licebit per intelligibiles homines placiti," c. xxxi § 4.
[5] " Presentibus itaque Justiciariis in curia, et in recordo bene concordantibus, necesse est eorum recordo stare sine contradictione alterius partium ut predictum

both of the contrast between courts of record and courts not of record,[1] and of this branch of the doctrine of estoppel. All matters recorded by the king's court, and authenticated by his seal—not only judgments, but also other transactions enrolled thereon—were records, and were accorded the same conclusive effect.[2]   Hence in later law both recognizances and fines gave rise to this species of estoppel; and this effect has been in modern times extended to the judgments of courts which, in earlier days, were not accorded the status of courts of record,[3] and to courts, like the ecclesiastical courts,[4] which were not so directly the king's courts as the courts of common law.   In all these cases the sealed record amounts to proof as incontrovertible as any of the older modes of proof, and therefore the parties are estopped from disputing it.

This conclusive effect of the facts recorded by a court of record is abundantly illustrated in the reports, from the days of the earliest Year Books.   In 1293 it was said that a judgment of the king's court could not be proved by the country, but only by the rolls [5]—i.e. they were in themselves a proof which needed no other proof.   In 1307 it was said that "a thing which can be averred by the judgment and record of the court is not to be tried by an inquest" [6]—i.e. the production of the record was so conclusive that there was no need for a further trial.   In 1308-1309 a defendant to an assize of novel disseisin successfully pleaded a fine, and the record of a judgment in an assize of mort d'ancestor, between the same parties—"it was awarded by the Court that the plaintiff took nothing by his writ, for he showed no title of later date than the previous actions in which he had taken

---

est. . . . Sciendum tamen quod nulla curia recordum habet generaliter preter curiam domini Regis. In aliis enim curiis si quis aliquid dixerit unde cum poenituerit, poterit id negare contra totam curiam tertia manu cum sacramento id se non dixisse, affirmando vel cum pluribus vel cum paucioribus, secundum consuetudinem diversarum curiarum," Bk. viii c. 8.

[1] Vol. v 157-158.

[2] " Necesse est enim quod id quod aliquis in curia domini regis coram domino rege vel ejus justiciariis recognoverit, vel quod se facturum in manum ceperit, tenetur is qui id cognovit vel in manum capit," Glanvil Bk. viii c. 5; and see Y.B. 21, 22 Ed. I. (R.S.) 146 where it was said by Gosefeld arg., " An acknowledgement of debt or other contract made in court has so great force in itself that he who makes the acknowledgement cannot go against it, but it shall stand good "; Salmond, op. cit. 62-63, where both these authorities are cited.

[3] Vol. v 160 n. 3; see Smith, Leading Cases (10th ed.) ii 753, 761-765.

[4] Smith, op. cit. ii 753-761; note that even in Glanvil's day there was a tendency to extend the doctrine even to local courts exercising royal jurisdiction—" in quibusdam tamen casibus habent comitatus et aliæ curiæ minores recordum per assisam de consilio regni inde factam," Bk. viii c. 8.

[5] Y.B. 20, 21 Ed. I. 406; " if such a record be alleged, and it be pleaded that there is no such record, it shall be tried only by itself," Co. Litt. 260a; cp. Y.B. 6 Ed. II. (S.S.) 1312-1313, 20-26.

[6] Y.B. 33-35 Ed. I. (R.S.) 528 per Toudeby, arg.

nothing."[1] In 1425 it was admitted that a fine, which showed that land had been conveyed by the ancestor of the plaintiff to the ancestor of the defendant, could be pleaded as an estoppel to an action by the plaintiff against the defendant for a trespass upon the same land.[2] Coke in several places emphasizes the fact that a record cannot be contradicted either by the verdict of a jury, or, a fortiori, by an averment of the parties to an action.[3]

But in Coke's day the reason given for this incontrovertibility of matter of record, and for the estoppel which resulted from it, was different from that which was given in the twelfth and thirteenth centuries. In *Hynde's Case* in 1591 the conclusiveness of matter of record was said to be "for the avoiding of infiniteness which the law abhors";[4] and this, as we have seen, was the chief reason for the conclusive effect of the fine, which, during the Middle Ages and later, was one of the most important of matters of record.[5] This would seem to show that, with the change in men's ideas as to the nature of a trial, it was coming to be thought that this species of estoppel was based, not so much upon the idea that the production of the record is a mode of proof, but rather upon the idea, which was present to the mind of the Roman lawyers,[6] that there ought to be a decent finality about the decisions of courts. The result to the parties was the same whichever reason was adopted; but, in fact, some parts of the doctrine of estoppel by record fitted in better with the old than the new reason.[7] The new reason, however, supplied the doctrine with a more rational basis, and was obviously more suited to modern ideas about matters procedural. In fact, the evolution of the rules governing this species of estoppel during the Middle Ages, shows that this more rational basis was emerging concurrently with the emergence of

---

[1] Y.B. 1, 2 Ed. II. (S.S.) 139-141; cp. Y.B. 6 Ed. II. (S.S.) 1312-1313, 52-53.

[2] "*Babington.* Il pled un Fin par lequel vostre ancestor luy devestit de meme le terre, lequel est de si haut record come un record est. Purque etc. *Strange* passa oustre, et dit que al temps del Fin levie et devant le pleintif fuit seisi de le terre dont le lieu etc., sans ceo que meme ceux qui furent parties al Fin rien avoient," Y.B. 3 Hy. VI. Hil. pl. 9.

[3] Goddard's Case (1584) 2 Co. Rep. at f. 4b; Co. Litt. 260a.

[4] 4 Co. Rep. at f. 71a; cp. Co. Litt. 260a—"and the reason hereof is apparent; for otherwise (as our old authors say and that truly) there should never be any end of controversies, which should be inconvenient."

[5] Vol. iii 240-244.

[6] "Singulis controversiis singulas actiones unumque judicati finem sufficere probabili ratione placuit, ne aliter modus litium multiplicatus summam atque inexplicabilem faciat difficultatem, maxime si diversa pronuntiarentur. Parere ergo exceptionem rei judicatæ frequens est," Dig. 44. 2. 6.

[7] E.g. the rule that such acts in the law as letters patent, recognizances, imparlances, warrants of attorney, and admittances, created an estoppel by record, Co. Litt. 352a; fines and recoveries also were valuable rather in helping to avoid litigation, and in settling titles, than in creating a finality in the decisions of the courts, vol. iii 240-244; vol. vii 383.

these modern ideas about matters procedural. Just as the jury, though it was at first regarded as a mode of proof,[1] could not be treated merely as a mechanical test, because it was in fact a body of rational men ;[2] so the conditions under which matter of record was allowed to operate as an estoppel, were settled by rational considerations which were based on the contents of the record, and the need to harmonize the rules governing this species of estoppel with other rules of law. We shall now see that the rules thus evolved, as restated and developed during the sixteenth and seventeenth centuries, are the basis of our modern law.

Just as the doctrine of estoppel by record is the result of the manner in which the proceedings of the king's courts were recorded, so the judicial activity of these courts gave rise to a number of detailed rules as to the manner of its application. At the end of the mediæval period the law had acquired a number of these rules (a) as to the statements which would give rise to an estoppel, (b) as to the parties bound by the estoppel, and (c) as to the qualities which a statement must possess to create an estoppel.

(a) It was settled law in 1434 that a statement made by a court, which had no jurisdiction, would create no estoppel, since the proceedings were merely void.[3] It was also settled that statements in pleadings, on which no judgment had been given, would not estop[4]; nor would a mere verdict on which no judgment had been given.[5]

(b) It was, from a very early period, the accepted rule that only the parties to an action were estopped by a judgment in that action.[6] This really follows from the primitive conception of the mode in which this species of estoppel operated. The record of an action between two parties operates as conclusive proof of the matters decided therein ; but it cannot affect the rights of other persons who were not parties to the action. As against them it is no proof, and therefore no estoppel arises. But it soon became clear that a judgment in a real action, which decided a right to

---

[1] Vol. i 317, 320.   [2] Vol. iii 613, 633.

[3] Y.B. 10 Hy. VI. Mich. pl. 43, where it was said, "si les justices de Banc le Roy veulent recevoir un Fin devant eux, nient contristant les parties al Fin ne seront pas estoppes en apres"; Rolle, Ab. *Estoppell* D.

[4] Brooke, Ab. *Estoppell* pl. 62 = Y.B. 11 Hy. IV. Mich. pl. 56; but, in case of a nonsuit before judgment, there were differences between matters alleged by way of supposal in a count and in other pleadings, Co. Litt. 352b; cp. Y.BB. 3 Hy. VI. Mich. pl. 21 ; 21 Hy. VII. Trin. pl. 16; Rolle, Ab. *Estoppell* i 867.

[5] Brooke, Ab. *Estoppell* pl. 189 = 21 Ass. pl. 9.

[6] "He alleges a judgment to which we were not a party; so it behoves that we should be allowed our averment," Y.B. 1, 2 Ed. II. (S.S.) 113 *per* Passeley *arg.*; consistently with this, it was argued in 27 Ass. pl. 57 that a confession of guilt at the king's suit, was no estoppel in an action; but this was over-ruled—though the reporter dissented; and the same law was laid down in Y.B. 11 Hy. IV. Pasch. pl. 21; but the contrary and more correct view prevailed in Y.BB. 9 Hy. VI. Hil. pl. 8; 33 Hy. VI. Hil. pl. 22.

possession, must have a more extensive effect. It must bind not only the parties to the action, but the land which was the subject of it; and so it was admitted that not only parties but privies would be bound. It was held, therefore, that in an action in which the right to possession had come into question and had been decided, both privies and parties were bound;[1] and that privies included, not only privies in blood, but privies in estate, such as feoffees or lessees, and privies in law, such as lords taking by escheat, and tenants in dower and by the curtesy.[2] An estoppel, therefore, could be said to run with the land;[3] and the better opinion was that this rule applied whether the action in which the matter had been decided was real or personal, provided that same right to possession based on the same title was in issue.[4] But it soon became obvious that some judgments must have an even more extensive effect. From the earliest period it was clear that excommunication, outlawry, villeinage, or attaint, estopped the persons so affected from denying their status as against all the world;[5] and in 1410 it was admitted that the certificate of the bishop that a person was bastard was conclusive as to his status, and that a certificate that he was legitimate was only not conclusive because a person might, if born before the marriage of his parents, be legitimate by ecclesiastical law and bastard by the common law.[6] Similarly, opinion was inclining to the view that if a person had proved that he was not a villein in a law suit, his status could not be again called in question,[7] though in Edward IV.'s reign there was some doubt whether such a proof in an action in which he was claimed as villein regardant, could be pleaded as an estoppel to an action in which he was claimed as villein in gross.[8] There was thus authority for

---

[1] Y.B. 33 Hy. VI. Hil. pl. 22, Pasch. pl. 13.

[2] Co. Litt. 352a.　　　　　　　　　[3] Ibid; Brooke, Ab. *Estoppell* pl. 15.

[4] "Auxy haut est l'issue en bref de trespass, s'il soit pris en le realty, come en Assise, et si celuy or plaintif en le bref de Trespass eust traverse le descent come il fist, et ust este trove ove le plaintif, et le plaintif ust port auter bref de Trespass, seroit il receu a voider le descent par tiel descent come il ad fait a or? Jeo di que non: nient plus sera il receu en cel Assise quand le pleint est fait de memes les tenements," Y.B. 7 Hy. VI. Mich. pl. 14 (p. 4) *per* Martin and Cottesmore, JJ.; Anon. (1587) 3 Leo. 194; the history of this matter and all the authorities will be found in the elaborate judgment of Lord Ellenborough, C.J., in Outram v. Morewood (1803) 3 East at pp. 352-366.

[5] Y.B. 33 Hy. VI. Pasch. pl. 13—"Sont divers estoppels; ascuns al person, et auters al terre quecunque soit tenant, al person come d'alleger villeinage etc., chescun estranger aura avantage encounter son person etc.," *per* Littleton *arg.*; "Les cases de Attaint et bastardie le matiere est determina come ad este dit qu'il estoppera chescun estranger, et un utlargarie est le ple personel va al person," ibid per Moile, J.

[6] Y.BB. 11 Hy. IV. Trin. pl. 32; 33 Hy. VI. Hil. pl. 22; Co. Lttt. 352b; for this rule see vol. i 622.

[7] Y.BB. 9 Hy. VI. Hil. pl. 12 *per* Paston; 13 Ed. IV. Mich. pl. 4 (p. 3) *per* Choke, J.; vol. iii. 498.

[8] Y.B. 13 Ed. IV. Mich. pl. 4 and 11; vol. iii 509.

the proposition that judgments declaratory of status had a more
extensive effect than other judgments, in that they were binding
as against all the world and not only inter partes.   This effect of
judgments declaratory of status was clearly stated by Coke,[1] and
forms the basis of the modern distinction between judgments in
rem and in personam.[2]   The growth of maritime law has added
to these older judgments in rem as to the status of a person, the
judgment in rem as to the status of a ship.[3]

(c) The rules as to the qualities which a statement must possess
in order to create an estoppel seem to me to be partly due to the
influence of procedural rules, partly to the influence of the rules
of the substantive law, and partly to considerations of obvious
common sense.   The influence of procedural rules can, I think,
be seen in the rules that words creating an estoppel must be
material to the point decided, and that the estoppel must be
reciprocal.   The first rule was well established in the fifteenth
century;[4] and Coke's statement that "a matter alleged that is
neither traversable nor material shall not estoppe,"[5] is supported
by abundant authority.   Probably it is due to the influence of the
rules of pleading.   Any statement in a pleading which was not
material to the issue was a departure,[6] so that it was only reasonable to hold that a statement in a record, which was immaterial
to the issue before the court, could not create an estoppel.   The
second rule that "every estoppel ought to be reciprocal, that is,
to bind both parties,"[7] was equally well established.[8]   It is, as
Coke points out, a direct result of the rule that the judgment in
an action bound only the parties and privies;[9] and this, as we
have seen, is probably due to the fact that the record of an action,
which created the estoppel, was regarded as a conclusive proof of
the matter in dispute, which must therefore bind both the parties
to it.[10]   The influence of the rules of substantive law can be seen
in the rules that a record will create no estoppel, if to allow an
estoppel would facilitate the perpetration of an illegal act;[11] or
if the person sought to be estopped was under some personal

---

[1] " When the record of the estoppel doth run to the disability or legitimation of
the person, there (those that) are strangers shall take benefit of that record, as outlawry, excommengment, profession, attainder of præmunire, of felony, etc., bastardy
mulierty, and shall conclude the party, though they be strangers to the record," Co.
Litt. 352b.

[2] Smith, Leading Cases (10th ed.) ii 734-737, 753-762.   [3] Ibid ii 762.

[4] Y.BB. 33 Hy. VI. Pasch. pl. 13 per Danby, J.; 37 Hy. VI. Pasch. pl. 10;
10 Ed. IV. Trin. pl. 7; though what was mere matter of supposal, and what was not,
might be difficult to decide, see Y.B. 21 Hy. VII. Trin. pl. 16.

[5] Co. Litt. 352b,   [6] Vol. iii 634; below 274-275.   [7] Co. Litt. 352a.

[8] " Jeo entend que nul sera recu de pleder estoppel envers l'auter, mes cesty que
plede puit estre estoppe per mesme le plaintiff," Y.B. 33 Hy. VI. Mich. pl. 35 per
Prisot, C.J.

[9] Co. Litt. 352a.   [10] Above 147-148, 150.

[11] Y.B. 42 Ed. III. Pasch. pl. 27.

disability—e.g. coverture—which made it legally impossible for such person to do the act, which it was sought to prove that he or she had done, by means of the doctrine of estoppel.[1] Considerations of obvious common sense are the basis of the rule, stated in a curious case of 1443, that if contradictory statements were produced, both of which would, if they had stood alone, have worked an estoppel, the matter was at large[2]—or, as Coke put it, "estoppel against estoppel doth put the matter at large."[3] This principle, though expressed in technical language, is a common-sense principle which is applied to presumptions generally,[4] and is recognized by the civilians.[5] Similar considerations are at the root of the rule, probably stated clearly for the first time by Coke, that, if the truth appear on the record, the party who would otherwise be estopped by the record can take advantage of it.[6]

The basis of these rules is sound and sensible; but in the Middle Ages they were obscured by the technicalities of two of the most technical branches of the mediæval common law. As these estoppels often ran with the land, they were often involved in some of the more esoteric parts of that law—e.g. the doctrines of remitter,[7] warranty,[8] and the rules as to relation between the various grades of real actions—the assizes, the writs of entry, and the writs of right;[9] and, as used by litigants, they were also involved in the technicalities of pleading—more especially as it was recognized in the fifteenth century that a plea by way of estoppel must be certain to every intent.[10] When the real actions

---

[1] In Y.B. 15 Ed. IV. Trin. pl. 6 it was said by Littleton, *arg.*, and Brian, C.J., that a married woman was not estopped by a fine unless she was separately examined; but note that in Y.B. 9 Ed. IV. Trin. pl. 44 Littleton had asserted that, though a married woman could not be estopped by deed, she might be estopped by such matter of record as a fine or a recovery; the two cases really represent two different views as to the reason why a fine or a recovery bound a married woman, vol. iii 245 n. 7.

[2] The rector of Edington, on being asked to pay a 15th granted by Parliament, pleaded a grant of Henry IV. to the rector and his successors freeing them from such taxes—Markham said in the course of his argument, " Le Roy sera estoppe per le grant fait a luy a demander cel parcel del xv, auxy bien come il sera estoppe vers le Roy per son grant en dernier Parlement a demander etre discharge, et donc j'entend ou chaque est estoppe vers auter, nul aura availe de tiel estoppel," Y.B. 19 Hy. VI. Pasch. pl. 1.

[3] Co. Litt. 352b.

[4] " The bringing forward of unusual facts often discharges the whole matter from the operation of presumptions, and, like Coke's estoppel against estoppel, ' doth put the matter at large,' " Thayer, Evidence 351.

[5] Ibid n. 1 citing a dictum of Alciatus that " alia præsumptio aliam tollit."

[6] Co. Litt. 352b.

[7] See Brooke, Ab. *Estoppell* pl. 41=46 Ed. III. Hil. pl. 14; for this doctrine see vol. ii 587.

[8] Syms's Case (1609) 8 Co. Rep. at f. 53b.

[9] See vol. iii 5-14, 91; and for the difficulties so caused see Outram v. Morewood (1803) 3 East at pp. 355-359 *per* Lord Ellenborough, C.J.

[10] " Plee que sera pris per voy d'estoppel doit estre certain a chescun entent," Y.B. 21 Ed. IV. Hil. pl. 36 (p. 83) *per* Brigges, *arg.*; Co. Litt. 352b,

became things of the past, the doctrine was relieved of much
technical rubbish which had accumulated round it; and when,
in the course of the nineteenth century, many of the technicalities
of special pleading were abolished, the justice and good sense of
the principle became more obvious. It became in effect a doctrine
which gave effect to the maxim *nemo debet bis vexari pro eadem
causa*.[1] We shall now see that the doctrine of estoppel by deed,
though it started from the same principle as that which originally
underlay the doctrine of estoppel by record, was likewise tending,
as early as the sixteenth century, to acquire a new basis, very
different from the new basis on which estoppel by matter of record
was coming to rest—a basis which foreshadows the modern development of estoppel by conduct.

(ii) *Estoppel by deed.*

A statement made by the parties to a sealed writing was
conclusive proof of the facts contained therein. If, therefore, one
of the parties to a litigation could produce a sealed writing which
showed that the other was bound, he produced a proof as conclusive as a record.[2] The other party was estopped by his deed.
That estoppel by deed grew naturally out of estoppel by matter
of record is very clearly explained by Professor Wigmore.[3] He
says: "the legal value of the seal was the result of a practice
working from above downwards, from the king to the people at
large. It is involved, in the beginning, with the Germanic principle
that the king's word is indisputable. . . . The king's seal to a
document makes the truth of the document incontestable. This
leads . . . to the modern doctrine of the verity of judicial
records. . . . For private men's documents, its significance is
that the indisputability of a document sealed by the king marked
it with an extraordinary quality, much to be sought after. As the
habitual use of the seal extends downwards its valuable attributes
go with it . . . this extension of the seal (from the king to private
persons) begins in the eleventh and is completed by the thirteenth

---

[1] Thus Smith, Leading Cases (10th ed.) ii 752, after discussing the question
whether estoppel must be pleaded, says, "If the law of estoppel be founded on
justice and good sense—if it be true that *nemo debet bis vexari pro eadem causa*—it
would be strange to say that the accidental form of an issue should deprive a party of
the benefit of it, and force him to litigate the same question twice over"; but, strange
as it might appear to a modern lawyer, this seems to have been the law, see Trevivan
v. Laurance (1705) 1 Salk. at pp. 276-277.

[2] "Anything contained in the writing cannot by any exception of the parties be
removed," Y.B. 21, 22 Ed. I. (R.S.) 436; cp. Y.BB. 1, 2 Ed. II. (S.S.) 68-69;
3 Ed. II. (S.S.) 171 *per* Herle *arg.;* Salmond, Essays in Jurisprudence 51-52. The
old custom of summoning the attesting witnesses with the jury, Thayer, Evidence 97-99,
and vol. i 334, illustrates the transition between the older idea that the deed properly
attested is a form of proof, and the newer idea that the proof is to be made by the
verdict of the jury, see Thayer, op. cit. 504-505; below 167-168.

[3] Evidence iv 3414, § 2426.

century." We shall see that the effects of the rule that the party is estopped by his deed, had no small influence upon the growth of the law as to documentary evidence in general.[1] And its effects were felt in other branches of the law besides the law of evidence. We have seen that the fact that this effect was ascribed to a deed had important effects both upon the law of property and the law of contract. In the law of property it helped to establish the rule that certain incorporeal things could be created or conveyed by deed.[2] In the law of contract it accounts for the early appearance of the specialty contract, and, consequently, for the idea that an agreement could give rise to a legal liability.[3]

The fact that a deed was regarded as proof, and for that reason produced an estoppel, was, as Stephen has pointed out,[4] the origin of the common law rules as to necessity of making profert of a deed. The pleader, who was relying on a deed as an estoppel, was suggesting a mode of proof. He must therefore proffer this proof, just as he must proffer any other mode of proof —a record, compurgation, battle, or a jury—which he thought proper to select. If the deed thus proffered bore out, when produced, the pleader's view of its effect, it proved his case, because it estopped the other party as effectually as a record. Profert of a deed continued in many cases to be necessary till the Common Law Procedure Act of 1852;[5] and the question when it was and when it was not necessary, gave rise to a mass of technical pleading rules.[6] But long before that date its original rationale had been forgotten. In the sixteenth century the rule was supposed to be based on the necessity of allowing the court to see the deed, that it might judge of its sufficiency;[7] and we shall see that, thus explained, it has influenced the development of the law as to the manner of bringing documentary evidence before the court.[8]

Since a deed produced an estoppel because, like a record, it amounted to proof, it was only natural that the lawyers should apply similar rules to both kinds of estoppel. Thus, just as there could be no estoppel by record unless the court from which the record emanated had jurisdiction,[9] so the deed must be valid and

[1] Below 163, 177.   [2] Vol. iii 98-99.   [3] Ibid 417-420.
[4] "By an ancient rule all affirmative pleadings were formerly required to be supported by an offer of some mode of proof. As the pleader therefore of that time concluded in some cases by offering to prove by jury, or by the record, so in others he maintained his pleading by producing a *deed* as proof of the case alleged. In so doing he only complied with the rule that required an offer of proof," Pleading (5th ed.) 485-485; and see the references cited, ibid note 86.
[5] 15, 16 Victoria c. 76 § 55.
[6] See Stephen, Pleading (5th ed.) 483-485; cp. Day, Common Law Procedure Acts (2nd ed.) 52-53; vol. vii 346-348; below 170-172.
[7] Doctor Leyfield's Case (1611) 10 Co. Rep. at f. 92b, cited below 170-171.
[8] Below 172-173.   [9] Above 150.

operative in order to work an estoppel.   As Vavisor said in 1490,
"if a deed be made bearing date the first day of May, and it was
delivered twenty days after, and the obligee made a release the
second day of May and delivered it the same day, the release is no
bar to an action on the deed."[1]   The reason is that, as the deed
takes effect by delivery, and not from its date,[2] it was not in
existence as a valid deed when the supposed release was made.
On the same principle no one was estopped from showing that
the deed produced was not his deed,[3] or that for any reason—e g.
by reason of infancy—it was invalid.[4]   Similarly, the statement
in the deed relied on must be material;[5] and the certainty
required in pleading an estoppel by record[6] had its counterpart in
the rule, recognized in the sixteenth century, that the statement
in the deed must be precise and particular.[7]   Just as estoppel by
record might bind the land and run with it,[8] so might estoppel by
deed;[9] just as estoppel by record bound as a rule only parties
and privies,[10] so did estoppel by deed;[11] and just as estoppel by
record must be reciprocal, that is, must bind both the parties,[12]
so must an estoppel by deed.   Hence it followed that neither
a recital in a deed, which was the statement of one of the
parties only,[13] nor a statement in a deed poll,[14] created an
estoppel.

Thus, to a large extent, the rules relating to estoppel by deed
were developed upon lines similar to those upon which the rules
relating to estoppel by record were being simultaneously developed.
But the differences between a deed and a record necessarily gave

[1] Y.B. 5 Hy. VII. Pasch. pl. 8 (p. 27).

[2] " Si Vavisor soit oblige a moy le premier jour de May, et jeo delivrai a luy
acquit portant date devant l'obligation, et ceo delivrai apres, si jeo port action de Det
vers luy, il pledera cel releas portant date devant, et coment il fuit premierement
delivre apres, et ne prendra nul travers ; et uncore prima facie il sera entender que
fuit deliver accordant al purport del fait : mes quand tout le mater est monstre, or
l'entendement est destruy," ibid per Townsend and Brian.

[3] Y.B. 37 Hy. VI. Mich. pl. 8 per Prisot, C.J.

[4] Y.B. 35 Hy. VI. Mich. pl. 26 (p. 18) per Laicon ; cp. Bracton f. 396b.

[5] Anon. (1570) Dyer 289b.   [6] Above 153.

[7] Co. Litt. 352b ; Rolle, Ab. Estoppell P. i 872-873.   [8] Above 151.

[9] " Where an estoppel works on the interest of the lands, it runs with the land
into whose hands soever the land comes, and an ejectment is maintainable upon the
mere estoppel," Trevivan v. Laurance (1705) 1 Salk. at p. 276.

[10] Above 150-151.

[11] " If H. of Westcote holds of you, and I make him a confirmation, can I
estrange you from the seignory by my deed ? Not so," Y.B. 3 Ed. II. (S.S.) 173 per
Friskeney arg.

[12] Above 148, 150.

[13] Y.B. 9 Hy. VI. Pasch. pl. 22 (p. 9) per curiam ; Co. Litt. 352b ; Rolle, Ab.
Estoppell M. i 870 ; Shep. Touch. 53 ; below 158-159.

[14] Brooke, Ab. Estoppell pl. 8—" Nota in Littleton tenures tit. tenant pur terme
dans, que home qui lease per fait poll pur ans ou per paroll, poet void ceo lease adire
que il navoit rien en le terre tempore dimissionis, contrarie sur lease per indenture car
cest estoppel, quod nota," citing a case of Pasch. 38 Hy. VIII. ; Shep. Touch. 53 ;
below 158-159.

rise to some differences in the mode in which the doctrine of estoppel was applied. Thus it was said in 1584 that, though the parties might be estopped by a deed, the jury were not estopped ; and that, in this respect, an estoppel by deed differed from an estoppel by record, which bound both the parties and the jury.[1] It would seem also that it was in connection with estoppel by deed that the rule that an interest, when it accrues, "feeds the estoppel," was developed as a distinct rule, consequential upon the rule that an estoppel could run with the land and bind it in the hands of a successor in title.[2] But, what was more important than these minor differences, was the fact that a different theory was emerging as to the reasons why the statements in a deed created an estoppel.

Just as the old idea that estoppel by record operated like one of the older modes of proof, was inapplicable to, and unintelligible in, a changed order of procedural ideas ;[3] so, for the same reason, this old idea ceased to afford satisfactory explanation of the operation of estoppel by deed. We have seen that a new explanation of the doctrine of estoppel by record was ultimately found in the principle that there ought to be a decent finality to litigation.[4] Obviously this explanation could not be applied to estoppel by deed. It was gradually coming to be seen that this form of estoppel was based on the act of the party in authenticating by his seal a document which placed him under some liability to another. That this idea was beginning to emerge at an early date, we can see from the rules laid down, in the twelfth and thirteenth centuries, as to the liability of the owner of a seal upon deeds sealed with his seal by other persons, to whom he had entrusted it, or who had got possession of it.[5] No doubt these older rules were based partly on those very primitive conceptions of liability for dangerous acts, which appear in the Anglo-Saxon laws.[6] But in the days of Glanvil and Bracton they were being rationalized, and made to depend on the negligent conduct of the owner of the seal in losing it, or entrusting it to a careless person.

---

[1] Goddard's Case (1584) 2 Co. Rep. at f. 4b ; this case later gave rise to a good deal of discussion as to whether an estoppel, to be conclusive, must be pleaded, see Smith, Leading Cases (10th ed.) 748-752 ; above 154 n. 1.

[2] Rawlyn's Case (1588) 4 Co. Rep. 52a ; and see Doe d. Christmas v. Oliver (1829) 10 B. and C. at pp. 187-190, where this and other cases are commented on by Bayley, J.

[3] Above 149-150. [4] Ibid.

[5] "Ubi sigillum suum esse publice recognoverit in curia, cartam illam præcise tenetur warrantizare, et conventionem in ipsa carta expressam sicut in ea continetur omnino servare sine contradictione. Et suæ malæ custodiæ imputet si damnum incurret per sigillum suum male custoditum," Glanvil x 12 ; Bracton f. 396b ; and see Mayor of Merchants of the Staple v. Bank of England (1887) 21 Q.B.D. at pp. 166-167 per Wills, J., for an account of these and other older authorities on this question.

[6] Vol. ii 52.

This was as yet too refined a conception for a common law, which had not attained to the conception of negligence.[1] But it did help to introduce the idea that estoppel by deed was based upon act of the party who had put his seal to a document. In fact, the manner in which a deed is pleaded as an estoppel in the thirteenth and early fourteenth centuries, is quite as consistent with this view as to the nature of its operation, as with the older view that it operated as a mode of proof.[2]

There are some indications that this conception was beginning to come to the front in the fifteenth century. Take, for instance, the following passage from the Year Book of 35 Henry VI.:[3] "*Ashton*. If a man has an obligation from me, which was never my deed, and I make an indenture in defeasance of it, will this indenture in defeasance of the obligation be good, and so my original deed good, though it was not good before? I think not. *Prisot, C.J.* No Sir, it will not make it good, but it will estop you." Clearly we have reached the idea that the operation of an estoppel is based upon the principle that "a man's own act or acceptance stoppeth or closeth up his mouth to allege or plead the truth."[4] But if this was the basis of estoppel by deed, it is obvious that it rested upon a basis very different from that upon which estoppel by record rested. It followed that some of the rules regulating it, which had been evolved before this difference was perceived, were no longer applicable. Thus it was difficult to see why such an estoppel should necessarily be reciprocal, and why a recital in a deed, or a deed poll, should not create an estoppel. As early as 1481 Brian, C.J., said that a man might be estopped by a recital in an indenture.[5] But the old rule that an estoppel must be reciprocal, and its consequences, were in Coke's day too well established to be upset by an as yet scarcely realized change in the principle upon which this species of estoppel was being based;[6] and in some cases—e.g. in the case of an estoppel as between landlord and tenant—it was clearly just that the estoppel should be reciprocal, whether the estoppel arose by deed or by matter in pais.[7] It was not till a later period, and under the influence, both of the idea upon which estoppel by matter in pais

---

[1] Vol. iii 375, 379-382; vol. viii 449.

[2] Above 154 n. 2; "against your deed you cannot be received to disclaim. Also your deed witnesses that the tenements are ' of your fee,' and that you ought to acquit him; so against your deed you cannot disclaim in the seignory," Y.B. 3 Ed. II. (S.S.) 173 *per* Stanton, J.

[3] Y.B. 35 Hy. VI. Mich. pl. 26 (p. 18).   [4] Co. Litt. 352a.

[5] " Il dit que en nul cas jeo serai estoppe per le rehercel d'un condicion, mes auter est d'un endenture, come si jeo reherce en endenture que ou jeo ay tiel accion vers J.H. que jeo serai devant tiel jour nonsue de cel, jeo serai estoppe a dire que jeo n'avais tiel accion," Y.B. 21 Ed. IV. Mich pl. 16.

[6] Above 156 nn. 13, 14.   [7] Below 160.

had from the first been based, and of the idea which ultimately gave birth to the modern estoppel by conduct, that these particular consequences of the old rule of reciprocity were got rid of.[1]   As we shall now see, the development of estoppel by matter in pais, helped the lawyers to realize more distinctly the changed basis upon which estoppel by deed had come to rest, and paved the way for the recognition of the modern principle of estoppel by conduct.

(iii) *Estoppel by matter in pais.*

The examples which Coke gives of estoppel by matter in pais are livery of seisin, entry, acceptance of rent, partition, and acceptance of an estate—all acts more or less notorious, of which "the *pays*" might be expected to have cognizance.[2]   Probably the earliest distinct recognition of this species of estoppel is to be found in a case of 1445, in which it was said by Newton that acceptance of rent, exchange, or partition, might work an estoppel.[3] The principle itself was probably new, since Littleton, after putting a case of an estoppel arising from the acceptance of an estate, thinks it worth while to note that the case shows that "a man shall be stopped by matter in fact, though there be no writing by deed indented or otherwise."[4]   It is clear, too, from Littleton's statement of the case that, from the first, it was recognized that this species of estoppel depended on the principle that it was the estopped person's own act which prevented him from setting up a different state of facts; for he says that, though a husband might be estopped by the acceptance of an estate from one to whom he had conveyed his wife's fee simple, the wife is not estopped, because "no folly can be adjudged in the wife which is covert in such case."[5]   In other words, it is not and cannot be her act because she is covert.   Probably the recognition of the principle underlying estoppel in pais was the easier, because in many cases the conveyance of an estate would be by deed, so that its acceptance could be based upon the principle of estoppel by deed.   But, as it was clear that estoppel by matter in pais depended on the principle

---

[1] As to estoppel by a recital, see Bowman v. Taylor (1834) 2 A. and E. 278; as to estoppel by a deed poll the law is not perhaps wholly clear, see Halsbury, Laws of England xiii 365 n. (a); in the note to the 4th ed. of Shep. Touch. 53 it is said that an estoppel may be created by a deed poll, though no very satisfactory reason is given; and this is assumed to be true by Cotton, L.J., in Cropper v. Smith (1884) 26 C.D. at p. 705, though a dictum of Bowen, L.J., at pp. 708-709 is opposed to this conclusion; it is difficult to see why a statement in a deed poll should not, in an appropriate case, have the same effect as a recital; in fact, the doubt is due historically to the same cause that long produced the uncertainty as to a recital, namely the survival of an archaic view as to the basis upon which estoppel by deed is based.

[2] Co. Litt. 352a.   [3] Y.B. 21 Hy. VI. Hil. pl. 5 (pp. 24-25).

[4] § 667; and see the case of Pasch. 38 Hy. VIII. cited above 156 n. 14, where it seems to be assumed that the mere relation of landlord and tenant will not create an estoppel.

[5] § 666.

that it was the estopped person's own act which prevented him from setting up a different state of facts, it helped to teach the lawyers that estoppel by deed really depended also upon this principle. And it is clear from Coke's statement in *Syms's Case*, that he was beginning to see that estoppels, which depended on this principle, had a wider operation than some of those estoppels by matter of record, which ran with the estate in the land.[1]

The principle upon which these estoppels by matter in pais rested was a broad and sensible principle. But, in the sixteenth and seventeenth centuries, it failed to develop on broad lines. As Coke's illustrations show, it was applied only in connection with the land law; and in relation to the land law it was developed with some minuteness. In particular, it was well established that a tenant is estopped from disputing his landlord's title while he is in possession under, and during the continuance of, the lease,[2] though he may show that the title, which the landlord once had, has expired;[3] and, conversely, that the landlord is estopped from repudiating such a tenancy.[4] There is, indeed, in 1603 a slight hint, but no more than a hint, that the position of a bailor of chattels with respect to his bailee, is analogous to that of a land-lord in relation to his tenant;[5] but no attempt was made, till long afterwards, to apply, as between bailor and bailee, the principle of estoppel by matter in pais, which it was well settled applied as between landlord and tenant. In fact, it was not till 1865 that it was clearly decided that, as between bailor and bailee, a similar estoppel arises, so long as the bailee is in pos-session under the bailment.[6] We shall now see that, as it was with the common law generally, so it was with the doctrine of estoppel in pais—it was necessary to bring new influences to bear, before the doctrine could be lifted out of the technical ruts in which it had become imbedded, and so fitted it to enter the service of the modern common law. As was the case with many other

---

[1] "If an abator marries with the right heir, and has issue by her, and the abator makes a lease for life rendering rent, and he and his wife die, in this case the issue has the mere right of the part of his mother; and yet if he accepts the rent, and makes acquittance, it shall estop him and his heirs to avoid the said lease, in respect of the acceptance of the recompence. . . . But an estoppel which accrues by admittance etc. of record, shall not conclude the heir who claims not the right by the same ancestor," (1609) 8 Co. Rep. at f. 54b.

[2] The principle is admitted in Y.B. 14 Hy. VI. p. 22 pl. 64; and for the modern cases see Smith, Leading Cases (10th ed.) ii 808-809.

[3] Brooke, Ab. *Estoppell* pl. 221, citing an opinion of Hales and Montague; Smith, op. cit. ii 810.

[4] This conclusion would follow from the rule that the estoppel must be reciprocal, and it was expressly stated by Lord Denman, C.J., in Downs v. Cooper (1841) 2 Q.B. at pp. 262-263.

[5] Shelbury v. Scotsford Yelv. 23, as explained by Blackburn, J., in Biddle v. Bond (1865) 6 B. and S. at pp. 232-233.

[6] Biddle v. Bond 6 B. and S. 225.

branches of the common law, these new influences were found in the rules which the chancellor was developing at the end of the seventeenth century, and in the developments which, in the eighteenth century, were occurring in the sphere of mercantile law.

(2) *The growth of the modern doctrine of estoppel by conduct.*[1]

It is in one or two cases decided by the chancellor in the latter half of the seventeenth, and the beginning of the eighteenth centuries, that we can see one of the origins of the modern doctrine of estoppel by conduct. In 1649, in the case of *Hunt v. Carew*,[2] the facts were as follows: A father was tenant for life of land, remainder in tail to his son. The plaintiff, thinking that the father had the fee simple, applied to the defendant, his son, to get his help in procuring the grant of a lease from the father. The defendant, affirming falsely that the father had power to grant the lease, procured a lease which the plaintiff accepted, and received a sum of £300. It was held that the defendant, who had led the plaintiff on to purchase the lease by the statement that the father had power to grant it, must join with the father to confirm the lease. The decision was grounded expressly on the fact that the fraudulent affirmation of the son had led to the expenditure of money by the plaintiff.[3] It would seem that at first this principle was applied only to a fraudulent affirmation, since, in 1682, Lord Nottingham refused to apply it to a false statement as to title, made in bona fide ignorance of the title.[4] It does not appear from the report whether or not Lord Nottingham considered that this ignorance was the result of negligence, and, if so, whether the presence of negligence would have made any difference to his decision. But, later in the same year, Lord North held that a defendant was estopped by a negligent mis-statement as to title,[5] though the distinction between fraud and negligence was pressed upon him;[6] and this decision was followed in 1717.[7]

The principle of these decisions was, as Dr. Ashburner has pointed out,[8] imported into the common law by Lord Mansfield. In 1762, in the case of *Montefiori v. Montefiori*,[9] the facts were as follows: Joseph Montefiori, being engaged in a marriage treaty,

---

[1] The best short account is to be found in Ashburner, Equity 628-629.

[2] Nels. 46.

[3] " The Court ordered, that since the plaintiff was not acquainted that the father had exceeded his power, and he relying on the affirmation of the son (who had most of the money) that the lease would be good without his joining, by which he was deceived; that therefore both should join at their own costs to make an assurance and confirm the lease to the plaintiff during the estate thereby granted," Nels. at p. 48.

[4] Dyer v. Dyer 2 Ch. Cas. 108.

[5] Hobbs v. Norton (1682) 1 Vern. 136. [6] S.C. 2 Ch. Cas. 128.

[7] Mocatta v. Murgatroyd 1 P. Wms. at p. 394.

[8] Equity 629. [9] 1 W. Black 363.

got his brother Moses to help him, by representing him to be a man of fortune. Moses gave him a note for a large sum of money, which he acknowledged to have in his hands on account of his brother, though no such money was due. Joseph refused to give up this note after the marriage, and Lord Mansfield held that he was not bound to do so. He said, "the law is that where, upon proposals of marriage, third persons represent anything material, in a light different from the truth, even though it be by collusion with the husband, they shall be bound to make good the thing in the manner in which they represented it. It shall be as represented to be." This decision was cited with approval by Lord Thurlow in 1782, in a case which involved an application of the same principle;[1] so that it may be said that the root principle of estoppel by conduct was in effect recognized both by the courts of common law and by the court of Chancery in the latter part of the eighteenth century.

But, though the principle of estoppel by conduct had been grasped by Lord Mansfield, he was in this, as in other respects, somewhat in advance of his time. However, in this case the principle which he laid down was not directly opposed to the rules of the common law.[2] On the contrary, it was fundamentally in harmony with the principle underlying the rules as to estoppel by matter in pais; and therefore, although it lay dormant, it was not overruled. And, at the end of the eighteenth and the beginning of the nineteenth centuries, the influence of mercantile law was making for its recognition. It was then that those rules as to the estoppels arising as between drawers, acceptors, and indorsers of bills of exchange were being recognized,[3] which are now contained in the Bills of Exchange Act.[4] The ground was thus well prepared for the clear enunciation of the principle by Lord Denman in 1837 in the case of *Pickard v. Sears.*[5]

This sketch of the history of estoppel shows how a principle, originating in the early days when the main interest in an action centred round the modes of proof, was gradually adapted to a changed order of ideas upon matters procedural. In one of its forms—estoppel by matter of record—it was adapted to the purpose of securing a decent finality to litigation; and in its other

[1] Neville v. Wilkinson 1 Bro. C.C. at p. 548.
[2] For his attempts to rationalize the rule in Shelley's Case see vol. iii 109-110; for his attempts to recognize purely equitable titles see vol. vii 19-20; for his ideas as to seisin see ibid 43-46; for his attempts to revolutionize the doctrine of consideration see vol. viii 26-31, 34.
[3] See Collis v. Emett (1790) 1 H. Bl. 313, at p. 319; ex pte. Clarke (1791) 3 Bro. C.C. 238; Cooper v. Meyer (1830) 10 B. and C. 468.
[4] 45, 46 Victoria c. 61 §§ 54, 55.
[5] 6 Ad. and E. at p. 474 cited above 146 n. 5.

forms it was adapted to secure the honest fulfilment of representations, a belief in which had induced another person to take action. Here, as in other branches of the law, traces still remain of the stages by which this result has been accomplished. The doubts long entertained as to whether estoppel by deed could be raised by a recital in a deed or by a deed poll, testify to the original influence of the oldest kind of estoppel—estoppel by matter of record; and the accepted classification of the various forms of estoppel indicates the milestones which mark the road by which the law at length reached the broad principle which underlies the modern doctrine of estoppel by conduct.

Documentary Evidence

We have seen that the practice of recording the proceedings of the king's court had led to the establishment of the doctrine of estoppel by matter of record. The record authenticated by the king's seal was conclusive.[1] We have seen, too, that this naturally led to the establishment of the doctrine of estoppel by deed. Other matters stated under the seal, either of the king, or of private persons, were equally conclusive.[2] In other words, both matter of record and documents under seal were proofs—proofs as conclusive as the older proofs by which in former days men were wont to try the truth of their respective allegations. It may thus be said that the efficacy of these kinds of estoppel was derived, partly from the new fashion of recording pleas and of authenticating the record by the king's seal, and partly from the application of this new idea to the old conception of a trial. But, as the jury superseded these older modes of trial, it gradually came to be seen that these sealed documents might have another effect. The jury was a body of reasonable men, whose verdict could be guided by the evidence put before them. And so the difference between the jury and these older modes of trial, which, as we have seen, had a decisive influence on the development of the common law system of pleading,[3] had an influence equally great on the law of evidence; for it gradually gave rise to the idea that these sealed documents could be used, not only as providing an absolute proof by creating an estoppel, but also as evidence. Hence we get the growth of the idea that a deed can be used, not only to estop the party as against whom it is produced, but also to give the jury evidence as to the truth of the matters in issue. Gradually this idea that a deed can be used as evidence, is applied to other writings, and so we get the modern conception of documentary evidence. But, from the first, the judges had exercised a strict control over the

---

manner in which this evidence must be produced to the court;[1] and they had always been careful to instruct the jury as to its effect, and as to the weight which they ought to attach to it.[2] Therefore, contemporaneously with the rise of this documentary evidence, we get the growth of rules which govern both its admissibility, and its use and effect.

In tracing the history of these rules I shall deal, firstly, with the introduction of the modern conception of documentary evidence; secondly, with the rules governing its admissibility; and, thirdly, with the rules governing its effect when produced.

(1) *The introduction of the modern conception of documentary evidence.*

That deeds could be adduced, not only as affording an absolute proof by way of estoppel, but also as evidence, is shown by the earliest of the Year Books.[3] That this was so clearly seen, is, to a large extent, due to the fact that the courts had refused to allow that a deed could transfer seisin; and had insisted that seisin could only be transferred by a real livery.[4] This rule, which was very necessary to a legal system which worked with a mediæval jury,[5] was, as we have seen, a reversion to a very primitive set of legal ideas;[6] and, as Professor Wigmore has shown, to an order of legal ideas in which the deed established nothing conclusively. "If the truth of its statement is disputed—the amount of money loaned, the area of land conveyed, the conditions of tenure annexed—the terms of the transaction may and must be proved by calling the witnesses to it, regardless of any contradiction of the writing. The attendant witnesses continued to be, as they had been, the main reliance for the proof of a disputed transaction. The procedure for disputing by the witnesses' oaths the correctness of the document was elaborate and well settled, and its ultimate settlement might turn upon a wager of battle."[7] It followed, therefore, that the statements in a deed as to livery of seisin were not conclusive. They merely amounted to evidence which might be rebutted.[8] Thus in 1292,[9] when a defendant to an assize of mort d'ancestor pleaded a deed,

---

[1] Below 167-173.   [2] Below 173-177.

[3] Thayer, Evidence 106; and see e.g. Y.BB. 20, 21 Ed. I. (R.S.) 258, cited below 164-165; 21, 22 Ed. I. (R.S.) 186; 33-35 Ed. I. (R.S.) 444; 2, 3 Ed. II. (S.S.) 185.

[4] Vol. iii 224.   [5] Ibid 95, 224.

[6] Vol. ii 76-77; vol. iii 221-224.

[7] Wigmore, Evidence iv 3413, § 2426, and authorities there cited.

[8] See Salmond, Essays in Jurisprudence 52-54.

[9] Y.B. 20, 21 Ed. I. (R.S.) 258, cited by Wigmore, loc. cit.; cp. Y.B. 33-35 Ed. I. (R.S.) 50—"Ink and parchment without delivery and acceptance do not make a presentation," *per* Scoter *arg.*; "a charter is worth nothing without seisin," *per* Roubiri, J.

showing that the father of the plaintiff had enfeoffed him, the plaintiff was allowed to prove that seisin had been delivered subject to a condition which the defendant had not fulfilled; and, on his proving this, the court held that he was entitled to succeed. In 1314 Scrope, J., said,[1] "If I make you a charter in fee and deliver you seisin for the term of your life, the charter vesteth in you naught more than an estate in accordance with the terms of the livery of seisin; and the reason of that is that the charter is not an enfeoffment, but evidence only; and you will certainly be received to aver a feoffment at variance with it."

The rule, therefore, that a deed was only evidence of a livery of seisin, brought prominently before the court the distinction between the effect of the deed in creating an estoppel, and the effect of the deed in merely supplying evidence. It is clear from the Year Books of Edward II.'s reign that this distinction was well understood, and that practical consequences were deduced from it. Let us look at one or two cases. In 1310 it was held that a tenant in possession could aver the facts showing the nature of his estate, and, without showing a charter, prove them by battle or the grand assize.[2] "Charter," it was said, "is no proof of tenancy; it is only evidence of tenancy"; and, "the law is founded not on charter but on livery of seisin which lies in the cognisance of the country."[3] In 1314 Scrope *arguendo* said that "the words of the writing are but evidence of the tenant's estate, of which the manner of the livery of seisin is the decisive fact; and I put the case that I make you an unconditional charter, and give you livery of seisin for the term of your life only. You have only a freehold";[4] and we have seen that Scrope, J., upheld this view.[5]

It followed that the effect of a deed in producing an estoppel, and its effect merely as evidence, were very different.[6] This difference was reflected in the rule that, if a deed was relied upon as producing an estoppel, it must be brought forward before the jury or assize was summoned, because it was then a bar to the

---

[1] Y.B. 8 Ed. II. (S.S.) (1315) 48.

[2] "When he is 'in' the country may have better knowledge of his entry and of his tenancy than if he were 'out,' and were demanding as a stranger by way of remainder that of which neither he nor his ancestors were seised. Besides, in that case might he not join battle or the grand assize and all without charter? Yes, he might," Y.B. 2, 3 Ed. II. (S.S.) 171 *per* Bereford, C.J.

[3] Y.B. 2, 3 Ed. II. (S.S.) 171 *per* Friskeney *arg.*

[4] Y.B. 8 Ed. II. (S.S.) (1315) 43; cp. Y.B. 6 Ed. II. (S.S.) (1312-1313) 12, 14, 89-90.

[5] Above n. 1.

[6] The case reported in Y.B. 8 Ed. II. (S.S.) 36-51 depended largely on the question whether the deed produced operated as an estoppel, or whether it was merely evidence, and thus capable of being modified by a writing executed contemporaneously.

action, and therefore precluded the need for the verdict of an assize or a jury; but that, if it was relied upon as evidence, it must be brought before the assize or the jury. In 1312-1313 this rule was clearly stated by Bereford, C.J., " In a writ of *ael* the parties descended to an inquisition. On the day when the inquisition should have passed the party put forward a fine in evidence to the inquisition, and he was not received to put the fine into evidence, because it (the fine) would have been a bar if it had been put forward (before) without the need for the joinder of the inquest." [1] On the other hand, if a fine would not be a bar as between the parties it was well recognized that it could be used merely as evidence. [2]

It seems to me, then, that it was this rule, that a deed was merely evidence of the intent with which seisin was made, which brought out clearly, in the later thirteenth and early fourteenth centuries, the idea that a deed can be used as evidence only of a transaction. As the law relating to estoppel became more elaborate, this distinction was emphasized. Thus in 1481 Brian, C.J., asked why a record, which might have been pleaded as an estoppel, because the person as against whom it was produced was a party to it, was only put forward as evidence. [3] Similarly, in 1463, a distinction was drawn between a deed in which a simple contract was merged, and a deed which merely evidenced a simple contract, and so left the simple contract subsisting. [4]

Thus, by the close of the mediæval period, the modern conception of documentary evidence had been reached. But as yet it was applied mainly to sealed writings; [5] and we shall see that,

---

[1] Y.B. 6 Ed. II. (S.S.) (1312-1313) 199; cp. the following passage from the Eyre of Kent (S.S.) iii 52: " *Warrington*. Does he tender the charter in bar or as evidence ? *Mallory, J.* As evidence. *Warrington*. The Court ought never to receive evidence before the party has pleaded to the assize or has assigned cause why the assize should not pass; and when he has pleaded to the assize he should then tender evidence and not before; but if he tender the deed in bar the Court ought to receive it. Therefore if they want to use this charter in bar we will reply to it."

[2] Y.B. 6 Ed. II. (S.S.) (1312-1313) 71, 73, 75.

[3] " Et Brian disoit, pur que ne fuit ceo record pled envers le dit plaintif per voye d'estoppel, pur ce que il est privie, *ad quod non fuit responsum*," Y.B. 21 Ed. IV. Mich. pl. 1.

[4] " Sicome on fait un obligation sur un contract, le contract est determine per ceo; et si on recovere det sur contract, le contract est determine per ceo: mes issent n'est icy, car n'est ascun oblige a cesty que mettra mes un papier tesmoinant le contract. Et si jeo baile biens per fait indente, et puis port bref de Detinue pur cause, jeo ne counte or sur le fait indente, pur ce que n'est que chose tesmoinant le bailement. Et meme la Ley si jeo face contract per fait indente, jeo ne sera coarcte a counter sur le fait indente, pur ce que le contract n'est determine sur le fait indente . . . et il poiet eslire comment il veut porter son action," Y.B. 39 Hy. VI. Mich. pl. 46 *per* Prisot, C.J.—*ad quod omnes justiciarii concesserunt;* this case is cited by Thayer, Evidence 394-395.

[5] Thayer, Evidence 104; in Y.B. 2, 3 Ed. II. (S.S.) 185 it is clear from a statement by Bereford, C.J., that both " a writing " and " a deed " had been put forward as evidence; for the use of tallies as evidence see Fleta II. 63, 12; note that a tally, though sealed, did not operate as a deed, and could be met by wager of law, Y.B. 8 Ed. II. (S.S.) 179-182.

when unsealed writings were produced, they were treated very differently from deeds.[1] But, in the new age which opened in the sixteenth century, it was inevitable that other writings should be brought more frequently before the courts. Wills of land were required by Henry VIII.'s Statute of Wills to be in writing;[2] and the growth of commercial law was acquainting the lawyers with many different kinds of written documents. We shall see that, in the latter part of the sixteenth and in the seventeenth centuries, the change in the character of the jury, which made their verdicts much more dependent on the evidence produced in court than on their own knowledge,[3] coupled with their power still to decide cases on their own knowledge,[4] induced the courts to attach very great importance to documentary evidence;[5] and we have seen that the Legislature gave effect to this idea in the Statute of Frauds.[6] All these causes combined to get rid of the wide distinction which the mediæval common law recognized between sealed and unsealed writings, and to produce the beginnings of our modern law as to the manner in which all documentary evidence must be produced, and as to its effect when produced. As we shall now see, the rules governing the first of these topics are derived almost directly from the mediæval rules as to the manner in which deeds must be produced in evidence and proved; and the rules governing the second of these topics, though not so directly influenced by these mediæval ideas, indirectly owe something to them.

(2) *The rules governing the admissibility of documentary evidence.*

If documentary evidence is put in, the document itself must as a general rule, be produced for the inspection of the court, accompanied by the production of an attesting witness, in cases where the evidence of such a witness is required.[7] This rule, as Professor Wigmore has pointed out,[8] can be traced back to the beginnings of our legal history. In fact, it takes its rise in the period when a sealed and attested document was regarded as a mode of proof.[9] A document thus put forward as proof must necessarily have been produced; and, when produced, the genuineness of the document was proved by the evidence of the attesting witnesses given to the jury, or sometimes by these witnesses and the jury acting together.[10] Till 1318 the presence of these

---

[1] Below 172-173.   [2] Vol. iv 465.   [3] Vol. i 334-335.
[4] Ibid 336, 346.   [5] Below 176-177.   [6] Vol. vi 388-390.
[7] Stephen, Digest of the Law of Evidence 72.
[8] Evidence ii 1385, § 1177.   [9] Above 154-155.
[10] Thayer, Evidence 97-102, 503-505; below 168, 169; for an illustrative case see Y.B. 6 Ed. II. (S.S.) 1312-1313, 104.

witnesses was a necessity. In that year it was enacted that, though they must still be summoned, the case could proceed without them if they did not appear;[1] and in 1472 it was said that process would not issue to secure their appearance unless it was asked for.[2] They were, however, still summoned with the jury till the end of the fifteenth century;[3] but, in the course of the sixteenth century, the practice of thus summoning them became obsolete.[4]

We have seen that the idea that a sealed document was a mode of proof chosen by the party, is the origin of the rule that a party relying on such a document must make profert of it—that is, he must offer to produce it.[5] This rule was naturally applied, not only to cases where the sealed document was relied on as giving rise to an estoppel, but also to cases where it was adduced as evidence. Indeed, as might be expected, these two uses of a deed were sometimes confused.[6] In both cases, therefore, profert must be made, and the other party could "have oyer," that is, demand that it be read in court. Similarly, the genuineness of a deed must be proved by the attesting witnesses, who, as we have seen, were originally summoned with the jury.[7] We have seen that the rule as to profert continued, in a modified form, to be a rule of the common law till the Common Law Procedure Act of 1852;[8] and, though the attesting witnesses ceased to be summoned with the jury,[9] the rule as to the necessity of calling an attesting witness lasted till the Act of 1854.[10] The long life of these rules is due to the fact that, during the fourteenth and fifteenth centuries, they had come to rest upon a new basis, in harmony with that new conception of a trial to which the extension and development of the jury system was giving rise. This fact also explains why the principle underlying the rule as to profert was extended, in a somewhat altered form, to all documents; and gave rise to the rule that, if documentary evidence is adduced, the document itself must as a rule be produced for the inspection of the court. It follows that it is necessary, in relating the history of this branch of the law, to deal firstly with the modern development of the rules

---

[1] 12 Edward II. st. 1 c. 2.

[2] Y.B. 12 Ed. IV. Pasch. pl. 9 *per* Catesby and the Court.

[3] Thayer, Evidence 102, citing Y.B. 5 Hy. VII. Mich. pl. 19; he points out that Brooke, in his argument in Reniger v. Fogossa (1549) Plowden at p. 12, assumes that it was still possible that the witnesses might be joined to the inquest.

[4] "Such process against witnesses is vanished," Co. Litt. 6b.

[5] Above 155.

[6] Thus in Y.B. 8 Ed. II. (S.S.) (1314) 132 Denham *arg.* says, "Take your stand on the deed and let the averment go, or hold to the averment and waive the deed; for you are not entitled to avail yourself of both"; clearly he is confusing the use of a deed as a form of proof which operated as an estoppel, with the use of the deed merely as evidence; as Scrope, replying to him, pointed out, he might well use both since "the one doth support the other."

[7] Above 167; below 169.

[8] Above 155.

[9] Above n. 4.

[10] 17, 18 Victoria c. 125 § 26.

as to profert, and as to the necessity of summoning an attesting witness ; and, secondly, with the extension of the principle underlying the rule as to profert to all documents.

(i) *The modern development of the rules as to profert, and as to the necessity of summoning an attesting witness.*

As the second of these two rules is of comparatively minor importance, and has left very slender traces in modern law, I shall briefly dispose of it before dealing with the more important rule as to profert.

(*a*) Down to the passing of the Common Law Procedure Act 1854, a deed or other document attested by a witness or witnesses, could not be proved unless at least one of the attesting witnesses was called.[1] As Thayer has pointed out, this rule goes back to the days of the preappointed transaction witnesses, who, by their attestation, had consented, and therefore could be compelled, to testify, if called upon.[2] When the old process of summoning these witnesses with the jury died out, they came to be regarded in the light of ordinary witnesses who, by the statute of 1562-1563,[3] could be compelled to testify. But a trace of the old law, which regarded their presence as necessary to prove the deed, survived in the rule that they must be produced,[4] unless their production was proved to be impossible.[5] If they were not produced the document could not be proved at all ;[6] but if they were produced and their testimony was adverse, it was settled, by the middle of the eighteenth century, that their testimony could be rebutted, and that the document could be proved by other evidence.[7] But the rule in this form was hardly rational—why should not an attested document be proved by other evidence without their presence ? It had, however, become so fixed a rule by the eighteenth century that Lord Mansfield did not dare to disturb it ;[8] and Lord Ellenborough said that it was a rule "as fixed, formal and universal as any that can be stated in a court of justice."[9] Various unsatisfactory reasons were found for it.[10]

---

[1] Wigmore, Evidence ii 1589-1590, § 1304.   [2] Evidence 502.
[3] 5 Elizabeth c. 9; below 185.   [4] Thayer, Evidence 503.
[5] For various causes where excuses for non-production were allowed, see Wigmore, Evidence ii 1600-1609, §§ 1311-1319; their recognition dates generally from the end of the seventeenth, and the eighteenth and nineteenth centuries.
[6] See the Second Report of the Common Law Procedure Commission 23, cited Wigmore, Evidence ii 1571, § 1290.
[7] Wigmore, op. cit. ii 1587, § 1302, and cases cited in n. 2; cp. Thayer, op. cit. 503; Abbot v. Plumbe (1779) 1 Dougl. 216.
[8] "To be sure this is a captious objection ; but it is a technical rule that the subscribing witness must be produced, and it cannot be dispensed with unless it appear that his attendance could not be procured," Abbot v. Plumbe (1779) 1 Dougl. 216.
[9] R. v. Harringworth (1815) 4 M. and S. at p. 354.
[10] E.g. that the parties were supposed to have agreed that the deed should not be given in evidence unless the witness was called, Whyman v. Garth (1853) 8 Ex.

But, as Professor Wigmore points out, the only real justification for it is in those cases in which the law requires attestation to prevent forgery or fraud. As, in these cases, "the attestation itself must in any case be proved as an element in the validity of the document, there seems to be no special hardship in obtaining the witness rather than in obtaining evidence of his signature."[1] It is to these cases that the rule was restricted by the Act of 1854.[2]

(b) It is clear from the Year Books of the fourteenth and fifteenth centuries, that the reasons, then assigned for the doctrine of profert, were giving to it a new and a more rational meaning. The rule that profert must be made in the pleading secured, in the days of oral pleading, when evidence was generally pleaded,[3] that the document relied upon was brought to the notice of the court in a regular way.[4] It gave the court an opportunity of considering its relevancy,[5] and it gave the other party an opportunity of urging any defences which he might have to it.[6] Moreover, it was a considerable check upon the power of the jury to give a verdict from their own knowledge or enquiries; for it helped to prevent them from taking cognizance of documents put forward by the parties which had not been produced in court.[7] These reasons for requiring profert of a deed were summed up by Coke in *Doctor Leyfield's Case:*[8] " It appears that it is dangerous to suffer any one who by the law in pleading ought to show the deed itself to the Court, upon the general issue to prove in

803; or that if he was not called the other side would be deprived of the right to cross examine, Abbot v. Plumbe (1779) Dougl. 216; see Wigmore, op. cit. ii 1568-1569, § 1288, for a criticism of these reasons.

[1] Op. cit. ii 1569-1570, § 1288. [2] 17, 18 Victoria c. 125 § 26.

[3] Vol. iii 635, 638; cp. Y.B. 20, 21 Ed. I. (R.S.) 20, cited Thayer, op. cit, 106.

[4] In Y.B. 11 Hy. IV. Mich. pl. 41 it appeared that a deed had been given by the plaintiff to a juror, and by him communicated to his fellows, so that it had not been brought to the notice of the court; "Gascoigne et Hulls disoient que le jury apres ceo que ils fuerent jures, ne devient veier ne porter ovesque eux nul auter evidence, sinon ceo que a eux suit livere per le Court, et per le party mis en Court sur l'evidence monstre, et entant que ils fierent le contrary ceo fuit suspicious, per que il ne duist judgment aver"; cp. Thayer, op. cit. 110-111; but as late as 1598, in Graves v. Short Cro. Eliza. 616, the fact that a juryman had shown his fellows an escrow not produced in court, and not furnished by one of the parties, was held to be no ground for a writ of error; cp. Thayer, op. cit. 111-112; below 172 n. 7.

[5] In Y.B. 21 Ed. IV. Mich. pl. 1 Brian, C.J., refused to allow the jury to have a writing as it was not "testimonial"; and, at the end of the case, he "delivera touts les evidences de l'un party et de l'auter, queux poient inducer le jure al verite del issue, et touts les evidences que ne fuerent my material, il ne voille suffrer eux d'estre delivres."

[6] "Ceo fait (a release) n'est forsque la privie entent d'un home, que ne puit estre conus, sinon per escript solement, et cel escript, s'il soit monstre, puit estre voide en plusors maners per le ley, si non sane memorie, deins age, imprisonment, ou pur ceo que il fuit fait devant le mort son auncestor, *et similia*, quel le partie ne puit pleder, s'il n'ayt oyer del fait, et que le fait soit monstre," Y.B. 7 Hy. V. pl. 3 at p. 8 *per* Huls, J.

[7] Above n. 4. [8] (1611) 10 Co. Rep. at f. 92b.

evidence to the jury by witnesses that there was such a deed, which they have heard and read; or to prove it by a copy; for the viciousness, rasures, or interlineations, or other imperfections in these cases, will not appear to the court; or peradventure the deed may be upon condition, limitation, with power of revocation, and by this way truth and justice, and the true reason of the common law would be subverted."

At the same time it had been recognized in the sixteenth century that it might, for various causes, be impossible to make profert. As early as 1537 the Court was equally divided, as to whether the fact that the document was in the hands of some one, whom the party seeking to rely on it could not compel to produce it, was admissible as an excuse;[1] and in *Doctor Leyfield's Case*[2] it was allowed that "in great and notorious extremities, as by casualty of fire, that all his evidences were burnt in his house, then if that should appear to the judges, they may in favour of him who has so great a loss by fire, suffer him upon the general issue to prove the deed in evidence to the jury by witnesses, that affliction be not added to affliction." This principle was easily extended to the loss of a document by any casualty or accident;[3] and at the end of the eighteenth century, in order to prevent applications to the court of Chancery, it was further extended to cases where the document could not be found.[4] Five years before *Doctor Leyfield's Case* it had been held that, unless a deed was required by law, a profert need not be made of a deed by which no interest was claimed; if, for instance the deed operated merely as a defence to a claim, and so was only collateral to an interest.[5]

The doctrine of profert was a rule of pleading—unless the proffer was made in the pleading the deed could not be produced in evidence. And, as a rule of pleading, it had a limited application. It applied only to deeds and records,[6] because it was originally an offer of proof;[7] and only deeds and records could

---

[1] Dyer 29b; but the fact that it was an excuse seems to have been conceded in 1568, see Estofte v. Vaughan Dyer 277a; see also the cases cited by Wigmore, Evidence ii 1437 n. 1, § 1211; this was extended in the seventeenth century to the case where the deed was in the hands of the opposite party, ibid ii 1419, § 1199, and cases cited in n. 2.

[2] (1611) 10 Co. Rep. at f. 92b; and see Wigmore, op. cit. ii 1404, § 1193.

[3] Wigmore, op. cit. ii 1404, § 1193, and the cases cited in n. 4.

[4] "It was said that the strict rule would not be attended with hardship as the party had a remedy in a Court of Equity. Now it is not a very pleasant thing for a Court of Law to say, that they cannot administer justice on legal titles because they are fettered with certain forms," Read v. Brookman (1789) 3 T.R. at p. 156 *per* Lord Kenyon, C.J.; this move was not regarded with favour by the court of Chancery, see Princess of Wales v. Earl of Liverpool (1818) 1 Swanst. at pp. 119-120 *per* Lord Eldon; Ashburner, Equity 16 n. (z); vol. vii 346-347.

[5] Bellamy's Case (1606) 6 Co. Rep. 38a; Wigmore, op. cit. ii 1562, § 1252.

[6] Ibid 1387, § 1177, citing Aylesbury v. Harvey (1685) 3 Lev. 204, and Tidd, Practice (9th ed.) 587, 590.

[7] Above 155.

operate as proof, just as for the same reason in modern law it is only these classes of writing that can produce an estoppel.[1]   Moreover, it applied only to civil and not to criminal cases.[2]   But, as explained and qualified by the cases of the fifteenth, sixteenth and seventeenth centuries, it did embody the general principle applicable to the law as to the production of all documentary evidence, that documents relied upon in evidence should be produced. Hence, though the doctrine of profert had become merely a rule of pleading, and was abolished by the Common Law Procedure Act of 1852,[3] the rule of evidence to which it had given birth is still a fundamental principle of the law.   To this adaptation of the rule of profert we must now turn.

(ii) *The extension of the principle underlying the rule of profert to all documents.*

The rise of the system of written pleadings,[4] and the consequent distinction between deeds which were pleaded and of which profert must be made, and deeds merely given in evidence, tended at first to restrict the rule of profert to those deeds or records which were pleaded.[5]   Thus, it is clear from the case of *Newis v. Lark*,[6] that in 1571 the rule was applied neither to records, nor, a fortiori, to deeds which were only given in evidence, and were not pleaded.   It was not till the following century that the modern rule, that all documentary evidence must be produced, was established.   During that century no such rule was regularly applied in civil cases;[7] and it is certain that in criminal cases material documents were not produced, and that copies were admitted.   It is true that on the trial of Strafford in 1640 the Lords, after "a very hot contestation," refused to admit the copy of a record.[8]   But it is not till after the Revolution that we get

---

[1] Above 147-148, 154-155.   [2] Wigmore, loc. cit.
[3] Above 155.   [4] Vol. iii 639-653.
[5] " In civil cases it is plain that during the sixteenth century no independent rule of evidence yet required the production of writings in general.   At this period whatever document was not brought in by virtue of the profert rule in pleading might be established without any production ; and this might sometimes suffice even for a record," Wigmore, op. cit. ii 1388, § 1177.
[6] Plowden at p. 411 ; the majority of the court said, " Upon the general issue, as this is here, the jury may find things which prove or disprove the seisin or disseisin, whether they be matters of record or otherwise, if so be they precede the seisin or disseisin.   For such records may be the cause of the seisin or disseisin, for they make and destroy a right, as fines and recoveries and such like do ; and therefore if the parties don't discover them in the pleading, the jury could not give a right verdict if they could not find them, and whatever they may take consusance of themselves may be given in evidence by parol or by copies, or by other argument of truth.
[7] Graves v. Short (1599) Cro. Eliza. 616 ; Wigmore, op. cit. ii 1388, § 1177, citing Anon. (1699) 1 Ld. Raym. 731, Geery v. Hopkins (1702) 2 Ld. Raym. 851, and later cases of the eighteenth century where the rule was applied.
[8] 3 S.T. at pp. 1434.

any clear indication that the rule was applied in civil cases to documents other than deeds or records,[1] or that it was regularly applied in criminal cases.[2] It was well established by the middle of the eighteenth century in both classes of cases; and it may well be that the substantial reasons assigned in the sixteenth century for the doctrine of profert, the fact that the jury were being restricted to evidence produced in court,[3] and the parallel rule against hearsay applied to oral evidence, which was becoming established almost contemporaneously,[4] all had something to do with its final settlement. At the same time, the same exceptions which were admitted to the rule of profert, were, with one exception, admitted to this generalized rule that a document relied upon in evidence must be produced.[5] In 1750 Lord Hardwicke laid it down that the fact that the document was only evidence collateral to the issue, was no excuse for its non-production.[6] But, with this exception, the other excuses for non-production, which were applicable to the doctrine of profert, were applied to this rule of evidence. It is clear that the establishment of the rule and its exceptions at the close of the seventeenth century, will give rise, in the eighteenth century, to rules as to the secondary evidence admissible in the excepted cases, and an elaboration of the law as to the scope of these cases.

In this way the law acquired a body of doctrine as to the manner in which documentary evidence must be produced to the court. We must now turn to the history of the rules as to the effect of this evidence when admitted.

(3) *The rules governing the effect of documentary evidence.*

In our modern law it is the rule that, if the parties to any transaction have embodied their intentions in a document or a series of documents, no evidence may be given of the terms of the transaction except the document itself, or secondary evidence of its contents, when such evidence is admissible. Nor can the terms of the document be contradicted, altered, added to, or varied, by oral evidence.[7] This is not a primitive principle. In fact it was

---

[1] Above 172 n. 5.

[2] "Under Lord Holt the first quarter of the eighteenth century finds the rule (coincidently with its progress in civil cases) regularly acknowledged in practice, and applied to all kinds of writings," Wigmore, op. cit. ii 1389-1390, § 1177, and cases cited in n. 22.

[3] Vol. i 336; Wigmore, op. cit. ii 1388, § 1177.

[4] Below 217-219; as Wigmore says (op. cit. ii 1388, § 1177), "the contrast would come to be between a document actually produced by a witness and a document merely spoken of by him; and the latter practice would be regarded as irregular."

[5] Wigmore, op. cit. ii 1387-1388, § 1177.

[6] Cole v. Gibson 1 Ves. Sen. at p. 505, cited Wigmore, op. cit. ii 1502, § 1252.

[7] Stephen, Digest of the Law of Evidence 95.

not fully established much before the latter half of the seventeenth century; and the provisions of the Statute of Frauds had something to do with the modern scope of the rule.[1]

That it was not a primitive principle is shown by the rules as to the effect of the production of the sealed documents—the records and the deeds—which have been already described. If these documents were adduced as a conclusive proof, they were much more than mere evidence. The party who was not prepared to deny their genuineness was absolutely bound—he was estopped.[2] If, on the other hand, they were adduced as evidence merely, they could be rebutted by other evidence. We have seen that the contrast between the use of these documents as proof which produced an estoppel, and their use merely as evidence, was brought out by the rule that, if they affected to witness a conveyance, they did nothing more than furnish rebuttable evidence as to the livery of seisin, which was the essential feature of the conveyance.[3] Hence it followed that, whatever were the provisions of the deed, the circumstances accompanying the livery of seisin could be proved by other evidence.[4] Thus Littleton says[5] that "if a man make a deed of feoffment to another, and in the deed there is no condition etc., and when the feoffor will make livery of seisin unto him by force of the same deed, he makes livery of seisin unto him upon certain conditions; in this case nothing of the tenements passeth by the deed, for that the condition is not comprised within the deed, and the feoffment is in like force as if no such deed had been made." On the other hand, it is clear from other passages in Littleton that, if it was necessary to prove that a person holding an estate in fee in tail or for life, held it subject to a condition, he must produce a record or a deed. This, Littleton said, was "common learning."[6] It is true that it was still possible that a jury might find that there was such a condition; and that, if they so found, the condition would be enforced.[7] But it is clear that, when he wrote, the law

---

[1] Wigmore, op. cit. iv 3411, § 2426.

[2] Above 147-148, 154-155.   [3] Above 164-165.

[4] "The essential working conception is the livery of seisin, not the charter. Whatever virtue there is in the writing is testimonial only. It furnishes one sort of proof but it is not a necessary kind of proof, and the main thing is something done apart from the writing. *This indenture* merely *witnesseth;* and the now time-worn phrase was once the actual conception," Wigmore, op. cit. iv 3415, § 2426.

[5] § 359.

[6] "Also a man cannot plead in any action that an estate was made in fee, or in fee tail, or for term of life, upon condition, if he doth not vouch a record of this, or shew a writing under seal, proving the same condition. For it is a common learning that a man by plea shall not defeat any estate of freehold by force of any such condition, unless he showeth the proof of the condition in writing, unless it be in some special cases," § 365; possibly Littleton had in his mind the distinction drawn in Y.B. 6 Ed. II. (S.S.) 1312-1313 (vol. xiv) 95 that "the tenant might aver the assignment without showing a deed, but in case of a demandant it would be necessary for him to show specialty."   [7] § 366.

was tending to require that all such conditions should be proved by a record or a deed.[1]

Probably the technical reason, by which this result was reached, was the idea that mere words or unsealed writings were inferior to deeds or records; and that nothing of an inferior kind should be allowed to interfere with the contents of documents of a superior kind.[2] This principle, as Professor Wigmore has pointed out, took many forms. As applied to the dissolution of contracts, it had been connected, since the days of Bracton, with the Roman principle "quod eisdem modis dissolvitur obligatio quæ nascitur ex contractu vel quasi, quibus contrahitur."[3] As applied to the law of evidence, it obviously prevented the variation of deeds by extrinsic evidence. "The sealed instrument will not merely *prove* the transaction, but rather by replacement will now *be* the transaction."[4] And this idea was the more easily applied in this way since, in some cases, the deed might operate as an estoppel, in which case it was conclusive proof.[5] Both the idea that the deed was the transaction, and the analogy of the effect of a deed in producing an estoppel, would naturally help towards the establishment of the rule that no extrinsic evidence could be admissible to vary its contents.

It may well be that, in the fifteenth century, this result had not been fully established. Littleton's somewhat inconsistent dicta would seem to indicate that the law was not quite settled.[6] But the technical reasons in favour of the rule that no extrinsic evidence was admissible were strong; and they were backed up by even stronger substantial reasons. Firstly, "the community was becoming more generally lettered, and this in its turn had resulted from the spread of the printing process in the late fifteenth century. Reading and writing were no longer the mysterious arts of a few. It was natural to hold that a man was bound by his written version of the transaction, when he might easily guard himself against the writings being deficient in some of the agreed terms."[7] Secondly, mercantile custom was making for the modern rule.[8] The parties were not allowed to offer evidence to dispute those bills and notes and policies which, in the sixteenth century,

---

[1] "Jeo scay bien que si jeo face a vous un fait sur certein condition, et livre le fait a vous, et vous usez le fait envers moy contrarie al condition, jeo n'aurai jamais avantage de les conditions, sans que j'ay eux en escripts, et ce sera adjuge ma folie demesne que jeo ne voulois le avoir fait escrier," Y.B. 8 Hy. VI. Hil. pl. 15 *per* Babington, J.

[2] Wigmore, op. cit. iv 3418, § 2426.

[3] Vol. ii 277 and n. 10; in the Countess of Rutland's Case (1605) 5 Co. Rep. at f. 26a this aspect of the matter is put forward as another reason against allowing a deed to be varied by parol evidence, see below 176 n. 3.

[4] Wigmore, op. cit. iv 3418, § 2426.

[5] Above 174; Wigmore, op. cit. iv 3416, § 2426.

[6] Ibid, and authorities cited in n, 24.

[7] Ibid.

[8] Above 154-155.

were beginning to be known to the lawyers.[1] Thirdly, the fact
that, during the sixteenth and seventeenth centuries, the jury was
in a transition stage, emphasized the need for such a rule. The
jury had ceased to have a first hand aquaintance with the facts
in issue, and yet they could still find a verdict from their own
knowledge.[2] The same reasons which made it expedient that all
documents should be produced openly in court, made it expedient
that they should not be allowed to be varied by oral testimony.
The judges could control the admission and the interpretation of
written evidence. They could not control the effect upon the
mind of the jury of loose oral averments, which might be merely
stated by the pleader.[3]

It is clear that, just as considerations of policy had led the
courts to extend the principle underlying the doctrine of profert,
and to develop from it the rule that documents given in evidence
must be produced;[4] so, similar conditions led them to apply the
rule that a deed could not be varied by the extrinsic evidence of
unsealed documents. In the sixteenth century the provisions of
the statute of Wills[5] brought such unsealed documents more prominently before the courts; and, in the seventeenth century, the
growth of the commercial jurisdiction of the common law courts
multiplied their number. A further large addition was made by
the Statute of Frauds;[6] and we have seen that it was the need
to get some certain evidence, which was the main reason for
requiring writing as the condition of the validity of the large and
varied list of transactions dealt with by the statute.[7] Among
other things, the statute rendered it impossible to create a freehold interest in land by livery of seisin unaccompanied by a
writing; and thus it abolished the possibility of the situation
which, in older days, had helped to emphasize the merely
evidential character of a sealed document, and the possibility of
proving by extrinsic evidence that it was wholly inoperative.[8]
Thus it is clear that in this and the other cases to which the statute applied, it made for the extension of the rule that the contents
of written documents cannot be varied by oral evidence. As

---

[1] Vol. viii 168, 175.   [2] Vol. i 336, 346.

[3] " The will concerning lands ought to be in writing, and the constructions of wills
ought to be collected from the words of the will in writing, and not by any averment
out of it; for it would be full of inconvenience, that none should know by the written
words of a will, what construction to make or advice to give, but it should be controlled
by collateral averments out of the will," Lord Cheyney's Case (1592) 5 Co. Rep. at
f. 68b *per* Wray and Anderson, C.JJ.; " it would be inconvenient that matters in writing
made by advice and on consideration . . . should be controlled by averment of the
parties to be proved by the uncertain testimony of slippery memory," Countess of
Rutland's Case (1605) 5 Co. Rep. at ff. 26a, 26b; see also Altham's Case (1611) 8 Co.
Rep. at ff. 155a, 155b.

[4] Above 173.   [5] Vol. iv 465.   [6] Vol. vi 384-386.
[7] Ibid 388-390.   [8] Above 164-165, 174.

Professor Wigmore has pointed out, "the moral and logical influence of the Statute was wide and immediate"; for it "now began to be appealed to in all questions of 'parol evidence,' as setting an example and typifying a general principle."[1] The result of this was that the rule began, in the eighteenth century, to be extended from cases where writing was required by law, to cases where the parties had voluntarily put their transactions into writing;[2] and so it attained its modern dimensions.

From the first, however, the rule admitted of exceptions and modifications. "Non est factum" was always a good plea to a deed;[3] and, in the sixteenth century, it was admitted that the effect even of the sacred fine could be nullified by the proof of fraud or illegality.[4] Moreover, as the practice of merely averring facts in the pleadings decayed, and the practice of summoning witnesses to give oral evidence on oath spread;[5] and as the idea that the jury could find a verdict from its own knowledge decayed, and as the fact that it relied solely on evidence documentary or oral became more obvious;[6] there was not quite the same objection to allowing modifications of the strict rule as in the earlier days. Hence, in the late sixteenth and seventeenth centuries, we begin to get some small development in the law as to the facts which could be proved by extrinsic evidence, though the transaction had been reduced to writing. But we cannot usefully consider this development, till we have considered the growth of the modern rules as to the competence and the compellability of the witnesses by whom this evidence was given, and as to the admissibility of the evidence which they offered. These two matters will be dealt with in the two succeeding sections.

Witnesses—how far Competent and Compellable

Early law knows the preappointed witness—the secta which appears to back a plaintiff's claim,[7] the witnesses who have affixed their seals to a writing,[8] and the official transaction witnesses.[9] All these witnesses will appear to testify to the facts to which they have agreed or have been appointed to testify—to the genuineness of the plaintiff's claim, to the genuineness of the writing, or to the fact of the sale or other disposition of property. But early law knows no witnesses of the modern type—no witnesses who can be compelled to disclose facts known to them, in order to assist the

---

[1] Op. cit. iv 3420, § 2426; see Falkland v. Bertie (1696) 2 Vern. at p. 339, and Strode v. Russell (1708) ibid at pp. 624-625, cited by Wigmore, loc. cit. n. 43.

[2] Ibid op. cit. iv 3421, § 2426, citing Lilly's Practical Register 48—a book of the year 1719.

[3] See Y.B. 8 Hy. VI. Hil. pl. 15; below 220.

[4] Vol. vii 33-34.   [5] Below 183-185.   [6] Vol. i 335-336.

[7] Ibid 300-301.   [8] Above 167-168.   [9] Vol. ii 81.

court to come to a conclusion as to the facts in issue in a case. For, as we have seen, such a conclusion was reached, not by a process of reasoning from evidence, but by some one of several alternative forms of proof selected by the plaintiff or the court, after the parties had stated their respective cases in the right form, and in accordance with the elaborate rules of procedure.[1] There was therefore no place for witnesses of the modern type in early law. And though, with the legal renaissance of the thirteenth century, and with the replacement of the older modes of proof by the jury, evidence of the modern type became possible; though, as we have seen, the documentary evidence of sealed writings was already common in the earliest of the Year Books,[2] the oral evidence of witnesses does not begin to make its appearance with any frequency till the sixteenth century. The reason for this phenomenon must be sought, partly in the survival of old ideas as to a trial which were fostered by the part played by the jury during the mediæval period,[3] and partly in the disordered state of the country in the fourteenth and fifteenth centuries.[4] It was not until the jury had obviously ceased to give a verdict from their own knowledge, it was not until the peace of the country had been restored by the Tudors, that witnesses of the modern type were recognized as the ordinary accompaniment of a jury trial, and that legislative provision was made for compelling them to appear and testify.[5] It was not till then that a body of law could be developed as to the competency of witnesses, and as to the circumstances under which exceptions could be made from the now general rule, that a person could be compelled to testify to facts which were within his knowledge. Therefore, before the history of these rules can be related, it is necessary to trace the steps by which the changed ideas as to the nature of a trial, which came with and were developed by the substitution of the jury for the older modes of proof, at length gave rise to the oral evidence of witnesses, as it had already given rise to documentary evidence.

The functions of the old pre-appointed witnesses were rigidly defined. The secta swore to their belief in the plaintiff's claim; the witnesses to the deed to its genuineness; and the transaction witnesses to the sale which they had been called to witness. "When the witness was adduced he came merely in order that he might swear to a set formula. His was no promissory oath to tell the truth in answer to questions, but an assertory oath."[6] They did not supply evidence upon which the court could decide, but proof of the particular facts to which they were called upon to

---

[1] Vol. i 302-311; vol. ii 520-521, 554. [2] Above 164-166.
[3] Below 181. [4] Below 181-183.
[5] Below 184-185. [6] P. and M. ii 599.

WITNESSES

testify. The best illustrations of this manner of regarding them can be found, firstly in the fact that a trial by witnesses was recognized in the older law,[1] and secondly in the practice, to which I have already alluded, of joining the witnesses to a deed to the jury when the point at issue was the genuineness of the deed.[2] The existence of the trial by witnesses was a recognition of the fact that they were a mode of proof as conclusive as battle, compurgation, or ordeal; and, since the testimony of these witnesses supplied a proof of the genuineness of the deed, since therefore its effect could hardly be distinguished from the verdict of the jury, it was natural to take a joint verdict from both jury and witnesses.[3]

There was thus no place for the modern witness in the old system of procedure, according to which trials were conducted by means of fixed methods of proof. And this fact was emphasized by two connected principles which rendered the modern use of witnesses legally impossible. The first of these principles was that no one ought to be convicted of a capital crime by mere testimony.[4] The second was that a witness was neither competent nor compellable to testify to a fact, "unless when that fact happened, he was solemnly taken to witness."[5] Both profoundly influenced the development of the mediæval common law on this topic.

The first of these principles is at the root of that refusal to compel directly an accused person to submit the question of his guilt or innocence to a jury, which gave rise to the clumsy and barbarous expedient of the peine fort et dure.[6] It was too serious a break with tradition to punish a man capitally, who, without his own consent, "had been allowed no chance of proving his innocence by any of the world-old sacral processes."[7] The second of these principles is illustrated by a case of 1291-1292,[8] in which the king attempted to compel certain magnates to take an oath as to the existence of certain facts. All of them asserted that it was a thing unheard of that they should be thus compelled to swear; and, in spite of repeated attempts to get them to change their minds, they persisted in their refusal to take the oath without a consultation

---

[1] Vol. i 302-305.   [2] Above 167, 168, 169.

[3] "They were summoned with the jurors, and they did not testify openly in court, but went out with the jurors to deliberate and give information to them; so that they bore the character for a long period of half jurors half witnesses," Wigmore, op. cit. iv 2959, § 2190.

[4] "Nemo de capitalibus placitis testimonio convincatur," Leg. Henr. xxxi 5.

[5] P. and M. ii 599; Wigmore, op. cit. iv § 2190.   [6] Vol. i 326-327.

[7] P. and M. ii 647; the idea that a conviction by a jury was a conviction by the testimony of witnesses comes out strongly in Fortescue's De Laudibus c. 26, when, after explaining the system of trial by jury, he commends it as a trial by witnesses, who are substantial men "of good name and fame and of honest report, not brought into court by the partie, but by a worshipful and indifferent officer chosen and so compelled to come before the judge," below 203-205, 210; cp. also the Mirror of Justices v 5 §§ 19, 126, 127, cited Thayer, op. cit. 57.

[8] Plac. Abbrev. 227b, cited Thayer, op. cit. 56.

with their peers.[1] As late as 1455 it was said in argument that "no one can compel another to swear with him."[2] This, indeed, was said in reference to compurgators; but it is clear that it was equally applicable to ordinary witnesses. The only witnesses that appear to have been compellable in the later mediæval period were the witnesses to a deed—that is witnesses who by appending their signatures to the deed had agreed to testify.[3]

There is nothing remarkable in the existence of these principles at an early period in the history of the common law. What is re-markable is their long survival. It is probable, indeed, that if the influence of lawyers of the school of Bracton had continued, they would not have survived. We have seen that Bracton was quite prepared to override the older rules and compel a man to be tried by a jury;[4] and it would seem that he and his fellows tried to rationalize the secta by treating them as witnesses and examining them,[5] and that they tried also to make something of the old trial by witnesses.[6] It is clear that the canonist theories of evidence were in the air—Bracton knew something of the full and the half proof which was recognized in that law.[7] No doubt if these in-fluences had continued English law would have acquired a set of rules as to witnesses and their evidence at a much earlier date than it actually did acquire them.

But, if it had thus acquired this set of rules, it could hardly have escaped a procedure modelled on that of the canon law, which would have left no room for the jury. The jury would have been treated as witnesses; and, at a later date, the wish to reconcile the rules as to the strict proof required by the law, with the need to suppress crime, would have introduced into England, as into other states, the use of torture as a regular part of the judicial pro-cedure.[8] Fortunately this danger was avoided; but at the price of a much slower development of the use of witnesses and their testimony than would otherwise have been the case. Hence, in the first half of the seventeenth century, we get the phenomenon

---

[1] " Dictum est ex parte Domini Regis Johanni de Hastinges et omnibus aliis mag-natibus supra nominatis quod, pro statu et jure regni et pro conservacione dignitatis coronæ et pacis suæ apponant manum ad librum ad faciendum id quod eis ex parte Domini Regis injungeretur, qui omnes unanimiter respondent quod inauditum est quod ipsi vel eorum antecessores hactenus in hujus modi casu ad præstandum aliquod sacrum coacti fuerunt etc. Et licet præfato Johanni et aliis magnatibus expositum fuisset . . . ac pluries eisdem magnatibus ex parte ipsius Regis conjunctim et separa-tim, libroque eis porrecto, injunctum est quod faciant sacramentum, responderunt de-mum omnes singillatim quod nichil inde facerent sine consideracione parium suorum," Plac. Abbrev. 227b.

[2] Y.B. 33 Hy. VI. Hil. pl. 23 (p. 8) *per* Nedham.   [3] Above 167, 169.
[4] Vol. i 326.   [5] P. and M. ii 607 n. 7.
[6] Bracton's Note Book, Case 1115; P. and M. ii. 635; vol. i 303-304.
[7] Vol. ii 284.
[8] Vol. i 304, 315-316, 318, 320; vol. v 170-175; P. and M. ii 656-657.

noted by Hudson[1] that "the books of the common law do yield small direction for examination of witnesses, and the civilians are therein far too copious." That this, or indeed almost any price, would have been trivial compared with the evil avoided was the opinion of Fortescue;[2] and it is obvious to all who know anything of the history of progressive deterioration of the continental criminal procedure.[3]

The jury, therefore, and not the canonical procedure, took the place of the old forms of proof; and the jury was treated by the judges as they treated those proofs.[4] Thus, though in a sense the jurors were witnesses, they were much more than witnesses. They were a test to which the parties had consented; and they represented the voice of the country-side. Therefore, they could not be separately examined.[5] They could only be asked to give a verdict which would conclude the case. How they got their knowledge it was not the business of the court to inquire. It is clear that this method of treating the jury will make for the preservation of many of the old ideas as to the nature of a trial, and will prevent any borrowing from the canonist rules of evidence. It will therefore entail a relatively slow development of a law of evidence.

But, it will be said, this does not wholly account for the late appearance in the common law of the modern witness, and the oral testimony of these witnesses. We have seen that the fact that the jury was a body of reasonable men, made it impossible to treat them quite in the same way as the older modes of proof, and produced those changes in the law of pleading,[6] and that use of documentary evidence,[7] which substituted the modern for the old conception of a trial. We shall see also that these changes led to the use of witnesses of the modern type, and of oral evidence, in certain cases.[8] It is significant that, in old collections of oaths, a witnesses' oath to tell the truth in answer to questions is found.[9] But it is quite clear that they did not lead, in the mediæval period, to any change in the old principle that a person could not be compelled to testify, nor to any such general use of oral as was made in that period of documentary evidence. The reason for this difference is, I think, to be found in the fact that the development of the law, in the direction of the free admission of the oral evidence of witnesses, was retarded by the disorderly state of the country in the fourteenth and fifteenth centuries. These conditions reacted, both on the double position of the jury as

[1] Star Chamber 210. [2] De Laudibus c. 22. [3] Vol. v 170-175.
[4] Vol. i 318. [5] Vol. i 317; P. and M. ii 624-651, 655-656.
[6] Vol. iii 613, 633. [7] Above 168. [8] Below 183-184.
[9] P. and M. ii 625 n. 6, citing the Court Baron (S.S.) 77.

witnesses and finders of the facts, and on the absence of any rules
as to how the jurors could inform themselves, and so gave rise to
all sorts of irregular methods of influencing the jury.[1]   In their
endeavour to cope with this evil the courts laid down rules which
tended to discourage oral testimony, and so retarded the growth
of this branch of the law.

We have seen that maintenance and conspiracy were crying
evils of the time ;[2] and that, by these practices, persons were able
to use the law courts, instead of the arms of their retainers, to
prosecute their feuds whenever they thought this course desirable.[3]
Nothing was easier than to get a partial jury ; and, as the verdict
of the jurors was given as the result of their own knowledge or inquiries, it was natural that they should get their instructions from
the side whom they favoured.[4]   The remedy for this state of
things, suggested in a Parliamentary petition of 1354, was that
all the evidence should be openly produced at the bar, and that,
after the jury had been charged and had departed from the bar,
no person should be allowed to confer with them.[5]   But this
remedy was plainly insufficient.   In the first place, it did not
prevent the jury from giving a verdict in accordance with its
pre-conceived ideas.   In the second place, it did not prevent
persons, who were in a position to intimidate the jury, from
coming forward and giving evidence at the bar in such a way as to
make it quite plain to the jury what the consequences of a hostile
verdict might be.   To meet this difficulty we have seen that the
courts so stretched the conception of maintenance, that a witness
who, without having any interest or cause to meddle in the
litigation, volunteered his testimony, rendered himself liable to be
proceeded against for this offence.[6]

The result was that the survival of the old ideas relating to
trials, combined with these measures taken by the courts to
suppress maintenance, to retard the appearance of the modern
witness.   In fact, the causes which operated to produce this effect
are very similar to the causes which led the common law to refuse

[1] Vol. i 334-335.
[2] Vol. iii 394-407 ; vol. v. 201-203 ; vol. vii 524-525 ; vol. viii 397-398.
[3] Vol. ii 416.   [4] R.P. ii 259 (27 Ed. III. no. 30).
[5] Ibid, cited Thayer, op. cit. 124-125.
[6] Vol. i 335; vol. iii 398 ; Thayer, op. cit. 125-129 ; see Y.B. 11 Hy. VI. Pasch. pl.
36 (p. 41) *per* Cheyne, C.J., cited Thayer, op. cit. 126-127 ; in Y.B. 22 Hy. VI. Mich. pl.
7 (p. 5) Paston said, " A ce que est dit il n'est maintenance de mettre al Jure le verity
del matter ; *casu quod sic et casu quod non* : car si celui que rien ad a meler ove le
matter, et que n'est erudite de le Ley veut mettre al Jure ou al party meme, ou a son
counsel le verity del matter, et apprent evidence de le matter, et ce sibien et circum-
stancialment come un que fuit erudite de Ley scavoit, uncore ce est un maintenance
en son person ; " clearly it was only if a person had the sort of interest in the proceedings which would be a defence to an action for maintenance that he could give
evidence.

to allow any relaxation of its rule that choses in action were not assignable. In both cases primitive juridical ideas combined with the fear of maintenance to preserve in the common law rules and institutions which were fast ceasing to correspond with the more advanced juridical needs and ideas of the time.[1] We have seen that, at the close of the Middle Ages, the merchants had begun to circumvent the rule of the common law that choses in action of a contractual kind could not be assigned, by the device of making the assignee the attorney of the assignor; and that, in the fifteenth century, the validity of this device had been recognized by the common law courts.[2] Similarly, as we shall now see, all through the mediæval period, the courts, in certain cases, were beginning to make use of the testimony of witnesses of the modern type. These cases illustrate the manner in which the old ideas were being gradually undermined, and pave the way for the recognition by the Legislature in 1562 of the necessity for compelling witnesses to come forward to testify to the court.

Firstly, the court, from an early period, would sometimes hear witnesses on matters which turned on its own procedure, or on the conduct of its officers. Thus, challenges to jurors were tried in this way. The triers of the challenge, "generally two of the unchallenged jurors, might question the challenged men on oath, and might be sworn and charged to say whether these were telling the truth."[3] As early as Edward I.'s reign, there is a case in which the evidence of a gaolor and fellow prisoners was taken on the question whether a confession had been extorted by duress.[4] Secondly, we have seen that evidence was, in the Middle Ages and later, constantly averred by counsel in their pleadings;[5] and both Fortescue[6] and the Year Books[7] show that these averments were sometimes backed up by the oral evidence of witnesses. The court sometimes expressly allowed a witness to testify,[8] and this permission was a defence to subsequent proceedings for

---

[1] Vol. vii 524-525, 532-534.　　　　　　　[2] Ibid 534; vol. viii 147.

[3] Thayer, op. cit. 123.

[4] P. and M. ii 651, citing Y.B. 30, 31 Ed. I. (R.S.) 543.

[5] Vol. iii 638; as Thayer, op. cit. 121, points out, in 1571 (Newis v. Lark Plowden 407) in a famous demurrer upon evidence in an assize of novel disseisin, there is a long set of recitals of what William Bendloe, the plaintiff's serjeant, "said in evidence," and "gave in evidence," and "showed in evidence."

[6] De Laudibus c. 26—"then may either party bring before the same justices and sworn men all and singular such witnesses on his behalf as he will produce, who by the justices being charged upon the holy gospel of God, shall testifie all things proving the truth of the fact whereupon the parties contend."

[7] See the analysis of the case in Longo Quinto 58 given by Thayer, op. cit. 133-134.

[8] E.g. in Y.B. 21 Ed. IV. Mich. pl. 1 the reporter tells us that, "un home offra luy destre jure que il fuit present al temps del liverie d'un des releases," and that Brian, C.J., said, "jeo ne voille luy compeller a ceo, mes s'il voille de gree il sera resceu—per que il fuit jure et appose, et il testifie come devant,"

maintenance.[1]　It is only gradually that these averments made by counsel in their pleadings, and the oral evidence of witnesses, were disintegrated.[2]　But it is clear that, either through the statements of counsel, or through the testimony of witnesses, oral evidence was brought to the notice of the court at the latter part of the mediæval period.　We should note, too, that the idea that the court could permit witnesses to testify, and that this permission protected them from proceedings for maintenance, helped to give the court a strict control over them.　The court naturally wished to keep them under its eye, so that it was not difficult to hold at a later period that evidence given to a jury out of court avoided the trial.[3]　Thirdly, there is one instance from the year 1235, in which, in a criminal case, evidence was collected from witnesses.　In that year an inquiry was made into the murder of Henry Clement, who had been sent as an envoy from some Irish nobles to the king; and evidence was taken on oath from a large number of persons.[4]　But this comes from a period when trial by jury in criminal cases was hardly as yet a settled institution; and, if this practice had become common, "indictment and trial by jury would have had to struggle for existence, and would very possibly have been worsted in the conflict."[5]　But we have seen that the procedure by way of indictment and trial by jury soon became common; and that, in the fourteenth and fifteenth centuries, Parliament frequently objected to the application to criminal cases of a different procedure by the Council.[6]

It was the application of the criminal procedure of the Council to a mass of cases in which the common law was defective or could not be enforced,[7] and the great extension of this jurisdiction in the Tudor period,[8] which familiarized the law with a criminal procedure in which the oral evidence of witnesses was freely used.　At the same time the system of procedure in the Chancery was familiarizing the law with the use of such witnesses in civil cases;[9] and since both the Council and the Chancery made use of the testimony of witnesses, they used the efficient process of subpœna, which had been invented by the Chancery in the course of the fourteenth century, to secure their attendance.[10]　There is at least one case in which a plaintiff asked the chancellor to subpœna a witness, in order that this subpœna might protect the witness from proceedings for maintenance.[11]　And so, when the evils which had led to the

---

[1] Y.B. 28 Hy. VI. Pasch. pl. 1 *per* Fortescue, C.J., cited vol. i 335.
[2] Vol. iii 648-650.　　　　[3] Metcalf's Case (1592) cited Cro. Eliza. at p. 411.
[4] P. and M. ii 653.　　　　[5] Ibid.　　　　[6] Vol. i 486-487.
[7] Ibid 405-406, 487.　　　[8] Ibid 504-508; vol. iv 84-87; vol. v 197-214.
[9] Ibid 285-287.　　　　[10] Wigmore, op. cit. iv 2963-2964, § 2190.
[11] Calendars of Proceedings in Chancery (R.C.) xix, cited Thayer, op. cit. 129.

undue extension of the offence of maintenance had been diminished,[1] when the testimony of witnesses had even been rendered necessary by the Legislature to secure a conviction for treason,[2] it became possible for the Legislature to recognize the importance which the oral evidence of witnesses had assumed in litigation, by providing that witnesses should be compelled to appear and testify.

The method by which the Legislature effected this change, was suggested, as Professor Wigmore has said, by the existing state of the law, "The lead was furnished by the existing qualification already noted that 'what a man does by compulsion of law cannot be called maintenance.' . . . Let an order of the judge commanding such a person's appearance be obtainable as of course before the trial, and the risk of a charge of maintenance would be removed, and no man need fear to come forward as a witness."[3] This was the course adopted. The Act of 1562-1563,[4] which, as we have seen, created the statutory offence of perjury,[5] enacted that witnesses served with process to attend and testify should be liable to a penalty if they did not appear.[6] And, though the common law courts had no compulsory process, the weapon of subpœna, which had been used by the Council and the Chancery for upwards of a century, was ready to hand, and was adopted by them.

This statute begins a new epoch in the law of evidence. Now that witnesses could be compelled to attend and testify, questions soon arose as to their competency, and as to the admission of exceptions to the general rule of compulsion. It was inevitable, also, that the more extensive use of the oral testimony of witnesses would soon bring into prominence the question of the conditions under which this testimony should be admitted. With the first of those questions I must now deal. The second will be dealt with in the ensuing section.

I shall deal firstly with the question of the competency of witnesses; and secondly with the rule that persons may generally be compelled to give evidence, and with the exceptions to that general rule.

(1) *Competency.*

In the twelfth and thirteenth centuries the canon law was developing a number of detailed rules as to the classes of persons

---

[1] Note that in Y.B. 20 Hy. VII. Mich. pl. 21 Rede, J., seems to think that, if a witness has been sworn to speak the truth, the mere fact that he has given evidence will not expose him to proceedings for maintenance; but that he will only be so liable if he has "laboured" the jury; clearly the old strictness is being somewhat relaxed.

[2] 1 Edward VI. c. 12 § 22; 5, 6 Edward VI. c. 11 § 12.

[3] Wigmore, op. cit. iv 2961, § 2190.   [4] 5 Elizabeth c. 9.

[5] Vol. iv 518.   [6] 5 Elizabeth c. 9 § 12.

whom it accounted incompetent to be witnesses ; and it was almost inevitable that many of these causes of incompetency should be applied to jurors. The general principle that these causes of incompetency could be applied to jurors is expressly recognized by Glanvil[1] and Bracton ;[2] and, as Sir John Salmond points out, the list of causes for which a juror could be challenged, which are given by Bracton, Fleta, and Britton, have obviously been influenced by the rules of the canon law.[3] Thus, "the canon law rejected the testimony of all males under fourteen and females under twelve, of the blind and the deaf and dumb, of slaves, infamous persons, and those convicted of crime, of excommunicated persons, of poor persons and women in criminal cases, of persons connected with either party by consanguinity and affinity, or belonging to the household of either party, of the enemies of either party, and of Jews, heretics and pagans."[4] Bracton tells us[5] that jurors can be challenged because they are infamous, that is if, on account of a conviction for perjury, they have "lost their law";[6] because they are friends or enemies of the parties ; because they have themselves made some claim in the subject matter of the suit ; because they are slaves ; because they are related to the parties by ties of consanguinity or affinity, or are in fact treated as one of the family of either of the parties, or are their dependants or counsellors or advocates. The application of some of these rules of the canon law to the jury, introduced some of the ideas on which these rules were founded into the common law. But, naturally, they were not applicable in their entirety, as the jury were something more than mere witnesses. Hence, as the jury developed, these rules as to the competency of jurors also developed on native lines.[7] But the fact that some of these rules, primarily applicable to witnesses, had been thus acclimatized, naturally led the lawyers of the fifteenth and sixteenth centuries to apply certain of them to the new class of witnesses who were then beginning to appear in the courts.[8]

Thus these rules of the canon law were not directly borrowed. For the most part they filtered through the rules as to the competency of jurors, which had been developed from the basis of

[1] " Excipi autem possunt juratores ipsi eisdem modis quibus et testes in curia christianitatis juste repelluntur," Bk. ii c. 12.

[2] " Eisdem enim modis amoveri possunt a sacramento quibus etiam testes amoventur a testimonio," f. 185a.

[3] Essays in Jurisprudence, 29, citing Bracton f. 185 ; Fleta Bk. 4 c. 8 ; Britton c. 53.

[4] Salmond, op. cit. 29.　　　　　[5] At f. 185a.

[6] Below 191 n. 8.

[7] Thus we get the development of rules to ensure that the jury came de visineto, vol. i 332.

[8] Salmond, op. cit. 29 ; it should be noted that Coke, Co. Litt. 6a and 6b, treats together of the disqualification of witnesses and jurors.

these rules in the Middle Ages. It is true that certain of the ideas of the civilians and canonists were introduced into the procedure of the Star Chamber[1] and the Chancery.[2] But English lawyers never attempted to borrow them wholesale; and it is clear that the rules of evidence which the civilians and canonists had developed were, certainly in criminal cases in which torture was freely used,[3] wholly alien to the feelings of Englishmen.[4] Thus, when the frequent use of witnesses compelled the courts to consider the question of their competency, they were able to assume a very free hand in shaping the law on this matter. Both with respect to the question of the competency of witnesses, and with respect to the rules as to the admissibility of their evidence,[5] they developed the law on native lines. Hence, although through the rules relating to the disqualification of jurors, some of the ideas of the canonists reappear at second hand, there was never any attempt to borrow directly from their rules, and to introduce the long list of disqualifications which had been elaborated by them. Rather, the various causes of incapacity recognized in the case of jurors, were reconsidered, and applied with important modifications to witnesses.[6] Thus a new and original set of rules as to the varieties of persons incompetent to testify, was gradually elaborated during the sixteenth and seventeenth centuries.

These rules can be grouped under two main heads : (i) Cases of natural, and (ii) cases of artificial incapacity.

(i) *Cases of natural incapacity.*

English law recognized fewer cases of natural incapacity than the canon law ; and their history can be briefly related.

(*a*) Unlike the laws of countries which followed the civil and canon law, English law has never known any general disqualification of women. It is possible, indeed, that they were excluded in certain cases—e.g. "to prove a man to be a villein."[7] But this probably refers to the old trial by witnesses ;[8] and, as Professor Wigmore points out, Coke, when he is enumerating the various cases of incapacity,[9] does not include among them any incapacity

---

[1] Vol. v 184, 191, 193.　　　　[2] Ibid 285.　　　　[3] Ibid 174-175.

[4] Ibid 185, 194 ; and see the preamble to the statute of 28 Henry VIII. c. 15, cited vol. i 550-551.

[5] Below 211-219.

[6] "But oftentimes a man may be challenged to be of a jury that cannot be challenged to be a witness," Co. Litt. 6b.

[7] "In some cases women are by law wholly excluded to bear testimony, as to prove a man to be a villein," ibid.

[8] Wigmore, op. cit. i 646, § 517 n. 2.

[9] "Regularly he that loseth liberam legem becometh infamous and can be no witness. Or if the witness be an infidel, or of non sane memorie, or not of discretion, or a party interested, or the like, . . . Though the witness be of nearest alliance or

based on sex. (*b*) Insanity, in Coke's day, created an absolute bar to testimonial capacity;[1] and Hale lays down the same general rule.[2] There was also a rebuttable presumption, when Hale wrote, that a deaf and dumb person was insane.[3] But this presumption disappeared in the nineteenth century;[4] and, in the course of the same century, the absolute disqualification of an insane person gave place to the more rational rule, that he is only disqualified if he is prevented by his insanity, "from recollecting the matter on which he is to testify, from understanding the question put to him, from giving rational answers to those questions, or from knowing that he ought to speak the truth."[5] (*c*) Infants below a certain age were, like insane persons, absolutely incapable because they "wanted discretion."[6] It would seem that Coke put this age at fourteen. Probably it was fixed by analogy to other branches of the law;[7] and the same analogy tended to produce the belief that a child below the age of seven was as incapable of being a witness as of incurring criminal liability.[8] The impossibility of *mens rea* was thought to connote the impossibility of understanding the nature of an oath. But, when Hale wrote, the law was being modified. As early as the sixteenth century, the evidence of infants in certain offences against the person of a sexual character, had been allowed;[9] and, though Hale repeats the rule that "regularly an infant under fourteen years is not to be examined upon his oath as a witness,"[10] he adds that "the condition of his person, as if he be intelligent, or the nature of the fact, may allow an examination of one under that age"; and he cites cases where this had been allowed in cases of treason and witchcraft.[11] Moreover, though he did not approve of a child under twelve being examined upon oath,[12] he approved of hearing their testimony without oath, "which possibly being fortified with concurrent evidences may be of some weight, as in cases of rape, buggery, witchcraft, and such crimes which are practised upon children."[13] It seems to have been partly the influence of the practice in crimes of this character, and partly the growing appreciation of the fact that an infant under fourteen may well be able to understand the

kindred or of counsel or tenant or servant to either party (or any other exception that maketh him not infamous, or to want understanding or discretion, or a party in interest) though it be proved true, shall not exclude the witness to be sworn, but he shall be sworn, and his credit upon the exceptions taken against him left to those of the jury who are triers of the fact," Co. Litt. 6b.

[1] Co. Litt. 6b; Wigmore, op. cit. i 630, § 492.

[2] P.C. ii 278—he adds, "it is a difficulty scarcely to be cleared what is the *minimum, quod sic* disables the party."

[3] Ibid i 34.   [4] Wigmore, op. cit. i 635, § 498.

[5] Stephen, Digest art. 107; Wigmore, op. cit. i 630, § 492.

[6] Co. Litt. 6b.   [7] Wigmore, op. cit. iii 2356, § 1821.

[8] Vol. iii 372.   [9] Hale P.C. i 302.   [10] Ibid.

[11] Ibid.   [12] Ibid ii 283.   [13] Ibid; cp. ibid i 634.

nature of an oath, which, when Blackstone wrote, had given rise to the more flexible rule that "infants of any age are to be heard ; and if they have any idea of an oath to be also sworn; it being found by experience that infants of very tender years often give the clearest and truest testimony."[1] Thus in the case of infants the law arrived at the conclusion that incapacity must depend upon the individual—that it must be subjective rather than objective—sooner than in the case of the insane. It should be noted, also, that infancy was one of the first cases in which the lawyers seem to have perceived the impolicy of a rule which incapacitated a witness on account of some defect, when all that was required was a due attention to the manner in which this defect might affect the weight of his evidence. Blackstone points out this distinction in this connection;[2] but, as we shall now see, it was not till the legislation of the nineteenth century that this principle was applied to some of the most important of the cases of artificial incapacity.

(ii) *Cases of artificial incapacity.*

The fact that oral evidence has always been given under the sanction of an oath, has, at many different times and in many different places, imported a religious or a moral element into the law, which has led to the disqualification, at different periods, of several distinct classes of persons. It is true that the theory of the precise nature of the sanction of the oath has varied. "The theory of the oath in modern common law may be termed a subjective one, in contrast to the earlier one, which may be termed objective. The oath is not a summoning of Divine vengeance upon false swearing, whereby, when the spectators see the witness standing unharmed, they know that the Divine judgment has pronounced him to be a truth teller ; but a method of reminding the witness strongly of the Divine punishment somewhere in store for false swearing, and thus of putting him in a frame of mind calculated to speak only the truth as he saw it."[3] The earlier view was well to the fore in the seventeenth, but the later view had practically prevailed by the beginning of the nineteenth century.[4] But, whichever view is adopted, it is clear that the solemnity of the religious sanction imports a reference to religion and morals, which cannot but affect men's ideas as to the competency of witnesses. It is due directly to this cause that we get incapacities

[1] Bl. Comm. iv 214.
[2] "There may be therefore in many cases of this nature witnesses who are competent, that is who may be admitted to be heard ; and yet, after being heard, may prove not to be credible, or such as the jury is bound to believe," ibid ; Coke, above 187 n. 9, had pointed out the distinction in connection with the rule that witnesses, who were related to the parties, were competent.
[3] Wigmore, op. cit. iii 2349, § 1816.
[4] Ibid, and see note 2 for some belated instances of the older view.

based on religious grounds, and on the ground of the moral character of the proposed witness. Indirectly also this cause helped to extend, and to secure the long duration of the incapacity, based upon the fact that the proposed witness was a party to or interested in the litigation; for, though the canonical reason that persons ought not to be put under the temptation of committing the mortal sin of perjury, may not have been the direct cause of this kind of incapacity,[1] a similar idea probably helped to establish it;[2] and the canonical reason was given for it in the eighteenth and nineteenth centuries.[3]

We can see nowadays clearly enough that, though all these various causes may affect the weight of a witness's evidence, they should not render him incompetent to testify. But that was not the point of view of the canon law, and, as we have seen, the canon law rules had influenced many of the rules as to the incapacity of jurors. It is true that if jurors are regarded as judges of fact, these causes afford valid reasons for incapacitating persons affected by them. But, in the sixteenth, and even in the seventeenth century, jurors had not wholly put off their character of witnesses.[4] It was therefore almost inevitable that the courts, when they were called on to consider the question of the competency of witnesses, should apply to them some of the rules which had been applied to determine the competency of jurors. The fact that these rules were in substantial agreement with the rules of the civil and canon law naturally seemed to confirm their reasonableness. It was not realized that this agreement was due, historically, to the manner in which most of the rules as to the competency of jurors had, in the twelfth and thirteenth centuries, been derived from the canon law; and the double capacity of jurors as witnesses and judges of fact prevented the lawyers from realizing that what were good grounds for incapacitating a man from serving as a juror, were not equally good grounds for refusing to allow him to testify as a witness. Thus these various causes for the incompetency of witnesses gained a foothold in the law, became the centres of bodies of technical learning, and lasted in most cases till the statutory changes of the nineteenth century.

Let us examine briefly the incapacities based (*a*) on religious grounds; (*b*) on moral grounds; and (*c*) on the ground of interest in the litigation.

(*a*) It seems to have been the opinion of Coke that it was only a person who could call on the God believed in by the Christian to attest his veracity, who could take a valid oath; and that, therefore, it was only a Christian who could be a competent wit-

---

[1] Below 193-195.
[2] Below 194-195.
[3] Below 196.
[4] Vol. i 336, 346.

ness.[1] But Coke's intellectual outlook was often very mediæval; and shortly after he wrote commercial considerations helped to give a decisive weight to the counter considerations of reason and tolerance. "I take it," says Hale,[2] "that altho' the regular oath, as it is allowed by the laws of England, is *tactis sacrosanctis Dei evangeliis*, which supposeth a man to be a Christian, yet in cases of necessity, as in forein contracts between merchant and merchant, which are many times transacted between Jewish brokers, the testimony of a Jew *tacto libro legis Mosaicae* is not to be rejected, and is used, as I have been informed, among all nations." Even in Spain the oaths of infidels who swore by their gods were admitted.[3] "And it were a very hard case if a murder committed here in England in presence only of a Turk or a Jew, that owns not the Christian religion, should be dispunishable, because such an oath should not be taken, which the witness holds binding, and cannot swear otherwise, and possibly might think himself under no obligation, if sworn according to the usual style of the courts of England."[4] These principles were finally sanctioned by Lord Hardwicke and Willes, C.J., in 1744 in the case of *Omichund v. Barker*.[5] And so, in this case, as in the case of the infant, the relaxation of the rule of absolute incapacity, had led the lawyers to see that the fact that a witness was not a Christian, was an objection, not to his competence as a witness, but to the weight of his evidence. "But then," says Hale at the conclusion of his argument in favour of the competency of such witness,[6] "it must be agreed that the credit of such a testimony must be left to the jury."

(*b*) That the commission of certain crimes renders a man so infamous that his testimony should be excluded was a principle which had its roots both in Roman and Germanic law. The rules of the Roman civil law were borrowed by the canon law, and were applied by Bracton and Britton to the competency of jurors.[7] But it was also an old principle of Germanic law that in certain cases a man "lost his law."[8] This "loss of law" followed if a man were

---

[1] Co. Litt. 6b, cited above 187 n. 9; hence no one ever questioned the proposition that a Roman Catholic might be a good witness, see Whitehead's Trial (1679) 7 S.T. at p. 379 *per* Scroggs, C.J.; Wigmore, op. cit. i 646-647, § 518; iii 2352, § 1818.

[2] P.C. ii 279.   [3] Ibid.   [4] Ibid.

[5] 1 Atk. 21—at p. 48 Lord Hardwicke said, " all that is necessary to an oath is an appeal to the Supreme Being as thinking him the rewarder of truth, and avenger of falsehood "; and at p. 50 he pointed out that, " if we did not give this credence courts abroad would not allow our determinations here to be valid."

[6] P.C. ii 279.

[7] Salmond, Essays in Jurisprudence 34-37; above 186.

[8] " Repellitur autem a sacramento infamis scilicet qui alias convictus fuerit de perjurio, quia legem amittit, et ideo dicitur quod non est ulterius dignus lege quod Anglice dicitur, He ne es othes worthe that es enes gylty of oth broken," Bracton,

reduced to villeinage,[1] and in earlier days as a punishment for perjury.[2] Thus a champion defeated in the trial by battle,[3] or a jury convicted of a false verdict,[4] lost their law, and became incompetent to testify. Later it was settled that the same consequence followed from a conviction of conspiracy at the suit of the king.[5] The combination of these two streams of doctrine produced a varied mass of offences, condemnation for which made a person incompetent to testify.[6] But whether it was the judgment of condemnation for an infamous offence, or the judgment of condemnation to an infamous punishment, was long an unsettled question.[7] The latter theory was held by Britton[8] and Coke,[9] and the former by Bracton[10] and Holt;[11] and it is the former opinion which has prevailed. On either theory it is the judgment of the court and not the commission of the offence which produces the disqualification. This indeed was a necessary rule in the interest of the administration of the law; for, if it had been the commission of the offence which produced the disqualification, the evidence of accomplices would have been excluded; and this was never the law.[12] But this was not the only difficulty to which this species of disqualification gave rise. Its operation was in many cases complicated by the intricacies of the criminal law. If a man had his clergy, this operated as a pardon, and rendered him competent as a witness—a decision which practically confined the operation of the doctrine to misdemeanours; for those who did not get the benefit of clergy were hanged.[13] Whether or not a pardon restored a man's competency to be a witness was at one time a matter of debate. It was settled in Hale's times that it did restore his competency;[14] but it was

---

f. 185a. It was the rule in Bracton's time that a juror must be a legalis homo, which excluded aliens who had not taken the oath of allegiance; it was attempted to extend this disqualification to alien witnesses in the Duke of Norfolk's Case (1571) 1 S.T. at p. 1002 on the authority of Bracton; but the Court ruled that an alien was not disqualified, ibid at p. 1026; cp. Coke, Fourth Instit. 279.

[1] Glanvil Bk. v c. 6, cited Salmond, op. cit. 38.

[2] Above 191 n. 8.   [3] Glanvil Bk. ii c. 3; Co. Litt. 6b.

[4] Glanvil Bk. ii c. 19; vol. i 337, 341.

[5] Y.B. 24 Ed. III. Mich. pl. 34 *per* Shardelowe.

[6] For the complete list of eleven cases see Hale, P.C. ii 277-278.

[7] Salmond, op. cit. 36-37.   [8] Cap. 53.   [9] Co. Litt. 6b.

[10] " Ictum enim fustium infamiam non irrogat, sed causa propter quod id plecti meruit," Bracton f. 101b.

[11] " It is not the nature of the punishment, but the nature of the crime and conviction that creates the infamy," R. v. Ford (1701) 2 Salk. at p. 690; see also R. v. Davis and Carter (1696) 5 Mod. at pp. 74-75; Pendock d. Mackender v. Mackender (1755) 2 Wils. 18.

[12] Tong's Case (1663) Kelyng 17-18, Hale dissenting; R. v. Charnock (1696) 12 S.T. at pp. 1403-1404; Wigmore, op. cit. i 656, § 526.

[13] Salmond, Essays in Jurisprudence 27; for the benefit of clergy see vol. iii 294-302.

[14] Hale, P.C. ii 278, dissenting from the opinion of Coke, C.J., in Brown v. Crashaw (1614) 2 Buls. 154, who applied the same rule to witnesses as to jurors.

thought that, if the disability to testify was not merely a consequence of the conviction and judgment, but was annexed by statute as the consequence of the commission of the crime, a pardon would not restore competency;[1] and at one time it was held that a witness, who by his own confession had committed perjury on a former occasion, was incompetent.[2] Indeed the old Germanic idea that the commission of perjury had an especially incapacitating effect, was so natural an idea that it appears in the seventeenth century;[3] its consequences lived long in the law;[4] and it still exists in some of the United States of America.[5] For all these reasons the application to the technical fabric of the English criminal law, of the principle that the commission of certain crimes renders a man incompetent to testify, had produced a mass of complex and uncertain rules; and the confusion was not diminished by one or two statutory modifications of the eighteenth and early nineteenth centuries.[6] But it was not till Bentham had demonstrated the fallacy of the premises on which the principle rested, and had shown that moral turpitude should be regarded as an objection, not to the competence of the witness, but to the weight of his evidence,[7] that the Legislature in 1843 finally swept it away.[8]

(c) The disqualification of parties, and other persons interested in the litigation, has a curious history which has been finally elucidated by Professor Wigmore.[9] It cannot be traced back to mediæval times; but it originates in the sixteenth and seventeenth centuries, contemporaneously with the appearance of the modern witness. It is due partly to accidental historical causes, and partly to the same set of ideas which made for a similar exclusion of this testimony in the canon law. But it is not probable that the ideas of the canon law exercised any direct influence. It is recognized first in civil cases, and then gradually becomes operative in criminal cases. I shall therefore deal separately with these two classes of cases.

[1] "If one be convict of perjury upon the statute, he cannot be restored to his credit by the King's pardon: for, by the statute, it is part of the judgment that he be infamous and lose the credit of testimony; but he may by a statute pardon. But in other cases where the infamy is only the consequence of the judgment, the King's pardon may restore the party to his testimony," R. v. Ford (1701) 2 Salk. at p. 691 *per* Holt, C.J.; cp. Anon. (1698) 3 Salk. 155.

[2] R. v. Oates (1685) 10 S.T. at p. 1185; Wigmore, op. cit. i 657, § 527.

[3] R. v. Castlemaine (1680) 7 S.T. at p. 1083 *per* Scroggs, C.J.; Wigmore, op. cit. i 654, § 523.

[4] 9 George IV. c. 32 §§ 3 and 4 enacted that enduring the punishment for a felony not punishable with death, or for a misdemeanour, should have the same effect as a pardon, except in the case of perjury or subornation of perjury.

[5] Wigmore, op. cit. i 654, § 524.

[6] 4 George I. c. 11 § 2; 31 George III. c. 35; 9 George IV. c. 32; 3, 4 William IV. c. 42 §§ 26, 27.

[7] Rationale of Judicial Evidence Bk. ix Pt. iii c. iii, cited Wigmore, op. cit. i 649-650, § 519.

[8] 6, 7 Victoria c. 85.   [9] Op. cit. i 688-698, § 575.

It was in the course of the sixteenth century that the parties to an action were definitely ruled to be incompetent as witnesses. The fact that they were incompetent was an established rule in 1582;[1] and it is recognized in the early years of the seventeenth century both by the Star Chamber,[2] the Chancery,[3] and the courts of common law.[4] Indeed, it was so well established that litigants joined persons unnecessarily as parties, in order to "take away their testimony."[5] What then was its origin? The suggestion made by Professor Wigmore, which is probably correct, is as follows:[6] Mediæval law knew a mode of trial, quite separate from trial by jury, in which the matter at issue was tried by the party's own oath assisted by compurgators;[7] it had also known in the thirteenth century the "serment décisoire,"[8] that is the procedure derived from the Roman civil law, by which the plaintiff put himself on oath of the defendant; and we have seen that witnesses to deeds were sometimes joined to the jury because their testimony was regarded as a mode of proof.[9] In the first two of these cases the oath of the party was a mode of proof—it decided the issue; and in the third case the oath of the witnesses was also regarded as decisive. "The hesitancy in admitting ordinary witnesses to testify was probably due in part to a sense of the incongruity of an oath which had in it no flavour of decisiveness;" and partly to the feeling that to allow the party to swear as a witness, would be a mixture of another mode of trial with a trial by jury. "A verdict was one kind of 'proof'; deed witnesses might be another kind; and the party's oath was still a different kind; there could not be two kinds of 'proof' together, i.e. two ways of testing and settling the truth. The party's oath, then, had no place in trial by jury; its appropriate place was in a distinct mode of trial, wager of law."

But, though this was the historical origin of the exclusion of parties, it can hardly be supposed that the minds of the lawyers were wholly uninfluenced, firstly by the fact that the ecclesiastical law, and other systems of law founded on the Roman civil law, recognized the same disqualification, and secondly by the reasons assigned by those laws for it. The fact that this influence was felt, and, consciously or unconsciously, operated upon their minds, is illustrated by Coke's words in *Slade's Case*.[10] "Experience,"

---

[1] Dymoke's Case, Savile 34 pl. 81.

[2] Manning's Case (1612) 2 Brown. and Golds. 151; Hudson, Star Chamber 205.

[3] Hollingworth v. Lucy (1580) Cary 91; cp. Phillips v. Duke of Bucks. (1683) 1 Vern. at p. 230.

[4] Smith's Case (1611) 12 Co. Rep. 69.

[5] Dymoke's Case (1582) Savile 34 pl. 91; Hudson, op. cit. 205, says that this practice had "grown exceedingly common."

[6] Op. cit. i 694-695, § 575.   [7] Vol. i 305-308.

[8] For this see P. and M. ii 634.   [9] Above 167-168.

[10] (1602) 4 Co. Rep. at f. 95a.

he says, "proves that men's consciences grow so large that the respect of their private advantage rather induces men (and chiefly those who have declining estates) to perjury; for *jurare in propria causa* (as one saith) *est sæpe-numero hoc seculo præcipitium diaboli ad detrudendas miserorum animas ad infernum.*" But, if this reason for the disqualification of parties is accepted, it will naturally lead to the conclusion arrived at by the civil and canon law, that not only parties, but also any persons interested in the litigation, should be excluded. That they were excluded is stated by Coke;[1] but, it would seem, that before Coke the law knew no such cause for exclusion,[2] and had in fact admitted interested persons as witnesses.[3] Here, as in many other cases, Coke's statement made law. This form of disqualification was well established in the latter half of the seventeenth century;[4] and it was accepted by the court of Chancery as well as by the courts of common law.[5]

In criminal cases the rule was not established till later. The accused was not allowed the help of counsel in cases of treason or felony, and so was obliged to defend himself in person. "His statements, therefore, covered without distinction whatever he had to say of law, of evidence, and of argument."[6] As we shall see, there was much informality in the actual conduct of the trial.[7] But, as the consequences of the rule that both the party and all interested were disqualified became clearer, we find, in the latter half of the seventeenth century, the judges ruling distinctly that a prisoner's statements were not evidence because he could not be sworn.[8] It is probable that the later application of the disqualification by reason of interest to criminal cases, was due to the fact that it was not till the latter half of the seventeenth century that the prisoner was allowed to call any witnesses on his behalf.[9] A strict application of the rule, therefore, could only affect the witnesses for the prosecution; and there was a general feeling that it was not safe to admit rules which might hamper the prosecution.[10] But during the Commonwealth the prisoner was allowed to call witnesses, who testified[11] without being allowed to be sworn;[12]

---

[1] Co. Litt. 6b, cited above 187 n. 9.

[2] In fact, as Wigmore points out, op. cit. i 690-691 it was the disinterested witness who ran the most risk of being proceeded against for maintenance; see as to this vol. i 335; above 182.

[3] Y.B. 27 Hy. VIII. Trin. pl. 10; Anon. (1613) 1 Bulstr. 202, cited Wigmore, op. cit. i 693 notes 16, 17.

[4] Ibid 692-693.   [5] 1 Eq. Cas. Ab. 223-225.

[6] Wigmore, op. cit. i 697.   [7] Below 225-226.

[8] R. v. Coleman (1678) 7 S.T. at p. 65, and R. v. Colledge (1681) 8 S.T. 681, cited Wigmore i 698 note 42.

[9] Vol. i 336; vol. v. 192-193; below 224.   [10] Vol. v. 189-190; below 223-224.

[11] Macguire's Trial (1645) 4 S.T. at p. 666; Faulconer's Trial (1653) 5 S.T. at p. 357; R. v. Hulet (1660) 5 S.T. at p. 1191; and other cases cited Wigmore, op. cit. i 698 n. 46.

[12] R. v. Hulet at pp. 1191-1192; R. v. Turner (1664) 6 S.T. at p. 570.

after the Restoration the court sometimes allowed him to compel their attendance;[1] and, by statutes of 1695[2] and 1702,[3] his witnesses were allowed to be sworn. The result was that, from the end of the seventeenth century, the principle of disqualification by interest was applied in criminal as well as in civil cases.

In the eighteenth and early nineteenth centuries this exclusion was based upon the probability that persons interested were likely to commit perjury. "It is founded," said Starkie in 1824,[4] "on the known infirmities of human nature, which is too weak to be generally restrained by religion or moral obligations, when tempted and solicited in a contrary direction by temporal interests. There are, no doubt, many whom no interests could seduce from a sense of duty, and their exclusion by the operation of this rule may in particular cases shut out the truth. But the law must prescribe general rules; and experience proves that more mischief would result from the general reception of interested witnesses than is occasioned by their general exclusion." The fact that this reasoning so long prevailed was due, as Professor Wigmore has pointed out,[5] partly to the greater violence of party feeling in the seventeenth and eighteenth centuries, which tended to lead otherwise truthful persons to distort the truth; and partly to the fact that juries were much more in the habit of counting witnesses than of weighing their credibility—a survival from the primitive idea that any one oath was as credible as any other oath, regardless of the position of the swearer.[6] But the fallacies which underlay it were exposed by Bentham,[7] and were brought to the notice of the public by Denman and Brougham.[8] The result was that, during the nineteenth century, the disqualification of persons interested and parties was gradually got rid of both in civil and criminal cases.[9] In the cases of parties and interested persons the Legislature has at length grasped the truth which had, in the case of some of the other disqualifications, been grasped at an earlier date[10]—that interest in the result of the litigation is a valid objection, not to the competence of the witness, but to the weight of his evidence.

---

[1] R. v. Twyn (1663) 6 S.T. at 516—the court promises to see that the witnesses come in; R. v. Turner (1664) 6 S.T. at p. 570—the court denies that it can summon witnesses; R. v. Reading (1679) 7 S.T. at p. 278—North, C.J., said the prisoner might have had subpœna at any time; all these cases are cited by Wigmore, op. cit. i 698 n. 47.

[2] 7, 8 William III. c. 3.　　　　　　　　[3] 1 Anne st. 2 c. 9, § 3.

[4] Evidence 83, cited Wigmore, op. cit. i 699, § 576; he only puts in shorter form what had been said by Gilbert in 1727, see Wigmore, loc. cit.

[5] Op. cit. i 703-704, § 576.

[6] See below 208 for the influence of this primitive idea in criminal procedure.

[7] Rationale of Judicial Evidence Bk. ix Pt. iii c. iii cited Wigmore, op. cit. i 700-701, § 576.

[8] Ibid 704.

[9] 6, 7 Victoria c. 85—persons interested; 14, 15 Victoria c. 99 § 2—parties in civil cases; 61, 62 Victoria c. 36—parties in criminal cases.

[10] Above 187 n. 9, 189.

We must probably bring under this category of exclusion the disqualification of husband and wife to testify on one another's behalf. It is the one case in which relationship is allowed to disqualify; and this fact is quite sufficient to negative any derivation from the civil or canon law, which disqualified many other relations, and even servants.[1] On the contrary, it is probably derived from, and accepted as a natural consequence of, the disqualification of the parties and persons interested. It appears at about the same period as this disqualification;[2] it is justified by Coke, partly on the ground that husband and wife are one flesh, and partly on the ground that a permission to testify might stir up dissension;[3] and later Gilbert explained that it was merely a corollary from the rule excluding interested persons.[4] The same reasons which induced the Legislature to abolish the disqualification of parties and persons interested, induced it to abolish also this disqualification of husband and wife.[5]

(2) *The rule of compulsion and its exceptions.*

When the statute of 1562 had established the general rule that all competent persons could be compelled to testify,[6] the question soon arose whether there were any, and, if so, what exceptions to the general rule of compulsion. It is obvious that there is no necessary connection between the causes which render a witness incompetent, and the causes which may make it fair that he should be exempted from the general rule of compulsion. But in some cases these two very different sets of exceptions to a general rule seem to have exercised some influence upon one another. This attractive influence is most marked in the case of husband and wife. The rule that the husband or wife cannot be compelled to testify against the other is stated by Coke in the same sentence as that in which he states their incompetence to testify on one another's behalf;[7] and, it would seem, that the privilege is better attested in the earlier cases than the disability.[8] It was justified, as the rule of incompetence was justified, on the ground that any

---

[1] Wigmore, op. cit. i 728-729, § 600.

[2] Coke's statement, Co. Litt. 6b, is one of the earliest, and indicates that the law was then new, see next note.

[3] " Note it hath been resolved by the justices that a wife cannot be produced either against or for her husband, *quia sunt duæ animæ in una carne*, and it might be a cause of implacable discord, and dissension between the husband and wife, and a means of great inconvenience; " Coke says nothing about the production of the husband against the wife; perhaps he is thinking of a case of 1613 1 Brown. and Golds. 47, which was the case of a wife's privilege; but his reasoning clearly applied to both cases, and the law is so stated by Hale, P.C. ii 279.

[4] Evidence 133, cited Wigmore, op. cit. i 729, § 601.

[5] 16, 17 Victoria c. 83—civil cases; 61, 62 Victoria c. 36—criminal cases.

[6] Above 185.   [7] Co. Litt. 6b cited above n. 3.

[8] Wigmore, op. cit. iv 3034-3035, § 2227.

other rule "might be a cause of implacable discord and dissension between the husband and the wife." From that time onwards it was accepted as an absolute rule in civil cases, and, subject to one or two exceptions, as the general rule in criminal cases.[1] The same attractive influence is also apparent in the closely connected rule as to the incompetence of the parties to litigation. Just as a party was incompetent as a witness, so, at common law, a party could not be compelled to appear and answer questions addressed to him by his opponent. It is true that this had always been possible in the court of Chancery[2] and in the ecclesiastical courts.[3] But it was this questioning of the parties to which the common lawyers had always objected; and so it was natural that they should regard the incompetence of the parties as witnesses, as carrying with it the privilege of not being liable to be called upon to answer at the suit of their opponents. It was probably because this was so obvious that no explicit statement of the rule occurs till the latter part of the eighteenth century.[4] The two rules might, as Professor Wigmore has pointed out, have been severed.[5] But they were not; and the inconvenience thereby caused was noted by Blackstone, as one of the principal defects of the common law system of procedure.[6] It was not removed till the passing of the series of statutes which rendered the parties competent to be witnesses.[7]

It is possible that this decision of the common law to allow a party the privilege of refusing to answer questions at the suit of his opponent, assisted indirectly the establishment of the privilege of parties and witnesses to refuse to answer incriminating questions —a privilege which made its appearance in the middle of the seventeenth century. At any rate, as we shall now see, the introduction of this privilege was helped forward by the hostility of the common law courts to the opposite methods pursued by the ecclesiastical courts in the exercise of their criminal jurisdiction.[8]

It is obvious that, in the early Middle Ages, a party accused had no privilege to refuse to answer incriminating questions. The

---

[1] R. v. Audley (1631) 3 S.T. at p. 414; R. v. Ivy (1684) 10 S.T. at p. 644; Cole v. Gray (1688) 2 Vern. 79—all cited by Wigmore, op. cit. iv 3036 n. 12.

[2] Vol. v 281, 285; below 337, 340. [3] Vol. i 609, 610, 620; below 199-200.

[4] Wigmore, op. cit. iv 3008, § 2217. [5] Ibid 3009.

[6] "It seems the height of judicial absurdity, that in the same cause, between the same parties, in the examination of the same facts, a discovery by the oath of the parties should be permitted on one side of Westminster Hall, and denied on the other: or that the judges of one and the same court should be bound by law to reject such a species of evidence, if attempted on a trial at bar; but when, sitting the next day as a court of equity, should be obliged to hear such examination read, and to found their decrees upon it," Comm. iii 382.

[7] Above 196 n. 9.

[8] The history of this privilege has been told very fully and clearly by Wigmore, op. cit. iv 3069 seqq., § 2250; see also Stephen, Juridical Soc. Papers i 456.

older modes of proof, such as compurgation and ordeal, forced the accused to a direct denial of the charge under oath; and in the sixteenth century the Legislature had no hesitation in sanctioning forms of procedure which involved an examination of accused persons. The Act Pro Camera Stellata of 1487,[1] and many other Acts,[2] sanctioned such an examination; and we have seen that Acts of 1553 and 1555 required accused persons to submit to examination by the justices of the peace.[3] We shall see, in fact, that, right down to the middle of the seventeenth century, the examination of the accused is the central feature of the criminal procedure of the common law.[4] Nor do we read anywhere that a witness could refuse to answer on the ground that his answer might incriminate him.[5] It is not till the Commonwealth period that this privilege to refuse to answer incriminating questions is accorded to accused persons.[6] Its existence was well established after the Restoration;[7] and it was then extended to ordinary witnesses.[8] How and why did it originate?

The answer seems to be that it is the somewhat illogical outcome of the disputes between the common law and the ecclesiastical courts in the early years of the seventeenth century; of the use made by the common law judges in these conflicts of the canonist maxim *nemo tenetur prodere seipsum;* and of the odium excited by the proceedings of the Star Chamber, in which the examination of the accused upon oath was a central feature.

The inquisitory procedure of the canon law had explained away the old maxim *nemo tenetur prodere seipsum.* A person suspected *per famam* or *per clamosam insinuationem* could be compelled to prove his innocence; and this easily led to proceedings under which he was arrested, and compelled to answer a series of searching interrogatories.[9] But there was a tendency, both in England and elsewhere, in proceedings against religious nonconformists, to neglect the conditions of common report or vehement suspicion, which should have existed before a person could be thus arrested and questioned. This was specially apparent when, in

[1] 3 Henry VII. c. 1.
[2] 13 Elizabeth c. 7 § 5—bankrupts; 35 Elizabeth c. 2 § 11—Jesuits; 43 Elizabeth c. 6 § 1—those who abused warrants; all these statutes are cited by Wigmore, op. cit. iv 3084.
[3] 1, 2 Phillip and Mary c. 13; 2, 3 Phillip and Mary c. 10; vol. i 296; vol. iv 529.
[4] Below 227.
[5] The first instance of this seems to have been R. v. Reading (1679) 7 S.T. at p. 296; Wigmore, op. cit. iv 3089.
[6] King Charles' Trial (1649) 4 S.T. at p. 1101; Lilburn's Trial (1649) ibid at pp. 1292-1293, 1341.
[7] R. v. Scroop (1660) 5 S.T. at p. 1039, and the long list of cases cited by Wigmore, op. cit. iv 3088 n. 105.
[8] R. v. Reading (1679) 7 S.T. at p. 295; R. v. Rosewell (1684) 10 S.T. at p. 169.
[9] Vol. v 170-175; Wigmore, op. cit. iv 3075.

1583, Whitgift devised the *ex officio* oath, which he proceeded to apply to all kinds of persons suspected of holding heretical views.[1] It was these proceedings which brought on a series of conflicts with the common law courts,[2] in which the maxim *nemo tenetur prodere seipsum* was produced to prove the illegality of such questioning by the ecclesiastical courts.[3] It would seem from Hudson's treatise on the Star Chamber, that some were inclined to think that this maxim was generally applicable both to parties and to witnesses in that court.[4] It is clear, however, from Lilburn's trial before that tribunal that the practice of the court was different.[5] But Hudson's statements are significant of the hold which the maxim was getting upon the minds of the lawyers; and it is clear that, about the same period, it was beginning to be heard of in the courts of common law.[6] It is not surprising, therefore, that, when the ecclesiastical courts and the court of Star Chamber were abolished by the Long Parliament, that abolition should have seemed to sanction the truth of the maxim which the procedure of those courts had disregarded. It is for these reasons that the privilege makes its appearance in the second half of the seventeenth century.

The privilege was thus introduced almost as the accidental result of a series of political causes. It is therefore not surprising to find, firstly, that it was not wholly consistent with certain parts of the English criminal procedure, and, secondly, that its meaning and limitations were not at first well understood.

(i) In spite of the rule that a person need answer no question which tended to incriminate him, the statutes which required the justices of the peace to examine persons charged with crime, and the witnesses for the prosecution, were still in force.[7] No one seems to have suggested that the privilege was inconsistent with these examinations of an accused person till the eighteenth century;[8] and it was not till 1848-1849 that the Legislature enacted that magistrates and justices of the peace should caution prisoners

---

[1] Wigmore, op. cit. iv 3078.

[2] Ibid 3078-3080: vol. i 609, 610; vol. v 429-431.

[3] This maxim was cited by Coke as counsel in Collier's Case (1590) 4 Leo. 194, Cro. Eliza. 201; and as judge in Burrowes and Others v. the High Commission Court (1616) 3 Bulstr. at p. 50.

[4] " Neither must it question the party to accuse him of a crime," Hudson, Star Chamber 208; "if a witness conceive that the answering of a question may be prejudice to himself, it seemeth that he need not answer," ibid 209.

[5] (1637) 3 S.T. 1315 seqq.

[6] " It was true the law did not oblige any man to be his own accuser," R. v. Fitz-Patrick (1631) 3 S.T. at p. 420 *per* Hyde, C.J. It may be noted that the court of Chancery would not compel a witness to answer a question which would expose him to a forfeiture, Tothill, 7, 10, 18; but this, as Professor Wigmore has pointed out, op. cit. iv 3086-3087, has little to do with the main rule, as the court of Chancery had no jurisdiction over criminal cases.

[7] Above 199.   [8] Wigmore, op. cit. iv 3084-3085.

that they need not say anything in answer to the charge unless they pleased.[1]

(ii) During the latter half of the seventeenth century no very great extension was given to the privilege—it was contrary to too many received ideas as to the conduct of criminal trials. " Until well on into the time of the English Revolution the privilege remained not much more than a bare rule of law which the judges would recognize on demand. The spirit of it was wanting in them. The old habit of questioning and urging the accused died hard—did not disappear indeed till the eighteenth century had begun." [2] On the other hand, there was a continuous current of authority down to the nineteenth century, in favour of extending the privilege so as to excuse a witness from answering questions, not only if they might expose him to a criminal charge, but also if the answer would expose him to disgrace.[3] This would seem to have been the view of Hudson,[4] and it was certainly the view of Treby, C.J., in 1696.[5] Starkie in 1824 argued against the existence of such a privilege;[6] but the Common Law Procedure Commissioners in 1853 treated it as still subsisting, " unless the misconduct imputed has reference to the cause itself." [7] They admitted, therefore, that there is no such privilege if the question is directly relevant to the issue. If it is only collateral to the issue, it would seem that the court at the present day assumes a discretion as to whether it will compel an answer.[8] We shall now see that this extension of the privilege against self-incrimination, is not wholly unconnected with the ideas which originally gave rise to the second of the leading exceptions to the rule of compulsion— the privilege given to legal advisers with respect to communications passing between themselves and their clients.[9]

This privilege was recognized in Elizabeth's reign,[10] so that its establishment was almost contemporaneous with the creation by

---

[1] 11, 12 Victoria c. 42 § 18 ; Stephen, H.C.L. i 220.

[2] Wigmore, op. cit. iv 3090, and note 109.

[3] Ibid ii 1124.

[4] Above 200 n. 4; in his book on the Star Chamber at p. 209 he says, "if the question concern not the cause he need not answer it, whether it be scandalous to himself or to any other, if not concerning the crime in question."

[5] " Men have been asked whether they have been convicted and pardoned for felony, or whether they have been whipped for petit larceny; but they have not been obliged to answer ; for though their answer in the affirmative will not make them criminal or subject them to a punishment, yet they are matters of infamy ; and if it be an infamous thing, that is enough to preserve a man from being bound to answer," R. v. Cook 13 S.T. at pp. 334-335, cited Wigmore, op. cit. ii 1124.

[6] Evidence i 193, cited Wigmore, op cit. ii 1119.

[7] Second Report 22, cited Wigmore, loc. cit.

[8] Stephen, Digest of the Law of Evidence Art. 129.

[9] Wigmore, op. cit. iv 3193, § 2290.

[10] Berd v. Lovelace (1577) Cary 62 ; Dennis v. Codrington (1580) ibid 100; cp. Waldron v. Ward (1654) Style 449, and other cases cited by Wigmore, op. cit. iv 3193 note 1.

the Legislature of the general rule of compulsion. But, though this exception was thus early established, the theory upon which it rested was not settled till the beginning of the eighteenth century; with the result that the scope and conditions of the privilege were not settled till the middle of the nineteenth century. In the sixteenth and seventeenth centuries the privilege was based upon the theory that the honour of the legal adviser was involved, and that therefore he must be privileged not to answer.[1] It belongs essentially to the same order of ideas as the privilege to refuse to answer questions, the answer to which would expose the witness to injury; and, this being the case, the privilege was naturally extended to other relations besides that of client and legal adviser. In several trials in the seventeenth century persons objected to give evidence on the ground that they had made a vow, or an oath of secrecy, or that they were bound in honour not to reveal information;[2] and there was some inclination to hold that this was a valid excuse. Hudson, for instance, seems to have been of this opinion.[3] It was not till 1776 that it was decisively ruled that " the point of honour " was no excuse.[4] If the privilege accorded to communication between a client and his legal advisers had rested merely upon " the point of honour," it might have disappeared along with the other suggested privileges.[5] But, before that time, it had come to be based also on the ground that it was a privilege necessary to secure a client's freedom of action in his dealings with his advisers.[6] The result of this conflict of theories was that the rules relating to the application of the privilege were confused. Thus, according to the older theory, the privilege was the adviser's: according to the newer, the client's. Therefore, according to the older theory the adviser could waive it, but according to the newer, the client. Again, the older theory limited it to the litigation then before the court; while the newer gradually extended it to all professional

[1] Wigmore, op. cit. iv 3194.

[2] Countess of Shrewsbury's Case (1613) 12 Co. Rep. at p. 94; Jones v. Countess of Manchester (1673) 1 Vent. 197; Bulstrod v. Letchmere (1676) Free. Ch. 5; R. v. Grey (1682) 9 S.T. at pp. 175-176; all these cases are cited by Wigmore, op. cit. iv 3188 notes 9 and 10.

[3] After stating that a witness cannot be asked questions which will prejudice him, he proceeds, " yet in the Dutch cause the goldsmith apprentices refused to give answer to their examinations, alleging that they were sworn not to reveal the mysteries of their trade; and they were committed until they were examined. But that Case was a Case of State, Wherein the Commonwealth was much interested, and I hope will be no precedent to future times," Star Chamber, 209.

[4] Duchess of Kingston's Case 20 S.T. at pp. 572-573, 586-588.

[5] Wigmore, op. cit. iv 3194.

[6] The mixture of the old and the new view comes out clearly in Gilbert, Evidence (1726) 136, cited Wigmore, op. cit. iv 3195 n. 3; it is also apparent in Blackstone's statement, Comm. iii 370, that " no counsel, attorney or other person entrusted with the secrets of the cause by the party himself *shall be compelled or perhaps allowed to* give evidence etc."

communications, irrespective of any litigation.[1] But since the gradual settlement of the new theory and its consequences was the work of the eighteenth and nineteenth centures, its treatment must be reserved for the following Book of this History.

Oral Evidence

During the whole of the mediæval period, the view which the law took of the oral evidence offered by witnesses, was affected, as many other legal rules and institutions were affected, both by the theories which underlay the rules of the canon law, and by survivals of some very primitive ideas as to the functions of witnesses. In this, as in other branches of the law, these theories and these ideas diverged widely from one another, because they represented two very different periods of legal development. But in one respect they tended, for very different reasons, to coincide. Both laid down the rule that a certain number of witnesses was requisite for proof. Of this rule, therefore, and its causes and effects I must speak, in the first place. In the second place, I must say something of the effects which it has had upon English law. We shall see that some of the reasons for the smallness of its direct effects upon English law, will help to explain why the most important branch of this part of the law of evidence has taken the form of certain rules, which definitely refuse to admit certain kinds of testimony. In the third place, therefore, I shall deal with these excluding rules.

(1) *The rule that a certain number of witnesses is requisite for proof.*[2]

The rule that at least two witnesses were needed for proof is found in the classical Roman law;[3] but it gained its great authority in mediæval Europe from the fact that it became a rule of the canon law,[4] justified, not only by the civil law, but by the authority of the Old [5] and New Testaments.[6] It is not surprising that, under these circumstances, the maxim *testis unus testis nullus* should be regarded almost as a provision of the Divine law. Its position is well illustrated by the objection to the system of trial by jury, which Fortescue in his *De Laudibus* puts into the mouth of the Prince. "Though," says the Prince,[7] "we be greatly delighted in

---

[1] Wigmore, op. cit. iv 3195-3196.

[2] On this topic generally see Wigmore, op. cit. iii 2695-2707, § 2032.

[3] Dig. 22. 5. 12; Code 4. 28. 4; 4. 20. 9.

[4] Decret. Greg. 2-20 c. 23; Decret. pars ii causa iv qu. ii and iii c. iv § 26; both passages cited by Wigmore, op. cit. iii 2696 note 5.

[5] Deut. xvii 6, and xix 12.   [6] Mat. xviii 16; John viii 17.

[7] De Laudibus c. 31.

the form which the laws of England use in sifting out the truth in matters of contention, yet whether the same law be contrary to Holy Scripture or not, that is to us somewhat doubtful.   For our Lord saith to the Pharisees in the eighth chapter of Saint John's Gospel, ' In your law it is written that the testimony of two men is true;' and the Lord, confirming the same, saith, ' I am one that bear witness of myself, and the Father that sent me beareth witness of me.'   Now Sir, the Pharisees were Jews, so that it was all one to say : It is written in your law, and it is written in Moses law, which God gave to the children of Israel by Moses.   Wherefore to gainsay this law is to deny God's law : whereby it followeth, that if the law of England swerve from this law, it swerveth also from God's law, which in no wise may be contradicted.   It is written also in the eighteenth chapter of Saint Matthew's Gospel . . . ' But if thy brother hear thee not, then take yet with thee one or two, that, in the mouth of two or three witnesses, every matter may be established.'   If the Lord have appointed every matter to be established in the mouth of two or three witnesses, then it is in vain for to seek for the verdict of many men in matters of doubt. For no man is able to lay any other or better foundation than the Lord hath laid."

This rule that more than one witness was needed to prove the truth of a matter in issue, also assorted well with some very primitive notions as to the nature of the probative force of the testimony of witnesses.[1]   That probative force was attached, not so much to the matter to which they testified under the sanction of an oath, as to the act of swearing to the truth of a fact under the prescribed forms.   We have seen that the proofs by compurgation[2] and by witnesses[3] both illustrate this point of view.   The law paid hardly any attention to the matter sworn to, provided it was sworn to in the proper form.   It concentrated its attention on the fact that a number of persons had sworn to the fact in that form. Hence the efficacy attached both in the Anglo-Saxon period[4] and and later[5] to the number of the swearers.   As Professor Wigmore says,[6] "since the performance of the act is in itself efficacious, the multiple performance of it . . . must multiply its probative value proportionately.   The numerical conception is inherent in the general formalism of it. . . .   That is, a greater degree of certainty is thought to be attained, not by analyzing the significance of each oath in itself and relatively to the person, but by increasing the number of oaths."   It is true that the older modes of trial, in which this conception was prominent, decayed during the mediæval period, and gave place to trial by jury.   But this by no means

---

[1] Wigmore, op. cit. iii 2696-2701.
[2] Vol. i 305-308.
[3] Ibid 302-305.
[4] Vol. ii 109, 112.
[5] Vol. i 303, 306.
[6] Op. cit. iii 2698-2699.

destroyed the primitive idea that an oath *per se* has a formal value, and that therefore a multiplication of oaths will produce greater certainty.   The jury themselves were witnesses; and their verdict amounted to an assertion backed by the oaths of twelve men.   This idea comes out clearly in the answer made by Fortescue to the Prince's objection.   He points out that, though the law of God forbids proof by less than two witnesses, it does not forbid the law to exact a proof by more than two;[1] and that, in effect, the law which requires the verdict of twelve men exacts a proof by twelve witnesses.[2]   He adds, moreover, that if for any reason the proof by twelve jurors is not available, e.g. if the matter alleged be done upon the high seas or abroad, the law of England provides that proof must be made by more than one witness.[3]

Thus both lines of thought led to the rule that a certain number of witnesses were necessary for proof.   Let us now examine the effect of this rule upon the development of the modern law.

(2) *The effects of this rule upon the development of English law.*

It was inevitable that a rule, backed by such authority as this, would leave its marks upon the law.   What is remarkable is not the fact that its influence can be traced, but the fact that its direct influence has been so small.   We shall see that, subject to two important exceptions, English law has rejected the rule that there can be no proof without more than one witness. At the same time we can trace its indirect effects in different directions.   I shall consider, firstly, the direct influence of the rule; secondly, its indirect influence; and thirdly, the reasons why it was, as a general rule of the law of evidence, rejected by English law.

(i) The idea that the evidence of one witness is not enough to prove the fact in issue emerges, during the sixteenth and seventeenth centuries, sometimes in the provisions of statutes, and sometimes in arguments and judicial dicta.   Various statutes of the sixteenth and seventeenth centuries, which required the evidence of two witnesses for a conviction of the offences created by them, show that the Legislature was convinced of the danger of allowing a conviction on the unsupported testimony of one person.[4]   But

---

[1] " That law must thus be understanded that by a lesser number of witnesses than two the truth in matters doubtful ought not to be searched for, as appeareth by Bernard, assigning divers cases, wherein by the Laws more than three witnesses must needs be produced," De Laudibus c. 32.

[2] " This law [the law of England] never determineth a controversy by witnesses only that may be determined by a jury of twelve men. . . .   For this form of proceeding cannot in any cause fail for want of witnesses, nor the testimony of witnesses, (if any be) cannot choose but come to their due end and effect," ibid.

[3] Ibid.

[4] 1 Elizabeth c. 1 § 37; 39 Elizabeth c. 20 § 10; 3 Charles I. c. 2; 1 William and Mary c. 18 §§ 14, 18; 3 William and Mary c. 11 § 5; all these statutes are cited by Wigmore, op. cit. iii 2702 note 21.

it is in the arguments and judicial dicta of these centuries that we get the clearest evidence of the survival of the old idea. In 1551, in the case of *Reniger v. Fogossa*,[1] the attorney-general argued that the testimony of one witness was "not sufficient in any law," because it was contrary to the law of God;[2] and he was answered by Brooke on exactly the same lines as Fortescue answered the Prince.[3] In the proceedings on Bacon's impeachment in 1620, Coke thought necessary to combat the idea that more that one witness was necessary;[4] and in 1632, in *Sherfield's Case*, Heath, C.J., commented on the fact that there was only one witness to prove one part of the charge.[5] Indeed, it would seem from the two cases of *Adams v. Canon*[6] and *R. v. Newton*,[7] that it was almost an accepted rule of the court of Star Chamber that a charge must he proved by two witnesses; though, from what was said by Lord Cottington in the *Bishop of Lincoln's Case*,[8] it would seem that it was not an invariable rule. It was stated in the widest terms by Strafford on his impeachment. He is reported as saying "that the testimonies brought against him were all of them single, not two one way; and therefore could not make faith in matter of debt, much less in matter of life and death."[9]

But, before this date, the common law had come to the conclusion that it would reject any rule requiring more than one witness as a general rule of the law of evidence. As Professor Wigmore points out,[10] the decision in *Reniger v. Fogossa* was in favour of the defendant, though he only produced one witness. Coke's speech in the proceedings on Bacon's impeachment shows that he rejected it;[11] and, as we have seen, even in the Star Chamber the rule requiring more than one witness was not invariable. After the Restoration the rule that one witness is

---

[1] Plowden 1.   [2] Ibid at p. 8.

[3] " As to that which has been said by the King's Attorney, that there ought to be two witnesses to prove the fact; it is true that there ought to be two witnesses at least where the matter is to be tried by witnesses only, as in the civil law, but here the issue was to be tried by twelve men, in which case witnesses are not necessary, for in many cases an inquest shall give a precise verdict, although there are no witnesses, or no evidence given to them," ibid at p. 12.

[4] " It is objected that we have but one single witness; therefore no sufficient proof. I answer that in the 37th of Eliz. in a complaint against Soldier-Sellers, for that having warrant to take up soldiers for the wars, if they pressed a rich man's son they would discharge him for money, there was no more than singularis testis in one matter," 2 S.T. at p. 1093.

[5] 3 S.T. at p. 545.   [6] (1622) Dyer 53b note 15.   [7] (1623) Dyer 99b note 68.

[8] " It is not always necessary in this court to have a truth proved by two or three witnesses. . . . And *singularis testis* many times shall move and induce me verily to believe an act done when more proofs are shunned," (1637) 3 S.T. at p. 786.

[9] (1640) 3 S.T. at p. 1450.   [10] Op. cit. iii 2702 note 22.

[11] Above n. 4.

sufficient is stated as a positive rule of law.[1] The only two exceptions admitted, other than exceptions introduced by express statutes, were in the case of high treason and in the case of perjury. We have seen that the requirement of two witnesses in the case of high treason rested upon a strained construction of the combined effects of statutes of Edward VI.'s and Mary's reign, and was not wholly freed from doubt till it was put upon a statutory basis by the statute of 1696.[2] The requirement of two witnesses in the case of perjury is due to two main causes. In the first place, the offence was developed in the court of Star Chamber, where the tendency to the adoption of the civil and canon law rule had always been stronger.[3] In the second place, the requirement of more than one oath against another oath is a particularly obvious measure of justice;[4] and it was a requirement which, in the shape of the attaint procedure against a perjured jury,[5] had a native tradition behind it.

The most beneficial effect of the rejection of the rule requiring more than one witness, was that it led the court to lay more stress upon the character of the evidence offered, than upon the number of the witnesses produced. Just as the abandonment of artificial rules as to the competency of witnesses forced to the front the question of the weight of the evidence,[6] so the refusal to require more than a single witness made it necessary, as Hale pointed out, to consider more carefully the character, the means of knowledge, and the demeanour of the witness, in order to estimate the value of his evidence.[7] The result was that the witness's character was always a fact relevant to the issue; and, in the latter part of the seventeenth century, witnesses were called to speak for or against his credibility.[8] But it was not till quite the end of the seventeenth century that we hear of the rule that evidence of specific

---

[1] R. v. Tong (1662) Kelyng at p. 18; R. v. Vaughan (1696) 13 S.T. at p. 535; Hale, History of the Common Law (6th ed.) 346—"they (the jury) may and do often pronounce their verdict upon one single testimony; which thing the civil law admits not of."

[2] Vol. iv 499.

[3] Wigmore, op. cit. iii 2720-2722, § 2040.

[4] "He that travaileth to convince witnesses of perjury must of necessity bring forth many more than they were, so that the testimony of two or three men shall not ever be judged true," De Laudibus c. 32.

[5] Vol. i 339.

[6] Above 196.

[7] History of the Common Law (6th ed.) 346-348.

[8] R. v. Earl of Stafford (1680) 7 S.T. at p. 1457; Duke of Norfolk's Divorce Suit (1692) 12 S.T. at p. 919; both these cases are cited by Wigmore, op. cit. iii 2631, § 1982. The modern rule that, in a criminal case, the fact that the accused has a good character is relevant was recognized in R. v. Turner (1664) 6 S.T. at pp. 606-607; but in this period the other modern rules as to when the evidence of the character of a party to litigation is relevant were as yet undeveloped.

acts of misconduct must be excluded, and that only evidence of general reputation can be given.[1]

(ii) Though the direct influence of the rule requiring more than a single witness has been small, the ideas which underlay it have had a certain amount of indirect influence in different directions. Firstly, though the rejection of the rule caused the court to pay more attention to the weight of a witness's evidence, we shall see that juries still continued for a long period to attach much weight to an oath merely as an oath. Even the judges in the latter part of the seventeenth century made very few attempts in criminal cases to weigh the evidence ;[2] and, according to Stephen,[3] this is still the prevailing habit of juries. Secondly, the influence of the same set of ideas can be seen in certain outlying branches of the law of evidence. If evidence given on oath must be believed because it is so given, the witness who has sworn to it cannot be allowed to retract it. This gave rise to the unsuccessful attempt to establish a rule that an attesting witness cannot be allowed to repudiate his attestation ;[4] and to the rule, which prevailed down to the end of the eighteenth century, that a person who by his signature has acknowledged an instrument to be valid, cannot be allowed to give evidence to show that it is invalid—"allegans suam turpitudinem non est audiendus."[5] It also seems to be answerable for the rule that a person cannot impeach the the competence or credit of his own witness. So long as the only witnesses known to the law were literally "oath helpers," "it was inconceivable that a party should gainsay his own witness."[6] This tradition survived, perhaps because it had been recognized in a modified form by the civil and canon law ;[7] and it was applied very illogically to the modern witness. It was stated as a general rule of law in the latter part of the seventeenth

---

[1] R. v. Rookwood (1696) 13 S.T. at p. 211 *per* Holt, C.J.—"look ye, you may bring witnesses to give account of the general tenor of his conversation ; but you do not think sure that we will try now at this time whether he be guilty of robbery or buggery," cited Wigmore, op. cit. ii 1103, § 979 ; ibid ii 1121, § 986 note 2.

[2] Below 232-233.

[3] H.C.L. i 400.

[4] Wigmore, op. cit. i 658, § 528, citing Hudson's Case (1683) Skin. 79 ; Dayrell v. Glascock (1680) ibid 413, and other later cases.

[5] Ibid i 658-659, § 529 ; the maxim was cited along with others to illustrate the as yet meagre rules of the law of evidence by Coke, Fourth Instit. 279 ; it was confused in the earlier cases with objections based on the disqualification of the witness from interest, Co. Litt. 6b ; but the general principle, based on the maxim cited, was accepted by Lord Mansfield in Walton v. Shelley (1786) 1 T.R. at pp. 300-301 ; but the idea was finally repudiated in Jordaine v. Lashbrooke (1798) 7 T.R. 601.

[6] Wigmore, op. cit. ii 1018, § 896.

[7] Ibid note 2, citing Code 4. 20. 17 ; Hudson, Star Chamber 201, says, "this is a firm and constant rule, as well in this court as in all laws, that no man shall be received to except against a witness as incompetent, if he examine him also himself."

century;[1] it was accepted as an established rule in the eighteenth century;[2] and it was not modified till 1854,[3] though by the end of the eighteenth century, it had been admitted that other evidence could be produced by a party to contradict his own witness.[4] Rationalistic reasons were found for it;[5] but its historical origin seems to have been the result of the survival of these primitive ideas as to the functions of a witness, and the probative effect of his testimony.[6]

(iii) The question now arises, why did this universal rule of "testis unus testis nullus" have so small an effect upon our modern law? The first and chief reason was the total rejection of the system of procedure worked out by the civilians and canonists. The rule of the canon law, that there could be no full proof without the concurrent testimony of two witnesses, had led, in the sphere of the criminal law, to the reinforcement of defective proof by means of admissions and confessions extracted by torture. The revolting brutality of this system had been exposed by Fortescue. But we have seen that in the sixteenth century it had become even more revolting in many continental states.[7] Naturally, as was shown by the statute which altered the criminal procedure of the Admiralty,[8] Englishmen in the sixteenth century were opposed to any borrowings from a system which led to these results. A second reason can be found in those conflicts of jurisdiction between the common law and its rivals, which became acute at the end of the sixteenth century. The common lawyers, though they recognized the legality of the different rules of procedure of the ecclesiastical courts and the court of Star Chamber, when these courts were acting within their proper sphere, though occasionally they even took hints from them,[9] had no desire, even in the sixteenth century, to adopt their technical rules.[10] And the victory of the common law after 1640 ensured the prevalence of common law rules and methods. These two reasons, it seems to me, got

---

[1] In R. v. Colledge (1681) 8 S.T. at p. 636 North, C.J., said, "look you Mr. Colledge I will tell you something for law, and to set you right; whatsoever witnesses you call, you call them as witnesses to testify the truth for you; and if you ask them any questions, you must take what they have said as truth: therefore you must not think to ask him any questions, and afterward call another witness to disprove your own witness"; it is said in Adams v. Arnold (1700) 12 Mod. 375 that Holt, C.J., "would not suffer the plaintiff to discredit a witness of his own calling, he swearing against him."

[2] Wigmore, op. cit. ii 1018, § 896.

[3] 17, 18 Victoria c. 125 § 22; as to this section see Stephen, Digest Art. 131 and note xlvii.

[4] Wigmore, op. cit. ii 1038, § 907.   [5] Ibid 1019-1024, §§ 897-899.

[6] "The modern rule as to impeaching the character of one's own witness is historically merely the last remnant of the broad primitive notion that a party must stand or fall by the utterance of his witness," ibid ii 1020.

[7] Vol. v 174-175.   [8] 28 Henry VIII. c. 15; vol. i 550-551.
[9] Vol. v 189-195.   [10] Vol. iv 285-289.

rid of the immense influence and prestige which, all through the Middle Ages, attached to a rule which was sanctioned by the civil and canon law.

They do not, however, account for the fact that the authority of the Bible, and the influence of primitive ideas as to the nature of the probative force of oral evidence, were also apparently ignored. For an explanation of these facts we must look primarily to the explanation which Fortescue gave to the Prince. The jury were the witnesses to whom this rule applied ; and they were twelve men.[1] We have seen that this explanation was repeated in 1551 ;[2] and the desire to circumvent the rule in this way, is probably at the root of Coke's laboured attempt to explain that the evidence of witnesses was no part of the trial, but the trial was by verdict of twelve men.[3] This reason carried weight in the sixteenth century, both because the jury had not as yet lost their character of witnesses, and because the practice of summoning witnesses to testify to them was as yet comparatively new. It therefore gave the lawyers a chance to evade the force of the rule, during a century when the authority of the Bible, and of primitive ideas, would otherwise have almost compelled its acceptance. During the seventeenth century it was beginning to be seen that the important matter to consider was, not the number of the witnesses, but their credibility. And so, though the jury were obviously ceasing to be witnesses, though they found their verdict on the evidence of witnesses, it was possible to ignore a rule which, owing to the older character of the jury, had never been received ; and to refuse to require any particular number of witnesses for the establishment of the facts in issue.

The rule "testis unus testis nullus" permeated the continental procedure, and tended to preserve those primitive ideas which led men to count witnesses, rather than to weigh their testimony.[4] The abandonment of this rule by the common law, which was due in part to the small influence of the civil and canon law, in part to the peculiar character of the jury, and in part to the late arrival of

---

[1] Above 205.   [2] Above 206.

[3] Arguing that the statute of Mary had not repealed the statute of Edward VI. (see vol. iv 499) he says, " the indictment is no part of the trial, but an information or declaration for the king, and the evidence of witnesses to the jury is no part of the trial, for by law the trial in that case is not by witnesses, but by the verdict of twelve men, and so a manifest diversity between the evidence to a jury and a trial by jury," Third Instit. 26-27 ; but, ibid 26, he quotes the Bible to prove that the rule of two witnesses in case of treason is grounded on the law of God.

[4] " All our old collections of customary law emulate each other in reminding us that a single witness cannot suffice, but that proof is made as soon as two at least are found to testify to the same effect. Curiously enough this bizarre system was accepted by our jurists down to the Revolution without the least protest," Glasson, Histoire du droit et des institutions de la France vi 543, cited Wigmore, op. cit. iii 2699 note 12 ; cp. Best, Evidence (12th ed.) 56-63.

the modern witness, helped English law to a far more rational treatment of the law of evidence than was possible in most continental states. Stress could be and was laid far more exclusively upon the character of the evidence. We shall now see that the need to guide the jury to a right judgment upon the character of this oral evidence, has led to the formation of those excluding rules, which are the most salient and peculiar characteristics of the common law.

(3) *The rules which exclude certain classes of oral evidence.*

The three leading rules which were beginning to emerge during this period, were the rules that the contents of a written document cannot be varied by oral evidence, that mere opinion is not generally admissible, and that " hearsay " is not evidence. Of the first of these rules I have already said something ; and I shall have more to say of it in the following section.[1] At this point I propose to say something of the beginnings of the two latter rules.

(i) *Opinion.*

The rule of our modern law on this subject is thus stated by Stephen:[2] " The fact that any person is of opinion that a fact in issue, or relevant or deemed to be relevant to the issue, does or does not exist is deemed to be irrelevant to the existence of such fact." But, "when there is a question as to any point of science or art, the opinions upon that point of persons specially skilled in any such matter are deemed to be relevant facts." Both the general rule and its modification have a long history.[3]

It was a very old rule, applied to the secta and the pre-appointed witnesses, that witnesses must testify " de visu et auditu," that is to matters which had come under the personal observation of their own senses ;[4] and this also was the general rule of the civil and canon law.[5] This rule, as we shall see, is not the same thing as the rule which excludes hearsay—though it probably had something to do with its establishment.[6] But it evidently made for the exclusion of mere opinion, and it appears that it was so

---

[1] Above 173-177; below 219-222.
[2] Digest (4th ed.), Arts. 48, 49.
[3] Wigmore, op cit. iii 2541, § 1917.
[4] Salmond, Essays on Jurisprudence 81-83, and the passages from Glanvil and Bracton there cited; thus Glanvil ii c. 3 says the demandant in a writ of right alleges that he is ready to prove his case by a free man, "qui hoc vidit vel audivit," or whose father on his death bed, " in fide qua filius tenetur patri, quod si aliquando loquelam de terra illa audiret, hoc diracionaret sicut id quod pater suus vidit et audivit "; Bracton f. 438a says that the birth of issue should be proved, " per sectam sufficientem quæ audivit clamorem in propria persona, et non ex relatione aliorum vel auditu."
[5] Salmond, op. cit. 81.   [6] Below 214-215.

interpreted in the Year Books.[1]   Coke, therefore, was justified in ruling in 1622[2] that "it is not satisfactory for the witness to say that he thinks or persuadeth himself . . . 1st because the judge is to give an absolute sentence, and therefore ought to have more sure ground than thinking; 2dly, the witness cannot be prosecuted for perjury; 3d, that judges, as judges, are always to give judgment *secundum allegata et probata*, notwithstanding private individuals think otherwise."

On the other hand, as early as the fourteenth century, the court had recourse to the opinions of experts in order to aid them to come to a conclusion as to the facts in issue.[3]   In 1353 surgeons were summoned by the court to give their opinion on the question whether a wound amounted to a mayhem;[4] and in the fifteenth century grammarians were summoned to testify as to the meaning of a Latin word.[5]   It would seem, therefore, that Saunders, J., in 1554, had good warrant for his opinion that, " if matters arise in our law which concern other sciences or faculties, we commonly apply for the aid of that science or faculty which it concerns."[6] These witnesses were regarded as expert assistants to the court; and the fact that they occupied this status "had naturally prevented any question from being raised as to their information in the aspect of testimony to the jury."[7]   But in the seventeenth century, when witnesses had begun to be commonly called to testify, these experts were naturally regarded merely as witnesses. They had always been admitted, and continued to be admitted. The result was that, in the course of the eighteenth century, the law begins to be stated in its modern form of a general exclusive rule, subject to a wide exception.[8]

In course of time many of the cases on which a witness's opinion was admissible became the centres of bodies of law.   At this point it is only necessary to allude to one of these cases— opinion as to handwriting—as round this topic some law was beginning to gather at the close of the seventeenth century.

It would seem that, right down to the end of the seventeenth

---

[1] " Les testmoignes doivent rien testmoigner fors ceo que ils soient de certein i.e. ceo que ils verront ou oyront," 23 Ass. pl. 11; cf. Y.B. 20 Hy. VI. Hil. pl. 16 where a statement of an essoiner, that " he was informed " that one was in the king's service, was held to be insufficient.

[2] Adams v. Canon Dyer 53b n. 15.

[3] Thayer, Cases on Evidence 672 *n.*, cited Wigmore, op. cit. iii 2543, § 1917.

[4] 28 Ass. pl. 5.

[5] " Brian allege un president, et le cas fuit tiel.   Un home fuit oblige in un obligacion sur tiel condicion que il paya v. *l. de fine gold*, et donques etc, et l'obligacion fuit *puri auri*.   Et fuit bien debate s'il etc., et nemy adjuge, et les Maistres del grammaire furent mis pur a doner lour consail quel Latin fuit pro *fine* et ne sceurent dire," Y.B. 9 Hy. VII. Hil. pl. 8.

[6] Buckley v. Rice Thomas, Plowden at p. 124.

[7] Wigmore, op. cit. iii 2543.   [8] Ibid iii 2543-2544.

century, it was very doubtful whether any evidence to prove that X had written a given document was admissible, other than the evidence of a witness who had actually seen him write the document in question.[1]   But it is clear from the trials of the last quarter of the seventeenth century, that it was beginning to be thought that the evidence of a person, who had, at some time, seen the person write, whose handwriting was in issue, was admissible— but only if he had seen him write.   This evidence was admitted on the trial of Sidney;[2] but Hawles said that such evidence had never before been admitted in a criminal case.[3]   Hawles' language,[4] however, and other cases[5] show that it was admitted in civil cases; and Holt, C.J., admitted it in criminal cases as confirmatory evidence, when other circumstances, such as the fact that the papers were found in the prisoner's possession, pointed to his authorship.[6]   The rule was generally stated in this way in the eighteenth century;[7] but, before the beginning of the nineteenth century, the rule for civil was applied to criminal cases, and this evidence was unconditionally admitted.[8]   In the eighteenth century the older rule was also relaxed in another direction.   The court no longer insisted, as it had done in the seventeenth century,[9] that the witness must have seen at some time or other the person write, whose handwriting was in issue.   It was allowed that he might have acquired his knowledge from other sources.   During the greater part of the eighteenth century, however, this evidence would seem to have been admissible, only if the evidence of those who had seen the person whose handwriting was in issue write, was not to be had.[10]   But, at the beginning of the nineteenth century, this limitation disappeared; and the evidence of persons who knew the handwriting in question from the receipt of correspondence, or from some such similar source of knowledge,[11] was unconditionally admitted.   The result was that the only evidence

[1] Wigmore, op. cit. iii 2648, § 1991.

[2] (1683) 9 S.T. at p. 854.   [3] Ibid at pp. 1002-1003.

[4] "An evidence never permitted in a criminal matter before."

[5] Bath and Mountague's Case (1693) 3 Ch. Cas. at pp. 58, 80, and Blurton v. Toon (1695) Skin. 639, cited Wigmore, op. cit. iii 2649 note 5.

[6] In the case of R. v. Crosby (1695) 12 Mod. 72 Holt, C.J., ruled that comparison of hands "is not sufficient for the original foundation of an attainder, but may be well used as a circumstantial and confirming evidence, if the fact be otherwise fully proved; as in *My Lord Preston's Case*, his attempting to go with them into France, and principally where they were found on his person; but here, since they were found elsewhere, to convict on a similitude of hands was to run into the error of *Colonel Sidney's Case.*"

[7] Wigmore, op. cit. iii 2650.

[8] Ibid, citing R. v. de la Motte (1781) 21 S.T. 810.

[9] R. v. Culpeper (1696) Skin. 673.

[10] Wigmore, op. cit. iii 2651, citing Ferrers v. Shirley (1731) Fitzgibbon at p. 196 *per* Lord Raymond, C.J.; Lord Eldon in Eagleton v. Kingston (1803) 8 Ves. at pp. 473-475 stated that the admission of this evidence was a new thing.

[11] Wigmore, op. cit. iii 2651.

excluded was the evidence of persons who merely got their knowledge from a comparison of the disputed document with genuine documents for the purposes of the trial.[1] It was not till 1854[2] that the Legislature modified this rule, and allowed this evidence to be given—with the result that the opinion of experts in handwriting is now as admissible as the evidence of experts in any other art or science.

(ii) *Hearsay.*[3]

" In England," said Lord Blackburn,[4] " hearsay evidence, that is to say, the evidence of a man who is not produced in court and who therefore cannot be cross-examined, as a general rule is not admissible at all." This is the rule excluding hearsay—the most famous and characteristic of all the rules of the English law of evidence.[5] In this, its modern form, it was not fully established till the end of the seventeenth century.

This rule is distinguishable, as Professor Wigmore has pointed out,[6] from the very much older rule that a witness must speak " de visu et auditu "[7]—that is from his own personal knowledge. The modern rule rejects all testimony as to the assertions of any person who is not called as a witness, because such assertions would, if they were admitted, be neither subject to cross-examination nor given under the sanction of an oath. The older rule would not necessarily reject such assertions. It would admit an assertion as to matters which the witnesses testifying had actually heard. It would only exclude assertions as to matters which rested, not upon a basis of things seen or heard by the witness, but upon rumours or opinions or information. At the same time, though the modern rule is far more strict than the older rule, though its basis and rationale are different, it sometimes led to similar results. In the latter half of the seventeenth century Vaughan, C.J., stated the older rule in this form: "a witness swears to what he hath heard or seen—generally or more largely to what hath fallen under his senses."[8] But we shall see that when Vaughan, C.J. uttered this dictum the modern rule was taking shape. It is not surprising,

---

[1] Wigmore, op. cit. iii 2652, 2654.

[2] 17, 18 Victoria c. 125 § 27; Stephen, Digest Art. 52.

[3] The history of this rule is fully related by Wigmore, op. cit. ii 1680-1695, § 1364, whose account I have followed.

[4] Dysart Peerage Case (1881) 6 A.C. at p. 503; the principle of course applies, not only to the oral statements of a man not produced in court, but also to documents emanating from persons not so produced, see Doe d. Wright v. Tatham (1838) 5 Cl. and Fin. at p. 720 *per* Alderson, B.; and this fact was recognized at an early date, see R. v. Sherfield (1632) 3 S.T. at p. 536.

[5] "A rule which may be esteemed, next to jury trial, the greatest contribution of that eminently practical legal system to the world's jurisprudence of procedure," Wigmore, op. cit. ii 1695.

[6] Ibid ii 1680-1681.   [7] Above 211.

[8] Bushell's Case (1670) 6 S.T. at p. 1006.

therefore, that the two rules should sometimes have been confused ; for the requirement that the witness must only speak "to what hath fallen under his senses," could sometimes be used to explain what evidence it was that was rejected as hearsay. Thus Holt, C.J., said in his summing up in *R. v. Charnock :* [1] "But then, gentlemen, as to what they say that the witnesses do testify by hearsay, that is not evidence ; but what they know themselves or heard from the prisoners ; and so Mr. Charnock insists upon it that what Mr. De La Rue says against him is mostly what captain Porter told him. . . . It is true, and therefore I did omit repeating a great part of what De La Rue said, because as to him it was for the most part hearsay. But whatsoever evidence has been given of any fact done within the witness' own knowledge, or of any consult or discourse of the prisoners themselves, that you are to take notice of as good evidence."

It may be that, when the modern rule against hearsay was developing, its development was helped by the memory of this older rule. It is true that the older rule applied to a class of witnesses very different from the modern witness. But we have seen that some of the rules, e.g. as to competency, originally applied to these older witnesses, were taken over and applied to the modern witness.[2] At any rate, the passage which I have just cited from Holt's charge to the jury in *R. v. Charnock,* shows that the two ideas sometimes almost coincided in their application. However that may be, we shall now see that the modern rule is only beginning to be heard of in the seventeenth century, that it is heard of only in connection with the modern witness, and that its rationale is based on the modern practice of examination and cross-examination which came with this type of witness.

It is clear that in the Middle Ages no such rule existed. Modern witnesses were unknown ; and jurors gave their verdicts, either from their own knowledge, or from any information which they could pick up.[3] Some of their verdicts must have been founded "on hearsay and floating tradition."[4] But, during the sixteenth century, it was gradually coming to be evident that juries based their verdicts neither upon their own knowledge, nor upon their own inquiries, but upon the oral evidence of witnesses given in open court ;[5] and we have seen that this fact was recognized by the statute of 1562-1563, which provided a compulsory process for witnesses.[6] It was therefore inevitable that more attention should

---

[1] (1696) 12 S.T. at p. 1454.   [2] Above 186, 191-193.

[3] That they were expected, even in the fifteenth century, to make inquiries, is clear from what Fortescue, C.J., said in Y.B. 28 Hy. VI. Pasch. pl. 1—"et si les Jurors venirent a un home, ou il demurre en le pais pur avoir le conusance de verite del matier, et il eux enforme, il est justifiable"; cp. P. and M. ii 625.

[4] P. and M. ii 622.   [5] Vol. i 335-336.   [6] Above 185.

be paid to the nature of the evidence by which juries were led. "Much begins to be thought and said, in statutes and otherwise, about having witnesses 'good and lawful,' 'good and pregnant,' 'good and sufficient.'"[1] We have seen that it was by no means certain that the common law would not follow the lead of the civil and canon law, and attempt to solve the problem of the sufficiency of proof by requiring a certain number of witnesses.[2] We have seen that this solution of the difficulty was ultimately rejected.[3] But, as we shall now see, it left its traces on the evolution of the rule against hearsay; and it is not improbable that it was discussions arising out of one of the cases, in which more than one witness was required, that helped toward its final establishment.

It was in the sixteenth century, and as a part of the general question as to the kind of evidence that would suffice for proof, that we begin to hear of an objection to hearsay evidence. As yet, however, there was no thought of excluding it; and it was in fact admitted both in civil[4] and criminal cases.[5] But it was beginning to be realized that it was inferior to evidence given from a party's own knowledge; and accused persons protested against its admission. Thus in 1554 Throckmorton says, "Master Crofts is yet living, and is here this day; how happeneth it he is not brought face to face to justify this matter, neither hath been all this time";[6] and in 1603 Sir Walter Raleigh said, "if witnesses are to speak by relation of one another, by this means you may have any man's life in a week; and I may be massacred by mere hearsay as Sir Nicholas Throckmorton was like to have been in Queen Mary's time."[7] And in other cases, down to the latter part of the seventeenth century, objections were often made to its admission.[8] But though objections were made to its admission, and were sometimes acceded to, though it was conceded that it was evidence of an inferior kind, it was nevertheless admitted.[9] In fact the judges seem to have adopted the view that such evidence, though plainly inferior to direct evidence given from the witnesses' own knowledge, was admissible as corroboration of other evidence. This point of view comes out very clearly in a ruling of Popham, C.J., in the course of Raleigh's trial. Cecil is reported as saying, "Sir Walter Raleigh

---

[1] Wigmore, op. cit. ii 1683.   [2] Above 205-206.   [3] Above 206-207.
[4] Rolfe v. Hampden (1541) Dyer 53b—proof of a will, two deposed upon the report of others, and the third "deposed of his own knowledge"; Stransham v. Cullington (1591) Cro. Eliza 228.
[5] Thomas's Case (1553) Dyer 99b, cited below 217 n. 7; Trial of Duke of Norfolk (1571) Jardine, Criminal Trials 157, 158, 159, 179, 201, 206, 210, cited Wigmore, op. cit. ii 1685 note 28; on Raleigh's Trial, 2 S.T. at p. 25, one Dyer deposed to what a person had said to him in a merchant's house at Lisbon.
[6] 1 S.T. at pp. 875-876.   [7] Jardine, Criminal Trials i 429.
[8] The cases are collected by Wigmore, op. cit. ii 1685 note 28.
[9] See e.g. R. v. Cole (1692) 12 S.T. at p. 876, cited Wigmore, op. cit. ii 1687 note 33.

presseth that my lord Cobham should be brought face to face. If he asks things of favour and grace, they must come only from him who can give them. If we sit here as commissioners, how shall we be satisfied whether he ought to be brought, unless we hear the judges speak."[1] To this Popham, C.J., replied, "where no circumstances do concur to make a matter probable, then an accuser may be heard, but so many circumstances agreeing and confirming the accusation in this case, the accuser is not to be produced."[2] This idea that hearsay was admissible as corroborative evidence, persisted down to the end of the seventeenth century;[3] and, as Professor Wigmore has pointed out, survived still longer in the rule that a witness's own prior statements could be proved to show that he had always told the same tale, and so ought to be believed.[4] As we shall now see, it was the growth of the idea that hearsay was wholly inadmissible, which got rid of the idea that it could be used in corroboration of other evidence.

It was, as Professor Wigmore has shown, in the second decade after the Restoration that the modern rule that hearsay is wholly inadmissible comes to be generally recognized. "There are occasional lapses; but it is clear that by general acceptance the rule of exclusion had now become a part of the law as well as of the practice. There is even found a counsel for the prosecution stopping 'for example's sake' its violation by his own witness. No precise date or ruling stands out as decisive; but it seems to be between 1675 and 1690 that the fixing of the doctrine takes place."[5] That the law was then settled in this way was, I think, partly due to a strong dictum of Coke's, and partly to the reflex action of the rejection of the rule requiring more than one witness.

We have seen that a statute of Edward VI.'s reign required a charge of high treason to be proved by two witnesses.[6] It had been held in *Thomas's Case* in 1553[7] that "of two accusers, if one be an accuser of his own knowledge, or of his own hearing, and

---

[1] 2 S.T. at p. 18.

[2] Jardine, Criminal Trials i 427—the reason assigned was that, "for having first confessed against him voluntarily, and so charged another person, if we shall now hear him again in person, he may for favour or fear retract what formerly he hath said, and the jury may be by that means inveigled"—the judge is thinking partly of the danger to the state if dangerous criminals got off in this way (see vol. v 189-190), and partly of the difficulty of weighing oath against oath; later Cecil suggested an adjournment to see if the king would allow Cobham to be produced, but the judges rightly ruled that this was impossible, ibid 435.

[3] "*Pemberton, C.J.* As to this the giving evidence by hearsay will not be evidence . . . *Attorney Gen.* It is not evidence to convict a man, if there were not plain evidence before; but it plainly confirms what the other swears," R. v. Lord Russell (1683) 9 S.T. at p. 613; and see the other cases cited by Wigmore, op. cit. ii 1687 n. 33.

[4] Op. cit. ii 1687, citing Gilbert, Evidence (ed. 1725) 149.

[5] Op. cit. ii 1686, and notes 29-32.

[6] Vol. iv 499. [7] Dyer 99b.

he relate it to another, the other may well be an accuser." But Coke in his third Institute denounces this case as erroneous—" the strange conceit that one may be an accuser by hearsay was utterly denied by the justices in *Lord Lumley's Case.*"[1]   Coke's third Institute was published in 1641, and was at once accepted as an authoritative statement of law.[2]   I cannot help thinking, therefore, that this statement of his had a good deal to do with fixing the attitude of the post-Restoration judges in criminal cases.   And obviously the rule for criminal cases would easily be applied to civil cases also.   Then, too, we have seen that it was just about the same period that the rule requiring more than one witness was decisively rejected;[3] and that one result of this rejection was to give added importance to the consideration of the question of the weight of the evidence offered.[4]   It may well be that this helped to call attention to the admitted inferiority of this evidence, and induced the judges to agree to its total exclusion.   It may well be also that the judges, seeking to justify this new excluding rule, recalled the old rules which required the pre-appointed witnesses of the older law to speak "de visu et auditu."[5]

When this result had been reached, and a general rule of exclusion had been made, its logical consequences soon made for its expansion.   We have seen that it got rid of the rule that hearsay could be used as corroborative evidence.[6]   It also affected the existing rule as to the admissibility of statements under oath made by persons not produced as witnesses.   Throughout the sixteenth and early seventeenth centuries, the main part of the case for the prosecution was contained in the depositions under oath of witnesses, who had been examined, sometimes by the justices of the peace, sometimes by the Council, and sometimes by the judges themselves.[7]   But, as the objections to hearsay gathered weight, it began to be thought that these depositions ought only to be read if the witness could not be produced—Raleigh was prepared to admit the legality of reading Cobham's deposition if he could "not be had conveniently."[8]   After the Revolution, when the rule excluding hearsay had come to be well established, it was finally settled in *R. v Paine*[9] that it applied equally to statements made under oath ; and this was admitted to be law in the case of *Sir John Fenwick.*[10]   The reason assigned by the court in *R. v. Paine*

[1] Third Instit. 25.   [2] Vol. v 471-472.   [3] Above 206-207.
[4] Above 207.   [5] Above 211.   [6] Above 217.
[7] Vol. v 191; below 223-224, 226-227.
[8] 2 S.T. at p. 19; and see a long list of cases civil and criminal in Chancery and at common law where this view seems to be adopted, cited Wigmore, op. cit. ii 1690 n. 47.
[9] (1696) 5 Mod. 163.
[10] (1696) 13 S.T. 618 seqq. where the matter was fully debated on the bill for Fenwick's attainder.

was that, "the defendant not being present when they (the depositions) were taken before the mayor, had lost the benefit of a cross-examination."[1] It was the logic of this reason which led, at the end of the eighteenth century, to the exclusion of the sworn depositions of witnesses before the justices of the peace, acting under the statutes of Philip and Mary's reign;[2] and, in the nineteenth century, to the exclusion by the Legislature of all depositions of accused persons taken by justices of the peace, except under very stringent conditions, the most important of which are that the deponent is dead or too ill to travel, and that an opportunity for cross-examination has been given.[3]

Thus, by the end of the seventeenth century, the modern rule had become fully established, and the development of its logical consequences had begun to get rid of usages or rules inconsistent with it. Soon, however, it began to be recognized that certain exceptions to its operation must be admitted. But, as the elaboration of these exceptions is the work of the eighteenth and nineteenth centuries, their history must be dealt with in a subsequent Book of this History.

The Relations between Documentary and Oral Evidence

The rudimentary state of the law as to oral evidence in the sixteenth and early seventeenth centuries, sufficiently accounts for the growth, in the seventeenth century, of the rule that the contents of written documents cannot be varied by oral evidence.[4] The manner in which that rule is phrased in the earlier authorities, indicates its origin in the days when the summoning of witnesses to testify to a jury was as yet a new thing. A written document, it is said, cannot be varied by mere averment[5]—an expression which clearly goes back to the days when evidence was stated in the pleadings.[6] And this conclusion was strengthened by the fact that the disallowance of these averments, or in later days the refusal to admit this oral evidence, kept the interpretation of these documents under the control of the court.[7] From this point of view, it was a rule which operated in a somewhat similar manner to the doctrines of colour in pleading, and the demurrer

---

[1] 5 Mod. at p. 165. [2] Wigmore, op. cit. ii 1694; ibid 1713, § 1375.

[3] 11, 12 Victoria c. 42 § 17; Wigmore, op. cit. ii 1712, § 1374; Stephen, Digest Art. 140; for depositions taken before a coroner see ibid at p. 155 n. 1 to Art. 141, and Art. 32.

[4] Above 173-177.

[5] Above 176 n. 3; below 221; cp. Doctor and Student i. c. 12 where the Student, explaining that a plea of payment without a written discharge is no answer to an action on an obligation, says, "that is ordained by the law to avoid a great inconvenience that else might happen to come to many people; that is to say that every man by a nude parol, and by a bare averment, should avoid an obligation."

[6] Vol. iii 638. [7] Thayer, op. cit. 409.

to evidence.[1]   And the fact that this rule, which prevented documentary from being varied by oral evidence, was helped by the desire of the common law courts to keep the interpretation of documents in their own hands, is illustrated by the fact that, in the seventeenth century and later, the court of Chancery admitted this evidence more freely.[2]

For these two reasons this rule was strictly enforced in the seventeenth century ; and it led, as we have seen, to the evolution of strict rules for the construction of written documents, which paid little heed to the real meaning intended by their framers.[3] It is true that it was coming to be admitted that fraud was a good defence even to a fine ;[4] and the admissibility of the plea of "non est factum" showed that, from the first, it was always open to the parties to show that an instrument had never had any operation.[5]   But it was not till 1767 that it was held that illegality could be pleaded as a defence to a bond.[6]   In fact, the lawyers were very reluctant to travel far outside the words of the document, and tried to interpret it with as little reference to outside facts as possible.   In 1702 Holt, C.J., declined to consider the knowledge of a testatrix as to the manner in which the property she was devising was settled, in order to ascertain whether she meant to devise a life estate or a fee simple.   "The intent of a testator," he said, "will not do, unless there be sufficient words in the will to manifest that intent ; neither is his intent to be collected from the circumstances of his estates, and other matters collateral and foreign to the will, but from the words and tenor of the will itself, and if we once travel into the affairs of the testator, and leave the will, we shall not know the mind of the testator by his words, but by his circumstances ; so that if you go to a lawyer, he shall not know how to expound it."[7]   But Holt was in a minority of one, and the opinion of the majority of the court was upheld by the Exchequer Chamber and the House of Lords.   It was the example set by the courts of equity during the eighteenth century, which went far to modify the rigidity of the common law rules, and to introduce the modern rule as to the sort of evidence which may be looked at in interpreting documents—the rule that, "in order to ascertain the relation of the words of a document to facts, every fact may be proved to which it refers, or may probably have been intended to refer, or which identifies any person or thing mentioned in it."[8]

There was, however, one case in which, even in the sixteenth

---

[1] Vol. iii 639 ; below 298.   [2] Thayer, op. cit. 429 seqq.
[3] Vol. vii 392-394.   [4] Ibid 33-34.   [5] Above 177.
[6] Collins v. Blantern 2 Wils. 347 ; Thayer, op. cit. 406.
[7] Cole v. Rawlinson 1 Salk. at pp. 234-235 ; Thayer, op. cit. 426-429.
[8] Stephen, Digest Art. 91.

century, the common law had relaxed the strictness of its rules. In 1591, in *Lord Cheyney's Case*,[1] the court laid it down that the intent of a testator was, as a general rule, to be gathered from the words of his will; and that, if no meaning could be attached to these words, the will was void for uncertainty. But they held that in one case direct evidence could be given of the testator's intent: "If a man has two sons both baptized by the name of John, and conceiving that the elder (who had been long absent) is dead, devises his land by his will in writing to his son John generally, and in truth the elder is living; in this case the younger son may in pleading or in evidence allege the devise to him; and if it be denied he may produce witnesses to prove his father's intent, that he thought the other to be dead; or that he at the time of the will made, named his son John the younger, and the writer left out the addition of the younger."[2] In other words, in a case of equivocation parol evidence of intention may be given. Though Coke cites for this rule a Year Book case of 1374, in which this evidence was admitted in the case of a fine, it was probably new law, and a modification of the older law.[3]

Bacon made this case the foundation of his celebrated rule that, though *ambiguitas patens* (i.e. an ambiguity appearing on the face of the document) "is never holpen by averment," *ambiguitas latens* (i.e. an ambiguity which arises, not on the face of the document, but from collateral matter arising out of the facts to which it is to be applied) can be so helped.[4] Both his phrasing, and his reasons for the rule as to *ambiguitas patens*, illustrate the manner in which this parol evidence rule had grown up.[5] The expression "averment" takes us back to the time when oral evidence was usually pleaded; and the statement that one reason for the rule is that "the law will not couple and mingle matter of specialty, which is of the higher account, with matter of averment, which is of inferior account in the law," carries us back to one of the reasons for the establishment of the rule.[6] Bacon probably intended simply to sum up and explain the application of the rule laid down in *Cheyney's Case*. But, in the latter half of the eighteenth century, it was given prominence by the use made of it in a book on "The Theory of Evidence" written by Mr. Justice Bathurst, which was embodied in his

---

[1] 5 Co. Rep. 68a. [2] At f. 68b.
[3] See Thayer, op. cit. 420 n. 1.
[4] Maxims of the Law, Regula XXV.
[5] "*Ambiguitas patens* is never holpen by averment: and the reason is, because the law will not couple and mingle matter of specialty, which is of the higher account, with matter of averment which is of inferior account in the law; for that were to make all deeds hollow and subject to averments, and so, in effect, that to pass without deed, which the law appointeth shall not pass but by deed."
[6] Above 175.

nephew Buller's "Trials at Nisi Prius."[1] The maxim only applied to the case of equivocation; but it was used as if it were a rule which could be used to explain all the cases, in which extrinsic evidence was or was not permissible, to aid the interpretation of a written document. And though Wigram in 1831, and many other writers since, have shown that it is useless for this purpose, "it still performs a great and confusing function in our legal discussions."[2]

The use made of this maxim of Bacon's, and the development of the "best evidence" doctrine through the use made of it in Gilbert's book on evidence,[3] represent premature attempts by the lawyers of the eighteenth century to give a systematic form to the principles of this new body of law, which had been developing in the seventeenth century.[4] In fact, the main line through which its further development proceeded, was not by reasoning from the doctrines propounded by Gilbert and Buller, but by the rulings on points of evidence which arose in trials at nisi prius.[5] When, at the end of the eighteenth century, these cases began to be reported, great developments in the law were rendered possible. The new material thus made available showed that the law had come to be far fuller and more detailed than it was at the end of the seventeenth century. It opened the way for new treatises which summed up the modern developments of this branch of the law; for an analysis and discussion of its contents by Bentham and others, which paved the way for the statutory reforms of the nineteenth century; and for its further developments from this new basis by the courts.[6]

These developments belong to the following period of legal history. At the end of the seventeenth century the foundations only of our modern law had been laid; and, though some of its most characteristic features were plainly discernible, it was as yet comparatively scanty. But we shall now see that the developments already made had revolutionized the mediæval system of common law procedure and pleading, and had been mainly instrumental in producing the new system which lasted till the reforms of the nineteenth century.

§ 2. COMMON LAW PROCEDURE AND PLEADING

The Criminal Law

In the preceding Book of this History I have given an account of the development of the main features of the criminal procedure

---

[1] Thayer, op. cit. 476.　　　　[2] Ibid 472.

[3] Ibid 490-491; as Thayer points out, ibid 489-490, the phrase "best evidence" first appears in the cases in Holt's time; see Ford v. Hopkins (1699) 1 Salk. 283; Altham v. Anglesea (1709) 11 Mod. at p. 213.

[4] Wigmore, op. cit. i 26 § 8.　　　　[5] Ibid 26-27.　　　　[6] Ibid 27-29.

of the common law;[1] and in Part I. of this Book I have said something of the introduction of those new ideas as to criminal procedure, which were needed for the protection of the state in the sixteenth century, and were suggested by the very different ideas as to criminal procedure which had become or were then becoming universal on the continent.[2] At this point I shall, in the first place, sketch briefly the history of the way in which the criminal procedure of the mediæval common law, the new ideas which were introduced in the sixteenth century, and the growth of a law of evidence, were, during the sixteenth, seventeenth and eighteenth centuries, combining to create the criminal procedure of our modern common law. In the second place, I shall say something of the origins and development of a new form of criminal procedure—the Information—which came into common use during this period.

(1) *The growth of the criminal procedure of the modern common law.*

On this matter I can fortunately be brief. I have already dealt with the effects which ideas derived from the continental procedure had upon the common law in the sixteenth century;[3] and the manner in which those ideas were blended with the mediæval ideas, so as to form our modern criminal procedure, have been so admirably described by Stephen in his account of the trials of the sixteenth, seventeenth, and early eighteenth centuries,[4] that it is necessary to do little more than summarize his results. In the first place, I shall briefly summarize the effect of the new ideas which were introduced into the law of criminal procedure in the sixteenth century; and, in the second place, I shall show how they were modified, partly by the predominance after the Great Rebellion of common law principles, partly by the independence of the judges which was secured at the Revolution, and partly by the growing precision of the rules of evidence.

(i) We have seen that public opinion in the sixteenth century demanded and approved of changes in criminal procedure, which gave advantages to the crown in its struggle with lawbreakers and traitors. Hence it was possible to pass statutes which made it more difficult for accused persons to get released on bail, to introduce the practice of issuing warrants to arrest suspected persons, and to introduce an inquisitorial examination of suspected persons by the justices of the peace, the Council, or the judges.[5] We have seen, too, that it was the need to protect the state against its enemies, which made it possible for the Council to imitate the continental practice, by employing torture to extract information

[1] Vol. iii 597-623.   [2] Vol. v 168-197.
[3] Ibid 188-197.   [4] H.C.L. i 324-427.
[5] Vol. iv 527-528, 529-530; vol. v 190-192; see also vol. i 294-297; above 199.

from the persons whom it arrested, and by disregarding, in important cases, the ordinary rules of procedure and the ordinary rules of law.[1] It was for the same reason that all the features of the mediæval procedure, which told in favour of the crown, were emphasized; and that, when the law was doubtful, the crown was always favoured. Thus, as under the old law, persons accused of treason or felony were denied the help of counsel,[2] and they were refused a copy of the indictment.[3] The law as to oral evidence was, as we have seen,[4] very new. Though the crown was beginning to call witnesses, there was no clear rule that the prisoner could call them; and continental analogies could be invoked for the proposition that he should not be allowed to call them. Therefore he was at first refused this right; and when, at the beginning of the seventeenth century, this refusal began to shock public opinion, the illogical expedient was adopted of allowing him to call them and refusing to allow them to be sworn.[5] Similarly, the absence of clear rules as to admissibility of evidence, and as to the conduct of a trial, were used to give advantages to the crown. The witnesses were not confronted with the prisoner, the evidence of accomplices was not only not suspected, but was even regarded as especially cogent,[6] and the prisoner himself was closely questioned by the examining magistrate, the judge at the trial, and the prosecuting counsel.[7] As we have seen,[8] the privilege of refusing to answer incriminating questions was only established for witnesses at the end of this period; and, even then, it had hardly been extended to the prisoner himself.

We have seen that in all these ways the criminal procedure of the sixteenth century had been immensely strengthened against accused persons. On the other hand, we have seen that, even in this period, both the survival of the mediæval conception of a trial, and the existence of a jury, made the English criminal procedure very much fairer to the accused than the continental procedure. Trials were public; the crown must make out its case to the satisfaction of the jury; the prisoner, though prevented from properly preparing his defence, could say what he could in court; the court generally put the issue fairly enough to the jury; the judges still professed the belief that it was better to let many guilty escape than to convict one innocent person.[9] And, though in important state trials, for offences which imperilled the safety of

---

[1] Vol. v 184-188. [2] Vol. ii 107, 312; vol. iii 616; vol. v 192.
[3] Vol. iii 615. [4] Above 184-185. [5] Vol. v 192-193; above 195.
[6] Thus Cecil, writing to Winwood as to Raleigh's trial, said that the main reason for his condemnation was the evidence of the accomplice Cobham—"the accusation of Cobham being of that nature that it implied the accusing of himself withal, *than which proof the law regarded none greater*," Jardine, Criminal Trials i 458; vol. v 193.
[7] Vol. v 193. [8] Above 200-201. [9] Vol. v 195-196.

the state, the accused had a very slender opportunity of making an effective defence; though the punishment of the jury in *Throckmorton's Case*, in which the jury indorsed the exceptionally able defence which the accused, in spite of all his disadvantages, managed to put up, must have inclined juries to convict if they were so directed by the court; there is reason to think that in ordinary cases the judges held the scales fairly, gave proper weight to all that the accused could urge, and did not attempt to punish juries who acquitted.[1]

The mediæval trial was a curious mixture of formality and informality. The arraignment of the prisoner, the wording of the indictment, the challenges to and the swearing of the jury, the giving of the verdict, and the judgment—were all formal matters governed by very precise rules. On the other hand, there were few rules which regulated the actual hearing of the case. There were no rules of evidence[2]—the knowledge of the jury being mainly relied on; and, though the judge generally summed up the case to the jury,[3] they were free to return what verdict they liked, subject only to the risk of proceedings being taken against them if they gave a verdict of which the court disapproved,[4] and possibly of proceedings in attaint if they acquitted.[5]

It is clear from Sir Thomas Smith's description of an ordinary criminal trial, that this mixture of formality and informality characterized the criminal procedure of the sixteenth century.[6] The formal parts of the trial, as he describes them, were all much as they were in the Middle Ages, and much as they are at the present day. The actual trial was still informal—it consisted of an altercation between the accused, and the prosecutor and his witnesses. But it is clear that the preliminary examination of the witnesses, and the evidence given at the trial, were beginning to take a very much more important place. After the jury had been sworn, and the cryer had made proclamation for all to come who could give evidence or say anything against the prisoner, then, "if no man come in, the Judge asketh who sent him to prison, who is commonly one of the Justices of peace. He if he be there [he] delivereth up the examination which he tooke of him, and underneath the names of those whom he hath bound to give evidence, although the malefactor hath confessed the crime to the Justice of the peace, and that appeare by his hande and confirmation, the xii men will acquite the prisoner, but they which should give evidence pay their recognizaunce. Howbeit this doth seldome chaunce, except it be in small matters, and where the

---

[1] Vol. v 195; vol. vi 630-631.　　　[2] Above 179-183.　　　[3] Vol. iii 616.
[4] Vol. i 343-344.　　　[5] But this is doubtful, see vol. i 340.
[6] De Republica Anglorum, Bk. II. c. 23.

Justices of peace, who sent the prisoner to the gaole, is away. If they which be bound to give evidence come in, first is read the examination, which the Justice of peace doeth give in: then is heard (if he be there) the man robbed what he can say, being first sworne to say trueth, and after the Constable, and as many as were at the apprehension of the malefactor: and so many as can say anything being sworn one after an other to say truth. These be set in such a place as they may see the Judges and the Justices, the enquest and the prisoner, and heare them, and be heard of them all. The Judge first after they be sworne, asketh first the party robbed, if he knowe the prisoner, and biddeth him looke upon him: he saith yea, the prisoner sometimes saith nay. The partie pursuivaunt giveth good ensignes *verbi gratia*, I knowe thee well ynough, thou robbest me in such a place, thou beatest mee, thou tookest my horse from mee, and my purse, thou hadest then such a coate and such a man in thy companie: The theefe will say no, and so they stand a while in altercation, then he telleth al he can say: after him likewise all those who were at the apprehension of the prisoner, or who can give any *indices* or tokens which we call in our language evidence against the malefactor. When the Judge hath heard them say inough, he asketh if they can say any more: if they say no, then he turneth his speeche to the enquest. Good men (saith he) ye of the enquest, ye have heard what these men say against the prisoner, you have also heard what the prisoner can say for himselfe, have an eye to your othe, and to you duetie, and doe that which God shall put in your mindes to the discharge of your consciences, and marke well what is said."

That Smith's description of an ordinary criminal trial is substantially true, is clear from the State Trials of this period. Necessarily in these trials the evidence against the prisoner was carefully prepared by the depositions of witnesses taken before the Council or the judges; and, if the judge who tried the case had taken the evidence, he sometimes used his knowledge to explain it—thus, on Raleigh's trial, Popham, C.J., gave the court information as to the circumstances under which Cobham's examination had taken place, and the manner in which he had induced him to sign his deposition.[1] The king's counsel laid all this evidence before the court, generally making an opening speech to explain the general nature of the case,[2] which the prisoner sometimes

---

[1] Jardine, Criminal Trials i 415.

[2] In Throckmorton's Case (1554) 1 S.T. 869 no such speech is reported; but it became the practice to make such a speech in Elizabeth's reign, see the Trial of the Duke of Norfolk (1571) 1 S.T. at p. 968; the Trial of Campion (1581) 1 S.T. 1051; the Trial of Raleigh (1603) 2 S.T. 5.

criticized as it proceeded.[1] If, as was usually the case, there were several counsel, each was entrusted with some particular part of the case.[2] But the main part of the trial consisted in laying the evidence before the court, in questioning the prisoner upon it and upon the answers which he made to it, and in listening to the remarks and answering the replies made by the prisoner.[3] Thus the trial was substantially, as Smith says, an "altercation" between the king's counsel, the judges, and the prisoner. The prisoner was questioned by the prosecution, he replied to the evidence as it was given, and he raised any points of law that occurred to him as the case proceeded. Thus, in *Throckmorton's Case*, Staundford, the king's serjeant, began by questioning the accused as to a confession made by one Winter, which was adduced to prove that he knew and approved of Wyat's rebellion.[4] After a witness had been called for the crown, Throckmorton made a speech to show that the witness's evidence was not credible; and this speech was followed by an altercation between the prisoner, the counsel for the crown, and the court.[5] The reading of other depositions were followed by similar altercations.[6] Then Throckmorton raised a point of law on Edward III.'s statute of treason; and this was followed by a similar dispute on the question of law, in which he proved himself a better lawyer than the king's counsel and judges.[7] Apparently he was allowed both to interrupt the judge's summing up, when he was unfairly stating his answers to the evidence of the crown,[8] and to make a speech to the jury after the summing up was concluded.[9] So, too, in *Raleigh's Case*,[10] the trial was, for the most part, made up of an altercation between the prisoner, the court, and the king's counsel. Raleigh, like Throckmorton, claimed to have the last word; but Coke claimed the last word for the king.[11] Raleigh interrupted Coke's address; and, on Cecil's interposing to protect Raleigh, there occurred the famous scene between Coke and the court.[12]

---

[1] See the Trial of the Duke of Norfolk 1 S.T. at pp. 969, 970; Trial of Raleigh 2 S.T. 6-8.

[2] Stephen, H.C.L. i 325, 330-331.   [3] Ibid 325-326.

[4] 1 S.T. at pp. 872-875.   [5] Ibid at pp. 878-882.

[6] Ibid at p. 883-887.   [7] Ibid at pp. 887-895.

[8] "Then the Chief Justice Bromley remembered particularly all the depositions and evidences given against the prisoner, and either for want of good memory or good will the prisoner's answers were in part not recited: whereupon the prisoner craved indifferency, and did help the judge's old memory with his own recital," ibid at p. 897.

[9] Ibid at p. 898. In fact he had turned the tables and cowed the king's counsel; at one point the attorney-general was even reduced to appeal for protection to the court—"some of us will come no more at the bar an we be thus handled," ibid at p. 893.

[10] (1603) 2 S.T. 1; but the best account of the case is in Jardine, Criminal Trials i 400; there is also a good summary in Gardiner, History of England i 127 seqq.

[11] 2 S.T. at p. 26.   [12] Ibid; vol. v 427 n. 1,

There was a good reason why Raleigh should wish to have the last word, for he had in his pocket a letter from Cobham which completely exonerated him.   But Coke countered this move by the production of a letter written only the day before, in which he retracted his letter to Raleigh, and stated that it was written at his request.[1]   This piece of evidence, though it did not prove the treasonable acts alleged in the indictment, was a stronger proof of a connection between Raleigh and Cobham than any that had yet been produced;[2] and it was no wonder that Raleigh was much amazed,[3] and that the Chief Justice remarked, " I perceive you are not so clear a man as you have protested all this while."[4] " Yet bye and bye he seemed to gather his spirits again."[5]   In spite of Coke's objections,[6] he got Cecil,[7] who knew Cobham's handwriting, to read the letter in which he retracted his charges against him.   But Coke proved that the letter, which he (Coke) had read, was not extracted from Cobham by a promise of pardon,[8] and forced Raleigh to admit a fact that he had previously denied.[9]   This admission, and the letter produced by Coke, deprived Cobham's letter of retraction of any effect which it might otherwise have had.   It was, in fact, fatal to Raleigh. After a deliberation of only a quarter of an hour the jury brought in a verdict of guilty.

It is clear that this new fashion of examining witnesses for the crown, and, in the light of their depositions, elaborately prepar- ing the case against the prisoner, enormously increased the severity of the rules which refused him a copy of the indictment, refused him professional advice, and refused to allow him to call witnesses.   And these advantages possessed by the crown pressed all the more hardly on him, because, as we have seen, the modern rules of evidence hardly as yet existed.   Let us recall one or two instances of the way in which the unsettled state of this branch of the law handicapped the accused.   The crown was not bound to produce its witnesses to be cross-examined by the accused—both Throckmorton and Raleigh asked in vain that persons, whose depositions had been read against them, should be produced.[10]

---

[1] 2 S.T. at pp. 27-28.

[2] " This confession of Lord Cobham seemed to give great satisfaction, and clear all the former evidence which stood very doubtful." Jardine, op. cit. i 446.

[3] "At this confession of Lord Cobham Sir Walter Raleigh was much amazed," Jardine, op. cit. i 446.

[4] 2 S.T. at p. 28.   [5] Jardine, op. cit. i 446.

[6] On Coke objecting, Cecil said, " Mr. Attorney you are more peremptory than honest."

[7] Cecil was one of the commissioners of oyer and terminer who was trying the case, and he seems honestly to have tried to get fair play for Raleigh.

[8] 2 S.T. at p 29.

[9] Jardine, op. cit. i 448-449—" this made the rest of the Lord Cobham's accusa- tion the better credited."

[10] Above 216, 217.

Hearsay evidence was freely allowed; and, though it was beginning to be objected to at the end of the sixteenth century,[1] nothing like the modern rule emerged till the latter part of the seventeenth century.[2] The rule that a witness could object to questions on the ground that they tended to incriminate him, was not established till the end of the seventeenth century; and this rule was not applied to the prisoner till the beginning of the eighteenth century.[3] In fact, as Stephen has pointed out, the jury was left, as under the older system, to form their opinion as they could, and on any fact or facts which they chose to consider evidence.[4] But the crown had come prepared with evidence written and oral. The prisoner, kept in ignorance of the details of the case which he was expected to meet, could make no similar preparation, and could produce no evidence. It is clear, therefore, that the informality of the trial, the irresponsibility of the jury, and the chance that they might be fined or imprisoned if, in an important state case, they gave a verdict displeasing to the court, gave the crown all the advantages it could wish for.

No doubt, as we have seen, these trials were far fairer to the accused than trials under the inquisitory system of the Continent.[5] They were public; and the prisoner could say what he liked in his defence. The preservation of a form of trial with these characteristics was, as we have seen, largely due to the fact that the mediæval accusatory trial, by presentment indictment and trial by petty jury, had become an effective criminal proceeding,[6] which was capable of being adapted to the new needs of the state in the sixteenth century. It was capable, as the development just described shows, of being strengthened by the introduction of some of the ideas derived from the continental procedure. But it was a trial by jury; and it could not shed those mediæval characteristics which made for fairness to the accused—its accusatory form, its publicity, its oral character, its liberty to the accused to defend himself as he could. We shall now see that, from the middle of the seventeenth century onwards, the growing strength of the common law, the growth of more settled rules of evidence, and, at the end of the century, the new impartiality of the judges, modified without destroying the effect of the continental ideas which had been introduced in the sixteenth century; and thus gave to the criminal procedure of the modern common law a combination of fairness and efficiency which it had never before possessed.

(ii) The beginnings of this process of modifying the harshness of the criminal procedure of the sixteenth century must be dated,

---

[1] Above 216-217. [2] Above 217. [3] Above 200-201.
[4] H.C.L. i 336-337. [5] Vol. v 195-196. [6] Vol. iii 620-622.

Stephen says, from the year 1640[1]—that is from the date when Parliament and the common law began to assert their supremacy in the state. "The whole spirit and temper of the criminal courts, even in their most irregular and revolutionary proceedings, appears to have been radically changed from what it had been in the preceding century to what it is in our own days. In every case, so far as I am aware, the accused person had the witnesses against him produced face to face, unless there was some special reason (such as sickness) to justify the reading of their depositions. In some cases the prisoner was questioned, but never to any greater extent than that which it is practically impossible to avoid when a man has to defend himself without counsel. When so questioned the prisoners usually refused to answer. The prisoner was also allowed, not only to cross-examine the witnesses against him if he thought fit, but also to call witnesses of his own."[2]

That these tendencies should be manifest at this time is not strange. We have seen that the inquisitory methods of the Star Chamber, had had a good deal of influence upon the criminal procedure adopted in the common law courts in the sixteenth century.[3] But it was exactly these methods, as applied to the suppression of the opponents of prerogative government, which the leaders of the Long Parliament were determined to suppress.[4] Thus it was natural that the practice of questioning the accused, and its concomitant, the use of torture, should disappear. It was inevitable, therefore, that the humaner methods of the common law should come to the front, both because they were the only alternative, and because the common lawyers and the Parliamentary party were old allies. Even before the meeting of the Long Parliament, it was clear that the nation was objecting to some of the harsher practices of the sixteenth-century procedure. We have seen that, in the middle of the seventeenth century, the accused had been allowed to summon witnesses.[5] Sir Thomas Smith had testified both to the national repugnance to torture,[6] and to the feeling aroused by the punishment of jurors for returning verdicts displeasing to the court;[7] and Sir Walter Raleigh,[8] and, at a later date, Hawles,[9] solicitor-general in 1695, in his

---

[1] H.C.L. i 358.   [2] Ibid.   [3] Vol. v 188-195.
[4] See above 200, for the analogous effects of these causes on some of the rules of evidence.
[5] Vol. v 193; above 195.   [6] Bk. ii c. 24.   [7] Bk. iii c. 1.
[8] "*Raleigh.* You try me by the Spanish Inquisition if you proceed only by circumstances without two witnesses. *Attorney.* This is a treasonable speech," 2 S.T. at p. 15.
[9] "The truth is, when I consider the practice of later times, and the manner of usage of the prisoners, it is so very much like, or rather worse than the practice of the inquisition, as I have read it, that I sometimes think it was in order to introduce popery, and make the inquisition . . . seem easy in respect of it," 8 S.T. at pp. 733-734.

criticism of the trials of the latter part of Charles II.'s reign, complained that the practices of the crown savoured of the methods of the inquisition. All these feelings and tendencies came to the front in 1640. And just as the informality and the fluidity of the rules of criminal procedure, had enabled some of the harsher methods of the continental procedure of the sixteenth century to be introduced gradually and without legislative change; so this same cause enabled a humaner practice to be introduced in a similar manner. Thus, as Stephen has pointed out, the procedure on Strafford's impeachment was "conspicuously fair" to the accused;[1] and the formal and pedantic proof offered, on the trial of Charles I., to prove his presence at different battles in the civil war, and the fact that persons had been killed in those battles, "shows how deeply men's minds had been impressed with the importance of proceeding upon proper and formal evidence in criminal cases."[2]

During the period from the Restoration to the Revolution these humaner methods of procedure were in the main followed; and, after the decision in *Bushell's Case*, a jury who chose to return a verdict of acquittal, contrary to the direction of the court, had nothing to fear.[3] We have seen that on the trials for ordinary crimes the procedure was as fair to the accused as the existing rules allowed.[4] Nor was the conduct of these trials by the judges unduly harsh. Indeed harshness was not needed; for the existing rules of procedure, and the absence of any fixed rules of evidence, still put enormous powers into the hands of the crown.[5] Naturally these powers were exercised in important state trials; and the unfairness of these rules in these trials was aggravated by the bitterness of party spirit which, at the end of Charles II.'s reign, was manifested in the Popish plot, the Exclusion controversy, and the Rye House plot. At the same time, the deterioration in the character of the bench, which was the direct result of this growth of bitter party feeling, caused many of the actual trials to be conducted with a brutality to the accused which has never been surpassed. The frenzy of unreasoning fear aroused by Oates's disclosures, so biassed public opinion that judges and juries were swept off their feet, and combined to refuse a fair trial to any person accused of complicity in the plot.[6] This is sufficiently illustrated by the accusations made against Scroggs, C.J., who quite properly and justly had procured the acquittal of Sir George Wakeman and three others. The existence of a state of public opinion which prevents a fair trial is a danger to which the jury system is always open; and it is a danger against which there is

---

[1] H.C.L. i 361.   [2] Ibid 364-365.   [3] Vol. i 345-346.
[4] Vol. vi 630.   [5] Stephen, H.C.L. i 382.   [6] Vol. vi 183-184.

no remedy except the existence of an impartial, a humane, a courageous, and a learned bench. It is obviously aggravated when, as in the latter part of Charles II.'s and in James II.'s reigns, there was a bench conspicuous for the absence of these qualities.[1] Let us look at one or two of the results of the existing rules of procedure, and of the absence of any fixed rules of evidence.

Firstly, the prisoner was kept in close confinement till the day of his trial. "He had no means of knowing what evidence had been given against him. He was not allowed as a matter of right, but only as an occasional exceptional favour, to have either counsel or solicitor to advise him as to his defence, or to see his witnesses and put their evidence in order. When he came into court he was set to fight for his life with absolutely no knowledge of the evidence to be produced against him."[2] Thus, on the trial of Colledge, it appeared that he had been allowed to have legal advice while in the Tower;[3] but, notwithstanding that fact, the counsel for the crown took away his papers; and the court refused to let him have back a paper which contained instructions for his defence, on the ground that this would be tantamount to allowing him professional assistance.[4] Though, as we have seen,[5] the court was beginning to allow process to issue to compel the production of the prisoner's witnesses, it was not every prisoner who could get this privilege. Ireland, on his trial called a witness, but, when he called him, he said, "It is a hundred to one if he be here, for I have not been permitted so much as to send a scrap of paper";[6] and it appeared on Oates's second trial for perjury that Ireland could, if he had had the opportunity, have established a perfectly good alibi.[7]

Secondly, "there was an utter absence of any conception of the true nature of judicial evidence on the part of the judges, the counsel, and the prisoners."[8] We hear of objections to hearsay evidence,[9] and to the necessity for two witnesses in cases of treason; "but, subject to these small rules, the opinion of the time seems to have been that if a man came and swore to anything whatever, he ought to be believed, unless he was directly con-

---

[1] Vol. vi. 503-511.
[2] Stephen, H.C.L. i 398; cp. Hawles's remarks in 8 S.T. 734-735.
[3] 8 S.T. 549-563.
[4] North, C.J., after examining the papers said, "for that which contains the names of the witnesses, that you have again : for the other matters, the instructions in point of law, if they had been written in the first person, in your own name, that we might believe it was your writing, it would have been some thing ; but when it is written in the second person, you should do so and so, by which it appears to be written by another person, it is an ill precedent to permit such things; that were to give you counsel in an indirect way, which the law gives you not directly," 8 S.T. at p. 585.
[5] Above 196.   [6] 7 S.T. 121, cited Stephen, H.C.L. i 388.
[7] Stephen, H.C.L. i 388 n. 3.
[8] Ibid 399.   [9] Above 217.

tradicted. The greater part of the evidence given in the trials for the Popish Plot consisted of oaths of Oates, Bedloe, and others, that they heard this man or that say he would kill the King, or that they read letters to the same effect, which, upon mentally comparing them with letters written by the accused, they perceived to be in the same handwriting."[1] The rule that the evidence of an accomplice needs corroboration was still not accepted. There was no idea of weighing the credit of a witness. His competency could be and was sometimes objected to; but, if he was competent, the court still adhered to the very primitive idea that his oath had, as a rule, "a mechanical value," which entitled it to be believed unless it was contradicted.[2] There could be no effective cross-examination, partly because the prisoner was not represented by counsel, and partly because he was kept in ignorance of the names of the witnesses and the evidence against him till the day of the trial. Under these circumstances, the only effective pieces of cross-examination could be those made by the counsel for the crown or by the judge; and they were as often as not directed to securing the conviction of the prisoner.[3]

Thirdly, the crown rigidly insisted on all the advantages which the older rules gave to it. I have already noted the strict way in which, in the case of Colledge, it interpreted the rules that the prisoner must have no professional assistance. The prisoner was still allowed no copy of the indictment. And though allowing a copy of the indictment might have enabled prisoners to waste the time of the court, or even to escape, by means of objections which the irrational rules as to the certainty required in indictments made possible;[4] yet it must be remembered that these objections must be proposed by the prisoner himself without professional aid;[5] and that the possibility of making these objections was almost the only point in which the law gave an advantage to the prisoner over the crown. Moreover, there had been a change, both in the practical conduct of the trial and in the law, which had given the crown additional advantages. The change in the practical conduct of the trial relates to the manner in which the crown's evidence was given. We have seen that in the sixteenth century the prisoner answered the king's witnesses as they were produced;[6]

---

[1] Stephen, H.C.L. i 399-400.   [2] Ibid 400-401; above 208.

[3] See e.g. Jeffreys' cross-examination of Dunne on the trial of Lady Lisle which, in Stephen's opinion, was masterly, H.C.L. i 413.

[4] This seems to be the view of Stephen, ibid 398-399; for the rules as to indictments see vol. iii 617-620.

[5] North, C.J., told Colledge, " for counsel you cannot have it, unless matter of law arises, and that must be propounded by you; and then if it be a matter debateable, the court will assign you counsel, but it must be upon a matter fit to be argued. For I must tell you a defence in a case of high treason ought not to be made by artificial cavils, but by plain fact," 8 S.T. at p. 570.

[6] Above 226-227.

but in the latter part of the seventeenth century, Hawles tells us, "he must hear all the witnesses produced to prove him guilty together, without answering each as he comes, for that is breaking in upon the king's evidence as it is called, though it (the trial) hold many hours."[1] The change in the law relates to the power of the court to discharge a jury after it had been charged with the prisoner, and to remand the prisoner in order that he might be tried at a later date. In the fourteenth century it was the rule that, if the jury had been sworn and charged with the prisoner, they could not be discharged till they had given a verdict;[2] and Coke repeated this rule.[3] But in the seventeenth century this rule had, with the approval of Hale,[4] been changed for obvious reasons of public policy.[5] If the evidence was such as to give the court reason to suspect the guilt of the prisoner, and yet was not sufficient to convict, the court could discharge the jury, and remand the accused to prison, till further evidence could be got.[6] After the Revolution, as was perhaps natural, Coke's view for a time prevailed;[7] but, in the course of the eighteenth century, the law as stated by Hale was followed,[8] and was finally settled to be correct in 1866.[9]

The development of the law of criminal procedure was brought back by the Revolution to the lines on which it was beginning to proceed, before the political passions of the last years of Charles II. and of James II.'s reigns, had subordinated its administration to the desire to use it as a party weapon. This phenomenon is apparent in other branches of the law; but naturally it is more strikingly apparent in this branch of the law than in any other. The scandalous miscarriages of justice which occurred in the trials for complicity in the Popish plot, the manner in which the criminal law had been used against the Exclusionist party in the closing years of Charles II.'s reign, and the excesses of Jeffreys in the trials arising out of Monmouth's rebellion, had convinced all parties of the need of some reform.[10] Public opinion demanded developments of the law of criminal procedure along the same lines as those which had

---

[1] 8 S.T. at p. 734.   [2] Y.B. 21 Ed. III. Hil. pl. 25.

[3] Co. Litt. 227b ; Third Instit. 110.

[4] P.C. ii 294-295—"the contrary course hath for a long time obtained at Newgate . . . and accordingly it hath been practised in most circuits of England."

[5] "Otherwise many notorious murders and burglaries may pass unpunished by the acquittal of a person probably guilty, when the full evidence is not searched out or given."

[6] This course was pursued on the trial of Whitebread and Fenwick in 1678, 7 S.T. 119-120; they were afterwards tried and convicted, ibid 315 ; see Stephen, H.C.L. i 395.

[7] R. v. Perkins (1698) Carth. 465.

[8] Kinlock's Case (1746) Foster, Crown Law 27-28.

[9] Winsor v. the Queen (1866) L.R. 1 Q.B. 289.

[10] Stephen, H.C.L. i 416.

begun to be apparent in 1640. Something was done by the Legislature. We have seen that in 1695 [1] considerable advantages were given to persons accused of high treason. They were allowed to have a copy of the indictment five days before trial, to be defended by counsel, and to have their witnesses on oath. The treason charged against them must be proved by two witnesses, either to the same overt act, or to different overt acts of the same kind of treason. In 1708 it was enacted that not only the copy of the indictment, but also a list of the witnesses for the crown and of the jury should be given to the prisoner ten days before trial. [2] In 1702 it was enacted that in cases both of treason and felony the prisoner's witnesses should be sworn. [3] But very much more was done by the change in the character of the bench which occurred after the Revolution, by the growing precision in the rules of evidence, [4] and, as the result of these influences, by the growth of humanity to accused persons. So much was this the case, that Stephen has said that perhaps the most striking feature in the political trials of the first part of the eighteenth century, is the fact that the statutory changes made so little difference. [5] The best illustration of the changed spirit which animated the bench is to be found in the gradual relaxation of the rule that persons accused of felony could not be defended by counsel. In fact, counsel came to be allowed to examine and cross-examine witnesses, and to do everything for the prisoner except address the jury. [6] The result was that when in 1837 the Prisoners' Counsel Act [7] gave to persons accused of felony the right to be defended by counsel, the change made was not nearly so great as that made by the Act of 1695, which had given the same privilege to persons accused of high treason.

In these ways the criminal procedure of the Middle Ages— strengthened by the changes of the sixteenth century; humanized, partly by the preservation of some of those mediæval characteristics which were secured by the victory of the common law in the seventeenth century, and partly by the abilities of the judges of the eighteenth century; rationalized by the growth of definite rules of evidence—developed into the unique criminal procedure of our modern law. The constitutional and political influences which have made it what it was are, at bottom, the same as those which gave England her unique system of local government, and her unique Parliamentary system. Like these institutions, it stood out as a model to the nations of Western Europe at the end of the eighteenth century; and, as with these institutions, so with the

---

[1] 7 William III. c. 3; vol. vi 233-234. [2] 7 Anne c. 21 § 11.
[3] 1 Anne st. 2 c. 9 § 3.   [4] Above 200-201, 217-219. [5] H.C.L. i 417.
[6] Stephen, H.C.L. i 424.   [7] 6, 7 William IV. c. 114 § 1.

English system of criminal procedure, most of these nations have, during the nineteenth century, adopted some of its characteristic features, and some of the ideas which underlie it.

(2) *The criminal information.*

The criminal information is almost as old as the indictment; and, like it, it has been affected by the course of the political and constitutional history of the English state. Nor is the antiquity of these criminal informations surprising; for the idea underlying the procedure by information, criminal or civil, came very naturally to the centralized royal justice of the thirteenth century. It was a very natural mode of putting the law in motion that the king, by his counsel, should "inform" his courts of some fact which had legal consequences. Thus if some one had got possession of property to which the king was entitled, or had committed some offence, the king could inform his courts, and ask them to act. Moreover, such a procedure was in accord with the ideas of an age which considered that all men, including the king, were subject to law. The mediæval king was no Austinian sovereign, who could *motu mero* assert his rights, or punish those who had broken his laws. He must take the proper steps to see that the law which had been broken was enforced; and the natural way to do this was to inform his courts.[1]

But naturally this vague general notion of an information developed as time went on. It was, so to speak, caught up into the technical procedure of the common law, the different cases in which the king might proceed by information were classified, and thus we get many different kinds of information, each governed by its own technical rules. Further complications arose from the fact that this procedure by information was taken up and developed on somewhat different lines by the common law courts, by the Council and Star Chamber, and by the court of Chancery. The Council allowed other persons besides the king to give information to the court, on which it could be asked to take action; and this idea was taken up and largely developed by the Legislature. Many penal statutes were enforceable by *qui tam* informations, as well as by *qui tam* actions; and we have seen that the abuses arising from these invitations to informers to take these proceedings, had given rise to legislation in Elizabeth and James I.'s reigns.[2] In one case this procedure by information was extended in a manner analogous to some of the extensions of the action of trespass. On account of the greater convenience of this procedure, the old writ of quo warranto was, in the sixteenth century, superseded by an information in the nature of a quo warranto.[3]

---

[1] Vol. ii 253-255, 435-436.
[2] Vol. iv 356-357; below 240-241.　　　[3] Below 237.

It is not therefore surprising to find that in the developed common law there are many kinds of informations. Firstly, there are the informations by which the crown asserts its right to money or chattels, or to damages for an intrusion on lands belonging to the crown; and the information *in rem*, by which property seized as having no owner, was adjudged to belong to the crown.[1] To these informations at common law by Latin bill, there were added later, informations in equity by English bill.[2] All of these informations are essentially civil proceedings. Secondly, there is the information in the nature of a writ of quo warranto, which superseded the old writ. It was originally a criminal proceeding, designed to punish the usurper of a franchise, as well as to seize the franchise for the crown. But, in the course of the sixteenth and seventeenth centuries, it developed into a purely civil proceeding;[3] and it is now provided that it shall be so exclusively regarded.[4] Thirdly, there are the criminal informations. These fall under two heads—those brought by a subject on a penal statute on behalf of himself and the crown, which "are a sort of *qui tam* actions, only carried on by a criminal instead of a civil process"; and those brought solely at the suit of the king.[5] The latter variety again fall under two heads: "first, those which are truly and properly his own suits, and filed ex officio by his own immediate officer, the attorney-general; secondly, those in which, though the king is the nominal prosecutor, yet it is at the relation of some private person or common informer; and they are filed by the king's coroner and attorney in the court of King's Bench, usually called the master of the crown office, who is for this purpose the standing officer of the public."[6]

It is with the informations falling under this third head that I am dealing here. But since this classification of informations is the result of a long historical development, it will be necessary, in tracing the history of these criminal informations, to say something of the other informations which have become distinct varieties. As I said at the outset, the history of the criminal information has been coloured by political and constitutional influences coming from different periods in the history of the law; and, as has happened with other institutions of English law, the legality of ex officio informations was made a matter of constitutional and legal controversy at the end of the seventeenth and in the eighteenth century.

[1] Bl. Comm. iii 261-262.
[2] Robertson, Civil Proceedings by and against the Crown 234; Halsbury, Laws of England x 20-26.
[3] Bl. Comm. iii 262, iv 307-308; vol. i 230; the proceedings on this information were regulated by 9 Anne c. 20.
[4] 47, 48 Victoria c. 61 § 15.
[5] Bl. Comm. iv 303.
[6] Ibid 304.

It will be necessary, therefore, in tracing their history to follow, a chronological arrangement. I shall deal firstly with the mediæval and early Tudor period; secondly with the sixteenth and seventeenth centuries; and thirdly with the settlement of the modern law in the seventeenth and eighteenth centuries.

(i) *The mediæval and early Tudor period.*

It seems to be quite clear that, in Edward I.'s reign, the king could, by information to his court, put a man on his trial for treason or felony.[1]   But, probably before the close of the mediæval period, this right to put a man on his trial by information, without the process of presentment and indictment, had been restricted to offences under the degree of felony, that is to misdemeanours.   It is, I think, probable that we must look for the cause of this restriction to the extensive use made by the Council of the process of information, and to the mediæval statutes passed to restrict the jurisdiction of the Council in criminal cases.   There seems to be no doubt that the Council habitually proceeded criminally against persons, on the information, not only of the king and his counsel, but also of any private person.[2]   We have seen that the decay of the criminal appeal had created the need for a criminal proceeding begun at the suit of the injured person; and that the action of trespass helped to fill this gap.[3]   There was, however, room for this other expedient of an information to the Council.[4]   But, considering the way in which all the forms of law were abused by the litigious and unscrupulous in the latter part of the mediæval period,[5] it was inevitable that this procedure should be turned to evil uses.   And "as the proceedings were secret, the way was opened for all kinds of false and malicious accusations."[6]   But we have seen that it was this abuse of the Council's procedure, coupled with the professional jealousy of the common lawyers, which led Parliament to pass that series of statutes which effectually debarred the Council from hearing cases of treason or felony.[7]   It is reasonable therefore to conjecture, that this restriction of the Council's jurisdiction, and therefore of its power to proceed by information, reacted on the proceedings at the suit of the crown by way of information in the common law courts.   There can be little doubt that the sphere of informations was thus restricted in the mediæval period, and later. But it would be as difficult to find an express authority for this

---

[1] P. and M. ii 658-659, and the references cited 659 n. 1.
[2] Baldwin, The King's Council 286; Select Cases before the King's Council (S.S.) xxxvi-xxxviii.
[3] Vol. ii 257, 360.
[4] Select Cases before the Council (S.S.) xxxvii.
[5] Vol. ii 415, 416, 457-459.
[6] Baldwin, The King's Council 286.
[7] Vol. i 486-488; vol. v 188-189.

proposition[1] as to find an authority for the equally obvious proposition that the Council, certainly in the Tudor period, and probably from the latter part of the fourteenth century, had no jurisdiction to try a case of treason or felony;[2] and perhaps this lack of express authority lends further probability to the view, that the restriction upon the competence of the information at the king's suit in the common law courts, is the indirect result of the legislation which insisted, as against the Council, that accusations for capital offences must be begun by presentment and indictment.

There is, however, no reason to think that the king was unable to proceed by information for offences under the degree of felony. It is clear that in civil cases he could proceed by information to recover property to which he was entitled.[3] It is clear, too, that he could proceed in this way in the Exchequer for customs duties which had not been paid;[4] and it would seem that there are a series of precedents, which Hale recognized to be authorities, showing that an information also lay for such offences as nuisance, contempt, rescous, and the like.[5] There are also cases of information for trespass, maintenance, champerty, and forestalling.[6] It is true that there are certain cases in the fourteenth century in which, because the king had sued by ordinary writ, it was agreed that he need not be answered, because he should have proceeded by indictment.[7] But the cases are conflicting;[8] and, if they mean anything, it would seem they intend only to assert the proposition that, though the king can sue for a wrong done to himself by ordinary writ, he cannot, merely because A has sued B for a wrong, himself take proceedings by writ for that wrong.[9] He must prove by

---

[1] Thus Hawkins, P.C. ii 260, can only say, "I do not find it anywhere holden that such an information will lie for any capital crime or for misprison of treason"; and he only cites so recent an authority as Shower's argument in R. v. Berchet (1690) 1 Shower at pp. 109-110.

[2] Vol. i 488; vol. v 188-189.   [3] Above 237.

[4] See e.g. Reniger v. Fogossa (1549) Plowden 1.

[5] See the cases cited from the Hale MSS. in Lincoln's Inn 1 Shower at pp. 118-119; cp. Y.B. 39 Hy. VI. Hil. pl. 4 (p. 41) = Brook Ab. *Surmise* pl. 3.

[6] 1 Shower 117, 118.

[7] Y.BB. 7 Ed. III. Trin. pl. 12; 26 Ed. III. Mich. pl. 20.

[8] See Y.B. 5 Ed. III. Trin. pl. 19.

[9] In Y.B. 7 Ed. III. Trin. pl. 12 the king sued a sheriff on a statute of Edward II.'s reign: "*Hill.* Sir, nous entendons que le Roy ne voet estre respondu a cesty bref, sans ceo qu'il fuist aprise de ceo per enditement ou en auter maner. *Parning.* Le Roy est aprise per le suggestion de *Thomas*, et tout fuist le bref *Thomas* abatu, le Roy voet estre response. *Herle.* En Eire le Roy ne mettra nul home a respondre a chose fait encontre les articles, s'il ne soit aprise per enditement, ou per process etc., mez en cas ou le Roy prent son accion de tort fait a luy meme, de que auter n'ad accion forsque le Roy, en tiel cas le Roy serra rescu tout sans estre aprise: mes la ou le Roy prent suite per reason de tort fait principalment a auter le Roy ne serra my respondu sans estre aprise etc. *Gayn.* En un attachement sur la prohibition le Roy voet estre respondu tout soit le party non suy a son bref. *Herle.* La le Roy prent action de Trespass fait encontre luy meme *Contra Coronam et Dignitatem suam*, de que il voet estre response sans estre aprise etc."; it would seem that the case in Y.B. 26 Ed. III. Mich. pl. 20 turned on an application of the same principle; cp. Theloall, Digest Bk. I c. 3 §§ 9-11.

presentment and indictment or in some other way, that the wrong
has been done; and, in the last sentence of the Y.B. of 7 Ed.
III., it seems to be admitted that he can take proceedings for a
trespass without indictment. It is true, also, that there are other
cases in which it was decided that certain commissions, issued from
the Chancery to take a man and his goods, without indictment
or suit of the party or other due process, were void.[1] We shall
see that both these lines of cases were appealed to at the end of
the seventeenth century to prove that criminal informations were
illegal at common law.[2] They were cited in conjunction with the
statutes passed to restrict the criminal jurisdiction of the Council,[3]
to prove that the common law recognized no criminal procedure
except that of indictment or appeal. It may well be, as we have
seen, that the effect of these statutes has been to limit the scope
of the criminal information to misdemeanours.[4] But there is
nothing in them, or in the cases cited, which justifies us in saying
that the due process of law, contemplated by the statutes and the
cases, does not include informations, which, as we have seen, were
well enough known.[5] Moreover, as we shall now see, so far was
the Legislature from wishing to condemn informations root and
branch, that it made use of them for the enforcement of statutes.

Several mediæval statutes provide that the penalty for the
breach of the statute shall be recovered by action or information,
at the suit either of the king, or of any other person who chooses
to sue.[6] Thus for instance, a statute of 1424 imposed a penalty
of three times the value of the merchandise on custom-house
officers who embezzled the duties paid by a merchant, and gave
a third of the penalty to an informer who sued on behalf of himself and the king.[7] Similarly, Edward IV.'s statutes against the
giving of liveries were to be enforced by information at the suit of
any person who would take proceedings;[8] and in the famous Act
of 1487 Pro Camera Stellata,[9] it was provided that the statutory
committee of the Council, constituted by it, should have power to
proceed "upon bill or information put to the said Chancellor for
the king or any other." In fact, Henry VII. considered, and
perhaps rightly, that in the existing state of the country more
speedy justice was likely to be done by the use of the machinery

---

[1] 42 Ass. pl. 5.—"Les justices disoient que cest commission fuit contre le Ley
de prendre un home et ses biens sans endictement ou suit de party, ou auter due process"; see also 41 Ass. pl. 13; these would seem to be the cases referred to in
Winnington's argument in Prynn's Case (1691) 5 Mod. 459—but the references are
wrongly given.

[2] Below 243-244.   [3] Vol. i 468-488.   [4] Above 238-239.

[5] See 1 Shower 120, 122, 123-124.   [6] Vol. ii 453; vol. iv 356-357.

[7] 3 Henry VI. c. 3.   [8] 8 Edward IV. c. 2.

[9] 3 Henry VII. c. 1; in the Act of 32 Henry VIII. c. 9 against maintenance there
was a permission to common informers to proceed for penalties by information, as
Holt, C.J., pointed out in Prynn's Case (1691) 5 Mod. at p. 464; below 244.

of an information than by the use of the machinery of presentment and indictment. It was therefore enacted in 1495[1] that the judges of assize and justices of the peace should have power, upon information given for the king, to try any offence (not being a capital offence) against any statute, and punish the offender as provided by that statute. This Act was supposed to have facilitated the extortions of Empson and Dudley,[2] and it was repealed in 1509.[3] Clearly neither its passage nor its repeal affected the right of the king to sue by information in the King's Bench. The repeal of the Act simply left the law as it was before it was passed.[4]

(ii) *The sixteenth and seventeenth centuries.*

The law, as it stood at the beginning of Henry VIII.'s reign, gave the king a somewhat indefinite power of proceeding by way of information for offences under the degree of felony, either in the court of King's Bench, or before the Council and Star Chamber. Further, a growing number of statutes gave to any one who liked to sue, the power to inform on behalf of himself and the king for the breach of these statutes. We have seen that the proceedings of informers gave rise to such abuses, that informations of this nature were regulated by statutes of Elizabeth and James I.'s reigns.[5] But of these informations I need say no more. The main interest lies with the informations initiated either ex officio by the attorney-general, or by the master of the crown office on behalf of some member of the public.

There seems to have been a large number of both varieties of information in the King's Bench in Henry VIII.'s reign. There are also instances in Edward VI.'s, Mary's, Elizabeth's, and James I.'s reigns;[6] but they were not then so numerous, as the Star Chamber was now taking cognizance of many offences which formerly would have been brought before the King's Bench. In 1630 occurred the famous information against Eliot, Holles, and Valentine;[7] and in Calthorpe's argument for Valentine we get the first hint of the theory that an information is not a legitimate mode of proceeding in a criminal case.[8] The argument was based partly on the theory that "informations ought not to be grounded on surmises, but upon matter of record." But this theory was founded upon dicta in cases connected with informations in civil cases to assert the king's proprietary rights, which had no application to criminal informations. Partly it was grounded

[1] 11 Henry VII. c. 3.
[2] See Coke, Fourth Instit. 198-199; Bl. Comm. iv 306.
[3] 1 Henry VIII. c. 6.   [4] 1 Shower 123; 5 Mod. at p. 464.
[5] Vol. iv 356-357.   [6] See cases cited in 1 Shower at pp. 114-116.
[7] 3 S.T. 294.   [8] Ibid at p. 302.

upon the mistaken theory that the mediæval statutes, passed primarily to restrict the jurisdiction of the Council, prevented any criminal procedure but that of presentment and indictment. The argument is historically important from the point of view of the later controversy on this subject; but it clearly rests upon mistaken analogies, and a false interpretation of mediæval statutes. The Court paid no attention to it; and the fact that it was disregarded, was not assigned as an error when this decision was questioned in 1641, and finally overruled in 1667.[1] In fact, throughout the reign of Charles I., there are very many precedents of these criminal informations;[2] and, as Blackstone points out, "in the same Act of Parliament which abolished the court of Star Chamber,[3] a conviction by information is expressly reckoned up, as one of the legal modes of conviction of such persons as should offend a third time against the provisions of that statute."[4]

Their legality was asserted under the Commonwealth. In Style's Practical Register[5] some rules relating to them are collected; and these rules are said to have emanated from Rolle, who was chief justice of the Upper Bench when this book was composed. In fact, the abolition of the Star Chamber had made it necessary for the Upper Bench (which had taken the place of the King's Bench) to exercise alone a jurisdiction which the King's Bench had formerly shared with the Star Chamber. That the Upper Bench regarded itself as exercising a similar jurisdiction to safeguard the state, can be seen from the following entry based on a case heard in 1649:[6] "An information may be preferred in this court against the inhabitants of any town or village in England for the not repairing the Highways which by law they are bound to repair. For this court may punish offences done against the weal publick all England over." The same reason made for the continuance of these informations in Charles II.'s reign. "They were so common in Charles II.'s time, that they are got into our precedent books of pleading. In Vidian's Entries is one exhibited by *Sir Thomas Fanshaw v. Justinian Paggit Senior* for neglects and abuses in his office of *custos brevium*, as for an offence at common law; and fol. 215 are

---

[1] See 1 Shower at pp. 112-113.

[2] Ibid at p. 112, citing the case of Hobert and Stroud (1632) Cro. Car. 209; R. v. Wingfield (1633) ibid 251; R. v. Mayor of London (1633) ibid 252; R. v. Warde and Lyne (1633) ibid 266; Stevens' Case (1640) ibid at p. 567; Freeman's Case (1641) ibid at p. 579.

[3] 16 Charles I. c. 10 § 6 (3).   [4] Bl. Comm. iv 306.

[5] Regestum Practicale or the Practical Register, consisting of Rules, Orders, and Observations concerning the common laws, and the Practice thereof. But more particularly applicable to the proceedings of the Upper Bench, as well in matters criminal as civil. Taken for the most part during the time that Lord Chief Justice Rolle did sit and give the rule there. Ed. 1657.

[6] Ibid at p. 187.

two more of a like nature; one of which is against Wilkinson the Six Clerk for cheating Sir John Marsh, Longvil, and Bluck of a deed of articles and cancelling it: all of which shows the opinion of the lawyers in this point; for the last was at the instance of lawyers; and Vidian was well known to be a good clerk, and a curious observer of what past here."[1]

But at the latter part of Charles II.'s reign, and in James II.'s reign, the procedure by ex officio information was used for purely political objects. There were the cases of Barnardiston,[2] of Pilkington Shute and others,[3] and other similar cases;[4] and it was upon an information that the Seven Bishops were tried.[5] Naturally, the nature of the cases in which these ex officio informations had been used, called attention to the question of their legality; and it was pointed out that, besides the political objection based upon the use made of them by Charles II. and James II., the procedure upon them inflicted many hardships on accused persons. Thus, the accused person, even if he were acquitted, could get no costs against the king, "but after an expensive troublesome suit must sit down contented with his own loss, and be glad he escape so."[6] He must plead instantly, "though he cannot possibly be prepared for it, having never before heard the information"[7]—a hardship which, as we have seen, was also experienced in the case of the procedure by indictment.[8] The master of the crown office did not follow the advice given by Style,[9] and take care to see that the plaintiffs had a probable cause of complaint, before he allowed them to exhibit an information.[10] This want of care in effect enabled "all private persons to prosecute criminally any person who had offended them by any act, which could be treated as a misdemeanour, without the sanction of a grand jury."[11] And, as might be expected, litigants abused this power to prosecute. An information was exhibited; the defendant pleaded to issue; and then the prosecution was abandoned.

It is not surprising, therefore, that a party in the House of Commons should wish to end this procedure.[12] In several cases an attempt was made to prove that all criminal informations were

---

[1] 1 Shower at p. 111.   [2] (1684) 9 S.T. 1334.   [3] (1683) 9 S.T. 187.
[4] See Winnington's argument in 5 Mod. at p. 461; 1 Shower at p. 110.
[5] (1688) 12 S.T. 183.   [6] 5 Mod. at p. 461.   [7] Ibid.
[8] Above 232, 233.
[9] " The Clerk of the Crown ought not to set his hand to an information without examining the cause for which it is preferred. For if there be not (at least in probabilities) good matter in law to ground an information upon, the party that doth prefer it is not to be so assisted and encouraged in it; for the law doth abhor vexatious and causeless suits," Practical Register (ed. 1657) 187.
[10] 4, 5 William and Mary c. 18 Preamble.
[11] Stephen, H.C.L. i 296.   [12] See the King v. Abraham (1690) 1 Shower 49.

illegal.[1]   The argument used was, in effect, an expansion of the argument used in *Eliot's Case*.[2]   Like that argument, it rested partly on the same erroneous construction of Edward III.'s legislation, partly on a misreading of inconclusive dicta in the Year Books, partly on a wholly erroneous assertion of the absence of precedents, and partly on quite baseless gossip that Hale considered them to be illegal.   The fallacies of these contentions were exposed in Sir Bartholomew Shower's very able argument, which he had intended to deliver in *Berchet's Case*.[3]   But, even without the help of that argument, Holt, C.J., found no difficulty in exposing them.   "The matter," he said,[4] "truly seems not of any great difficulty, for we shall hardly now impeach the judgment of all our predecessors; it would be a reflection on the whole bar. In Lamb and Wingfield's information there were learned counsel who would certainly have taken exceptions to the information had they thought it did not lie.   My Lord Chief Justice Hale complained of the abuse of informations, but not that they were unlawful."   He pointed out that the repeal of the Act of 1495 did not affect the question.   "Notwithstanding the repeal of 11 Hen. 7 c. 3 by the 1 Hen. 8 c. 6 yet afterwards the statute 32 Hen. 8 c. 9 of Maintenance, supposes that informations still lay; and if it had been a new thing, that statute would have said, that there shall be an information for that crime, and not that it shall be punished by information, which supposes informations to lie.   A man may make a better argument against *writs of enquiry* and *new trials* than against *informations*."   This was really decisive.   It is true that a Mr. Earbery wished in 1737 to contend that informations were illegal.   His undelivered argument is published in the State Trials;[5] but it is little more than a reproduction of the arguments which had been rightly rejected in 1691.

(iii) *The settlement of the modern law.*

But, though the legality of criminal informations was established, the Legislature did something to mitigate the hardships which resulted from those exhibited by the master of the crown office at the suit of private persons.[6]   For the future no such informations were to be exhibited without an express order of the Court, and without taking a recognizance for effectual prosecution.   If the information was not effectually prosecuted within a year, or a nolle prosequi was entered, or the defendant got a verdict, the Court could award the defendant costs.   A check was thereby

---

[1] See the King v. Abraham (1690) 1 Shower 49; Prynn's Case (1691) 5 Mod. 459; the King v. Berchet (1691) 1 Shower 106.
[2] Above 241-242.   [3] 1 Shower 106.   [4] 5 Mod. at pp. 463-464.
[5] 20 S.T. 856.   [6] 4, 5 William and Mary c. 18.

imposed upon the exhibition of baseless or frivolous informations; for, as Stephen has pointed out,[1] a motion for an information made to the court in substance operates, like a preliminary proceeding before the magistrates, to stop at the outset merely frivolous prosecutions. But of course much depends upon the manner in which the court exercises its discretion; and on this matter its practice has fluctuated.[2] At the end of the eighteenth and the beginning of the nineteenth centuries its practice had come to be somewhat lax.[3] But, in the latter part of the nineteenth century, there was a return to the stricter practice followed at the beginning of the eighteenth century.[4] That practice was in substance described by Blackstone, when he said that the objects of this species of information were the suppression of "gross and notorious misdemeanours, riots, batteries, libels, and other immoralities of an atrocious kind, not peculiarly tending to disturb the government (for those are left to the care of the attorney general) but which on account of their magnitude or pernicious example, deserve the most public animadversion."[5] This sentence was quoted with approval in 1884,[6] and represents the modern law.

It is, perhaps, hardly necessary to add that, throughout its history, the difference between the procedure by way of presentment and indictment, and by way of criminal information in the King's Bench, was only a difference as to the method by which the proceedings were initiated. "The same notice was given, the same process was issued, the same pleas were allowed, the same trial by jury was had, the same judgment was given by the same judges, as if the prosecution had originally been by indictment."[7]

The Civil Law

At the end of this period the common law system of procedure and pleading showed, perhaps more clearly than any other branch of the common law, the marks of the various stages through which the history of that law had passed. We have seen that the main outstanding features of the law of procedure and pleading had been fixed by the end of the thirteenth and the beginning of the fourteenth century.[8] This system of procedure centred round the original writs. The suitor must, at his peril, select the writ appropriate to his cause of action. He must then get the defendant before the court by means of the process prescribed for the particular writ which he had selected. When he had got him before the court he must "declare" or "count" against him.[9] The

---

[1] H.C.L. i 295.　　　[2] See the Queen v. Labouchere (1884) 12 Q.B.D. at p. 324.
[3] Ibid at pp. 325-326.　　　[4] Ibid at pp. 326-327.　　　[5] Comm. iv 304-305.
[6] 12 Q.B.D. at p. 330.　　　[7] Bl. Comm. iv 305.　　　[8] Vol. iii chap. vi § 2.
[9] The word "declare" was generally used in a personal, and the word "count" in a real action, Stephen, Pleading (1st ed.) 36.

defendant must then plead; and the plaintiff must reply. By means of this oral altercation at the bar, which was recorded as the case proceeded, an issue of law or of fact was reached. The issue of law was decided by the court, and the issue of fact in almost all cases by a verdict of a jury. On the verdict of the jury the court gave the judgment which, having regard to the record and the law applicable thereto, appeared to be just.

It was a system of procedure suited only to a primitive society, in which archaic ideas as to law and law suits still survived, and in which it was necessary, in the interests of justice, that process should be slow. It was suited only to a system of law which was still in an early stage of development. Before the close of the mediæval period, it was already becoming inadequate to the new needs of a more complex society, and a more developed system of law. Both its archaic traits and its cumbersome character were beginning to be a serious impediment to the administration of justice. We have seen that its rules of process afforded abundant opportunities to the dishonest litigant;[1] that both the growing elaboration of the law, and the more complex transactions which formed the subject matter of litigation, necessarily made the pleadings of the parties more complex; and that the new pleading rules laid down by the courts, were combining with the older rules both of process and pleading, to make the art of pleading a very technical and a very complex branch of the law.[2] The Legislature did very little to remedy these evils. Hence it was that, at the close of the mediæval period, we can see the beginnings of changes in practice which will, without directly changing the old system, gradually modify it; and, in the end, under cover of numerous fictions and tortuous devices, completely undermine it.

Thus, in the course of the sixteenth and seventeenth centuries, many of the older writs dropped out of use. As we have seen, trespass and its offshoots usurped the place occupied by the older real and personal actions.[3] Partly owing to this cause, and partly by the direct action of the Legislature,[4] the mesne process upon these writs was shortened and assimilated. For the oral altercation in court between the parties, in which the issue was settled, the system of written pleadings was substituted.[5] The practice of summoning witnesses to testify to the court, and the consequent growth of a law of evidence, revolutionized the conduct of a trial.[6] It also changed the whole position of the jury; and the growth of

[1] Vol. ii 458-459; vol. iii 623-627.
[2] Ibid 627-639, 641-642.
[3] Vol. vii 7 seqq.; 402 seqq.; vol. viii 89 seqq.
[4] Vol. iii 626-627; vol. iv. 534; vol. viii 231.
[5] Vol. iii 640-653.   [6] Ibid 654; above 223-224, 226-229, 232-234.

new methods of controlling the jury in the latter part of the seventeenth century emphasized their changed position.[1] But, as all these processes had been proceeding almost silently, and without any direct change of the older system, the procedure which resulted was perhaps the most artificial, and the most encumbered with fictions, that any legal system has ever possessed. In all its branches the older machinery and the older rules survived ; but they were overlaid by a mass of technical rules of practice, in which was contained the real working rules which guided the suitor. In fact, in the eighteenth century, the real working rules of procedure consisted mainly of the conventions of the law courts, just as truly as the real working rules of our public law were coming to consist mainly of the conventions of the constitution.

Of the beginnings of the growth of a law of evidence, I have already spoken.[2] Here I propose to say something, firstly, of these conventions of the law courts, which were substituting a new system of procedure for the older mediæval procedure ; and, secondly, of the characteristics of that new system of written pleadings, which was coming into use in the sixteenth century. In both cases the rules and principles introduced during this period form the transition stage between the mediæval system, and the modern system under which we are now governed. Like many of the rules and principles of the substantive law, they lasted unchanged till the reforms which began in the second quarter of the nineteenth century. Therefore in describing their evolution I shall pursue the same course as I have pursued in dealing with some parts of the substantive law, and not confine myself to the period which ends with the seventeenth century.

THE NEW SYSTEM OF PROCEDURE FOUNDED UPON THE CONVENTIONS OF THE LAW COURTS

It would be both tedious and useless to discuss in detail the complicated rules of procedure set out in the many books of practice which appeared in the seventeenth and eighteenth centuries.[3] All that I shall attempt is to show how the principal mediæval rules as to the stages in and the conduct of an action, had been superseded by a mass of conventional practices, which had, in effect, substituted a wholly new system ; and how these changes were illustrated by, and reflected in, the manner in which the formal record of the proceedings was drawn up.

In order to illustrate the manner in which these conventional

---

[1] Vol. i 225-226, 346-347. [2] Above, § 1.
[3] For the sixteenth and seventeenth century books see vol. v 379-387 ; vol. vi 598-600, and App. IV. (1).

practices had superseded the older rules, I shall give a brief description of certain rules relating to the following stages in an action:—The issue of the original writ; the appearance of the defendant; the pleadings in the action; trial by jury and the nisi prius system; judgment and execution; the manner of recording the proceedings.

The issue of the original writ.—We have seen that in theory all actions must be begun by their appropriate original writ;[1] and, right down to the nineteenth century, the choice of the wrong writ involved the loss of the action, even though all the merits were with the plaintiff. In fact, even though he had got a verdict or judgment, this objection could be raised by a motion to enter judgment non obstante veredicto, or by a writ of error.[2] And although, owing to the supersession of many of the older writs by writs of trespass and their offshoots, and by the fact that the cause of action might be redressible by either one of several writs, the risk of failure from this cause was reduced, it was still a real risk —more especially in cases where the facts disclosed a cause of action which was on the border line between trespass and case.[3] It might well be that after a plaintiff had declared in trespass, the facts proved disclosed a cause of action in case; and if that happened he lost his action. On the other hand, the judicious choice of a form of action, by precluding a defendant from defences which he might have urged had another form been chosen, might enable the plaintiff to recover.[4]

But, by the end of the seventeenth century, these failures of justice were generally due, not to the choice of a wrong writ, but to the choice of a wrong form of action. The form of action was determined by the manner in which the plaintiff's pleader chose to frame his declaration, and not by the form of the writ, which in some cases was supposed to exist, but which was never in fact issued, and in other cases was not even supposed to exist. The mediæval system of separate writs, each originating a separate

---

[1] Vol. ii 512, 520-521.

[2] "A mistake of one form of action for another is not only a source of failure on the trial; it may also present itself in such a shape as to be ground for general demurrer, or motion in arrest of judgment, or writ of error," Third Report of Commissioners on Courts of Common Law, Parlt. Papers 1831 x 8.

[3] "In no respect perhaps are they more objectionable than in the indistinctness, in some instances, of the lines of demarcation which determine the bounds and competency of each different form of suit; the effect of which is, that it is sometimes difficult to ascertain upon a given state of facts, which is the proper mode of remedy, and that a very trifling variation in the state of facts as proved from that originally supposed, will also sometimes suffice to make the action chosen inapplicable to the case, and frustrate the plaintiff's proceedings. It is in reference to trespass and trespass on the case that these inconveniences principally occur," ibid 7.

[4] "By a judicious choice of the remedy the defendant may be frequently precluded from availing himself of a defence he might otherwise establish," Chitty, Pleading 231, cited Spence, Equitable Jurisdiction i 250 n. (f).

cause of action, had given rise to separate forms of action. But the manner of beginning an action had come to be extraordinarily various; and probably the least common of all these various ways was the issue of an original writ. This was due to the fact that the use of an original writ was not only more expensive and dilatory than any other method of beginning an action,[1] but also exposed the plaintiff to greater risks of failing by reason merely of a formal defect. "Being a special statement of the plaintiff's demand or complaint, to which he is afterwards bound to conform, it requires to be framed with as much care and consideration as any of the pleadings in the cause, and the plaintiff therefore finds himself obliged, before he can take out the writ, to instruct a special pleader to prepare a draft of it in the proper technical form."[2] This was specially necessary in framing writs in assumpsit, and in actions on the case; for, though some forms of writ, e.g. writs of debt and covenant, were short and simple, writs in assumpsit and in actions on the case "stated the cause of actions as fully as the declaration itself, and consequently extended to an indefinite number of law folios."[3]

The Common Law Commissioners in 1829 stated that it was possible to begin an action in the different common law courts in the following ways :—[4]

In the King's Bench

By Original.
    Original writ adapted to the action.
By Bill.

1. Attachment of Privilege	{	1. With ac etiam or bailable.
		2. Not bailable.
2. Bill of Middlesex.	{	1. Bailable.
		2. Not bailable.
3. Latitat.	{	1. Bailable.
		2. Not bailable.
4. Bill and Summons.		

---

[1] The costs of a writ were from £3 14s. to £5 4s. 11d.; the cost of a non bailab'e latitat, which was just as efficacious, was £1 5s. 8d., First Report of Commissioners on Courts of Common Law, Parlt. Papers 1829 ix 81; moreover, "great inconvenience and in some cases delay is produced by certain rules relative to the teste and return of original writs as distinguished from other process," ibid.

[2] Ibid.

[3] Ibid 73; when Coke said in Boyton's Case (1592) 3 Co. Rep. at f. 44b that "writs are more compendious than counts, and counts than other pleadings, for writs comprehend the effect and substance without circumstances of time or place and other circumstances," he was clearly thinking of the former class of writs.

[4] Parlt. Papers 1829, ix 74.

In the Common Pleas

By Original.

    1. Original Writ adapted to the Action.

    2. Original Writ Quare clausum fregit.

    3. Common Capias   { 1. Bailable.
                              { 2. Not bailable.

By Bill.

    1. Attachment of Privilege.

    2. Bill and Summons.

In the Exchequer

    1. Venire ad Respondendum.

    2. Subpœna ad Respondendum.

    3. Quo minus Capias.

    4. Venire of Privilege.

    5. Capias of Privilege.

    6. Bill and Summons.

As the commissioners said, this complexity was due mainly to three causes—the desire to avoid the expense and inconvenience of the original writ; the desire of the King's Bench and the Exchequer to encroach on the domain of the Common Pleas; and the privilege, allowed to attornies and other officers of the courts, of suing and being sued in the courts to which they were officially attached.[1]

Of all these methods of beginning an action the most common was a *capias ad respondendum*, i.e. a writ directing the sheriff to arrest the defendant. This process was possible in all the most usual personal actions; and, where it was possible, it became the practice, in the course of the eighteenth century, to " resort to it in the first instance, and to suspend the issuing of the original writ, or even to neglect it altogether, unless its omission should afterwards be objected by the defendant. Thus the usual *practical* mode of commencing a personal action by original writ is to begin by issuing, not an original, but a capias."[2] As the author of the Pleader's Guide said :—

> " Still lest the Suit should be delayed,
> And Justice at her Fountain stayed,
> A *Capias* is conceived and born
> Ere yet th' ORIGINAL is drawn,
> To justify the Courts proceedings,
> Its Forms, its Processes, and Pleadings,

[1] First Report of Commissioners on Courts of Common Law, Parlt. Papers 1829 ix 77.

[2] Stephen, Pleading (1st ed.) 27; it would seem that this practice was coming into regular use in the latter part of the sixteenth century, see Reeves, H.E.L. iii 757-758.

> And thus by ways and means unknown
> To all but Heroes of the Gown,
> A Victory full oft is won
> Ere Battle fairly is begun ;
> 'Tis true, the wisdom of our Laws
> Has made Effect precede the Cause,
> But let this Solecism pass—
> *In fictione æquitas.*" [1]

But the original was always supposed ; and the defendant could always object to its absence, and compel the plaintiff to procure it from the office of the cursitor.[2]   It should be noted also that in the procedure by bill against persons actually privileged, or supposed to be privileged, there was necessarily no original.   The bill took the place of the original, and also operated as the plaintiff's declaration.[3]

It will be clear that this manner of using a capias, and thus of dispensing with original writs, tended to introduce a greater uniformity of process than was possible under the older system, when each action was begun by its separate original writ, which was subject to its own peculiar rules.   No doubt the tendency in this direction had been rendered possible by the spread of trespass and its offshoots ; and it had been helped by the legislation, which had tended in the direction of assimilating the process in personal actions, by extending the power to arrest on mesne process.[4]   But it was greatly strengthened by the practice of dispensing with originals, and allowing the uniform process of capias as the first step in the action.   It was thus possible in 1833[5] to introduce a uniform writ of summons in place of the complex system, which had gradually undermined the old scheme, based on the separate original writs.   On the other hand, though by devious routes the practice of the courts had been making for the elimination of separate writs for the beginning of an action, it had, as we have seen, in no way weakened the separation between the forms of action.[6]   These separate forms of action were too

[1] The Pleader's Guide, A Didactic Poem, by the late John Surrebutter, Esq. (1796) pp. 40-41 ; the poem was written by John Anstey who died in 1819.

[2] Stephen, op. cit. 27 ; "if the action be in the Common Pleas, and if the plaintiff has proceeded upon a common capias, and has obtained judgment by default, on demurrer, or confession, or nul tiel record, the defendant may bring a writ of error for want of an original, and the plaintiff will then find himself obliged to procure one from the Cursitor's Office ex post facto, for which purpose he has to encounter the trouble and expense of a petition to the Master of the Rolls," First Report of Commissioners on Courts of Common Law, Parlt. Papers 1829 ix 81-82 ; moreover, the process of capias was not possible in real or mixed actions, or in certain personal actions, Stephen, op. cit. 27.

[3] Ibid 55-57 ; for an instance of an action of ejectment begun by bill, see Bingham's Case (1598-1600) 2 Co. Rep. 82b.

[4] Vol. iii 626-627 ; vol. iv 534 ; vol. viii 231.

[5] 2, 3 William IV. c. 39.

[6] In the form of writ introduced in 1833 it was necessary to state the nature or subject matter of the action ; it was not till the Common Law Procedure Act of 1852, 15, 16 Victoria c. 76 § 3, that this requirement was dropped, on the recommendation of the Common Law Procedure Commissioners, Parlt. Papers 1851 xxii 2.

closely bound up with the system of pleading to be so easily abolished by a body of Commissioners who were firmly convinced of the essential excellence of that system.[1]   And, even after the passing of the Common Law Procedure Act of 1852, "the form of action remained of vital importance to the pleader, for each action retained its own precedents, and although the choice of the proper form of action need no longer be made in the choice of writ, it is merely deferred until the declaration." [2]   But it is clear that the introduction of uniformity in the writ of summons, the way for which had been paved by the conventional rules of practice sanctioned by the courts, was the first step towards the abolition of the forms of action, and the introduction of the modern system of procedure introduced by the Judicature Acts.

The appearance of the defendant.—It is clear that the evolution of the rules, which have just been described, for beginning an action, is intimately bound up with the evolution of the rules for securing the appearance of the defendant.   Just as in legal theory an action was begun by an original writ, so in legal theory both plaintiff and defendant must appear personally in court by themselves or their attornies ; [3] but in both cases theory was widely divorced from the actual facts.   Though a personal appearance was still in theory required, " it exists," says Stephen,[4] " in fiction or contemplation of law " only.   " In fact appearance is effected on the part of the defendant (where he is not arrested) by making certain formal entries in the proper office of the Court expressing his appearance, or, in case of arrest, it may be considered as effective by giving bail to the action.   On the part of the plaintiff, no formality expressive of appearance is observed, but, upon appearance of the defendant, effected in the manner above described, both parties are considered *as in Court*."   Similarly, when the party appeared, as he generally did, by attorney, "there ought regularly, and there is always supposed to be, a warrant in writing executed by him for that purpose." [5]   Thus in the rules as to appearance, as in the rules as to the existence of an original writ, there were abundant traces of the older law beneath the mass of conventional rules by which they had been overlaid.

---

[1] " To those who have observed the inconveniences which, in other systems of judicature, are found to flow from the want of fixed forms of action, it will scarcely be doubtful that they are an invention of real merit and importance.   They tend most materially to secure that certainty in the right of action itself which is one of the chief objects of jurisprudence ; they form a valuable check to vagueness and prolixity of statement ; and in this and other respects they are essential to the convenient application of the rules of pleading. . . . To innovate to any considerable extent upon this part of our juridical system would, in our judgment, be to disturb foundations, and to endanger the safety of the whole structure," Third Report of Commissioners on Courts of Common Law, Parlt. Papers 1831 x 6; as to their views on the system of pleading see below 324-325.

[2] Maitland, Forms of Action 375.   [3] Vol. ii 311-312, 315-317.
[4] Pleading (1st ed.) 32.   [5] Ibid.

This characteristic was even more marked in the complicated rules as to the enforcement of appearance. We have seen that it was a very old principle of the law that there could be no proceedings against an absent defendant.[1] Naturally, from an early date, the law was much concerned with the steps which a plaintiff could take to make a defendant appear, and with the possibility of realizing his claim in the defendant's absence.[2] At the beginning of the eighteenth century the ground was already cumbered by many complex rules, as to different expedients, which were applicable to different forms of action. In certain cases, indeed, it had been provided in 1725 that the plaintiff might, on affidavit that a copy of the process had been personally served, enter an appearance for the defendant.[3] But, if this procedure was not possible, the plaintiff must choose, according to the nature of his action, or the person who was defendant, or the court in which he brought his action, between distringas, i.e. distraint, capias, i.e. arrest, or attachment and commission of rebellion.[4] The process of capias was by far the most common;[5] and it gave rise to a most complex body of law as to the bail below, i.e. bail which the defendant must give to the sheriff who had made the arrest, for his appearance at the return of the writ; and the bail above, i.e. bail which he must give in court, that he will satisfy judgment.[6] On the acceptance of bail above, the bail below was vacated. But, if the persons accepted by the sheriff as bail below were insolvent, the plaintiff could call on the sheriff to produce the defendant; and if the sheriff then failed to cause sufficient bail above to be taken, he was personally liable to the plaintiff.[7] As author of the Pleader's Guide says :—

> " But let the Plaintiff, ere he sue
> In *debt* or *case* for money due,
> Swear to the sum, the writ indorse,
> And let the Shrieve said writ enforce,
> Be quick to execute, but slow
> To take the proffer'd bail *below*,
> Lest with the Plaintiff's Suit embroil'd,
> The Shrieve at his own weapons foil'd,
> The bond assign'd, the Debtor fled,
> Himself Defendant in his stead,
> Be doomed with curses to bewail
> The horrors cf insolvent Bail,
> His folly to his Cost expose,

---

[1] Vol. ii 105.　　　　　　[2] Ibid 104-105; vol. iii 624-626.

[3] 12 George I. c. 29; extended by 45 George III. c. 124 § 3, and 7, 8 George IV. c. 71 § 5.

[4] " The ulterior process upon the original in the King's Bench and Common Pleas, is either by *distringas* or *capias*. On the venire in the Exchequer, and on the summons against persons having privilege of Parliament in any court, it is by distringas only; upon subpœna in the Exchequer, it is by *attachment* and *commission of rebellion*," First Report of Commissioners on Courts of Common Law, Parlt. Papers 1829 ix 86.

[5] See vol. viii 231-232 for some account of how this came about.

[6] Parlt. Papers 1829 ix 88-90, 101 seqq.; Bl. Comm. iii 290-291, and App. II. § 5.

[7] Bl. Comm. iii 291.

> And bear the weight of others' woes;
> Till by the Plaintiff vex'd and sped,
> Fresh suits impending o'er his head,
> He feels in dreams, or seems to feel
> His own Bum-bailiff at his heel,
> Flies his own writs, and strives to shun
> Th' ideal form of frightful Dun."

It was this state of the law which led to the growth of a set of men called "sham bail," who would, for a consideration, be bail for anyone—a practice which Mr. Pickwick called perjury, but which Mr. Perker preferred to regard merely as a legal fiction.[1]

All these methods, however, presupposed that the defendant was within the jurisdiction. If he was neither within the jurisdiction, nor had any fixed abode there, nor any property which could be distrained, the plaintiff's only recourse was to proceed to outlawry.[2] And the manner in which he could thus proceed, affords one of the most striking illustrations of the way in which an institution of early law had been perverted and overlaid with a mass of conventional rules. " In its original design it [outlawry] was intended to give the most ample and reiterated notice of the suit, and its penal operation attached only on the contumacious or fraudulent, who after such notice chose to set the king's authority at defiance, by refusing obedience to the exigency of his writs.[3] But in its modern form it can scarcely be said to have any tendency even to apprize the defendant of the action, much less to warn him by distinct and repeated summons. In fact, he is never summoned during the whole course of the proceeding. The original writ, capias, alias, and pluries are not even delivered to the sheriff to be executed, but are returned as a mere matter of form, and the exactions

---

[1] " Bail you to any amount, and only charge half-a-crown. Curious trade, isn't it? said Perker. . . . What! Am I to understand that these men earn a livelihood by waiting about here, to perjure themselves before the judges of the land, at the rate of half-a-crown a crime! exclaimed Mr. Pickwick, quite aghast at the disclosure. Why I don't exactly know about perjury, my dear sir, replied the little gentleman. Harsh word, my dear sir, very harsh word indeed. Its a legal fiction, my dear sir, nothing more."

[2] Parlt. Papers 1829 ix 90.

[3] The process of outlawry is thus summed up in the Pleader's Guide 56-58 :—

> " But first *attach him*, and attend
> With *Capias ad Respondend.*
> Let loose the Dogs of War and furies,
> TESTATUM, ALIAS, and PLURIES;
> But if at length *non est invent,*
> At him again with *Exigent.*
> Proclaim him by the Act's direction
> (*Act* 31*st Eliz.* 3*rd Section*)
> Then smite him as a *Coup de Grace*
> With *Utlagatum Capias.*
> *Exacted*, outlaw'd, and embruted,
> His head to head of Wolf transmuted,
> Compell'd by writ of *Exigenter*
> The Lists against his will to enter."

in London are not very likely to come to the defendant's knowledge, even if he be resident there, much less in the ordinary case of his being in another county at the time.   Nor does any greater effect in general attend the proclamations, unless the defendant should reside at the time in the parish in which proclamation is made, or in its vicinity; but this can seldom happen, for at the time of awarding the exigent he is commonly abroad, or, if in England, his existing place of abode there is unknown.   A defendant against whom judgment of outlawry passes has therefore in general had no previous notice that the suit has been commenced, and may probably have had no opportunity of becoming acquainted with that fact, and it is quite possible that even his property may be seized and sold, and the proceeds paid over to the plaintiff, before he is aware that any action is pending against him." [1]

It is obvious, therefore, that the use of outlawry as mesne process to enforce appearance might work very serious oppression. Moreover, though it might have this result, it was also quite possible that it might not effect the purpose for which it was instituted.   If a defendant had been outlawed, he could always get it set aside or reversed.[2]   This was the inevitable result of a collision between the rule of the common law that no man could be outlawed who was not within the kingdom; and the conventional rule, resting on the practice of the court, not to allow process to issue to outlaw the defendant, unless it was proved that he was out of the kingdom.   It is true that, if an application were made to set aside the outlawry, he must pay the costs of the outlawry, and enter an appearance, so that the object of the outlawry was secured.   But, if he chose to take proceedings to get it reversed by a writ of error, he need neither pay costs nor enter an appearance; so that "the plaintiff was left in a worse position than he was before the proceedings to outlawry were instituted."   As the Common Law Procedure Commissioners said in 1851, the proceedings were "from beginning to end founded on fiction and built up on technical forms."   But, in spite of the recommendations of the Common Law Commissioners in 1829, nothing had been done; and this mischievous procedure was in 1851 still part of the law.   But, in spite of this survival, and in spite of the complexity of the various courses which were open to a plaintiff to compel the defendant's appearance in the eighteenth century, it is fairly obvious that the general use of the process of capias, was paving the way for a uniformity both in the writ and process, which could

---

[1] First Report of Commissioners on the Courts of Common Law, Parlt. Papers 1829 ix 93-94.

[2] Common Law Procedure Commission, Parlt. Papers 1851 xxii 5-7; and see Mathew v. Erbo (1698) 1 Ld. Raym. 349, there cited.

never have been attained under the older system of separate writs, with their separate rules of process.

The pleadings in the action.—Of the characteristics of the system of pleading I shall speak directly.[1] Here I am only dealing with it as a stage in the procedure of an action. From this point of view, it is only necessary to note that the actual mode of exchanging the written pleadings in the action, was as unlike the mediæval mode of oral pleading, as the mediæval mode of beginning an action by original writ, was unlike the modern mode of beginning it by writ of capias.[2] But in both cases the law still retained many traces of the older system. Just as an actual writ was sometimes necessary, and could always be required by a defendant;[3] so, some of the rules as to the exchange of these written pleadings, recalled the period when the pleadings, were settled by an oral altercation in court between the parties. Thus, when the pleadings were conducted viva voce in open court, it was only in term time that they could be conducted, or any judgment got. But the law terms were short;[4] and the rule that these steps in the action could only be taken in term time, was obviously meaningless when applied to the new method of delivering written pleadings out of court, and to the entry of a judgment which might have been got or delivered out of term. Therefore the practice had grown up of filing and delivering the pleadings, and of signing and entering judgments, in vacation as well as in term. But, said the Common Law Commissioners in 1830,[5] "There still remain considerable relics of the ancient plan of proceeding. All writs (including those to compel appearance) must be made returnable in term; every paper pleading and every entry of judgment, even when in fact delivered or entered in vacation, must always be entitled of some current or antecedent term; a plaintiff, though at liberty to declare in vacation, cannot in that case compel the defendant to plead until the subsequent term; and a party obtaining a verdict in vacation, on the trial of any issue, or on an inquisition of damages, must also wait until the term next following before he can obtain final judgment, or take out execution."

The adherence to these rules, from which all real meaning had

---

[1] Below 262 seqq.

[2] For the change from the system of oral to the system of written pleadings see vol. iii 640-653. For some time the King's Bench tried to ensure that the attornies did not deliver pleadings to each other till each pleading had been filed in the office of the Clerk of the Papers, see Cooke, Rules and Orders of the King's Bench and Common Pleas, King's Bench Orders Trin., 1604, Trin., 1664, Mich., 1690; this clearly marks the latest stage of the transition; that the attornies entered the pleas on the roll is assured by the orders of the King's Bench of Easter, 1699, and Mich. 1706, ibid.

[3] Above 251.　　　　　　　　　　　[4] Vol. iii App. VII.

[5] Parlt. Papers 1830 xi 27-28.

departed, produced quite unnecessary delays in the conduct of the litigation. As the plaintiff could not compel appearance except by a writ returnable in term time, he might not be able to declare for a period which varied from two to four months; and a similar delay was interposed between a verdict, and judgment and execution on that verdict.[1] Worse hardship than mere delay was sometimes inflicted by the last mentioned of these two rules. The defendant against whom a verdict had been got might become insolvent, or abscond, or conceal his property, with the result that the plaintiff who had proved his case lost both his damages and his costs.[2] "In ejectment," said the Commissioners,[3] "the case is often particularly galling. For by the delay in obtaining execution, the plaintiff is not only exposed to the danger of being ultimately left without effective remedy for the mesne profits and costs, but frequently encounters the vexation in the meantime of seeing his property remain for months after the verdict, in the possession of his adversary, who is at liberty to avail himself of that interval to remove every article of value, and to gratify his vindictive feelings by committing any kind of waste or spoliation."

Trial by jury and the nisi prius system.—The procedure which centred round the summoning of the jury, the rules of venue, and the sending of the case for trial at nisi prius, was likewise filled with obsolete forms of great historical interest; but productive of delay and expense to the litigant, and even risk of unmerited failure by reason of non-compliance with some meaningless form.

The Common Law Commissioners reported in 1851 that the jury process (*distringas* in the king's bench and *habeas corpora* in the common pleas)[4] were "forms useless and expensive, and a source of irregularities which sometimes defeat justice. The party desirous of having the cause tried prepares two writs, by one of which, the *venire*, the sheriff is directed to summon a jury to Westminster by a certain day; this, however, it is not intended he should do: the other writ, viz., the *distringas* or *habeas corpora*, supposes that he has done so, and that the jurors have made default, and commands the sheriff to distrain their goods or take their bodies so as to have them at Westminster, unless before that day the Chief Justice or Judge of Assize come to a certain place where the cause is to be tried; it is to this place the jurors are summoned. In practice, the sheriff without reference to any particular writ or cause, summons a sufficient number of persons to serve as jurors in all causes to be tried, and has their names inserted in a printed panel. A copy of this panel is annexed

---

[1] It will be remembered that in the great case of Bardell v. Pickwick an interval of two months elapsed between the verdict and the issue of execution.

[2] Parlt. Papers 1830 xi 28.   [3] Ibid.

[4] Stephen, Pleading 105.

to each of the writs above mentioned, and the sheriff makes a return, stating that he has obeyed the writ. It is manifest that these writs are useless, and have no operation, and that such a panel might as well be attached to the record as to the writs; yet, within a recent period, a plaintiff who had recovered a verdict, lost the benefit of it because the panel was not annexed, and no return had been made, to one of these writs."[1]

The rules of venue carry us back to the early days of the jury system, when the jury were as much witnesses as judges of the fact. Even in the sixteenth and seventeenth centuries these rules were becoming, in personal actions, merely obsolete survivals. Indeed, if their ancient stringency had not been evaded, it is difficult to see how the common law courts could have succeeded in wresting from the court of Admiralty its jurisdiction over commercial cases.[2] But the old rules had only been evaded, not repealed. The result was that they had given rise to a body of law filled with all sorts of intricate and minute distinctions, which not only filled no useful purpose whatever, but also put it into the power of a defendant to delay the action, and even exposed the plaintiff to risks of failure on mere points of form, even after the expense of a trial had been incurred.[3]

Before the case went for trial at nisi prius the Nisi Prius Record must be made up and passed. This record was a copy of the record, supposed to be made by the officers of the court from which the record came, but really made by the attornies of the parties. We shall see that the legal theory upon which this record was made up, differed widely from the practice actually followed. It was not, as that theory supposed, made up from day to day as the case proceeded, but only came into existence when an issue had been reached.[4] Thus the Nisi Prius Record, and the record of which it was a copy, really came into existence practically simultaneously.[5] But, as it was a copy, the correctness of which it was necessary to certify, the Nisi Prius Record must be "passed"; and this ceremony was made the occasion of many

[1] Common Law Procedure Commission, First Report, Parlt. Papers 1851 xxii 42-43.

[2] Vol. i 554; vol. v 117-119, 140-142.

[3] "It affords to the defendant the means of vexation and delay; for it is notorious that the motion to change the venue is generally made with a dilatory or unfair purpose. It has also the effect of exposing the plaintiff to defeat upon points of form, even after the expense of a trial has been incurred, for it frequently happens that he is nonsuited on account of a mistake of venue, and sometimes because he is unable to give material evidence, arising in the county where the action is laid," Third Report of Commissioners on Courts of Common Law, Parlt. Papers 1831 x 14.

[4] Below 275.

[5] In fact rules of the King's Bench, Trin. 1685, and Mich. 5 Anne, Cooke, op. cit., were made to provide that the copy should not come into existence before the original had been completed; these rules provide that the record of Nisi Prius is not to be sealed till the issue has been entered on the Roll.

forms and fees which remained long after any real occasion for them had ceased. "The passing of the Nisi Prius Record," said the Commissioners in 1831,[1] "is an expensive ceremony. It appears also to be a useless one, for the officers have long ceased to perform the duty of the actual transcription of the pleadings upon the record made up for trial, or even that of comparing them with the record; and their official allowance of it has no tendency therefore to secure its accuracy. Indeed this object is found to be quite sufficiently attained without any official intervention; for the incorrectness of the record may always be ascertained by comparison with the pleadings filed or delivered, and a party who should make it up incorrectly would therefore ultimately obtain no advantage from that circumstance, but might suffer loss and inconvenience. It is consequently the interest of the party who prepares the record to be accurate, and he is found in fact to be so. It is to be observed, too, that the passing of the record serves to entitle the officers to fees for services actually performed by other persons, namely, by the attornies, and for which the latter receive remuneration in another shape; so that the client is doubly charged."

Judgment and Execution.—There was a similar conflict between legal theory and actual practice in the delivery of judgment, and the manner of getting execution on the judgment. "Judgments (like the pleadings) were formally pronounced in open court; and are still always supposed to be so. But, by a relaxation of practice, there is now, in general, except in the case of an issue in law, no actual delivery of judgment, either in court or elsewhere. The plaintiff or defendant, when the cause is in such a state that, by the course of practice, he is entitled to judgment, obtains the signature or allowance of the proper officer of the court, expressing, generally, that judgment is given in his favour; and this is called signing judgment; and stands in place of its actual delivery by the judges themselves."[2] It is obvious from what was said in the controversy between Coke and Ellesmere, on the jurisdiction of the court of Chancery, that this practice goes back at least as far as the sixteenth century.[3] Similarly, "like the judgment, writs of execution are supposed to be actually awarded by the judges in court; but no such award is in general actually made."[4] The attorney, after signing judgment, sued out the writ of execution to

---

[1] Third Report of Commissioners on Courts of Common Law, Parlt. Papers 1831 x 50-51; the same abuses were apparently still existing in 1851, Common Law Procedure Commission, First Report, Parlt. Papers 1851 xxii 42.
[2] Stephen, Pleading 132.
[3] "Not one judgment of a hundred is pronounced in court, nor the case so much as heard or understood by the judges, but entered by attornies," Reports of Cases in Chancery vol. i App. 43, cited vol. i 461 n. 7.
[4] Stephen, Pleading 138.

which he considered himself entitled—"upon peril that, if he takes
a wrong execution, the proceeding will be illegal and void, and
the opposite party entitled to redress."

The manner of recording the proceedings.—Right down to the
nineteenth century, the actual record of the case read as if it had
proceeded in strict accordance with the mediæval procedure, and
as if entries had been made on the roll of the various steps in the
cause as it proceeded in court. But, long before the nineteenth
century, the form in which the record was drawn up was nothing
but an elaborate and circumstantial lie. Nothing whatever was
recorded till an issue had been reached by the exchange of the
written pleadings between the parties. When the issue was
reached and not till then, the pleadings, which to the end retained
the form of extracts from a non-existent record, were entered;
and, in order to maintain the deception, there was likewise entered
an account of various stages and steps in the action which were
supposed to have taken place in court, but which never in fact took
place.[1] "These acts in Court have the general name of *continuances*, because their effect is to *continue* or carry on the history of
the suit regularly from term to term, without chasm or interrup-
tion, as the ancient rigour of practice prescribed. The entries of
them are of various kinds and appellations, according to the nature
of the case; among the principal are the entry of continuance by
imparlance, curia advisari vult, vicecomes non misit breve, and
jurata ponitur in respectu."[2] Historically, the most interesting of
these continuances was that by imparlance. It was a survival of
the days of oral pleading in court, when each pleader was expected
to answer his adversary's pleading at once, unless the court would
grant him an imparlance, that is a delay to talk the matter over.[3]
In spite of the rise of written pleadings, the law as to imparlances
was in full vigour when Stephen wrote the first edition of his book
in 1824, and, as might be expected, had given rise to a maze of
minute rules.[4]

Naturally it required some experience to make these and other
necessary entries of the proceedings in the action in this way; and,
before 1664,[5] the most trifling inaccuracy in the most unessential detail might render the whole proceedings liable to be upset on a writ of
error.[6] After this statute, and later statutes of Anne and George I.,[7]
the need to insert these continuances on the formal record

---

[1] Stephen, Pleading 30-32, 95-97, 98-99; Second Report of Commissioners on
Courts of Common Law, Parlt. Papers 1830 xi 31-32.

[2] Ibid 31.   [3] Stephen, Pleading 90, 91.

[4] Ibid 93.   [5] 16, 17 Charles II. c. 8.

[6] The following cases are a few out of many illustrations in the reports:—Kirke
v. Barrat (1559) Dyer 173b; Blunt v. Snedston (1607) Cro. Jac. 116; Robins v.
Sanders (1616) Cro. Jac. 386.

[7] For this legislation see below 264 n. 9, 315-316, and cp. Bl. Comm. iii 406 n. t.

served, as the Common Law Commissioners said in 1830, "merely to commemorate an antiquated system of practice." It caused great expense to the parties, " by entitling the officers of the Court to fees for entries in respect of which they performed no real duty or service"; and, in spite of statutes of Henry VIII.'s and Anne's reigns,[1] and of the other statutes just mentioned, a neglect of these obsolete forms might even cause loss of the action.[5] In fact Henry VIII.'s statute, which provided that no miscontinuance or discontinuance should, after verdict, have the effect of reversing the judgment, showed that, even in 1541, they had lost any usefulness they may once have possessed. But the manner in which they survived till the second quarter of the nineteenth century, and the mode in which they were pieced on to the new mode of making up the record, which had come with the introduction of written pleadings in the sixteenth century, are a striking illustration of the manner in which the new conventional rules of practice had been joined up with, and reconciled to, the rules of the mediæval common law.

These few illustrations will show the nature of the elaborate conventional rules of practice, with which the older rules were being overlaid, in the course of the sixteenth, seventeenth and eighteenth centuries. Their complication and their irrational character would have been bad enough if one set of rules had applied to all three common law courts. They were rendered three times as bad by the fact that the practice of all these three courts differed.[3] Moreover, these bodies of practice were nowhere completely collected in any official compilation or code of rules, but existed only in a few rules and orders, a few statutes, many decided cases, and the tradition of the officials and practitioners.[4] And yet all this mass of rules was part of the law, of which the courts were bound to take judicial notice.[5] The only guide to it was the books of practice which, as we have seen, were beginning to increase in number during the latter part of the seventeenth

---

[1] 32 Henry VIII. c. 30 ; 4 Anne c. 16.   [2] Parlt. Papers 1830 xi 32.

[3] " One of the points on which it is most open to exception, is the variety which exists between the different courts ; in respect of their rules and forms of proceeding ; a variety which is far beyond that which is necessarily occasioned by the differences in their juris.iction or constitution," Third Report of Commissioners on Courts of Common Law, Parlt. Papers 1831 x 37.

[4] " The Courts have no code of Practice. The authorities by which the course of proceeding is governed consist of Rules of Court, of statutable provisions, of adjudged cases, and the usages of particular offices, as certified upon reference to the officers themselves. On such authorities are founded a vast variety of detached and promiscuous rules, devised at various periods as occasion has required, and not connected as parts of a general or preconceived system," ibid.

[5] " The customs and courses of every of the King's Courts are as a law, and the common law, for the universality thereof, doth take notice of them ; and it is not necessary to allege in pleading any usage or prescription to warrant the same," Lane's Case (1596) 2 Co. Rep. at f. 16b.

century.[1] The best illustration of the complexity of the rules is, as the Common Law Commissioners pointed out in 1829, the length and elaboration of these books. They pointed out that, in the eighth edition of Tidd's Practice, 154 closely printed large octavo pages were required to carry the proceedings only so far as the stage where the defendant first appeared to the action.[2] It was no wonder that in 1831 they recommended the compilation of a single official book of practice for the three common law courts.[3]

But it was long before anything like this ideal could be realized. The procedure of the common law, as it emerged at the close of the eighteenth century, consisted of so complicated a mass of rules of all dates, and of so many fictions and dodges to evade inconvenient rules, that the task of erecting upon its foundations a rational system was long and complicated. It taxed the strength and ability of three able bodies of commissioners; and it was not till the reforms effected by the Judicature Acts, that the uniform code of procedure, foreshadowed in 1831, was in substance obtained.[4] The work was difficult because, amidst the infinite details and complications and historical survivals of the existing procedure, very few guiding principles were to be found. What principles there were were mediæval, and had long been overlaid by a luxuriant mass of un-coordinated conventional rules. But we shall now see that one branch of this law of procedure—the branch concerned with pleading—did possess and always had possessed some very definite principles, which show a continuous development from the end of the thirteenth century right down to the middle of the nineteenth century. Like other branches of the law of procedure, it was cumbered by survivals from past stages in the history of the law ; but, unlike them, some of its principles had been developed into a set of rules more logical and more scientific than those of any other branch of the law—so logical and so scientific that they had ended by defeating the ends for which they had been created.

THE CHARACTERISTICS OF THE SYSTEM OF WRITTEN PLEADINGS

I have already sketched the history of the introduction of the common law system of pleading, and of the change from the older system of oral pleading in court to the modern system of exchanging written pleadings between the parties or their attornies, till an issue of law or fact had been reached.[5] I have also indicated the

---

[1] Vol. vi 598-599.   [2] Parlt. Papers 1829 ix 78.
[3] Ibid 1831 x 38.   [4] Vol. i 646-647.   [5] Vol. iii 627-653.

large effects upon procedure and other matters connected therewith which were caused by or accompanied this change.[1] At this
point it is necessary to say something of the characteristics of the
very unique body of law which, from the sixteenth to the eighteenth centuries, was growing up round these written pleadings.
Like many other branches of the common law, and especially those
branches which are concerned with procedure, it is remarkable
both for the continuity of the principles which underlay it, and for
the number of historical survivals from earlier periods in the history
of the law. But its most salient characteristics come from this
period. It was the developments then made, under the regime of
this system of written pleadings, which gave to its principal rules
their salient characteristics of such extreme precision, technicality,
and subtlety, that it became the most specialized and the most
esoteric of all the branches of English law. It was these developments which made the law of special pleading "the most exact, if
the most occult, of the sciences." [2]

In relating the history of this branch of the law, there is a
difficulty which is not felt to anything like the same degree in
respect to other branches of law. As I have already indicated, the
qualities of precision, technicality, and subtlety, which marked this
science of special pleading, became so great a hindrance to the
administration of justice, that its technical rules and phraseology
were swept away. Our modern system of pleading is so unlike
the older technical system, that not only the detailed rules of that
older system, but even its more general rules, and the terms used
to describe them, are unknown to all but a few modern lawyers.
There is not, as we shall see, an entire breach of continuity between
the older and the modern system ; but there is a greater breach of
continuity than exists in any other branch of the common law.
Therefore, in order to make even a short and summary account of
the history of the older system intelligible to modern readers, it
will be necessary to begin by stating in outline the chief features
of that system. It will then be possible to discuss the influences
which, at different periods, contributed to its formation ; the
attempts made at different periods by the Legislature and the
courts to remedy its defects ; and its effects on the development of
the common law. I shall therefore deal with this topic under the
following heads :—(1) The common law system of pleading ; (2)
the influences which have contributed to its formation ; (3)
attempts made to remedy its defects ; and (4) the effects of this
system of pleading on the development of the common law.

---

[1] Vol. iii 654-656. [2] P. and M. ii 609.

(1) *The common law system of pleading.*[1]

We have seen that the object of pleading is to produce an issue, i.e. some specific question of law or fact for decision by the court or jury, which is agreed upon by the parties as the question in dispute between them.[2] We have seen, too, that the production of such an issue by the pleadings of the parties is peculiar to the common law.[3] At this point I shall try to sketch, in the briefest possible outline, the way in which this object was effected under the old system of pleading.

The pleadings began with the plaintiff's declaration or count. In personal actions, and in some real actions, it began by a recital of the original writ.[4] This recital was not essential to the validity of the declaration; and therefore an erroneous recital did not vitiate the declaration.[5] But it was essential that the declaration should conform to the original writ;[6] so that, if a writ of detinue were brought for £20 and the declaration demanded £40, it was held that judgment for the plaintiff could be reversed on a writ of error.[7] But, in the course of the eighteenth century, this particular objection was practically done away with, partly by the practice of the courts,[8] and partly by the operation of the statutes of jeofail.[9] The old practice had, however, one permanent result. It fixed the "frame and language of the declaration in conformity with the original writ in each form of action."[10]

---

[1] This sketch is based mainly on the First Edition of Stephen's Pleading, and the precedents cited are taken from that book.

[2] Vol. iii 627-628.

[3] Ibid 628.

[4] Stephen, op. cit. 420-422.

[5] Ibid 422; but as late as 1561 (Plowden at p. 228) Brown, J. (dissenting from his brethren) thought that the wording of the original writ ought to be slavishly followed, even though the words were inapplicable to the case in hand, so that, e.g. in ejectment, the plaintiff must allege that the defendant had taken his goods and chattels, though in fact he had not done so.

[6] " Ita quod narratio brevi conveniat, a quo si discordet et brevi non conveniat narratio, amittit petens, quia non admittitur variatio," Bracton f. 431a ; "item datur exceptio . . . ita quod narratio non sit consona brevi, vel quod non dicat quod tantundem valeat," ibid f. 435b, cited Stephen, op. cit. 423-424.

[7] Young v. Watson (1593) Cro. Eliza. 308.

[8] The Common Pleas in 1739, and the King's Bench in 1769, by making rules that no oyer should be granted of an original writ, prevented any plea in abatement " founded on facts that could only be ascertained by examination of the writ itself," Stephen op. cit. 69; see Gray v. Sidneff (1803) 3 B. and P. at p. 399; for a very subtle plea founded on this rule see White v. Howard (1810) 3 Taunt 339.

[9] Some account of these statutes will be found in vol. iii 650; vol. iv 535-536; vol. vi 409; and I shall have something more to say of them below 315-316; it may be convenient at this point to have a list—14 Edward III. c. 6; 9 Henry V. c. 4; 4 Henry VI. c. 3; 8 Henry VI. c.c. 12, 15; 32 Henry VIII. c. 30; 18 Elizabeth c. 14; 21 James I. c. 13; 16, 17 Charles II. c. 8; 4 Anne c. 16; 9 Anne c. 20 § 7; 5 George I. c. 13.

[10] Stephen, op. cit. 425; for inconveniences which resulted when the declaration did not, in consequence, give sufficient information to the defendant, and the way in which these inconveniences were obviated see below 286 and n. 4.

The following is an example of a declaration in covenant on
an indenture of lease for not repairing :—

In the King's Bench.[1]
    —Term in the   year of the reign of King George the Fourth.
    —To wit. C.D. was summoned to answer A.B. by a plea that he keep
with him the covenant made by the said C.D. with the said A.B. according to
the force, form and effect of a certain indenture in that behalf made between
them.   And therefore the said A.B. by   his attorney, complains : For
that, whereas heretofore, to wit, on the   day of   in the year of our
Lord   at   in the county of   by a certain indenture then and
there made between the said A.B. of the one part, and the said C.D. of the
other part (one part of which said indenture, sealed with the seal of the said
C.D. the said A.B. now brings here into court, the date whereof is the day
and year aforesaid), the said A.B. for the consideration therein mentioned,
did demise, lease, set, and to farm let unto the said C.D. a certain messuage
or tenement, and other premises, in the said indenture particularly specified,
to hold the same, with the appurtenances, to the said C.D. his executors,
administrators and assigns, from the twenty-fifth day of March next ensuing
the date of the said indenture, for and during and unto the full end and term
of seven years from thence next ensuing, and fully to be complete and ended,
at a certain rent payable by the said C.D. to the said A.B. as in the said
indenture is mentioned.   And the said C.D. for himself, his executors,
administrators, and assigns, did thereby covenant, promise and agree, to and
with the said A.B. his heirs and assigns (amongst other things), that he the
said C.D., his executors, administrators, and assigns, should, and would, at all
times during the continuance of the said demise, at his and their own costs
and charges, support, uphold, maintain, and keep the said messuage or
tenement and premises in good and tenantable repair, order, and condition ;
and the same messuage or tenement and premises, and every part thereof,
should and would leave in such good repair order and condition, at the end
or other sooner determination of the said term.   As by the said indenture
reference being thereunto had, will among other things fully appear.   By
virtue of which said indenture, the said C.D. afterwards, to wit on the twenty-
fifth day of March, in the year aforesaid, entered into the said premises, with
the appurtenances, and became and was possessed thereof, and so continued
until the end of the said term.   And although the said A.B. hath always, from
the time of the making of the said indenture, hitherto done, performed, and
fulfilled all things in the said indenture contained on his part to be performed
and fulfilled, yet protesting, that the said C.D. hath not performed and
fulfilled anything in the said indenture contained, on his part and behalf to
be performed and fulfilled, in fact, the said A.B. saith, that the said C.D.
did not, during the continuance of the said demise support, uphold, maintain
and keep the said messuage or tenement and premises in good and tenantable
repair, order, and condition, and leave the same in such repair, order, and
condition, at the end of the said term ; but for a long time, to wit, for the
last three years of the said term, did permit all the windows of the said
messuage or tenement to be, and the same during all that time were, in
every part thereof ruinous, in decay, and out of repair, for want of necessary
reparation and amendment.   And the said C.D. left the same, being so
ruinous, in decay, and out of repair as aforesaid, at the end of the said term,
contrary to the form and effect of the said covenant so made aforesaid.   And
so the said A.B. saith, that the said C.D. (although often requested) hath not

---

[1] Stephen, op. cit. 41.

kept the said covenant so by him made as aforesaid, but hath broken the same ; and to keep the same with the said A.B. hath hitherto wholly refused, and still refuses, to the damage of the said A.B. of   pounds, and therefore he brings his suit [1] etc.

When the plaintiff had delivered his declaration the defendant must either (i) demur, or (ii) plead.

(i) If, admitting the plaintiff's facts to be true, it appears that in point of law he is not entitled to the redress which he seeks, the defendant can demur ; and this point of law may be raised either in respect of a matter of substance, as where the declaration shows no case on the merits, or in respect of a matter of form, as where the declaration violates the rules of pleading.[2] "The law," said Hobart, C.J., in 1613,[3] "requires in every plea two things; the one that it be in matter sufficient, the other that it be deduced and expressed according to the forms of law ; and if either the one or the other of these be wanting, it is cause of demurrer."

If the objection was matter of substance a general demurrer was sufficient. The following is an example :—[4]

General Demurrer to the Declaration

In the King's Bench.
—Term in the — year of the reign of King George the Fourth.
C.D.⎫ And the said C.D. by—his attorney, comes and defends the wrong
ats.[5]⎬ and injury, when etc. and says that the said declaration and the
A.B.⎭ matters therein contained, in manner and form as the same are above stated and set forth, are not sufficient in law for the said A.B. to have or maintain his aforesaid action against him the said C.D., and that he, the said C.D. is not bound by the law of the land to answer the same. And this he is ready to verify. Wherefore, for want of a sufficient declaration in this behalf, the said C.D. prays judgment, and that the said A.B. may be barred from having or maintaining his aforesaid action against him.

If the objection was matter of form a special demurrer was necessary. This was the result of statutes of 1585 and 1705,[6] which, in substance, provided that the judges were not to regard defects of form, "except those only which the party demurring shall specially and particularly set down and express together with his demurrer as causes of the same." This meant that the party demurring must set out the nature of the informality on which he

---

[1] The English form of "inde produxit sectam," for which archaic formula see vol. i 300-301.
[2] Stephen, op. cit. 61, 158-159 : thus the misrecital of an Act of Parliament might be ground for a special demurrer, the Prince's Case (1606) 8 Co. Rep. at f. 28a ; and the question when such misrecital could thus be taken advantage of, gave rise to a mass of complex rules, see the note to Holland's Case (1597) 4 Co. Rep. 77a.
[3] Colt and Glover v. the Bishop of Coventry Hob. at p. 164.
[4] Stephen, op. cit. 61.   [5] I.e. at the suit of.
[6] 27 Elizabeth c. 5 ; 4 Anne c. 16 ; Stephen op. cit. 159-160.

relied.   A mere general statement that the declaration was informal and insufficient (though generally added) was useless.[1]

Holt, C.J.'s view, which is very likely right, was that the need for these statutes was caused by the change from oral to written pleadings.   He said:[2] " Upon a *general demurrer* he might take advantage of all manner of defects, that of *duplicity* only excepted ; and there was no inconvenience in such practice, for the pleadings being at Bar *viva voce*, and the exceptions taken *ore tenus*, the causes of demurrer were as well known upon a general demurrer as upon a special one ; therefore after the Reformation, when the practice of pleading at the Bar altered, the use of general demurrers still continued, and thereby this public inconveniency followed, that the parties went on to argue a general demurrer not knowing what they were to argue, and this was the occasion of making the statute 27 Eliz., by which it is enacted that the causes of demurrer should be known in all cases ; " the fact that a general demurer disclosed nothing as to the point which the demurring party intended to take was, from that party's point of view, a desirable characteristic.   Therefore Stephen tells us,[3] " when a general demurrer is plainly sufficient, it is more usually adopted in practice ; because the effect of the special form, being to apprize the opposite party more distinctly of the nature of the objection, is attended with the inconvenience of enabling him to prepare and maintain his pleading in argument, or of leading him to apply the earlier to amend."

The following is an example of a special demurrer : —[4]

SPECIAL DEMURRER TO THE DECLARATION

In the King's Bench.

—Term, in the — year of the reign of King George the Fourth.

C.D.⎫
ats. ⎬
A.B.⎭ As in previous precedent with the addition of the following clause ; —And the said C.D. according to the form of the statute in such case made and provided, states and shows to the court here the following causes of demurrer to the said declaration : that is to say, that no day or time is alleged in the said declaration at which the said causes of action, or any of them, are supposed to have occurred.   And also that the said declaration is in other respects uncertain, informal, and insufficient.

Under a special demurrer the party demurring could take substantial as well as formal objections ; so that it was generally

---

[1] " Now the moderation of this statute (27 Elizabeth c. 5) is such, that it doth not utterly reject form ; for that were a dishonour to the law, and to make it in effect no art : but requires only that it be discovered, and not used as a secret snare to entrap. And that discovery must not be confused or obscure, but special, therefore it is not sufficient to say, that the demurrer is for form, but he must express what is the point and speciality of form, that he requires," Heard v. Baskerville (1615) Hob. at p. 232, cited Stephen op. cit. note 45.

[2] Anon. 3 Salk. 122.   [3] Op. cit. 160-161.   [4] Ibid 62.

the safer course to demur specially, unless it was quite clear that there was a substantial objection.[1]

Since a question of law was raised by the demurrer, the party demurring must (as will be seen from the examples given) refer the question to the proper tribunal—the Court. This he did by praying the Court's judgment, and thus tendering an issue in law.[2] Such an issue the opposite party must accept; and he accepted it by a joinder in demurrer, as follows : —[3]

JOINDER IN DEMURRER

In the King's Bench.

—Term, in the   year of the reign of King George the Fourth.

A.B. ⎫ And the said A.B. says, that the said declaration and the matters
v. ⎬ therein contained, in manner and form as the same are above pleaded
C.D. ⎭ and set forth, are sufficient in law for him the said A.B. to have and maintain his aforesaid action against him the said C.D. And the said A.B. is ready to verify and prove the same as the Court here shall direct and award. Wherefore inasmuch as the said C.D. hath not answered the said declaration, nor hitherto in any manner denied the same, the said A.B. prays judgment, and his debt aforesaid, together with his damages by him sustained, by reason of the detention thereof, to be adjudged to him.

(ii) If a defendant did not demur he must plead. The main division between pleas is between those which are (a) dilatory, and those which are (b) peremptory or in bar of the action.[4]

(a) Dilatory pleas are either to the jurisdiction of the court, or in suspension of the action—e.g. demurrer of the parol, or in abatement.[5] The last named of these dilatory pleas is the most important. It is a plea which "shows some ground for abating or quashing the original writ; and makes prayer to that effect".[6] It may relate to the person of the plaintiff or defendant, e.g. that the plaintiff is an alien enemy; or to the declaration, e.g. a variance between the declaration and the writ; or to the writ, e.g. that the wrong form of writ has been chosen, or that all the proper parties are not named in it.[7] The following is an example of a plea in abatement of the writ : —[8]

(In Assumpsit)

In the King's Bench.

—Term, in the   year of the reign of King George the Fourth.

C.D. ⎫ And the said C.D. by   his attorney, comes and defends[9] the
ats. ⎬ wrong and injury when etc.[10] and prays judgment of the said writ and
A.B. ⎭ declaration, because he says that the said several supposed promises

---

[1] Stephen, op. cit. 160-161.   [2] Ibid 73-74.
[3] Ibid 75.   [4] Ibid 63.
[5] Ibid ; for demurrer of the parol see vol. iii 513-516.
[6] Stephen, op. cit. 65.   [7] Ibid 65-67.   [8] Ibid 68.
[9] For the formal " defence " see vol. iii 629, 630-631 ; below 282-283.
[10] The full form is as follows: "And the said C.D. by E.F. his attorney, comes and defends the force and injury when and where it shall behove him, and the

and undertakings in the said declaration mentioned (if any such were made), were made jointly with one G.H. who is still living, to wit, at   , and not by the said C.D. alone. And this the said C.D. is ready to verify. Wherefore inasmuch as the said G.H. is not named in the said writ, together with the said C.D., he, the said C.D. prays judgment of the said writ and declaration, and that the same may be quashed.

On any of these dilatory pleas there might be further pleading. The other party might demur, or he might plead, either by way of traverse, or by way of confession and avoidance.[1] If the party putting forward the plea succeeded, the writ or declaration was quashed; but the other party could start a new action, if and when the particular objection was removed.[2]

In earlier days pleas in abatement might be founded on objections raised, either to the original writ, or to the declaration. But we have seen that, in the course of the eighteenth century, the practice of using an original writ was dropping out; and that in 1739 and 1769 the courts practically stopped all such objections founded on the original writ, by refusing oyer of it.[3] The result was that these pleas were for the future founded only on objections to the declaration.

(b) Peremptory pleas, or pleas in bar of the action, are "distinguished from all pleas of the dilatory class, as impugning the right of action altogether, instead of merely tending to divert the proceedings to another jurisdiction, or suspend them, or abate the particular writ."[4] They must either traverse, i.e. deny all or some essential part of the averments of fact in the declaration, or they must confess these averments and avoid their effect by the averment of new facts. A plea which attempted both to traverse and confess and avoid was bad.[5] Hence "pleas in bar are divided into pleas *by way of traverse*, and pleas *by way of confession and avoidance.*"[6]

The following are examples of pleas in bar by way of traverse, and confession and avoidance :—[7]

---

damages, and whatsoever else he ought to defend," Stephen, op. cit. 433; for the distinction between the " full defence," and the " half defence," based on the words of this formula see vol. iii 630 n. 5; below 282 n. 5.

[1] Stephen, op. cit. 76-77, 239; for the pleas by way of traverse, or confession and avoidance see below 270.

[2] Stephen, op. cit. 68.

[3] Above 264 and n. 8.

[4] Stephen, op. cit. 70-71.

[5] " Where the plea is fully confessed and avoided, and then a traverse moreover is taken, this traverse vitiates the whole plea," Lambert v. Cook (1698) 1 Ld. Raym. at p. 238 *per* Curiam.

[6] Stephen, op. cit. 71.

[7] Ibid 71-72.

Plea in Bar

By Way of Traverse

(See the Declaration above 265-266)

C.D. ⎱
ats. ⎰ And the said C.D., by   his attorney, comes and defends
A.B. ⎰ the wrong and injury when etc., and says that the said A.B. ought
not to have or maintain his aforesaid action against him, the said
C.D., because he says that the windows of the said messuage or tenement
were not in any part thereof ruinous, in decay, or out of repair, in manner
and form as the said A.B. hath above complained against him the said C.D.
And of this he puts himself upon the country.

Plea in Bar

By Way of Confession and Avoidance

(See the Declaration above 265-266)

C.D. ⎱
ats. ⎰ and the said C.D., by   his attorney, comes and defends the
A.B. ⎰ wrong and injury when etc., and says that the said A.B. ought not to
have or maintain his aforesaid action against him, the said C.D.,
because he says that, after the said breach of covenant, and before the commencement of this suit, to wit, on the   day of   in the year of our
Lord   at   aforesaid, in the county aforesaid, the said A.B. by his
certain deed of release, sealed with his seal, and now shown to the court here
(the date whereof is the day and year last aforesaid), did remise, release, and
for ever quit claim to the said C.D. his heirs, executors and administrators,
all damages, cause and causes of action, breaches of covenant, debts and
demands whatsoever, which had then accrued to the said A.B., or which the
said A.B. then had against the said C.D. ; as by the said deed of release,
reference being thereto had, will fully appear.   And this the said C.D. is
ready to verify.   Wherefore he prays judgment if the said A.B. ought to have
or maintain his aforesaid action against him.

Let us consider firstly the case where the plea is by way of
traverse, and secondly the case where it is by way of confession
and avoidance.

Traverse.—The oldest form of Traverse is the " general issue."
That is, to use Stephen's words, "an appropriate plea fixed by
ancient usage as the proper method of traversing the declaration,
in cases when the defendant means to deny the whole or the
principal part of its allegations." [1]   Thus in formedon the general
issue was "ne dona pas"; in debt on a specialty "non est
factum," and on a simple contract "nil debet"; in trespass or
case "not guilty"; in assumpsit "non assumpsit."   The effect of
pleading the general issue was thus to contradict generally the
plaintiff's allegations, and to put a summary close to the pleadings,
thus, as Stephen has said, "narrowing very considerably the
application of the greater and more subtle part of the science
of special pleading." [2]   We shall see that, because it had this

---

[1] Op. cit. 172 seqq.   [2] Ibid 176.

effect, it was given a wide application by the judges, and helped materially to mitigate some of the evils arising from the subtleties of special pleading.[1]

It should be noted that the general issue does not merely deny facts, it also denies the legal effect of those facts as understood by the pleader; and this was true also of the whole system of common law pleading.[2] Probably this manner of pleading originated in the days when the distinction between issues of fact and issues of law was not clearly drawn; and it became permanent in mediæval law because, as we have seen,[3] statements of fact, the legal conclusions arising from those facts, and the evidence for the facts stated, could not be clearly distinguished under the mediæval system of oral pleading. The growth of a law of evidence separated a pleader's statement of facts from the evidence for those facts; and the new system of written pleadings would have made it possible to plead the facts rather than the legal effect of the facts. But this change was not made—probably because the introduction of those written pleadings came gradually, informally, and almost without acknowledgment.[4] And so this manner of pleading survived till the Judicature Acts.[5]

An ordinary traverse, it will be seen from the example given, raises at once a question of fact between the parties; the plaintiff has stated facts which the defendant has denied. The defendant, having raised this question of fact, must refer it to some mode of trial. This he does (as the example just given shows) by "putting himself on the country." If the plaintiff "does the like" they are at issue. The following is an example of a joinder in issue.[6]

JOINDER IN ISSUE

(Upon the Traverse at p. 270.)

A.B.⎫
v. ⎬ And the said A.B. as to the plea of the said C.D. above pleaded, and
C.D.⎭ whereof he has put himself upon the country, doth the like.

But the plaintiff need not necessarily "do the like." He might demur to it for insufficiency in substance or in form. In that case the defendant would have no option but to join in demurrer.[7]

Confession and Avoidance.—If the defendant has pleaded by

---

[1] Below 319-322.

[2] "The pleadings are regarded, not as statements by the respective parties of what they claim to be the truth of the case in point of evidence, . . . but as statements by their counsel of what they claim to be the legal effect of the evidence to be produced," Langdell, Equity Pleading, Essays A.A.L.H. ii 772; Odgers, Pleading (4th ed.) 81.

[3] Vol. iii 638.   [4] Ibid 640-641.   [5] Below 329.

[6] Stephen, op. cit. 76.   [7] Ibid 75-76; above 268.

way of confession and avoidance, the plaintiff may either demur, or make a replication by way either of traverse or of confession and avoidance. If his replication be by way of traverse, he must tender issue, as explained in reference to the defendant's traverse. But if it be by way of confession and avoidance, the defendant may in his turn either demur, or make a rejoinder by way either or traverse or of confession and avoidance.[1] The following are examples of such pleadings :—[2]

REPLICATION

By Way of Confession and Avoidance

(Upon the plea by way of Confession and Avoidance at p. 270)

A.B.⎫ And the said A.B. says, that, by reason of anything in the said plea
v. ⎬ alleged, he ought not to be barred from having and maintaining his
C.D.⎭ aforesaid action against the said C.D. because he says that he the said A.B. at the time of making the said supposed deed of release, was unlawfully imprisoned and detained in prison by the said C.D. until, by force and duress of that imprisonment he the said A.B. made the said supposed deed of release, as in the said plea mentioned. And this he the said A.B. is ready to verify. Wherefore he prays judgment, and his damages by him sustained by reason of the said breach of covenant, to be adjudged to him.

REJOINDER

By Way of Traverse to the above Replication

C.D.⎫ And the said C.D. saith, that by reason of anything in the said
ats. ⎬ replication alleged, the said A.B. ought not to have or maintain his
A.B.⎭ aforesaid action against him the said C.D., because he says, that the said A.B. freely and voluntarily made the said deed of release, and not by force and duress of imprisonment, in manner and form as by the said replication alleged. And of this the said C.D. puts himself upon the country.

DEMURRER TO THE ABOVE REPLICATION

C.D.⎫ And the said C.D. says, that the same replication of the said A.B. to
ats. ⎬ the said plea of him the said C.D., and the matters therein contained,
A.B.⎭ in manner and form as the same are above pleaded and set forth, are not sufficient, in law, for the said A.B. to have or maintain his aforesaid action against the said C.D. ; and that he the said C.D. is not bound by the law of the land to answer the same. And this the said C.D. is ready to verify. Wherefore, for want of a sufficient replication in this behalf, the said C.D. prays judgment, if the said A.B. ought to have or maintain his aforesaid action against him.

" In the same manner," says Stephen,[3] "and subject to the same law of proceeding, viz. that of *demurring*, or *traversing*, or pleading *in confession and avoidance*, is conducted all the subsequent altercation, to which the nature of the case may lead ; and the order and denominations of the alternate *allegations of fact* or *pleadings* throughout the whole series, are as follows : *declaration*,

---

[1] Stephen, op. cit. 77. [2] Ibid 79-80. [3] Ibid 77-78.

plea, replication, rejoinder, surrejoinder, rebutter, and *surrebutter.* After the surrebutter, the pleadings have no distinctive names; for beyond that stage they are very seldom found to extend. To whatever length of series the pleadings may happen to lead, it is obvious that, by adherence to the plan here described, one of the parties must, at some period of the process, more or less remote, be brought either to demur or to traverse; for, as no case can involve an inexhaustible store of new relevant matter, there must be somewhere a limit to pleading in the way of *confession and avoidance.*"

The foregoing is the normal and regular course of the pleadings. But there are one or two matters which might occur in their course, to which allusion must be made, because they illustrate the care which the law took to ensure the correctness of the issue reached.

Firstly, if after the delivery of a preceding plea new facts had arisen, which, e.g., gave a defendant a new matter of defence, the defendant could withdraw his first plea, and substitute another. This was called a plea of "puis darrein continuance," because it dealt with matters arising since the last continuance or adjournment.[1]

Secondly, it might happen that a defendant misunderstood the allegation in the declaration, and therefore pleaded a plea quite inapplicable to the facts upon which the plaintiff was suing. Suppose, e.g., that the plaintiff was twice assaulted by the defendant, and that the first assault was justifiable because in self-defence, and that the second was not; suppose the plaintiff sued for the second assault, and the defendant, thinking or pretending to think that the first assault was meant, pleaded "son assault demesne"; it would be necessary for the plaintiff to "new assign," that is "to correct the mistake occasioned by the generality of his declaration,"[2] by showing that he referred to the second assault. The following is an example of such a plea;—[3]

REPLICATION

To a Plea of Son Assault Demesne by Way of New Assignment

And as to the said plea of the said C.D., by him secondly above pleaded, as to the said several trespasses in the introductory part of that plea mentioned, and therein attempted to be justified, the said A.B. says that, by reason of anything in that plea alleged, he ought not to be barred from having and maintaining his aforesaid action thereof against the said C.D., because he says that he brought his said action, not for the trespasses in the said second plea acknowledged to have been done, but for that the said C.D. heretofore, to wit, on the day of   in the year of our Lord   with force and arms,

---

[1] Stephen, op. cit. 81-82; for these " continuances " see above 260.
[2] Ibid 241-243.   [3] Ibid.

at   aforesaid in the county aforesaid, upon another and different occasion, and for another and different purpose than in the said second plea mentioned, made another and different assault upon the said A.B. than the assault in the said second plea mentioned, and then and there beat, wounded, and ill-treated him in manner and form as the said A.B. hath above thereof complained ; which said trespasses above newly assigned, are other and different trespasses than the said trespasses in the said second plea acknowledged to have been done. And this the said A.B. is ready to verify. Wherefore inasmuch as the said C.D. hath not answered the said trespasses above newly assigned, he, the said A.B. prays judgment, and his damages by him sustained by reason of the committing thereof, to be adjudged to him etc.

Thirdly, the pleadings of the parties must present consistent stories leading up to a definite issue. It would be impossible to attain this result within any reasonable time, if a party, having taken up one ground in an earlier pleading, was allowed to take up another inconsistent ground in a later pleading. A party who did this was said to have made a " departure " in pleading ; and such a departure made the pleading bad.[1] The following illustrations will show how this rule was applied :—" In trespass, if the defendant will plead a descent to him, and the plaintiff says that after the descent the defendant infeoffed him, and the defendant says, that this feoffment was upon condition, for the breach whereof he entered, this is a departure from the bar,[2] for it contains new matter." [3]   In the case of *Roberts v. Mariett*[4] a bond was made conditioned to perform an award, provided that the award was delivered by a certain time. To an action on the bond, the defendant pleaded that the arbitrators made no award. The plaintiff replied that they did make an award which was tendered in proper time. The defendant rejoined that the award was not so tendered. This was held to be a departure from his plea in which he had alleged that no such award was made. In the case of *R. v. Larwood*[5] an information was brought against the defendant for not serving the office of sheriff, being duly elected thereto. He pleaded that he was a Protestant dissenter and had not received the sacrament, and that therefore he was, by the Corporation Act of 1661, incapacitated from holding office. The attorney-general replied that he ought not to take advantage of his own wrong. The defendant rejoined that he was protected by the

---

[1] " A departure in pleading is said to be when the second plea containeth matter not pursuant to his former, and which fortifieth not the same, and thereupon it is called *Decessus* because he departeth from his former plea," Co. Litt. 304a ; see generally, Stephen, op. cit. 405-411.

[2] I.e. from the plea in bar.

[3] Reniger v. Fogossa (1551) Plowden at p. 8 *per* Bradshaw, A.G., *arg.*; for other illustrations see Fulmerston v. Steward (1554) Plowden at p. 105; Anon. (1537) Dyer 31b; Anon. (1566) ibid 253b; and cp. Chapman v. Chapman (1628) Cro. Car. 76.

[4] (1670) 2 Saunders, 188.   [5] (1694) 1 Ld. Raym. 29.

Toleration Act of 1689. To this rejoinder the attorney-general demurred ; and the court upheld the demurrer, on the ground that " the rejoinder was a perfect departure, because it did not strengthen the bar, and it ought to have been pleaded at the beginning.[1]

When the issue had been reached by the pleadings of the parties, the record was, as we have seen,[2] made up ; and the case went for trial to the court if the issue was one of law, and to the jury if the issue was one of fact. The following are examples of the record on an issue of law, and an issue of fact respectively :—[3]

ENTRY OF ISSUE

On Demurrer

With an Imparlance[4]

(In the King's Bench—by original—in an action of covenant.)

As yet of   -   Term, in the   year of the reign of King George the Fourth, Witness Sir Charles Abbott Knight.

— to wit, A.B. puts in his place E.F. his attorney against C.D. in a plea of breach of covenant.[5]

— to wit, C.D. puts in his place G.H. his attorney, at the suit of the said A.B. in the plea aforesaid.

— to wit, C.D. was summoned to answer (*as in the declaration above* 265-266).

And the said C.D. by   his attorney, comes and defends the wrong and injury when etc., and prays a day thereupon to imparl to the said declaration of the said A.B.; and it is granted to him etc. And upon this a day is given to the parties aforesaid, before our Lord the King, until wheresoever etc., that is to say, for the said C.D. to imparl to the declaration aforesaid, and then to answer the same. At which day before our said Lord the King at Westminster, come the parties aforesaid, by their attorneys aforesaid ; and the said C.D. says that the said A.B. ought not to have or maintain (*as in the plea above* 270).

And the said A.B. says that by reason of anything in the said plea alleged, he ought not to be barred (*as in the replication above* 272).

And the said C.D. says that the said replication of the said A.B. to the said plea of him the said C.D., and the matters therein contained, in manner and form as the same are above pleaded and set forth, are not sufficient in law (*as in the demurrer above* 272).

And the said A.B. says that the said replication, and the matters therein contained, in manner and form as the same are above pleaded and set forth, are sufficient in law for him the said A.B. to have and maintain his aforesaid action against the said C.D. And the said A.B. is ready to verify and prove the same, as the Court here shall direct and award. Wherefore, inasmuch as the said C.D. hath not answered the said replication, nor hitherto in any manner denied the same, the said A.B. prays judgment, and his damages, by him sustained by reason of the said breach of covenant, to be adjudged to him.[6]

---

[1] (1694) 1 Ld. Raym. at p. 30.   [2] Above 258.
[3] Stephen, op. cit. 99-101.   [4] For imparlances see above 260.
[5] For the early formalities attending the appointment of an attorney see vol. ii 315-317.
[6] Joinder in Demurrer, see above 268.

But because the Court of our said Lord the King now here, are not yet advised what judgment to give of and upon the premises, a day is given to the parties aforesaid, before our Lord the King, on   , wheresoever etc., to hear judgment thereon, for that the said Court of our said Lord the King now here are not yet advised thereof.[1]

ENTRY OF ISSUE
On an Issue of Fact to be tried by a Jury
Without an Imparlance

(In the King's Bench—by original—In an action of Covenant.)

As yet of the   Term, in the   year of the reign of King George the Fourth, Witness Sir Charles Abbott, Knight.

— To wit, A.B. puts in his place E.F. his attorney, against C.D. in a plea of breach of covenant.

— To wit, C.D. puts in his place G.H. his attorney, at the suit of the said A.B., in the plea aforesaid.

— To wit, C.D. was summoned to answer (*as in the declaration above* 265-266). And the said A.B. by   his attorney comes and defends the wrong and injury, when, etc., and says (*as in the plea above* 270).

And the said A.B. says, that, by reason of anything in the said plea alleged, he ought not to be barred from having and maintaining his aforesaid action against the said C.D., because he says (*as in the replication above* 272).

And the said C.D. saith, that, by reason of anything in the said replication alleged, the said A.B. ought not to have or maintain his aforesaid action against him the said C.D. because he says (*as in the rejoinder above* 272).

And the said A.B. does the like.[2] Therefore it is commanded to the Sheriff that he cause to come before our Lord the King,[3] on   wheresoever our said Lord the King shall then be in England, twelve etc., by whom etc., and who neither etc., to recognize etc., because as well etc. The same day is given to the parties aforesaid etc.

We have seen that trials of issues of fact generally took place at the assizes.[4] When the jury gave their verdict it was drawn up in proper form, and entered on the Nisi Prius Record. This entry is called the " Postea " from its initial word.[5] The following is an example :—[6]

POSTEA.

For the plaintiff on the issue (in the last cited precedent) if tried at Nisi Prius in London or Middlesex.

Afterwards, that is to say, on the day and at the place within contained, before the Right Honourable Sir Charles Abbott, Knight, the Chief Justice

---

[1] This entry of " curia advisari vult " is a variety of continuance, as to which see above 260.

[2] The Rejoinder concludes to the country ; and this is an abbreviated form of joining an issue of fact ; for the longer form see above 271.

[3] The writ of Venire Facias ; for the procedural rules connected with the summoning of the jury see above 257-258.

[4] Vol. i 278-280.   [5] Ibid 281-282.   [6] Stephen, op cit. 109-110.

within mentioned ; (John Henry Abbott, Esquire, being associated to the said Chief Justice, according to the form of the statute in such case made and provided) come as well the within named A.B. as the said C.D. by their respective attornies within mentioned ; and the jurors of the jury, whereof mention is within made, being summoned, also come, who, to speak the truth of the matters within contained, being chosen, tried and sworn, say, upon their oath, that the said A.B. was, at the time of the making of the said deed of release within mentioned, unlawfully imprisoned and detained in prison by the said C.D. until, by force and duress of that imprisonment, he the said A.B. made the said deed of release, in manner and form as the said A.B. hath within alleged. And they assess the damages of the said A.B. by reason of the said breach of covenant within assigned, over and above his costs and charges by him, about his suit in this behalf expended, to fifty pounds ; and for those costs and charges to forty shillings. Therefore etc.

After the verdict of the jury it remained for the court to give judgment. As with the pleading of the general issue,[1] so with the giving of judgment, there were certain ancient formulæ adapted to judgments on different kinds of pleas, and to judgments in different courts.[2] Thus, in case of judgment for the plaintiff on an issue in law arising from a dilatory plea, there was judgment of "respondeat ouster," i.e. "answer over." If the issue was one of fact or any other issue in law, the judgment was "quod recuperet," i.e. "that the plaintiff do recover."[3] In case of judgment for the defendant on any kind of dilatory plea, the judgment was "quod breve cassetur," i.e. "that the writ be quashed" ; and on any other plea the judgment was "nil capiat," i.e. "that the plaintiff take nothing by his writ, and that the defendant go thereof without day" ;[4] and the judgment was the same if, after verdict, the defendant moved successfully in arrest of judgment.[5]

It did not, however, follow that judgment would be given in accordance with the verdict ; or that, if given, it would stand. We have seen that there were various ways of questioning the verdict of a jury both before and after judgment—before the judgment by motion for a new trial, after the judgment by bill of exceptions or writ of error. With these matters I have already

---

[1] Above 270.   [2] Stephen, op. cit. 126-131.

[3] If the action sounded in damages, and the trial was on an issue in law, the judgment was interlocutory ; a writ of inquiry issued to assess the damages, and, on the return of the writ, final judgment issued for the damages thus assessed, ibid 126-127.

[4] There were similar forms for judgments in cases in which the pleadings had not proceeded regularly to issue—e.g. judgment by "nil dicit," i.e. if the defendant, after appearing, failed to plead or to continue the pleadings ; or judgment by "confession relicta verificatione," i.e. if the defendant withdrew his plea and confessed the action ; or judgment by "non prosequitur," i.e. if the plaintiff failed to plead, or to take any necessary step in the action ; or judgment by "nolle prosequi," or "retraxit," i.e. where the plaintiff refused to go on, or withdrew his suit ; or judgment by "nonsuit," i.e. when, on a trial by jury, the plaintiff, being called to hear the verdict, failed to appear, ibid 129-131.

[5] Thomas v. Willoughby (1621), Cro. Jac. 587.

dealt;[1] and I need not refer to them again, as they are only remotely connected with the law of pleading. But there were other ways of questioning the verdict—motion to arrest the judgment, to give judgment non obstante veredicto, or to award a repleader[2] —which turn at bottom upon a very fundamental principle of the common law, which had important effects upon the principles of pleading. It was the duty of the court to give judgment according to the law applicable to the facts of the case. Now the facts of the case were, after the verdict, all upon the record. They were ascertainable, partly from the pleadings, and partly from the verdict. It followed, therefore, that the court must give judgment according to the law applicable to the facts there set out, and according to no others.[3] But it might well happen that, if the whole record was examined, the party in whose favour the verdict was given, was not entitled to judgment. Thus, if an error appeared on the face of the record which vitiated the proceedings, a motion might be made in arrest of judgment;[4] and, till the statutes of jeofail,[5] the error might be one of mere form. Or if, on examination of the record, it appeared that a plea of the defendant was bad in substance; so that, even though the jury had found the facts to be as he pleaded them, he was not entitled to judgment, the plaintiff might move for judgment non obstante veredicto.[6] Or if, owing to mispleading, the issue joined was not proper to decide the action, the court might award a repleader, that is, order the parties to begin their pleading anew. Thus, "if in an action of debt on bond, conditioned for the payment of ten pounds ten shillings, at a certain day, the defendant pleads payment of ten pounds, according to the form of the condition, and the plaintiff, instead of demurring, tenders issue upon such payment, it is plain that, whether this issue be found for the plaintiff or the defendant, it will remain equally uncertain whether the plaintiff is entitled or not to maintain his action; for, in an action for the penalty of a bond conditioned to pay a certain sum, the only material question is, whether the exact sum were paid or not, and a payment in part, is a question quite beside the legal merits."[7]

---

[1] Vol. i 213-214, 222-224, 225-226. [2] Stephen, op. cit. 115.
[3] Ibid 140-141; below 280-282. [4] Ibid 117.
[5] Above 264 n. 9; below 315-316. [6] Stephen, op. cit. 117-118.
[7] Ibid 119; cp. the following illustration taken from Plowden's note to Hill v. Grange (1558) Plowden at p. 179—"If the bar had been insufficient to convey the land to the defendant by the lease made by Pate, then the demurrer being upon the replication made to the bar, as it is here, the judgment thereupon ought to be that the parties should replead as to the land. For if the bar is naught, and a replication is made to it, and a demurrer is upon the replication, the judgment ought to be that they shall replead"; for a case in which a repleader was awarded see Jones v. Weaver (1555) Dyer 117b; for general rules relating thereto see Staple v. Hayden (1704) 2 Salk. 579; Reeves, H.E.L. ii 651-652.

Such then, in very bare outline, was the scheme of the common law system of pleading. As stated in this bare outline it seems sensible, and well adapted to fulfil its purpose—the attainment of an issue of law or fact, for the consideration of the court alone, or of the court and jury. We shall see that it had in fact some very considerable merits, and that it has conferred much service both on litigants and on the development of the common law.[1] But we shall see also that the main scheme and ground work of principle were overlaid with a mass of technical rules taken from all periods in the history of the law ; and that, under the regime of the system of written pleadings, its main principles had been developed by decided cases, and by the skill of the pleaders, into so logical, so scientific, and so technical a system, that they had lost touch with the illogical facts of life, and with the practical needs of litigants. We shall see that, in consequence, its defects had come, at the end of the eighteenth century, to be far more conspicuous than its merits. The reasons for this will appear from the history of the manner in which it was gradually developed, and of the ineffectual attempts made by the Legislature and the courts to remedy its defects. With the history of these two matters I shall deal in the two following sections.

(2) *The influences which contributed to the formation of the common law system of pleading.*

From the historical point of view, the influences which contributed to the formation of the common law system of pleading, can be grouped under the four following heads: (i) There are a set of rules which must be regarded partly as survivals from the very archaic period in the history of procedure, which prevailed in the tenth and eleventh centuries; and partly as the product of these archaic ideas, as modified and influenced by the newer ideas as to procedure, which were growing up under the influence of the royal judges, and of the new system of the enrolment of pleas, which was coming into use in the twelfth and thirteenth centuries. (ii) A far more important set of rules comes from the fourteenth and fifteenth centuries, when the judges, in order to force the parties to arrive at an issue which a jury could try, laid down the rules directed to secure the production of such an issue, and its singleness, certainty, and materiality. These rules form the backbone of the common law system of pleading. (iii) The rules, thus devised, came, as the law grew more elaborate, to fetter unduly the work of the pleaders in stating their clients' cases. Hence we get the rise of a number of technical devices designed to supplement, or evade, or even to pervert these rules, which came, in

---

[1] Below 327-335.

course of time, to be the centres of important bodies of technical doctrine.   (iv) All these rules, new and old, were elaborated by the decisions of the courts under the system of written pleadings, which was introduced in the sixteenth century.   As the result of three centuries of continuous work of this character, the common law system of pleading assumed its character of a pseudo-exact science, which attempted to justify its claim to be an exact science, by ruthlessly sacrificing the claims both of common sense and convenience, to the claims of minute verbal, and strict logical, accuracy.

(i) The earliest rules.

Till the reforms of the nineteenth century, the common law system of pleading retained many traces of ideas and rules derived from that primitive condition of legal procedure, which prevailed in Anglo-Saxon England.[1]   Some of these ideas and rules preserved archaic conceptions as to the administration of justice, which, under the changed conditions of the thirteenth century, were beginning to give rise to new principles and rules, destined later to assume great importance in this branch of the law. Others preserved archaic forms, which seemed strange and useless to pleaders who had come to regard this branch of the law as a science, the principles of which were dictated by pure reason and logic, and as an art, upon the rules of which the right application of the principles of the common law depended.[2]   Others were founded on archaic rules as to the manner in which litigants must state their case, which, even in the thirteenth century, were becoming rationalized, and thereby fitted to take their place in the new system of pleading, which the common lawyers devised in the fourteenth and fifteenth centuries.   Let us glance at one or two of these ideas and rules under these three heads.

(a) We have seen that it was an old principle that it was the business of the court, which was trying an action, merely to see that the law adjective and substantive was observed by the litigants.   The strict rules of law determined the rights of the litigants; and its administrators were passive agents—umpires— set there to see that the law was observed by both parties, and that the final decision was arrived at, and executed, in accordance

---

[1] Vol. ii 102-117.

[2] Thus Stephen, op. cit. 434, speaking of the formal "defence" (vol. iii 630-631; below 282-283) says, "this formula can perhaps be considered in no other light than as one of these verbal subtleties, by which the science of pleading was in many instances anciently disgraced.   It is at least difficult to discover in what solid view much consideration could be attached to the use of these technical words.   Yet they have been formerly held to be essential; are still constantly used; and cannot in general with safety be omitted."

therewith.[1] Moreover, a party aggrieved by the fact that these umpires had not observed the strict rules of the game, might even have a right of action against them.[2] This conception of the nature of an action or a trial, and of the duty of a judge, dominated men's minds in the thirteenth century. But, necessarily, it somewhat changed its shape, when the practice of enrolling all the proceedings in the action, and all the pleadings of the parties, was established.[3] The record thus made was incontrovertible evidence of the course of the proceedings;[4] and it was the duty of the judge to give effect to the law applicable to the state of facts which appeared on the record. It followed, therefore, that if any error, verbal or substantial, appeared on the record, no judgment could be given for the plaintiff, even if he had got a verdict in his favour; and, even if judgment had been given it could be reversed on a writ of error. Thus, in *Piggott's Case*,[5] Piggott was the administrator durante minore aetate of Longfield. As such, he sued two defendants for debt, averring that Longfield was under twenty-one years of age. The defendants pleaded an insufficient plea, to which the plaintiff demurred. It was held that, though the demurrer was good, judgment must be given against the plaintiff because his declaration was insufficient. It was insufficient, because, for this purpose, the question when minority ceased was governed by the civil law, and the civil law rule was that it ceased at seventeen. It followed that, for all that appeared in the declaration, Longfield might be seventeen, and so the plaintiff had no title to sue. As Stephen puts it,[6] "if, on demurrer to the replication, the court think the replication bad, but perceive a substantive fault in the plea, they will give judgment, not for the defendant but the plaintiff, provided the declaration is good; but if the declaration also be bad in substance, then, upon the same principle, judgment would be given for the defendant."[7]

This is a sensible and sound principle; and so far as it applies to the substantial rights of the parties, it would be accepted to-day. But since, right down to the middle of the nineteenth century, it was applied to the smallest verbal objections, both to any part of the elaborate machinery of process, and to the form of the pleadings,

---

[1] Vol. i 299-302; vol. ii 105-107; vol. iii. 612.   [2] Vol. i 213-214.
[3] Above 278.   [4] Vol. v 157-158.
[5] (1598) 5 Co. Rep. 29a; see also Y.B. 7 Ed. IV. Hil. pl. 18 *per* Choke; Gewen v. Roll (1607) Cro. Jac. at pp. 132-133; Le Bret v. Papillon (1804) 4 East at p. 509 *per* Lord Ellenborough, C.J., citing Dive v. Maningham (1551) Plowden at p. 66.
[6] Op. cit. 162.
[7] A good illustration will be found in Tippet v. May (1799) 1 B. and P. 411; the following is the head note: " Assumpsit against three: two pleaded a debt of record by way of set off: the plaintiff replied nul tiel record, and gave a day to the two defendants, but entered no suggestion respecting the third: held on demurrer that the action being discontinued, judgment must be given against the plaintiff, even though the pleas of the defendants were bad."

it produced the grossest miscarriages of justice, by causing litigants to fail, though they had all the substantial merits on their side. Something, it is true, was effected by the statutes of jeofail;[1] but these statutes still left it open to litigants to take these objections by a special demurrer. "The result has been," said the Common Law Procedure Commissioners in 1851,[2] "that almost all these ancient technicalities have been preserved and still exist. The reports abound in instances of objections of the most technical description, which have been held fatal on special demurrer; and the subtlety and ingenuity of pleaders are constantly exercised in raising points of a purely formal nature, more especially when it is desired to avoid a substantial issue in fact." Something also was effected by the greater liberality of amendment, which the courts showed in the eighteenth and nineteenth centuries. But we shall see that this remedy could sometimes be defeated by the ingenious plan of not taking the objection at once, but of passing it over and taking advantage of it at a later stage, when amendment was impossible.

Thus the rigid application of this principle has had a very long life in English law. And, as historians, we should note that, though the form which it took in our modern law was dictated and shaped by the new fashion of enrolling pleas which came in the twelfth and thirteenth centuries, it depends at bottom on the very archaic idea that the only duty of the court is to apply the law, adjective and substantive, to the facts as stated by the parties; and that either party can take advantage of any fault, whether of form or of substance—*qui cadit a syllaba cadit a tota causa.* It is perhaps the most striking example of a phenomenon (of which this branch of the law will furnish us with many examples) of the manner in which primitive principles have taken a new technical shape in later periods of the history of the law. We shall now see that some, but not all, of these old rules, have been similarly adapted to the system of pleading, developed by the mediæval, and elaborated by the modern common law.

(*b*) Right down to the nineteenth century the declaration always stated that the plaintiff produced suit, and gave the names of his pledges to prosecute;[3] and the defendant's plea always contained a formal defence,[4] which, in Coke's day, might be either firstly of the wrong and force only, or secondly of the damages as well, or thirdly of the wrong and force and damages and of all that he ought to defend.[5] Even at the latter part of the mediæval period these

---

[1] Below 315-316.   [2] Parlt. Papers 1851 xxii 20.

[3] Stephen, op. cit. 427; vol. i 301; vol. ii 106 and n. 3.

[4] Vol. iii 630-631; for the Latin forms see Co. Litt. 127b; Reeves, H.E.L. ii 622-623.

[5] Coke explains (Co. Litt. 127b) that the effect of the first part of the defence is to make the defendant "a party to the matter," and to enable him to plead to the juris-

forms were in effect but forms. But they could not be safely neglected, as, to the end, their omission might have been made the ground of a special demurrer. As late as 1617 the omission of pledges to prosecute was held to be sufficient ground to reverse a judgment on a writ of error.[1] Coke, at the beginning of the seventeenth century, explained that if no defence were made the defendant must fail.[2] As late as 1697 the court was talking about "full defences" and "half defences," and what pleas could be used after a "full," and after a "half" defence;[3] and it was not till 1698 that the court of Common Pleas came reluctantly round to the opinion of the court of King's Bench, that the omission of a defence was merely matter of form.[4] Similarly, the question when a pleader must offer to verify, and when he must conclude the country, had hardened into the fixed rule that, if he advanced new matter he must conclude with an offer to verify, but if by his allegation an issue was reached, he must conclude to the country.[5] As Stephen points out, these forms dated from the period when the pleader must always tender some mode of proof of the averment which he had made.[6] This was clearly the rule when Bracton wrote; and it probably prevailed down to the end of the thirteenth century[7]—as we have seen, this rule as to tender of proof explains the operation of the doctrine of estoppel, when it first makes its appearance.[8] But, as Stephen says,[9] "soon after that period the process of pleading began to be conducted with a more distinct and single view to the development of the particular question in controversy, or production of an issue; and when so conducted, the offer of evidence in support of any allegation would naturally be

---

diction of the court; that the effect of the second part is to admit the ability of the plaintiff to sue; and that the effect of the third part is to admit the jurisdiction of the court.

[1] Hussey v. More Cro. Jac. 413.

[2] "And of such necessity is it for the tenant or defendant to make a lawful defence, albeit he appeareth and pleads a sufficient bar without making a defence, yet judgment shall be given against him," Co. Litt. 127b.

[3] Britton v. Gradon 1 Ld. Raym. 117; vol. iii 630 n. 5.

[4] Bellasis v. Hester (1698) 1 Ld. Raym. at p. 282.

[5] Stephen, op. cit. 437.

[6] "It was a doctrine of ancient law, little if at all noticed by modern writers, that every pleading affirmative in its nature must be supported by an offer of some mode of proof; and the reference to a jury . . . was considered as an offer of proof within the meaning of that doctrine. When the proof proposed was that by jury, the offer was made in the viva voce pleading by the words *prest d'averrer* or *prest etc.*, which in the record was translated *et hoc paratus est verificare*. On the other hand, when other modes of proof were intended, the record ran—*et hoc paratus est verificare per recordum*, or *quoquo modo curia consideraverit*. But while these were the forms in general observed, there was the following exception: that on the attainment of an issue to be tried by a jury, the record marked that result by a change of phrase, and substituted for the verification the conclusion ad patriam," ibid 437-438.

[7] Bracton ff. 307b, 373b, and the other references cited by Stephen in notes 84 and 85.

[8] Above 145.   [9] Note 84.

284 EVIDENCE, PROCEDURE, PLEADING

considered as premature, till it was ascertained that such matters
came into debate. The rule in question appears therefore to have
suffered a silent abrogation; yet vestiges of it to this day remain
in the production of suit, and in the formal verification."

(c) These, then, are instances in which the old forms remained
merely as dry forms, from which all meaning had departed. But
it was not so with all of these formulæ. We have seen that the
forms of the general issue on different writs,[1] and the forms of the
judgment of the court in various events,[2] had become stereotyped,
and continued to be the necessary forms right down to the end.
Indeed, we shall see that the fact that the formulæ for the general
issue had been thus stereotyped, helped to mitigate some of the
defects of the common law system of pleading.[3] Similarly, at an
early date, the formulæ for the commencement and conclusion of
different sorts of plea had become fixed;[4] and these formulæ were
very far from being merely dry forms. They indicated the nature
of the plea, and therefore fulfilled a useful purpose in later law.
"The commencement and conclusion of a plea," says Stephen,[5]
"are in such forms as to indicate the view in which it is pleaded,
and to mark its object and tendency, as being either to the
jurisdiction, in suspension, in abatement, or in bar. It is therefore held that the class and character of a plea depend upon these
its formular parts; which is ordinarily expressed by the maxim
conclusio facit placitum." Thus, if a defendant were sued on a
deed, and his contention was that the deed was void, he ought to
conclude his plead "et sic non est factum"; on the other hand, if
the deed was valid, but for other reasons the defendant contended
that he was not bound, he ought to conclude his plea with a
prayer for judgment that the plaintiff could not maintain his
action.[6] Similarly, where to an action for debt on a judgment,
the defendant pleaded in abatement that a writ of error had been
brought in the Exchequer Chamber on the same judgment, and
concluded his plea with the words "quod eat sine die quousque";
the plea was held bad on demurrer, as he ought to have pleaded
"quod breve cassetur."[7]

In fact it was not only in the commencement and conclusion
of a plea that the judges adhered closely to established forms. If
once a form of plea had become stereotyped, they would uphold
it, even if it might otherwise have been more clearly expressed;[8]

---

[1] Above 270. [2] Above 277. [3] Below 319-322.
[4] For some of the Latin forms of commencement and conclusion see Reeves,
H.E.L. ii 623-624.
[5] Op. cit. 402.
[6] Dive v. Maningham (1551) Plowden at p. 66 *per* Mountague, C.J.
[7] Prinn v. Edwards (1696) 1 Ld. Raym. 47; cp. Nowlan v. Geddes (1801) 1 East
634.
[8] See Buckley v. Rice Thomas (1554) Plowden at p. 123 *per* Staunford, J.; and
cp. above 264 n. 5.

and they regarded any departure from that form with suspicion. This process of creating fixed forms was very evident in the later mediæval period;[1] and it continued to the end, largely because the extreme precision, upon which the courts insisted, made it risky to use any other forms.[2] In 1820 defendants, who wished to set up the statute of limitations to an action on the case, instead of pleading in the usual way that the cause of action did not accrue within six years, pleaded that they were not guilty within six years. Their plea was held bad; and Abbot, C.J., said,[3] " It is important to the administration of justice that the usual and established forms of pleading should be observed, in order that the parties to the suit may know with certainty what is the point intended to be tried, and that the judge and jury may not be perplexed at nisi prius by controversy and argument upon the effect and import of the issue joined on the record." But this statement shows us that the need for adherence to fixed forms had come, in the modern common law, to rest upon a somewhat different ground from that upon which it had rested in very early times.

It is probable that, in early days, the rule that the parties must adopt certain fixed formulæ, was based on the fact that these formulæ had a sacramental significance. We have seen that the rules as to the wording of appeals and indictments long retained abundant traces of this primitive phase in the history of pleading;[4] and there is no reason to think that similar forms were not at one time essential in civil cases.[5] But in the thirteenth century these rules were being relaxed and rationalized. Thus Bracton gives reasons for the different averments which the demandant in a writ of right must make;[6] and he rationalizes the rule which required great particularity in the statement of a plaintiff's claim.[7] Both

---

[1] Vol. iii 642; as Reeves, H.E.L. ii 645-646, says, " It was impossible that a set form of expression could be designed for every matter that might become the subject of a declaration or a plea. But many modes and circumstances of property recurred so often in judicial enquiries as to obtain apt and stated forms of description and allegation, which were established by long usage; the experience of them having shewn them preferable to all others."

[2] "The extreme precision required is scarcely practicable, except in pleadings of well-known character and daily occurrence, in which former generations of suitors, having paid costs for the settlement of the law, the pleadings have become easy and intelligible," First Report of the Common Law Procedure Commission, Parlt. Papers 1851 xxii 20; below 297, 309.

[3] Dyster v. Battye 3 B. and Ald. at p. 453.

[4] Vol. ii 108-109, 198; vol. iii 612, 616-618.

[5] See vol. ii 105-106. [6] At ff. 373 a and b.

[7] "Oportet igitur inprimis quod petens rem designet quam petit, videlicet qualitatem, ut sciatur utrum petatur terra vel redditus cum pertinentiis. Item quantitatem, utrum videlicet sit plus vel minus quod petitur . . . Specificare autem poterit sic, ut si dicat : Peto versus talem tot maneria, quandoque cum pertinentiis, quandoque sine. Item tot foeda militum cum pertinentiis. Item tot carucatas terræ, tot virgatas, tot acras, tot selliones. Item tot libratas terræ, tot solidatas, tot bovatas, secundum diversitatem tenementorum," f. 431a.

the thing which he is demanding, he says, must be made certain, and its quantity or amount—e.g. so many manors and whether with or without appurtenances, so many knight's fees, so many carucates, virgates, or acres. "For that which is made the subject matter of litigation ought to be certain, lest the judgment be illusory or obscure, because, if the subject matter of the litigation be uncertain, no certain judgment can be given—though sometimes it may be that an action is brought for an uncertain thing."[1] These rules laid down by Bracton became fundamental rules of the common law system of pleading. "The declaration," it was said in *Playter's Case*,[2] "ought to reduce the generality of the writ to particularity, and to declare *that* which is briefly touched in the writ to certainty, to which the defendant may have a certain answer, and on which a certain judgment may be given, *quia oportet quod certa res deducatur in judicium.*" In the eighteenth century,[3] in the case of declarations, e.g. in assumpsit or debt for goods sold, which did not disclose the nature of the plaintiff's demand, the judge would make an order for the delivery of particulars[4]—a practice which was evidently designed to give effect to this principle.

The Latin quotation in *Playter's Case* perhaps shows that the court had Bracton's words in their minds. But, long before the date of that case, Bracton's principles had been applied to all pleadings; and by reason of their adaptation to the ideas underlying the system of pleading, which the judges of the fourteenth and fifteenth centuries were elaborating, they had become the centre of a mass of detailed rules.

(ii) The fundamental principles of the system of pleading developed in the fourteenth and fifteenth centuries.

We have seen that it was during the fourteenth and fifteenth

---

[1] "Certam enim rem oportet deducere in judicium, ne contingat judicium esse delusorium vel obscurum, quia de re incerta in judicium deducta certa fieri non poterit sententia, licet quandoque de incerta re agatur," f. 431a.

[2] (1584) 5 Co. Rep. at f. 35a; cp. Harpur's Case (1615) 11 Co. Rep. at f. 25b; Savel's Case (1615) ibid 55a; Slade v. Dowland (1801) 2 B. and P. 570; in Nevil v. Soper (1699) 1 Salk. 213 we get a good example of the verbal precision with which the rule was applied—"In covenant against an apprentice the plaintiff assigned for breach that the apprentice, before the time of his apprenticeship expired, *et durante tempore quo servivit*, departed from his master's service. The defendant demurred and had judgment, because the declaration was repugnant, for it should have been *durante tempore quo servire debuit.*"

[3] Bentham, Works v 12, said that this plan had been invented within the last half-century.

[4] Tidd, Practice (8th ed.) i 642-646; cp. Le Breton v. Braham (1763) 3 Burr. 1389—when Lord Mansfield approved of the practice, and said that it should be applied in all cases and not only when attornies were plaintiffs; Holland v. Hopkins (1800) 2 B. and P. 243. It was said in Brown v. Watts (1808) 1 Taunt. at p. 355, that it was a contempt of court to give particulars so generally that they conveyed no more information than the declaration.

centuries that the problems raised by the survival of the older ideas as to a trial, the introduction of new ideas as to pleading derived from Roman law, and the need to adapt those new ideas as to pleading to trial by jury, determined the shape which the principles of pleading took, not only in the mediæval period, but throughout the history of the common law.[1] We have seen that the dominant feature in this system is the formulation of an issue of law or fact by the allegations of the parties;[2] and that it was the need to formulate this issue in a precise and intelligible form which gave rise to the principal rules of pleading.[3] I have already given one or two illustrations from the Year Books of the rules which were devised to effect these objects.[4] At this point it will be necessary to speak of them in a little more detail, and show how they continued to be applied throughout the history of this branch of the law.[5] In the first place, I shall illustrate the rules which were directed to ensure that the parties, by their respective allegations, reached a definite issue. In the second place, I shall illustrate the rules as to the form which these allegations must take.

(a) *Rules directed to ensure that the parties reached a definite issue.*

I have already mentioned some of the more general of these rules—the rule that the litigant must either demur or plead,[6] the rule that, if he pleaded, he must either traverse or confess or avoid,[7] the rule that there must be no departure in pleading;[8] and in a preceding volume I have alluded to some of the more particular rules directed to secure the same object.[9] At this point I propose to take some of these more particular rules, and show how they were applied in practice. The rules which I have selected are the following :—Each pleading must contain an answer to the whole of what is alleged in the count or in the preceding pleading, otherwise it is demurrable or there is a discontinuance ; pleading must not be argumentative; a pleading which involves a negative pregnant is bad; a pleading must not be double.

The rule that each pleading must contain an answer to what is alleged in the count or in the preceding pleading, is illustrated by the following cases: In 1429[10] the plaintiff brought a writ of

---

[1] Vol. iii 628-629, 630-633.
[2] Ibid 628, 632.
[3] Ibid 633.
[4] Ibid 633-634.
[5] Reeves says that, " almost everything substantial in pleading, which was practised from this time down to the present, was settled by judicial determinations in the reigns of these kings [Henry VI. and Edward IV.]. The precedents of this period became ever after the standards of good pleading, and the rules and maxims of plead-ing now settled have governed ever since in our courts," H.E.L. ii 623.
[6] Above 266.
[7] Above 269.
[8] Above 274.
[9] Vol. iii 633-634.
[10] Y.B. 7 Hy. VI. Mich. pl. 8.

account against the defendant, and counted that he was his receiver during the preceding seven years, and that during that time he had received £10 by the hands of such a person. The defendant pleaded that he had fully accounted on such a day before certain auditors. But the day was in the fifth year. The plaintiff traversed this plea, and a verdict was given for him. But it was held that he was not entitled to judgment—"the plea pleaded by the defendant was no plea, and issue joined on it is nothing but a jeofail; for the plaintiff counts that he was his receiver for seven years, and he (the defendant) alleges an account in the fifth year, so two years are not answered, so that issue taken on such a plea is bad."[1] The same law was laid down in 1589 in *Herlakenden's Case*;[2] and in 1701, in the case of *Weeks v. Peach*,[3] Holt, C.J., laid down rules to determine when a partial answer of this kind was a discontinuance of the whole action, when it gave the plaintiff the right to a judgment on a *nil dicit*, and when it was demurrable. The report runs as follows :—"Replevin for taking chattels *in quodam loco vocat. A. ac etiam in quodam alio loco vocat. B.* The defendant avowed the taking *in praedict. loco in quo etc.*, for that such a one was seised of the *locus in quo etc.* To this the plaintiff demurred. *Et per Cur.* The *locus in quo* relates only to one place, so that there is a discontinuance, the avowry not being an answer to the whole declaration; and this difference was taken *per* Holt, C.J. If a plea begin with an answer to the whole, but in truth the matter pleaded is only an answer to part, the whole plea is naught, and the plaintiff may demur; but if a plea begin only as an answer to part, and is in truth but an answer to part, it is a discontinuance, and the plaintiff must not demur, but take his judgment for that, as by *nil dicit*; for if he demurs or pleads over the whole action is discontinued."[4] These few illustrations show us the manner in which a comparatively simple principle was elaborated by its application to the facts of concrete cases. They also show us that this method of developing the law is the main cause for the subtlety and precision of the rules of pleading. As we shall now see, this fact is abundantly illustrated by the development of all the other leading principles of this branch of the law.

The rule that pleading must not be argumentative meant, as we have seen, that the plaintiff and defendant must clearly state

---

[1] *Per* Rolf. *arg.*, whose argument was accepted by the court; as Cokayn, J., said " Quand il fuit vostre recevor per vii ans *ad merchandizandum*, vous avez accompt aussi bien des profits come del summe, et par nul entendement il ne peut accompter al fin de v ans des profits ne del encrease de ii ans a venir: issint son ple adeprimes nient sufficienter. Purque il est bon que ,vous repledes etc. "; for repleader see above 278.

[2] 4 Co. Rep. at f. 62a.   [3] 1 Salk. 179.
[4] This was what happened in Y.B. 7 Hy. VI. Mich. pl. 8, above 287 n. 10.

their cases, and not leave their meaning to be gathered by argument or inference.[1] Thus, "in an action of debt against a lessee for years, the defendant cannot say that the disseisee entered upon him, and that the plaintiff is a disseisor; but he ought to plead that he owes nothing."[2] "In an action of trespass for depasturing another's grass, it is no plea to say *quod non depascit herbas*, for this is merely an argumentative plea; but he ought to plead not guilty."[3] We have seen that difficulties sometimes arose when a defendant, instead of denying a plaintiff's statement, pleaded other facts inconsistent with it; and we have seen that it was to meet these difficulties that the courts laid it down that every affirmative proposition must, as a general rule, be answered by a direct negative—a special traverse—which began with the words "absque hoc," or, in French, "sans ceo que."[4] Thus, "when the declaration was for rent for the occupation of twenty acres of land, and the defendant pleaded a lease for twenty acres and twelve more, he was bound to traverse the lease for twenty acres."[5] The parties would thus soon arrive at precise negative and affirmative statements upon which issue could be joined—a consummation which was assisted by the rule that no traverse upon a traverse of a material point was possible.[6] In simple cases, where a single affirmative fact was pleaded, the application of the rule was easy. It was by no means easy of application where the story set out in the plea was long and complicated. The facts selected to be traversed were the facts upon which the issue was to be joined; and it was often a matter of difficulty to select rightly. As an illustration, take the case cited by Reeves, from Edward IV.'s reign:[7] "A formedon in the descender was brought on a gift to the father and mother of the demandant in tail. The tenant pleaded that he, long before the donors had anything in the land, was seised thereof in his demesne as of fee; and, being so seised, and being within the age of twenty-one years, he infeoffed the donors to have and to hold to them and their heirs; and the donors, being so seised, made a gift to the donees in tail, who had issue the demandant and died; and that the tenant, being within age, entered; by force of which entry he was seised in his remitter,[8] and so he demanded judgment of the action. To this the demandant replied that the donors made the gift to the donees, as had been stated in the declaration, *sans ceo que* that the

---

[1] Vol. iii 633-634.

[2] Doctrina Placitandi 44, citing Y.B. 20 Hy. VI. Hil. pl. 15.

[3] Ibid 42, citing Y.B. 22 Hy. VI. Hil. pl. 2.   [4] Vol. iii 634.

[5] Reeves, H.E.L. ii 625, citing Y.B. 32 Hy. VI. Mich. pl. 1.

[6] Digby v. Fitzharbert (1616) Hob. at p. 104—a rule which, as this case shows, gave rise to all sorts of fine distinctions; Thorn v. Shering (1640) Cro. Car. 586.

[7] Reeves, H.E.L. ii 625, citing Longo Quinto Ed. IV. 9-12.

[8] For remitter see vol. ii 587.

tenant infeoffed the donors in the manner they had pleaded. It was objected to this replication that the feoffment was only the conveyance to the (plea in) bar, and that it was not the conveyance, but the matter and substance of the bar which should be traversed, or confessed and avoided ; and there was great debate whether the seisin or the feoffment should in this case be traversed." This was for some time a vexed question ; but, ultimately it was held that either might be traversed.[1] But this rule as to the need for a special traverse, which was originally designed to obviate the inconveniences of argumentative pleading, caused continual questions as to what matters were traversable in different kinds of pleas ; and so became "one of the nicest and most curious parts of the science of pleading."[2] Naturally it gave rise to much complex law, and to many subordinate rules, to some of which I shall have occasion to allude later.[3]

We have seen that what was called a "negative pregnant" was a plea affected by a similar but opposite defect to the defect of argumentativeness. Just as an argumentative plea was an affirmative plea implicitly pregnant with a negative, so a "negative pregnant" was a negative plea implicitly pregnant with an affirmative.[4] There are many instances of pleas held bad for this reason in the Year Books.[5] A good instance in later law is afforded by the case of *Myn v. Cole*.[6] The report runs as follows : "Trespass for entering his house and taking his goods. The defendant pleads as to the goods not guilty ; as to the entry into the house that the plaintiff's daughter licensed him etc., and that he entered by that licence. The plaintiff saith *quod non intravit per licentiam suam :* and issue was joined thereon. The first issue was found for the defendant ; and the second issue for the plaintiff, that he (the defendant) did not enter by licence ; and damages were assessed to eighty pounds. Whereupon it was moved in arrest of judgment that he ought to have traversed the licence, and not the entry by the licence ; for that is pregnant in itself and an ill issue : and he ought to have traversed the entry by itself, or the licence by itself, and not both together." Williams and Yelverton, J.J., were of this opinion ; but Popham, C.J., while he agreed that that was the common law, thought that after trial the defect was

---

[1] Reeves, H.E.L. ii 626 ; cp. Read's Case (1600) 6 Co. Rep. 24a.

[2] "When the pleadings were long and special, they of course drove one of the parties to a traverse, and occasions were continually furnished to inquire what matters were traversable, and what not, whether in pleas or in declarations. This made one of the nicest and most curious parts of the science of pleading," Reeves, H.E.L. ii 626-627.

[3] Below 302-304.   [4] Vol. iii 634.

[5] Doctrina Placitandi 256-257 ; Reeves, H.E.L. ii 627 ; vol. iii 634.

[6] (1606) Cro. Jac. 87 ; see also Lea v. Luthall (1619) ibid 559.

remedied by the statute of 1541.[1]   Just as the difficulties arising out of an argumentative pleading were met by a special traverse, so the difficulties arising out of a negative pregnant were met by the same device—a special traverse of the affirmative which would otherwise have been implied.   This was another reason for the employment of a special traverse, which accounts for its prevalence, and therefore, as we shall see,[2] for the complexity of the law relating to it.

We have seen that, in order to arrive at a single issue, the rule that a plea must not be double, had been laid down and applied from the beginning of the fourteenth century.[3]   The following is an illustration of the application of the rule : " In detinue of an obligation, where the defendant entitles himself to have it because an award was made that the plaintiff shall make partition of certain land, and shall pay ten marks to the defendant, or otherwise that the defendant shall retain the writing ; and he (the defendant) says that the plaintiff has neither made partition nor paid that money ; seeing that each of these matters is a breach of the condition, the Court ruled it to be a double plea.   So in debt for £10 by several obligations, the defendant as to one pleaded a release of all actions, and as to the other said that it was made by duress ; that is double because the first matter pleaded is an answer to the whole."[4]   Only one matter of defence, which went to the whole action, could be pleaded.[5]   If the defendant wished to avoid the conclusion that he admitted the other matters, he must exclude this conclusion by a protestation.[6]   The rule as thus stated seems simple ; but its application in practice was difficult, firstly, because it was not universal, secondly, because it was not every plea which alleged two defences that was bad for duplicity, and thirdly, because it required much subtlety to appreciate its effect upon pleadings of a complex kind.   Firstly, the rule applied as a rule only to peremptory pleas, and not to dilatory pleas ;[7] but there were exceptions to both branches of this rule.[8] Secondly, the rule did not apply so as to prevent a defendant

---

[1] 32 Henry VIII. c. 30; above 260, 264 n. 9; below 315-316.
[2] Below 302-304.   [3] Vol. iii 633.
[4] Doctrina Placitandi 136, citing Y.B. 21 Hy. VI. Mich. pl. 33; cp. also Y.B. 22 Ed. IV. Mich. pl. 5 and 13.
[5] " The plea that contains duplicity or multiplicity of distinct matter to one and the same thing, whereunto several answers (admitting each of them to be good) are required, is not allowable in law," Co. Litt. 304a.
[6] " Protestatio is an exclusion of a conclusion that a party to an action may by pleading incur; or it is a safeguard to the party, which keepeth him from being concluded by the plea he is to make, if the issue be found for him," Co. Litt. 124b; Doctrina Placitandi 295-296; Reeves, H.E.L. ii 627; vol. iii 634.
[7] Co. Litt. 304a; Doctrina Placitandi 295.
[8] Doctrina Placitandi 145; Plowden 86; in Trevelian v. Seccomb (1688) Carth 8-9, the court drew a distinction between a plea of outlawry in disability, to which it said the objection of duplicity did apply, and other pleas in abatement.

pleading one matter in bar of part of a declaration, and another matter in bar of another part[1]—as when, for instance, A brought trespass against B for cutting down and carrying away his trees, B could plead not guilty as to the cutting down, and justify as to the carrying away.[2] Nor did the rule apply if the additional matter alleged was either necessary,[3] or mere surplusage which added nothing substantial to the plea—though what was substantial and what was not often turned on very fine distinctions, which involved a very accurate perception of the principles of the law substantive and adjective.[4] Thirdly, the fact that much subtlety was required to appreciate its effect upon pleadings of a complex kind, is best illustrated by *Crogate's Case*[5]—a famous case in the law of pleading, to which I shall refer again in other connections.[6] In that case Crogate brought an action of trespass against R. Marys for driving his cattle. R. Marys pleaded that W. Marys had, as a copyholder of a certain manor, a right of common in the place where Crogate had put his cattle, and that he by the command of W. Marys had driven out the cattle. Crogate replied *de injuria sua propria absque tali causa*. The defendant demurred to this replication on the ground of duplicity. The demurrer was upheld, partly because this replication attempted to put in issue two things viz., the right of the defendant to his common, and the command of W. Marys, either of which would have been an answer to the plea ; and partly because, to allow the replication of *injuria sua propria*, where the defendant claimed an interest in the property, would encourage not only duplicity but multiplicity.[7] But since a plaintiff could put several causes of

---

[1] Co. Litt. 304a.   [2] Anon. (1572) Dyer 305a.

[3] See Wrotesley v. Adams (1558) Plowden at p. 194.

[4] "So in 22 H. 6 a man alleged two continual claims to avoid a descent, viz., that his predecessor and himself made continual claims, and that is there held to be double, because his own continual claim would have been sufficient to avoid the descent, if the dying seised was in his own time, and then the other was unnecessary. So if one will plead in bar two descents in fee, this makes the plea double *causa qua supra* : but to allege two descents in tail does not make the plea double, for one answer, viz., *ne dona pas*, makes an end of the whole ; so that the descents there are not the most substantial parts of the matter, but the gift, and in shewing the gift he must shew how it came to the last issue, and for as much as he is necessarily compelled to do that, it is not double," Browning v. Beston (1553) Plowden at p. 140 *per* Brook *arg*.

[5] (1609) 8 Co. Rep. 66b.

[6] Below 310-311, 316, 326 ; and see App. I (2) for "Crogate's Case, A Dialogue in ye Shades on Special Pleading Reform" by George Hayes, privately printed in 1854, and reprinted in Hayesiana in 1892 ; for this dialogue see Pollock, Genius of the Common Law 27-37 ; the parties to the Dialogue are Baron Surrebutter and Crogate ; the original of Baron Surrebutter is Baron Parke, whose decisions upon the new pleading rules of 1834 had considerably aggravated all the existing hardships inflicted by the rules of special pleading ; for these rules and their effect see below 324-327.

[7] "Lastly it was resolved that in the case at Bar, the issue would be full of multiplicity of matter, where an issue ought to be full and single, for parcel of the manor, demisable by copy, grant by copy, prescription of common etc., and commandment, would all be parcel of the issue," 8 Co. Rep. at f. 67b.

complaint in his declaration, and since a defendant was by this rule prevented from using all the means of defence open to him, the justice of the rule was not immediately obvious; and when it was applied in this technical fashion, it is not surprising that, even in this age of strict pleading, it should have been "misliked." [1]

We shall now see that some of the rules as to the forms which the pleadings must take, had become as elaborate and as technical as these rules which were directed to ensure that the parties reached a definite issue.

(b) Rules as to the form which the pleadings must take.

The two rules of which I propose to say something are the rules that the allegations in a pleading must be material to the issue, and that they must be sufficiently certain.

Materiality.—The need to secure that the pleading should be material to the issue gave rise to rules which took many different forms. I propose to illustrate the sort of rules which this need inspired, by certain rules relating to traverses.

Firstly, as a traverse was a plea which raised an issue of fact, it was only matters of fact, and not matters of law, which were traversable—if this rule had not been enforced, no clear line could have been drawn between issues of fact and issues of law.[2] Thus, in the case of *Kenicot v. Bogan*,[3] the defendant pleaded in bar to an action of trover for taking two tuns of wine, that he had taken it as agent for the king, who was entitled to it as prisage. One exception taken to his plea was that the defendant had not traversed the conversion supposed by the plaintiff, viz. a conversion by the defendant; but had only justified a conversion to the use of the king, which was a different conversion. This exception was overruled, because "the coming to the hands, and intermeddling with the two tuns, supposed by the plaintiff, is confessed by the defendant to be to the use of the king, and that is matter in law on the plea in bar, which the Court is to adjudge, and the matter in law shall never be traversed." [4] Similarly, it was agreed by the court in 1490 that, in a *Praecipe quod reddat* a man should plead simply that the land is ancient demesne, and pleadable and impleded by little writ of right close from time immemorial, and that he should not traverse the conclusion, viz. that the *Praecipe quod reddat* does not lie.[5] Obviously that was merely a conclusion of law from the facts pleaded.

---

[1] "The law in this point is by them that understand not the reason thereof misliked, saying, *Nemo prohibetur pluribus defensionibus uti,*" Co. Litt. 304a.
[2] Above 269.   [3] (1611) Yelv. 198.   [4] At p. 200.
[5] Y.B. 5 Hy. VII. Hil. pl. 4 (p. 13) *per* Curiam; Coke, it may be noted, states the rule in terms of formal logic: "As in logic the conclusion of a syllogism cannot be denied, but the major or minor proposition; so it holds in law which is the perfection of reason; and therefore in a *praecipe*, if one pleads that the manor of Dale is ancient

Secondly, as a litigant must either traverse or confess and avoid,[1] a plea which attempted to do both was bad. Thus, in the case of *Bedel v. Lull*,[2] to an action of ejectment on a lease made by Elizabeth James it was pleaded that, before Elizabeth had anything in the land, Martin James was seised in fee, that the land descended to his son Henry James, that Elizabeth entered and was seised by abatement, and that the defendant entered by command of Henry James. The plaintiff, by way of replication, confessed the seisin of Martin James, alleged that he devised the land to Elizabeth, and traversed her seisin by abatement. On this replication the defendant demurred, and the demurrer was upheld, because " the plaintiff needed not both to confess and avoid and to traverse the abatement: for the plaintiff made a title to his lease under Elizabeth, the devisee of Martin James, and so her entry legal, and not by abatement as the defendant supposeth." In fact this traverse was taken, not on a point material to the issue, viz. the devise, but on a point not material to the issue, viz. the abatement— a reason which illustrates what has been said above about the difficulty of picking out the right point to traverse.[3]

Thirdly, as the traverse of a matter not material to the issue made the pleading bad, so *a fortiori* did the traverse of a matter not previously alleged. Thus, when to a writ of maintenance the defendant pleaded facts which showed that he was guilty of no maintenance, with a special traverse of the maintenance, the court held that the special traverse was bad, as no maintenance had been confessed in the plea.[4] In debt on a bond against an executrix, the executrix pleaded that she was an administratrix, to which plea the plaintiff demurred, on the ground that she should have traversed the fact that she had intermeddled as executrix. But Holt, C.J., held that, as this was not alleged in the declaration, it would have been a bad traverse, because it was against the rule that matters not thus alleged cannot be traversed.[5] A traverse bad on this ground was sometimes said to be too large;[6] but this

---

demesne; and the land in demand is parcel of the manor, and so ancient demesne; the demandant cannot say that the land in demand is not ancient demesne, for that is the conclusion upon the two precedent propositions; " and " it is not only a conclusion, but a conclusion of law," Priddle and Napper's Case (1613) 11 Co. Rep. at f10b; it was this sort of logical reasoning which helped to give this branch of law its very " scientific " form, see below 311-312.

[1] Above 269.   [2] (1610) Cro. Jac. 221.   [3] Above 289-290.

[4] Y.B. 22 Hy. VI. Mich. pl. 54—" Et puis *Markham* pleda tout ut supra, *sans ceo que il fuit culp d'ascun auter maintenance*. A qui fuit dit per le Court que ce ne fuit ple clerement, entant que nul maintenance fuit confesse. Purque *Markham* ut supra *sans ceo que il fuit culp de maintenance suppose par le breve. Brown.* Or rien sera entre que de rien culp."

[5] Powers v. Cook (1696) 1 Ld. Raym. at p. 64.

[6] See Crosse v. Hunt (1699) Carth. at p. 100—" that the traverse in the bar is ill, because 'tis too large, for the defendant had traversed more than was alleged in the declaration."

expression was generally used with regard to traverses which were bad for another reason, which I must now explain.

Fourthly, the rule was laid down that a traverse must be neither too "large" nor too "narrow." A traverse was too large if it denied all the facts alleged by the other party in so general a way that it was possible, consistently with this general denial, that that party was entitled to recover something. Thus in the case of *Osborne v. Rogers*,[1] the plaintiff brought assumpsit for wages from March, 1647, to November, 1664. The defendant pleaded that he served him from March 21, 1647, to December 31, 1658, and traversed his service till November 1, 1664. This was held to be a bad traverse, because, "if the plaintiff had taken issue upon it, he would have been bound to prove the service for the *whole* time, otherwise he could not recover anything ; whereas, if he had in fact served for any part of the said time, he ought to have recovered pro tanto. And upon issue joined upon this traverse, if the plaintiff proved that he had served for one two three or more years, yet if he does not prove that he served till November 1st 1664, the issue would be against him, although the merits of the case were for him."[2] A traverse was too narrow if it did not sufficiently deny all the material facts alleged by the other party. Thus in *Buckley v. Wood*[3] the plaintiff brought an action on the case for words against the defendant. The defendant justified the speaking of certain of the words on the ground that he spoke them as counsel, and traversed the speaking of the other words before or after the day mentioned in the declaration. This traverse was too narrow—"he excluded the day itself, and answered not to it, for which cause the bar was held insufficient."

Certainty.—The rules last cited illustrate also the rule that a pleading must be sufficiently certain. We have seen that this was a very old-established principle. The result was that, even in the mediæval period, it had begun to give rise to a number of very detailed and very complicated rules, applicable to different kinds of pleadings. In some of these rules it is difficult to see either logic or sense. Thus, Reeves tells us[4] that it was held in the fifteenth century, that "in a [plea in] bar, and where a title was to be pleaded, it was not sufficient to say that such a one made a lease or a gift to the defendant, but it should be stated

---

[1] (1669) 1 Wms. Saunders 267.
[2] At p. 269; see also Goram v. Sweeting (1670) ibid 205; as appears from the note to the case last cited, the question whether a traverse was too large often turned on very fine distinctions.
[3] (1591) 4 Co. Rep. 14b.
[4] H.E.L. ii 647-648; cp. Co. Litt. 303b where a number of these and other rules are collected.

that such a one was seised, and being so seised, he made the lease
or gift; yet in a writ or declaration it was enough to say he made
the lease or gift, without suggesting that he was seised. . . . If a
man was under an obligation to make a feoffment of a certain
manor, and he pleaded that he had made the feoffment, he should
show where the manor was, because, said they, the feoffment could
not be made except on the land.   On the other hand, if he was
bound to make a release, he need not show where the manor
was. . . . In trespass, if a person justified under the command
of a stranger, he was required to show the place where the
command was given; but if he justified as servant under the
command of a master, he need not show the place."   Other rules
turned upon a desire to get a precision of statement, which, as the
Common Law Procedure Commissioners said in 1851,[1] was over-
refined and quite unnecessary.   Let us look at one or two concrete
cases.

In the case of *Codner v. Dalby*[2] the plaintiff brought an action
of debt upon an obligation, the condition of which was the defendant was to save him harmless from his obligation as bail in a
certain action.   "The defendant pleaded, *quod libere et absolute
exoneravit* him of the said bail; and it was thereupon demurred,
because it doth not show how he discharged him.   And without
argument it was adjudged for the plaintiff; for always when one
pleads a discharge, and that he saved him harmless, he ought to
show how, that the Court might adjudge thereof.   But he may
plead generally *non damnificat*, without showing how, because he
pleads in the negative, and the other ought to show damnification."[3]
In the case of *Holme v. Lucas*,[4] the declaration and writ in an
action of assumpsit " were, *quod cum indebitatus fuit* to the plaintiff
in fifteen pounds; in consideration whereof he assumed to pay
unto the plaintiff the said fifteen pounds."   After verdict for the
plaintiff, it was moved in arrest of judgment "that this declaration
is not good, because it is generally *indebitatus assumpsit*, and doth
not show for what cause, viz., for merchandise sold, or money lent,
or for other causes which lie in contract : for if it was *indebitatus*
by judgment, or by specialty, which lies not in contract, an assumpsit in consideration thereof would not lie; because damages

---

[1] Above 285 n. 2.   [2] (1615) Cro. Jac. 363.
[3] Cp. the following rule taken from the Doctrina Placitandi 57-58—" Si home
soit tenus de performer touts les covenants en un Indenture, si touts sont in le
affirmative, il poit plead generall performance de touts ; mes si ascuns sont in le
negative, al tants il doit plead specialment (car un negative ne poit estre performe)
et al rest generalment.   Issint si ascuns d'eux sont en le disjunctive, il poit monstrer
queux d'eux il ad performe; et si ascuns sont destre faits de record, il doit monstrer
ceo specialment, et ne poit ceo involve in generall pleading "; cp. Nevil v. Soper
(1699) 1 Salk. 213, cited above 286 n. 2.
[4] (1625) Cro. Car. 6.

recovered in an assumpsit cannot be a bar to a debt upon a record or specialty." On the other hand, it was held in *Poynter v. Poynter*[1] that, on an assumpsit to pay so much if the plaintiff married the daughter of the defendant at his request, an allegation that he had married her, without alleging the defendant's request, was sufficient.

When we compare these and other cases, in which the leading principles of this branch of the law were applied, with the principles themselves, we can see that it is easy enough to lay down general rules as to the kind of statements which the parties must make in order to arrive at an issue, and as to the way in which they must be made ; and we can see that these general rules may be sensible and even obvious. But we can also see that it is not so easy to apply these rules to individual pleadings, and to determine whether the pleadings have or have not complied with the rules. In fact it was almost inevitable that, when a given pleading came to be closely scrutinized "with eagle's eyes" by the opposite party, some fault should be found ; and when the judges, in the interests of logic and precision, upheld these objections, it became increasingly difficult to draw a pleading which would stand this ordeal. In fact the situation of a pleader, thus confronted with his antagonist, was somewhat like the situation to-day of a writer on law or general jurisprudence, who ventures on a definition of some well-known legal concept, such as a trust or a contract. His statement is merely a target for the critics ; and the subsequent discussion of the criticisms, and of the merits of the original definition, generally leaves the definition not a little ragged. In the same way, the discussions of the pleadings in court, and the allowance of often captious objections, gave rise to a mass of decisions upon the meaning of particular pleas, which too often added to the intricacy of the law without giving very much light to future pleaders. It is not therefore surprising that the lawyers should have welcomed fixed forms, which had acquired one technical and unquestionable meaning, and should have been reluctant to sanction any form of words which departed from them.[2]

As some of the cases which have just been cited show, this striving after an impossible precision, was aggravated by the introduction of written pleadings in the sixteenth century. But of the effects of this change I cannot speak fully, till I have said something of the manner in which the lawyers, both during the mediæval period and later, were elaborating a number of technical devices designed either to supplement or evade the rules which I have just described ; or to give full effect, in the interests of their

[1] (1631) Cro. Car. 194.   [2] Above 284-285.

clients, to the many opportunities which the technicality of the rules of pleading afforded.

(iii) The technical devices designed to supplement or evade the principal rules of pleading.

The mediæval development of the law of pleading is a striking illustration of a phenomenon, which is evident in many other branches of the common law—the evil results of the premature fixing of its principles. Many of the rules of pleading were designed for a simpler body of law than the common law had become in the fifteenth century. The rule that the parties must either raise an issue of law by demurrer, or an issue of fact by pleading, caused inconveniences which, as we have seen, were met by the device of a demurrer to the evidence, or by the doctrine of colour.[1] The rule that all matters not denied were admitted was got round by the device of a protestation.[2] The rule against argumentativeness was evaded by the device of a special traverse.[3] At a later period in the history of the law other devices were used. Thus, to meet the difficulty that the evidence given might not support the declaration as drawn, the device was resorted to of stating the same facts in different forms in different counts. To secure time to answer, and often for mere purposes of delay, recourse was had to sham pleas. When, at the latter part of the eighteenth century, the device of a demurrer to the evidence and the doctrine of colour began to go out of use, other devices were used to counter the rule that a litigant must either demur or plead.[4] All these devices, mediæval and modern, added immensely to the complication of the law; and some became the centre of large bodies of technical rules. I propose to take as illustrations of their effect (a) the two mediæval devices of colour, and special traverses; and (b) the two more modern devices of the multiplication of counts, and sham pleas.

(a) *The two mediæval devices.*

The two mediæval devices of colour and special traverses, as well as the device of a demurrer to evidence, got over the difficulty

---

[1] Vol. iii 639.   [2] Ibid 634.   [3] Above 289-291; below 302-304.
[4] The Commissioners on the Courts of Common Law, Parlt. Papers 1831 x 25, after pointing out that, after argument on demurrer, a party was generally allowed to amend, by withdrawing the demurrer and pleading over; and that, after pleading, he could take any substantial objection in point of law by motion in arrest of judgment, said: "The defendant occasionally resorts to the expedient of pleading in addition to some plea sufficient in point of law, another plea which he knows to be insufficient, but to contain a true statement of facts. He thus sometimes succeeds in compelling the plaintiff to take issue in fact upon the first plea, and to demur to the second; and, as upon the argument of the demurrer, the Court looks to the whole record, and decides against the party first in fault, the defendant, instead of supporting his second plea, attacks the declaration, and thus, in effect, both demurs and pleads to the declaration."

that, if the parties pleaded, the pleading must end in an issue of fact to be tried by a jury.   Obviously, with the growing complication of the law, points of law might arise on the pleadings, which it was most inadvisable to leave to a jury of laymen; with only such instruction as the court could give them at the close of the trial.   To this extent, therefore, all these devices had a common object.   But both the doctrine of colour and the special traverse had another similar object, which they met in different ways.   We shall see that, from an early period, the courts had strongly insisted on the rule that if a plea amounted to the general issue, the general issue must be pleaded; and that a special plea in these circumstances was bad for argumentativeness.[1]   The doctrine of colour got over the difficulty that a particular plea merely amounted to the general issue, by inventing facts which made a plea in confession and avoidance appropriate.   The special traverse got over the rules that an affirmative proposition must be answered by a direct negative, and that an inconsistent affirmative proposition was bad as an argumentative denial, by allowing the inconsistent affirmative proposition to be made, with a direct denial of the affirmative proposition advanced by the other side. Both these devices, therefore, originated from the inapplicability to a more complex body of law, of the simple rules adopted by the common law in the fourteenth century, to secure that the parties arrived at an issue of fact or law.   Both operated by means of a modification of one or other of the two alternative methods of pleading which the parties could adopt—the plea in confession and avoidance and the traverse.   The doctrine of colour was founded on a fiction which made a plea in confession and avoidance appropriate; and the special traverse was a variation of the ordinary traverse, which allowed the introduction of new affirmative facts.

Every plea in confession and avoidance must give colour— that is must admit that the plaintiff has a prima facie case.   The confession amounts to such an admission, and the avoidance nullifies its effect.   Therefore such a confession was sometimes said to give "implied" colour.[2]   We have seen that the doctrine of "express" colour was an improvement upon this, designed to give so good a prima facie case to the plaintiff, that, on the facts as stated in the pleadings, a serious question of law arose as to which of the two had a legal right to succeed.[3]   A question of law having thus been raised, the court and not the jury must decide it. Thus, in a case in which a demurrer would have been impossible, the parties were enabled to raise on the pleadings a question of

---

[1] Below 319-320.   [2] Stephen, op. cit. 220.   [3] Vol. iii 639.

law for the court.   To make this clear I will repeat the illustration given by Reeves, which I have cited in an earlier volume.[1] Suppose A enfeoffed B of land, and an assize was brought by a stranger against B, B could not plead these facts simply, as such plea would amount only to the general issue; he would be obliged to plead the general issue, and the case would be left to the jury.   He, therefore, by a wholly fictitious averment, gave the plaintiff *colour*, i.e. a prima facie cause of action.   Thus, after pleading that A had enfeoffed him, he would further plead, "that the plaintiff claiming by colour of a deed of feoffment made by the said feoffor, before the feoffment made to the said tenant (by which deed no right passed) entered, upon whom the said tenant entered. This left a point of law for the court, i.e. the validity of the first deed, and thus the case was withdrawn from the jury.   If the plaintiff did not demur, so that no point of law was raised on the pleading, he was obliged to take issue on "one certain point," so that the matter was not left "at large to the jury," as it would have been left if the general issue had been taken.[2]

That the doctrine was in full working order in the year 1440 appears from a note in a Year Book of that year.[3]   That note shows also that the conditions, which such a colourable plea must satisfy, were determined strictly by its original object.   It must be a plea which raised a difficulty which the jury could not fairly be expected to determine.   Thus, if "I bring an assize against you, and you say that you yourself leased the same land to a man for his life, and then granted the reversion to me, and that then the tenant for life died, then that I, claiming the reversion by force of this grant, though the tenant had never attorned, entered; this special matter is allowable, since it is perilous to plead 'Nul tort,' for the jury may find that the reversion passed by force of the grant without attornment."   On the other hand, "if the tenant says that he was seised until the plaintiff disseised him, on whom he entered, this plea is not allowable, because everyone knows well enough that the tenant in such a case is no disseisor."[4]   It was the fact that this manner of pleading tended to prevent the jury from unwittingly committing something like perjury, that the Student used to combat the objection of the Doctor to allowing

---

[1] Vol. iii 639 n. 1.

[2] Doctor Leyfield's Case (1611) 10 Co. Rep. at f. 90a.

[3] Y.B. 19 Hy. VI Mich. pl. 42.

[4] In later law the fictions adopted became stereotyped—" though originally various suggestions of apparent right might be adopted, according to the fancy of the pleader, and though the same latitude is still perhaps allowable, yet, in practice it is unusual to resort to any, except certain known fictions, which long usuage has applied to the particular case.   Thus, in trespass to land, the colour universally given is that of a defective *charter of demise*," Stephen, op. cit. 230-231 ; for a further refinement designed to protect the tenant see Reeves, H.E.L. ii 630.

a party to an action to plead a plea that was notoriously untrue.[1] As this fictitious manner of pleading was allowed by the courts, they necessarily refused to allow the fictitious matter alleged to be traversed, since to have allowed this would have frustrated the attainment of the purpose for which the fiction was invented.[2]

During the fifteenth century this doctrine of colour gave rise to a mass of decisions, as to the conditions under which the use of this device was permissible. Their complexity, and the difficulty of finding any rational ground for many of them, will appear from Reeves' summary:[3] "It was said that when such matter was pleaded as bound the *possession* only, the defendant should give colour ; as in case of a dying seised, and descent to the defendant. But when the *right* was bound, as by feoffment with warranty, by fine, and the like, there no colour need be given. Again, if a defendant pleaded liberum tenementum, he need not give colour, nor when he justified as servant to one who had the freehold ; the same when one justified for a distress : because, says the book, where no property was claimed, there no colour need be given. It was held, at one time, that in justification for taking as wreck, or as the goods of felons, the defendant should give colour : but afterwards it was laid down, that in those cases, and also in justification for tithes, for waif and stray, or as a purchaser in market overt, no colour need be given ; though in the case of goods sold in market overt they made this distinction : If the defendant said simply, that A sold them to him, he need not give colour, but if he had said, that A was possessed of goods *as of his proper goods*, and sold them to him, colour should be given ; because in this latter case, he fully stated, that no property was in the plaintiff, and therefore that he had no colour of action ; but in the former there might still be a property in the plaintiff ; which distinction seems analogous to that of the two cases before mentioned, where the *right* and where the *possession* only was bound." Many of these rules were summed up and explained by Coke in *Dr. Leyfield's Case.*[4]

During the eighteenth century there was a tendency to drop some of these refinements, and to simplify the rules relating to colour. The rules relating to this doctrine, as stated by Stephen, are far less elaborate than the rules prevailing in the fifteenth, sixteenth, and seventeenth centuries ; and the more important rules

---

[1] "There is no default in the party that pleadeth such a special matter to avoid from his neighbour the danger of perjury, nor yet in the court, though they induce him to it, as they do sometime for the intent before rehearsed," Doctor and Student, Bk. ii c. 53.

[2] Stephen, Pleading 229.

[3] H.E.L. ii 631-632, citing Y.BB. of Henry VI. and Edward IV.'s reigns.

[4] (1611) 10 Co. Rep. 88a.

were intelligible. Thus it was laid down that the plea "must contain such matter as, if it were effectual, would maintain the nature of the action";[1] so that where an assize was brought for disseisin of a freehold, the tenant should not suggest by way of colour a demise for years to the demandant, as such a demise gives no ground at all for bringing an assize.[2] Similarly the colour must not give a good right to the plaintiff as, if it does, he is able to recover on the defendant's own showing. Thus, when trespass was brought for taking one hundred loads of wood, and the defendant pleaded that I.S. was possessed of them ut de bonis propriis, and the plaintiff claiming "by colour of a deed of gift by the said I.S. afterwards made" took them, and the defendant re-took them; the plea was bad, because the plaintiff, who had taken under a deed of gift from the owner, had only done what he was entitled to do.[3] In fact, when the verdict of a jury had come to be capable of correction by a new trial,[4] there was less need to have recourse to the doctrine; and, though still occasionally used at the beginning of the nineteenth century,[5] it was falling into disuse. I must now deal with the second of these mediæval devices —the special traverse.

I have already said something of the nature and objects of special traverse. We have seen that it differed from the ordinary traverse, in that it did not simply deny the facts stated by the opposite party, but introduced new facts coupled with a denial of those asserted by the opposite party.[6] Thus, suppose an action of covenant for non-payment of rent, brought by A.B., the heir of E.B. the lessor, against C.D. the lessee, in which the lessee wishes to plead that the lessor was seised for his life only, so that the term ended at his death. The lessee, if he used a common traverse, would plead as follows: "and the said C.D. says that the said A.B. ought not to have or maintain his aforesaid action against him, because he says, that after the making of the said indenture, the said reversion of the said demised premises did not belong to the said E.B. and his heirs, in manner and form as the said A.B. hath in his said declaration alleged. And of this the said C.D. puts himself upon his country." If, on the other hand, he used a

---

[1] Stephen, op. cit. 231.　　　　[2] Keilway 103; cf. 10 Co. Rep. at f. 91b.

[3] "Colour ought to be such a thing which is good colour of title, and yet is not any title; as a deed of a lease for life because it hath not the ceremony viz. livery. So grant of a reversion without attornment is not good; but a deed of goods and chattels without other act or ceremony is good," Radford v. Harbyn (1607) Cro. Jac. 122.

[4] Vol. i 225-226, 346.

[5] "Though now rather of rare occurrence, it is still sometimes practised," Stephen, op. cit. 225.

[6] Above 289; see generally Stephen, op. cit. 188-192, and the illustrations given ibid at pp. 192-197.

special traverse, he would begin with a statement of the new matter he wished to plead, i.e. the fact that E.B. was seised only for his life. This statement was called the inducement. Then, beginning with the words "absque hoc," he denied the plaintiff's statement. Lastly, instead of concluding to the country, he offered to verify the new matter alleged, and prayed judgment. Thus a special traverse "always consists of an inducement, a denial, and a verification";[1] and its effect "is to postpone the issue to one stage of the pleading later than it would be attained by a traverse in the common form"[2]—an effect in causing delay which helps to account for its popularity in the sixteenth and seventeenth centuries, and its use in cases in which a common traverse would have met all purposes.[3] In fact, the question when a special traverse could be used in place of a common traverse, when no new matter was alleged, was never precisely fixed; and in the eighteenth century somewhat arbitrary rules were laid down as to when it was allowable in these circumstances.[4] At the end of that century the fashion began to set against its use in cases of this kind; and even in cases where new matter was alleged it was going out of use.[5] The inducement tended to disclose the nature of the case of the party using it;[6] and both the pleaders and the courts were turning against it.[7] But down to the middle of the nineteenth century it was still a possible, and sometimes, perhaps, even a necessary form of plea.[8]

Naturally a large number of minute rules gathered round it, and more especially round the qualities that an inducement must have. Into these rules it is unnecessary to enter. Their character is sufficiently described by the following passage from the First Report of the Common Law Procedure Commission : " The rules

---

[1] Stephen, op. cit. 192.   [2] Ibid 198.

[3] " The special traverse grew so much into fashion as to be frequently adopted even in cases to which the original reasons of the form were inapplicable—that is to cases where the intended denial was, in its nature, simple and absolute, and connected with no new matter," ibid 203.

[4] " When the whole substance of the last pleading is denied, the conclusion must be to the country, or, in other words, the traverse must be in common form ; but where one of several facts only is the subject of denial the conclusion may be either to the country or with a verification, that is the traverse may be either common or special at the option of the pleader," ibid 205.

[5] " It now rarely occurs in any instance where there is no inducement of new matter, although the denial relate to one out of several facts only. This change of practice however is very recent, having been effected within the memory of many living practitioners," ibid 206.

[6] Ibid 206-207.

[7] " It has been discountenanced by the courts, and is disapproved of by Mr. Serjeant Williams in the first edition of his notes on Saunders' reports," First Report, Common Law Procedure Commission, Parlt. Papers (1851) xxii 26.

[8] " Where allowable, it should still be occasionally adopted in a view to the various grounds of necessity or convenience by which it was originally suggested," Stephen, op. cit. 207.

which govern the form and application of the special traverse are so technical and artificial as to perplex the practitioner; for instance, the inducement must not be a direct denial, but it must be a sufficiently indirect one, and it must not be in confession or avoidance. The rules also as to when an inducement may or may not be traversed, and how the pleading may be answered by the opposite party, are extremely difficult and abstruse."[1]

It will be observed that, though these two mediæval devices were going out of use at the beginning of the nineteenth century, they were by no means obsolete. Hence the large bodies of law, which had grown up round them during the three centuries when they flourished, were still necessary to be known by the pleader—indeed ignorance of them might prove fatal to a litigant, if his pleader was called on to deal with a case in which either of these devices had been used. We shall now see that his burden had been increased by the two modern devices which I must now describe.

(b) The two modern devices.

Of the two modern devices—the multiplication of counts and sham pleas—the first was occasioned by difficulties which had resulted from the new practice of written pleadings, and of calling witnesses to support the statements in the pleadings; and the second was occasioned by the desire of the defendant to gain time, and thereby to delay the signature of judgment against himself.

We have seen that under the mediæval system the pleadings were oral, and that the modern practice of summoning witnesses to testify to the facts was unknown. Counsel took upon themselves the responsibility for the truth of the facts pleaded; and, by means of imparlances, taken for the purpose of examining their clients on the fresh facts, which emerged as the debate in court as to the real issue proceeded, the form of the pleadings could be adjusted to the facts as finally elicited by them.[2] This became impossible under the new system. The pleadings were closed and the issue was settled before the parties got into court; while the truth of the facts alleged in the pleadings was proved or disproved by the witnesses summoned to testify. Thus it might easily happen that the facts as proved did not support the facts as alleged in the pleadings—there was a variance. And a variance, however slight, might prove fatal to the success of the party who had all the substantial merits on his side.

The arbitrary way in which this doctrine of variance operated, is very clearly explained by the Common Law Procedure Com-

---

[1] Parlt. Papers 1851 xxii 26; Stephen op. cit. 208-210.
[2] Vol. iii 635-638.

missioners in 1830:[1] "At the trial of the cause a material variance between the allegation in the pleading, and the state of facts proved, is a fatal objection, and decides the suit in favour of the objecting party, and a variance is often considered in this technical sense as material, though to common sense it may appear to be very trifling, and though it may be wholly irrelevant to the merits of the case. Thus, in an action for a false charge of felony, when the declaration stated that the defendant went before Richard Cavendish, Baron Waterpark of *Waterfork*, a Justice of the Peace, and falsely charged the plaintiff with the felony, and it appeared in evidence that the charge was made before Richard Cavendish, Baron Waterpark of *Waterpark*, this variance was considered as fatal, and the plaintiff was nonsuited. So in a case where the plaintiff brought his action on the warranty of a horse, stating the warranty to be that the horse was sound, and it appeared upon the proof that the warranty was that the horse was sound, except for a kick on one of its legs, this was also held to be a ground of nonsuit, though the unsoundness which was proved, and for which the action was brought, had no relation to the leg. In another case where the plaintiff brought his action on a contract to deliver goods, though he took the precaution of stating it in two different ways; viz. in one count, as a contract to deliver within fourteen days, and in another, as a contract to deliver on the arrival of a certain ship, yet he was nonsuited, because at the trial it was proved to be a contract in the alternative; viz. to deliver within fourteen days, *or* on the arrival of the ship; and he had no count stating it in the alternative. The cause of action however was the non-delivery of the goods after the expiration of the fourteen days, and also after the arrival of the vessel, so that the variance was wholly immaterial to the real merits of the case."

To meet this difficulty, the practice arose of stating in the declaration the plaintiff's cause of action in several distinct ways, in several distinct counts, in order to meet every possible variety in the proof. It is probable that this practice arose during the seventeenth century;[2] and, when by a statute of 1705,[3] it became possible, with the leave of the court, to plead several pleas, each of these counts was met by its appropriate plea. In 1830 the Commissioners said that, "though in other respects the prolixity of allegation once prevalent has been materially retrenched, this particular kind of redundance has never perhaps prevailed more remarkably than at the present day. Records containing from

---

[1] Parlt. Papers 1830 xi 35. [2] Ibid.
[3] 4 Anne c. 16 § 4; below 316-317.

ten to fifteen special counts or pleas are by no means rare, and fail to excite remark. Of these the greater proportion, and frequently the whole, relate to the same substantial cause of action or defence. They are merely different expositions of the same case, and expositions of it often inconsistent with each other."[1] This device no doubt helped to meet the extraordinarily strict way in which the doctrine of variance was applied; but it met it at the cost of an enormously increased complication in the pleadings; and it was not always successful. In 1830 it was said that this doctrine was "one of the most frequent sources of miscarriage in the suit."[2]

The second of these devices—sham pleading—was a device to gain time. The gaining of time is always especially desired by the litigant with a bad case; and many of the devices which I have just described, and others, which this artificial system of pleading made possible, were used or rather abused for this purpose. Thus the popularity of the special traverse was no doubt partly due to the fact that it delayed the reaching of an issue to one stage later in the pleadings;[3] the doctrine of variance was much insisted on with the same object;[4] and the extreme precision of statement exacted by the courts gave opportunity for purely formal objections interposed merely for the purpose of delay.[5] The device of sham pleading was a device which aimed directly at securing the object which the other devices only secured indirectly. The device was of comparatively late introduction. It was not, it would seem, tolerated at the beginning of the seventeenth century;[6] and the courts always in theory held to the view that pleadings must be true. In fact, it was always possible on motion, supported by affidavit of the falsity of the plea, to allow judgment to be signed for want of a plea.[7] Possibly the clause in the statute of 1705,[8] which made it necessary for the party pleading a dilatory plea to prove its truth or probability by affidavit, testifies to the growth of the practice of using sham pleas. Certainly at the latter part of the eighteenth century it was a common practice to plead a sham plea or demurrer, with the object of giving the party pleading it

---

[1] Parlt. Papers 1830 xi 34.

[2] "This kind of objection [variance] is naturally looked out for by a party whose case has no foundations on the merits, and is consequently of very frequent occurrence; so that, notwithstanding the protection from it afforded by the use of several counts and pleas, it is one of the most frequent sources of miscarriage in the suit," ibid 35.

[3] Above 303.   [4] Above 304-305.

[5] Above 282, 297; below 315-316.

[6] "This [pleading] is the principal art of law, for pleading is not talking; and therefore it is required that pleading be true; that is the goodness and vertue of pleading; and that it be certain and single, and that is the beauty and grace of pleading," Slade v. Drake (1618) Hob. at p. 295.

[7] Stephen, op. cit. 445.   [8] 4 Anne c. 16 § 11.

more time;[1] and the courts had come to tolerate certain common forms of pleas—e.g. that of judgment recovered—though all the parties knew that they were false.[2] It is obvious, however, that the permission to use this way of securing time might defeat the claims of substantial justice. If an unprincipled pleader pleaded a tricky or subtle plea, and its falsity was not discovered, it was quite possible that, in the course of the subsequent pleading, his adversary might make some formal mistake, which would enable the pleader to snatch a judgment on special demurrer.[3]

The history which I have just related of the sources of the main rules of pleading, shows that, at the end of the eighteenth century, these rules were derived from all periods in the history of English law. The main body of them, like the main body of other older branches of the common law, came from the fourteenth and fifteenth centuries. But they were supplemented by archaic rules which came from an earlier period in the history of the law, and by devices originated, both by mediæval pleaders and by pleaders of later ages, to meet new needs occasioned by the development of the law. And both because the law of pleading is necessarily closely connected with procedure, and because the law of procedure retained more archaic traits than any other branch of the common law, these archaic rules continued to possess great practical importance for the pleader. Disregard of them might mean failure of the action; and a skilful use of them might enable a just claim to be delayed, if not defeated. Thus the law had come to be made up of a large number of detailed rules, a minute knowledge of which was essential to the practitioner. When we consider the complexity of these rules, it is not surprising that special pleading had become a distinct branch of the law, and the class of special pleaders a distinct order in the legal profession.[4]

---

[1] "It is very usual for the purpose of delay to plead what is termed a *sham plea*. This practice, though it still prevails, is discountenanced by the courts, and difficult questions of law ought not to be pleaded for this purpose," Chitty, Pleading (ed. 1817) i 506.

[2] Stephen, op. cit. 445; for a case where another form of plea was used see Solomons v. Lyon (1801) 1 East 369; the Commissioners on the Courts of Common Law in their Third Report, Parlt. Papers 1831 x 30, said, "the character of these proceedings is notorious both in and out of the profession, and is sufficiently indicated by the appellation which belongs to them."

[3] In the case of Blewitt v. Marsden (1808) 10 East at pp. 237-238, "the Court said that there might be occasions where they would not enter into any question as to the truth of a plea of judgment recovered, pleaded in the usual form, upon motion, but await the time for producing the roll, when such a plea would be regularly disproved; but they expressed great indignation against the abuse which had grown up of late and was continually increasing, of loading and degrading the rolls of the court with sham pleas of this nonsensical nature; . . . by which it sometimes happened that the time of the court . . . was taken up in futile investigations of nice points which might arise on demurrer to such sham pleas;" see also Charles v. Marsden (1808) 1 Taunt. at pp. 226-227 *per* Lawrence, J.

[4] Vol. vi 446.

We shall now see that it was under the regime of the system of written pleadings, which had come in the sixteenth century, that all these rules were first elaborated and given their modern form; and then co-ordinated into a system which, in the opinion of its practitioners and many other lawyers, gave it the character of an exact science.

(iv) The effect of the introduction of written pleadings.

I have already dealt with the larger effects of this change upon the law and legal institutions.[1]   At this point I must say something of its effects upon the form and contents of the law of pleading. One of these effects I have already alluded to.   The fact that under this system of written pleadings the form and course of the pleadings, and therefore the issue to be tried, were settled by the counsel of the parties before the parties came into court, made it much more difficult for them to avoid a fatal mistake before it was too late.   Under the earlier system of oral pleadings the issue to be tried was settled by a debate in court, which gave the counsel opportunities to avoid such mistakes, and to adopt the form of pleading which would allow the substantial matter at issue to be tried.   Under the later system each party prepared his pleading; and, not till an issue had been reached, did the case normally come before the court.   Then, and not till then, was the court asked to pronounce upon the validity of the various criticisms which each side could make to the other's pleading.   Obviously the chances of a fatal error—sometimes of the most formal description—were enormously increased; and we have seen that this effect of this change has been noted by all our legal historians from Hale to Maitland.[2]   At the same time, the evil results of this particular effect were aggravated, firstly, by the growth of the precision and the complexity of the rules of pleading which came in its train; and, secondly, by growing firmness with which the lawyers held that these rules were a logical and a scientific system, in which it would be dangerous, if not impossible, to make any radical changes. Since it was these two results of this change which gave the law of pleading its modern shape, they can be regarded as the two most important elements which went to the making of the modern law.   At this point, therefore, I must explain how they operated to produce this result.

(a) The cases cited in the preceding sections sufficiently illustrate the manner in which decisions upon the construction and effect of pleadings developed and elaborated the law.   We can distinguish three main directions in which this development proceeded.

---

[1] Vol. iii 653-656.   [2] Ibid 655 n. 3.

In the first place there is a long line of cases which turns upon the construction of particular pleadings. The court construed these pleadings just as it construed other documents which came before it ; and very many cases were concerned solely or chiefly with the meaning and legal effect of particular pleadings. And just as the cases which turned on the construction of conveyances helped forward the development of the law, by showing the conveyancers what forms of expression they must use to obtain particular results,[1] so these cases helped to instruct the pleaders as to the forms of words which they should employ. They thus helped to establish those recognized forms of pleas, the existence of which, as we have seen, mitigated the uncertainty as to the construction which the court would put on any particular pleading—an uncertainty due to that craving for absolute logical accuracy, which led the courts to look sympathetically upon the most captious objections.[2] In so far as these decisions secured this result they did good service. But often they were merely records of the misplaced ingenuity of the judges and pleaders in picking holes in particular pleadings. The repetition of these decisions led to an anxiety to make the pleadings so clear that they could not be misunderstood by the most hostile and ingenious critic ; and this desire was, as the Common Law Procedure Commissioners pointed out in 1851, to a large extent answerable for the tautology, verbosity, and length, which disfigured pleadings during the sixteenth and later centuries.[3]

In the second place, the different rules applicable to the pleadings in different classes of actions were elaborated and settled. We have seen that the forms of action differed from one another, both in the writ by which they were begun, and in the mesne process upon that writ. From the fourteenth century onwards, the kinds of pleas open to the parties also differed. All these differences were elaborated by the many cases decided on points of pleading in the sixteenth and seventeenth centuries. Thus the Doctrina Placitandi devotes some paragraphs to such headings as the proper pleas in a writ of entry, a quare impedit, an action for false imprisonment, an action for maintenance, and others ; and the largest half of Comyns's title on pleading is taken up with an account of the pleadings in particular actions. This gave rise to a mass of detailed rules, the general result of which was summarized in

---

[1] Vol. vii 397-398.   [2] Above 284-285, 297.

[3] "The redundant and tautological modes of expression which disfigure legal pleadings, and the repetition of the same thing in different ways, are in great measure to be ascribed to the rigour with which pleadings are construed, which has introduced verbosity and length, from a desire to omit nothing, to be strictly precise, and to put everything in so many shapes that some one at least shall be found to square with the facts," Parlt. Papers 1851 xxii 17.

Hayes's Dialogue on *Crogate's Case*[1] as follows: "The forms of pleading are more or less strict, according to the nature of the action; and in many actions there is, in substance, no special pleading at all.   In actions on *contracts*, if the facts are such as to render it necessary, according to the established rules of the court, to declare specially, great strictness and particularity are enforced, and the simplest questions are often involved in much complication of pleading ; but if the case admits of the use of certain general or common counts (which indeed are applicable in the great majority of ordinary actions) the whole matter is left pretty much at large, and the most complicated questions are tried on simplest statements.   So in actions on *torts*, you may have more or less special pleading, entirely according to the form of action which you elect, or are obliged to adopt.   Thus, if your goods are taken away, and you sue the wrongdoer in *trespass* you will have special pleading in all its strictness ; but if you choose to sue in *trover*, and make a fictitious statement that you casually lost your goods, and that the defendant found and converted them ; here he is allowed to deny the fictitious loss and finding, and may set up almost any possible defence, under a denial of the alleged ownership and conversion of the goods ; or if you prefer to sue in *detinue* and state a fictitious delivery or bailment of the goods to the defendant (which fiction he is not allowed to deny) you will have rather more special pleading than in *trover*, but considerably less than in *trespass*.   If you are assaulted and beaten, you cannot escape special pleading by any fictitious allegation, but you are obliged to sue in *trespass*, and the defendant to justify specially.   If you sue for a *trespass* to your land, however small the injury the greatest strictness of pleading is required, but if you are actually turned out, you may recover the land itself by a fictitious mode of proceeding called ejectment, without any special pleading at all."

In the third place, as the cases already cited show, certain forms of pleading, e.g. special traverses, gave rise to a mass of detailed rules.   Thus, in Hayes's Dialogue, Baron Surrebutter says that the cases upon the question whether a replication de injuria was permissible could be classified as follows : firstly, when it was clearly permissible, secondly, when it was clearly not permissible, thirdly, when it was probably permissible, fourthly, when it was probably not permissible, and fifthly, when the question was wholly doubtful.[2]   Then, after dealing with the elaborate commentary with which the resolutions in *Crogate's Case* had been overlaid, he said,[3] "A multitude of other points and distinctions will also demand our attention ; and amongst others I shall have to show you that, when this replication is clearly allowable, yet, if

---

[1] App. I (2) p. 428.   [2] Ibid p. 430.   [3] Ibid p. 430-431.

the pleader does not use the proper and accustomed form of words, but introduces some new-fangled allegation, such as that the opposite pleading is *untrue in substance*, this will be clearly bad, because (as we settled in a recent case) by alleging a plea to be *untrue in substance* you necessarily put in issue immaterial and unsubstantial matters ; but by denying the truth of the whole plea in the common form *de injuria*, only material and substantial matter are put in issue." Obviously questions of this kind can only be described, in Lord Bowen's words,[1] as "the merest legal conundrums which bore no relation to the merits of any controversies except those of pedants."

(*b*) These and similar decisions by which the law was developed and elaborated, tended to convince the lawyers that the rules of pleading were a logical and a scientific system, in which it would be dangerous, if not impossible, to make any radical changes. That this was so is illustrated by the literature of the subject.

From the earliest period the lawyers and judges have spoken with the utmost respect and reverence for the art of pleading ;[2] and it was natural that they should do so. It was a branch of the law of procedure ; and it was from the law of procedure, and around the forms of action, that the principles of the common law were being developed. Since the maintenance of these forms of action was, right down to the beginning of the nineteenth century, regarded as a vital necessity for the being of the common law,[3] it is not surprising that a subject, so intimately bound up with these forms of action, should be regarded in much the same light.[4] But, though the extreme importance of the art of pleading had been well recognised from the earliest period in the history of the law, it was not till the latter part of the eighteenth century that the lawyers began to insist that its rules were so logical as to be inevitable ; and that the system was so scientific that any radical change must be for the worse, because it would inflict damage, not only on the law of pleading, but on the common law as a whole.[5]

---

[1] Administration of the Law in the reign of Queen Victoria, cited vol. i 645.

[2] For Littleton's words in § 534 of his tenures see vol. ii 521.

[3] Thus, in Bryant v. Herbert (1878) 3 C.P.D. at p. 390, Bramwell, L.J., said that the Common Law Commissioners did not abolish the forms of actions in words. They "recommended that ; but it was supposed that, if adopted, the law would be shaken to its foundations ; so that all that could be done was to provide as far as possible that, though forms of action remained, there should never be a question what was the form."

[4] Thus the Commissioners on the Courts of Common Law said in their Third Report, Parlt. Papers 1831 x 6, that much confusion and uncertainty as to the right of action would be generated if the forms of action were abolished, "and so much of our course of pleading would also be unsettled by it that in this point of view alone more advantage would be lost than gained " ; see the whole passage cited above 252 n. 1.

[5] Thus Coke says, First Instit. 303a, " when I diligently consider the course of our Books of years and terms from the beginning of the reign of Edw. III., I observe that more jangling and questions grow upon the manner of pleading, and exceptions to form, than upon the matter itself, and infinite causes lost or delayed for want of good pleading "—there is no idolatry here of the art of pleading.

It is, I think, probable that the growth of this feeling was rendered possible by the treatises which summarised, and linked up with the Year Book cases, the numerous decisions of the sixteenth and seventeenth centuries.[1]   One of the most important of these books was the Doctrina Placitandi, published in 1677, which grouped these rules under alphabetical headings.   A still more important work was contained in the article on Pleading in Comyns's Digest.   It was, says Stephen,[2] "a more systematic compilation upon this subject than had previously appeared; comprising the substance, not only of the authorities collected in the Doctrina Placitandi, but also of the cases subsequently decided, and reducing the whole, under different heads, upon a plan peculiarly scientific and masterly."   A similar work of digesting and arranging the rules of pleading was done by Chitty's work, which was published in 1817, and, with respect to some of the rules of the subject, by Williams' notes to Saunders' reports.   These works were in the nature of digests of the rules; but, by showing the connection between the various parts of the subject, they made it possible to represent it as a collection of well-conceived principles, logically worked out into detailed rules.   We can see the growth of this manner of regarding it in the latter part of the eighteenth and at the beginning of the nineteenth century.   In 1757 Lord Mansfield could say that "the substantial rules of pleading are founded in strong sense and the soundest and closest logic."[3]   In 1768 Blackstone could talk of the science of pleading.[4] In 1820 Runnington, the editor of Hale's History of the Common Law, said, "the science of pleading (however those who do not understand may affect to despise it) is admirably calculated for the purposes of analysing a cause; of extracting, like the roots of an equation, the true points in dispute, and referring them with all imaginable simplicity to the court or to the jury. It is reducible to the strictest rules of pure dialectic."[5]   The way was thus prepared for Stephen's work—the first work as he points out ever written on the principles of pleading—which was published in 1824.   He did more than anyone else to demonstrate the logical and scientific character of its chief principles; and, as we shall see later,[6] to postpone any radical reform of the system.

At first sight, it is not immediately obvious why the elaboration of the law, which was proceeding from the sixteenth to the nineteenth century, should have resulted in this widespread belief that the system of pleading was so logically and scientifically perfect, that no radical reform was necessary or desirable.   It

[1] For this literature see vol. v 386-387; vol. vi 567-568, 569-571, 600.
[2] Pleading, Preface to the 1st edition.
[3] Robinson v. Raley 1 Burr. at p. 319.
[4] Comm. iii 305.   [5] Hale, H.C.L. 212.   [6] Below 324

was due, I think, to two main causes. In the first place, this elaboration of the law was effected through the agency of decided cases. Now, as Sir F. Pollock has pointed out, the mental operations, which result in the production of a body of case law, " have a truly scientific character," since the decision of each case involves an inference as to the rule of law applicable to the facts, just as the explanation of a natural phenomenon involves an inference as to the particular scientific law which may have produced it.[1] And just as the observation and explanation of different natural phenomena lead to the discovery of new and the elaboration of old scientific laws, so the decision of new cases leads to an elaboration of the rules of law. But the decision of each of these new cases is justified as the logical consequence of the cases previously decided. Hence the law assumes a logical and a scientific form. It may be that the premises from which these rules of law are deduced are arbitrary or archaic, as was the case with many of the older rules of the law of pleading. But the deductions drawn from them were logical deductions; and so the superstructure raised on their foundation took a scientific form. Those who were concerned in erecting this logical superstructure somewhat easily forgot the dubious character of some of the premises on which it was founded; and, in their admiration of the processes of reasoning by which it was erected, they also forgot the harmful results which followed from it. They became the slaves of technicalities which had ceased to have any real meaning.[2] " It is plain to me," said Crogate to Baron Surrebutter,[3] " that you can't understand half of your own decisions; and that with all your fine spun distinctions and crochets you have got into a mystification and confusion, from which you can find no straightforward way out." These technical rules could not be " put into sensible English "; and that, as Sir F. Pollock has said,[4] is the test of the soundness of a technical rule. In the second place, this danger was much increased in the case of the law of pleading, because a great number of its more important rules were eminently sound and sensible rules, logically well designed to produce the effect for which they were intended—the formulation of an issue. Stephen,

---

[1] Essays in Jurisprudence and Ethics 246-249.

[2] " The technical terms of every language are convenient symbols, but their very convenience is dangerous, and the facility given by them is always in danger of abuse. When one is operating with symbols it is often a good thing to forget what the symbols mean during the process, but one must always be prepared to remember it at the end. Now a fixed habit of operating with a certain number of symbols is apt to induce one to forget this very thing, the result of which is that the operator becomes the slave of his symbols instead of their master, and thinks he is thinking when he is only playing with counters. . . . In our case law there has been a good deal of this kind of diseased technicality," ibid 258-259.

[3] App. I (2) p. 431.   [4] Essays in Jurisprudence and Ethics 259.

speaking of its leading principles, could say with some justice that, "when properly understood and appreciated. it appears to be an instrument so well adapted to the ends of distributive justice, so simple and striking in its fundamental principles, so ingenious and elaborate in its details, as fairly to be entitled to the character of a fine juridical invention." But naturally those who spoke of it in these terms, tended to slur over the distinction between those parts of it which were sensible and well adapted to get the facts at issue before the court, and those parts of it which consisted, either of a series of elaborate rules founded on ideas which had long lost any meaning which they had once possessed, or a series of shifts and devices to circumvent rules which had lost their usefulness. They were inclined to cherish all parts of their science, and to cut down all projects of change to a minimum.

Two of the results of these ideas upon the development of the law were most unfortunate. In the first place, both the system of pleading, and the system of procedure in which it played so important a part, tended to grow more elaborate and more rigid as time went on. Now a rigid system of procedure is no doubt necessary in an early stage of legal development. As both Roman and English law show, there is need at such a stage of a stable framework of actions, round which the substantive rules can take shape, and give rise to distinct legal doctrines. But, as these legal doctrines grow in number and complexity, they should be able to emancipate themselves from the leading strings of the old forms of action. That is what happened at Rome when the Legis Actio procedure gave place to the formulary procedure, and when that in its turn gave place to the extraordinary procedure. In England, on the other hand, right down to the middle of the nineteenth century, the substantive law was still cramped by the forms of action; and it only developed because, under cover of numerous fictions, these forms of actions had been largely extended. But, in spite of these extensions, suitors could only get redress if they could put their pleadings into a shape which was determined by a mass of technical rules, coming from all periods in the long history of English law. We have seen that many regarded the preservation of these forms of action as essential to the continued existence of English law.[1] Similarly, most lawyers regarded the rules of pleading as a science so perfect that it was dangerous to tamper with any but the most unimportant of its rules. Thus the fetters both of an obsolete system of procedure, and of an unduly rigid and elaborate system of pleading, seemed to be firmly riveted upon the common law. In the second place, as we shall now see, this manner of regarding these rules of pleading, tended to diminish

[1] Above 252 n. 1, 311 n. 4.

the usefulness of certain measures which had been taken both by the Legislature and the courts to reform some of their most obvious abuses.

(3) *The attempts made to remedy the defects of this system of pleading.*

From time to time these attempts were made both by the Legislature and by the courts; but perhaps the most effectual mitigation of all was the common law rule as to the manner in which the old plea of the general issue could be used to prevent the necessity for any special pleading. I shall deal with the history of this topic under these three heads.

(i) The attempts made by the Legislature to remedy these evils are contained in the statutes of jeofail; in the statute of 1705,[1] which allowed a defendant with the leave of the court to plead several pleas in his defence; and in several statutes which expressly permitted defendants to plead the general issue. Of the last class of statutes I shall say something under my third head.[2] At this point I shall deal with the two first classes of statutes.

Various statutes of jeofail were passed between the years 1340 and 1718.[3] Though they effected some good, they were on the whole very ineffective to remedy the principal evils which flowed from this system of pleading. This was due mainly to three causes. In the first place, the earlier statutes dealt simply with defects in process, and left untouched formal defects in pleading.[4] In the second place, the later statutes, which did deal with certain formal defects in pleading, dealt, for the most part, only with the most formal parts of the pleading.[5] Moreover, they proceeded by the method of simple and particular enumeration,[6] so that fresh cases of hardship were always coming to light. Thus till 1705[7] they only applied to formal errors discovered after verdict and judgment. It was not till that year that this series of statutes was extended to judgments on demurrer and *nil dicit*.[8] In the third place, owing to their limited application arising from this particularity of statement, all these formal objections could be taken by a party before judgment by special demurrer.[9] We have seen that the result of

[1] 4 Anne c. 16 § 4.   [2] Below 321.
[3] For the list see above 264 n. 9.
[4] E.g. 14 Edward III. c. 6; 9 Henry V. c. 4; 4 Henry VI. c. 3; 8 Henry VI. cc. 12 and 15.
[5] E.g. 32 Henry VIII. c. 30; 18 Elizabeth c. 14; 21 James I. c. 13.
[6] See especially 16, 17 Charles II. c. 8 which enumerates in detail a large number of formal defects in process and pleading.
[7] 4 Anne c. 16 §§ 1 and 2.
[8] For further extensions of the statute see 9 Anne c. 20 § 7; 5 George I. c. 13.
[9] The Common Law Procedure Commissioners pointed out in 1851, Parlt. Papers 1851 xxii 19, that the operation of this series of statutes "was limited to providing that certain technical objections should be cured by pleading over, or after verdict; when particularized or pointed out by special demurrer, these objections are still allowed to prevail"; cp. Heard v. Baskervile (1615) Hob. 232.

this was that justice was defeated by means of all these technical and formal objections right down to the middle of the nineteenth century.[1] In fact, this series of statutes is a typical illustration of the worst features of English enacted law. It was not till a grievance had been disclosed that the Legislature was roused to act; and then all it did was to remedy that particular grievance, without ever troubling to make any comprehensive inquiry into the state of that branch of the law in which the grievance had arisen, in order to provide a measure of reform which would go to the root of the evil.[2]

The second of these measures, which allowed a defendant with the leave of the court to plead several pleas in his defence, was a clause in a statute of 1705 for the amendment of the law.[3] The common law, though it allowed a plaintiff to state his whole complaint in his declaration, compelled the defendant to admit all the allegations except one, and to confine his defence to that one point. The object of this rule was to facilitate the reaching of a single issue; but it obviously worked great hardship, and was logically hardly justifiable. Crogate remarks in Hayes's Dialogue,[4] " I always supposed the object of justice was to get at the whole truth, but it seems that the special pleading way of doing justice is to shut out the truth upon all points but one "—a statement which Baron Surrebutter admitted was accurate. The result therefore was, as Crogate said, that "if a man tells a dozen lies against me anywhere else I may deny them all," but that this is not allowed in a court of justice. Baron Surrebutter then explained that the rule was founded historically on reasons of convenience—"nothing can be more convenient for judge and jury than to bring all causes, by the statements and counter-statements of the parties, to one plain intelligible point." "That," said Crogate, "might be all very well if people went to law for the convenience of the judges and juries, and not to get justice for themselves. If they have only one point in dispute, they don't want more than one tried; but if they dispute about several, it is a wicked injustice, that the law should refuse to try more than one."

It was probably for these somewhat obvious reasons that the law was changed in 1705; but the statute did not go to the root of the evil. In the first place, it only extended to pleas. It did not extend to replications and subsequent pleadings. The result was that "where several facts were comprised in a plea, the plaintiff

---

[1] Above 281-282.

[2] As Sir F. Pollock has said, Genius of the Common Law 34, " after the common fashion of English public business reforms were introduced piecemeal and without any settled plan, and so, while they lightened some of the most pressing grievances, they raised fresh difficulties almost at every turn."

[3] 4 Anne c. 16 § 4.   [4] App. I. (2) p. 424, 425.

was in many cases restricted to the denial of some one of them, and was obliged to admit the rest, although they might be untrue; and in no case could a plaintiff reply twofold matter of answer."[1] Thus all the old evils remained with respect to all the pleadings subsequent to the defendant's plea. In the second place, the law applied its old rules as to duplicity with the same rigidity to each of the different pleas allowed by the statute, as it had formerly applied them to the single plea permitted before the statute. "Though the statute," said the Common Law Procedure Commissioners in 1851,[2] "permitted several pleas, it did not alter the rule that each plea should state a single defence only. The result is, that captious objections of duplicity are sometimes made to pleadings; and, in the endeavour to avoid such objections, it occasionally happens that a necessary statement or denial is omitted, and the pleading for want of it is insufficient." Crogate's comment on this state of the law was very apposite.[3] "Well, Mr. Judge, this seems to me very like swallowing a camel and straining at a gnat. If the law can manage to swallow twenty separate pleas, it need not be very squeamish about a little of what you call *duplicity* in one of them. But, for the life of me, I can't conceive why, when a man is allowed to deny the whole case of the other side, and to set up any other answer he may have to it, he should not be allowed to do so, in the shortest and simplest manner, so as to make one story of it. Why really, Mr. Judge, it must be arrant nonsense to make a man split his case into I don't know how many different parts, in order to make what you call separate pleas of it; and there can be no reason for this, except to puzzle and create expense."

Neither of these measures therefore had succeeded in materially diminishing the evils of special pleading; and in some respects the latter of these two statutes had increased its complications. The same remark, as we shall now see, applies to some of the attempts at amelioration applied by the courts.

(ii) Two of these measures adopted by the courts will serve as illustrations—firstly, a greater liberality in amending pleadings, and, secondly, a device to evade the extreme precision of statement required in pleadings.

Firstly, we have seen that in the mediæval period a pleader was at liberty to amend the roll at any time in the same term as that in which he had pleaded; but that after the term the roll became a record, and (apart from the statutes of jeofail) no amendment was possible.[4] But, before the time of Blackstone,

---

[1] First Report of the Common Law Procedure Commissioners, Parlt. Papers 1851 xxii 19.
[2] Ibid.   [3] App. I. (2), p. 426.   [4] Vol. iii 643.

the courts had become more liberal, and "when justice required it would allow of amendments at any time while the suit is depending, notwithstanding the record be made up, and the term be past."[1]   This more liberal practice no doubt afforded some relief; but it was not liberal enough.   It in fact suffered from a similar, but opposite, defect to that from which the statutes of jeofail suffered.   We have seen that those statutes afforded no protection to a formal objection taken by special demurrer.[2]   Conversely, the power of amendment could not be exercised, in the case of some objections if they were taken after verdict, and in the case of others if they were taken after judgment.   It was possible, therefore, for a pleader, by passing over an objection, and by waiting to raise it, sometimes till after the verdict, and sometimes till after the judgment, to render nugatory the court's power to amend.   We have seen that the possibility of thus raising these objections, even at the last stage of the case, can be traced ultimately to the primitive rule that the judges were umpires, set to see that all the rules of law adjective and substantive were observed by the parties; and that, for that reason, they could not give judgment for the plaintiff, if the least defect occurred on the record, which set out the facts to which the law was to be applied.[3]   This particular consequence of this old idea was denounced as a great scandal by the Common Law Procedure Commissioners in 1851; and their statement shows very clearly how unfairly it was used:[4]   "For instance, through inadvertence a party omits a material averment in a declaration, as e.g. in an action against the drawer of a bill of exchange the averment of the notice of dishonour. The defendant observes the omission, but keeps his objection secret and pleads over. . . .   The cause is tried and a verdict found for the plaintiff, and the defendant then takes his objection by a motion in arrest of judgment.   The objection when taken at that stage is fatal, because no amendment is allowed after trial; whereas, if the defect had been pointed out at any earlier period, the omitted fact if capable of proof might have been supplied by amendment, and if it were not capable of proof the costs of the trial might have been saved.   But this is not the greatest evil. A plaintiff may have apparently passed the ordeal of all objections to his pleading, and have successfully opposed an application for a new trial which has delayed his judgment for a considerable period; when, on the eve of issuing execution, he may be met by a writ of error on a point which might have been raised by demurrer, or on motion in arrest of judgment, and which, though

[1] Comm. iii 406.　　　　　[2] Above 315.
[3] Above 278.　　　　　[4] Parlt. Papers 1851 xxii 52.

possibly a sound objection in point of law, would, if raised before, have been amended as a matter of course."

Secondly, we have seen that extreme precision of statement was required in all pleadings.[1] The parties must state in detail all matters affecting time, space, and quantity, and everything affecting the description of the subject matter of the litigation. But, as it was found impossible to tie the parties to the proof of all these minute statements, a compromise was arrived at, "whereby the theoretic principle of pleading was preserved while the go-by was given to it in practice."[2] This was to aver all these precise statements under a "*videlicet.*" The pleading was thereby made to look precise, but statements so made would be satisfied by the proof of details differing from those inserted under the *videlicet.* But even this expedient did not wholly meet the difficulty, because, if a plaintiff omitted to insert an essential fact under his *videlicet,* his declaration would be bad on special demurrer. The result was that the plaintiff was obliged to insert useless details under his *videlicet,* in order to prevent objections to his declaration, though he was not bound to prove a single one of the details so inserted. Thus, "if a plaintiff were to sue for wrongfully taking away his household furniture, without stating what sort of articles, or their number, or their value, his declaration would be objectionable on special demurrer; but if he were to insert a description including every sort of article, and stating them to be of any assignable number, and of any value, however extravagant, this, while it made his declaration valid, would in no respect oblige the plaintiff to prove the number or value alleged. Thus parties are compelled to make allegations which are useless, but the omission of which may be fatal."[3] It would seem, therefore, that this expedient to avoid the consequences of the rule as to precision of statement, greatly added to the length of the pleadings, without necessarily ensuring the attainment of the result which it was intended to produce.

(iii) I have already explained the nature of the general issue.[4] We have seen that the effect of this plea was to contradict generally the plaintiff's allegation, and to put a summary close to the pleadings. It was because it had this effect that it gave to litigants the most effectual relief from the risks to which the system of special pleading exposed them. It was the more efficacious because, from an early period, the courts held that a special plea, which only amounted to the general issue, was bad. In other words, they refused, as a general rule, to allow special pleading if the general issue would serve. This rule was well recognized in the Year

---

[1] Above 285, 297. [2] Parlt. Papers 1851 xxii 18.
[3] Ibid. [4] Above 270.

Books;[1] and it was maintained throughout the history of this branch of the law.[2] It is true that the rule was never inflexible. In the Middle Ages it was sometimes relaxed in order that the true state of the case might be brought to the notice of the jury;[3] it did not apply if the special plea disclosed matter in law;[4] and in other cases the court had a discretion.[5] But, subject to these modifications, there is no doubt that it was a rule which was generally adhered to. Possibly at the outset it was established because the court preferred to use the old formulæ.[6] In later times, it is true, it was sometimes justified and explained by saying that the use of a special plea, when the general issue was sufficient, would be a breach of the rule that a plea must not be multifarious or argumentative.[7] But probably Stephen is right, when he says that the real reason why the courts, from the days of the Year Books onwards, continued to favour the rule, was the fact that it prevented prolixity.[8] In 1436 Juyn, J., when pressed to admit a special plea which amounted to the general issue, said, " I will not say that we cannot enter the whole matter, but if we do so it will result in a great burdening of the Court; for if we do, it in this case we must do it in all others; and if we enter pleas in this fashion, we shall not have enough clerks in this place."[9] "The reason of pressing a general issue," it was said in 1616,[10] " is not for insufficiency of the plea, but not to make long records when there is no cause, which is matter of discretion."

We have seen that this rule sometimes gave rise to inconvenience; and that, with a view to allowing the parties to raise a question of law on the pleadings, when it would have been dangerous to leave the whole matter to the jury, the courts invented the device of express colour.[11] But the rule stood its ground;

---

[1] See e.g. Y.B. 10 Hy. VI. Mich. pl. 53—" En un breve de *trespass d'entre en son garren et ses leverets et conyngs pris* ove force et armes. *Chant.* Il n'ad nul tiel garren. *Prest. Newton.* Ces n'est pas ple. *Bab.* Votre ple n'est ple; car il amount a nient plus sinon Rien culp, car si n'ad pas garren vous n'estes pas culp. Purque respondez. *Chant. Rien culp; et alii e contra.*"

[2] See e.g. Lynner v. Wood (1630) Cro. Car. 157; Gifford v. Perkins (1676) 1 Sid. 450; Saunders' Case (1702) 12 Mod. 513-514.

[3] See Y.B. 11 Hy. IV. Hil. pl. 27 *per* Hankford, J.; note that it was said in Birch v. Wilson (1673) 2 Mod. at p. 277 that to allow a special plea when matter of law arose was " on the same reason as giving of colour "; we have seen, vol. iii 639, above 298-299, that the doctrine of colour originated in the desire to withdraw cases from the jury.

[4] Comyns, Digest, *Pleader* E. 14; Warner v. Wainsford (1616) Hob. 127; Birch v. Wilson (1673) 2 Mod. at pp. 276-277.

[5] Comyns, Digest, *Pleader* E. 14; Warner v. Wainsford (1616) Hob. 127.

[6] Above 285.

[7] Gifford v. Perkins (1676) 1 Sid. 450; Stephen, op. cit. 414.

[8] Op. cit. 414.   [9] Y.B. 14 Hy. VI. p. 23 pl. 67.

[10] Warner v. Wainsford Hob. 127.

[11] Above 298-299; thus in Saunders' Case (1702) 12 Mod. at p. 514 the Court said, " he should here either have pleaded the general issue or given colour to the plaintiff."

and, as we have seen, there was the less need to evade it by the doctrine of express colour, when a more effective control over the verdicts of juries was established.[1] Since the court had, as we have seen, a discretion as to when it would hold a special plea to be bad as amounting to the general issue, it was possible for the court either to enlarge or to restrict the scope of the rule; and, as the art of special pleading grew more complex, the tendency of the courts to use their discretion to insist on the use of the general issue whenever possible and to allow it more and more scope, became more pronounced.[2] This tendency was seconded by the Legislature. An Act of 1650 allowed the general issue to be pleaded in any case whatsoever;[3] and, though this sweeping change did not outlive the period of the Commonwealth, there are a number of statutes of the seventeenth and eighteenth centuries, which expressly allow the general issue to be pleaded in certain actions in which it would not otherwise have been applicable.[4]

The history of this tendency to favour the general issue, and the reasons for the larger scope given to it in the eighteenth century, are admirably summed up by Blackstone in the following passage:[5] "Formerly the general issue was seldom pleaded, except when the party meant wholly to deny the charge alleged against him. But when he meant to distinguish away or palliate the charge, it was always usual to set forth the particular facts in what is called a *special* plea; which was originally intended to apprize the court and the adverse party of the nature and cir-cumstances of the defence, and to keep the law and fact distinct. And it is an invariable rule, that every defence, which cannot be thus specially pleaded, may be given in evidence, upon the general issue at the trial. But, the science of special pleading, having been frequently perverted to the purposes of chicane and delay, the courts have of late in some instances, and the Legislature in many more, permitted the general issue to be pleaded, which leaves

---

[1] Above 302.

[2] Thus in Paramour v. Johnson (1701) 12 Mod. at p. 377 Holt, C.J., said, " it is indulgence to give accord with satisfaction in evidence upon *non assumpsit* pleaded; but that has crept in, and now is settled."

[3] Acts and Ordinances of the Interregnum (Firth and Rait) ii 443-444, an Act of Oct. 23, 1650; Shepherd also proposed that the general issue should be allowed in all personal and mixed actions, and that the defendant should give notice in writing " of the things he will stand upon at the tryal," England's Balme 75; for this book see vol. i 430, vol. vi 421-422.

[4] Thus by 21 James I. c. 12 § 5 the general issue was allowed to be pleaded in actions against certain officials; by 11 George I. c. 30 § 43 the Royal Exchange and London Assurance Companies were allowed to plead the general issue in actions against them on their policies; and it is stated in the Act that " by reason of the necessity of pleading specially in such cases the whole merit of the case in question cannot oftentimes come into consideration"; see Stephen, op. cit. (5th ed.) 189 n. (c); Bentham, Rationale of Judicial Evidence, Works vii 325-326.

[5] Comm. iii 305-306.

everything open, the fact, the law, and the equity of the case; and have allowed special matter to be given in evidence at the trial." That the large scope thus given to the general issue, was the best corrective to the defects of special pleading, was the opinion of Runnington, who said in 1820 that "nothing would more prevent 'the many miscarriages of causes,' or more promote the ends of justice, than to enact that the defendant shall in all actions, on giving previous notice of his intended defence to the plaintiff, be permitted to plead the general issue, and give the merits of his case in evidence."[1]   We shall appreciate the reasons for these views expressed by Blackstone and Runnington, and endorsed by the Legislature, if we look at the large scope given to the general issue in two of the commonest classes of actions brought before the courts—the action of assumpsit and the action on the case.

If the defendant in an action of assumpsit pleaded the general issue "non assumpsit," he put in issue, not only the question whether or not the promise had been made, but also any fact which tended to impeach the validity of the promise, and any matter of defence which showed that he was not liable; so that, though the words "non assumpsit" literally only traversed the promise, the fact, for instance, that the promise had been made and released could be given in evidence under this issue.[2] Similarly, the general issue "not guilty" in actions on the case was literally only a traverse of the facts alleged; but a defendant who pleaded it was allowed to prove any matter of defence tending to show that the plaintiff had no right of action.[3]   Likewise a defendant, who pleaded "not guilty" to an action of trespass *quare clausum fregit*, could deny both that the land was the plaintiff's, and that he had committed the trespass alleged, and could compel the plaintiff to prove both these facts.[4]   In fact, a defendant who pleaded the general issue, disputed, and therefore put the plaintiff to the proof of, every averment in the declaration. As Sir F. Pollock has said, a defendant who adopted this course "said in effect, 'I admit nothing and want to see what you can make of it.'"[5]   Obviously the adoption of this course, whenever possible, was the wisest plan to pursue; and it was generally adopted.   It was, says Runnington, "the uniform practice" in the action of ejectment, and in personal actions on mercantile contracts, such as insurances and bills of exchange; and it was very generally adopted in the action of assumpsit.[6]

It was perhaps not unnatural that the extended scope thus given to the general issue should have offended the scientific

---

[1] Hale, H.C.L. 212 n.
[2] Stephen, op. cit. (1st ed.) 179-181.
[3] Ibid 182-183.
[4] Ibid 278.
[5] Genius of the Common Law 37.
[6] Hale, H.C.L. 212 n.

pleader. We have seen that Stephen's work on the principles of pleading, coming as it did at the close of a long period in which the rules of the art had been logically developed by the courts, had done more than any other work to demonstrate the scientific character of its principal rules.[1]   Though he admits that the system of special pleading had its defects, the whole tendency of his work is to minimize them, and to insist on its strong points, as compared with the methods adopted by other systems of law to bring cases before the courts.[2]   He is inclined to reserve his severest animadversions for pleas like the general issue, which did not conform to the principles of the science, and restricted its scope.[3]   Nor was it difficult to make a plausible case against the extended scope which had been given to the general issue ; for, though it was by far the most efficacious remedy for the evils of the system of special pleading, it had its defects—defects which had been emphasized by Brougham in his great speech on the state of the courts of law in 1828.[4]   The issue was not clearly defined. Issues of fact were not distinguished from issues of law ; and the parties did not know exactly what were the issues of fact upon which the case really turned.   It followed from this that the parties incurred expense by reason of the "unnecessary accumulation of proof"—often of facts which turned out at the trial to be undisputed.   Moreover, the questions of law which arose were not argued, as they would have been argued on demurrer, before the court *in banc*, but before a single judge at nisi prius, who had no previous intimation of the point, and no adequate opportunity to refer to the authorities.   Hence applications for new trials were multiplied.[5]   Bentham epigrammatically summed up the situation when he said,[6] "general pleading [by which he meant the general issue] conveys no information, but there is an end to it: if any information is conveyed by pleading, it is by special pleading, but there is no end to it."   That is the gist of

---

[1] Above 312.   [2] See especially his concluding chapter.

[3] Thus, op. cit. 181, speaking of the extension given to the plea of "non assumpsit," he points out that the effect is that "in an action which has become of all others the most frequent and general in its application, the science of pleading has been in a great measure superseded by an innovation of practice, which enables the parties to come to issue before the plea (the second step in the series of allegations) in a great variety of cases, which would formerly have led to much remoter or more specific issues."

[4] Hansard xviii 201—"in the indebitatus assumpsit the general issue is non assumpsit. Now under that plea no less than eight different defences may be set up ; as, for instance, a denial of the contract, payment, usury, gaming, infancy, accord and satisfaction, release, and coverture. All these defences are entirely different, and yet they are all stated in the selfsame words."

[5] This is in effect a short summary of the Second Report of the Commissioners on Courts of Common Law, Parlt. Papers 1830 xi 45 seqq. ; this part of the report is also printed in Stephen, Pleading (5th ed.) lix-lxvi.

[6] Rationale of Judicial Evidence, Works vii 274.

the matter. The general issue did ensure that the case came at once before the court, and that it was tried on the merits; and that was an advantage which, by comparison with the system of special pleading, outweighed all its defects. What Stephen and other lawyers of his day did not see, and what perhaps they could not be expected to see, was that the defects of the general issue were small in comparison with the enormous risk that, in cases where the parties specially pleaded, the action would be decided without any reference to the substantial merits of the case, and that the proceedings might be unduly prolonged by objections and appeals on mere matters of form. They had not realized the truth pointed out by Bentham that the extended permission to use the general issue given by the Legislature, and the fact that litigants always availed themselves of this permission, were so many recognitions of the fact that "the practice of special pleading was a nuisance." [1]

Unfortunately the views of Stephen, which were backed up by a large body of professional opinion, had a large and a disastrous effect upon the development of the law of pleading. He was one of the Commissioners appointed to consider the practice and procedure of the courts of common law; and it is clear from their Second Report issued in 1830, that he and those who thought with him had brought round his fellow Commissioners to his views on the subject of special pleading. In that report the defects of the system of special pleading are minimized,[2] and the evil results which flowed from the extended scope allowed to the general issue are exaggerated. The recommendations of the Commissioners on the subject of pleading were left to the judges to carry out; and they were directed by the Legislature to make and submit to Parliament what alterations they saw fit.[3] The judges, with the acquiescence of Parliament, adopted the recommendations of the Commissioners; and a principal effect of their new Regulæ Generales of the Hilary term 1834 was to restrict drastically the

---

[1] "So many hundred times as the Legislature gives this authority, so many hundred times has it recognized the practice of special pleading to be a nuisance: so many times as professional lawyers . . . have concurred in giving to their clients the benefit of this authority, so many times have they, by their conduct and deportment, subjoined their attestation to the same unquestionable and important truth," Rationale of Judicial Evidence, Works vii 326.

[2] "We conceive that considerable misapprehension popularly prevails upon the subject of *special pleading*. That system was characterized no doubt, at former periods of our legal history, by a tendency to prolix and tautologous allegation, an excessive subtlety, and an overstrained observance of form; and notwithstanding material modern improvements, it still exhibits too much of the same qualities. These its disadvantages are prominent and well understood; its recommendations are, perhaps, less obvious, but when explained, cannot fail to be recognized as of far superior weight," Parlt. Papers 1830 xi 45.

[3] 3, 4 William IV. c. 42 § 1; Stephen, op. cit. Pref. to the 4th ed.

scope of the general issue.[1] For instance, the plea of "non assumpsit" was for the future to operate only as a denial of the
promise; so that, "in an action on a warranty, the plea will
operate as a denial of the fact of the warranty having been given
on the alleged consideration, but not of the breach; and in an
action on a policy of insurance, of the subscription to the alleged
policy by the defendant, but not of the interest, of the commencement of the risk, of the loss, or of the alleged compliance with
warranties." In actions on bills of exchange and promissory
notes the plea of "non assumpsit" was wholly excluded. In all
actions of assumpsit matters showing that the transaction had been
discharged, or was void or voidable—e.g. fraud, infancy, coverture,
release, payment, performance, illegality—must be specially
pleaded. The plea of "nil debet" was abolished. In actions
on the case the plea of "not guilty" was to operate as a denial
only of the breach of duty or wrongful act alleged, and all other
pleas in denial must be specially pleaded. Thus, in an action on
the case for obstructing a right of way, the general issue only
denied the obstruction, and not the plaintiff's right of way; and
in an action for conversion it denied the conversion only, and not
the plaintiff's title to the goods. In trespass *quare clausum fregit*
the plea of not guilty only operated to deny that the trespass had
been committed in the place mentioned, and not that the plaintiff
was in possession, or had a right to possess that place—if it was
wished to deny these facts there must be a special traverse.

The Commissioners in 1830 admitted that there might be some
objection to this extension of the system of special pleading, and
anticipated some difficulties as to the settlement of the proper
forms of pleas. But they considered that "the principles of the
science of pleading have been so successfully cultivated, and are
at the present day so well understood, that the extent of such
embarrassment would probably be small, and we should expect
the whole law on this subject to be permanently settled within
a short period, and at the expense of a few adjudged cases."[2]
That was in effect the view of Stephen; and never was a more
disastrous mistake made. "Under the common law system the
matter was bad enough with a pleading question decided in every
sixth case. But under the Hilary rules it was worse. Every
fourth case decided a question on the pleadings. Pleading ran
riot."[3] The broad effect of the new rules were, as may be seen
from the report of the Common Law Procedure Commissioners

---

[1] Those of the rules which deal with this matter will be found in Stephen, op. cit.
(5th ed.) lv-lix.

[2] Parlt. Papers 1830 xi 51.

[3] C. B. Whittier, Notice Pleading, H.L.R. xxxi 507—this conclusion is reached
after an examination of selected volumes of law reports from 1830 and 1846.

in 1851,[1] pretty accurately summed up in the following passage in Hayes's Dialogue:[2] "*Crogate*. Oh! you've been making new rules about pleading have you; then, I suppose, as a matter of course, that you've pretty nearly done away with the whole thing. *Surrebutter, B.* Done away with special pleading? Heaven forbid! On the contrary, we adopted it (subject to the relaxation introduced by the Statute of Anne) in even more than its original integrity; for we have enforced the necessity of special pleas in many actions in which the whole case was previously left at large, on the merits, under the general issue. And we framed a series of rules on the subject, which have given a truly magnificent development to this admirable system; so much so, indeed, that nearly half the cases coming recently before the Court, have been decided upon points of pleading. *Crogate.* You astonish me. But pray how do the suitors like this sort of justice? *Surrebutter, B.* Mr. Crogate that consideration has never occurred to me, nor do I conceive that laws ought to be adapted to suit the tastes and capacities of the ignorant.[3] At first, to be sure, we found that in consequence of our having restored the ancient strictness of pleading, when it had been relaxed, and applied it to several of the most common forms of action to which it had never previously been applied, plaintiffs were put into considerable perplexity by special pleas. If they denied too much a demurrer for duplicity followed; and if they only denied one point, and consequently admitted the rest, they sometimes traversed the only allegation which could be proved, or, to use your language, they took the wrong sow by the ear. In this state of things, though justice was by no means uniformly defeated, yet this result took place more frequently than was convenient, and some obloquy was beginning to attach on the New Rules. In this emergency, Mr. Crogate, we fell back on the replication *de injuria* with the happiest success. . . . And thus we were enabled to bring the system of pleading as near to perfection as I believe to be possible."[4] Very few persons will be found to question the

---

[1] Parlt. Papers 1851 xxii 20.   [2] App. I. (2) p. 427.

[3] This sentiment put into the mouth of Baron Surrebutter may seem extravagant; but that it is not can be seen from the view expressed by Lord Redesdale in his tract on the Chancery Commission of 1826: "whoever," he said, "considers the administration of justice by courts of civil jurisdiction of any description with a view only to the personal interests of the parties engaged in litigation, has taken a very imperfect view of the subject. In very few cases comparatively ought the parties litigating to be considered as the only persons interested in the result," Parkes, Chancery 520, citing The Times, Aug. 31, 1826.

[4] Compare this with the finding of the Common Law Procedure Commissioners: "So long as in the three principal kind of actions, viz.: assumpsit, debt on simple contract, and trespass on the case (which constitute a very large majority indeed of all the actions which are brought), it was competent for the defendant to raise almost all defences under the old plea of the general issue, the evil was not so much felt. . . . But when the new rules compelled the use of special pleas in these actions, the technical

justice of the judgments of Radamanthus against Surrebutter, B.,
or Edmund Saunders, though they may sympathize with the
astonishment of those eminent pleaders at the neglect which those
judgments showed of the most elementary rules of pleading.[1]

Nearly a hundred years before Hayes's Dialogue was written,
Blackstone had said that, though it might have been supposed
that "confusion and uncertainty" would follow from the greatly
extended scope allowed to the general issue, experience had shown
it to be otherwise."[2] Baron Surrebutter admitted that in his day
such was the popularity of the new county courts, in which no
special pleadings were allowed, that suitors were anxious to have
their cases tried there whenever possible—"and it remains to be
seen whether the effect will not be to transfer to them the great
bulk of the civil business of the country, and to leave the superior
courts without employment; a result which will be obviously fatal
to the law of England." The moral was, as Crogate said, that
special pleading should be eliminated also in the superior courts.[3]
Something was done in this direction by the Common Law
Procedure Acts. But it was not till the advent of the new
procedure introduced by the Judicature Acts, that the old system
disappeared, and was replaced by the modern system under which
litigation is now conducted.

(4) *The effects of this system of pleading on the development of
the common law.*

A history of special pleading necessarily stresses the unhappy
results following from the accumulated technicalities which it had
gathered about it during its long and varied development. It
had long been a burdensome anachronism; and when, after the
passing of the Judicature Acts, it was replaced by the modern
system, its technical rules and technical phraseology speedily
passed into an oblivion as complete as that which overtook the

and formal defects of the system . . . became extended to all (actions), and the
inconvenience was increased in proportion. Special demurrers for want of form, and
for objections of a technical nature, were much increased. From the necessity of
specially pleading all defences to actions in most general use, new pleas were introduced; and defendants who had no real defence availed themselves of a chance of a
temporary success, by pleading subtle and tricky pleas to invite special demurrers for
the mere purpose of delay," Parlt. Papers 1851 xxii 20; in fact the replication *de
injuria*, as used after the New Rules, was in itself a condemnation of those Rules; the
objection to it taken in Crogate's Case, based on multiplicity (above 292 n. 7), was
almost abandoned, see W. T. Kime, Replication de Injuria 59-60; so that it was
made to perform somewhat the same service as the general issue—thereby, as Surrebutter said, mitigating some of the harsh results of the New Rules.
 [1] App. I. (2) pp. 418, 419.
 [2] "And though it would seem as if much confusion and uncertainty would follow
from so great a relaxation of the strictness anciently observed, yet experience has
shown it to be otherwise; especially with the aid of a new trial, in case either party
be unfairly surprised by the other," Comm. iii 306.
 [3] App. I. (2) p. 429.

technical rules and phraseology which had centred round the real actions. But it is well to remember that the main principles which underlay the art of special pleading were sound and sensible —as Lord Mansfield said they were founded in strong sense, and were developed by the soundest and closest logic.[1] It is therefore not surprising to find that these principles still exercise a very considerable influence on our modern system of pleading; and that they have had effects on the general development of the common law, which may not be so apparent, but which are none the less real. Let us examine their effect under these two heads.

(i) Our modern system of pleading, like the older system, still aims at the production of an issue by the allegations of the parties to the action.[2] This, as Stephen pointed out, was the feature of the common law system of pleading which distinguished it from all other systems.[3] And, as the general object of the modern system is the same, and as it is still secured by the alternate allegations of the parties, it follows that many of its principal rules are in substance the same. They appear, indeed, in a changed form. The old names are gone, and, with the old names, the technical subleties which clung round these names. And over these rules the court has far larger powers. They are not rigid rules which the parties can appeal to, and the court must enforce, regardless of the merits of the case. "Law has ceased to be a scientific game, that may be won or lost by playing some particular move."[4] For all that, many of the rules which the modern pleader must obey, are in essence the same as under the older system; and many of the older cases, which illustrate these principles, are still the best guides to correct pleading.[5] One or two illustrations from Dr. Blake Odgers' well-known work on pleading will make this clear.

---

[1] Above 312.

[2] "The whole object of pleadings is to bring the parties to an issue; and the meaning of the rules of Order XIX. was to prevent the issue being enlarged, which would prevent either party from knowing, when the cause came on for trial, what the real point to be discussed and decided was. In fact the whole meaning of the system is to narrow the parties to definite issues, and thereby to diminish expense and delay, especially as regards the amount of testimony required on either side at the hearing," Thorp v. Holdsworth (1876) 3 C.D. at p. 639 *per* Jessel, M.R.

[3] See the passage cited vol. iii 627-628.

[4] Bowen, Administration of the Law in the Reign of Victoria, cited vol. i 647; Mr. Whittier, H.L.R., xxxi 507, after an examination of recent reports, says, "What a successful reform the Judicature Acts were! In only one case in seventy-six can a pleading point be found. Reversals on questions of pleadings drop from one in forty-four under the common law, and one in thirty-three under the Hilary Rules, to one in six hundred and five: one reversal in all the cases under the Judicature Acts which were examined."

[5] "So long as written pleadings remain, the best masters of the art will be they who can inform the apparent licence of the new system with that spirit of exactness and self-restraint which flows from a knowledge of the old," Address of Montague Crackanthorpe to the American Bar. Ass. 1896, cited Essays A.A.L.H. ii 681.

The different possible courses open to the litigant are the same as under the old system.   He may either traverse, confess and avoid, or demur—though a demurrer is not now called a demurrer, but an objection in point of law.[1]   But a litigant can no longer hang up the trial of the action by taking such an objection ; [2] and special demurrers on points of form were abolished by the Common Law Procedure Act of 1852.[3]   Similarly, the rules that the parties must plead material facts,[4] that they must not plead evidence,[5] that a traverse must not be too wide or too narrow,[6] that a negative pregnant is bad because it is evasive,[7] that there must be no departure in pleading,[8] are all essentially the same as under the older system.   And though there is now no such plea as a plea " puis darrein continuance," [9] or a " new assignment," [10] under those names, the things themselves are recognized under other names ; for matters of defence which have arisen after a defence has been delivered may be subsequently pleaded,[11] and matters formerly alleged by new assignment can be introduced by an amendment of the statement of claim or by way of reply.[12]

Thus many of the fundamental principles of the modern system of pleading are the same as those of the older system.   But they differ in two important respects.   In the first place, the parties must plead the facts on which they intend to rely, and not legal conclusions which they put upon those facts.   No such plea as the general issue is now possible.[13]   In the second place, the enforcement of this rule has been made possible by the very different manner in which the rules of pleading are enforced and applied. In fact, it is the manner in which these principles are enforced and applied that is so utterly different from the older system, that, at first sight, there seems to be little in common between them. Let us look at one or two illustrations : the abolition of forms of action has necessarily entailed the disappearance of all the fine distinctions between the pleas applicable to different classes of actions.[14]   The parties are not bound to elect between a traverse, a plea in confession and avoidance, or an objection in point of law.[15] They are not bound to put their pleadings in any particular shape, provided that they contain a clear and concise relation of the

---

[1] Odgers, op. cit. (4th ed.) 137-138.   [2] Ibid 138 n.
[3] 15, 16 Victoria c. 76 § 51—" No pleading shall be deemed insufficient for any defect which could heretofore only be objected to by special demurrer."
[4] Odgers, op. cit. 87; that is, material at the present stage of the action—there is no need to anticipate the answer of the other side, for that, as Hale, C. J., said in Bovey's Case (1678) 1 Vent. 217, is like leaping before one comes to the stile, ibid 93.
[5] Ibid 103, citing Dowman's Case (1584) 9 Co. Rep. at f. 9b.
[6] Ibid 153-156.   [7] Ibid 156-157.   [8] Ibid 239-240.
[9] Above 273.   [10] Above 273-274.
[11] Odgers, op. cit. 223-224.   [12] Ibid 243-245.   [13] Ibid 81.
[14] Above 309-310.   [15] Odgers, op. cit. 138-139.

material facts necessary to decide the particular case.[1] But they must state all these facts clearly—no vague pleas, such as the general issue, which merely stated in a short form a conclusion of law—are permissible.[2] And now that the rules of pleading have been rationalized, now that liberal powers of amendment have been given to the court, now that all courts have power to enforce discovery, and to compel the parties to disclose further particulars of matters stated in the pleadings—this exclusion of the general issue works no hardship.

These changes have effected the object with which they were introduced; for they have enabled the courts to realize that "the relation of rules of practice to the work of justice should be that of handmaid rather than mistress"; and that the court ought not to be so tied by its procedural rules "as to do what will cause injustice in the particular case."[3] That many of the basic principles of the common law system of pleading, should thus have been transplanted into the new informal system, which was introduced by the Judicature Acts, is the highest testimony to the technical skill of the judges who made the Rules of the Supreme Court, which have carried out the intentions of the framers of these Acts.

(ii) Of the more general effects upon the development of the common law of this system of special pleading, by means of written pleadings delivered out of court, I have already said something. I have shown that it had extensive effects upon the mechanism of legal institutions, upon the manner of reporting cases, and upon the law.[4] But, necessarily, at an earlier stage of this history I could only indicate these effects in a summary way. Now that we have examined in some detail the later history of this system, it is possible to state more precisely its effects upon the development of the law. Its influence can be seen in three main directions. Firstly, it had a principal share in introducing

---

[1] Odgers, op. cit. 167; as Cotton, L.J., said in Phillips v. Phillips (1878) 4 Q.B.D. at p. 139, "What particulars are to be stated must depend on the facts of each case. But in my opinion it is absolutely essential that the pleading, not to be embarrassing to the defendants, should state those facts which will put the defendants on their guard, and tell them what they have to meet when the case comes on for trial."

[2] "A variety of matters are set forth in the statement of claim shewing the plaintiff's cause of action, namely, that the agreement was made, that it was in writing, and that it was made by an agent properly authorized. Under the old common law system of pleading all these matters . . . might have been put in issue by pleading the general issue. . . . But that system of pleading, while it tended to raise clear issues, had the disadvantage that the plaintiffs had no means of knowing what the point to be tried was. The new rules were expressly framed to prevent that, and to make the defendant take matter by matter and traverse each of them separately," Byrd v. Nunn (1877) 7 C.D. at p. 287 per Thesiger, L.J.

[3] In re Coles and Ravenshaw [1907] 1 K.B. at p. 4 per Colins, M.R., cited vol. i 647.

[4] Vol. iii 653-656.

our modern view as to the binding force of decided cases, and it ensured the success of this method of developing the law. Secondly, it has helped the lawyers to build up logical and coherent bodies of doctrine on the foundation of the forms of action. Thirdly, the searching technical training which it imposed, gave to the best lawyers a very complete mastery of the principles of the common law, to which was due in no small degree the success with which they have from age to age developed and adapted them to the needs of the age. These are large claims; but I think that a short examination will show that they can be substantiated.

Firstly, we have seen that it was in the sixteenth century that the modern theory as to the binding force of decided cases grew up.[1] Though at an earlier period very considerable respect was paid to the decisions of the courts, it was hardly possible to treat reports of the arguments which led to the formulation of an issue, in the same way as reports of decisions upon an issue which the parties had formulated before they got into court. The system under which the parties exchanged written pleadings, and formulated the issue for the decision of the court, changed the whole character of the proceedings in court, and therefore the character of the report. The reporters could report, not arguments leading to the formulation of an issue, but a decision upon an issue already formulated. It therefore became possible to cite a case for a definite ruling upon a definite point of law.[2] And, as this system of pleading ensured that the precise issue upon which this ruling was founded was before the court, it became possible to distinguish accurately between the authoritative ruling and the obiter dictum. Each decided case could thus be regarded as an authority for the decision on the issue developed by the pleadings. Mere speculation on matters not in issue could be eliminated.

This tended to keep the law in touch with the needs of practical life—the decisions which were given were decisions on facts which had actually occurred. Moreover, this system of pleading tended to ensure that the decisions so given should harmonize with the doctrines which had been laid down in previous decisions. A pleader who was ignorant or forgetful of these doctrines, soon found that his opponent would call the attention of the court to the fact that the statements in his pleadings led to consequences, which failed to substantiate the defence which he was trying to make. Thus, if a defendant wished to maintain that the deed on which he was being sued was void ab initio, he must conclude his plea with the allegation "non est factum." If, instead, he concluded it by praying judgment "si actio," i.e.

---

[1] Vol. v 372-373.   [2] Vol. iii 654.

whether there was any right of action on it, the plea was bad, because such a plea would only be maintained if it could be proved that the deed was originally good, but had been avoided by matter ex post facto, such as a release.[1]   A sheriff's officer, who was sued for assaulting beating and wounding a prisoner whom he was directed to arrest, must plead the justification of his warrant for the assault, and not guilty as to the beating and wounding; because the warrant would not justify these acts except in self-defence, or in resisting an attempt to escape—matters which could be given in evidence under the plea of not guilty.[2]   It follows, therefore, that a pleader who forgot these rules of law, and merely pleaded the justification of the warrant, would certainly fail. Similarly, a pleader who alleged that the defendant, having received money of the plaintiff by the hands of the plaintiff's wife, had promised to pay and had failed to do so, "ad damna eorum," was non-suited, because the wife "cannot have goods with her husband."[3]

Thus, whether we look at the precision with which the issue was formulated for the decision of the court, or at the manner in which the legal effects of the statements in the pleadings were criticized, we can see that this system of pleading ensured a decision on a definite problem in accordance with ascertained principles.   The science of pleading, by ensuring the elimination of immaterial facts, and of cases in which the pleaders were, on their own showing, clearly unable to substantiate their pleas, caused the decision of each case to partake of the nature of a scientific inquiry into a carefully isolated phenomenon.   And there can be no doubt that the rules against duplicity, which, as we have seen, worked so great hardship to suitors,[4] helped to ensure the success of this method of developing law by decided cases; for it tied down the court to the solution of a simple problem, and prevented it from wandering too widely over different fields of law. It made the development of the law slow, but it made it sure, because it made it the easier to ensure the logical dependence of each decision upon preceding decisions; and, if it was a case of first impression, it made it easier to envisage the relation of the different solutions proposed by the parties, both to the ascertained doctrines governing the particular branch of the law, and to public policy.   It is worthy of note that the strictness of pleading, which was the result of the restriction of the liberty to plead the general issue made by the Rules of 1834, was followed by an increased attention to the scope of and distinctions between the forms of

[1] Dive v. Manningham (1551) Plowden at p. 66.
[2] Note to Greene v. Jones (1669) 1 Wms.' Saunders 296.
[3] Abbot v. Blofield (1623) Cro. Jac. 644.   [4] Above 316-317.

action, which the rationalism of the eighteenth century had tended to obscure. The most conspicuous effect of this influence can be seen in the history of the doctrine of consideration in the nineteenth century.[1] It can also be seen in the modern development of the distinctions between trover and trespass,[2] and in the judgment of the majority of the court of Appeal in *Phillips v. Homfray*.[3] But of this effect I must speak further under the succeeding head—the influence of this system of pleading upon the evolution of the doctrines of the common law.

Secondly, if a systematic body of doctrine is to be evolved from the decision of isolated cases, there must be some principle or principles of division to settle the category under which a particular rule must be grouped. Such principles of division are in fact necessary to the orderly development of any body of knowledge. These principles of division will, of course, differ as a legal system develops; but it is generally true to say that in a primitive system they will be dictated by the law of actions. In the common law it was the differences between the forms of action which contained the main principles of division. Right down to the end of the system of special pleading the plaintiff must choose his form of action, and his choice determined many of the pleading rules which he must obey. Other differences between these forms of action tended to disappear; but the pleading differences remained.[4] Now it seems to me that the rule that a case must be brought within one or other of these categories was no small help, in an early stage of legal development, to the construction of an orderly body of rules on the basis of decided cases. Just as the pleading rules against duplicity tied down the court to the decision of a precise point, and prevented discursive ramblings over large fields of law, so the rule that the action must fall within a definite category brought the case under its appropriate heading in the legal system. In that way it was the more possible to develop logically separate bodies of principle. It is true that the time came when the principles so developed could no longer be confined within the strait limits of the forms of action. The working of these actions had developed the substantive law, and had given rise to bodies of principles which demanded a freer development, and a restatement from the new point of view of the contents of the principles themselves, and not from the old point of view of the remedies by which they were enforced. It is true that the recognition of this fact was too long delayed by the unfortunate

---

[1] Vol. viii 38-42.   [2] Vol. vii 420.

[3] (1883) 24 C.D. 439; vol. iii 582; see a paper by the author in Cambridge Law Journal i 273-278.

[4] Above 252 n. 1, 311 n. 4.

prolongation of the life of the strict system of special pleading. But let us not forget that, in an earlier stage in the history of the law, this division into somewhat arbitrary categories had its uses, in helping the common law to develop a logical set of principles by decided cases.   Moreover, it is well to remember that it has left its permanent traces on our modern law.   "The forms of action," says Sir F. Pollock,[1] "were only the marks and appointed trappings of causes of action; and to maintain an action there must still be some cause of action known to the law. . . . The question, therefore, whether any cause of action is raised by given facts is as important as ever it was."   That the traces are still so distinct is, it seems to me, due in no small measure to the long life of this system of pleading.

Thirdly, though in its last days this system of pleading suffered from a diseased technicality, though throughout its history it gave too small an opportunity for bringing before the court the substantial merits of the case, it cannot be denied that it helped to train accomplished lawyers.   Any lawyer, who had become a good special pleader, was bound to have an accurate acquaintance with the rules of law, and a power of very exact statement.   It is true that some of these pleaders never rose above the pleader's point of view, and regarded the maintenance of the rules of correct pleading as an end in itself.   But, when a man with great capacity had been thus trained, it gave him a technical mastery of his subject, which enabled him to deal with broad questions of principle in a manner which ensured the logical development of the common law.   Sir F. Pollock has said of Baron Parke, who was the original of Baron Surrebutter in Hayes's Dialogue, that, "when there was not any point of pleading before the court, no man could handle matters of principle with greater clearness or broader common sense."[2]   And it is clear that the same thing can be said of such great lawyers as Coke and Hale and Holt, all of whom graduated in the strict school of special pleading, and all of whom showed remarkable capacity for adapting old rules to new uses.   In fact, if we look at such episodes in our legal history as the development of an original theory of contract by gradual extensions of the action of assumpsit, and the creation of a flexible set of principles of civil liability by the application of the actions on the case, it is clear that the common law owes much to the strict technical training which its system of pleading imposed on all who studied and practised it.   What its weak points and its bad points were I have already explained in some detail.   Its strong points still live, not only in our modern system of pleading, but also in

---

[1] Torts (12th ed.) 540.   [2] Genius of the Common Law 28.

the principles and rules of the common law itself; for, as I said in an earlier volume, it was under its regime that these principles and rules were developed. It is therefore true to say that, "until the whole system of English law shall be recast and codified," some acquaintance with the old learning "will be indispensable to all who wish to be sound common lawyers"; since, "without it a great deal of quite recent authority will remain obscure, and, the old books in a great measure unintelligible."[1]

§ 3. Equity Procedure and Pleading

We have seen that, by the end of the seventeenth century, the principles of equity had begun to develop into a fixed system.[2] But this development had only just begun; and it was not till the following century that this process was completed. Equity, however, was no exception to the general rule that the adjective part of the law is developed before the substantive. It is significant that Blackstone found that the most essential difference between law and equity consisted in the different modes in which they administered justice—"in the mode of proof, the mode of trial and the mode of relief."[3] It is therefore possible to relate the history of equity procedure at this point, because this procedure had attained substantially its final form at the end of this period. And this course is desirable for two reasons: In the first place, it will help us to understand the history of the development of the principles of equity which will be related in the following Book of this History. In the second place, it will enable us to compare and contrast it with the system of common law procedure which has just been described; and so to get a clearer idea of the manner in which it has influenced our modern code of procedure which was introduced by the Judicature Acts.

These two systems of procedure differed firstly in respect of their historical antecedents, and secondly in their fundamental principles. Firstly, while the common law system was a purely native development, the equity system owed much to that summary procedure, which the mediæval canon lawyers were developing and applying to mercantile transactions.[4] Secondly, the two fundamental differences in principle, which determined the very different form taken by these two procedures, turned firstly upon the different machinery by means of which the plaintiff brought his case before the court, and secondly upon the different objects aimed at by the rules of pleading—by the rules, that is, which prescribed the manner in which the parties must state their respective cases. We

---

[1] Address of Montague Crackanthorpe to the American Bar. Ass. 1896, cited Essays A.A.L.H. ii 681.
[2] Vol. vi 640-671.　　　[3] Comm. iii 436.　　　[4] Vol. v 81-83.

have seen that under the common law procedure a plaintiff must choose some one of the forms of action, and that the procedural rules which he must obey were determined largely by his choice. Under the equity procedure, on the other hand, the procedure was generally by bill and answer, and uniform for all sorts of cases.[1] We have seen that the common law rules of pleading aimed at the production of an issue by the mutual allegations of the parties. In equity, on the other hand, the rules of pleading aimed, not at the production of an issue, but at getting all the facts before the court in so complete a fashion that the court could do complete justice to the parties.[2]

The differences in the character of the relief sought by plaintiffs in equity, necessarily entailed many differences between the rules of procedure governing an action at law, and those governing a suit in equity. But the systems of pleading prevailing in the two jurisdictions, though fundamentally divergent, were never completely distinct. In the mediæval period the system of equity pleading was very informal;[3] it was modelled, not upon the elaborate solemn procedure of the Roman civil and canon laws,[4] but upon the summary procedure recognized by those laws;[5] and the counsel who practised before the chancellor were common lawyers.[6] Thus, although the chancellors set their faces against the importation into the chancery of the technical formalities of the common law system of pleading, though in equity mistakes in pleading never had the same fatal effect as at common law, some of the ideas and technical terms of the common law were received. Equity knew such pleas as demurrers, replications, and rejoinders; and it sometimes adopted common law rules as to the manner in which these pleas should be drawn.[7] And so, when the fusion of jurisdiction came with the Judicature Acts, it was possible to create a more uniform system of pleading than of procedure.[8] As in the preceding section, therefore, I shall deal separately with procedure and pleading.

Procedure

We have seen that in the fifteenth century the procedure of the court of Chancery was simple and speedy. The plaintiff sent in his bill, which was quite untechnical in its form, and sometimes even illiterate. When the defendant appeared, he must answer

---

[1] For certain exceptional cases where the procedure was otherwise see below 343 n 6.

[2] Below 338, 369 373. [3] Below 337; vol. v 285-286.

[4] For a good short account of this system see Langdell, Equity Pleading, Essays, A.A.L.H. ii 753-764.

[5] Vol. v 81-83. [6] Vol. iv 277.

[7] Below 378, 382-383, 387, 390-392, 405. [8] Below 347-348, 407.

the complaint. Both the defendant and the plaintiff, and any witnesses which they might produce, were examined by the chancellor or other person deputed by him. It is true that certain pleas were open to a defendant who wished to avoid giving an answer on the merits. He might, for instance, plead that the proper parties had not been joined, or he might demur to the bill. But we have seen that the chancellor refused to give effect to the technical rules of special pleading; and we shall see that a decision on a demurrer or a plea did not put a final end to the case. If it was determined against the defendant he must answer on the merits. If it was determined against the plaintiff it generally only meant that he would be obliged to supply the defect by amending his bill.[1]

This procedure, used by the ecclesiastical chancellors of the Middle Ages, was necessarily influenced by the summary procedure of the canon law;[2] and that summary procedure was, to some extent, influenced by the solemn procedure of the civil law. Moreover, in the Middle Ages and later, some of the masters were civilians;[3] so that procedural rules and ideas, drawn from the Roman civil and canon law, have had some influence in shaping the later equitable procedure. Thus the idea that witnesses should be examined privately and by an official of the court, and that their evidence should be reduced to writing and not divulged till published;[4] the idea, which prevailed in the sixteenth and early seventeenth centuries, that, after publication, fresh evidence could be given to inform the conscience of the court;[5] the idea that all the steps in the cause were under the superintendence of the officials of the court, who must record them, and from whom the parties must take office copies;[6] the position and duties of the Registrar in relation to the drawing up of decrees;[7]—all show signs of these influences. Then, too, we shall see that the system of pleading in equity by bill, and by an answer to which the defendant

---

[1] Vol. v 285-286; below 383, 392, 405.   [2] Essays, A.A.L.H. ii 776.

[3] Vol. i 417; vol. v 257-259, 261.

[4] Below 354-356; vol. v 174-175, 180-184; see Essays, A.A.L.H. ii 762-764 for the practice of the civilians, and ibid pp. 768-769, 772 for the practice in the ecclesiastical courts.

[5] Spence, i 380-381, says, "a strange practice which then (i.e. in the sixteenth and early seventeenth centuries) prevailed of examining witnesses to inform the conscience of the judge only, deserves particular notice. The depositions taken for this especial purpose were delivered to the judge, sealed up. In some cases these depositions were taken by consent of both parties. Sometimes the witnesses were examined for this purpose after publication of the regular depositions"; the practice which Spence found strange was also the practice of the Star Chamber, vol. v 183, and was derived from the continental procedure, vol. iv 278 n. 2; see below 354.

[6] Essays, A.A.L.H. ii 773-774, 775 n. 1; as Langdell says, the pleadings were less under the control of the court in the Chancery procedure, and the system was more like that of the common law; but I think we can see the influence of the continental system in the supervision of the officers of the court, below 369-370, which gave rise to the abuse of office copies, vol. i 426-427, 441-442.

[7] Essays, A.A.L.H. ii 775 n. 1; below 366-368.

was sworn,[1] and the other rules of pleading,[2] had affinities with the continental system, in which the "mutual allegations are allowed to be made at large—that is, with no view to the exposition of the particular question in the cause by the effect of the pleading itself."[3]   As might be expected from these differences, the form taken by the judgment of the court resembled that taken by the judgment in courts which followed the procedure of the Roman civil or canon law, rather than that taken by the judgment in the common law courts.   We have seen that in the common law courts the court simply decided the specific issue raised by the pleadings.[4]   In equity, on the other hand, the court considered the whole circumstances of the case made by the bill and answer, and tried to make a decree which would give effect to the rights of all the parties according to the circumstances of the case.[5]   In this respect it resembled far more the procedure of the Roman civil law; for, unlike the common law, where everything alleged in the pleading was admitted except the single point on which issue was joined, nothing need be admitted on the pleadings, so that the court could much more readily adapt its judgment to the facts as proved by the parties.[6]   On the other hand, while at common law a party was not bound by the allegations in his pleadings, by the civil law and in the court of Chancery, a party was held to admit the truth of the facts which he alleged, "the rule being *qui ponit fatetur*."[7]

These resemblances to Roman civil law procedure lived long in the procedure of the court of Chancery.   But that procedure, as it developed in later days under the guidance of the common lawyers, acquired other characteristics, some of which were

---

[1] Below 383-386, 402-404.   [2] Below 383, 392.

[3] Stephen, Pleading (5th ed.) 494 ; Stephen points out, in the note to this passage, that, though in equity pleading " the common replication offers a formal contradiction to the answer—a contradiction which imitates in some measure the form of an issue in the common law, and borrows its name, yet in substantive effect the two results are quite different ;—for the contradiction to which the name of an issue is thus given in the equity pleading, is of the most general and indefinite kind, and develops no particular question as the subject for decision in the cause."

[4] Above 264, 275.

[5] " The judgments of the common law, following the writ on which the action was founded, were uniform simple and invariable, according to the nature of the action, as that the said William recover seisin, or his term of years, or his damages. . . . In the court of Chancery no writ or formula of action imposed any fetter of form ; and the court, not being tied to forms, was able to modify the relief given by its decrees to answer all the particular exigencies of the case fully and circumstantially," Spence, op. cit. i 390.

[6] " All the essential differences between a trial at common law and by the civil law, arise from this ; namely, that by the common law a cause goes to trial with everything alleged in the pleadings on either side admitted, except the single point on which issue is joined, while by the civil law it goes to trial with nothing admitted," Essays, A.A.L.H. ii 760; in the Chancery the form of the Answer makes this difference clear, below 384-385, 402-403.

[7] Essays, A.A.L.H. ii 771.

reminiscent of the common law, but most of which were quite peculiar to itself. We shall see that the process used to get the defendant before the court resembled the dilatory processes employed by the common law;[1] and that the system of equity pleading borrowed certain of the terms and rules of the common law system.[2] We have seen that sinecure officials and saleable offices were even more common in the Chancery than in the common law courts.[3] But these are superficial resemblances. In fact, the procedure of the court developed into an independent system;[4] and, in the process, it gradually became as slow, elaborate, and technical as it had formerly been speedy, simple, and common-sense. The general nature of this development will appear from a comparison of the procedure of the fifteenth century, which I have just outlined,[5] with the procedure of the court in its last days.

Bentham, in his Introductory View of the Rationale of Evidence,[6] sketched, picturesquely, but with substantial accuracy, the condition of this procedure in the eighteenth and early nineteenth centuries: " Under the name of a *bill*, a volume of notorious lies delivered in, with three or four months' time for a *first answer*, and after *exceptions* taken of course, two or three months for a *second*—then *amendments* made to the bill, with more such delays, and more succeeding answers—then a *cross bill* filed on the other side, and a *second* such cause thus mounted on the shoulders of the *first*—then volumes heaped upon volumes of *depositions*—then after years thus employed, a *decree* obtained, by which nothing is decided—then the whole matter, and everything that has been made to grow out of it, sent to be investigated in the hermetically sealed closet of a sort of under judge called a *Master*—with days of attendance separated from each other by days or weeks—length of attendance each day nominally an hour really half or a quarter of the time. . . . The judge paid for *three* attendances and bestowing one. . . . The party whose interest or purpose is served by delay, attending or not attending, according as by attendance or non-attendance that interest and that purpose are best served—then in the course of a few more years thus employed out of a dozen or two of parties, one carried off by death and then another—and upon each death another bill to be filed, and the same or a similar course of retardation to be run."

That Bentham's critical sketch was in fact substantially accurate, is, as we shall see, borne out by the books of practice, and by the reports of royal commissions. Let us compare it with the picture

---

[1] Below 348-351.   [2] Vol. v 285; below 382-383, 390-392.
[3] Vol. i 424-425, 439-442.   [4] Essays, A.A.L.H. ii 773.
[5] Above 336-337; vol. v 285-286.
[6] Works (Ed. Bowring) vi 43; this Treatise is contained in vols. vi and vii of this edition.

drawn by the Chancery Commissioners of 1850 in their first report.[1]

The plaintiff began his suit by addressing a bill to the chancellor, praying process against the defendant to compel him to appear and put in an answer. The bill asked for relief, and required the defendant to make discovery, i.e. to give on oath an answer to the matters stated in the bill. To get this discovery the bill contained an interrogating part, which converted each statement into a series of interrogatories, framed on the principle that the defendant might be dishonest and might therefore answer evasively.[2] The bill was then engrossed on parchment and filed with the proper officer of the court. A subpœna then issued, requiring the defendant to appear and answer. This subpœna contained no intimation of the object of the suit. The defendant must then appear and get an office copy of the bill. Having obtained this copy, the defendant must decide whether he would demur or plead or answer. He might demur, either on the substantial ground that no case had been made out for the interference of the court, or by reason of a technical objection to the form of the bill. A plea was generally a statement of matters not appearing on the face of the bill, which showed a reason why the suit should be either barred or delayed.[3] The answer, which was generally given on oath, both answered the plaintiff's interrogatories and set out other facts essential to the defendant's defence.[4] Unless the defendant lived within twenty miles of London, a special commission issued to take the answer. This involved office fees, charges by the London solicitor who took it out, and fees to the Commissioners for swearing. Often there were frequent applications to a master for more time to answer, and appeals from his decision to the court.[5] Omission to put in an answer in the proper time was punished by attachment; and, if the defendant was attached, all applications for time must be made to the court. After a sufficient answer[6] was filed, a motion was made by the plaintiff for the production of documents in the defendant's possession. This order was also the occasion of considerable expense.[7] It often happened that the

[1] Parlt. Papers, 1852, xxi 5-10; see also the extract from C. P. Cooper's book on proceedings in Parliament relative to the court of Chancery printed in App. II. (1).

[2] For the bill and its various parts see below 379-382, 394-402.

[3] For these pleas see below 382-383, 390-393.

[4] For the answer and its preparation see below 402-404.

[5] Apparently time could always be got by motion of course on the following scale, if the defendant lived within 20 miles of London: on the first motion 28 days, on the second 21 days, on the third 14 days; and if the defendant lived over 20 miles from London, the times were 42, 21 and 14 days, Bentham, Rationale of Judicial Evidence, Works (Ed. Bowring) vii 216; Maddock, Chancery (ed. 1815) ii 208-209.

[6] For the procedure to get a sufficient answer, if the first answer was insufficient, see below 405-406.

[7] " There are fees to counsel, office fees for the order of the court, and charges by the solicitors for the briefs and for attendances on counsel, the Court, and the Registrar,

answer of the defendant made it necessary for the plaintiff to amend his bill, in order either to traverse the facts stated in the answer, or to introduce new facts. Further answers were then called for; and the case could then either be heard on these answers, or the plaintiff could put in a formal replication denying the answers. The pleadings being thus at an end, the next step was to lay them before counsel to advise on the evidence, and to prepare interrogatories for the examination of witnesses. On these interrogatories the witnesses were examined in private, none of the parties or their agents being present. As the interrogatories were framed by counsel without knowing what witnesses would be forthcoming, or what answers they would give, it was necessary to frame questions to meet many possible contingencies. It is obvious that, in these circumstances, no effective cross-examination was possible, so that it was seldom resorted to.[1] It was necessary to issue a special commission to take the evidence of witnesses in the country —a process which was at once expensive and slow.[2] When all the evidence had been taken it was published; and the parties could get copies on payment of fees. The case was then ripe for hearing; but it could be delayed by motions to suppress depositions, or to issue another commission to take further evidence. When the case was set down for hearing, there were often further delays, by reason of objections taken on account of the misjoinder of a party, or non-joinder of necessary parties, or the death of a party, or the emerging of new facts. This was the occasion of bills of revivor or supplement, which often meant that the same tedious course of procedure must be started anew.[3] Even if all these defects were cured, it was often still not possible for the court to pronounce a final judgment unless it was a judgment dismissing the bill. It was often necessary to send the case to a master to take accounts or to make inquiries. Again, if at the hearing a question of law arose, a special case might be sent to a court of law, or the court might require a plaintiff to test his legal right by bringing an action at law.[4] Moreover, if on the depositions the court could not come to a clear conclusion as to the facts, it might direct that an issue should be tried by a jury in a court of common law. Even if final judgment were at length given, many more delays

and for serving the orders. The actual expenses of the documents is necessarily a proceeding of considerable expense, as the solicitor inspecting must be paid his professional charges for attending to inspect, and for the extracts and copies which he makes, and the other solicitor must be paid for attending at the examination," Parlt. Papers 1852 xxi 7.

[1] Below 355.

[2] For this cumbrous and ineffective process of taking evidence see below 354-355.

[3] See below 344-347.

[4] For instances where this was done in 1589 and 1600 see Monro, Acta 591, 744.

might be interposed by a successful petition for a rehearing, or by an appeal.[1]

Even if all had been well with the constitution of the court, the possession of such a procedure must have made its proceedings very slow. But we have seen that, from the sixteenth century onwards, all the defects of its procedure were aggravated by its defective constitution.[2] The court was understaffed; as in the common law courts, obsolete forms and machinery had remained long after they had lost their usefulness; and the chancellor exercised no adequate control over his officials. It is true that the nature of the jurisdiction exercised by the court of Chancery made it inevitable that there should be greater delays in a suit in equity than in an action at law. The Chancery Commissioners in 1826 pointed out that, both by reason of subject matter of the equitable jurisdiction, and by reason of the nature of the relief given, "its proceedings cannot be rendered short or summary; and that, in considering its rules of practice, little analogy can be drawn from courts of common law."[3] Thus to unravel a long chain of fraud and to counteract its effects; to investigate accounts; to enforce agreements for the conveyance of property in which many people were interested, and the title to which was complicated; to administer a large property, and adjust the rights of creditors and beneficiaries—were necessarily tasks that demanded time. Moreover, a large number of suits in Chancery were concerned with the administration of trusts; and they necessarily lasted as long as the trust endured.[4] But delays due to these causes were trivial matters, compared with the delays caused by the combined results of the defective procedure and the defective constitution of the court. We have seen that, as the combined result of all these causes, the Chancery procedure became a byeword for dilatoriness and inefficiency. I propose, in the first place, to trace briefly the history of this gradual deterioration of its procedure; and, in the second place, to compare the defects in its procedure with the defects in the procedure of the common law.

(1) *The deterioration of the procedure of the court of Chancery.*

It was during the sixteenth century that we can see the beginnings of our later system of equity.[5] The court of Chancery was established in its final form;[6] and its procedure began to be elaborated. In fact, in the case of its procedure, much the same

---

[1] Vol. i 438; below 368-369.
[3] Parlt. Papers 1826 xv 9.
[5] Vol. v 299-338.
[2] Vol. i 423-428, 435-442.
[4] Ibid.
[6] Vol. i 409-412.

process was taking place as was taking place in the case of the procedure of the court of Star Chamber;[1] and, as we have seen in an earlier volume, it is probable that Lord Ellesmere had a good deal to do with the settlement of the procedure of both courts.[2] It would be obviously both tedious and unnecessary to trace in detail the stages by which this procedure became progressively more elaborate, more dilatory, and more ineffective. It would, moreover, be a very difficult task, as the rules of procedure were, throughout the eighteenth century, becoming a very esoteric body of knowledge, known only to the officials of the court, and known imperfectly to them. Very few general orders were made during that century;[3] and it was admitted that a contrary course of practice might deprive orders of their legal effect.[4] Obviously this tended both to make the existing practice uncertain, and to sanction changes which often tended to benefit the officials of the court at the expense of the suitors. I shall, therefore, as in the case of the common law procedure, illustrate its development by taking as instances the rules governing the procedure in a suit in equity upon a few selected topics. The topics which I have selected are—The machinery by which a suit in equity was begun and continued; process; the mode of taking evidence; motions; references; hearing and judgment; rehearings and appeals; the conduct of a suit in equity.

The machinery by which a suit in equity was begun and continued.

There was a great contrast between the mode of beginning a suit in equity, and the mode of beginning a common law action. We have seen that at common law the plaintiff must, at his peril, select the form of action suited to the facts of his case, and that if the facts proved showed that he had chosen the wrong form, he was non-suited.[5] In equity, on the other hand, proceedings were, in nearly all cases,[6] begun by a bill, in which the plaintiff stated his cause of complaint. In equity, therefore, there was much more uniformity in the manner of beginning proceedings, and no risk that the selection at the outset of the wrong form would cause

---

[1] Vol. v 178-184.   [2] Vol. i 501; vol. v 232-233.   [3] Vol. i 436.

[4] " From a manuscript book containing all the written Orders, which was presented by *Mr. Dickens* to *Lord Loughborough*, who handed it to me, as I shall to my Successor, I can see that it is impossible for this Court in many instances to support its present practice upon the notion that a continual practice does not nullify a written Order," Boehm v. De Tastet (1813) 1 V. and B. at p. 327 *per* Lord Eldon.

[5] Above 248.

[6] An information was used " if the suit was instituted on behalf of the crown, or of those who partake of its prerogative or whose rights are under its particular protection as the objects of a public charity," Mitford, Pleading (2nd ed.) 7; Maddock, Chancery (ed. 1815) ii 135.

failure. On the other hand, in the course of the various vicissitudes through which a suit in equity might pass before a final decree was made, the need arose for distinguishing between bills which originated such a suit, and bills brought to obviate difficulties which arose in the course of the suit. A considerable body of law gradually gathered round the different varieties of these bills, and the occasions upon which one or other was necessary; and we shall see that the delay and expense caused by the necessity of having recourse to these bills, was hardly inferior to the delay and expense caused by the choice of a wrong form of common law action, and the consequent need to start proceedings afresh.

The necessity for the growth of bills, other than those which originated a suit, was caused, firstly, by the desire of the court to get before it all the parties whom a decree might affect, in order that the decree might be complete and final; and, secondly, by its desire to get all the facts before the court, so that the justice done by that decree might be as nearly perfect as possible. In order to effect the first object a bill of revivor was generally filed; and in order to effect the second a supplemental or a cross bill. These were the principal types of bill filed with these objects; and they were well known in the fifteenth century.[1]

Naturally, in course of time, variations on these types sprang up. Consequently, there emerged a body of rules as to which of these various types of bill it was proper to file in different circumstances, and as to when it was desirable to have recourse to a new bill—rules which may be compared with the common law rules as to the differences between the forms of action. In the first place, therefore, I shall say a few words as to these types of bill; in the second place, I shall say something of the later variations on these types; and, in the third place, I shall show how the need to file these bills increased the delay and expense of a suit in equity.

(i) The number of parties to a suit in equity, for the purpose e.g. of administering an estate, was necessarily large; and the court required all the parties, who might be affected by the decree, to be before the court. Moreover it was a rule that, "if any person joined as co-plaintiff should, by any act, or by conduct amounting to assent or acquiescence, have disentitled himself to relief, all the co-plaintiffs were bound by it, and deprived in that suit of the relief they might otherwise have had."[2] To obviate this inconvenient result it was the practice to have only a single plaintiff, and make the other parties defendants. If possible an infant was selected as plaintiff, because he could not "by any act

---

[1] Spence, Equity i 374-375, and the precedents cited from the calendars of Henry VI. and Edward IV.'s reigns.

[2] Parlt. Papers 1852 xxi 8-9.

or omission have prejudiced his right to relief." [1] But, in the twenty or thirty or more years that a suit in equity might last, it was inevitable that among these parties there should be deaths and marriages.   That meant that new parties—personal representatives, heirs, or devisees, or husbands must be brought before the court. Whenever any of these events occurred after the close of the pleadings, so that the defect could not be supplied by amendment,[2] it was necessary that a bill of revivor should be filed.   The cases where the bringing of such a bill was a proper or a necessary course came to turn on a number of fine distinctions; and the rules as finally ascertained were thus stated by Mitford; [3] "wherever a suit abates by death, and the interest of the person whose death has caused the abatement is transmitted to that representative which the law gives or ascertains, as an heir-at-law, executor, or administrator; so that the title cannot be disputed, at least in the court of Chancery,[4] but the person in whom the title is vested is alone to be ascertained; the suit may be continued by bill of revivor merely.   If a suit abates by the marriage of a female plaintiff, and no act is done to affect the rights of the parties by the marriage, no title can be disputed; the person of the husband is the sole fact to be ascertained, and therefore the suit may be continued in this case likewise by bill of revivor merely."

A supplemental bill, on the other hand, was proper where some new matter had arisen after the close of the pleadings, so that the defect could not be supplied by amendment.[5]   Its scope was therefore wide, and covered considerably more ground than that covered by a bill of revivor.   Thus it could be filed "to obtain a further discovery from a defendant, to put a new matter in issue, or to add parties, when the proceedings are in such a state that the original bill cannot be amended for the purpose." [6]   Its use for the last named of these purposes brings it near to a bill of revivor.   But whereas the latter species of bill only lay when there had been a devolution of interest by operation of law, the former was needed where the devolution was otherwise occasioned.   Thus, if the birth of a tenant in tail gave rise to a new interest in the

---

[1] Parlt. Papers 1852 xxi 8-9; it is also pointed out by the Commissioners that all this large body of defendants might "all appear by separate solicitors, and all put in separate answers, and against whom all the proceedings must ordinarily be taken."

[2] Mitford, op. cit. 53.　　　　　[3] Ibid 63-64; Maddock, op. cit. ii 396-404.

[4] The title of the heir-at-law could only be decided by a court of common law, and the title of the executor or administrator could only be decided in the ecclesiastical courts. For the rules which governed the procedure when the chancellor sent a case to the common law courts to get advice on a question of law, see Maddock, op. cit. 364-369; it occasioned great delays, especially if the chancellor, being dissatisfied, sent the case to another court for a second opinion, see vol. i 451.

[5] Mitford, op. cit. 53.　　　　　[6] Ibid 59; Maddock, op. cit. ii 405.

property, which was the subject of the suit, a supplemental bill was necessary.[1]

A cross bill was filed by a defendant to an original bill, and gave him somewhat similar advantages as were given to a plaintiff by the power to file a supplemental bill. It is defined by Maddock[2] as "a bill brought by a defendant to a former bill which is depending, against the plaintiff in such bill, or the parties thereto, touching the matter of the bill, or the facts set out in the defendant's answer to such bill." It was necessary, as the Chancery Commission of 1850 pointed out, to give the defendant the relief to which it might appear from the course of the suit he was entitled;[3] and it might operate, as is pointed out both by Maddock[4] and Mitford,[5] somewhat in the same manner as a plea of "puis darrein continuance" at common law.[6] Thus a release got after issue joined could be put in issue by such a bill.[7] Moreover, if it appeared that the interests of co-defendants were opposite, the court, in order to do complete justice, might order that one set of these co-defendants should file a cross bill against the plaintiff and the other co-defendants.[8]

(ii) These were the main types of bill which it might become necessary to file during the course of a suit in equity. Naturally a large and technical body of law grew up as to when it was proper to make use of each variety; and further sub-varieties were developed. Thus, in some cases, a bill of revivor and supplement was needed. "If," says Mitford,[9] "a suit becomes abated, and by any act besides the event by which the abatement happens the rights of the parties are affected, as by a settlement or a devise under certain circumstances; though a bill of revivor merely may continue the suit so as to enable the parties to prosecute it, yet to bring before the court the whole matter necessary for its consideration the parties must by supplemental bill, added to and made part of their bill of revivor, show the settlement or devise or other act by which their rights are affected." Thus if a female plaintiff had married, and had settled her property on herself and her issue, a bill of supplement and revivor was necessary. In other cases

---

[1] Mitford, op. cit. 60.   [2] Op. cit. ii 327.

[3] "It frequently happens that a defendant to a bill in equity is advised to become himself a plaintiff in what is called a cross bill. He may require from the plaintiff in the original suit admissions of facts or the production of documents necessary for his defence. The original case may be founded on a deed or instrument which he may be entitled to have set aside for fraud or error; or he may on other grounds . . . be entitled not merely to resist the plaintiff's demand, but to have a decree giving him relief in respect of the property or transactions the subject of the original suit. He is not however able to obtain any such discovery or production of documents, or any such relief, without a cross bill," Parlt. Papers 1852 xxi 10.

[4] Op. cit. ii 328.   [5] Op. cit. 76.
[6] For this plea see above 273.   [7] Mitford, op. cit. 76-77.
[8] Ibid 77.   [9] Op. cit. 65-66.

original bills in the nature, according to the circumstances, of a bill of revivor or a supplemental bill, were needed. For instance, if the property in dispute were devised, the devisee could not continue the suit by bill of revivor. An original bill must be filed which had some of the characteristics of a bill of revivor.[1] Similarly, if the interest of the person in the property in dispute determined, and vested in another person who did not claim under him (e.g. in the case of a remainderman becoming entitled on the death of a tenant for life), an original bill in the nature of a supplemental bill was needed; and this had many more of the characteristics of an original bill than an original bill in the nature of a bill of revivor.[2]

Other varieties of bills will be considered when I come to deal with proceedings which could be taken to question a decree.[3]

(iii) The fact that the need to file these bills increased the delay and expense of a suit in equity will be at once obvious, if we remember that these bills must, as a general rule, proceed through the same preliminary stages as an original bill. When a case at length came on for hearing,[4] it was not improbable that some one of the defendants took the preliminary objection that all the necessary parties were not before the court. "After a technical argument, which in some cases is known to be wholly beside the merits, the court may be compelled to yield to the objection, and to direct the cause to stand over in order that the plaintiff may, by new proceedings, bring the absent party before the court, against whom it may be necessary to prove the whole case *de novo*."[5] The same thing often happened when a cross bill was filed. "The same interrogatories which are administered in the one suit, are sometimes administered over again to the same witnesses in the other; and the duplicate depositions, not only occasion in the first instance greatly increased expense, but by swelling the copies and briefs, very much enhance the costs in all the subsequent stages of the litigation."[6]

In fact, these rules are an illustration of the manner in which the desire of the chancellors to do absolutely complete justice often

---

[1] Mitford, op. cit. 66-67.

[2] Ibid 67-68; cp. Parlt. Papers 1852 xxi 20—"If there be a devise; or a marriage settlement; or a bankruptcy or insolvency; or a change of office, as in the case of a bishop or incumbent or the like; or if a new person has come into existence interested in the subject of the suit, a bill is in that case filed, to which answers are required, and all the formalities of a hostile Chancery suit gone through, in order to obtain what is called the usual Supplemental Decree; that is, a decree directing that the proceedings in the original suit may be carried on between the parties in the supplemental suit in the same way as between the original parties."

[3] Below 368-369.

[4] For the delays before hearing see vol. i 439; above 339-342; below 360-361; App. II. (1).

[5] Parlt. Papers 1852 xxi 9.

[6] Ibid 10.

defeated itself. With this object in view the court had bound itself by the rigid rule that, if it acted at all, it must assume entire control. It would not decide a single doubtful point connected with the administration of a trust or the estate of a deceased person, without administering the whole estate; and, even if all the parties were friendly, it would not dispense with the forms of a contested action. It is true that at the hearing these friendly causes could be treated as short unopposed causes.[1] "But," said the Chancery Commissioners in 1852,[2] "the preliminary proceedings are nevertheless of the same cumbrous and expensive character as in hostile suits. A bill with long statements and interrogatories, subpœnas, answers, and frequently amendments and evidence, succeed each other. For example, in a creditor's suit, when the executor does not feel himself justified in admitting the debt; or where the real estate has to be administered and there is an infant heir; or where there are infants or unborn issue interested in the estate under devise or settlement, the form of a hostile suit is gone through, although no person really doubts that the plaintiff is a creditor, and although he will be obliged afterwards to satisfy the master of the existence and amount of his debt." When we consider the origin and the effect of these rules, we recall Maitland's description of another rule of common law procedure, which also did much injustice—"a respectable sentiment that has degenerated into stupid obstinacy."[3]

How great was the delay and expense occasioned by this striving after an unattainable ideal of perfection and completeness, will appear more clearly when we have considered the procedure followed in some of the other stages of a suit in equity.

Process.

The process of the court of Chancery to enforce appearance, to force a defendant who had appeared to answer, and to enforce obedience to a decree, was not, it is true, characterized by so many conventional fictions as the process of the common law; but, at the end of the seventeenth century, it had come to be quite as lengthy and complex as that process. I propose to deal shortly with the process used by the court for these three purposes.

(i) It was a rule of the court in the sixteenth century that no subpœna, and therefore no other process, could issue to enforce appearance, till a bill signed by counsel had been filed.[4] But, apparently, in the course of the seventeenth century, this rule was

---

[1] Parlt. Papers 1852 xxi 9.   [2] Ibid.   [3] P. and M. ii 592-593.
[4] Spence, op. cit. i 369, citing Wriothesley's orders, 37 Henry VIII.; the rule as to the signature apparently goes back to Henry V.'s reign, ibid n. (g); Sanders, Orders i 7d.

disregarded. It was therefore enacted in 1705 that, except in the case of "bills for injunctions to stay wastes or to stay suits at law commenced," no subpœna or other process to compel appearance should issue, till a bill was filed.[1]

In earlier days this process was short and speedy.[2] In the eighteenth century, as Blackstone's summary shows,[3] it had become lengthy and slow. In effect it was as follows : (1) attachment—"a writ in the nature of a capias directed to the sheriff, and commanding him to attach, or take up the defendant, and bring him into court."[4] (2) If the sheriff returned "non est inventus," attachment with proclamations. (3) If this be returned "non est inventus," a commission of rebellion—"four commissioners therein named, or any of them are ordered to attach him, wheresoever he be in Great Britain, as a rebel and contemner of the King's laws and government, by refusing to attend his sovereign when thereunto required." (4) If this was unavailing ,a serjeant-at-arms was sent to find him. (5) If the serjeant-at-arms could do nothing, "a sequestration issues to seize all his personal estate and the profits of his real estate."

It was probably in the latter years of the sixteenth century that this complicated procedure was introduced. The manner of, and the reasons for, its introduction are described both picturesquely and with substantial accuracy by Roger North :[5] "When the process was young, a *subpœna*, which was a legal writ, and attachment upon it for disobedience carried a great terror. But when the terror of that abated, and defendants came in but slackly, then addition was given to the terror, and proclamations were to be made upon the second attachment if the party hid away from the first; and if that second proclamation did not fright him in, then he was a rebel, and commissioners, that is a petit army, was raised to fetch him in, as standing out in rebellion, and there was an end. But if he was caught and escaped, then the king's serjeant at arms went to look for him. But sequestrations were not heard of till the Lord Coventry's time, when Sir John Read lay in the Fleet (with £10,000 in an iron cast chest in his chamber) for disobedience to a decree, and would not submit and pay the duty. This being represented to the Lord Keeper as a great contempt and affront put upon the court, he authorized men to go and break up his iron chest, and pay the duty and costs, and leave the rest to him, and

---

[1] 4 Anne c. 16 § 22.   [2] Vol. v 279-280, 285, 286.

[3] Comm. iii 443-444 ; that it had reached its final form at the beginning of the eighteenth century is clear from Gilbert's Forum Romanum chap. v, which was written before 1725.

[4] For the difference between an attachment and a capias see Gilbert, op. cit. (ed. 1758) 82-83.

[5] Lives of the Norths i 258.

discharged his commitment. From thence came sequestrations; which are now so established as to run of course after all other process fails." The only part of this account which is inaccurate would seem to be the dating of sequestrations from Lord Coventry's time. They were clearly in use in Francis Bacon's time, as he regulates them by his orders.[1] But it may well be that they did not come into general use, as a part of mesne process, till a little later; and, if this be so, North's account is substantially accurate.

It is clear, then, from North that the Chancery process to compel appearance was established in its final form by the middle of the seventeenth century. It suffered from three main defects. In the first place, it was unduly lengthy, as North himself allows.[2] In the second place, it gave rise to all sorts of captious objections as to the regularity of the manner in which, in any given case, the various steps had been taken. A writer of 1707[3] complains of "the great number of processes before you can come to a sequestration, and the many niceties in suing out and returning them, which frequently is adjudged irregular, and the plaintiff pays costs for it, and is forced to begin again." In the third place, as the same writer also complains, "there can be no decree against a defendant that has not appeared, though you have run out all process of contempt against him."

So obvious were these defects that the Legislature gave a partial remedy in 1732. If the defendant was suspected of leaving the realm, or of otherwise absconding to evade service of process, the plaintiff could, after certain formalities specified in the Act, apply to have his bill taken pro confesso, and the court could make such decree as appeared to it to be just;[4] and if a defendant was produced in court and refused to enter an appearance, the court could have an appearance entered for him.[5] But it was not always possible to make use of the procedure provided by this Act. In that case the old unsatisfactory process was alone available. How complicated and unsatisfactory it was was clearly

---

[1] "No sequestration shall be granted but of lands leases or goods in question, and not of any other lands or goods not contained in the suits. When a decree is made for a rent to be paid out of land, or a sum of money to be levied out of the profits of land, then a sequestration of the same lands, being in the defendant's hands, may be granted," orders 29, 30; order 29, like order 30, may only refer to process to enforce a decree; there is an instance of a sequestration for this purpose in 1616, Monro, Acta 240; North's instance is obviously a sequestration for this purpose; and they may well have become common as a part of mesne process later; Blackstone, Comm. iii 444, says that they were introduced by Nicolas Bacon, but, as the reference to 1 Vern. 421 cited by him shows, this is a mistake for Francis Bacon.

[2] "What signifies all the process between a *subpœna* and a sequestration, and the officers that depend thereon, when the former is a summons, and the latter a *distringas* answerable to the common law?" op. cit. 265.

[3] Cited Parkes, Chancery 282-283.   [4] 5 George II. c. 25 § 1.   [5] § 2.

shown by the evidence given by Mr. Bickersteth to the Chancery Commission which reported in 1826.[1] The two charts which he handed to the Commissioners, showing the complication of the process to compel appearance, and to compel an answer after appearance, will be found in the Appendix.[2]

(ii) It would seem that in the eighteenth century the complication of the process to compel an answer, was equal to, if not greater than, the process to compel appearance.[3] The chief point in which it differed was that, apart from statute, as against a defendant who stood out all process, an application might be made to take the bill pro confesso.[4] But, as will be seen from the Appendix, even if the defendant were in custody, repeated writs of habeas corpus to bring his body before the court were needed before such an order could be made.[5]

At this point also it should be noted that the delays of equity procedure pressed quite as hardly on a person who had been made defendant to a frivolous bill, as on a plaintiff who wished to compel an unwilling defendant to appear and answer. According to Bacon's orders, a bill not prosecuted for a term after all the defendants had answered was ipso facto dismissed.[6] Tothill states the time as two terms;[7] but in the course of the eighteenth century the period was silently lengthened.[8] The Commissioners of 1826 found[9] that, "after a defendant has fully answered the bill, although the plaintiff should take no step in the cause, the defendant is not entitled to call for a dismissal of the plaintiff's bill, for want of prosecution, until the expiration of a period, depending upon the length of the law terms, but which may generally be computed at about three-quarters of a year. To prevent the order to dismiss from being then obtained, the plaintiff may file what is termed a replication, by which he gains, without making any real advance in the cause, a further delay in the same period of about three-quarters of a year; and if, at the expiration of that period, the plaintiff upon a motion to dismiss the bill, will give an undertaking to speed his cause, he may prevent his bill from being even then dismissed. And, if, after this undertaking, he does not proceed before the expiration of another term, he is still allowed an opportunity of keeping his suit alive, by giving

[1] Parlt. Papers 1826 xv App. A 150-152.
[2] App. II. (2).   [3] Ibid.
[4] (1667) 2 Free. Ch. 128, where this difference is noted.   [5] App. II. (2).
[6] Order 17; but after replication a motion and order of the court was necessary.
[7] Beames, explanatory paper on the recommendations of the Chancery Commission, Parlt. Papers 1826 xv 75; West, Symboleography (ed. 1618) Part II. p. 195, states that, "the plaintife ought to reply the next terme after that the defendant hath answered, else may he give him day to reply: by which day if hee doe not reply the defendant may procure a dismission and get costs."
[8] Parlt. Papers 1826 xv 75.   [9] Ibid 13.

another undertaking to speed his cause with effect ; and it is only after this second undertaking, that he is under the necessity of proceeding to a hearing with due diligence ; or of altogether losing the benefit of that suit."

(iii) The process to compel obedience to a decree, which had taken its final shape at the end of the seventeenth century,[1] was even more complicated than the process to enforce an appearance or an answer ; and it was often quite as inefficacious. Probably the reason for this combination of complication and inefficiency, must be sought in the jealousy which existed between the common law courts and the court of Chancery at the end of the sixteenth and the beginning of the seventeenth centuries. It compelled the court of Chancery to move warily, and to develop the law by means of small changes, which resulted in the system in force in the eighteenth century.[2] The absurdity of that system was clearly exposed in Mr. Bickersteth's evidence to the Chancery Commission of 1826.[3] " I conceive," he said, " that the process to compel obedience to orders is extremely inefficient. Every order, before it can be enforced, must have its writ of execution served. In case of disobedience to the writ of execution, there must be an attachment. After the attachment, the course will vary according to the nature of the order. If the order be to deliver possession, there is a mandatory writ of injunction to deliver possession, and if that injunction be disobeyed, there is ultimately a writ of assistance directed to the sheriff, ordering him to give possession ; so that we have those several steps : the order, the writ of execution, the attachment, the writ of injunction, and the writ of assistance, before the defendant is compelled to obey ; and I apprehend that no sufficient reason can be given why the order should not be followed up by a writ, in the nature of a writ of possession, in the same manner that judgment in ejectment is followed up by a writ of possession at law. But if the order be to pay money, or to execute a deed, or do some act which must be personally done by the party himself, then, after the writ of attachment, you proceed to the writ of sequestration. The steps vary according as the party may happen to be taken into custody or not. If the party be taken and in prison, . . . and if there be no estate to sequestrate, or the commissioners of sequestration be in possession of such estate as they are able to seize, matters may

---

[1] Notes on the earlier fluctuations of practice will be found in Spence, op. cit. i 391-392.

[2] " The courts of law down to the time of Elizabeth uniformly denounced all these modes of enforcing decrees, excepting by simple imprisonment, as being illegal : but the Chancellors persevered, and the present practice is founded on the course which was then established," ibid 392.

[3] Parlt. Papers 1826 xv App. A. 150.

remain in that state; the man may continue in gaol during the whole of his life, and the order of the court not be in the meantime obeyed." Moreover, it was a question whether the death of the party in default did not discharge the sequestration.[1] On this view, the premature death of a defendant, against whom a decree had been made, might go far to deprive a plaintiff of its fruits.

The mode of taking evidence.

With the pleadings I shall deal in the following section.[2] After the pleadings were closed, the next step was to take the evidence; and it may safely be said that a more futile method of getting at the facts of a case, than the system in use in the court of Chancery from the seventeenth century onwards, never existed in any mature legal system. The method was, as we have seen, essentially the same as that employed in the canon law;[3] but it was carried out under such technical forms, and in such a manner, as to be productive of the most unconvincing testimony at the greatest possible expense.

We have seen that in the fifteenth century the practice as to the mode of taking evidence was not settled—viva voce evidence was sometimes heard by the chancellor.[4] It would seem too from Norburie's account, that, at the beginning of the seventeenth century, such evidence was not then finally excluded at the hearing of the case.[5] But the orders of the court show that written evidence was more usual; and it is clear from these orders that the method of taking it had assumed substantially its modern form. That form, Spence thinks, was finally fixed by the orders issued by lord keeper Coventry in 1635.[6] Witnesses who lived within a short distance of London, ultimately fixed at twenty miles, were examined by one of the official examiners of the court. Otherwise the examination took place in the country before special commissioners.[7] During the course of the seventeenth century, it was settled that all witnesses must be examined

---

[1] Maddock, Chancery ii 363 n. (*f*).
[2] Below 376 seqq.
[3] Above 337.
[4] Vol. v 285, 286.
[5] "The defendant being served with process *ad rejungendum* must either rejoine or lose the benefit of rejoining within other eight days, and then examine witnesses *either by commission or in court*," Abuses of the Court of Chancery, Harg. Law Tracts 436.
[6] Op. cit. i 402-403.
[7] There is an order of 1545 that a commission is not to issue except where the witness is impotent or lives at a distance, Sanders, Orders i 9; the examiners are alluded to in an explanation of an order of the court given by Crooke in 1554, ibid i 11; in 1537 there is an order as to delivery up of the copies of depositions by the examiners, ibid i 19; an order of Puckering and Egerton in 1596 shows that the procedure was fixed in substantially its final form, ibid i 70; and this seems to be the view of Spence, op. cit. i 379.

in this way. In 1737 the chancellor, on a motion to allow the examination of witnesses viva voce at the hearing, said, "I cannot allow the motion; the constant and established proceedings of this court are upon written evidence like the proceedings upon the civil or canon law. This is the course of the court, and the course of the court is the law of the court; and though there are cases of witnesses being so examined, yet they have been allowed but sparingly, and only after publication, where doubts have appeared in their depositions, and the examination has been to clear such doubts, and inform the conscience of the court. There never was a case where witnesses have been allowed to be examined at large at the hearing; and though it might be desirable to allow this, yet the fixed and settled proceedings of the court cannot be broke through for it."[1]

The following was the process by which evidence was taken under this fixed and settled system.[2]

The first step was to prepare the interrogatories. These were prepared by the plaintiff's and defendant's counsel.[3] As counsel could not tell what the answers of the witnesses would be, they were necessarily lengthy and minute;[4] and for the same reason the numbers of the witnesses were often multiplied unnecessarily.[5] Then, in a country cause, the commissioners must be appointed. Each party named one alternately up to the number of four. Then each party struck out two of the other's names, and the four left were the commissioners.[6] These commissioners and their clerks then repaired to an inn at the place where the examination was to take place. There they lived at the expense of the parties during the whole time that the examination took place. Each commissioner was paid at the rate of two guineas a day, and each clerk at the rate of fifteen shillings, in addition to his expenses at the inn.[7] There was also two guineas a day to each of the

---

[1] Graves v. Eustace Budgel (1737) 1 Atk. at p. 445.

[2] A clear short account is contained in the Report of the Chancery Commission of 1852, Parlt. Papers 1852 xxi 7-8; it is also abundantly illustrated by the evidence contained in App. A. to the first Chancery Commission, Parlt. Papers 1826 xv; see also Maddock, op. cit. ii 307-325.

[3] "The string of interrogatories thus drawn by an advocate, and an advocate who would take it as an affront if it was proposed to him to have any personal communication with his ultimate client—with the suitor—the only person who of his own knowledge is capable of affording him any information," Bentham, Rationale of Judicial Evidence, Works (Ed. Bowring) vi 444.

[4] Parlt. Papers 1852 xxi 7.

[5] Ibid 1826 xv App. A. 46—evidence of Mr. Vizard, who said, "I have no doubt that many unnecessary witnesses are examined, and much information taken which, with an expert examiner, and the attendance of some person understanding the course and nature of the examination, would never appear upon the depositions"; see also the evidence of Mr. Barnes, ibid 380.

[6] Maddock, op. cit. ii 308.

[7] Evidence of Mr. Barnes, Parlt. Papers, 1825 xv App. A. 381.

solicitors, and the expenses of the witnesses.[1]   At the examination
the witnesses were examined "without the presence of the solicitor,
or any one representing the parties, or any one acquainted with
the circumstances of the case, to see that all the information
wanted was drawn forth."[2]   The interrogatories were always
expressed in very technical language, so that often the witnesses
did not understand their meaning.[3]   As Mr. Plumer, one of the
examiners said,[4] "the same artificial interrogatory is constructed
for witnesses of all different capacities"; and the commissioners
were generally reluctant to offer any explanations.[5]   The evidence
given was put into the third person, and the phrasing was generally
that of the commissioners; so that there was every chance that,
in the course of this transposition, its effect would be materially
altered.[6]   At the close of the examination of each witness, his
depositions were engrossed and signed by him.   When all the
witnesses had been examined—a process which often took many
months—the depositions were sealed up and sent to the court;
and thus, as Bentham pointed out, the person who took the
evidence had nothing to do with the work of applying it to its
proper use.[7]   It is obvious that, under these circumstances, cross-
examination was useless if not dangerous.   It was in fact seldom
resorted to, "except when the witness was known to be friendly
to the cross-examining party, and had previously communicated
facts to be the subject of such cross-examination.[8]

After the depositions were all returned to the court an order
of the court was got for their publication.[9]   This might be delayed
by a motion to enlarge the time allowed for publication, if it
appeared that further evidence was needed.[10]   Further delays might
be caused by a motion, before publication, to suppress depositions

---

[1] Evidence of Mr. Winter, Parlt. Papers, 1826 xv App. A. 317.

[2] Evidence of Mr. Vizard, ibid 45.

[3] For an illustration of the effect of this see below 356.

[4] Parlt. Papers 1826 xv App. B. 543.

[5] Evidence of Mr. Vizard, ibid App. A. 45; evidence of Mr. Barnes, ibid 379.
It would seem from Peacock's Case (1612) 9 Co. Rep. 70b that in the Star Chamber
the commissioners were "not strictly tied to the words of the interrogatories,"
but they could inquire into "everything which necessarily ariseth thereupon for
the manifestation of the whole truth"; and that they could, after the examination
had begun, "take new instructions from the party to examine farther than he knew
before"; probably the practice had not become so fixed as it became later, but we
can see some of the causes of the defects of the developed system.

[6] Mr. Shadwell, Parlt. Papers, 1826 xv 197, said that, "you are almost morally sure
that you have not got upon the written deposition the answers the witness gave";
see also the evidence of Mr. Barnes, ibid 379-380, who described the acrimonious
discussions that used to take place as to what a witness meant, and how his meaning
should be phrased by the commissioners; he said that "it is always the case that the
answer is taken down in the words agreed upon by the commissioners, and not in
the words of the witness, unless he dictates his own answer"; this is corroborated
by the evidence of Mr. Plumer, one of the examiners, ibid App. B. 543-544.

[7] Op. cit. vi 444.   [8] Parlt. Papers 1852 xxi 7.

[9] Maddock, op. cit. ii 317-318.   [10] Ibid 318.

on the ground, e.g. that the interrogatory was leading ; and sometimes this led to an application for leave to examine the same
witness all over again by the same process.[1]   Generally no further
evidence could be taken after publication, as it was supposed that
if this was allowed it would lead to subornation of perjury ;[2] but,
even after publication, leave might be given on special motion to
take a fresh examination as to the credit of a particular witness.[3]

The slowness of this system is obvious.   It is equally obvious
that it was both costly and inefficient.   Unnecessary numbers of
witnesses were examined at great expense ; and their testimony
was often the reverse of satisfactory, because they did not understand the questions put to them.   Two concrete illustrations will
suffice to illustrate these two defects.   Mr. Lowe, in his evidence
to the Chancery Commission, cited a case in which, though there
was absolutely no dispute, the cost of examining wholly unnecessary witnesses to prove a will was £100.[4]   Mr. Vizard, another
witness, said,[5] " I had received a written statement from a witness
living in the county of Devon, as to information he could give ;
I had other means of ascertaining that the information he sent to
me was correct ; I, in consequence, brought him to town to be
examined at a very considerable expense ; he went before the
examiner and was examined ; and when the depositions came to
be published, I found the information which he had given directly
opposite to that I had expected ; upon which I sent him a copy
of his letter to me, and a copy of the evidence he had given, and
asked him to account for the difference ; the explanation I received
was that he had wholly mistaken the question as it was put to
him."

At the beginning of the eighteenth century, the House of
Commons had given very good reasons for thinking that the
common law system of taking evidence viva voce in court was
far preferable to this system ;[6] and in effect this was admitted
by the chancellors.   In the sixteenth and earlier part of the
seventeenth centuries they frequently allowed evidence, after
publication, to inform the conscience of the court ;[7] and even oral

---

[1] Maddock, op. cit. ii 313.

[2] Monro, Acta 254 (1617)—leave given to take further evidence in a case where
the defendant and his witnesses swore that they had not seen the depositions.

[3] Maddock, op. cit. ii 320-321.

[4] Parlt. Papers 1826 xv App. A. 167-168.   [5] Ibid 45.

[6] Commons Journals xv 198 (1705).   It was pointed out that, on a viva voce
examination in open court, cross examination was possible, that it was possible to
have regard to the demeanour of a witness, that perjury was more easily detected
and punished, and that " it may happen very often that the manner of wording such
depositions . . . may give a turn to the fact, very different from what the witnesses
meant, or from what might have appeared upon his examination *viva voce* in open
court."

[7] Spence, Equity i 380-381, cited above 337 n. 5 ; Bacon's Orders no. 74 ; Monro,
Acta 375 (1569).

evidence.[1] Though, as we have seen, this practice was alluded to
as late as 1737, it had by that time become obsolete.[2] Before
that date, the practice had arisen of settling a disputed question of
fact by sending an issue to be tried by a court of common law;[3]
and, at the end of the eighteenth century, the practice was
constantly resorted to by the chancellor.[4] "So sensible," wrote
Blackstone,[5] "is the court of the deficiency of trial by written
depositions, that it will not bind the parties thereby, but usually
directs the matter to be tried by a jury; especially such important
facts as the validity of a will, or whether A is heir-at-law to B.
. . . But as no jury can be summoned to attend this court, the
fact is usually directed to be tried at the bar of the court of
king's bench or at the assizes, upon a *feigned issue*. For, (in
order to bring it there, and have the point in dispute, and that
only, put in issue) an action is feigned to be brought, wherein the
pretended plaintiff declares that he laid a wager of £5 with the
defendant, that A was the heir-at-law to B; and then avers that
he is so; and brings his action for the £5. The defendant allows
the wager, but avers that A is not the heir to B; and thereupon
that issue is joined, which is directed out of Chancery to be tried;
and thus the verdict of the jurors at law determines the fact in
the court of equity." Bentham summed up the situation as
follows: "The prolific examination crawling on for ten, fifteen,
or twenty months, fees pullulating from it all the time. A suit in
equity, perhaps to do nothing but get the evidence; and then a
suit at common law, six, twelve, or eighteen months, to give
employment to the evidence."[6] We cannot say that there was
much exaggeration in this summary.

It is not surprising that those who advised suitors followed the
example of the court, and resorted to another means of getting
the necessary evidence. This was explained by Mr. Lowe. He
was asked, "Do you avoid going before the examiner whenever
you can?" He replied, "Certainly; and that is one of the reasons
that I amend my bills. I get from the defendant by answers all

---

[1] Above 353. [2] Above 354.

[3] In 1705 the Commons stated that "upon depositions taken in courts of equity,
if the witnesses differ as to matters of fact, or the credit of the witnesses is suspected,
the courts of equity are so far from relying on such depositions, that they direct issues
to be tried at law, in order that the witnesses may be then examined in open court,
when the credit of the witnesses will be considered," ibid.

[4] Evidence of Mr. Shadwell, Parlt. Papers 1826 xv App. A. 199.

[5] Comm. iii 452; in 1799 the Master of the Rolls said, 4 Ves. at p. 762, "it is
impossible to sit here any time without seeing that a viva voce examination of
witnesses is much more satisfactory than depositions, where a possibility of doubt can
be raised. . . . I should do a most dangerous thing if I was to decide this question
upon these depositions."

[6] Rationale of Judicial Evidence, Works (Ed. Bowring) vii 472.

the facts."[1] And, in answer to another question he said,[2] "it frequently happens that it is absolutely necessary to scrape the defendant's conscience by continuing to amend the bill: I have amended a bill against one of the first merchants in the city of London three times, in one of the plainest cases that ever was; for that I was very much abused; at last he could not evade the questions put to him, and paid my client the thousand pounds in dispute." It would appear from Bentham that this was generally considered to be a very much more efficient mode of extracting evidence than the regular mode of examining witnesses before an examiner or commissioners.[3] Norburie's Tract shows, indeed, that this practice was known and abused at the beginning of the seventeenth century;[4] and no doubt it was still abused in the eighteenth century.[5] But there can be little doubt that the inadequacy of the evidence taken on commission did render it a valuable means of getting at the truth. We shall now see that this absurd way of getting evidence, combined with other rules of the Chancery procedure, produced multitudes of interlocutory motions and references, which all contributed their quota to the expense and delay of a suit in equity.

Motions.

At all stages of the suit motions might be made to the court for various purposes—often, as Norburie pointed out in the early part of the seventeenth century, for the mere purpose of delay.[6] In fact, he was inclined to regard them as the chief cause for the delays in a suit in equity. "How oft have we seen ten or twelve orders in a cause, and perhaps half as many reports before hearing . . . and afterwards upon the motion of a grave and judicious counsellor all is overturned or set aside as impertinent, and the plaintiff ordered to proceed to his proofes

[1] Parlt. Papers 1826 xv App. A. 167.   [2] Ibid 165.

[3] "In general the interrogation by bill—the examination that extracts the testimony in the shape of an instrument called an answer . . . will be much more efficient than . . . the examination by which the testimony is produced in the shape of an instrument composed of depositions. . . . By bill the plaintiff, that is his law assistants, with the help of exceptions to the answer, and amendments to the bill, keep on examining the defendant till the plaintiff and his law assistants are satisfied with the completness at least (if not with the correctness) of the answer," Rationale of Judicial Evidence, Works (Ed. Bowring) vii 515.

[4] "We have seen when a plaintiff hath alleged in his bill, that he had no remedy but the defendant's confession, and that the defendant having been referred to better answer, hath in the end falsely denied the allegations, yet would the plaintiff afterwards fall as nimbly to his proofes as if he had never so alleged. . . . Let this be observed, that after the defendant hath been tortured by multiplicity of answers, little will be found in any of them either of proof or illustration for the good of the plaintiff; but all his proofes are taken out of the depositions, wherein consists the life of his cause," Harg. Law Tracts 442.

[5] Parlt. Papers 1826 xv App. A. 165-166.

[6] Harg. Law Tracts 443, cited vol. i 427.

and so to hearing."[1]   Matters were no better at the end of the
century. "The causes come often to a hearing," said Roger
North,[2] "with a file of orders in the solicitor's bundle, as big as
the common prayer book, for commissions, injunctions, publications,
speedings, delayings, and other interlocutories; all dear to the
client in every respect."

Necessarily, as the rules of procedure grew more elaborate,
these occasions of delay were multiplied.   Norburie says[3] that
the chief varieties of these motions were motions for staying suits
at law, for settling possession, for staying waste, and for amending
answers, besides petty motions for punishing contempts, grants of
dedimus potestatem, the renewing commissions and the like.   By
the end of the eighteenth century they had swelled to a much
greater bulk.   Maddock[4] gives the following list of motions which
might be made after the bill was filed, and before answer: Motions
which might be made on the part of a plaintiff were, 1. For an
injunction.   2. For a writ ne exeat regno.   3. For a guardian.
4. For a receiver.   5. For amendment of the bill.   6. That a
bill may be taken pro confesso.   7. That witnesses may be
examined de bene esse.   8. For payment of money into court.
9. For leave to prosecute as a pauper.   Motions which might be
made on the part of a defendant were, 1. For time to answer.
2. For a commission to take an answer.   3. To refer the bill
for scandal or impertinence.   4. That the defendant, a married
woman, may defend a suit separately.   5. For a reference to a
master on bills of foreclosure, specific performance etc.   6. For a
reference to inquire whether two suits are for the same matter.
7. That defendant may have a month's time to answer after payment of the costs by the plaintiff of a previous suit.   8. For an
order to defend in forma pauperis.   9. That the plaintiff may give
security for costs.   10. For leave to amend a plea.   11. To stay
proceedings on an original bill till a cross bill be answered.   12.
For a reference to a master to see if a bill filed on behalf of an
infant is for his benefit.   13. For a guardian to put in an answer.
The following motions might be made after demurrer plea or
answer, and before decree:[5] 1. Motion to refer for scandal or
impertinence.   2. Motion that the plaintiff may elect to sue at
law or in equity.   3. Motion on bills for specific performance
to see if a good title can be made.   4. Motion to dissolve an

[1] Harg. Law Tracts 437.

[2] Lives of the Norths i 262; at p. 260 he says, "I have heard Sir John Church-
hill, a famous Chancery practiser, say, that in his walk from Lincoln's Inn down to
the Temple Hall, where, in Lord Keeper Bridgman's time, causes and motions out
of term were heard, he had taken £28 with breviates, only for motions and defences
for hastening and retarding hearings."

[3] Harg. Law Tracts 437.   [4] Op. cit. ii 171-172.

[5] Maddock, op. cit. ii 277 seqq.

injunction. 5. Motions for amendments of pleadings. 6. Motion to discuss a bill. 7. Motion for the production of deeds or other writings. 8. Motion for payment of money into court. 9. Motion to take the bill and answer off the file in the case of a compromise. 10. Motion for a commission to examine witnesses. 11. Motion for the examination of defendant or plaintiff as a witness. 12. Motion to enlarge publication. 13. Motion for the examination of witnesses after publication. 14. Motion to prove exhibits viva voce at the hearing. Needless to say there accumulated round all these topics a mass of case law which afforded occasion for infinite argument.

References.

It will be seen that many of these motions gave occasion for references to the masters; and other matters, e.g. questions of account, were referred to them by interlocutory judgment of the court. One of the worst features of the procedure of the court of Chancery was, as a writer of 1707 pointed out, the "great charge and delay before the masters."[1] On this matter I have already said something.[2] Here I must deal with it in its bearings on the progress of a suit in equity. I shall say something, firstly, of the procedure before the masters; secondly, of their reports; thirdly, of the delays which might be caused by taking exceptions to their reports; and, fourthly, I shall give a concrete instance of some of these abuses taken from the evidence given to the Chancery Commission of 1826.

(i) The procedure before the masters was almost inconceivably dilatory. For every attendance at a master's office a warrant must be taken out, and a fee paid.[3] It was the custom, on leaving the papers to be copied, to take out a warrant for attendance. But, if the papers to be copied were long, the solicitor knew they could not be ready in time, and so the custom sprang up of never attending till the second, third, or even the fourth warrant.[4] It would seem from the report of a committee of the House of Commons in 1732, that this abuse was well known at that period.[5] Each attendance was only for an hour; and though, if all the

---

[1] Cited Parkes, Chancery 283; a good summary of the course of procedure before the masters will be found in the First Report of the Chancery Commission of 1850, Parlt. Papers 1852 xxi 28-30, which I have printed in App. II. (3).

[2] Vol. i 426, 441, 444.   [3] App. II. (3).

[4] Mr. Winter's Evidence, Parlt. Papers 1826 xv App. A. 278.

[5] "The masters in Chancery claim two shillings for every summons, which the committee admit to be reasonable; but are informed that abuses have been often committed by a great number of summonses issuing, without any attendance of the clerks or solicitors, who nevertheless may charge their clients for such summons and their attendance, because few bills are regularly taxed before the masters," Commons' Journals xxi 892.

parties were friendly, two or three successive hours might be arranged,[1] this was seldom possible owing to the engagements of the master.[2] If the parties were not friendly the hour would never be exceeded;[3] and the business might be infinitely protracted by failure to attend or to attend punctually.[4] For it would seem that the master's powers to deal with defaulters was very slight.[5] In particular, they had for a long time no power to proceed in the absence of the parties; and, when they got that power, they did not use it; so that if two out of three solicitors attended and the third did not, nothing could be done, though the client was obliged to pay the fees of the two who had attended.

"Whatever authority," said Mr. Winter,[6] a very competent solicitor, to the Chancery Commission, "the masters now have to proceed in the absence of solicitors, who, either because they represent parties that wish for delay, or for any other cause, do not attend, we know practically that their jurisdiction amounts to nothing: because at present, even up to the moment before signing a report, it is possible for a person wishing delay to create it in the master's office: there are no laches against a party in the master's office; it is never too late to bring evidence, it is never too late to bring discharges, I think it is never too late for anything, till the report is signed." In many cases it was directly to the interest of the parties to cause delay. Thus, if the debts of a deceased person, which bore no interest, were large, it was greatly to the benefit of the persons entitled to the residue to delay the master's report as long as possible. The executors took the interest which, if the delay were long enough, might suffice to pay the debts and the costs.[7]

The Chancery Commissioners in 1852 pointed out that this ridiculous system of procedure took its rise (like many of the other abuses of the court of Chancery) at the time when the master and his clerks were paid by fees.[8] Hence it followed that "every warrant, every copy, every report, indeed every proceeding carried its fee." I have already described the manner in which the abuse of compelling the suitor to take office copies permeated the whole system of Chancery procedure.[9] The following statement shows clearly the manner in which this

---

[1] Parlt. Papers 1826 xv App. A. 279.　　　　　[2] Ibid 299.

[3] "Any solicitor is quite in the power of the adverse party if he does not choose to proceed from hour to hour," ibid 279.

[4] Ibid 376, 377, 379; Bentham, Rationale of Judicial Evidence, Works vii 217-218, 219 n.; his strictures are borne out by the evidence given to the Chancery Commission.

[5] See the return of Master Stephen, Parlt. Papers 1826 xv App. B. 514-517, giving an account of the case of Silcox v. Bell, in which case a decree had been made in 1802, and the property was not divided till 1823.

[8] Ibid App. A. 280.　　　　　[7] Ibid 1826 xv 99.

[8] App. II. (3) p. 439.　　　　　[9] Vol. i 426, 441.

abuse increased the expense of proceeding before the master: Mr. Winter said:[1] "I select a single fact as an illustration, and similar ones are of every day occurrence. In a suit for specific performance of a contract of purchase, the usual reference was made to the master, to inquire whether the plaintiff could make a good title: I left the abstract of title with the master: the defendant, knowing that there was no objection to the title, did not appear in the master's office; but the abstract once having found its way there someone must pay for a copy of it; and as the defendant did not appear I was obliged to pay for that copy. So little occasion had my client for the copy, that in fact it was never made; but in lieu of it I took from the master's office a slip of paper indorsed 'copy abstract of title,' for which slip of paper I paid the master £8. Those slips of paper are known by the cant name of dead copies. I must request the Commissioners to remark the effect of this upon the suitor. First he paid his solicitor for the copy of the abstract left at the master's office; that copy was necessary, and the solicitor's charge for it was £5 6s. 8d., but then he was obliged to pay the master for another copy which he had no earthly occasion for. So that this copy, . . . which was utterly useless, and was in fact never made, cost him £8." Though this mode of remunerating the masters had ceased in 1833, the system still remained down to 1852. All that the earlier Act had effected was to transfer the former fees paid to the master to a fee fund; so that the old procedure and the old fees still remained.[2]

(ii) Necessarily this system affected the manner in which the master's report was drawn up, and its contents. It would seem from Lord Coventry's orders that, in the seventeenth century, the masters deliberately lengthened their reports by reciting needlessly the order of reference.[3] Similar abuses had not altogether ceased in the eighteenth century;[4] and in addition, the system of drawing up the report, and the system of taking accounts, gave the master still more ample means of remuneration. Let us listen again to Mr. Winter's evidence. He said:[5] "It is

---

[1] Parlt. Papers 1826 xv App. A. 282; this abuse had been pointed out by a committee of the House of Commons in 1732, Commons' Journals xxi 892.

[2] App. II. (3) p. 439.

[3] "Whereas the masters of the court do sometimes, by way of inducement, fill a leaf or two of the beginning of their reports, and sometimes more, with a long and particular recital of the several points of the order of reference: they shall forbear such iterations . . . and . . . shall fall directly into the matter of their report," cited Spence, Equity i 404.

[4] In 1824 Mr. Winter deposed that it was the custom for the masters to set out in their reports affidavits and states of facts, which merely increased their length, "without answering any one useful purpose," Parlt. Papers 1826 xv App. A. 286; cp. evidence of Mr. Lowe, ibid 222.

[5] Ibid 282-283.

now the practice to lay everything before the master in writing; and a solicitor, in drawing a state of facts, puts it in such a form that, provided the statement be correct, it shall answer the purpose at once of being transferred into the master's report, and, with a slight alteration of introductory matter, may constitute the report itself. I do admit that this gives great facility to the preparing of reports; but I must say that it is a facility which is procured at a vast expense to the suitors. . . . Now I propose to show the Commissioners how much unnecessary writing there is according to the present practice. I will first take the charge and discharge, and I will show how often the same items, which constitute the charge and discharge, are written over and over again, and how often they are written unnecessarily. First, the defendant carries in his examination to the master's office, that is one copy; then the plaintiff procures a copy of it from the master's office, that is a second copy. This examination states all the sums the defendant has received, and all the sums he has paid; then the plaintiff makes a transcript of all the sums the defendant, by his examination, admits himself to have received, and he takes that transcript into the master's office, which is called the charge against the defendant. The defendant's solicitor, on his part, transcribes from his examination the items which he alleges he has paid, and leaves that transcript at the master's office, which is called the defendant's discharge. This charge and discharge, therefore, constitute a third copy of the whole account; then the defendant takes a copy from the master of the plaintiff's charge, and the plaintiff takes a copy from the master of the defendant's discharge, and those constitute a fourth copy of the whole account. Then, when the charge and discharge have been allowed by the master, they are added by way of schedules to the master's report, and the plaintiff's solicitor procures a copy of that report; there is a fifth copy of the whole account. The defendant's solicitor does the like, and that is a sixth copy; then the report is transcribed with these schedules, which is a seventh copy of the account. The plaintiff's solicitor files the original report at the report office, and produces an office copy of it, which contains the eighth copy of the account; and when the cause comes on for further directions a ninth copy is made for the judge who hears the cause. I have supposed a cause in which there are only two solicitors; but in a cause in which there were five solicitors . . . the number of copies would amount to eighteen instead of nine. I will now state to the Commissioners what proportion of those copies I think necessary, and how many of them are unnecessary. The original examination clearly is unavoidable. The second copy, that is the copy of the examination which the plaintiff's solicitor procures from the master, is also necessary; the third and fourth copies (that is the charge and discharge carried in by the plaintiff and defendant to the master's office, and the copy which each takes of the paper left by the other) are quite unnecessary; and for this reason: the master has already in his office the original examination, and each of the solicitors have their copies of it; the plaintiff's solicitor has already procured a copy from the master, the defendant's solicitor has the draft of the examination in his own office." [1]

Then, too, we must remember that it was to the interest of everyone concerned to increase the length of all these documents, because increased length meant increased profit. "The solicitor," as Mr. Winter said, "is paid for drawing these statements by the length; the master's fees for copies are paid by the length; the attendances of the adverse solicitors are regulated by the length; the consequence is that nobody has any interest in talking about there being too much length; and, without supposing any person concerned in it to be otherwise influenced by his own interest than all mankind are, one cannot help seeing that the present practice affords no inducement to any of the parties to bind his conscience down very strictly with regard to length." [2]   In effect this witness suggested a new mode of taking accounts,[3] which was to a large extent indorsed by the recommendations of the Chancery Commission in 1852.[4]

(iii) Further delays could be caused by taking exceptions to the master's report when it came up for confirmation. This was an old standing abuse. Roger North tells us [5] that his brother, when he became chancellor, "found very great mischief by errors in master's reports, which, shown to him, had been set right: but the parties craftily let the report go and depended to bring it back by exceptions, and so torment the court with abundance of frivolous matters for experiment, and come off at last with such a slip which carries the costs, and is an immense vexation to the parties."

---

[1] It will be seen from App. II. (3) that this system was substantially unchanged in 1850.

[2] Parlt. Papers 1826 xv App. A. 282.   [3] Ibid 285.

[4] "We are of opinion that the system of proceeding to take accounts by charge and discharge, state of facts, and counter-state of facts [see App. II. (3)] should be entirely abolished. We think that an account should be taken in the court of Chancery in the same way in which it would be taken by any man of business. The accounting party should bring in his account, and should furnish a copy to the opposite party. This account should be gone through, not, as at present, from time to time, and at considerable intervals, but as far as practicable continuously. The accounts should be kept in the office for reference when necessary, and should not be annexed to the Report in the form of Schedules . . . the Report stating the results merely, not the materials upon which these results were arrived at," Parlt. Papers 1852 xxi 34.

[5] Lives of the Norths i 261.

North tried to remedy this by a rule which, as his brother explains, made the evil much worse; "for it introduced two reports instead of one and multiple attendances." In the eighteenth and at the beginning of the nineteenth centuries, this evil was aggravated by the possibility of appealing from a decision on these exceptions from court to court—from the master of the Rolls or the vice-chancellor to the chancellor, and from him to the House of Lords.[1]

(iv) As a concrete instance of the effects of this system let us take the bill of costs in the case of *Morgan v. Lord Clarendon*,[2] which was analysed by Mr. Winter in his evidence before the Chancery commission. This case had begun in 1808, and in 1824 it was still proceeding. The whole of the bills of costs up to that date amounted to £3,719 19s. 2d. Deducting the stamp duties, it amounted to £3,590 18s. 10d. The expenses of the master's office alone were £1,716 8s. 10d., being nearly half the expenses of the whole suit. In this case no counsel had been employed before the master, so that these expenses included simply the expenses of the master, his clerk, and six solicitors, for ordinary routine work. Of this sum £799 19s. 6d. was paid to the master, and £39 18s. as gratuities to his clerk; so that the fees paid to the master and his clerk were nearly half as much as were paid to the whole of the six solicitors in the case. Moreover, it appeared that the fees paid to the master were only £249 less than the fees paid to counsel and all the other officials of the court put together. It would seem, therefore, that, at the beginning of the nineteenth century, as at the beginning of the eighteenth century, the procedure in the master's offices was the "very worst part of the business of the court."[3]

Hearing and Judgment.

The actual hearing of the case was a lengthy business. The number of parties to be heard was often very large—let us recall a passage from the immortal scene in the court of Chancery with which Bleak House opens: "'Mr. Tangle,' says the Lord High Chancellor, latterly somewhat restless under the eloquence of that learned gentleman . . . 'have you nearly concluded your argument?' 'M'lord, no—variety of points—feel it my duty t'submit—ludship,' is the reply that slides out of Mr. Tangle. 'Several members of the bar are still to be heard, I believe?' says the Chancellor with a slight smile. Eighteen of Mr. Tangle's learned friends, each armed with a little summary of eighteen hundred sheets, bob up like eighteen hammers in a pianoforte, make eighteen bows, and

---

[1] Report of a committee of the House of Lords in 1823, cited by Beames, Parlt. Papers 1826 xv 90.

[2] Ibid App. A. 155, 276-277.

[3] Parkes, Chancery 283, citing a writer of 1707.

drop into their eighteen places of security." Moreover, as is indicated in this passage, the delay at the hearing was augmented
by the fact that there was apparently no limit to the number of
counsel that might be heard for one party.   An instance was adduced before the Chancery Commission in which eight or nine
counsel were employed on one side.   As Mr. Beames, the secretary to that Commission, pointed out, this was an abuse which
was tolerated neither in the House of Lords nor in the courts of
common law.[1]

But the worst delays were experienced in the office of the
registrars.   They could do much to impede or expedite a suit,
firstly by giving it a worse or a better place in the list, and secondly
by the slowness or speed with which they drew up the various
orders of the court, which were made in the course of a suit, and
the final decree.   Of the first point I have already spoken.   We
have seen that in the seventeenth century a regular trade was
carried on by the registrars in the placing of causes in the lists,
which was styled "heraldry."[2]   The abuse in this form seems to
have almost disappeared in the eighteenth century;[3] though, according to Mr. Lowe, the registrar sometimes manipulated the list;[4]
and a similar abuse had emerged in the form of concessions by the
chancellor to counsel to hear cases out of their turn.[5]   But the
second point—delays in drawing up the orders of the court and the
final decree—was a matter of complaint throughout the eighteenth
century, and was prominent in the evidence given to the first
Chancery Commission.

To a certain extent the delay in drawing up orders and
decrees was inevitable.   As the Commissioners pointed out, "the
judgment for a plaintiff in a court of equity is not, as in a court of
law, simply a decision upon a definite point in his favour; but, in
almost all cases in which he succeeds, the decree to which he is
entitled, embraces several points, finally disposes of some, and
directs various enquiries or accounts, with a view to the determination of others; and it is not easy nor always possible for the
Registrar to write down at once full minutes of such a decree as
ought to follow the judgment which the court has given."[6]
Moreover, there was no adequate increase of the number of deputy
registrars to cope with the increasing business of the court.   Even
after the appointment of a vice-chancellor in 1813, there was no
increase in their number, though the appointment of an additional

[1] Parlt. Papers 1826 xv 101; ibid App. A. 172.
[2] Vol. i 426; Lives of the Norths i 266-267.
[3] It hardly figures at all in the evidence given before the Commission of 1826.
[4] Parlt. Papers 1826 xv App. A. 171.
[5] Ibid.   [6] Ibid 1826 xv 16.

judge necessarily added greatly to their work.[1] But, even after
these allowances have been made, there can be little doubt that
needless and even wilful delays were caused. In the first place,
there is evidence that, in spite of specific and repeated orders[2] to
the contrary, the registrars stuffed the decrees with needless
recitals.[3] In the second place, there is evidence that solicitors
who did not complain and who took plenty of office copies, could
get preferential treatment.[4] In the third place, the drafting of
correct minutes of the judgment was often a difficult matter in
complicated cases, and occasioned much delay. North tried to
remedy this defect by drafting the minutes of his own judgments
in such cases.[5] Generally these minutes were drafted by the
registrar, and read to the court in the presence of the judges and
counsel.[6] But this practice does not seem to have been very
satisfactory. Motions to vary the minutes were common—so
common that orders were frequently made to prevent the abuse of
this procedure, and to fix a time within which such motions must
be brought.[7] Matters grew worse at the beginning of the nineteenth century. The custom of reading the minutes to the court
dropped, owing to increased pressure of business;[8] and the orders
fixing a time limit for motions to vary fell into disuse.[9] The
parties were left to settle them, with the result that there was
much delay in the drafting of decrees.[10] This led to the bringing

---

[1] Parlt. Papers 1826 xv 86-87.

[2] Sanders, Orders i 179-180 (Lord Coventry 1635); ibid ii 568 (Lord Hardwicke 1743).

[3] Mr. Winter said, " the expense of these orders is vastly augmented by the useless statements which are inserted in them. The Commissioners are aware that the registrar's regulated charge for drawing orders is 3s. 6d. a side. Now the original decree containing fifty-one sides, the introductory part of it sets forth (as it is now the custom to do) the bill and answers, and occupies forty-five sides. It is hardly neces- sary to observe that it is wholly useless to set forth any of those pleadings," Parlt. Papers 1826 xv App. A. 277; for earlier complaints of this kind see vol. i 441; and see Commons Journals xxi 892 for a similar complaint made by the House in 1732.

[4] See Mr. Lowe's Evidence, Parlt. Papers 1826 xv App. A. 168, an extract from which is cited vol. i 442.

[5] Lives of the Norths i 263—" To prevent the colour they used for delay in cases decreed upon points nicely decided, and also to prevent motions for settling such orders, which often was done to jog the matter again, and see if the opinion of the court would alter, his lordship has frequently ordered the registrar to attend him in the afternoon and take the ordering part penned by himself."

[6] There is an order to this effect in 1654, Sanders, Orders i 265; this practice apparently continued to the end of the eighteenth century, as Mr. Vizard said, " I can remember that when the hearing of a cause had arrived at its conclusion, the counsel and the solicitor standing by the registrar the court dictated to the registrar what in truth amounted to all the minutes of the decree," Parlt. Papers 1826 xv App. A. 47; but according to Gilbert, Forum Romanum 162-163, the decree was generally settled by the parties and the registrar, and it was only in case of a difference of opinion that an appeal was made to the court.

[7] See orders of 1657, 1721, and 1725 cited ibid 88.

[8] Ibid 16.   [9] Ibid 88.

[10] Mr. Vizard said, " I have experienced great delay in adjusting the minutes; I have had numerous attendances before the registrar . . . ; I have had frequent

of motions to vary, long after all concerned had any distinct recollection of what had really been decided ; and it produced so much confusion that even the Chancery Commission of 1826 recommended that a time limit should again be imposed on these motions.[1]

Rehearings and Appeals.

Even when the decree had been drafted, the suitor was by no means out of the wood.   At any time before enrolment a petition for rehearing could be made to the chancellor or other judge who had heard the case ;[2] and for that reason no one was in any hurry to enroll the decree.[3]   In some cases, even, it was possible to vacate the enrolment.[4]   If this was not possible, the aggrieved party could still proceed by bill of review.   " It," says Maddock,[5] "lies against those who were parties to the original bill and against them only, and must be either for error apparent on the face of the decree, or upon some new matter, as a release receipt etc., proved to have been discovered since."   It seems to have been thought, as early as 1536, that something in the nature of a bill of review for error in law could be brought before the chancellor ;[6] and that such a bill would lie for errors of this kind was settled at the beginning of the seventeenth century.[7]   Bacon's orders show that at that time it lay also where new matters of fact had emerged after the decree.[8]   Thus, in 1742, a bill of this kind was brought on the discovery of new matter, after two trials and a decree establishing a will.   In consequence of this new evidence another trial was ordered ; and, on a verdict for the heir,

attendances on my counsel on the subject, and sometimes meetings and conference with the different counsel, with a view to settle what the minutes were, the court not having given explicit directions; and I believe that this in many cases has led to the incurring of considerable expense " . . . and, " to delay of more than weeks on some occasions," Parlt. Papers 1826 xv App. A. 47 ; see also Mr. Winter's evidence, ibid 313.

[1] Ibid 18.

[2] Maddock, op. cit. ii 356 ; complaints of the delays so caused were common in the seventeenth century, Parkes, Chancery 126, 219 ; Lives of the Norths i 263 ; Spence, op. cit. i 393 ; on one occasion in 1620 Bacon made a decree with this note appended, " nevertheless, in regard I am so straightened for time, that I cannot now peruse my former orders, I reserve to myself to alter it, if I shall find cause," Monro, Acta 294-295.

[3] " The signing and enrolling of decrees with expedition is not encouraged, because if there is a small mistake in a decree, it occasions the expense of an appeal to the Lords or a bill of revivor," Maddock, op. cit. ii 356 ; but it would seem that the practice was not quite fixed in this way at the end of the sixteenth century, as in 1596 the Lord Keeper seemed to think a rehearing irregular after the decree had been drawn up and entered by the registrar, and before it had been " drawn up at large" and signed, Monro, Acta 687.

[4] Maddock, op. cit. ii 357-358.   [5] Ibid 409.

[6] Y.B. 27 Hy. VIII. Mich. pl. 6 (p. 15).

[7] Rolle, Ab. i 382, citing cases of 8 and 15 James I.

[8] Order 1 ; Spence, op. cit. i 398-399.

the former decree was reversed.[1] Even if a bill of review failed, it was still open to appeal—from the vice-chancellor or master of the Rolls to the chancellor, and from him to the House of Lords; and in all these appeals, except in the case of appeals to the House of Lords, new evidence was admitted.[2] Moreover, the chancellor could, like the judge of first instance, rehear a case brought to him on appeal.[3]

It thus appears that the impossible attempt of the court to produce a perfect decree prevented any kind of decent finality. So far was this carried that in 1686 it was held that a plaintiff, after his bill had been dismissed by the House of Lords, could bring another bill, which was partly original and partly a bill of review, for discovery of a deed, in order that he might again apply to the House of Lords;[4] and this case was cited as good law by Mitford[5]—though it was apparently conceded that no such bill would lie on an allegation of error in the decree itself.[6]

The conduct of a suit in equity.

At common law the parties employed their own attornies. We have seen that, during the Middle Ages, attornies, thus employed to conduct legal business, had become officers of the court.[7] But they were only officers of the court in a limited sense. The court admitted them and controlled them. They were not paid by the court. They lived by their own practice, which, subject to the rules of the court, they conducted in their own way. It is true that some parts of the proceedings in a common law action were at one time conducted by the paid officials of the court. We have seen that the clerks in the prothonotaries' offices had at one time a good deal to do with the settlement of the pleadings. But we have seen that, by the middle of the seventeenth century, this work had come to be done by the attornies, the pleaders under the bar, or by counsel.[8] But in the newer courts and councils, which had assumed a distinct existence in the Tudor period, a different system had been pursued. Both in the Star Chamber and in the court of Chancery there were officials who acted as the attornies of the parties.[9] In the court of Chancery these officials were at first the Six Clerks. During the seventeenth and eighteenth centuries their place was taken by the private solicitors of the parties and the sixty clerks;[10] and at the end of the eighteenth century, these private solicitors of the

---

[1] Attorney-General v. Turner Ambler 587.   [2] Vol. i 438.   [3] Ibid.
[4] Barton v. Searle 1 Vern. 416.   [5] Pleading (2nd ed.) 79.
[6] 1 Vern. at p. 418.   [7] Vol. ii 316-318; vol. vi 432-444.
[8] Vol. iii 652-653; vol. vi 445-446.   [9] Vol. i 421-422, 500; vol vi 454-456.
[10] Vol. vi 455.

parties had ousted the sixty clerks.[1] But, as might perhaps have been expected, considerable traces remained at the end of that century of the older system; and these survivals helped to increase the expense and delay of a suit in equity.

Every suitor in the court of Chancery must appoint a clerk in court, who was supposed to act as his solicitor in court, to advise his private solicitor, and from whom copies of the pleadings must be obtained.[2] Though the fees paid to these clerks in court amounted to an insignificant sum, compared with the vast sums which were spent in the master's offices, they all added to the expense; and they obviously tended to increase the delay of a suit.[3] One solicitor told the Commissioners that he paid them annually about £200 a year out of his client's money;[4] and many witnesses agreed that they were wholly useless.[5] That these witnesses were right can be seen from the fact that it was quite a usual occurrence for the same clerk in court to act for adverse parties;[6] and from Mr. Lowe's statement that a "Mr. Shaddick was a good clerk in court even when he was a lunatic."[7] Indeed, as he pointed out he had reason to regret the lunatic—"his successor has, since his declared lunacy, got my bills from the office, and has doubled the charges for attendance. It is shameful the way they get money from us and the suitors for ideal attendances."[8]

To this system of procedure we can apply the criticism which Gibbon, at the end of his forty-fourth chapter, applied to the Roman law under Justinian. It was "a mysterious science and a profitable trade," and "the innate perplexity of the study was involved in tenfold darkness by the private industry of the practitioners." The results also were the same. "The expense of the pursuit sometimes exceeded the value of the prize, and the fairest rights were abandoned by the poverty or prudence of the claimants.[9] Such costly justice might tend to abate the spirit of

---

[1] It would appear from the evidence of Mr. Lowe, Parlt. Papers 1826 xv App. A. 162, that, when he began to practice in London in 1785, "the sixty or under clerks had great skill in the course of the court; had a great part of the solicitation business of the suitors; and were in fact their 'attornies when so employed. Since then that state of the Six Clerks office is completely upset, and I do not know a sixty clerk of any considerable business as a practitioner, nor do I think that they know much of the business or course of the court; in consequence of which the solicitors have now become the attornies of the suitors, and do their business."

[2] Evidence of Mr. Forster, ibid 256-257.

[3] Evidence of Mr. Vizard, ibid 43.   [4] Ibid.

[5] Mr. Vizard, ibid; Mr. Lowe, ibid 169; Mr. Forster, ibid 256-257.

[6] Ibid 43.   [7] Ibid 169.   [8] Ibid.

[9] "What is obvious is, that many parties die after years of litigation, but before their rights are established; and that many suits end in compromises, by which some parties obtain advantages to which they are not entitled, whilst others sacrifice advantages to which they are entitled, in order to prevent the loss of the whole in costs," evidence of Mr. Bickersteth, Parlt. Papers 1826 xv App. A. 217; cp. vol. i 442.

litigation, but the unequal pressure serves only to increase the influence of the rich, and to aggravate the misery of the poor. By these dilatory and expensive proceedings the wealthy pleader obtains a more certain advantage than he could hope from the accidental corruption of his judge." It was in vain that the Chancery Commissioners tried to shift the blame on to the suitors and their advisers.[1] It was the system which was at fault, as Mr. Winter conclusively proved to the Commissioners in the following passage of his evidence:[2] "When it is said that the delays in the court of Chancery rest with the solicitors, the observation seems to imply, that a solicitor and an attorney are two different persons; for no one hears of the delays of attornies in the courts of law. But everyone knows that every attorney is a solicitor, and every solicitor an attorney. . . . To say therefore that the delays in equity are attributable to solicitors, is to assume that a solicitor is divided into two parts; the one all activity, the other all indolence; and that whilst he bestows all his energies on the court of law, he reserves all his sloth for the court of equity. But surely the obvious explanation of it all is to be found in the difference between the instrument which the solicitor has to use in the court of law, and the instrument he has to use in a court of equity; the essence of the practice of our courts of law is dispatch; and I have no difficulty in saying that the essence of that of our courts of equity is delay." But we have seen that the procedure of the common law courts was far from perfect. Let us now take a comparative view of the defects of these two instruments for the dispensation of justice.

(2) *The comparison between the defects of the common law and the equity procedure.*

There are certain points of similarity between the defects of the common law and the equity procedure, but there are more points of difference; and though, on the whole, the defects in the equity procedure were far more burdensome to the suitor than the defects in the common law procedure, there were certain points in which the equity procedure was superior to that of the common law. I shall consider, firstly, the points in which the two systems resembled, and, secondly, the points in which they differed from one another.

(i) Both systems were old systems which, at the end of the eighteenth century, were quite unsuited to modern needs. Both contained many survivals which had long lost all the meaning

---

[1] See the passage cited vol. i 442-443.
[2] Parlt. Papers 1826 xv App. A. 308; and cp. App. II. (1).

which they had ever possessed. At common law the need to insert continuances on the record,[1] in equity the existence of the Six Clerks[2] and the need to employ a clerk in court,[3] may be taken as examples. In both systems the rules of procedure were uncodified. They rested partly on a few orders of the court, which had in many cases been superseded by the silent growth of new rules, but mainly on its traditional practice. The authority for that practice was partly numerous decided cases, and partly the usage of the offices of the courts.[4] Both systems were needlessly expensive. Rules might become obsolete or be evaded in practice; but, if the working of any of these rules carried a fee to an official, the fee remained. At common law the old writs for summoning a jury, and the old fees payable for those writs, still remained, though the jury was summoned in quite another fashion;[5] and the ceremony of passing the nisi prius record was maintained, because it entitled officials to fees for work which had come to be done, not as formerly by themselves, but by the attornies.[6] The whole of the equity procedure was permeated with the pernicious system of extravagant payment for copies of documents which were not needed.[7] In both systems sinecure and saleable offices, the work of which was either not done at all or done by deputies, abounded.[8]

(ii) But, in spite of these resemblances, it is the points of difference which are the most remarkable. In three points, and I think in three points only, was the system of equitable procedure superior to that of the common law. Firstly, there was one uniform writ—the writ of subpœna—by which the defendant was summoned. This contrasted favourably with the multifarious and devious ways by which a common law action could be begun.[9] Secondly, we have seen that at common law the litigant must elect some one of the various causes of action;[10] and, when the cause of action had been selected, each litigant must elect, at different stages in that action, between some one of several expedients. He must either demur or plead; and, if he pleaded, he must either confess and avoid, or traverse.[11] And, not only must he elect some one of these different expedients, he must word his pleading so as to fit exactly the facts of his case.[12] His whole case, whatever might be its intrinsic merits, were staked upon the plan of campaign which his pleader chose to adopt, and

---

[1] Above 260.   [2] Vol. i 421-422, 440-441.   [3] Above 370.
[4] For the authorities for the common law practice see above 261-262; for the orders issued by the chancellors see vol. v 265-266; above 343.
[5] Above 257-258.   [6] Above 258-259.   [7] Vol. i 426-427, 441-442.
[8] Vol. i 246-251, 256-261, 424-425, 439-441.
[9] Above 249-250.   [10] Above 248.   [11] Above 266, 269.
[12] Above 304-305.

the words which he chose to employ. This, as we shall see, was never the case in equity. From the earliest times the chancellors had always tried to judge according to the substantial merits of the case;[1] and, though demurrers and pleas were known in the court of Chancery, it was always open to a defendant to demur to one part of the plaintiff's case, to plead to another, and to answer the rest. Moreover, failure to prove a plea or demurrer merely meant that he was thrown back on an answer; and bills and answers could always be amended.[2] We shall see that the rules as to the drafting of bills and answers came to be technical enough; and that they expressed in tortuous and artificial language, with a plentiful accompaniment of fiction, the real case of the parties.[3] But it was never the case that a mistake merely of word or form was irretrievable, and precluded any further examination of the case. Thirdly, we have seen that the common law methods of questioning the decision of the court, by means of a writ of error or a bill of exceptions, were extremely archaic; and that their inconvenience was only partially remedied by the growth of the practice of granting new trials.[4] On the other hand, equity had always adopted the straightforward method of questioning a decision by a rehearing of the case.[5]

In other respects, it seems to me, the advantage rests with the common law procedure.

The common law rules as to such matters as process,[6] the delivery of the pleadings,[7] and judgment,[8] were to a large extent conventional, and were permeated with legal fictions. But the conventions and the fictions were in the main directed towards the speedy conduct of the action in accordance with modern needs. On the other hand, the equity rules aimed at the doing of complete justice regardless of any other consideration. No doubt the administrative character of much of the equitable jurisdiction necessitated many more delays than the trial of a common law action. But we have seen that the delays need not have been so great if the ideal of completeness had not been so high.[9] By aiming at perfection the equity procedure precluded itself from attaining the more possible, if more mundane, ideal of substantial justice. And the ideal aimed at was made the more impossible by the very small control which the chancellor was able or chose to exercise on the machinery and the officials of his court.[10] As compared with the three courts of common law the judicial strength of the Chancery was ridiculously small. Necessarily

---

[1] Vol. v 285-286; cp. an extract from a decree of 1591, cited Monro, Acta 613-614.
[2] Below 383, 392.   [3] Below 394-398, 402-404.   [4] Vol. i 222-224, 225-226.
[5] Above 368-369.   [6] Above 253-255.   [7] Above 256.
[8] Above 259.   [9] Above 347-348.   [10] Vol. i 427-428, 435, 436.

control was stricter in the common law courts. It was not possible that general orders issued by the judges, and even statutes dealing with practice, should be so systematically disregarded in the common law courts as they were in the court of Chancery.[1] It was not so easy for abuses to grow up in the offices of the common law courts, and for these abuses to attain by lapse of time the status of established rules of practice.[2] Nor was there in the courts of common law the same temptation to delay as there was in the court of Chancery. In an ordinary common law action there were certain steps to be taken and certain fees to be earned —the sooner those steps were taken and those fees earned the better for all concerned. In many suits in equity large masses of property were in court, and the longer the suit lasted the more of it went to the officials of the court and the legal advisers of the parties. If it was a contested suit they probably absorbed the whole. "Cases have occurred within my own knowledge," said Mr. Bickersteth,[3] "in which the whole property sought to be administered in Chancery has proved insufficient to pay the costs of the suit; and in which the last question discussed in the cause has been how the deficient fund was to be apportioned amongst the different solicitors in part payment of their respective bills." The result of the case of *Jarndyce v. Jarndyce* was thus by no means unique.

The common law procedure was more archaic than the procedure of the Court of Chancery. The former was mediæval, and some of it quite early mediæval. The latter was developed into its modern technical shape in the sixteenth and seventeenth centuries.[4] Hence the need for admitting changes, whether by way of fiction or otherwise, was more apparent in the case of the common law procedure. Because the procedure of the court of Chancery was less archaic, the need was not so apparent; and fewer attempts were made to adapt it to modern needs. In point of fact the procedure of the court of Chancery was, at the end of the eighteenth century, as badly adapted to the needs of the day as the mediæval procedure of the real actions to the needs of the sixteenth century. But no attempt was made by the court to meet new needs, such as was made by the common law courts when they adapted the action of ejectment to the new role of trying the title to the freehold. The time of the chancellor was too

---

[1] Vol. i 426 and n. 4, 428; above 343.
[2] For this cause for the deterioration of the procedure of the court see vol. i 426 n. 4, and Spence, op. cit. i 401-402, there cited; vol. v 265-266.
[3] Parlt. Papers 1826 xv App. A. 217.
[4] "In the time of Elizabeth and her immediate successors, the common rules of practice of the court had become well settled, differing little in principle from those of the present day," Spence, op. cit. i 379.

much occupied, and his control was too lax. Too many officials had a vested interest in things as they were; and lawyers who understood a system which supplied them with an ample livelihood were likely to rally to its defence. In fact, all the abuses of the court found defenders when it was put upon its trial before the first Chancery Commission. Barristers spoke in defence of the system of pleading; and the usefulness of the clerks in court, and even of the Six Clerks, was defended. This evidence shows that the court and its officials and practitioners had become so close a body, that they had lost touch, in a way in which the common law courts and their officials and practitioners had never lost touch, with the common life and public opinion of the day. Hence, although there was stagnation enough and abuses enough in the common law procedure at the end of the eighteenth century, there was never acquiescence in any such systematic injustice as was perpetrated by the procedure of the court of Chancery, in its endeavour to accomplish, by means of an utterly inadequate staff and an obsolete machinery, an unattainable ideal of complete justice.

The largest part of this monstrous system of procedure, which "had its decaying houses and its blighted lands in every shire, its worn out lunatic in every madhouse, and its dead in every church-yard,"[1] was gradually swept away by the reforms of the nineteenth century. As was the case with the common law procedure,[2] something was done by the legislation which followed the Whig victory of 1830.[3] But, in spite of improvements in the machinery of the court, its system of procedure and pleading remained much as it was; and, as was the case with the system of common law procedure and pleading, a fuller measure of reform did not come till the middle of the century. In 1852 Acts were passed to amend the practice and procedure of the court,[4] which are the counterpart of the Common Law Procedure Act of the same year.[5] These Acts swept away the system of taking evidence;[6] and the cumbrous machinery of the masters' offices, and the masters themselves, were abolished.[7] The judicial duties of the masters were handed over to the judges at Chambers, and their other duties to their chief clerks.[8] Moreover, one of the Acts passed in 1852 to amend the practice of the court, and later Acts, went some way towards giving the common law courts powers which had formerly only belonged to the court of Chancery, and the court of Chancery powers which had formerly only belonged to the courts of common

---

[1] Bleak House.   [2] Above 251, 262.   [3] Vol. i 443-444.
[4] 15, 16 Victoria cc. 80, 86.   [5] 15, 16 Victoria c. 76.
[6] 15, 16 Victoria c. 86 § 28.
[7] 15, 16 Victoria c. 80; vol. i 444-445.   [8] Ibid.

law.[1] The court of Chancery, therefore, could no longer hang up a suit by sending a case for the consideration of a court of common law. The same Act of 1852[2] also carried somewhat further a tendency, which the Legislature had already approved,[3] of allowing certain cases to be heard without the necessity for the cumbrous bill and answer,[4] and of allowing the court to give in some cases partial relief,[5] or to make a merely declaratory order.[6] But it did not deal adequately with the objection that no satisfactory procedure was provided for getting the opinion of the court on some specific point arising in the administration of an estate, e.g. the construction of a will, without a decree for the administration of the whole estate. The first Chancery Commission seemed to think that this might have been done ;[7] but it never was done in practice ;[8] and no sufficient procedure was provided for this purpose till the Rules of the Supreme Court devised the procedure by way of originating summons.[9]

In equity, as at common law, the changes made by these Acts paved the way to the fusion of jurisdiction effected by the Judicature Act, and the formation of the modern code of procedure contained in the Rules of the Supreme Court. And, just as the older system of common law procedure has contributed something to those rules, so we can see in the uniform writ of summons, in the abolition of separate forms of action, and in the substitution for writs of error of appeals by way of rehearing, the influence of procedural ideas which have come from the court of Chancery. Similarly, we shall see that the new system of pleading, inaugurated by these rules, owes something to the system of pleading practised in that court.[10] To the history of that system we must now turn.

Pleading

The system of pleading developed by the court of Chancery was as unique as its system of procedure. Its unique character

---

[1] 15, 16 Victoria c. 86 §§ 61, 62; 17, 18 Victoria c. 125 §§ 68, 79, 83; 21, 22 Victoria c. 27; 25, 26 Victoria c. 42; vol. i 636-638.

[2] 15, 16 Victoria c. 86.

[3] See Parlt. Papers 1852 xxi 12-14; in addition to the Acts there specified it was pointed out that Lord Cottenham, in his General Orders of 1850, had allowed claims to be filed and proved or rebutted by affidavits, without formal pleadings.

[4] Thus 15, 16 Victoria c. 86 § 45 provided for a new procedure by way of summons.

[5] § 51—the court was allowed to decide between some of the parties without making others interested also parties.

[6] § 50.   [7] Parlt. Papers, 1826 xv 29.

[8] Mr. Birrell says, A Century of Law Reform 195-196, "it is now a feat of great difficulty to obtain in the Chancery Division a general decree for the administration of the estate of a deceased person. In the days even subsequent to 1852 such decrees with all the costs they entailed were matters of daily occurrence."

[9] Orders 54, 55.   [10] Below 407.

was, as I have already indicated,[1] due to the fact that it was influenced by the two very different conceptions of the methods and objects of pleading held by the Roman civil law and the common law.

The first set of conceptions led, as we have seen, to the idea that the parties should state the facts of their respective cases in their own way, that the defendant should be obliged to make any discovery in his power in order that the real facts might be ascertained, that both parties should have a large liberty to amend if they made a mistaken or inaccurate statement, and that on these statements—assisted by any evidence which the parties might adduce—the court should judge which of these rival contentions prevailed, and adjust the rights of the parties accordingly. These conceptions might also have led to the rule that the court should exercise a supervision over the statements made by the parties;[2] and there is some indication in earlier days of an attempt to exercise this supervision.[3] As at common law the pleadings were entered by the prothonotaries,[4] so in equity the pleadings were at first entered by the registrars;[5] to the end they continued to be filed with the Six Clerks;[6] and we shall see that, in the sixteenth and seventeenth centuries, the court exercised a strict control over their style and draftmanship.[7] This might easily have led to the adoption of the rule of the Roman civil law, which prevailed in the ecclesiastical courts, that the pleadings must be settled in court, and must be authenticated by it.[8] But this step was never taken. Both on this and on other matters there was, on the contrary, a reversion to the very different set of conceptions which were growing up in the common law.

We have seen that, at the end of the mediæval period, the pleading in a common law action was tending to be conducted out of court by the legal advisers of the parties; and that it was directed to raise some one clear and certain issue of law or of fact.[9] Both these ideas made their influence felt in the Chancery. Though the pleadings in a suit in equity were filed in court as the case proceeded, though the court exercised some control over their style and draftmanship, the parties were allowed to shape their statements in their own way. The bill of the plaintiff and

---

[1] Above 337-339.   [2] Essays A.A.L.H. ii 773-774, 775.

[3] Orders in Chancery made in Henry V.'s reign as to the duties of the registrars (Notarii sive Tabelliones), Sanders, Orders 7c; moreover, the master of the Rolls and one of the other masters are given power, in the absence of the chancellor, "causas dirigere et in ordinem disponere (videlicet) assignare terminos ad respondendum replicandum rejungendum testes producendum eorumque dicta publicandum dies ad causas audiendum et cetera brevia faciendum," ibid 7d; cp. Langdell, op. cit. 775 n. 1.

[4] Vol. iii 642-645.   [5] Note 3.

[6] Parlt. Papers 1826 xv App. A. 138, evidence of Mr. Vesey.

[7] Below 388-389.   [8] Langdell, op. cit. 767-768.   [9] Vol. iii 628, 633, 641-648.

the answer of the defendant were shaped by themselves. It is true that the court permitted a liberty of amendment which was unknown at common law. But, like the bill and answer, these amendments were applied for and made on the initiative of the parties. Similarly a defendant, instead of answering, was allowed to plead or demur to a bill; and we shall see that common law influences are traceable in some of the rules relating to these pleas and demurrers. After the answer there might be further pleadings —replications and rejoinders; and in form the parties were made nominally to come to issue as at common law. But nominally only, because equity set out to decide, not one single issue arrived at by a course of pleading directed to produce such an issue, but to do complete justice to the parties in respect of the matters set out in the bill.[1]

Thus, although certain of the common law rules and ideas were received, they were modified by their new environment. In fact, it would have been impossible to have received them in their entirety, unless the influence of the ideas derived from the Roman civil law had been wholly eliminated. This was very far from being the case; and so we can see in the system of equity pleading of the sixteenth and seventeenth centuries a curious mixture of opposite ideas. In the bill and answer, in the discovery which the defendant was obliged to give, and in the liberty of amendment, we can see one set of influences. In the system of pleading out of court, in the pleas and demurrers, and in the nominal issue, we can see the other set. Naturally the system which resulted was quite unique. But it was inevitable that, when the consequences of these very different conceptions came to be worked out, it would be necessary for the law to develop in accordance with either one or the other; and it was fairly clear that it could not, consistently with the substantive principles of equity, develop in the direction of any further assimilation of common law ideas; for the common law principles of pleading were unsuited both to the administrative work of the court, and to its avowed aim of doing justice in accordance with the actual facts of the case. And so we find, at the end of the eighteenth century, that the conceptions derived from the common law were tending to evaporate. Pleas and demurrers were being in practice deprived of their former importance, the joinder of issue was becoming a very formal affair, and all the pleading was coming to centre round the bill and answer.[2]

But this had been a gradual and almost an unconscious process; and it was never quite worked out to its logical conclusion. It was effected through the medium of a number of

---

[1] Above 338, 347-348.   [2] Below 392-393, 404-406.

changes in the structure of the bill and answer, in the growth of the practice of making exceptions to the answer, and, where necessary, of amending the bill. It resulted in making both the bill and answer documents very unlike anything that was ever produced in the sixteenth and early seventeenth centuries. The bill, as we have seen, became a "marvellous document which stated the plaintiff's ₁case at length and three times over"; [1] and this increase in the elaboration of the bill entailed a corresponding increase in the elaboration of the answer. It is true that neither bill nor answer wholly dropped the forms which they had assumed in the sixteenth and early seventeenth centuries, and the stereo-typed allegations which were then considered necessary to give the court jurisdiction. But there was added to the old forms a large amount of new matter, which, in effect, made for the partial elimination of many of those common law influences, which, in earlier days, had gone to the making of the system of equity pleading. And, though this effect tended to make that system of pleading more logical, it was not wholly beneficial; for, by de-priving the parties of short cuts which they had previously had to the termination of the suit, it lengthened the suit directly by making it necessary to go through the whole tedious procedure which has just been described; and it lengthened it indirectly by increasing the burden of work placed upon the inadequate staff of the court.

From this summary it is clear that the history of equity pleading falls into two fairly clearly marked chronological periods: (1) the sixteenth and early seventeenth centuries; and (2) the late seventeenth, the eighteenth, and the early nineteenth centuries.

(1) *The sixteenth and early seventeenth centuries.*

The first pleading of the plaintiff was the Bill. It is defined by West[2] as "a declaration in writing showing the plaintifes griefe, and the wrong which he supposeth to be done unto him by the defendant, and what damages he sustaineth by occasion thereof, praying process against him for redresse of the same"; and it is significant that West quotes some lines of Hostiensis to show what it contents should be.[3] In the developed system of equity pleading it consisted of nine parts: "the *first* part contains the address of the bill to the person or persons . . . holding the great seal. . . . The *second* part consists of the names of the

---

[1] Bowen, Administration of the Law in the reign of Queen Victoria, cited vol. i 646; below 394-402.
[2] Symboleography (ed. 1618) Pt. ii 194a, b.
[3] "Quis, quid, coram quo, quo jure petatur, et a quo,
Recte compositus quisque libellus habet."

plaintiffs and their descriptions.   The *third* is called the stating part of the bill and contains the plaintiff's case.   In the *fourth* place is a general charge of confederacy.   The *fifth* part (the charging part) consists of allegations of the defendant's pretences, and charges in evidence of them.   In the *sixth* part of the bill there is an averment that the acts complained of are contrary to equity, and that a court of equity alone can afford relief.   The *seventh* part (the interrogating part) consists of a prayer that the parties may answer the premises.   The prayer of the relief sought by the bill is the *eighth* part.   In the *ninth* part is a prayer of process."[1]   If this description be compared with the following specimen of a bill from the end of the sixteenth century,[2] it will be seen that all this elaboration is as yet in the future, and that the bills of that period corresponded much more closely with West's definition.

A BILL OF COMPLAINT FOR ENTRING INTO AND MAKING SECRET ESTATES OF COPYHOLD LANDES, WASTING PART THEREOF, AND MINGLING PART THEREOF WITH THE LANDES OF OTHERS, TO DISINHERIT THE PLAIN-TIFE BY HAVING THE COPIES THEREOF.

Humbly complaining sheweth unto your Honorable L. H.E. of B in the County of Yorke esquire :   That whereas H.E. late of S. Esquire deceased, father to your Orator, was in his lifetime by good and lawfull conveyance and assurance in the Law, lawfully seised to him and to his heires in fee simple, according to the custome of the Manor of W in the said Countie of Y, of one copyhold or customarie Mesuage or Tenement, and of certaine customarie lands, medowes, and pasture to the quantitie of 100 acres, or thereabouts : and the said H.E. your Orators father so being thereof seised as aforesaid, and being visited with sicknesse during the minority of your said Orator, by good and lawfull conveyance and assurance in the Law, and according to the custome of the said Manor of W, did convey, assure, and surrender the said copyhold or customarie Mesuage or Tenement, and other the premisses with the appurtenances, into the hands of A.B. the Lord of the said Manor, for the better maintenance, and to the use of your said Orator.   To have and to hold to your said Orator, and to his heires and assignes, at the will of the Lord, according to the custome of the said Manor : by force whereof, your Honors said Orator in the Court of the said Manor paid his fine, and was of the said copyhold and customarie tenements, with the appurtenances, by the then Steward of the said Manor of W. admitted tenant.   But so it is, if it may please your Honor, that all the Evidences and Copies, of, and con-cerning the said Mesuage, lands, tenements, and premisses, being left in the hands, custodie, and possession of your Orators said father whilest he lived, in right belonging unto your Lordships said Orator, are now by casuall and sinister meanes come to the hands and possession of one H.H. of D. in the said Countie of Y., who by colour of the having thereof, hath wrongfully entred into the said Mesuage, lands and premisses aforesaid, and hath made and conveyed unto himselfe, and to others to his use, divers and sundry secret

[1] Maddock, op. cit. ii 135-136; cp. Mitford, op. cit. 41-47; see below 394-398 for specimens of these bills.
[2] West, op. cit. Pt. ii 195-196, § 68.

Estates thereof, and doth pretend wholly to disinherit your Lordships said Orator of the same, notwithstanding your said Orator hath by divers and sundry meanes in friendly manner oftentimes sought to have the said Evidences and Copies, and requested the same at the hands of the said H.H. and also that he would yield unto your said Orator the quiet possession of the said Mesuage, lands, and premisses, to whom he doth well know the same in right to belong and appertaine : Yet that to doe, he hath not only denied and refused, and still doth deny and refuse to doe the same : but of his further malice against your said Orator, he doth threaten your Orator in such sort, that your Orator for want of the said Evidences and Copies, dareth not make his just and lawfull entry, in, and to the same : And also the said H. hath committed and doth continue daily great and outragious wastes and spoyles, in decaying of the Houses, felling downe of the Wood and Timber trees of the premisses, to your Orators great losse and disinherison, and contrarie to all right, equitie, and good conscience. In tender consideration whereof, and forasmuch as by the strict course of the common Lawes of this Realme, your L. said Orator hath not any ordinarie remedie for the obtaining and recovering of the said evidences and copies, for want of the certain knowledge of the contents and dates thereof, and what in them be contained, neither can your Orator learne against whom to commence any suit for the said mesuage, lands, and premisses, for that the said H.H. and others, to your Orator altogether unknown, have confederated themselves together against your said Orator, and have contrived and made amongst themselves divers secret estates and conveyances, and have so intermingled the same, to, and with other lands, tenements, and hereditaments, to, and with certaine of their owne freehold and inheritance, that your Orator knoweth not which the same be, nor how much thereof the said H.H. and other his confederates do severally hold, whereby to commence any action or suit, or make any lawful entry, into, or for the same, without your Orators great danger : and yet your Orator hopeth that upon the corporall oth of the said H.H. he will manifest such matter, whereby your Orator may the more better, easily, and readily, proceed and attaine to the recovering of his just and lawfull right and inheritance of the premisses ; for the furtherance whereof, it may please your good L to grant unto your said Orator, his Majesties most gracious Writ of Subpoena to be directed to the said H.H. commanding him thereby at a certaine day, and under a certaine paine therein to be limited, personally to be and appeare in his Ma. high Court of Chancery, then and there to answer to the premisses &c.

It will be clear from this specimen that the bill was a far more straightforward document than it afterwards became.   But, for all that, we can see, either in existence or in embryo, many of the parts of which the later bill consisted.   The first three parts—the address, the name and description of the plaintiff, and the stating part—are there.   The sixth part, in which the plaintiff avers that the acts are contrary to equity and that he can get no relief elsewhere, comes next ; and it is followed by and mixed up with the fourth part in which confederacy is charged.   Similarly the seventh and eighth parts are represented only by a general request for the examination of the defendant, and are not clearly distinguished from the fourth and sixth.   In fact, this general request for an examination of the defendant was all that was necessary, as, during the sixteenth century and down to the time of lord keeper Bridgeman (1667-1672), it was common for the chancellor to examine the parties in court.[1]   It was probably not till this practice ceased, at the end of the seventeenth or beginning of the eighteenth century, that the interrogating part of the bill assumed its modern form of detailed questions set out in the bill.   The ninth part which prays process is present.   The one part of which there is no trace is the fifth or charging part; and we shall see that there is reason to think that this is the latest addition to the bill, and that it is closely connected with the modern form assumed by the interrogating part.[2]   These developments were the work of the late seventeenth and eighteenth centuries.   We shall see that the change in the form of the interrogating part, and the addition of the charging part which followed this change, coupled with the later elaboration of both these parts, were the main factors in converting a comparatively simple statement into the artificial document of the later law.[3]

The bill having been filed, the defendant must meet it.   If he did not disclaim all interest in the subject matter,[4] he might adopt either (i) what may be called the common law methods of a demurrer or a plea, or (ii) what may be called the equitable method of an answer.

(i) If the defendant considered that the bill on its face disclosed no matter which called for an answer, he could demur.[5] There is an instance of a demurrer for want of proper parties as early as Edward IV.'s reign.[6]   If he wished to adduce some new matter, which was a defence to the bill, he could put in a plea.[7] A plea in equity was thus always in the nature of a plea in confession and avoidance.[8]   If the defendant proved his plea or

---

[1] Spence, op. cit. i 370 n. (b).

[2] Below 401.   [3] Below 400-402.

[4] " A defendant may disclaim all right or title to the matter in demand by the plaintiff's bill or by any part of it," Maddock, op. cit. ii 264; but, as he there points out, generally an answer was also required, so that a disclaimer would be part of the answer; this defence was known in the sixteenth century; it is first mentioned by Tothill, but not as a novelty, Spence, op. cit. i 372 n. (g).

[5] Bacon's Orders no. 58; in 1601 master Carew certified that, " it is required in all demurrers which are laid in to any bill exhibited in this court, that the causes alleged for the demurrer must be drawn out and grounded upon the assertions in the bill, in admitting the same to be true; and not upon any foreign matter that lieth not in the notice of the court, which must otherwise be averred by answer upon oath," Monro, Acta 22.

[6] Y.B. 8 Ed. IV. Trin. pl. 1, cited Spence, op. cit. i 373 n. (h); and cp. Y.B. 7 Hy. VII. Pasch. pl. 2, cited ibid n. (f)—a demurrer for want of equity.

[7] Bacon's Orders no. 58; Beek v. Hesill (Hy. IV.) Cal. (R.S.) ii xii.—a plea of the statute 4 Henry IV. c. 23; for this statute see vol. i 462.

[8] " A plea does not deny the equity, but brings forward a fact or a series of circumstances, forming, in their combined result, some one fact which displaces the equity," Maddock, op. cit. ii 238; for pleas in confession and avoidance see above 271-272.

demurrer there was an end of the case. Therefore the power to plead or demur gave the defendant a chance to put a summary end to the suit. The advantage of taking this course was recognized by Bacon who ordered that "demurrers and pleas which tend to discharge the suit shall be heard first upon every day of orders, that the subject may know whether he shall need further attendance or no."[1] But though the effect of successfully pleading or demurring was the same as at common law, the effect of a failure to support a plea or demurrer was very different. It did not mean that the plaintiff got judgment, but only that the defendant must put in another defence.[2] Moreover, in equity, the defendant was not, as at common law, restricted to a single alternative in his defence. It is true that a defendant would not both demur and plead, or demur and answer, to the whole bill, or on the same point.[3] But he could "demur to one part of a bill, plead to another, answer to another, and disclaim as to another."[4] We shall see, however, that, as the learning as to those pleas and demurrers grew more elaborate, some of the technical common law rules were applied to them.[5] We shall see that they might be overruled for want of form; and that then, in default of another demurrer or plea, the only recourse was to answer.[6]

(ii) Just as the bill was the statement of the plaintiff's case, so the answer was "that which the defendant pleadeth or saith in barre to avoid the plaintifes bill or action, either by confession and avoiding or by denying and traversing the materiall parts thereof."[7] At the beginning of the seventeenth century the answer was as plain a statement of the defendant's case, as the bill was of the plaintiff's. It was not till the interrogating part was added to the bill, that the answer necessarily assumed its later artificial and elaborate form;[8] and we have seen that this development probably did not take place till the end of the seventeenth or the beginning of the eighteenth century.[9] Take, for example, the answer given to the bill given above.[10] It runs as follows :—

---

[1] Order 57; cp. Chapman v. Turner (1739) 1 Atk. 54; cp. Mitford, Pleading 15.

[2] "After a demurrer has been overruled new defence may be made by a demurrer less extended, or by plea, or answer; and, after a plea has been overruled, defence may be made by demurrer, by a new plea, or by an answer; and the proceedings upon the new defence will be the same as if it had been originally made," Mitford, op. cit. 17.

[3] Maddock, op. cit. ii 225-226; Mitford, op. cit. 254.

[4] Ibid.   [5] Below 392.

[6] Below 392, 404.

[7] West, Symboleography Pt. II. 194b.

[8] Below 402-404.   [9] Above 379-380; below 399-401.

[10] West, Symboleography Pt. II. 196a-197b § 69.

The said defendant saith, that the said Bill of Complaint against him
exhibited into this honorable Court, is verie uncertaine, untrue, and insufficient
in the Law to be answered unto by the said defendant for divers and sundrie
apparant faults and imperfections therein contained : and devised and
exhibited into this honorable Court, partly of malice and evill will, without
any just cause conceived against the said def. to the intent thereby unjustly to
vexe and molest him with tedious travell, being an aged man, and to put him
to great expences, being verie poore : but chiefly to the intent and purpose to
wearie, impoverish, and terrifie him this defendant : Neverthelesse, if by the
order of this honorable Court, this defendant shall be compelled to make any
further or other answer unto the said untrue, incertain, and insufficient Bill of
Complaint, then and not otherwise the advantage of exception thereof to this
defendant, at all and everie time and times herafter saved, for further answere
thereunto, and for a full and plain declaration of the truth, touching so much
of the materiall contents of the said bill, as in any sort concerneth this
defendant, He for himselfe saith, That whereas the said complainant in his
said bill aleageth, that one H. E. his father deceased, was in his life time by
good and lawfull conveiance and assurance in the Law, lawfully seised to him
and his heires in fee simple, according to the custome of the said Manor of
W. in the said bill mentioned, of one copyhold or customary mesuage or
tenement, and of certaine customarie lands, medowes, and pastures, to the
quantitie of an hundred acres, or thereabouts : and that he being thereof so
seised, and visited with sicknesse, during the minority of the said complainant,
by good and lawfull conveyance and assurance in the Law, and according to
the custome of the said Manor of W. did convey, assure, and surrender the
same copyhold or customarie mesuage or tenement, and other the premisses,
with the appurtenances thereunto belonging, for his better maintenance, to
the use of the said complainant. To have and to hold to the said complainant, and to his heires and assignes, at the will of the said Lord,
according to the custome of the said Manor : And that by force thereof, the
said complainant in the Court of the said Manor paid his fine, and was of the
said copihold or customarie tenements with the appurtenances, by the then
Steward of the said Manor of W. admitted tenant. He this defendant saith,
that to his knowledge the said H. E. late father of the said complainant, was
never either lawfully seised to him and to his heires, according to the
custome of the said Manor of W. of the said tenements and premisses in the
said Bill mentioned, by any good and lawfull conveyance and assurance in
the Law, according to the custom of the said Manor : Nor did ever convey,
assure and surrender the said customarie tenements and other the premisses,
to the use of the said complainant, his heires and assignes : neither did the
said complainant ever pay his fine for the same in the said Court, neither was
he ever lawfully admitted tenant thereof, as he the said complainant in his
said Bill untruly pretendeth. And whereas the said complainant in his said
Bill also pretendeth, that the evidences and copies, of, and concerning the
said mesuage, lands, tenements, and premisses, being left in the hands,
custodie and possession of the said complainants father whilest he lived, in
right belonging unto this complainant, are now by casuall meanes commen to
the handes and possession of this defendant, and that he by colour of the
having thereof, hath wrongfully entred into the said mesuage, lands, and
premisses aforesaid, and hath made and conveied to himselfe, and to others
to his use, divers and sundrie secret estates therein, and doth pretend
thereof wholly to disinherit the said complainant. This defendant saith, that

none evidences or copies, of, or concerning the said mesuage, tenements and premisses, are by casuall meanes, or otherwise come to the hands or possession of this defendant, and that by colour of having thereof, he this defendant, neither wrongfully entred into the said mesuage, tenements and premisses, nor any part thereof, neither hath he this defendant conveyed, to himselfe, or to any other person to his use, divers and sundrie, or any secret estates therof, neither doth he pretend thereof wholy to disinherit the said complainant, as in the said Bill it is untruly alleaged : without that, that the said complainant by diverse and sundrie meanes in friendly maner hath oftentimes sought to have the said evidences and copies, and requested the same at the handes of this defendant : and also that he would yield unto your said Orator the quiet possession of the said mesuage, tenements, and premisses, or that he this defendant doth well know the same, in right to belong unto him the said complainant, as in the said Bill it is untruly alleaged : and without that, that he this defendant of malice against the said complainant doth threathen him the said complainant, in such sort, that he for want of the said evidences, dareth not make his just and lawfull entrie or clame, to and in the same premisses, or that he the said defendant hath or could commit, or doth or can continue daily committing great and outragious wastes and spoiles, in decaying of the houses, and felling downe of the woods and timber trees of the premisses, to the great losse and disherison of the said complainant, and contrary to all right, equity, and good conscience, as in and by his said Bill of complaint he hath most vainely and untruely alleaged.   For touching the said supposed threats this defendant saith, that he is a verie feeble poore old quiet man, verie desirous of the favor and good will of all men, and therefore neither willing nor able by his threats to terrifie or feare the said complainant, being a gentleman of worship, power, and living, having many kinsfolks, alies, friendes and servants, so that he this defendant, hath rather just cause to be afraid of the said complainant, then the said complainant to feare him.   And further touching the said wastes and spoiles, this defendant saith, that the said customarie or copihold lands in W. aforesaid, are holden of the Manor of W. aforesaid.   And without that, that the said complainant hath, or ever had any lawfull title to commence any action or suit, or to make any entrie, against or upon this defendant, for any lands, tenements or hereditament, in the said Bill of Complaint mentioned, as it is therein untruly alleadged : and without that, that this defendant can upon his corporall oth manifest such matter, whereby the said complainant may the more better, easily, and readily proceed and attain to the recovering of any just or lawfull right or inheritance or in any other maner then in this answer is set down, as the said complainant unwisely guesseth, and most vainely hopeth, as he in his said Bill alleageth : And without that, that any other matter, thing or things, clause, sentence, article or allegation in the said Bill of Complaint contained, materiall or effectuall in the Law to be answered unto by this defendant, and not herein confessed and avoided, denied or traversed, is true.   All which matters this defendant is readie to aver and proofe, as this honorable Court shall award : And therfore prayeth to be dismissed out of the same, with his reasonable costes and charges in this behalfe wrongfully and without cause sustained.

It will be observed that the answer begins by reserving all advantages that may be taken by exceptions to the bill.   This continued to the end to be the first clause in an answer.   It was, as Mitford has said, "probably intended to prevent a conclusion that the defendant, having submitted to answer the bill, admitted everything which by his answer he did not controvert, and especially such matters as he might have objected by demurrer or plea."[1] The answer then goes on to deny specifically and in detail the whole case of the plaintiff; and it concludes with a general traverse of all the allegations in the bill. This clause again was retained to the end, though as Mitford said,[2] it was unnecessary if the bill was otherwise fully answered.

Having now dealt with the possible courses open to the defendant, it remains to deal with the further steps that might be taken. I shall deal with them under the two heads of exceptions and references, and the further pleadings. Lastly, I shall say a few words as to the control exercised by the court over the pleadings at this period.

(i) *Exceptions and references.*—It was always open to the parties to take exceptions to the bill or answer; and such matters were referred to the master for his report.[3] A bill or answer was open to exception on two main grounds—firstly, that it did not contain a sufficiently clear statement, or, secondly, that its statements were impertinent or scandalous or both. I will cite one or two illustrations of these exceptions from Monro's collection. In 1598 a bill was referred for insufficiency to master Carew; and apparently there was reason to think that the name of the counsel who had signed it was forged.[4] In 1607 the same master made the following report as to an answer:[5] "I find the same faulty and peccant both in matter and form; wherein is unordinarily inserted much unnecessary and impertinent matter, drawing the said answer to unnecessary length by recrimination; and leaving the most material points, with which the defendants are charged, unanswered; wherefore, in my opinion, it were fit that the whole answer (being yet a rude and *indigesta moles*) should be committed to learned counsel, to be cast again by a perfect artificer into a new mould, and to be framed in a better form to answer the matter more effectively." In 1594 five de-

---

[1] Pleading 249.

[2] Ibid; for early instances of this clause see Spence, op. cit. i 373.

[3] Ibid 374.

[4] Monro, Acta 598—" This Court was this present day informed by Mr. Towse, being of the defendant's counsel, that the plaintiff hath lately put in a very insufficient bill against the defendant, whereunto the name of Mr. Edward Morrys, a counsellor of Gray's Inn, is subscribed, notwithstanding the same Mr. Morrys doth disavow the same "; cp. ibid 36 (1602), 628 (1592)

[5] Ibid 81; and for another similar report in 1615 see ibid 216; in 1622, to exceptions to a third insufficient answer, Williams, L.K., appended the following note : "I have perused the defendant's answer according to these allegations—find him to dally with the Court. To teach him and others better manners I do order him to pay the plaintiff £6 6s. 8d. costs : and if he do not answer directly, within three days after sight hereof, the costs to be doubled, and the defendant to stand committed," ibid 306.

fendants, having made five insufficient answers, contrary to the advice of their counsel, were ordered to pay 20s. costs for the first, and 40s. for the other four.[1] In 1607 master Tyndal found a bill impertinent, and directed it to be amended; and he also found the answer to it so impertinent and scandalous that he directed it to be taken off the file.[2] It would seem, therefore, that these exceptions resulted, sometimes in the whole bill or answer being quashed, and sometimes in a direction to amend. Apart from any exceptions, it was always open to a plaintiff to apply to amend his own bill.[3] In 1635 it was ordered that, if a demurrer was grounded on a merely verbal error, the plaintiff was, without motion, to be allowed a week to amend it.[4]

(ii) *Further pleadings.*—If the defendant demurred there could be no further pleading. It only remained to argue the demurrer. To a plea, on the other hand, there might be a replication. A replication admitted the legal validity of the plea, but denied the truth of the facts therein stated. A replication, there-fore, put the defendant to prove these facts.[5] If the defendant answered, the plaintiff might put in a replication. If this replication stated new facts, the defendant might rejoin generally or specially. In the time of Edward IV. there is even an instance of a surrejoinder.[6] But in Elizabeth's reign it was becoming the general practice to put in a general replication denying the answer, so that this replication in effect closed the pleadings.[7] This prob-ably points to the beginning of the practice of introducing new facts, not by way of replication, but by way of amendment of the bill.[8]

The following is an instance of a general replication of this kind made to the answer given above.[9]

---

[1] Munro, Acta 647-649.

[2] Ibid 72; in 1602 master Carew made the following certificate : " I have perused the plaintiff's bill and the defendant's answer, in both of which I find a course . . . renewed again, in scandalizing the one and the other ; and that the plaintiff by irritating the defendant, a gentleman of good credit and reputation, with unseemly words ; in his bill taxing him to be of a slippery and wavering disposition ; and to have little re-gard to his honest word and promise ; and with unhonest dealing ; the defendant hath repaid him with the like or even worse words in his answer; both which I think need to be suppressed ; and both bill and answer to be taken off the file on both sides," ibid 112.

[3] See instances from Edward IV.'s reign cited by Spence, op. cit. i 374 n. (d); this was not generally allowed after the examination of the witnesses, Mitford, op. cit. 258-259; cp. Monro, Acta 468 (1579), where this rule was applied to the amendment of an answer.

[4] Sanders, Orders i 180.

[5] Parker v. Blythmore (1695) 2 Eq. Cas. Ab. 79 ; Maddock, op. cit. ii 235-236.

[6] Spence, op. cit. i 374-375.

[7] Ibid 374 n. (i) ; below 388.

[8] Below 405.

[9] West, Symboleography Pt. ii 197b § 70.

THE REPLICATION OF H.E. ESQUIRE COMPLAINANT, TO THE ANSWER
OF H.H. DEFENDANT.

The said Complainant for Replication saith, that he will averre main-
taine and justifie, his said Bill of complaint, into this honorable Court exhibited, and everie matter and thing therein contained, to be certain, true,
and sufficient in the Law to be answered unto by the said defendant, and not
devised and exhibited into this honorable Court of any malice or evill will,
but upon just cause conceived against the said defendant, as the said defendant in his answer untruly hath alleaged.   And for further Replication saith,
that the said H.E. late father of this repliant, was lawfully seised to him and
to his heires, according to the custom of the said Manor of W. of the said
tenements and other things in the said Bill mentioned, by good and lawfull
conveyance and assurance in the Law, according to the custom of the said
Manor: And did convey assure and surrender, the said customarie tenements
and premisses to the use of the said repliant and of his heires, and the said
complainant did pay his fine therefore, and was lawfully admitted tenant
therof, as he the said complainant in his said Bill verie truly pretendeth.
And also he saith, that the evidences and coppies, of, and concerning the said
tenements and premisses, are come to the hands of the said def. and that by
colour therof, the said def. hath wrongfully entred into the said mesuage,
tenements and premisses, and hath conveyed to himselfe and to others to his
use, divers and sundrie secret estates therin, as in his said Bill of complaint
is also most truly declared: and that the said complainant hath oftentimes
sought and requested to have the said writings, coppies and evidences at the
hands of the said defendant: and also that he would yeeld unto him the quiet
possession of the said mesuage and premisses: and also that the said def. hath
and still doth commit, and continue daily committing great and outragious
wastes and spoiles, in decaying of the houses, and felling downe of the woods,
and timber trees of the premisses, to the losse and disherison of him this complainant as in the said Bill of Complaint is truely alledged: And without that,
that any other matter or thing contained in the said Answer, materiall or
effectuall to be replied unto, and not herein sufficiently confessed or avoided,
traversed or denied, is true.   All which this complainant is readie to aver and
prove, as this honorable Court shall award.   And prayeth as he before in
his said Bill of Complaint hath prayed.

(iii) *The control exercised by the court.*—During the whole of
this period the chancellors exercised a strict control over the
manner in which the parties or their counsel framed their pleadings.   They both issued general orders on this matter, and they
took effective steps to see that their orders were obeyed.   We
have seen that such orders were issued by Egerton.[1]   More
elaborate orders to the same effect were issued by Bacon and
Coventry.   Bacon's order deals more especially with slanderous
or libellous matter; and it is partly also directed to the semi-
political object of suppressing those references to conflicts of
jurisdiction which were common in his day.[2]   Coventry's order,

[1] Vol. v 232-233.
[2] " If there be contained in any bill answer or other pleading, or any interrogatory,
any matter libellous or slanderous against any that is not party to the suit, or against
such as are parties to the suit upon matters impertinent, or in derrogation of the settled

on the other hand, deals more especially with the needless verbosity of the pleadings, and aims at the restoration of the "ancient brevity and succinctness in bills and other pleadings."[1] Nor were these orders a dead letter. I have already referred to Egerton's punishment of Richard Mylward, who had filled 120 sheets with a replication which might have been contained in sixteen sheets;[2] and there are many other cases in which the parties or their counsel were punished for filing pleadings which were slanderous or vexatious.[3]

In the latter part of the seventeenth century the control of the court was much less strict. The court ceased to punish the parties or their counsel who drew pleadings which did not conform to its orders. It is true that exceptions could always be taken for scandal, impertinence, or insufficiency. These exceptions were referred to a master; and, if the exceptions were upheld, the offending party was mulcted in costs. But this was a method of securing obedience to the orders of the court, which was obviously far less effective than the more drastic methods pursued in the sixteenth and early seventeenth centuries. It merely increased the expense and delay of a suit; and there is reason to think that the parties referred pleadings to the masters with these objects.[4] Nor was the rule as to mulcting the guilty party in costs fairly applied. "If," said Beames,[5] "500 passages are before the master pointed out in succession as scandalous or impertinent, and the master should deem 499 to be neither the one nor the other, but should consider the remaining passage to be open to

---

authority of any of His Majesty's courts; such bills, answers, pleadings, or interrogatories, shall be taken off the file and suppressed, and the parties severally punished by commitment or ignominy, as shall be thought fit, for the abuse of the court: and the counsellors at law, who have set their hands, shall likewise receive reproof or punishment, if cause be," Order 56.

[1] "That bills answeres replications and rejoynders be not stuffed with repetitions of deedes or writings *in haec verba*, but the effect and substance of so much of them only as is pertinent and materiall to be sett downe, and that in breif and effectuall termes. That long and needles traverses of points not traversable, nor materiall causeles recitalls tautologies and multiplication of wordes, and all other impertinences, occasioning needles perplexitie be avoyded, and the auncient brevitie and succinctnes in bills and other pleadings restored," Sanders, Orders i 176-177.

[2] Vol. v 233.

[3] See e.g. a case of 1600, in which a scandalous bill was ordered to be taken off the file, and the plaintiff (who had been guilty of other contempts) fined £20 and committed close prisoner to the Fleet, Monro, Acta 743-744; and see other cases cited by Spence, op. cit. i 376-377.

[4] Mr. Beames said, "these references are obtained as of course, and there is reason to believe, that they have in some instances been had recourse to, with a view to the solicitor's own particular benefit, in the shape of costs, rather than with a serious intention of conferring any good on the party in whose name they are taken, as the costs to the party aggrieved by expunging the matter complained of, often exceed the costs occasioned such party by the insertion of the scandalous or impertinent matter," Parlt. Papers 1826 xv 89.

[5] Ibid.

the objection taken, this will carry the costs, though substantially the reference has failed."

But these developments belong to the period of the late seventeenth, the eighteenth, and the early nineteenth centuries, when the system of pleading, like the system of procedure, was acquiring all those characteristics which made it so great a hindrance to the administration of justice.   To this period we must now turn.

(2) *The late seventeenth, the eighteenth, and the early nineteenth centuries.*

During this period two developments can be traced.   Firstly, the rules as to what I have called the common law methods of equity pleading—the demurrers and pleas—became both more elaborate and more fixed.   Secondly, at the end of this period, developments in the more distinctly equitable methods of pleading —in the bill and answer—were depriving these demurrers and pleas of much of their former importance.   Thirdly, and consequently, these developments were altering the whole character of equity pleading.   I shall deal with the history of this period under these three heads.

(i) It is clear from the books on equity pleading and practice, which were published at the end of this period, (*a*) that equity had acquired a definite set of rules as to the kinds of demurrers and pleas by which a bill could be met, and as to their competence; (*b*) that in many respects these rules were influenced by the common law rules of pleading; and (*c*) that these rules were being evaded by developments in the drafting of bills, which made it impossible to meet them by demurrers or pleas.

(*a*) At the end of the eighteenth century, the various grounds upon which a defendant could demur to a bill could be classified as follows:[1] (1) that the subject matter of the suit did not fall within the jurisdiction of a court of equity.   (2) That some other court of equity, e.g. the counties palatine of Lancaster and Durham, and certain other courts, had jurisdiction.   But demurrers of this kind were rare; for, as Mitford said, "the want of jurisdiction can hardly appear upon the face of the bill, at least so conclusively as is necessary to deprive the Chancery, a court of general jurisdiction, of cognizance of the suit."[2]   (3) That the plaintiff was not entitled to sue by reason of some personal disability apparent on the face of the bill—e.g. infancy or coverture.   (4) That the plaintiff had no interest in the subject matter of the suit,

---

[1] Mitford, op. cit. 102-148; Maddock, op. cit. ii 224-235.
[2] Op. cit. 134.

or no title to institute such a suit—e.g. where a plaintiff claimed property under a will, and it was clear, on the construction of the will, that he had no title.[1] (5) That the plaintiff, though he had an interest in the subject matter of the suit, and a right to institute the suit, had no right to sue the defendant—e.g. "though an unsatisfied legatee has an interest in the estate of his testator, and a right to have it applied to answer his demands in a due course of administration, yet he has no right to institute a suit against the debtors to his testator's estate, for the purpose of compelling them to pay their debts in satisfaction of his legacy."[2] (6) That the defendant had no such interest in the subject matter of the suit as would make him liable to the plaintiff—e.g. a bankrupt could not be made a party to a bill against his assignees, as all his interest was transferred to his assignees.[3] (7) That all the persons interested had not been joined as parties. (8) That the plaintiff had demanded from several defendants several matters of such distinct natures that they ought to have been made the subjects of separate bills.

We have seen that a demurrer only lay for matters apparent on the face of the bill. But "it sometimes happened that a bill which, if all the parts of the case were disclosed, would be open to a demurrer, was so artfully drawn that it avoided showing upon the face of it any cause of demurrer."[4] The defendant must then resort to a plea. It followed that many of the cases in which a demurrer would be appropriate, if the defect had appeared on the face of the bill, would furnish occasion for a plea, if the defendant could prove *aliunde* the necessary facts.

Pleas were generally classified as follows :[5] (1) Pleas to the jurisdiction—e.g. that the property in question, or the acts done, or the party sought to be made liable, was or were outside the jurisdiction of the court. (2) Pleas to the person—e.g. that the plaintiff was an outlaw ; or an infant, married woman or lunatic ; or that he had not the character in which he was suing—for instance, if he was suing as heir, that he was not heir. (3) Pleas in bar—e.g. that there was a statutory bar, such as, in some cases, the statute of limitations ; matter of record, such as a judgment or a decree ; or matter in pais, such as a fine and nonclaim, a recovery, a release, or want of necessary parties. There were a special set of pleas to a bill brought for a discovery merely. They were that the discovery might subject the defendant to a penalty, or would be a breach of confidence, or that he was a purchaser for value without notice.[6]

---

[1] Mitford, op. cit. 136.   [2] Ibid 141.
[3] Ibid 142-143.   [4] Ibid 175.
[5] Maddock, op. cit. ii 239-259; Mitford, op. cit. 176-243.   [6] Ibid 221 seqq.

(*b*) As the capacity to stop a suit in equity by means of one of these pleas or demurrers was derived from the common law, it is only natural that some of the common law rules relating to them should be applied. Thus a demurrer which was argumentative—a "speaking demurrer" as it was called—was bad.[1] For instance, where a date mentioned in the bill was explained in a demurrer to be "upwards of twenty years before the bill was filed," the demurrer was overruled on this ground.[2] It was said in 1743, in reference to a plea of a fine and nonclaim, that "in pleading there must be the same strictness in equity as at law";[3] and it was laid down that the subject matter of a plea ought to be reducible to a single point.[4] We shall see, too, that in some of the rules applied to the composition of the answer, the influence of common law conceptions can be traced.[5] On the other hand, the law was not followed with absolute rigidity. A plea might be good in part and bad in part;[6] and in both demurrers and pleas the court allowed a liberty of amendment which was quite unknown at common law.[7] In one case, even after a demurrer to the whole bill had been allowed, an amendment of the bill was permitted;[8] but this decision went too far, and was disapproved by Mitford.[9] Moreover, as we have seen,[10] the effect of overruling a demurrer or a plea was not the same as at common law. It did not mean that the defendant lost his suit. It meant merely that he must have recourse to the more distinctly equitable mode of pleading—the answer. In fact, if a defendant had put in a plea as to one part of the bill and had answered as to another, and the subject matter of the plea and the answer was the same, the answer overruled the plea.[11] A plea which, by reason of informality or for some reason, was not good as a plea, might be allowed to stand as an answer;[12] and, if a plea was overruled, the defendant could always insist on the same matter by way of answer.[13]

(*c*) These rules show us that the common law conceptions, which had introduced these demurrers and pleas into the system of equity pleading, did not consort well in the strange environment in which they found themselves. And they were not popular with those suitors and practitioners in equity who

---

[1] Maddock, op. cit. ii 228.

[2] " There is a vice in the demurrer which is fatal at law. It is a speaking demurrer. There is argument in the body of it: viz. ' in or about the year 1770 *which is upwards of twenty years before the bill filed*,' " Edsell v. Buchanan (1793) 2 Ves. at pp. 83-84 *per* Lord Loughborough, L.C.

[3] Story v. Lord Windsor 2 Atk. at p. 632.

[4] Mitford, op. cit. 177.   [5] Below 405.

[6] Maddock, op. cit. ii 236.   [7] Ibid ii 294.

[8] Coningsby v. Sir J. Jekyll (1725) 2 P. Wms. 300.

[9] Op. cit. 15 *n.*; cp. Maddock, op. cit. ii 227.   [10] Above 383.

[11] Maddock, op. cit. ii 227; Parlt. Papers 1826 xv 29; below 393, 404.

[12] Mitford, op. cit. 242.   [13] Ibid 244.

wanted delay; for a successful plea or demurrer stopped the suit in its inception. Unfortunately the court, from a desire to do perfect justice, also leaned against them. "There is little disposition in courts of equity," said Mitford,[1] "to countenance those defences which tend to prevent the progress of a suit to a hearing in the ordinary way, whatever the expense of the proceeding may be." The Chancery Commissioners found that, in consequence of the strictness of the rule that any answer which covered any part of the same ground as a plea or demurrer, overruled the plea or demurrer, it was almost impossible to frame a plea or demurrer which would stand.[2] The result was that the plaintiff was driven to answer the whole bill; and that meant that, instead of the suit being stopped wholly or partially in its inception, the lengthy and expensive course of the equitable procedure must be pursued. In fact the equitable elements in the system of equity pleading had driven out the common law elements. We must now examine the process by which this result had been attained.

(ii) There is an analogy between this process which resulted in the victory of the equitable elements in the system of equity pleading, and the contemporaneous process which was reducing the common law system of special pleading to something approaching an exact science. Both represented the victory of the logical conceptions which underlay the respective systems—at common law, the desire to reduce the respective contentions of the parties to a single definite issue of law or fact; and in equity, the desire to give the parties the greatest possible latitude in the statement of their respective cases. In both cases the pursuit of the logical conception was carried out regardless of the consequences to the parties, with the result that its victory entailed, in a very large number of cases, the sacrifice of substantial justice. At common law, the subtleties of special pleading prevented the courts from ever knowing the real merits of the case. In equity, the system of pleading resulted in so artificial a statement of the case, and the system of procedure spun the suit out to such an interminable length, that the whole subject matter of the suit often went in costs before a conclusion was reached.

[1] Mitford, op. cit. 181-182.

[2] " If he answer any part of the bill which, by the plea or demurrer, he insists he ought not to answer, he is considered as having overruled, or in other words as having deprived himself of the benefit of his plea or demurrer; his answer being, in that respect, regarded as inconsistent with such plea or demurrer. In practice this frequently operates to embarrass the justice of the case, inasmuch as it imposes upon the pleader a degree of minute accuracy, which, with the greatest attention on his part, in difficult and complicated cases, may not always be attained; and the consequence of the slightest failure of strict technical nicety, in this respect, is, that the defendant is driven to the necessity of answering the whole bill," Parlt. Papers 1826 xv 29.

Under this system of equity pleading the whole interest centred on the bill and answer. I shall therefore deal with the subject under these two heads; and, in conclusion, I shall show how these developments destroyed the usefulness of demurrers and pleas, and reduced the later pleadings to mere formalities.

The Bill.—By the end of the seventeenth century the bill had become substantially a document consisting of the nine parts mentioned above.[1] This is clear from the two parts of the " Praxis Almæ Curiæ Cancellariæ," which were published in 1694 and 1695. But the precedents there collected show that, though the shape of the bill was rapidly assuming this form, the form was not as yet quite so elaborate as it afterwards became, or quite stereotyped. It is clear, however, from the precedents contained in the fourth edition of this book, which was published in 1725, that it had assumed almost its final form by the first quarter of the eighteenth century.[2] The character of the bill will be seen from the two following specimens. The first comes from the end of the seventeenth century, and the second from the latter part of the eighteenth century—from the period, that is, when it had assumed its final form.

(1)

(1) The address.

TO THE RIGHT HONOURABLE GEORGE LORD JEFFREYS ETC.[3]

(2) The names of the plaintiffs.

(3) The stating part.

Humbly complaining, sheweth unto your Lordship, your Orator and Oratrix VV.S. and S. his Wife, THAT his late Majesty King Charles the Second, did in or about the year of our Lord 1669 give the sum of 300*l.* to one S.S. (who afterwards married one T.J.) one of the Daughters of H.S. late of P. in the county of S. Gardner, and her Brothers and Sisters being five in number, to be equally divided amongst them. And that the said S.S.'s share amounting to the sum of threescore Pounds, the same was paid into the hands of R.S. your Oratrix S. her former Husband. And your Orator and Oratrix further shew unto your Lordship, That one R.N. being Trustee for the said S.S. did soon after the payment of the said 60*l.* to the said R.S. apply himself to the said R.S. and did request him to enter into Bond for securing the repayment thereof to the said S.S. when she should attain her Age of one and twenty years or be Married, which should first happen. And your Orator and Oratrix further shew unto your Lordship, That the said R.S. did enter into one Bond or Obligation, bearing date on or about the last day of February, in the said year of our Lord one thousand six hundred sixty nine, unto the said R.N. of the penalty of one hundred and twenty Pounds, conditioned for the payment of sixty eight Pounds twelve shillings, unto the said S.S. at or upon such day or time as the said S.S. should come to and attain her Age of one and twenty years or be Married, which of the said days and times should first come and happen. And in case the said S.S. should happen to die or depart this Life before she should attain the Age of one and twenty years or be married. That then the said S.S. his Executors, Admini-

---

[1] Above 379-380.
[2] See e.g. op. cit. i 342-346, 379-383; ii 156-168.
[3] Praxis Almæ Curiæ Cancellariæ (ed. 1695) ii 156-162.

strator or Assigns should pay the said sixty eight Pounds twelve Shillings to the said R.N. in trust for the Brothers and Sisters of the said S.S. or so many of them as should be then living, as in and by the said Bond or Obligation, and Condition thereof, had your Orator and Oratrix the same to produce, would more fully and at large appear. And your Orator and Oratrix further shew unto your Lordship, That the said S.S. when she was about three years of age was sent to the House of the said R.S. and dwelt at his House from her said age of three years, until she was eleven years of age or thereabouts, and was all that time maintained in Meat, Drink, Washing, Lodging, and Cloaths by Monies laid out by the said R.S. for her and for her use, and had several fits of Sickness, and particularly the small Pox, the charges whereof were paid by the said R.S. And at her age of twelve years or thereabouts, the said R.S. provided a Mistress for her the said S. one Mistress M.M. who was a Sempstress, and the said S.S. was bound to her as her Apprentice. And he the said R.S. paid to the said M.M. for the said S.S. the sum of 32*l.* and in the said eight or nine years, when she dwelt with him, the said R.S. expended and laid out for the said S.S. and for her use, much more than 60*l.* And your Orator and Oratrix further shew unto your Lordship, that the said R.S. died about fourteen years ago, and soon after his decease your Oratrix who was his Widow and Relict, took out Letters of Administration, but finding his Estate would not pay his Debts, gave up all his Estate whatever to his Creditors, who made not above nine Shillings in the Pound thereof, your Oratrix not knowing anything at that time of the Bond aforesaid. And your Orator and Oratrix did after that Intermarry, and the said S.S. did live unmarried till after she did attain her age of one and twenty years; and when she was about the age of twenty four, she the said S. did Intermarry with one T.J. who is since dead; and both the said S. when she was sole, and the said T.J. and S. after their Intermarriage, being very sensible of what Monies the said R.S. had expended on the account of and for the use of the said S. often declared (after they knew there was such a Bond) that they would never desire a Penny of it, nor would ever consent the same should be put in suit, but did promise often to procure the same to be delivered up to your Orator and Oratrix to cancel the same. And your Orator and Oratrix well hoped that the said Bond would have been delivered up, and that your Orator and Oratrix should not have been put to any trouble or charge by reason of the same standing out against your Orator and Oratrix. BUT NOW SO IT IS, MAY IT PLEASE YOUR LORDSHIP, That the said R.N. in whose Name the said Bond was taken in trust for the said S.S. now S.J. Combining and Confederating himself with the said S.J. and one A.S. one of the Brothers of the said S. and designing unjust advantages to himself, hath caused the said Bond to be put in suit against your Orator and Oratrix, and threatens to recover the penalty of your Orator and Oratrix, AND SOME-TIMES PRETENDING that he had directions so to do from the said S. before her Intermarriage with the said T.J. and sometimes pretending he was ordered so to do by the said T.J. and the said S. after their Intermarriage; and at other times pretending that he cannot perform the trust in him reposed, for and on the behalf of the said S. now she is a Widow, unless he prosecutes your Orator and Oratrix upon the said Bond : And at other times he pretends that the said Bond was assigned to the said A.S. the Brother of S. by the said T.J. in his Life-time ; and that the said A.S. did Order him to put the said Bond in suit against your Orator and Oratrix ; whereas the truth is, as is herein before charged. And the said R.N., S.J., and A.S. do well know in their Conscience, that the said S.J. received of the said R.S. and he did lay out for her much more Mony than the said 68*l.* 12*s.* which ought to be allowed in discharge of the said Bond ; neither did the said T.J. and S. during the

(1) The charge of confederacy.

(5) The charging part.

time they were Married, or the said S. either before or after her Intermarriage ever give any order or directions for suing of the said Bond; nor did the said T.J. ever assign the said Bond to the said A.S. or any other Person or Persons, but the said S.J. is willing the same should be delivered up and cancelled; and yet the said R.N. refuseth to deliver up the said Bond to be cancelled, and hath put the same in suit against your Orator and Oratrix. All which doings and pretences of the said R.N. and other the Confederates, are contrary to Equity and Good Conscience, and tend to the manifest wrong

(6) Allegation that all this is contrary to equity and can only be remedied by a court of equity. and injury of your Orator and Oratrix. IN TENDER CONSIDERATION WHEREOF, and forasmuch as your Orator and Oratrix are remediless in the Premises by the strict Rules of the Common Law of the Land, the said Bond being made iu the said R.N.'s Name: And your Orator and Oratrix having no way or means to obtain a discovery of what sum or sums of Mony the said S. received of the said R.S. and were laid out by him for her use, nor to compel the Allowance of the same in discharge of the said Bond, but by the aid of this Honourable Court; and the rather for that the said R.N. sues the Bond without the direction of the said S.J. for whom he stands intrusted as aforesaid. And your Orator and Oratrixes Witnesses are either dead, beyond the Seas, or in places remote, and to your Orator and Oratrix unknown. TO

(7) The interrogating part. THE END THEREFORE that the said R.N., A.S. and S.J. may upon their several and respective Corporal Oaths, true, full, distinct, direct, and perfect answer make to all and every the matters and things herein and hereby charged, as if they were particularly interrogated to every particular matter and thing. And that the said R.N. may particularly upon his Oath set forth whether he had any Order or Directions from the said T.J. in his Life-time, or from the said S., either before or since his death, and when or from whom else, and when and whether he was not ordered the contrary by the said T.J. and

(8) The relief sought. S. or one of them, AND that he be decreed to deliver up the said Bond to your Orator and Oratrix; and that your Orator and Oratrix may have such further and other relief in all and singular of the Premises as is usual in

(9) The prayer of process. Cases of this Nature. MAY IT PLEASE YOUR LORDSHIP to grant unto your Orator and Oratrix, etc.

(2)

(1) The address. TO THE RIGHT HONOURABLE EDWARD LORD THURLOW BARON THURLOW OF ASHFIELD, IN THE COUNTY OF SUFFOLK, LORD HIGH CHANCELLOR OF GREAT BRITAIN.[1]

(2) The names of the plaintiffs. Humbly complaining, sheweth unto your Lordship, your Orator, James Willis (son of John Willis, of Bablington, in the county of Essex, Esqr.) an Infant, under the age of 21 years; to wit, of the age of 6 years, or thereabouts,

(3) The stating part. by his said Father and next friend, and Samuel Dickenson of etc., THAT Thomas Atkins of Taunton in the county of Somerset Esqr. being seised and possessed of a very considerable real and personal Estate, did, on or about the fourth day of March, in the year of our Lord 1742, duly make and publish his last Will and Testament in writing; and thereby, amongst other things, devised and bequeathed as follows (*here are recited such parts of the Will as constitute the bequest, which was of £800*). AND that the said Testator departed this life, on or about the 20th day of December, 1748; and upon, or soon after, the death of the said Testator, to wit, on or about the 8th day of January 1750, the said Edward Willis and William Willis[2] duly proved the said Will

---

[1] This precedent is taken from C. Barton's Historical Treatise of a suit in Equity (1796) 29-43; for a collection of precedents in use in the latest period of the unreformed court of Chancery see F.M. Van Heythuysen, the Equity Draftsman (2nd ed. 1828).

[2] The Executors previously named in the parts of the will recited.

in the Prerogative Court of the Archbishop of Canterbury, and took upon themselves the burthen and execution thereof; and accordingly posssessed themselves of all the said Testator's real and personal estate, goods, chattels, and effects to the amount of £1500 and upwards. AND your Orator further sheweth unto your Lordship, that he hath by his said Father and next friend, at various times, since his said Legacy of £800 became due and payable, applied to the said Edward Willis and William Willis requesting them to pay the same, for the benefit of your Orator; and your Orator well hoped that they would have complied with such request as in conscience and equity they ought to have done. BUT NOW SO IT IS, MAY IT PLEASE YOUR LORDSHIP that (4) The charge of the said Edward and William Willis, combining and confederating together, confederacy. to and with divers other persons as yet unknown to your Orator, (but whose names, when discovered, your Orator prays may be inserted herein, as Defendants and parties to this your Orator's Suit, with proper and sufficient words to charge them with the premises) in order to oppress and injure your Orator, do absolutely refuse to pay, or secure for your Orator's benefit, the Legacy of £800 aforesaid, or any part thereof; FOR REASON WHEREOF, THE (5) The charging SAID CONFEDERATES SOMETIMES ALLEDGE AND PRETEND that the Testator part. made no such Will, nor any other Will, to the effect aforesaid: and at other times they admit such Will to have been made by the said Testator, and that they proved the same, and possessed themselves of his real and personal Estate; but then they pretend that the same was very small and inconsiderable, and by no means sufficient to pay and satisfy the said Testator's debts, legacies, and funeral expences: and that they have applied and disposed of the same towards satisfaction thereof; and, at the same time, the said Confederates refuse to discover and set forth what such real and personal Estate really was, or the particulars whereof the same consisted, or the value thereof, or how much thereof they have so applied, and to whom, or for what, or how the same has been disposed of particularly. WHEREAS your Orator chargeth the truth to be, that the said Testator died possessed of such real and personal Estate, to the full value aforesaid: and that the same was much more than sufficient to pay all the just debts, legacies, and funeral expences of the said Testator: and that the said Confederates, or one of them, have possessed and converted the same to their own uses, without making any satisfaction to your Orator for his said Legacy: (6) Allegation all which actings, pretences, and doings of the said Confederates, are contrary that all this is contrary to to equity and good conscience, and tend to the manifest injury and oppression equity and can of your Orator. IN TENDER CONSIDERATION whereof, and for that your only be remedied by a court of Orator is remediless in the Premises, by the strict rules of the Common Law, equity. and relievable only in a Court of Equity, where matters of this nature are properly cognizable; TO THE END, THEREFORE, that the said Confederates (7) The interro- may, respectively, full, true, direct, and perfect answer make upon their gating part. espective corporal Oaths, according to the best of their respective knowledge, information, and belief, to all and singular the charges and matters aforesaid; as fully, in every respect, as if the same were here again repeated, and they thereunto particularly interrogated; and more especially, that they may respectively set forth and discover, according to the best of their knowledge, whether the said Testator, Thomas Atkins, duly made and executed such last Will and Testament, in writing, of such date, and of such purport and effect, aforesaid: and thereby bequeathed, to your Orator, such Legacy of £800 as aforesaid; or any other, and what last Will and Testament, of any other and what date, and to any other, and what purport and effect particularly; and that they may produce the same, or the probate thereof, to this Honourable Court as often as there shall be occasion; and whether by such Will, or any other, and what Will, the said Testator appointed any and what other Executors by name ; and when the said Testator died, and whether he revoked or altered the said Will before his death, and when, and before whom, and in what manner ; and whether the said Confederates, or one, and which of them proved the said Will, and when, and in what Court ; and that they may respectively set forth, whether your Orator, by his said Father and next friend, hath not several times, since his said Legacy became due and was payable, applied to them to have the same paid, or secured for his benefit or to that purpose and effect, or how otherwise ; and whether the said Confederates, or one, and which of them, refused, or neglected, to comply with such requests, and for what reasons respectively, and whether such refusal was grounded upon the pretences herein before charged, or any, and

(8) The relief sought.

which of them, or any other, and what pretences particularly. *AND* that the said Confederates may admit assets of the said Testator come to their hands, sufficient to satisfy your Orator's said Legacy, and subject to payment thereof : And that etc. etc. (*requiring a full statement of the Effects come to their hands, and the disposal thereof etc., that the Plaintiff may be enabled to shew he has a right to the payment of his Legacy, in case it should be controverted*). AND, that they may be compelled by a decree of this Honourable Court to pay your Orator's said Legacy of £800. And that the same may be placed out at interest, for your Orator's benefit, until your Orator attains his age of 21 years ; and that the said £800 may then be paid him ; and that in the meantime the interest thereof may be paid to your Orator's said Father, John Willis, towards the maintenance and education of your Orator. AND that your Orator may have such further and other relief in the Premises as the nature of his case shall require, and as to your Lordship shall seem meet.

(9) The prayer of process.

MAY IT PLEASE YOUR LORDSHIP to grant unto your Orator his Majesty's most gracious writ, or Writs of Subpœna, to be directed to the said Edward Willis and William Willis, and the rest of the Confederates, when discovered, thereby commanding them, and every of them, at a certain day, and under a certain pain, therein to be specified, personally to be and appear before your Lordship, in this Honourable Court ; and then and there to answer all and singular the Premises aforesaid, and to stand to perform and abide such order, direction, and decree therein, as to your Lordship shall seem meet : and your Orator shall ever pray etc.

It is impossible to justify on logical grounds such a method of stating a plaintiff's case. Even Mitford admits so much. Thus he says that the general charge of confederacy, though " commonly inserted " " seems unnecessary " ;[1] and he admits that the indiscriminate use of all these parts in all bills, " has given rise to a common reproach to practisers in this line that every bill contains the same story three times told." But he maintains that, " in a bill prepared with attention," all these parts have a distinct and necessary operation.[2] In fact, the form which the bill came to assume admits of an historical explanation. It is true that it is not possible to speak very positively of the stages by which it assumed this form. If we had, for the end of the seventeenth and

---

[1] Op. cit. 42.

[2] " The indiscriminate use of these parts of a bill in all cases has given rise to a common reproach to practisers in this line, that every bill contains the same story three times told. In the hurry of business it may be difficult to avoid giving ground for the reproach; but in a bill prepared with attention the parts will be found to be perfectly distinct, and to have their separate and necessary operation," ibid 47.

the eighteenth centuries, a collection of excerpts from the records of the court, such as Monro made for the sixteenth and early seventeenth centuries, much would be clear that is now somewhat obscure. But we can, I think, gather enough from our authorities to tell the story, in outline. It will, I think, be found that the form assumed by the bill is due partly to the preservation of old forms; but chiefly to the growth of new expedients devised, either to meet new needs, or to preclude the possibility of putting a summary end to the suit by a plea or a demurrer. Let us look at the structure of the bill from these points of view.

The general charge of confederacy, occurring in the fourth part of the bill, which seemed to Mitford to be unnecessary, is doubtless a relic from the early days of the court, when its interference was asked for quite as often on the ground of the power of the defendant, as on the ground of the inadequacy of the law.[1] But, as often happens with these old rules, it was found to be useful for another purpose. Its insertion sometimes enabled a demurrer to be evaded; and it was probably for this reason that it was retained. "If," says Maddock,[2] "a bill be brought concerning things of distinct natures against several persons, or against one, it is demurrable; but not if combination is charged." It is true that if a demurrer were combined with a denial of the combination in the answer, the demurrer might stand. But we have seen that extreme nicety of pleading was needed to confine the answer to the denial of the combination merely.[3] If the answer did anything more, it overruled the demurrer.[4]

The two most important parts of the bill were the fifth and the seventh parts—the charging and the interrogating parts. We shall now see that it was the addition of these parts which both gave the bill its modern form, and the system of equity pleading its modern character.

As to the time when these two parts were added to the bill we have little distinct information. The most direct statement on this matter is contained in a statement of Lord Eldon in the case of *Partridge v. Haycroft*.[5] He said: "Formerly the bill contained very little more than the stating part. I have seen such a bill; with the simple prayer that the defendant may answer all the matters aforesaid, and then the prayer for relief. I believe the interrogating part had its birth before the charging part. Lord Kenyon never would put in the charging part; which does little more than unfold and enlarge the statement."

---

[1] Vol. i 405-406.   [2] Op. cit. ii 234.   [3] Above 393 n. 2.
[4] Hester v. Weston (1687) 1 Vern. 463.
[5] (1805) 11 Ves. at pp. 574-575.

Lord Kenyon was called to the bar in 1756 and became attorney-general in 1782. Therefore this statement of Lord Eldon would seem to imply that the interrogating part was well enough known before 1756, and that the charging part had come into general use in the last thirty years of the eighteenth century. This statement is not quite accurate. It is quite clear from the precedents contained in the Praxis Almæ Curiæ Cancellariæ that both these parts of the bill were being evolved at a much earlier date than Lord Eldon supposed.[1] These precedents show that both these parts had begun to be developed before the end of the seventeenth century—though it may well be that they did not attain their modern form till the beginning or even the middle of the eighteenth century.[2]

The fact that the interrogating part should have developed at the end of the seventeenth century, and that it should have been later elaborated, admits of an easy explanation. We have seen that the practice of interrogating the parties in open court was ceasing at that date.[3] It followed that a merely general request that the defendants should answer was no longer sufficient. It was as necessary that particular interrogatories should be administered to them as to the witnesses. It is therefore probable that the interrogating part of the bill originated in the disuse of the practice of viva voce examination of the parties in court, and the growth of the practice of getting a full reply in the defendant's written answer. But it was soon found that a general interrogation, such as we get in the earlier bills,[4] was not sufficient. Therefore the interrogating part naturally grew more and more detailed. As Mitford says,[5] since "experience has proved that the substance of the matters stated and charged in a bill may frequently be evaded by answering according to the letter only, it has become a practice to add to the general requisition that the defendants should answer the contents of the bill, a repetition by way of interrogatory of the matters most essential to be answered, adding to the enquiry after each fact, an enquiry of the several circumstances which may be attendant upon it, and the variations to which it may be subject, with a view to prevent evasion and compel a full answer." But, even before this stage had been

---

[1] See the precedent set out above 394-396.

[2] Thus the interrogating part was not so elaborate as it afterwards became—e.g. in the 1695 ed. of the Praxis ii pp. 75 and 90 there is a general request for an answer to the premises, "as fully and particularly as if the same were here again repeated and interrogated"; but it was beginning to get more elaborate, see the precedent set out above 394-396; and see a precedent of the time of Lord Nottingham in the fourth ed. of the Praxis ii 222-224; and a precedent of the time of Lord Jeffreys, ibid at pp. 237-238; see also ibid i 342-349 for a bill with both a charging and an interrogating part, which must be before 1725.

[3] Above 353-354.   [4] Above n. 2.   [5] Op. cit. 44.

reached, the need for further enlarging the bill had become apparent. It was a strict rule of pleading that every interrogatory must be founded on some statement in the prior part of the bill.[1] It is true that a number of questions might be founded on a single charge or statement in the bill.[2] But this rule hardly allowed sufficient latitude to a plaintiff who wished in his interrogatories, not only to examine, but also, by a process of cross-examination, to extract information from an unwilling defendant.[3] To conduct such a process, it was necessary to anticipate the kind of defence that such a defendant was likely to make, and to put questions, the answers to which would demonstrate its baselessness. It was therefore necessary to insert in the charging part an allegation of the various "pretences" of which the defendant was assumed to be guilty, and to charge their falsity against him. The insertion of these pretences, it was said in 1747,[4] sufficiently put the point in issue, and so justified the interrogatory. It was for this reason that counsel of great experience maintained before the first Chancery Commission that all these parts—the stating, the charging, and the interrogating parts—were absolutely necessary. The interrogatories could not be made particular enough without the charging part; and the stating part was necessary to lead up to the charging part.[5]

No doubt these pleading rules gave rise, justly enough, to the reproach that the bill contained a thrice told tale. No doubt also they were open to Bentham's gibe[6] that, "if, for example, to make good your title you want a deed, but know not where it is; if you tell the truth and say you don't know where it is, you will

---

[1] "No interrogatories can be put that do not arise from some fact charged in the body of the bill, or, if such interrogatories be put, the defendant may either demur to such interrogatories as having no foundation in the bill, or may omit to answer them; and if there be exceptions for want of an answer to such interrogatories, the exceptions on a reference will be overruled with costs," Gilbert, Forum Romanum 218-219; above 398 n. 2; Mitford, op. cit. 44.

[2] Maddock, op. cit. ii 137.

[3] Mr. Bell said in his evidence to the Chancery Commission, "the pleader is obliged to vary the manner of the question. It is very difficult to explain, unless a man is trying his skill as a draftsman against an unwilling defendant, how difficult it is often to extract the truth. I am certain in such cases the truth could not be extracted except by very particular interrogatories"; and again, "very often the defendants are so ignorant, and sometimes so prejudiced with their views of the case, that without a wish to disguise the truth, they will look at and consider the allegation in a very different way from that in which they would, if they were indifferent persons; and therefore rather state their own view of the case, than give a direct answer, if no question is put," Parlt. Papers 1826 xv App. A. 1, 2.

[4] "The former decree was on a bill brought by the plaintiff's wife, to have an account of her father's personal estate . . . ; that bill charges the defendant pretends the legacy of Margaret Molesworth was lapsed; this is the common and only way of bringing on the question, by setting forth the pretences of the defendant, and therefore sufficiently puts the point in issue," Gregory v. Molesworth 3 Atk. at p. 626.

[5] See Mr. Bell's evidence, Parlt. Papers 1826 xv App. A. 1.

[6] Rationale of Judicial Evidence, Works (Ed. Bowring) vi 308; cp. Mr. Bickersteth's Evidence Parlt. Papers 1826 xv App. A. 153.

never get it. You must begin by saying you *do* know where it is; you must say the defendant has it; and so, having complied with the condition, and said on your part what you know is false, you are allowed to call upon the defendant to declare on his part what is true." But, having regard to these pleading rules, the witnesses told the first Chancery Commission the truth, when they said that it was difficult to see how a bill could be framed in any other way. It was the rules which were at fault; and, when they had given rise to this artificial mode of framing a bill, bills of all kinds were framed in this way, whether or not all this superfluity of detail was really necessary. It was said, for instance, by Mr. Bickersteth[1] that, in very simple and uncontroversial suits for the administration of an estate, the bill need not be long. But he admitted that in many cases they were unnecessarily long. "I have seen them very long in very simple cases. I have seen very long unnecessary pretences and charges introduced in this sort of way: 'the defendant pretends that he has not received sufficient assets whereas your orator charges the contrary, and that he has received so and so (*enumerating several particulars*), and so the truth would appear to be if the said defendant would set forth particular accounts, the nature of which is stated at very great length'; and then in the interrogating part of the bill it is prayed that the defendant may set forth all that matter, which is then again repeated."

The Answer.—This increase in the complication of the bill necessarily entailed a corresponding increase in the complication of the answer. This will be seen from the following specimen of an answer to the second of the two bills given above:[2]

THE JOINT AND SEVERAL ANSWERS OF EDWARD WILLIS AND
WILLIAM WILLIS, TWO OF THE DEFENDANTS TO
THE BILL OF COMPLAINT OF JAMES
WILLIS, AN INFANT, BY JOHN
WILLIS, HIS FATHER
AND NEXT FRIEND
COMPLAINANT.

These Defendants now, and at all times hereafter, saving and reserving to themselves all manner of benefit and advantage of exception to the many errors and insufficiencies in the Complainant's said Bill of Complaint contained, for Answer thereunto, or unto so much, and such parts thereof, as these Defendants are advised is material for them to make Answer thereunto: they answer and say, they admit that Thomas Atkins, in the Complainant's

---

[1] Parlt. Papers 1826 xv App. A. 148.

[2] Barton, op. cit. 115-121; that the Answer had in substance reached its final form by the end of the seventeenth century is clear from the precedents in the Praxis Almæ Curiæ Cancellariæ, see a specimen in vol. ii of the 1695 ed. at pp. 433-441, which is so similar in its framework to the specimen here given that it is not worth while inserting it.

Bill named, did duly make and execute such last Will and Testament in writing, of such date, and to such purport and effect as in the Complainant's said Bill mentioned and set forth; and did thereby bequeath to the Complainant, James Willis, such Legacy of £800 in the words for that purpose mentioned in the said Bill, or words to a like purport or effect. And these Defendants, further answering, say, they admit that the said Testator, Thomas Atkins, did by such Will appoint these Defendants, Edward Willis and William Willis, Executors thereof; and that the said Testator died on, or about, the 20th day of December, 1748, without revoking or altering the said Will. And these Defendants, further answering, say, that they admit that they, these Defendants, sometime afterwards, to wit, about the month of January, 1750, duly proved the said Will in the Prerogative Court of the Archbishop of Canterbury; and took upon themselves the burthen of the execution thereof, and these Defendants are ready to produce the said probate as this Honourable Court shall direct. And these Defendants, further answering, admit, that the said Complainant, James Willis by his said Father and next friend, did several times, since the said Legacy of £800 became payable, apply to them, these Defendants, to have the same paid or secured for the benefit of the said Complainant, which these Defendants declined, by reason that the said Complainant was, and still is, an Infant under the age of 21 years. Wherefore these Defendants could not, as they are advised, be safe in making such payment, or in securing the said Legacy in any manner for the benefit of the said Complainant, but by order and direction, and under the sanction of this Honourable Court. And these Defendants, further answering say, that by virtue of the said Will, of the said Testator, they possessed themselves of the real and personal Estate, goods, chattels, and effects of the said Testator, to a considerable amount; and do admit that assets of the said Testator are come to their hands sufficient to satisfy the Complainant's said Legacy, and which assets they admit to be subject to the payment thereof, and are willing and desirous, and do hereby offer to pay the same as this Honourable Court shall direct, being indemnified therein; and these Defendants deny all unlawful combination and confederacy in the said Bill charged, without that any other matter or thing material or necessary for these Defendants to make Answer unto, and not herein, or hereby, well and sufficiently answered unto, confessed, or avoided, traversed, or denied, is true to the knowledge or belief of these Defendants. All which matters and things these Defendants are ready to aver, maintain, and prove, as this Honourable Court shall direct; and humbly pray to be hence dismissed with their reasonable costs and charges, in that behalf most wrongfully sustained.

It will be seen that the answer still retains, in its introductory and concluding parts, the same formulæ as were used in the sixteenth century.[1] But the main part consists of the detailed replies to the questions contained in the interrogating part of the bill. Necessarily it was hardly possible for a defendant to compose the answer to which he swore without professional aid. The manner in which it was prepared was thus described by the Chancery Commissioners, who reported in 1852 :[2] "The solicitor goes through all the interrogatories of the Bill with his client, and takes down his answers to the several questions; he assists in searching for and making out a list of all the documents relating

[1] Above 384-385.   [2] Parlt. Papers 1852 xxi 6.

to the matters in question, and in preparing all the other materials for the defence. These are laid before counsel, who from them prepares an Answer; which Answer is elaborate and minute; and with verbal exactness either admits, or traverses, or ignores all the minute interrogatories of the Bill. The Answer being drawn, is sent to the client for his perusal, that he may be satisfied that it is one which he can swear to. It is frequently so long and so technically framed, with so many references and qualifications as to be scarcely intelligible to the defendant, who is obliged to trust that his solicitor and counsel have, in the voluminous document to which he deposes, accurately translated the brief and somewhat bald notes which the solicitor took down from his mouth. The Answer is engrossed on parchment, and is frequently accompanied by long schedules containing accounts, and also lists of books and documents in the possession of the defendant." As Bowen said[1] truth found no difficulty in disappearing during the many complicated processes of its manufacture.

Moreover, just as the complication of the bill had been largely caused by the pleading rule that every interrogatory must be founded on some statement in the prior part of the bill,[2] so the complication of the answer was greatly increased by another pleading rule, that only those parts of the answer could be relied on which the plaintiff's counsel chose to read.[3] The result was, as one of the Chancery Commissioners put it, "great dexterity was exercised in so interweaving the parts of an answer as to prevent one part being read without the other."[4] Obviously this vastly increased both the labour of constructing the answer and its incomprehensibility when constructed.

(iii) These changes entirely changed the whole character of equity pleading.

Firstly, we have seen that it became very difficult to frame a bill that could be met by a demurrer or a plea. The rule that if any part of the answer covered the same ground as the demurrer or plea, the demurrer or plea was overruled, made these methods of pleading comparatively useless; for bills were so framed that they could not be met in their entirety by a demurrer or plea; and the attempt to answer those parts of them not covered by a demurrer or plea, generally meant that the demurrer as a demurrer, or the plea as a plea, was overruled, and accepted only as part of the answer.[5]

Secondly, the place of further pleadings was taken (a) by

---

[1] Administration of the Law in the reign of Queen Victoria 291, cited vol. i 646.
[2] Above 401.
[3] Maddock, op. cit. ii 335-336.
[4] Parlt. Papers 1826 xv App. A. 201.
[5] Above 392-393.

amendments of the bill, and (*b*) by exceptions to and amendments
of the answer.[1] (*a*) If "the plaintiff conceives from any matter
offered by the defendant's plea or answer that his bill is not
properly adapted to his case, he may obtain leave to amend his
bill, and suit it to his case."[2] The ease with which amendments
were allowed, led to the filing of what were called 'fishing bills'
—the case was stated as the plaintiff believed it to be; then, on
getting the answer, a new and better case was made by amending
the original bill.[3] It also led to the use of amendments for the
mere purpose of oppression and delay.[4] (*b*) We have seen that
the power of excepting to the answer was used to supply the
defects of the Chancery method of taking evidence. The answer
was excepted to till an adequate answer, which supplied the information required, was produced.[5] But, necessarily, this was a
lengthy business, as it involved a reference to the master, a report
from him, and a decision as to the validity of his report, which
might be taken by way of rehearing or appeal even as far as the
House of Lords. And, if the case was hotly contested, this was
not unlikely; for, as Bentham showed, there were no certain rules
for the amendment of answers.[6] There was, in fact, a curious
mixture of conflicting criteria applied to test the statements made
in answers. Without insisting on all the common law rules as to
the directness and plainness of statement required in a common
law plea, both the masters and the court sometimes used these
rules to test the validity of an answer; and, for instance, objected
to answers which were argumentative,[7] or involved something like
a negative pregnant.[8] Mitford said that this substitution of the
practice of amendment, for the old practice of introducing new
facts by the common law method of special replication and rejoinder, was due to a desire to avoid "inconvenience delay and

---

[1] "Special replications and all subsequent pleadings on the part of the plaintiff
have since been got rid of, by suggesting the defendant's case originally, or by way of
amendment in the bill, and making it by way of charge, to which the defendant may,
in the original or further answer, give the answer which originally would have been
contained in a rejoinder," Spence, op. cit. i 375 n. (*b*).

[2] Maddock, op. cit. ii 286.

[3] Mr. Lowe said in his evidence to the first Chancery Commission, "A man
never understands his case till he sees what his opponent says: then he states many
matters which were in his knowledge before, but which I should think it wholly immaterial to state in the first instance: we file very frequently (having a very good
case) what is called a fishing bill. . . . I put my client's case as I believe it to be,
but, subject to correction and amendment, if it afterwards turns out, upon seeing the
defendant's answer, that there is a new case to be made," Parlt. Papers 1826 xv App.
A. 166.

[4] Ibid App. A 22.　　　　　　　　　　　[5] Above 358.

[6] Rationale of Judicial Evidence, Works (Ed. Bowring) vi 456.

[7] Faulder v. Stuart (1805) 11 Ves. at p. 303 *per* Eldon, C.

[8] Munro, Acta 88-89 (1607)—a certificate of master Carew; and see Mr. Bell's
evidence, Parlt. Papers 1826 xv App. A. 4.

unnecessary length of pleading."[1] But it is quite clear that, having regard to the machinery provided for hearing exceptions and making amendments, the Chancery method came to be both longer and more expensive.

Thirdly, these developments made the joinder of issue a mere form. As a form, however, it survived. The plaintiff filed, as in the preceding period,[2] a general replication.[3] Then he served the defendant with a subpœna to appear to rejoin. This subpœna was obtained by order of course, was made returnable immediately, and was served on the defendant's clerk in court.[4] The case was then formally at issue, and the parties proceeded to the examination of witnesses.

In these ways, therefore, the influence of the conceptions derived from the common law system of pleading were gradually eliminated, or reduced to mere forms. The result was that a wholly original system of pleading was developed, which centred round the bill and answer, the practice of amending the bill, and the machinery for excepting to and getting amendments of the answer. Though it was free from the subtleties of the common law system of special pleading, it was quite as artificial and technical ; and it was infinitely more dilatory and expensive.

As with the system of equity procedure,[5] so with the system of pleading, no material change was made till the Act passed in 1852 to amend the procedure of the court of Chancery.[6] That Act provided that bills should "contain as concisely as may be a narrative of the material facts matters and circumstances on which the plaintiff relies, such narration being divided into paragraphs numbered consecutively, and each paragraph containing as nearly as may be a separate and distinct statement or allegation."[7] It was not to contain interrogatories [8]—they were

---

[1] Op. cit. 256.   [2] Above 388.

[3] The following is a specimen : " The Replication of James Wilis, Complainant, to the Answer of Edward Willis and William Willis, Defendants.   This Repliant saving and reserving to himself, all and all manner of advantage to Exception which may be had and taken to the manifold errors, uncertainties, and insufficiencies of the Answer of the said Defendants, for Replication thereunto, saith, that he doth and will aver, maintain, and prove his said Bill to be true, certain, and sufficient in the Law, to be answered unto by the said Defendants, and that the Answer of the said Defendants is very uncertain, evasive, and insufficient in the Law, to be replied unto by this Re-pliant ; without that that any other matter or thing in the said Answer contained material or effectual in the Law to be replied unto, and not herein and hereby well and sufficiently replied unto, confessed, or avoided, traversed, or denied, is true ; all which matters and things this Repliant is ready to aver, maintain, and prove as this Honourable Court shall direct, and humbly prays as in and by his said Bill he hath already prayed," Barton, op. cit. 144-145.

[4] Mitford, op. cit. 257 ; in Rodney v. Hare (1730) Mos. 296, the master of the Rolls said that the cause was at issue by the replication, and that a rejoinder was only a fiction of the court and was never actually filed.

[5] Above 375-376.   [6] 15, 16 Victoria c. 86.

[7] § 10.   [8] Ibid.

to be filed separately.[1] The answer might contain the replies to the interrogatories; but the statement of the case of the defendant, was, like the bill, to be divided into numbered paragraphs.[2] The practice of excepting to bills and answers for impertinence was abolished.[3] Issue was to be joined by filing a replication in the form then usual.[4]

Both this Act, and its fellow the Common Law Procedure Act,[5] while effecting valuable reforms in the systems of equity and common law procedure and pleading, left the two systems still very distinct from one another. But the prevailing tendency was in the direction of fusion;[6] and, when the fusion of the courts was decided on, it was necessarily accompanied by a new system of pleading, as well as a new system of procedure. Both the salient characteristics of the existing systems of common law and equity pleading, and the object aimed at by the new system which replaced them, are so clearly stated by the Judicature Commissioners in their first report,[7] that I shall copy their words. "Common law pleadings," they said, "are apt to be mixed averments of law and fact, varied and multiplied in form, and leading to a great number of useless issues, while the facts which lie behind them are seldom clearly discoverable. Equity pleadings, on the other hand, commonly take the form of a prolix narrative of the facts relied upon by the party, with copies or extracts of deeds, correspondence, and other documents, and other particulars of evidence, set forth at needless length. The best system would be one, which combined the comparative brevity of the simpler forms of common law pleading, with the principle of stating, intelligibly and not technically, the substance of the facts relied upon as constituting the plaintiff's or the defendant's case, as distinguished from his evidence." That is the gist of the matter. Our modern system of pleading endeavours, not unsuccessfully, to combine the brevity and the simpler forms of the common law, with the equity principle of stating facts and not the legal conclusion which the pleader puts upon the facts.[8] This principle is the main contribution which the equity system of pleading has made to our modern system.

In spite of the enormous abuses which this system of procedure and pleading developed in the eighteenth century, that century was the great formative period of our modern system of equity. These abuses no more stopped the development of its principles, than the parallel abuses in the system of common law

---

[1] § 12.   [2] § 14.   [3] § 17.   [4] § 26.
[5] 15, 16 Victoria c. 76; above 327, 375.   [6] Above 375-376; vol. i 638.
[7] Parlt. Papers 1868-1869 xxv 11.   [8] See above 328-330.

procedure and pleading stopped the development of the common law. But it can hardly be doubted that, if the equity procedure had been more speedy and less expensive, more cases would have been decided, and, consequently, the principles of equity would have been more fully worked out during that century. There would have been no such decline of the business of the court as that which took place at the beginning of the nineteenth century.[1] All this we shall see when, in the second Part of the succeeding and final Book of this History, I trace the development of the modern system of equity.

From the point of view of modern law, this period of the sixteenth and seventeenth centuries is the most important of all periods in the legal history of the states of Western Europe; for it was then that the modern state, and the law which governed it, took shape. It is no exaggeration to say that the course which the development of the law of these states then took, has affected the whole course of their subsequent history. During this period the course of English legal development was unique in its continuity; and it is at the causes and consequences of this unique continuity which we must look, if we would understand why the course of English legal history, and the condition of our modern English law, differ so widely from the history and law of other European states.

Far back in the Middle Ages the work of Henry II. and Edward I. had prepared the way for the possibility of this continuity. They gave to England a centralized government and a common law; and, during the latter part of the mediæval period, we can see in the growth of the English Parliament, in the elaboration of the machinery of central and local government, and in the development of the common law, further progress along the lines which they had marked out. But in the fifteenth century signs of deterioration were growing more and more obvious. The collapse of the institutions of government was made manifest by the wars of the Roses; and the development of the common law was hindered by the growth of an irrational technicality. The institutions and the law, which the kings of the twelfth and thirteenth century had founded, were saved by the Tudors. They not only rescued the English state and English law from

[1] Vol. i 438.

the impotent condition to which they had sunk, but gave them strength enough to meet the new needs of the age of the Renaissance and the Reformation. They accomplished this work, not by the wholesale destruction of mediæval institutions and mediæval law, but by adapting these institutions and this law to the new situation, by the development of new institutions and new law, and by skilfully piecing together the old and the new. That they were able to accomplish successfully this delicate task, was due partly to the fundamental soundness of English mediæval institutions and law, but mainly to their own tact and ability. It is due mainly to them that, in a century of change, English law was developed continuously from its mediæval bases.

Because the English state and English law were developed in this way during the sixteenth century, the differences between the English and the continental development, which were emerging at the close of the mediæval period, were intensified. The possession of mediæval institutions and mediæval law, adapted to the needs of the territorial state; and the retention of the mediæval ideal of the supremacy of the law, modified by a recognition of the supremacy of Parliament; sharply differentiated the English state from states which had attained national institutions through royal absolutism, and a national law by a more or less sweeping reception of Roman principles. But the English constitution with its mixture of old and new institutions, the English law administered in many separate courts old and new, were complex mechanisms, which only a dynasty with abilities equal to those of the Tudors could guide. The advent of a less competent dynasty was the signal for constitutional and legal struggles, the issue of which left England the one state in Europe in which some measure of constitutional government still existed, and left the common law supreme in the English state.

These constitutional and legal struggles, which occupied nearly the whole of the seventeenth century, left their marks on the development of English law. The victory of constitutional principles prevented any such extensive development of the law by direct legislative action, as was possible in those continental states where king and state were identified; and the victory of the common law meant the victory of a law which, though it was being modernized, still possessed many mediæval traits. At the same time, the establishment of the rival bodies of law administered in the Chancery and the Admiralty, prevented any approach to uniformity in the rules which made up the English legal system. But, though the institutions of the English state, and the machinery of English law, at the end of this period, were the reverse of logical, they were proving themselves to be workable. They were proving that they were capable of creating modern rules to meet modern needs. That this development of modern rules had already begun in 1700 is clear, if we look at any of the leading branches of English law—at the land law, at the law of contract, or at the law merchant; and, under the influence of the large sane rationalism of the eighteenth century, it proceeded apace. The principles of our modern law were settled during that century; and just as the leading principles of the mediæval common law proved to be capable of adaptation to the new needs of the sixteenth century; so the leading principles of the modern law, accepted and developed in the eighteenth century, were found by the reformers of the early nineteenth century to be capable of adaptation to the new demands, which the vast material and intellectual changes of that century made upon them.

But in the year 1700 it would hardly have been possible to foresee these results. A French critic, who looked at the condition of English law in that year, might well have called it a very insular system; and, if he had reflected upon the collapse of the machinery for teaching law and its effects, he might well have called English lawyers a learned race of unlearned men. That there would have been some truth in these criticisms can hardly be denied. Englishmen, unlike the men of France and of many other countries, had refused to purchase national unity, and an up-to-date legal system, by travelling down the broad road which led to royal absolutism, and the reception of the principles of Roman law. Our French critic might well have thought that they had rejected the two civilizing agencies of the modern world. Nevertheless such a criticism would have been essentially one-sided, as the Marquis of Halifax saw,[1] because it left out of account two large compensating considerations.

In the first place, it took no account of the fact that, in the sixteenth century, many new ideas had been received into the English legal system; and that English lawyers were assimilating them, and were using them to adapt their system to the needs of the modern state. Lawyers who were inventing the Trust concept, who were evolving an wholly original theory of contract, who were successfully adapting to their own use foreign principles of commercial law, had little to fear from the results of a comparison with their continental neighbours. Then, as in the days of Wycliffe,[2] "as much learning and philosophy were to be found in a judge of the common law as in a doctor of the civil law." In the second place, though the constitutional struggles and conflicts between

---

[1] Vol. vi 300.   [2] Vol. ii 407.

rival courts had retarded the development of English law; though its development by separate tribunals, acting on divergent principles, had been fatal to its uniformity; though it contained many mediæval survivals ill-suited to the needs of the seventeenth century; yet there were compensating advantages, albeit of a spiritual and impalpable sort, which were destined in the near future to take away the reproach of insularity. English legal and political institutions fostered the qualities of self-reliance and resource, taught Englishmen the art of self-government, and maintained the ideals of supreme and equal law for all members of the state. It was the lessons so taught and learned which enabled Englishmen, in the following century, to found an Indian Empire, and many Dominions beyond the seas; which enabled them to rule, and, by ruling, to educate many subject races; which ensured the vigorous growth of those Dominions which, by settlement or conquest, had come to acknowledge allegiance to the English Crown.

The foundation for these developments had been laid in the legal history of the sixteenth and seventeenth centuries, which I have endeavoured to relate in this Book of this History. The new life given to the English legal system by the assimilation and adaptation to native uses of the new ideas received in the sixteenth century, and the happy results upon the national character of the issue of the constitutional and legal struggles of the seventeenth century, were soon to show that English law, so far from being a merely insular system, was destined to divide with Roman law the empire of the modern civilized world.

APPENDIX

I

HUMOROUS PIECES ILLUSTRATING THE CONDITION OF COMMON LAW PROCEDURE AND PLEADING IN THE FIRST HALF OF THE NINETEENTH CENTURY.

It may at first sight seem remarkable that what is in many respects the most arid part of the common law, should have given rise to more humorous pieces, both in verse and prose, than any other legal topic. But the phenomenon is easily explicable. The contrast between the original significance and form of the existing institutions and rules of common law procedure, and the significance and form which had been given to them by the mass of conventional rules with which they had been overlaid, easily lent itself to humour and satire. And, similarly, humour and satire were obviously provoked not only by the contrast between the plain statement of the facts of a case which the parties themselves would have made, and the contorted statement imposed upon them by the rules of special pleading ; but also by the contrast between the decision which would obviously have been arrived at if such a plain statement had been permitted, and that arrived at as the result of stating it in accordance with these rigorous rules. I have here printed three of these pieces. The first deals with both procedure and pleading, the second with pleading only, and the third with one aspect of the old procedure—the activities of John Doe and Richard Roe.

For permission to print the first—" The Circuiteers : an Eclogue "—I am indebted to the Right Hon. Sir F. Pollock. The version here printed is taken from the first volume of The Law Quarterly Review, and was contributed by the Right Hon. Sir F. Pollock's father, Sir F. Pollock, sometime the Queen's Remembrancer—hence the initials—P.Q.R.—with which it is signed. That version has been collated by the Right Hon. Sir F. Pollock with the MS. in the handwriting of his father ; and, with one exception noted in the text, the two versions are identical. The commentary which the Queen's Remembrancer has supplied contains all that is needed to elucidate the text ; and the note which he has inserted at the end contains all the material information as to the author of the piece—John Leycester Adolphus. It may, however, be added that Adolphus, like Mr. Justice Whitelocke nearly two centuries earlier, was educated at Merchant Taylors' school, and St. John's College Oxford ; and, like him, held the post of steward of the manors of the College. His humour and literary ability is sufficiently illustrated by the piece here printed ; but I must add one other illustration, taken from the " Personal Remembrances of Sir F. Pollock," the Queen's Remembrancer (vol. i p. 100). " It was he who in Grand Court invented the names Fidelia Fanny and Caleb Samuel for the twins of an eminent pleader, in order that they might be affectionately called by the abbreviations of Fi. Fa. and Ca. Sa., and who wrote for their especial use the nursery rhyme :—

> Heigh ho !   Richard Roe !
> Why did you break the closes so,
> Which the bishop demised to poor John Doe ?
> Good Mr. Doe had done you no harm
> When you ejected him out of his farm ;
> Fie on you, naughty Richard Roe,
> How could you break the closes so ?

The two other pieces were written by George Hayes.   The following account of the author is taken from Edmund Macrory's biographical preface to Hayesiana, which was published in 1892.   Hayes was born in 1805.   He was admitted as a student to the Middle Temple in 1824, and, after practising for a short time as a special pleader, he was called to the bar in 1830.   He soon got an extensive practice at the Warwickshire Sessions and on the Midland Circuit.   He became serjeant-at-law in 1856, and was appointed a judge of the court of Queen's Bench in 1868.   Only fifteen months later, November 19, 1869, he was suddenly struck with paralysis as he was unrobing after the close of his day's work in court, and he died a few days later.   His literary gifts, and his rich vein of humour, sufficiently appear from the two pieces here printed.   His gifts as an advocate and a lawyer were equally conspicuous; but, owing perhaps to his modest and diffident nature, he never had so large a practice as might have been expected.   Mr. Justice Wills said of him as an advocate that, "a certain consciousness that he was passed by men who could hardly be considered his equals, either in legal learning or in general accomplishments, no doubt helped to give to some of his forensic performances in every-day cases a hesitating character which undoubtedly interfered with his success.   But he had all the power of advocacy within him, and you never knew when a brilliant display would not be forthcoming."   Speaking of his gifts as a lawyer, the same authority says that the extent of his learning was probably known only to his intimate friends.   "He belonged to two schools of lawyers.   He had learned his law in days when technicality was rampant, and when the influence of antiquity was supreme; and he was at the Bar for many years after the spirit of reform had thoroughly leavened the practice, and seasoned the administration of the law.   He had accumulated really vast stores of ancient learning, which never lost their attractions for him.   He was one of the best real-property lawyers of his day, and could hold his own in questions of real-property with men who spent their lives in dealing with them.   The mysteries of the systems of special pleading, which flourished both before and after the New Rules of H.T. 4 Wm. 4, were equally familiar to him."   It was the inadequacy of the reforms effected by these New Rules, "and the monstrous results arrived at by the inflexible logic of Baron Parke," which inspired the Dialogue here printed.   In that Dialogue Baron Parke (afterwards Lord Wensleydale) figures as Baron Surrebutter; and Hayes "used to say that Lord Wensleydale was the most forgiving of mortals.   He read 'Crogate's Case'—which had been privately printed—and having read it, invited the author to Ampthill, where he gave him the heartiest of welcomes."   But as Sir F. Pollock has said (The Genius of the Common Law 28), the Dialogue represents only "that half of Lord Wensleydale which was devoted to the technical side of process and pleading. . . . When there was not any point of pleading before the court, no man could handle matters of principle with greater clearness or broader common sense.

And now let us turn to the pieces themselves, the humour of which will, I hope, be intelligible to those who have read this and the preceding volumes of my History, and especially § 2 of the last chapter of this volume.

THE CIRCUITEERS.

An Eclogue.

SCENE—*The Banks of Windermere. Sunset.*

ADDISON.[1] SIR GREGORY LEWIN.[2]

The notes are by P.Q.R. except the two marked W.S.H. which I have inserted.

A. How sweet, fair Windermere, thy waveless coast !
   'Tis like a goodly issue well engrossed.
L. How sweet this harmony of earth and sky !
   'Tis like a well concerted *Alibi*
A. Pleas of the Crown are coarse and spoil one's tact,
   Barren of fees and savouring of fact.
L. Your pleas are cobwebs, narrower or wider,
   That sometimes catch the fly, sometimes the spider.
A. Come let us rest beside this prattling burn,
   And sing of our respective trades in turn.
L. Agreed ! our song shall pierce the azure vault :
   For Meade's[3] case proves, or my Report's in fault,
   That singing can't be reckoned an assault.
A. Who shall begin ?
L.   That precious right, my friend,
   I freely yield, nor care how late I end.
A. Vast is the pleader's rapture, when he sees
   The classical endorsement—" Please draw pleas."
L. Dear are the words—I ne'er can read them frigidly—
   " We have no case, but cross-examine rigidly."
A. Blackhurst[4] is coy, but sometimes has been won
   To scratch out " Hoggins "[5] and write " Addison."
L. Me Jackson[6] oft deludes ; on me he rolls
   Fiendlike his eye, then chucks his brief to Knowles.[7]
A. What fears, what hopes through all my frame did shoot
   When Frodsham's breeches, Gilbert, fouled[8] thy boot ![9]

[1] A special pleader.
[2] A criminal lawyer and reporter of " Lewin's Crown Cases."
[3] Meade and Belt's Case, I. Lewin's C.C. 184, *per* Holroyd, J.: " No words or singing are equivalent to an assault."
[4] An attorney of Preston.
[5] Hoggins, a barrister on the Northern Circuit—afterwards a Queen's Counsel.
[6] An attorney.
[7] C. J. Knowles, on the Northern Circuit—afterwards a Q.C.
[8] The version in the L.Q.R. i 232 reads " felt " ; but the word in the text is the reading in the MS. [W.S.H.].
[9] Frodsham, an attorney, was summarily ejected by Gilbert Henderson (Recorder of Liverpool) from his chambers, for some offensive words used by him during an arbitration. Afterwards Frodsham sued Henderson for damages for the assault. His counsel was Serjeant Cross. John Williams, afterwards a Judge of the Court of Queen's Bench, led for the defence, and concluded his speech to the jury by saying, " I vow to God, gentlemen, I should have done the same thing myself—an insult—a kick—and a farthing—all the world over ! " The jury accordingly found for the plaintiff with one farthing damages. Cross tied up his papers and remarked, " My client has got more kicks than half pence." But it was always a matter of doubt whether he knew that he was saying a good thing or not. He had never before said anything to provoke such a suspicion.

L. O ! all ye jail-birds, 'twas a day of sulks
   When Roger Whitehead flitted to the hulks.
A. Thoughts much too deep for tears subdue the Court
   When I *assumpsit* bring, and god-like waive a tort.[1]
L. When witnesses, like swarms of summer flies,
   I call to character, and none replies,
   Dark Attride [2] gives a grunt, the gentle bailiff sighs.
A. A pleading fashioned of the moon's pale shine
   I love, that makes a youngster new-assign.
L. I love to put a farmer in a funk,
   Then make the galleries believe he's drunk.
A. Answer, and you my oracle shall be,
   How a sham differs from a real plea?
L. Tell me the difference first, 'tis thought immense,
   Betwixt a naked lie and false pretence.
   Now let us gifts exchange ; a timely gift
   Is often found no despicable thrift.
A. Take these, well worthy of the Roxburghe Club,
   Eleven counts struck out in Gobble *versus* Grubb.
L. Let this within thy pigeon-holes be packed,
   A choice conviction on the Bum-boat Act.[3]
A. I give this penknife-case, since giving thrives ;
   It holds ten knives, ten hafts, ten blades, ten other knives.
L. Take this bank-note (the gift won't be my ruin),
   'Twas forged by Dade and Kirkwood ; see first Lewin.[4]
A. Change we the *Venue*, Knight ; your tones bewitch,
   But too much pudding chokes, however rich,
   Enough's enough, and surplusage the rest.
   The sun no more *gives colour* to the West,
   And, one by one, the pleasure boats forsake
   Yon land with water covered, called a lake.
   'Tis supper time ; the inn is somewhat far,
   Dense are the dews, though bright the evening star ;
   And Wightman [5] might drop in and eat our char.

These lines were written by John Leycester Adolphus, whose name is so well known as a reporter in conjunction first with Barnewall and afterwards for a much longer period with Ellis. He was appointed Judge of the Marylebone County Court in 1852. He was, beyond his law, a man of the finest literary accomplishment and taste, and wrote the " Letters to Richard Heber, Esq., containing critical remarks on the Series of Novels beginning with Waverley, and an attempt to ascertain their Author." This charming and ingenious little work was published in 1821, reached a second edition in 1822, and procured for its writer the friendship of Sir Walter Scott.

This eclogue formed part of the amusement provided after dinner in the festive Grand Court holden while the Northern Circuit was at Liverpool for the Summer Assizes in 1839.

---

[1] This line was cited by Scrutton, L.J., in Verschures Creameries v. Hull and Netherlands Steamship Co. [1921], 2 K.B. at p. 611 [W.S.H.].

[2] Sir Gregory Lewin's clerk.

[3] 2 Geo. III. c. 28. " An Act to prevent the committing of Thefts and Frauds by persons navigating Bum-boats and other boats upon the river Thames," rep. 2 and 3 Vict. c. 47, s. 24.

[4] I. Lewin C.C., 145.

[5] Afterwards a Judge of the Court of Queen's Bench.

The lines have already been printed, but many years ago, in Notes and Queries, 3rd Series, v 5, page 6 (January 2, 1864). No apology can be needed for reproducing in these pages so choice a specimen of legal humour, parts of which may now almost serve as a sort of valedictory address to the defunct science of Special Pleading.

P.Q.R.

(2)

CROGATE'S CASE : A DIALOGUE IN YE SHADES ON SPECIAL PLEADING REFORM.[1]

Speakers :—BARON SURREBUTTER, AND EDWARD CROGATE.

The Venue is in the Shades.

BARON SURREBUTTER. I am informed that you are the Shade of the celebrated Crogate, who, in his mortal state, gave rise to the great case reported in 8 Co. 66, and whose name is inseparably connected with the doctrine of *de injuria.*

CROGATE. I can't say that I quite understand you.

SUR. B. Why, did not you bring an action of *trespass* against a man for driving your cattle, in which judgment was given against you, because you had improperly replied *de injuria* ?

CROGATE. Oh, aye, to be sure ! I did go to law with a fellow who drove my beasts off Bassingham Common, where they had as good a right to be as any beasts in the county of Norfolk ; and as you say, it was given against me through some knavish quibble or other. The more shame for the Judges who decided it, say I. But pray, may I ask who may you be ?

SUR. B. (surprised) What ! Not know me, Mr. Crogate ? Why, I have done more to elucidate the doctrine of *de injuria* than any Judge since my Lord Coke's time. But I am afraid you have not taken in Meeson and Welsby here.

CROGATE. Why, we've taken in a pretty goodish number of all sorts, but I can't say I know the gentlemen you mention. But pray what brought you here, may I ask ?

SUR. B. I have just been sent here, Mr. Crogate, by a most erronous decision of the Judges of your Court below, which I would gladly carry to a Court of Error, if I could.

---

[1] Edward Crogate was a farmer in the county of Norfolk, who, in the sixth year of James the First, brought an action of trespass against Robert Marys, for driving his cattle off Bassingham Common. The defendant pleaded that a house and land in Bassingham were copyhold, and part of the Manor of Thurgarton ; that the Bishop of Norwich was seised thereof in fee, and prescribed to have common of pasture in Bassingham Common for him and his customary tenants of the said house and land ; that the Bishop at a Court, granted the house and land to William Marys ; and that the defendant, as servant and by command of William Marys, *molliter* drove Crogate's cattle off the common. To all this, Crogate, or rather his Pleader, replied, *De injuria sua propria absque tali causa* ; whereupon the defendent demurred at law ; and the case having been very learnedly argued, the Court decided against Crogate, and held his replication bad. In this case, as Coke says, divers points were resolved, which he has embodied in the shape of four Resolutions, which are among the curiosities of the Law, and have served as the foundation for a vast superstructure of technical learning, especially in modern times.

CROGATE. Well, I've tried both sorts of Courts in my time ; and, though it was given against me in both places, I think, that somehow or other, one gets more substantial justice down here. There is no risk of a man (or a ghost, as I should rather say,) being turned round on a quibble. But what ground have you for finding fault with our Court ?

SUR. B. Mr. Crogate, I am the unfortunate victim of their loose pleading, as you shall hear. I was busily engaged in the upper regions in preparing some elaborate Judgments in further elucidation of the New Rules, when I was summarily removed by *habeas corpus* before I could find time to question the regularity of the proceeding. I made the best of my way down below, and arrived on the banks of the Styx without accident. Here I found myself in the midst of a multitude of unhappy shades, whom I understood to be Charon's remanets, but upon a special application I was fortunately placed at the head of his paper, and ferried over with little delay. On reaching the further shore, I was considerably alarmed by Cerberus, whose multifarious head struck me as being decidedly bad on special demurrer. I had, however, fortunately prepared myself against this danger, by bringing with me a very special traverse, which I immediately threw out to him as a bait. He greedily caught it, and swallowed the inducement in a twinkling ; but the *absque hoc* stuck in his throat, and nearly choked him, and in the mean time I made my escape. As soon as I was out of his reach, I began to revolve in my mind whether an action on the case could be supported against his proprietor, for keeping a dog used to bite at shadows, when, upon a very short notice, I was summoned to take my own trial, which, as I had not been put under terms, struck me as a great irregularity.

CROGATE. I am sorry I was not by to see you tried.

SUR. B. Mr. Crogate, you would have derived very little benefit from witnessing the proceedings, which were more like the summary practice of one of the new-fangled county courts, than the regular procedure of a respectable superior, or even inferior tribunal. The pleadings were *ore tenus*, as in the early days of special pleading. Radamanthus took the case into his own hands, and acted both as Judge and Prosecutor ; and he declared against me *ex delicto*, in case, for breach of duty, by having systematically obstructed justice during my judicial career, with the frivolous technicalities of special pleading. I pleaded that special pleading was a wise and useful system, and that I had helped to remedy all its defects by the New Rules. This plea was perhaps bad in form, as an argumentative general issue ; but I was willing to run the risk of a special demurrer for the chance of entrapping my opponent into a denial of only one branch of my plea, and so of impliedly admitting either that special pleading was a wise and useful system, or that I had helped to remedy all its defects ; in either of which cases I should have stood well for judgment. But he replied by asserting that special pleading was an abominable system, and that I had made it much worse by the New Rules. To the replication I demurred specially on the ground of duplicity ; but to my astonishment, the Court, on my refusing to withdraw my demurrer, most unceremoniously set it aside as frivolous, and gave judgment against me. Now, Mr. Crogate, I consider the judgment to be wrong ; but the idea having occurred to my mind that the Judges may possibly have been misled by the doctrines laid down in your great case, I determined upon finding you out, in order that I might converse freely with you on the subject.

CROGATE. And pray, Mr. Judge, how did you discover me?

SUR. B. With considerable difficulty, Mr. Crogate. After I had been removed into these dismal regions according to my sentence, and had had time to recover a little from the surprise and mortification of this adverse judgment, I began to receive some consolation at finding myself in the very best society. I discovered, in short, that most of the magnates of the earth were no better off than myself. Kings, Emperors, and Statesmen surrounded me on all sides; and many of the greatest Heroes and Conquerors of antiquity were pointed out to me. I was anxious, of course, to see Caesar and Alexander, but was unable to get near them. I had, however, the good fortune to see the Persian monarch Darius; and I took the opportunity of informing him that we had recently decided in the Court of criminal appeal, that his name was not in the eye, or rather I should say in the ear of the law, *idem sonans*, with Trius,[1] a piece of news that appeared to afford him a melancholy satisfaction. Quitting this aristocratic region with regret, I was conducted to the Judicial Quarter, where I fortunately met with the ghost of Sir Edmund Saunders, who received me with great cordiality, and expressed much sympathy with my misfortune. This was natural enough, for he had, as he told me, been turned round pretty much as I was, in consequence of putting in what the Court said was a tricky plea. The fact was, that he had given *express colour* in his plea, and was astonished when issue was taken upon it, and he was required to prove its truth; and being of course unable to do so, or to convince the Judges that the allegation was not properly traversable, he was at once condemned for making a false defence, and thus became an illustrious victim to the ignorance of his Judges. This eminent Judge was kind enough to shew me some of the lions of the place; and to tell you the truth, Mr. Crogate, I was not a little shocked at much that I witnessed.

CROGATE. Aye, aye, Mr. Judge, I reckon that it was not very pleasant to see the way in which some of you lawyers are treated down here.

SUR. B. Mr. Crogate, I was horrified at witnessing some of the punishments of eminent special pleaders. I saw two illustrious men engaged in a complicated course of special pleading with each other, which resulted in everlasting new assignments. Another pair of pleaders similarly engaged, were subjected to the mortification of having eternal judgments of repleader awarded against one or the other of them. But the most lamentable case appeared to be that of the ghost of a special pleader of the old school, who was sentenced to draw an undemurrable plea to an action, brought after the New Rules, upon a bill of exchange, with counts for the consideration, interest, and the money counts, in which the defence was made up of part failure of consideration, part payment, a set-off as to part, and payment into court of the residue. This unhappy ghost had all the New Rules and the forms of the Judges, and the decisions of the Courts upon them, given to him to enable him to accomplish his task; but the more he read the more he was puzzled. Sir Edmund and I witnessed his abortive attempts with great interest; and he pointed out to us a *dictum* of a great pleading Judge to the effect that "there must be *some way of pleading* in such a case,"[2] though the court "was not bound to say what it was." Sir Edmund gave me a knowing wink, and whispered in my ear that it was all very well to say

---

[1] See 20 L.J. Rep. M.C. p. 207.　　　[2] See 16 M. and W. p. 762.

so, but that he took it to be clear that the thing could not really be done ; and we left the pleader at his work, without being able to give him any material assistance.

CROGATE. Well, but how came you to find me out, Mr. Judge ?

SUR. B. Why, Sir Edmund was kind enough to point out to me the region assigned to departed litigants ; though he was very shy of shewing his own face in that quarter, for fear of being ill-used. And truly, Mr. Crogate, as soon as I set my foot within its bounds, I was attacked and mobbed in the most unmerciful manner by a host of former plaintiffs and defendants, against whom I had given judgment in my life time, as they alleged, contrary to plain justice and upon technical quibbles. I endeavoured to justify my Judgments, by shewing that they were in strict conformity to former decisions, but this only irritated them the more, and brought new assailants upon me ; and at length they became so violent, that I was glad to make my escape to this comparatively tranquil spot, which appears to be chiefly peopled by litigants who have been long since removed from the earth.

CROGATE. I suppose you found out some here whose names you had heard of before ?

SUR. B. Oh, yes ! Mr. Crogate ; I was first accosted by a venerable-looking old gentleman, who told me his name was Twyne,[1] and that he had got into a world of trouble in the Star Chamber about some goods and chattels which he had taken for a debt, and good-naturedly suffered to remain for a short time in the possession of his debtor ; upon which ground the Judges decided that he was guilty of fraud. Mr. Twyne assured me that whatever the Judges might have held, it was a most honest and straight-forward transaction ; and that he thought it very hard that he should have been set down as a knave, and ruined, on account of a mere piece of good nature. I endeavoured to comfort the old gentleman by informing him, that although his case had given rise to much misconception, we had effectually set the matter right by recent decisions, and that he would be quite safe if ever the same thing should occur to him again ; but Mr. Twyne only shook his head, and said this was not likely. I was next accosted by a dismal-looking ghost, who came up to me and asked me in a solemn tone, if I had made my entry there for a condition broken ? I at once recognized him as the shade of Dumpor,[2] and was in hopes of getting into an interesting discussion with him ; but my attention was arrested by a miserable-looking ghost, surrounded by books and papers, which, with a bewildered countenance, he was vainly endeavouring to read through. Upon inquiry, I found that this was the shade of the celebrated Shelley,[3] who for some misdeeds committed upon earth, had been sentenced to read and understand all the decisions and books relating to the celebrated rule laid down in his own case.

CROGATE. Pray, did you happen to come across an impudent fellow named Bagg,[4] who was formerly one of the burgesses of Ipswich ?

SUR. B. Indeed, I did, Mr. Crogate ; and he conducted himself so disgracefully towards me, that I should have committed him instantly if I had had the power.

[1] See 3 Rep. 80   [2] See 4 Rep. 119.
[3] See 1 Rep. 88.   [4] See 11 Rep. 93.

CROGATE. Why, what did he do?

SUR. B. I am almost ashamed to say. He came up to me, and without the smallest ceremony (to use the language of the pleadings in his case), "Convertens posteriorem partem corporis sui more inhumano et incivili versus meipsum scurriliter contemptuose inciviliter et altâ voce dixit haec anglicana verba sequentia, videlicit,—COME AND KISS." [1]

CROGATE. Ha! Ha! Ha! I can guess pretty well what you mean, though I don't know much Latin. Bagg boasts, that the Judges decided that there was no harm in his acting in this polite way to the Mayor of Ipswich; and that it was against Magna Charta to disfranchise him for it; and so, whenever he meets with a Judge coming down here, he makes a point of saluting him in the same fashion. I wish you had been by to have seen how old Sir Edward Coke looked when Bagg accosted him in this manner.

SUR. B. I must find out Sir Edward, and confer with him as to the means of stopping this insolence. After escaping from Bagg, I fortunately met with a comfortable motherly-looking female ghost who turned out to be the shade of Mrs. Margaret Podger,[2] and she was kind enough to direct me to you; but just as I was about to accost you, I was stopped by half a dozen ill-manner'd shades, looking like the ghosts of drunken mechanics, who said they were old friends of mine, and that if I was a jolly fellow, I would treat them with something to drink.

CROGATE. Oh! I know those fellows well; they were the six carpenters,[3] who were sued by the landlord of the Queen's Head, at Cripplegate, because they got drunk in his house and refused to pay for their liquor. They contrived, however, to bamboozle the Judges, by setting up as a defence that the landlord was a relation of theirs, and the Judges said they would not allow the carpenters to be made trespassers by a relation; though, in point of fact, he was no more their relation than I was. However, they managed to win their suit on this ground, and I lost mine: but hang me, if I could ever find out upon what ground.

SUR. B. Mr. Crogate, your view of the Six Carpenters' Case is singularly inaccurate: no relation was referred to in it, except a relation to the original entry of the defendants into the Queen's Head. The Court held, and very properly, that drinking the landlord's liquor and refusing to pay for it amounted to a mere *non feasance*, and would not make the original entry unlawful, and the carpenters trespassers *ab initio*. But, however you may have misunderstood the Six Carpenters' Case, you surely can't pretend to be ignorant of the resolution of the Judges in your own.

CROGATE. I don't know what resolutions the Judges made; but I know one that I made myself, and that was never to go to law again. However, it was too late; my beasts were sold to pay the lawyer's bills, and I was a ruined man. More shame for my Judges! say I.

SUR. B. Mr. Crogate, I am astonished at your sentiments. The decision in your case was a most sound one; it has been admirably reported by Sir E. Coke; it has given the rule to countless decisions since; and has, in fact, constituted one of the great landmarks of special pleading; and yet you are so unreasonable as to complain of it.

---

[1] See 11 Rep. 97. [2] See 9 Rep. 104.
[3] See 8 Rep. 146.

CROGATE. Why, don't I tell you I was ruined by it?

SUR. B. What on earth can that signify, Mr. Crogate, if the decision was a sound one?

CROGATE. But I say it wasn't a sound one. My beasts, as I have told you, had as good a right to be on Bassingham Common as any beasts in the County of Norfolk, and the defendant had no right to drive them off.

SUR. B. Very likely; indeed we may assume this to be true.

CROGATE. Well, then, if I had all the right on my side, and the defendant had all the wrong on his, how came the Judges to give it against me?

SUR. B. For this plain, simple, and conclusive reason, that you had most improperly replied *de injuria*.

CROGATE. Will you be so good as to speak so that I may understand you.

SUR. B. Mr. Crogate, it is difficult to use plainer language; but in order to explain the point so as to make it perfectly clear to your uninstructed mind, you should have confined your replication to the traverse of some one material allegation in the plea, and should not have used the cumulative traverse *de injuria* in a case in which it was clearly inadmissible. My Lord Coke observes in the 4th resolution in your case, "that the issue raised by your replication would have been full of multiplicity of matter, where an issue ought to be full and single, for parcel of the manor demisable by copy, grant by copy, prescription of common, and commandment would all be parcel of the issue." I presume that you now fully comprehend the great principle upon which your case was decided.

CROGATE. Odzooks, man alive! (i beg your pardon for calling you so when you're dead), you seem to suppose that I was one of the builders of the Tower of Babel instead of a plain Norfolk farmer. I fancied I'd a sort of notion of what you were driving at before, but I'll be hanged if your last explanation has not driven it clean out of my head.

SUR. B. Mr. Crogate, I can go no further. I have used the very plainest terms which the science of pleading admits of, and if you can't understand me you must impute it to your ignorance. It is hopeless, I see, to attempt to explain the niceties of a science to a person who is ignorant of its rudiments. Read Stephen and Chitty and the Doctrina Placitandi and Com. Digest Title Pleader and the Notes to William's Saunders, and the New Rules, and my Judgments upon them, and particularly the sixteen volumes of Meeson and Welsby; and when you have mastered them I shall find no difficulty in explaining the matter to you. But I forgot that you may probably be unable to obtain these works in this inconvenient locality, and in that case I am afraid you must remain in ignorance of the grounds of the decision in your own case to all eternity, for it is not to be expected that I can find time to teach you the first principles of pleading.

CROGATE. Well, Mr. Judge, before I went to law I'd a notion that justice was a very plain and simple thing, but the end of my law-suit and your explanations have shewed me that I was mortally mistaken. However, as I don't think I am quite so stupid as you seem to suppose, and as you won't give me any more explanations of your own (which to be sure only make the matter worse), perhaps you'll answer a few questions of mine, for I confess I should like to get to the rights of the whole concern.

SUR. B. With great pleasure.

CROGATE. Well, then, let's start with this: My beasts were my own, and they had a right to be on Bassingham Common.

SUR. B. These points did not come in issue, and may be assumed to be as you state.

CROGATE. Well, the rascal that drove them off, set up as defence that he was acting under orders of another party, who, as he said, had a copyhold house and land, and a right of common, and beasts of his own on the common, and told the defendant to drive off my beasts.

SUR. B. You have correctly stated the substance of the defendant's plea of justification.

CROGATE. Well, to proceed. All this, d'ye see, was untrue from beginning to end; the man, whose title he set up, had no copyhold, no right of common, no beasts on the common, and gave no orders to the defendant to drive off my beasts. Now I told my lawyer to let the Court know the rights of all this; and he told me that his counsellor had pleaded that there was not a word of truth in the whole defence. What should I expect then? Why, of course, that my case would come on at our 'Sizes and that I should have won the day. But lo! and behold, a trial comes off, as I'm told, behind my back in London, and the Judges give it against me on all points without hearing a single witness, and I'm sold up and ruined!

SUR. B. A hard case. But hard cases make bad law.

CROGATE. I don't know what you mean by that, Mr. Judge, but I think bad law makes hard cases. But what I want to make out is, how the Judges came to give this rascally judgment against me? I always supposed that my lawyer did not let them know that the whole defence was untrue, and that the defendant got them to believe it.

SUR. B. Quite the contrary. The defendant by his demurrer expressly admitted, as I've told you, that all the facts, or what you absurdly enough call the rights of the case, were against him. The true reason for the decision was, that you denied the whole plea instead of denying a part of it only.

CROGATE. Why, have not I told you that there was not a word of truth in it from beginning to end?

SUR. B. That is immaterial. You should have denied only part of the plea, and admitted all the rest to be true.

CROGATE. What, admit lies to be true?

SUR. B. Yes, certainly, in such a case as yours.

CROGATE. Come, come, Mr. Judge, you're hoaxing me. This is no place for cutting your jokes.

SUR. B. Mr. Crogate, I am speaking in sober seriousness, and assure you that your case was decided against you solely and simply because your pleader had (most improperly) denied the whole of the defendant's plea, instead of confining his denial to some one part of it, and so admitting the rest to be true.

CROGATE. You astonish me! Pray, be so good as to explain it to me. For what reason on earth, or in the regions below (as I should rather say down here), I should be obliged to admit lies to be true?

SUR. B. Because it is an established rule that pleadings should not be double. When a plea consists of several distinct assertions (and whether true or false is immaterial), the plaintiff is bound to elect whether he would give an affirmative or negative answer to it, as he is not allowed to do both; and if he wishes to plead in denial, he must select some one assertion for denial, and admit the rest of the plea. An exception to this rule prevails where the plea consists of mere matter of excuse, and involves no question of title, interest, matter of record, or authority, derived mediately or immediately from the plaintiff, but this exception did not apply to your case.

CROGATE. Then, if my opponent tells two falsehoods, and I want to deny them both, the law will make me admit one to be true.

SUR. B. Certainly.

CROGATE. And if he tells ten I must admit nine of them to be gospel.

SUR. B. Exactly so; you reason correctly. If a plea (not amounting to mere matter of excuse) consists of twenty, or any greater number of distinct assertions, no matter whether true or false, you must still confine your denial to one, and consequently admit the rest.

CROGATE. Well, we live and learn (as I used to say before I was dead). Now, d'ye see, I had a notion in my own mind that in order to do justice you must first get at the truth; but it's a queer mode of getting at the truth to make people admit falsehoods. However, you say that this is a rule of that which you call special pleading.

SUR. B. It is one of the great fundamental rules of that admirable science. The whole object of special pleading is to bring the parties in every cause to issue upon some one single point, and this object could never be attained unless duplicity were strictly prohibited.

CROGATE. Well, I always heard that duplicity was a bad thing; but I never supposed before now that there would be any duplicity in denying a string of falsehoods.

SUR. B. I use the term *duplicity*, not in its ordinary sense, in which it is not opposed to good pleading, but in its scientific and technical sense; duplicity, in this sense, may consist either in telling too much truth, or in denying too much falsehood. The rules of good pleading do not prohibit falsehood when it is free from duplicity, but they do prohibit duplicity, even though it may be in strict accordance with the truth.

CROGATE. Mr. Judge, you're getting a great way out of my depth.

SUR. B. Mr. Crogate, I have explained to you that the object of special pleading is to bring the parties to trial upon some one point.

CROGATE. Well, I always supposed the object of justice was to get at the whole truth, but it seems that the special-pleading way of doing justice is to shut out the truth upon all points but one.

SUR. B. Exactly so, Mr. Crogate; you are now beginning to form a correct idea of the science of special pleading,—to know which, as the great Littleton says, "is one of the most honorable laudable and profitable things in our law."

CROGATE. Egad, Mr. Judge, I wish I'd known as much of it before I went to law, and that scamp should never have got the better of me.

SUR. B. How so, Mr. Crogate?

CROGATE.   Why, look you ; I'd have begun the game by telling lies against him, and making him admit them all but one ; according to the rules of special pleading I could have put him in a pretty fix, then.

SUR. B.   There is some originality and acuteness in your idea, but it would not have availed you ; for, if the defendant had succeeded in shewing the falsehood of the particular point upon which he had taken issue, he would have succeeded in the action, and all the admissions of other points would have gone for nothing ; so, in your case, if you had confined yourself, as you ought to have done, to the denial of part of defendant's plea, and had disproved that, you would have succeeded in your action.

CROGATE.   But suppose, Mr. Judge, that I had taken the wrong sow by the ear ; and that when the trial came on, either from bad information, or bad luck, or from my witnesses not coming up to the mark, or his witnesses swearing too strong, he was able to beat me on that one point, though all the rest of his story was untrue ?

SUR. B.   In that case he would undoubtedly succeed, as you would not be allowed to contest at the trial any point which you had admitted in pleading.

CROGATE.   Now, that is just what I complain of, Mr. Judge ; if a man tells a dozen lies against me anywhere else, I may deny them all ; then, why should I not be allowed to do so in a Court of justice ?

SUR. B.   Because the rules of good pleading prohibit it ; and if it were allowed, the whole object of pleading, which, as I have told you, was to bring the parties to an issue upon a single point, would be defeated.

CROGATE.   Mr. Judge, if parties have several points which they dispute about, why in the name of common sense should they not be allowed to try them ? If you determine to shut out the truth by making the parties admit all the points set up by their opponent, except one, you may as well go the whole hog at once, and make one side admit the whole case of the other, and so put an end to dispute.   To my simple mind, this would be every bit as right and just as the special-pleading rule, and a much shorter way of settling law-suits.

SUR. B.   Mr. Crogate, the rule which confines the parties to a single point, raised either by way of negation or affirmation, is as ancient as the science of pleading.   It originated, as my Brother Stephen states, in the practice of oral pleading, and was founded upon reasons of convenience ; nothing can be more convenient for Judge and Jury, than to bring all causes by the statements and counter-statements of the parties to one plain intelligible single point.

CROGATE.   That might be all very well, if people went to law for the convenience of the Judges and Juries, and not to get justice for themselves. If they have only one point in dispute, they don't want more than one tried ; but if they dispute about several, it is a wicked injustice, that the law should refuse to try more than one.   Really, Mr. Judge, this is as plain as that two and two make four, and so there's an end of it.

SUR. B.   There would be more weight in your objections, Mr. Crogate, if special pleading existed in its original integrity ; but it is proper that I should inform you, that since your time, a great relaxation of the system was made by a Statute passed in the reign of Queen Anne, and which enables defendants, with leave of the Court (which is seldom refused), to plead several matters, so that they may now deny any number of material allegations in the declaration, or set up any number of distinct affirmative defences.

CROGATE. Ah ! that makes a great difference ; and I suppose that, if my case had happened after this Act of Parliament, I should have been allowed to deny the whole of that fellow's trumped-up-plea.

SUR. B. Certainly not, Mr. Crogate ; the privilege of pleading several matters was confined, by the statute, to the pleas of defendants (except as to plaintiffs in replevin who are *quasi* defendants), and your replication would have been as bad after the statute as it was before.

CROGATE. Well then, all I can say is, that it was a rascally Act of Parliament. It is bad enough to deny justice to both parties alike ; but to give it to one, and deny it to the other, because one happens to be what you call plaintiff, and the other defendant, is really too bad.

SUR. B. You are unreasonable, Mr. Crogate. The policy of the Statute of Anne, in permitting an unlimited number of pleas, may, indeed, be very questionable, but surely a stand ought to be made somewhere. If several replications were allowed, we must allow several rejoinders, several surrejoinders, and so on to several surrebutters ; issues would be multiplied like the population, according to the theory of Malthus, in geometrical progression ; and a single action of *trespass* might so expand itself, as to require the skins of a flock of sheep for the *nisi prius* records. Now, however advantageous this might be for the agricultural interest, it would be, in other respects, an absolute evil ; and consequently the law, while it allows of an unlimited number of pleas, strictly prohibits duplicity in a replication. And even with respect to pleas, although a defendant may raise twenty or more different defences, each must form the subject of a distinct plea ; and the least duplicity in any one plea will make it bad on demurrer.

CROGATE. Well, Mr. Judge, this seems to me very like swallowing a camel and straining at a gnat. If the law can manage to swallow twenty separate pleas, it need not be very squeamish about a little of what you call *duplicity* in one of them. But, for the life of me, I can't conceive why, when a man is allowed to deny the whole case of the other side, and to set up any other answer he may have to it, he should not be allowed to do so, in the shortest and simplest manner, so as to make one story of it. Why, really, Mr. Judge, it must be arrant nonsense, to make a man split his case into I don't know how many different parts, in order to make what you call separate pleas of it ; and there can be no reason for this, except to puzzle and create expense.

SUR. B. This, Mr. Crogate, was a necessary consequence of the application of the established principles of pleading to the statutory privilege of pleading several matters. The Act of Parliament, in allowing this privilege, left special pleading in other respects as it previously existed ; and, consequently, each plea was treated as if it were the only one in the case, and the Court dealt with it upon the same principles that were applicable when the defendant was confined to a single plea.

CROGATE. And a pretty jumble you must make of it ; for, if I can make out your meaning, it seems to be this ; that the Act of Parliament having altered your special-pleading system, root and branch, and altogether put an end to your fine plan of chopping and lopping all questions, till you bring them to a single point ; you still went on with your foolish quibbling rules, just as if you had still only one point to try.

SUR. B.   Mr. Crogate, the Judges have only to administer laws, not to make them.   The Legislature might have remodelled the system of pleading, when the statute was passed, but it did not think proper to do so.   The Act was not a perfect measure,—it left some evils unremedied, and produced some defects and incongruities.   It was reserved to a later age to introduce more comprehensive improvements, and to bring the system of pleading to perfection by means of the New Rules.

CROGATE.   Oh ! you've been making new rules about special pleading have you ; then, I suppose, as a matter of course, that you've pretty nearly done away with the whole thing ?

SUR. B.   Done away with special pleading ?   Heaven forbid !   On the contrary, we adopted it (subject to the relaxation introduced by the Statute of Anne), in even more than its original integrity ; for we have enforced the necessity of special pleas in many actions in which the whole case was previously left at large, on the merits under the general issue.   And we framed a series of rules on the subject, which have given a truly magnificent development to this admirable system ; so much so. indeed, that nearly half the cases coming recently before the Court, have been decided upon points of pleading.

CROGATE.   You astonish me.   But pray how do the suitors like this sort of justice ?

SUR. B.   Mr. Crogate, that consideration has never occurred to me, nor do I conceive that laws ought to be adapted to suit the tastes and capacities of the ignorant.   At first, to be sure, we found that in consequence of our having restored the ancient strictness of pleading, where it had been relaxed, and applied it to several of the most common forms of action to which it had never previously been applied, plaintiffs were put into considerable perplexity by special pleas.   If they denied too much, a demurrer for duplicity followed ; and if they only denied one point, and consequently admitted the rest, they sometimes traversed the only allegation which could be proved, or, to use your language, they took the wrong sow by the ear.   In this state of things, though justice was by no means uniformly defeated, yet this result took place more frequently than was convenient, and some obloquy was beginning to attach on the New Rules. In this emergency, Mr. Crogate, we fell back on the replication *de injuria* with the happiest success ; and by a series of decisions, which I shall by and by explain to you, we gave it an application so extensive, as would have astounded my Lord Coke, and must be signally gratifying to you, considering the frequent reference that has necessarily been made to your great case in our recent decisions.   And thus, Mr. Crogate, we were enabled to bring the system of pleading as near to perfection, as I believe to be possible.

CROGATE.   Well, Mr. Judge, though I'm rather doubtful about your great improvements, it is, at all events, some consolation to think that, if my case had arisen after your New Rules, I should have been allowed to deny the whole of that fellow's trumped-up defence.

SUR. B.   You would have been allowed to do nothing of the sort, Mr. Crogate.   Your replication would have been just as bad after the New Rules, as it was before.

CROGATE (in a rage). Then I must tell you, Mr. Judge, that your New Rules, as you call them, can't be worth a farthing.

SUR. B. Really, Sir, I trust you will speak of the New Rules with more respect, otherwise I must close our discussion.

CROGATE. With all my heart, Mr. Judge, and the sooner the better, as we are not very likely to agree. But pray, may I ask, if there is no way of getting justice up above, without all this special pleading?

SUR. B. The forms of pleading are more or less strict, according to the nature of the action; and in many actions there is, in substance, no special pleading at all. In actions on *contracts*, if the facts are such as to render it necessary, according to the established rules of the court, to declare specially, great strictness and particularity are enforced, and the simplest questions are often involved in much complication of pleading; but if the case admits of the use of certain general or common counts (which indeed are applicable in the great majority of ordinary actions) the whole matter is left pretty much at large, and the most complicated questions are tried on simplest statements. So in actions on *torts*, you may have more or less special pleading, entirely according to the form of action which you elect, or are obliged to adopt. Thus, if your goods are taken away, and you sue the wrong-doer in *trespass* (as you did in your own case, Mr. Crogate), you will have special pleading in all its strictness; but if you choose to sue in *trover*, and make a fictitious statement that you casually lost your goods, and that the defendant found and converted them; here he is allowed to deny the fictitious loss and finding, and may set up almost any possible defence, under a denial of the alleged ownership and conversion of the goods; or if you prefer to sue in *detinue*, and state a fictitious delivery or bailment of the goods to the defendant (which fiction he is not allowed to deny), you will have rather more special pleading than in *trover*, but considerably less than in *trespass*. If you are assaulted and beaten, you cannot escape special pleading by any fictitious allegation, but you are obliged to sue in *trespass*, and the defendant to justify specially. If you sue for a *trespass* to your land, however small the injury, the greatest strictness of pleading is required, but if you are actually turned out, you may recover the land itself by a fictitious mode of proceeding called *ejectment*, without any special pleading at all.

CROGATE. Mercy upon us, what an embranglement! Surely, if special pleading is a good thing, you ought to have it in all actions alike; but at all events, a man ought not to be allowed to escape from it by telling all sorts of nonsensical falsehoods.

SUR. B. Mr. Crogate, the forms of action are of great antiquity; they are part and parcel of the law, and great confusion would no doubt be caused from any mad attempt to alter them. In framing the New Rules we adopted the principle of enforcing special statements as far as we could, consistently with the established forms of action; but we could hardly go further without a revolution in pleading. For, where a plaintiff is allowed the privilege of stating a pure fiction in his declaration, it would have been extremely inconvenient to compel the defendant to state the real facts of his defence. And, if the plaintiff's fictitious statements were prohibited, an evident absurdity must follow, unless the form of action itself were abolished. How could you have an action of *trover*, wherein loss and finding was not alleged! This would be *lucus a non lucendo*.

CROGATE. Well, well, Mr. Judge, I see how the whole thing stands pretty clearly.   The more you patch and mend a bad thing the worse you make it : and this is just what you have been doing by your New Rules.   But what I want to know is whether there are no courts, where you can get justice, or something like it, without any special pleading.

SUR. B.   Oh, yes.   In consequence of an idle and absurd clamour on the part of the public, some inferior courts were established a short time back to enable the common people to sue for small debts and damages under twenty pounds ; and in these courts, the proceedings are wholly free from the refinements of special pleading.

CROGATE.   But, if special pleading is a good thing, why is it done without in these courts?

SUR. B.   Because of the expense and delay which the forms of correct plead-ing would occasion, and because neither practitioners nor judges could be expected to understand the system properly ; and moreover, Mr. Crogate, in these trifling matters, the great object is to administer sub-stantial justice in the simplest form and at the least expense.

CROGATE.   Well, in my ignorance, I should have thought that would have been the object in great cases as well as small.   But, pray, what mode of proceeding do you use instead of special pleading ?

SUR. B.   The simplest process in the world.   The forms of action have been practically abolished.   The plaintiff gives a concise statement or notice of his claim, and the defendant of his defence (where it is con-sidered proper that he should do so) in plain English, unfettered by the technical rules of pleading.   If either party really stands in need of further information, the judge requires it to be given ; or if either party complains of surprise, and requires further time, he adjourns the trial upon just terms.   The case being understood and ready for trial, he decides it, and there is an end of the matter.

CROGATE.   And does this answer ?

SUR. B.   It has not been complained of.   In fact suitors were so well satisfied with these new-fangled courts, that they were anxious to go to them in cases which ought to have come to us ; and they began an im-proper practice of splitting their demands, which we endeavoured to put a stop to by *prohibitions ;* but this was all in vain, for the jurisdiction of these courts was speedily extended to fifty pounds, and beyond that amount by consent ; and it remains to be seen whether the effect will not be, to transfer to them the great bulk of the civil business of the country, and to leave the superior Courts without employment ; a result which will be obviously fatal to the law of England.

CROGATE.   But why, in the name of common sense, can't you proceed in your superior Courts, in pretty much the same simple and rational manner which has been found to answer in these inferior courts, and get rid of your special pleading ?

SUR. B.   What ? Mr. Crogate.

CROGATE.   Why, Mr. Judge, you have made it quite plain to me, that justice and special pleading can never get on together ; and as people go to your

courts for justice, and not for special pleading, the sooner you get rid of
your special pleading nonsense the better.

SUR. B. Heaven forbid! Mr. Crogate.   Why, if special pleading were
abolished, what would become of all the New Rules, and the valuable
decisions on them, in the sixteen volumes of Meeson and Welsby? Really,
Mr. Crogate, your mind has been most unfairly prejudiced against the
science by the decision of your own case; but you should recollect that
to this apparent misfortune you owe an immortality, for, never will the
name of CROGATE be forgotten while the replication *de injuria* continues to be drawn by the hand of a special pleader. Let me now
endeavour to unfold to you the magnificent series of decisions in which
the doctrine of *de injuria* has been elaborated since the New Rules; and
for the purpose of classifying these cases, I propose to consider,—First,
When *de injuria* may clearly be replied.   Secondly, When it clearly
cannot be replied.   Thirdly, When it is probable that it may be replied.
Fourthly, When it is probable it cannot be replied.   And, Fifthly, When
it is altogether doubtful whether it can or cannot be replied.   In the
course of this discussion, I shall have to point out and explain what
amounts to mere matter of excuse—a nice and difficult subject, and with
respect to which much variety of opinion has prevailed.   I shall also
have to consider and examine in detail all the resolutions of the Judges
as reported by Sir E. Coke in your case; and I shall shew you how this
third resolution, in so far as it refers to an authority given by the law, is
at variance with the instances given in his first resolution; and also how
his fourth resolution, so far as it refers to mere multiplicity of matter,
without reference to the nature and quality of such matter, being an objection to *de injuria*, is unfounded; both of which points were made
tolerably clear by the great case of *Bardons v. Selby*.[1]   I shall also have
to shew you that *de injuria* is inapplicable where the plea amounts to an
argumentative denial of the declaration,[2] or where the plea discloses
matter of subsequent discharge such as payment, accord and satisfaction,
as we settled in numerous cases,[3] or when the plea is in the nature of a
set-off; for this is not properly matter in excuse, but rather in the nature
of matter in extinguishment.[4]   We shall further see that *de injuria* is
inapplicable where the matter of excuse is not of an affirmative character,
but is a mere negative excuse, such as the non-delivery of an attorney's
bill.[5]   So also, where the plea is (according to the third resolution in your
case) founded upon authority mediately or immediately derived from the
plaintiff, a point of considerable nicety, and on which contradictory decisions were given.[6]   So where the plea claims any title or interest in the
goods or other subject-matter of the action (as laid down in the second
resolution in your case); with this limitation, however, that it must be a
title or interest prior to, and irrespective, and independent of, the act
complained of; for want of due attention to which distinction, much misconception has arisen.   A multitude of other points and distinctions will
also demand our attention; and amongst others I shall have to shew you
that when this replication is clearly allowable, yet if the pleader does not
use the proper and accustomed form of words, but introduces some new-
fangled allegation, such as that the opposite pleading is "*untrue in*

[1] See 3 B. and Ad. 2; s.c. 9 Bing. 756.
[2] See 3 M. and W. 230.
[3] See 2 C. M. and R. 159; 4 M. and W. 123, etc.
[4] See 7 M. and W. 314; 1 Q.B. 197.
[5] See 7 Q.B. 402.   [6] See 1 Q.B. 197.

substance," this will be clearly bad, because (as we settled in a recent case [1]) by alleging a plea to be *untrue in substance,* you necessarily put in issue immaterial and unsubstantial matters ; but by denying the truth of the whole plea in the common form, *de injuria* only material and substantial matters are put in issue.[2] But our especial attention will be directed to the long and important series of cases on the application of *de injuria* to pleadings on bills of exchange. In these actions, Mr. Crogate, before the New Rules, special pleas were wholly unknown ; but the cases that have been decided on pleading points arising out of them since the New Rules would fill volumes ; and a treatise might be written on the use and abuse of *de injuria* in these actions. The discussion on which I propose to enter cannot be compressed within very narrow limits, but as we have plenty of time before us, Mr. Crogate, there can be no reason why we should not go into the subject fully ; and I have no doubt that before we shall have finished, all your objections to special pleading will be removed. But you don't appear to be attending to me.

CROGATE. Attending ! Mr. Judge. Why, to tell you the plain truth, I have heard a great deal too much of you long since. It was no part of my sentence to be obliged to listen to such an abominable rigmarole. Oh ! Mr. Judge, I think of all the unhappy wretches who have come to your Courts for justice, and who have been turned round and ruined by such miserable quirks and quibbles as those with which you have been puzzling me for the last half hour. No wonder, indeed, that their ghosts should have made some little disturbance when they caught sight of you down here. Why, it is quite plain to me, that you can't understand half of your own decisions ; and that with all your fine-spun distinctions and crotchets, you have got into a mystification and confusion, from which you can find no straightforward way out. But the worst of all is, that my unhappy name has been mixed up with all this foolery and injustice. How many poor devils have learnt to curse the name of Crogate, through being ruined by quibbles which none of them could understand, but which, when explained, are shewn to be arrant nonsense. What have I, Edward Crogate, done that I should suffer this ? and what on earth could possess me, that, like an idiot, I should ever have thought of going to law with the scamp who drove my beasts off Bassingham Common ? Oh ! Crogate ! Crogate !

(Exit, in great anguish of mind.)

SUR. B. The ignorance and prejudices of this man are absolutely astounding ! But what could I expect down here after such an absurd decision of the Court ? I hardly know where to turn, or how to employ myself ; but I shall endeavour to find out the learned Editor of Saunders's Reports, in order to converse with him on a question which gave me great uneasiness when alive ; I mean whether a *Virtute Cujus* is traversable.[3]

(Exit.)

---

[1] See 10 M. and W. 367, 369.

[2] It seems hard to believe that, two years only by-gone (from 1853, when this Dialogue was first printed), this mode of legal "*wrangling*" was deemed and taken to be "excellent learning."

[3] [Some discussion of this point is contained in 1 Wms. Saunders 23 note 5, and note (*m.*) to note 5. W.S.H.]

(3)

TO THE MEMORY OF JOHN DOE AND RICHARD ROE (*lately deceased.*)[1]

Should Doe and Roe be e'er forgot,
　　And never brought to mind ?
Should John and Richard go to pot,
　　And not a mourner find ?
For auld lang syne, my friends,
　　For auld lang syne ;
We'll chaunt a dirge for Doe and Roe,
　　For auld lang syne.

Of old, when latitats were rife,
　　At grim misfortune's frown,
A shy defendant, half his life,
　　Went " running up and down "—
Then Roe deserted not his friend,
　　Who knew not where to dine,
But wander'd with him to the end,
　　For auld lang syne.

When served with writ, and brought at last,
　　Within the Law's dread pale,
No sad defendant then stuck fast,
　　For want of Common Bail ;
For Doe and Roe in goodly trim,
　　With charity divine,
Stood forth, and gave their bail for him
　　And auld lang syne.

When plaintiffs oft were sore perplex'd,
　　In term time or vacation,
For want of names to be annex'd
　　Beneath the declaration ;
Then Doe and Roe upheld the suit,
　　Like staunchest friends of thine,
And pledges gave to prosecute,
　　For auld lang syne.

When quarrels rose about the right
　　To houses or to lands,
Then John and Richard took the fight
　　Entirely in their hands,
And Richard, ever rash and brave,
　　To enter did incline,
And turn'd John out " with stick and stave "
　　For auld lang syne.

[1] On the 24th October, 1852. Forsaken by friends (the Common Law Commissioners, 1850) who, by the help of John Doe and Richard Roe, had reaped many a golden harvest, and thus " left naked to their enemies,"—

　　" Ingratitude, more strong than traitor's arms,
　　Quite vanquish'd them,"

and, at a good old age, hoary with years, this faithful pair, on the 24th day of October, 1852, died of broken hearts, the dissolution of the one following that of the other so rapidly that their departures may be said to have been simultaneous.

Then, sad to say, Doe sued poor Roe,
    For this his valiant part,
But Richard would not ward the blow,
    It almost broke his heart,
A letter of advice he penn'd
    In most pathetic line,
And signed himself " your loving friend,"
    For auld lang syne.

Now Doe and Roe—'tis grief to tell—
    For Law's Reform ye die,
And, as I bid ye both farewell,
    A tear bedims my eye—
Ye were my friends in life's first stage,
    But no one can divine
The use, in this enlightened age,
    Of auld lang syne.

Ye spread upon the page of Tidd
    A ray of Fancy's charm,
And if but little good ye did,
    Ye did but little harm ;—
And this is more than I can say
    For Law Reforms so fine,
And Law Reformers of to-day,
    And auld lang syne !

II

EQUITY PROCEDURE

(I)

SOME ACCOUNT OF THE PROCEEDINGS IN A COMMON CHANCERY SUIT, AND THE PROBABLE TIME OF ITS DURATION.

[C. P. Cooper, Proceedings in Parliament relative to defects in
the Court of Chancery, pp. 86-89.]

Every practitioner knows, that, in the present state of the Court,[1] a common
siut by legatees or creditors cannot be terminated in less than five years, even
supposing its duration be not prolonged by exceptions to the Master's report,
or appeals from interlocutory or final orders.

I will endeavour to explain this to the reader, who is not a member of the
profession of the law.

I will take one of the most common suits instituted in the Court of Chancery
—a suit against executors, the object of which is to recover legacies or enforce
the payment of debts. In about a year after the filing of the bill, the cause
will be ready to be heard, and it is then set down for hearing before the Vice-
Chancellor. Eighteen months must expire before the Vice-Chancellor has
disposed of the prior business on the list and its turn to be heard comes, and
then (two years and a half after the commencement of the suit) a decree is
made, directing one of the Masters of the Court to take an account of the
executors' receipts and payments, in order to see whether there are assets to
pay all the debts and legacies. The making this decree does not occupy the

---

[1] That is in the year 1828.

Court five minutes. Some little delay, however, generally occurs in drawing up the decree, which is then carried into the Master's office.

At the end of twelve months, the Master has taken the accounts and makes his report to the Court, and the executors upon a motion or summary application, made to the Vice-Chancellor for that purpose, pay into Court the balance found due from them. Indeed it frequently happens, that executors pay money into Court upon motion made at an earlier period of the cause. This money cannot, however, in either case, be disposed of until the Court gives what are technically called Further Directions, being an order to distribute the fund amongst the creditors and legatees pointed out by the Master's report, after payment of the costs of the suit. To obtain this order, the cause must, after the Master has made his report, be set down in the list of Further Directions and Exceptions, where it remains eighteen months before its turn to be heard a second time arrives, and then, in a lucky case, an order is made to pay the legatees and creditors. The order made to pay the money into Court, the decree made upon the first hearing of the cause, and the order made upon further directions to divide the fund, may all be made the subject of an appeal to the Lord Chancellor, and afterwards to the House of Lords. The Master's report, stating the result of the accounts, may also be excepted to, and the exceptions set down to be heard before the Vice-Chancellor ; and the Vice-Chancellor's decision upon the exceptions, in like manner, carried by appeal before the Lord Chancellor, and afterwards to the House of Lords. In fact, almost all the minor orders, deciding points of practice and other trifling matters incident to judicial proceedings, are subject to a double appeal ; and the pendency of an appeal, even on such subjects as these, renders it impossible to prosecute the suit with effect.

During all this time, the suit is liable to the delays occasioned by the events alluded to in a preceding part of this Chapter, namely, death, bankruptcy, insolvency, etc., of some of the parties ; new and unexpected points arise, cross or supplemental suits are frequently rendered necessary, the pleadings increase in bulk with the lapse of time, and a cause, which, if heard when first set down, might have been disposed of at a trifling expense, swallows up a large portion of the estate, for the administration of which it was instituted.

It is evident from this statement, that if the plaintiffs use the utmost diligence in the prosecution of their suit, if the defendants be not particularly litigious, if there be no exceptions, no appeal, still great delay is unavoidable, and that delay is with the Court, and not with the parties ; the cause, at two different stages of it, being inscribed on the list for hearing during a period of eighteen months, waiting its turn to be heard, and in this manner three years are altogether lost.

I am taking, however, a very favourable view of even a common Chancery suit, for the payment of a few wretched creditors and legatees, without exception or appeal, when I assume they will receive their debts at the end of five years, upon the suit coming on for the first time on Further Directions. From various causes, which it is not necessary here to explain, it seldom happens that the Court finds itself in a condition to divide the fund without directing a second reference to the Master to take some additional accounts, to make some further inquiries, to convert into money certain property still left unsold, etc. Take, for instance, the common case of the debts or legacies charged upon real estate, in case of the personal estate being insufficient to satisfy them. The Court but rarely does or can direct the real estate to be sold, until the Master reports there is a deficiency of the personal estate. There must, therefore, be a second reference to the Master, to carry on the accounts, to sell the real estate, etc. He must make a second report, the cause must be a second time set down on Further Directions, it must wait a third period of eighteen months before its turn to be heard arrives, and all the proceedings in this third stage may be delayed and embarrassed by the same events and incidents as in the two former stages.

It must not be forgotten, that during all this time the widow and children of the testator, who I will suppose to be his residuary legatees, are kept out of the enjoyment of the property which the testator intended should produce to them an immediate income. The residuary legatees cannot touch a sixpence until all the prior charges of debts and legacies are actually paid, unless, by some amicable arrangement between the parties, the Court can ascertain at an earlier period of the cause, that there are funds sufficient to pay all the debts and legacies, and the costs of the suit.

Legatees of particular sums of money are not in a much better situation than legatees of a portion of the residue, as the creditors must of course be satisfied before the legacies can be paid. A daughter, to whom a testator leaves a legacy of £10,000 for her fortune, charged upon his real estate, must wait eight years before she can receive interest or principal, and during more than half this time the cause remains on the lists of the Vice-Chancellor, waiting its turn to be heard.

But when I suppose that a legatee of £10,000, charged upon real estate, will receive the legacy at the end of eight years, I am putting a most favourable case. It rarely happens that a suit, to administer a large property, can be carried on without exceptions or appeal, and then the delay is presently doubled or trebled.

(2)

MESNE PROCESS IN CHANCERY. [Parlt. Papers, 1826, xv APP. A. at p. 152.]

No. 1.—*Process to compel Appearance.*

Subpœna :

Absconding Parties not served : — Order to Appear under Statute. — Publication of Order. — Pro Confesso.

Order to Appear, etc., to Pro Confesso ;
  or
Serjeant at Arms. — Commission of Sequestration.

Party served : — Attachment for want of Appearance :

Party not taken : — Attachment with Proclamation. — Commission of Rebellion. — Order to Appear, etc., to Pro Confesso ; or
Serjeant at Arms. — Commission of Sequestration.

Party taken : — Messenger.

Out on Bail. — Not taken : — Commit-ment to Fleet. — Order to enter Appearance.

In Custody : — Taken : — Habeas Corpus cum causis. — Commitment to Fleet. — Order to enter Appearance.

No. 2.—Process to compel Answer after Appearance.

Appearance.

Attachment for want of Answer.

Party not taken :
Attachment with Proclamation. | Commission of Rebellion. | Serjeant at Arms. | Commission of Sequestration. | Pro Confesso.

Party taken.

Out on Bail.
Messenger.
Not taken.
Serjeant at Arms. | Commission of Sequestration. | Pro Confesso.

Taken.
Commitment to Fleet. | Habeas Corpus. | Alias. | Pluries. | Alias Pluries. | Pro Confesso

In Custody.
Habeas Corpus.
Commitment to Fleet. | Habeas Corpus. | etc.

(3)

THE PROCEDURE OF THE MASTERS' OFFICES.

[Parlt. Papers, 1852, vol. xxi. pp. 28-30.]

Supposing the suit to be a creditor's suit, where the debtor has died intestate, leaving real and personal estate to be administered. The ordinary form of decree would be a reference to the Master, to take the following accounts, and make the following inquiries :—

1st. An account of the intestate's personal estate received by the administrator and his application of it.

2nd. An account of the intestate's debts and funeral expenses.

3rd. An inquiry what portion of the intestate's personal estate is outstanding.

4th. If the Master should find that the personal estate is deficient to pay the debts, an inquiry what real estate the intestate died seised of, and what charges and incumbrances affect it.

The decree does not ordinarily extend beyond this, but leaves it for further directions to direct a sale or mortgage of the real estate to satisfy the debts, and to direct an account of the rents and profits against the heir-at-law.

We suppose the simplest case, and that on the warrant to consider the decree, the Master or his chief clerk has directed an account to be brought in by the administrator within a limited time.

An account is left in the Master's office by the administrator at the time fixed, or probably not until some considerable time afterwards ; for though the Master is expressly authorised by one of the general orders of the Court to fix the time for proceeding, yet as the order prescribes no penalty consequent on disobedience to the Master's order, this authority is practically of little force. The account so left is verified by affidavit, and the party leaving it takes out a warrant on leaving, and serves a copy on the adverse solicitors, who thereby become aware that it is left ; and, in due course, go to the Master's office, and bespeak copies. The copies having been furnished, the plaintiff's solicitor converts one side of the account into what is called a *charge*, and carries it into the Master's office, taking out and serving a warrant on leaving as in the former case. The solicitor who brought in the account, and the solicitor of the heir-at-law respectively take copies of this charge, and the plaintiff's solicitor then takes out a warrant to proceed upon the charge. This warrant is attended, generally before the chief clerk, who, in the presence of the solicitors, checks the items in the charge with those in the account ; and when they are all gone through, the charge is marked and considered as allowed. A similar process is then gone through with respect to the opposite side of the account, which is converted into a *discharge*, brought in by the administrator's solicitor—the vouchers produced and examined before the chief clerk, and, in cases of dispute, before the Master himself—for which purpose separate warrants must be taken out until the discharge is either allowed in its original form—if sustainable in that form—or, if not, then with such modifications and deductions as the Master may have thought right to make in it.

The inquiry as to outstanding personal estate may now be prosecuted ; unless the defendant's answer in the cause is sufficient for this purpose, the plaintiff may require the defendant to bring in an affidavit or to be examined on interrogatories. The plaintiff's solicitor leaves in the Master's office a *state of facts*, taken either from the defendant's answer, affidavit, or examination. Upon this state of facts warrants on leaving and to proceed are taken out and served ; it is then proceeded on before the Master's clerk, who verifies it by comparing it with the document upon which it is grounded, and it is then allowed.

Pending these proceedings, the Master issues advertisements for the creditors to come in and prove their debts before him. There are usually two advertisements, the first directing the creditors to come in forthwith, the second directing them to come in before a limited time : the last is called the peremptory advertisement ; but in fact it is only so far peremptory that the Master does not make his report until the limited time is gone by. A creditor may always come in before the report is prepared, whatever time may have elapsed. Each creditor has to leave in the Master's office an affidavit of his debt, and to take out and serve a warrant on leaving, and another warrant to proceed. In some offices, as we are informed, arrangements are now made to take most of these claims at one time ; but this is not generally the case, each claimant selecting his own time, subject, of course, to the previous engagements in the office.

It will then appear from the accounts of personal estate received, and of outstanding personal estate, and also from the account of debts, whether the personal estate is or [is] not sufficient for payment of the debts.

The fourth inquiry has still to be prosecuted. For this purpose a state of facts containing the particulars of the real estate, and of the charges and incumbrances, if any, affecting it, is prepared, and brought in, and after fresh warrants on leaving and to proceed, is ultimately allowed, upon evidence verifying the statements.

The matter being now ripe for a report, the plaintiff's solicitor takes out a warrant to show cause why the Master should not prepare the draft of his Report. This warrant having been served upon the adverse solicitors, is attended before the Master, an opportunity being thus afforded to all parties of applying for time to supply any evidence which may have been omitted, or to correct any error which, inadvertently or otherwise, may have crept into the proceedings. If no cause be shown the Master then issues a warrant on preparing the draft of his Report. After the issuing of this warrant, no fresh evidence can be given on either side without leave of the Court.

The Master's chief clerk then, from the various charges, discharges, affidavits, and states of facts, prepares the draft of the Master's Report. This Report generally sets forth in the body of it the results of the accounts, as allowed by the Master, and contains in schedules complete transcripts of the accounts themselves. When the draft has been prepared by the chief clerk, a warrant on preparing is taken out and served, and a copy of the draft is taken by the solicitor prosecuting the decree, and generally by the solicitor for each party interested. Warrants to settle the draft Report are then taken out, served, and attended ; and when the draft is finally gone through, and it is seen that all the inquiries, as directed by the order, have been answered, another warrant issues for the Master to sign his Report. This is issued for the purpose of giving any of the parties an opportunity of taking objections to the draft. According to the ordinary practice of the Court, no party can except to the Report—in other words, appeal from the Master to the Court, without having taken such objection before the Master. Supposing no objection to be taken to the draft, the Report is transcribed, and signed by the Master, and, when signed, is delivered to one of the solicitors, ordinarily the solicitor having the carriage of the decree or order, who files it at the Report Office, and takes an office copy, for the purpose of being produced to the Court on the hearing on further directions, and of being used in the further progress of the cause.

We have thus explained the course of procedure in the Master's office in a simple case ; it is obviously calculated to cause unnecessary delay and expense. The system had its origin at a time when the Masters and their clerks were paid by fees. Every warrant, every copy, every report, indeed every proceeding carried its fee, small perhaps in individual amount, but the multiplication of which pressed heavily on the suitor, and yielded large emoluments to the officers. This method of remunerating the Masters and their chief clerks by fees has been put an end to by the Chancery Regulation Act ; but the system still remains, fees are still paid as heretofore, though the amount is carried to the fee fund, and the effects of the system still remain in the mode of procedure, of which we have given an example.

In estimating the evils arising from this system, it must not be forgotten that every warrant and every other step and proceeding which we have enumerated is attended with professional charges of the solicitors employed.

If in such a simple case as we have described it is the practice to proceed by so many steps and with so much delay, it is obvious what must be the course of a litigation carried on and prosecuted in a hostile manner, and in a case of complicated circumstances. Each item in an account may form the subject of a separate investigation, of a state of facts, and counter-state of facts, each of which may be supported by evidence on affidavit, deposition, or *vivâ voce* examination. Warrants are taken out at intervals according to the engagements of the Master or his clerk, and to suit the convenience of counsel or solicitors.

It is further to be observed, that an application may be made to the Master for a warrant to review any decision which he may have come to in the course of the proceedings before him. This warrant is generally granted without much difficulty, because until the warrant on preparing the draft of the Report issues, a party may generally adduce further evidence, and this evidence the Master would be bound to receive, and to state or refer to in his Report, although it might entirely displace the grounds on which the Master had proceeded. If the warrant to review were refused, the Report would, in many cases, state the Masters' finding on a state of circumstances, which he had not actually considered, and which might have led him to a different conclusion.

INDEX

A

ABATEMENT, pleas in, 268-269.

ABBOT, C.J., 285.

ABROAD, status of persons born, 75-76, 87-88, 89, 91.

ABSQUE HOC, 289.

AC ETIAM CLAUSE, 249.

ACCEPTANCE OF AN ESTATE, creation of an estoppel by, 159.

ACCOMPLICES, the evidence of, 192, 224, 233.

ACCOUNTS, mode of taking in Chancery, 363-364.

ACTIO PERSONALIS, etc., 6.

ACTIONS, effect of law of on the arrangement of substantive law, 333.

ACTS OF STATE, 98.

ADMIRALTY, alteration of the criminal procedure of the, 209.

ADVOWSONS, petitions of right for, 18.

AID PRAYER, 10.

ALIAS WRIT, 116, 121, 254.

ALIEN ENEMIES, 73, 98-99; children of born in England, 80; effect of a permission to reside in England, 98, 100-101, 102, 104.

ALIEN FRIENDS, 73; naturalization of, 76-77, 89-90, 91; denization of, 77, 90; incapacity to own land, 77, 79, 85-86, 92-93; limited capacity to take a lease, 97; disabilities of in public law, 91-92; in private law—in the Middle Ages, 92-96; modification of the mediæval rules, 96-97; effect on constitutional law, 97-98.

ALIENS, how different from subjects, 72; see *Alien Enemies, Alien Friends*.

ALLEGIANCE, doctrine of helps to define who are British subjects, 72; effect on of the rise of the conception of Enemy Character, 72-73, see *Enemy Character*; ideas underlying, 73; when the modern doctrine emerges, 74; its two bases, 74; compared with the tenurial tie, 75; its territorial basis, 75-76, 80-81, 89; its personal basis—indissolubility, 77-79; emphasized in *Calvin's Case*, 84-86, 86-87; effect of the lessor of territory on, 87; statutory changes, 91; due to the king in his personal capacity, 81-83; possibility of a double, 86; temporary, due from aliens, 81, 91; see *British Subjects*.

AMBIGUITIES, patent and latent, 221.

AMENDMENT, *of common law pleadings*, permission given for, 282; development of the law as to, 317-318; how the court's power over was evaded, 318-319; power of since the Judicature Acts, 330; *of equity pleadings*, 378, 379, 387, 392, 405-406.

AMOVEAS MANUS, judgment of, 17, 21, 40; remedy given by a petition of right not circumscribed by this form of judgment, 21, 40.

ANGARY, the right of, 44.

ANNUITIES, petitions of right for, 18, 20; the proprietary and contractual nature of, 17, 36; petitions to the Barons of the Exchequer for, 34, 35, 36; granted by Charles II. to the bankers, 33; payable to or by a corporation—effect of the dissolution of the corporation, 69.

ANSTEY, T.C., 39.

ANSWER, the, 336, 337-338, 340-342, 377, 378, 379; early form of, 383; a precedent from the end of the sixteenth century, 384-385; its contents, 385-386; development of, 402; a precedent from the eighteenth century, 402-403; effect on of the growth of the interrogating part of the bill, 403-404; effect on of the rules as to the parts of the answer which could be read, 404; exceptions to and amendments of take the place of further pleadings, 405-406; influence of common law rules as to the statements in, 405; effect of the Act of 1852, 407; of the Judicature Act, 407.

ANTE-NATI, the, 80.

APPEAL, unlimited licence of in the Chancery, 365, 369; system of in Chancery compared with that at common law, 373.

APPEALS from decisions granting or refusing to grant writs of habeas corpus, 122-124.

APPEARANCE, rules as to, 252; enforcement of at common law, 253-256; in the Chancery, 348-351.

ARGUMENTATIVE PLEAS, 288-290; how the rules against were avoided by special traverses, 299.

ARREST by the Chancery or Council, legality of, 111, 112-114, 115.

PRINTED IN GREAT BRITAIN AT THE UNIVERSITY PRESS, ABERDEEN

CPSIA information can be obtained at www.ICGtesting.com
Printed in the USA
LVOW02s0138060814

397657LV00016B/727/P